THE WORLD OF OLD EUROPE

THE CIVILIZATION OF THE GODDESS

Marija Gimbutas

EDITED BY JOAN MARLER

HarperSanFrancisco
A Division of HarperCollins Publishers

ACKNOWLEDGMENTS

In the course of thirty years of research and excavation in Europe, hundreds of archeologists wholeheartedly shared with me the new information essential for the process of reconstructing the Old European culture. Their names are in the notes and the bibliography and I am indebted to all of them. Much was learned through excavations of Neolithic sites (Obre in Bosnia, 1967–68, Anza and Sitagroi in Macedonia, 1968–70, Achilleion in Thessaly, 1973–74, and Scaloria in Southeastern Italy, 1978–80): heartfelt thanks to my collaborators Drs. Alojz Benac (Sarajevo), Sándor Bököny (Budapest), James Mallory (Belfast), the late János Nemeskéri (Budapest), Colin and Jane Renfrew (Cambridge), Daniel Shimabuku (Los Angeles), Santo Tinè (Genoa), and Shan M. M. Winn (Hattiesburg). The preparation of this book coincides with the beginning of the application of radiocarbon dating to the Neolithic materials and the calibration with the tree-ring chronology. For guidance in the complicated process of dating I am indebted to my colleagues at the University of California, Drs. Hans Suess and Rainer Berger. For inspiration and assistance warm thanks to my friends, Indo-Europeanists, and archeologists, Drs. Edgar C. Polomé, Wolfgang Meid, Martin Huld, Eric P. Hamp, Miriam Robbins Dexter, Elizabeth Barber, David Anthony, Michael Herity, Šarūnas Milišauskas, and Rimutė Rimantienė. And for invaluable help to my former students Dr. Karlene Jones-Bley, Patricia MacDonell, Michael Everson, Kristina Kelertas, Dr. Susan Skomal, Starr Goode, and the late Zipporah Sabsay. For the continuous assistance in drafting the illustrations many thanks to James Bennett and for grant-in-aid to the Ahmanson Foundation.

For the final shape of this book deepest gratitude belongs to my editor Joan Marler and to the editing and design staff of Design Office and HarperSanFrancisco.

Design and Production:
Design Office, San Francisco
Bruce Kortebein, Marilyn Perry

FIRST EDITION

Library of Congress Cataloging-in-Publication Data
Gimbutas, Marija Alseikaitė
    The civilization of the goddess : the world of Old Europe / Marija Gimbutas.—1st ed.
    p. cm.
    Includes bibliographical references and index.
    ISBN 0-06-250368-5 (hard : alk. paper)
    ISBN 0-06-250337-5 (pbk.)
    1. Religion, Prehistoric—Europe.
2. Goddesses—Europe.   3. Neolithic period—Europe.   4. Europe—Antiquities.   I. Title.
GN799.R4G54   1991
936—dc20   90-55792
                                      CIP

91 92 93 94 95 K.P. 10 9 8 7 6 5 4 3 2 1

This edition is printed on acid-free paper that meets the American National Standards Institute Z39.48 Standard.

CONTENTS

What Is Civilization?

My purpose in this book is to bring into our awareness essential aspects of European prehistory that have been unknown or simply not treated on a pan-European scale. This material, when acknowledged, may affect our vision of the past as well as our sense of potential for the present and future. We must refocus our collective memory. The necessity for this has never been greater as we discover that the path of "progress" is extinguishing the very conditions for life on earth.

This book examines the way of life, religion, and social structure of the peoples who inhabited Europe from the 7th to the 3rd millennia B.C., which I have termed Old Europe, referring to Neolithic Europe before the Indo-Europeans. During this period, our ancestors developed settled agricultural communities, experienced a large growth in population, and developed a rich and sophisticated artistic expression and a complex symbolic system formulated around the worship of the Goddess in her various aspects.

Substantial evidence for a rapidly growing Neolithic culture that began in the middle of the 7th millennium B.C. exists in the Aegean area, the Balkans, and in east-central Europe. A second area of focus is the central Mediterranean world. In the western Mediterranean coastal zone, the transition from hunting and food gathering to agriculture took the entire 7th millennium for a full transition. In western Europe, the transition from food gathering to agriculture took place only in the early 5th millennium B.C.

The first half of this book is dedicated to the definition, distribution, and chronologies of culture groups throughout the period of c. 6500–3500 B.C. (in western and northern Europe, somewhat beyond 3500 B.C.). Regional groups reveal a surprising variety of styles, inventiveness, and imagination in the arts and architecture. Subsequent chapters discuss religion, script, and social structure. The last chapter focuses on the decline of these cultures, the intrusions of alien people with a totally different economic, social, and ideological structure that gradually changed the face of the Old European world. These events not only explain the disintegration of the civilization of Old Europe but define the transition to patriarchal and belligerent societies. As interdisciplinary research (archeological data, linguistics, mythology, and early historic data) confirms, this transition coincides with the Indo-Europeanization of Europe.

The use of the word *civilization* needs an explanation. Archeologists and historians have assumed that civilization implies a hierarchical political and religious organization, warfare, a class stratification, and a complex division of labor. This pattern is indeed typical of androcratic (male-dominated) societies such as Indo-European but does not apply to the gynocentric (mother/woman-centered) cultures described in this book. The civilization that flourished in Old Europe between 6500 and 3500 B.C. and in Crete until 1450 B.C. enjoyed a long period of uninterrupted peaceful living which produced artistic expressions of graceful beauty and refinement, demonstrating a higher quality of life than many androcratic, classed societies.

I reject the assumption that civilization refers only to androcratic warrior societies. The generative basis of any civilization lies in its degree of artistic creation, aesthetic achievements, nonmaterial values, and freedom which make life meaningful and enjoyable for all its citizens, as well as a balance of powers between the sexes. Neolithic Europe was not a time "before civilization" (used as the title for Colin Renfrew's book on Neolithic and Copper Age Europe, 1973). It was, instead, a true civilization in the best meaning of the word. In the 5th and early 4th millennia B.C., just before its demise in east-central Europe, Old Europeans had towns with a considerable concentration of population, temples several stories high, a sacred script, spacious houses of four or five rooms, professional ceramicists, weavers, copper and gold metallurgists, and other artisans producing a range of sophisticated goods. A flourishing network of trade routes existed that circulated items such as obsidian, shells, marble, copper, and salt over hundreds of kilometers.

All of this was not *ex nihilo*. Next door, in Anatolia, a multitude of temples appeared in the town of Çatal Hüyük which had wall paintings of extraordinary richness and sophistication a thousand years earlier than the high-level architecture, wall paintings, sculptures, and ceramic art of Europe. Before Çatal Hüyük, there were three more millennia in which the evolutionary transition to agriculture and a settled civilized life took place. The rich display of religious symbolism which flowered in central Anatolia and in Old Europe is part of an unbroken continuity from Upper Paleolithic times.

It is a gross misunderstanding to imagine warfare as endemic to the human condition. Widespread fighting and fortification building have indeed been the way of life for most of our direct ancestors from the Bronze Age up until now. However, this was not the case in the Paleolithic and Neolithic. There are no depictions of arms (weapons used against other

Hamangian Stiff Nude, clay figurine from the Cernavoda graveyard, c. 4800 B.C.

humans) in Paleolithic cave paintings, nor are there remains of weapons used by man against man during the Neolithic of Old Europe. From some hundred and fifty paintings that survived at Çatal Hüyük, there is not one depicting a scene of conflict or fighting, or of war or torture.

Old European village sites are not remarkable for their defensive positions but were chosen for their convenient setting, good water and soil, and availability of animal pastures. Hill forts in inaccessible locations are not known to Old Europe, nor are daggers, spears, and halberds. Neolithic villages were occasionally encircled by ditches but seldom by palisades or stone retaining walls. Earthen ramparts and other defensive structures occur only in later Neolithic and Copper Age settlements when measures were taken to protect villages from an influx of human intruders. These changes became visible in central Europe only toward the end of the 5th and during the 4th millennium B.C.

The focus on religion is also significant here. Previous books on Neolithic Europe have focused on habitat, tool kits, pottery, trade, and environmental problems, treating religion as "irrelevant." This is an incomprehensible omission since secular and sacred life in those days were one and indivisible. By ignoring the religious aspects of Neolithic life, we neglect the totality of culture. Archeologists cannot remain scientific materialists forever, neglecting a multidisciplinary approach. A combination of fields—archeology, mythology, linguistics, and historical data—provides the possibility for apprehending both the material and spiritual realities of prehistoric cultures. Furthermore, Neolithic social structure and religion were intertwined and were reflections of each other.

Archeology of the last half of our century is plagued by extremes. "A balanced amalgam is needed," reminds James Mellaart, "one which combines the best of both schools (i.e., digs 'for rubbish' and digs 'for temples') and does not promote sectarian rivalry between the 'art' and 'science' based approaches to archaeology."[1]

The primordial deity for our Paleolithic and Neolithic ancestors was female, reflecting the sovereignty of motherhood. In fact, there are no images that have been found of a Father God throughout the prehistoric record. Paleolithic and Neolithic symbols and images cluster around a self-generating Goddess and her basic functions as Giver-of-Life, Wielder-of-Death, and as Regeneratrix. This symbolic system represents cyclical, nonlinear, mythical time.

The religion of the Goddess reflected a matristic, matrilineal, and endogamic social order for most of early human history. This was not necessarily "matriarchy," which wrongly implies "rule" by women as a mirror image of androcracy. A matrifocal tradition continued throughout the early agricultural societies of Europe, Anatolia, and the Near East, as well as Minoan Crete. The emphasis in these cultures was on technologies that nourished people's lives, in contrast to the androcratic focus on domination.

The Old European social structure was in direct contrast with the Indo-European system that replaced it. As archeological, historical, linguistic, and religious evidence shows, Old European society was organized around a theacratic, communal temple community, guided by a queen-priestess, her brother or uncle, and a council of women as the governing body. In spite of the revered status of women in religious life, the cemetery evidence throughout the 5th and most of the 4th millennia B.C. does not suggest any imbalance between the sexes or a subservience of one sex to the other. It suggests, instead, a condition of mutual respect. The primary grave goods for both sexes are symbolic of the sacred cycles of regeneration, although burial goods also honor personal achievements in the arts, crafts, trade, and other professions.

The Old European society lacked the centralized structure of a chiefdom of the Indo-European type. However, it was not simply composed of small-scale segmentary societies throughout the millennial duration of the Neolithic and Copper Age. The Old European society grew from small agricultural village communities in the earliest Neolithic, to expanded composites of social units in the 5th millennium B.C. East-central European settlements were larger than the largest proto-urban tells in the Near East. The Late Cucuteni culture, c. 4000–3500 B.C., reached an urban stage with towns of up to 10,000 inhabitants at the center of a district surrounded by medium and smaller size villages.

Note: The chronology used in this volume is radiocarbon, calibrated with tree-ring counting. The dates for each culture group from the 7th to the 3rd millennia B.C. are given in the appendix. (B.C. indicates a calibrated date, *b.c.* an uncalibrated date, while B.P. refers to years before the present.)

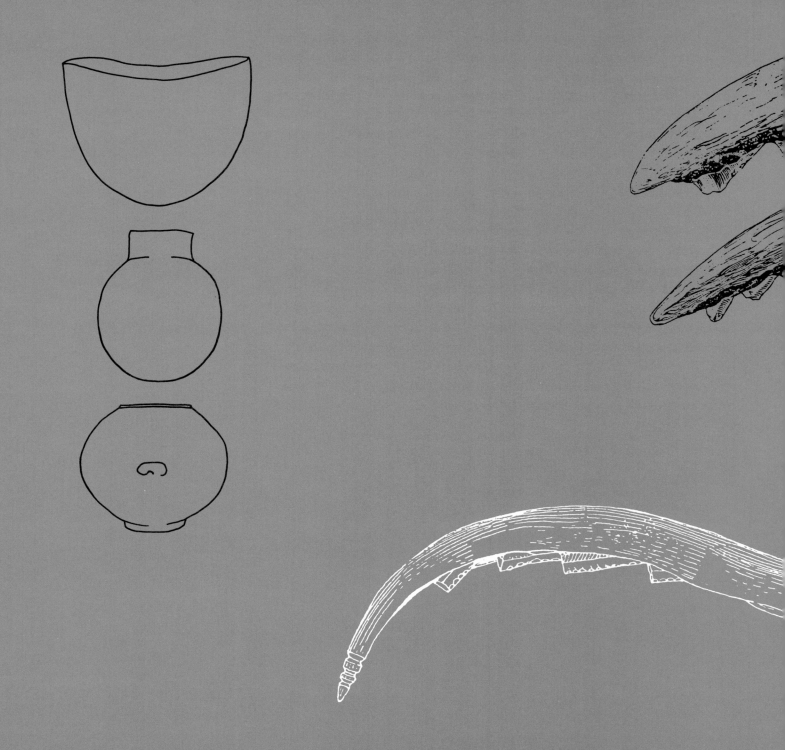

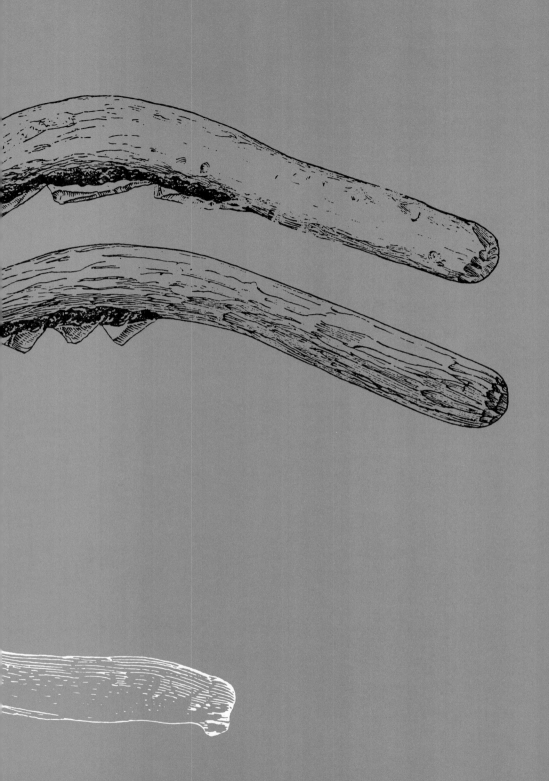

The retreat of the last ice age brought a warming of the world's climate which stimulated a rich abundance of wild plant and animal life and an increase in human populations. The transition from hunting and gathering to permanent settlements and the domestication of plants and animals was a gradual development between c. 9000 and 6500 B.C. The milder conditions of the Boreal period during the 8th millennium B.C., resulting in a dramatic rise of sea level, had a strong influence on plant and food resources for humans and animals. In the coastal regions and along inland lakes, marshes and peat areas were created that spawned a rich habitat for fish, molluscs, shellfish, and water birds. These concentrated food supplies and the spread of deciduous oak forests attracted humans toward a more settled life. In the Mediterranean region rose the exploitation of legumes and fruits.

Not all animals and cereals were domesticated at one time nor in the same region. The dog had already been domesticated from the wolf in central Europe by the Magdalenian period of the Upper Paleolithic.[1] Sheep were domesticated in the hilly flanks of the Zagros Mountains (Iran, Iraq) and in the Taurus Mountains (Turkey) before 7000 B.C. where they had previously been hunted in the wild. Cattle and pigs followed between 7500 and 6500 B.C. in Anatolia and domestication continued locally in Europe from 6500 to 5500 B.C.[2] The domesticated horse was unknown to the Near East and east-central Europe before the end of the 5th millennium B.C.

There were three domesticated grains on which the early agriculture was based: einkorn wheat (Triticum monococcum), emmer wheat (triticum dicoccum), and two-row barley (Hordeum vulgare ssp. distichum). These were domesticated during the 8th and 7th millennia in settlements between southeast Europe and Afghanistan. To this day wild wheat, both einkorn and emmer, is found between Greece and Afghanistan, and wild barley still grows between the Aegean basin and Baluchistan.[3]

Settled village life was also a gradual development. The precursors of sedentary farmers lived as semisedentary food gatherers several millennia before agriculture developed, providing a transitional link between the Upper Paleolithic and the Neolithic. Such were the Natufians who lived in caves as well as in open air settlements along the eastern Mediterranean coast, 10,000–8,000 B.C.

Natufians were biologically modern human beings, similar to modern Mediterraneans,[4] who harvested and stored the plentiful wild wheat and barley. Numbers of mortars and stones for grinding grains and seeds, and many toothed sickle blades of flint were found in their settlements. There were also tools made of bone: awls, needles, spatulae, reaping knives, fishhooks, and harpoons—tools that for millennia to come would typify Neolithic inventories. Their animal sculptures of bone represent a continuity of Upper Paleolithic traditions, while dentalium shells used for beads, imported from the Mediterranean and Red Seas, indicate their navigational communication with distant areas. They hunted gazelle, deer, and pigs, and kept domesticated dogs but no other domesticated animals.

By 8000 B.C. cereals were fully domesticated in the eastern Mediterranean area, and the Natufian culture was followed in the east Mediterranean and Anatolia by Pre-Pottery Neolithic (food-producing culture without pottery). By 7000–6500 B.C., the Near East and southeast Europe were sharing a full agrarian complex wherein all communities were dependent upon a rich variety of cereals, legumes (peas and lentils), sheep, goats, pigs, and cattle. It was in this period that the production of ceramics was discovered. Because it is virtually indestructible, pottery remained the most abundantly recorded fossil throughout the Neolithic.

The Spread of Agriculture in Europe

Several Theories

"Revolution"

The hypothesis that a ready-made agricultural complex was imported to Europe from the Near East is no longer acceptable. It was fashionable, in the days of V. Gordon Childe, to consider the introduction of agriculture as a "revolution," but the Neolithization of Europe is now seen to have been much more complex. The process was long and not uniform, and was dependent upon various geographical and natural conditions.

A Biological Model of Diffusion

Another hypothesis also became partially obsolete due to intensive research of Mesolithic and Early Neolithic strata in the western Mediterranean zone. In 1936, geneticist R.A. Fisher proposed a biological model of diffusion which was promoted by the book of A. J. Ammerman and L. L. Cavalli-Sforza entitled, *The Neolithic Transition and the Genetics of Populations in Europe* (1984). Its thesis sought to explain the spread of agriculture as a diffusionary process brought about by population growth and displacement. This model proposed that it is not the idea of farming that spread, but the farmers themselves. The authors stated that if an increase in population coincides with a local migratory activity, a wave of population explosion will ensue, progressing at a constant radial rate that can be measured mathematically. The distance of the migratory activity is taken to be eighteen kilometers for each generation of twenty-five years, or one kilometer per year. Although this method is theoretically sound, especially when population increases are associated with migratory movements, it cannot be applied in practice to all parts of Europe. We must base our views, instead, on actual archeological data combined with radiocarbon dating.

The Conversion of Food Gatherers to Agriculture and the Spread of Migrating Farmers

The earliest signs in Europe of a transition from hunting-gathering to a food producing economy are found in the Mediterranean area. The process of Neolithization took place in two ways: through the conversion of local food gatherers to agriculture in the western and central Mediterranean region; and through the spread of agriculture with migrating farmers from southeast to northwest in southeastern and central Europe in combination with the conversion of local populations.

Western and Central Mediterranean Zone

Gradual Adoption of Domestication by the Mesolithic Population in Southern France and Spain

For a long time it was believed that the Neolithic of this region started with the spread of Cardial or Impresso pottery (pottery impressed with the edge of *cardium edule* shells, widely found in the central and western Mediterranean area) from the east Mediterranean. In the 1980s it became clear that the Neolithization of coastal regions of the western Mediterranean was accomplished by a gradual adoption of domestication by the local Mesolithic Castelnovian culture in eastern Spain and southern France. In addition, a rather specialized proto-agricultural exploitation of pulse crops and greens began in southern France some 10,000 years ago. The use of legumes including lamb's lettuce, lentils, peas, bitter vetch, grass peas, and chick peas is evidenced in several Mesolithic sites in Provence and Languedoc.[5] The presence of sheep and goats and the use of legumes and greens as well as the continuity of Upper Paleolithic industries indicate no major dichotomy between the hunter-gatherers and incipient agriculturalists. The excavation of stratified cave and rock-shelter sites, in combination with radiocarbon dating in eastern coastal Spain and southern France, has shown that this process took place during the 7th millennium B.C.

(see discussion in chap. 6). Many factors played a part in this process: the amelioration of climate, the increased sedentism of fishermen and shell gatherers, and the natural environment.

Evidence from Iberia and France has shown that the domestication of animals began considerably earlier than the cultivation of cereals and the use of pottery. Sheep and even pigs and cattle appear in aceramic strata in the early 7th millennium B.C., and perhaps earlier. Pottery and grains are well attested in the strata dated between 6500–6000 B.C. Lithic complexes in these Mesolithic, or more accurately proto-Neolithic, layers indicate a gradual continuity with no breaks. Thus, the sum of accumulated data suggests that the western Mediterranean Neolithic was the result of a development by means of self-contained cultural mechanisms.

Although gradual cultural development cannot be disputed, influences from the East cannot be denied. Domesticated sheep and goats that are found in Mesolithic strata do not have direct local predecessors. The sheep are related to the Near Eastern mouflon and the goats developed, not from the local *Capra ibex* or *Capra pyrenaica*, but from the Near Eastern *Capra aegagrus*. This leaves archeologists in the realm of hypothesis. It is for future research to establish when and how these species arrived. One guess is that the caprovines arrived through the central Mediterranean coastal regions from the Aegean area and not directly from the Near East. It is known that the navigators with early pottery and caprovines from the Aegean area reached the islands west of Greece (the island of Corfu; see chap. 5). In the west Mediterranean zone, caprovines never achieved the high economic importance that they had in the Near Eastern, Aegean, and in all of southeast European Neolithic.

The Gradual Adoption of Agriculture in the Circum-Adriatic and Central Mediterranean

The circum-Adriatic region was settled by the Upper Paleolithic and Mesolithic food gatherers whose lithic industries show no break of tradition up to the beginning of the Pottery ("Impresso") Neolithic.[6] The importation of agriculture from the Near East or even the Aegean area is here also quite unlikely. Corsica and Sardinia were settled by pre-Neolithic groups no later than during the 8th millennium B.C. (the earliest radiocarbon dates of Corsica are from Strette 9140 B.P. and from Araguina Sennola at Bonifacio, 8650 B.P.). There, the Neolithic culture with pottery is dated to the end of the 7th millennium B.C. Soon thereafter, Sardinian obsidian was discovered and traded widely, becoming a true catalyst for the communication between the western central Mediterranean and the Adriatic regions (see chap. 5).

Southeast Europe

A food producing economy was established in the Aegean basin before the middle of the 7th millennium B.C. We do not know yet to what extent the Neolithic economy was spread by new immigrants or if these ideas were passed on from Anatolia over a period of generations without large scale migrations. Were the Mesolithic populations absorbed? The evidence suggests that all of these factors may have contributed to some extent. It is generally true that by this time the predominant farm stock animals, sheep and goats, were already fully domesticated in the earliest southeastern European Neolithic sites. The exceedingly high ratio of domesticated animals to wild fauna in the earliest known Neolithic sites argues for an initial intrusion from outside Europe of both stock and peoples.

Unfortunately, the period prior to the Neolithic is poorly represented in the archeological record. The climatic warming which accompanied the postglacial period caused a rise in sea level which may have submerged many Mesolithic deposits on the Aegean islands and coastal regions. Mesolithic and Neolithic habitation layers have been found only at Franchthi, a cave in the Argolid region of the Peloponnese, although, even here, a continuity of culture is not clear. Skeletal material found in the cave reveals two possibilities: the early population is either from local Mesolithic stock or is of eastern origin.[7]

Heterogeneous Physical Type

The physical anthropological material from farther north, from the Nea Nikomedeia site in Greek Macedonia, is taxonomically heterogeneous. According to Angel, several types were present: the Dinaric-Mediterranean and the so-called Basic White type with Cro-Magnon characteristics. This variability is explained in terms of gradual intermixing, over the centuries, of the farming populations with hunter-gatherers. The heterogeneous physical type is also attested in the Starčevo culture in the central and northern Balkans (see chap. 2).

In the Iron Gate region of the Danube, cultural continuity is evidenced from the Upper Paleolithic and through the Mesolithic shown by the continuous local European Cro-Magnon population, lithic industries, religion, and art. This is called "the Balkan-Danubian Epigravettian and Mesolithic culture" or "Lepenski Vir culture" (Lepenski Vir is one of the fourteen other excavated sites famous for its shrines and sculptures to which we shall return in chaps. 2 and 7). A food producing economy appeared here only with the arrival of central Balkan (Starčevo) Neolithic people around 6000 B.C.[8] The robust Cro-Magnons in this region were either replaced by the gracile Mediterraneans coming from the south or progressively merged with the newcomers.[9]

Navigation and Trade—Decisive Catalysts for the Rise of Culture

Navigational skills, trade, and barter creating increased human contact seem to have been very important catalysts for the unprecedented rise of Neolithic culture. From the 8th millennium B.C., even before the Neolithic, there is evidence of trade in flint and obsidian.[10] With the beginning of a food producing economy, a constant growth of communication is indicated by imported obsidian, marble, colorful stones, and spondylus shells. Obsidian—volcanic glass formed from silica rich lava—was ideal for sickle blades and other cutting tools. It was, therefore, in great demand and is found hundreds of kilometers from the original source areas. The principal source of obsidian for the Aegean area and for all of Greece was the island of Melos in the southern Aegean.[11] The sources for the central Mediterranean, the circum-Adriatic, and inland western Yugoslavia were Sardinia (Monte Arci) and the Lipari volcano north of Sicily. The source for the Carpathian basin and the Danubian lowlands were the Carpathian Mountains in northeastern Hungary and northwestern Romania. Marble, used for bowls, dishes, ornaments, and figurines, was available from many sources, but the Paros and Skyros islands in the southern and northern Aegean may have been the main suppliers since Neolithic sites have been found there. Aegean spondylus shells were in demand for the manufacture of beads, pendants, and bracelets. These were diffused in large quantities from the Aegean Sea northward to Bulgaria and Romania and then along the Danube to central Europe.[12] Shells from the Adriatic spread to western Yugoslavia and to southeastern Italy.

A Full-fledged Neolithic Economy in Greece by 6500 B.C.

By 6500 B.C., coastal Greece and the nearby inland plains supported a full-fledged Neolithic economy that produced ceramics as well as domesticated sheep, goats, cattle, pigs, and dogs. A complete set of domestic fauna occurred here about five hundred years earlier than in southwest Asia. Wheat, barley, vetch, lentils, peas, and flax were cultivated. Emmer wheat, bread wheat, and sheep had presumably been imported from Anatolia, while cattle and pigs were domesticated independently in southeastern Europe. Agricultural tools included hoes of stone and antler, sickles of wood or bone set with obsidian, chert, or flint teeth (FIGURE 1–1), and grinding stones, mortars and pestles.

The spread of Neolithic technology into east-central Europe was relatively rapid after a Neolithic economy became established in the Aegean and the Mediterranean zone. The Mediterranean climate of that time was wetter than it is today, creating favorable conditions for agriculture.

The Spread of Agriculture from Southeast to Northwest

The advance of agriculture in Europe as shown on the map (FIGURE 1–2) indicates that seaways were crucial for the accelerated diffusion of Neolithic ideas. Navigation across the Aegean and Adriatic Seas and along the Mediterranean coasts was not difficult. The trade in obsidian and shells testifies to this. Inland, communication was slower. It took about 500 years for agriculture to spread from the Aegean to the Danube, and another 500 years from the Middle Danube basin to eastern France and Holland. Northern Europe between Denmark and Lithuania was converted to agriculture only around 4000–3500 B.C.

Neolithic Towns in Anatolia (Turkey)

The earliest Neolithic culture in southeast Europe is tightly bound with that of Anatolia. Settlements in both areas have yielded similar tools, jewelry, statuary, and a related temple-building tradition with the same deities worshiped using the same symbolic language. In Anatolia, as in the east Mediterranean area, the developmental stages from the semi-sedentary Natufian to the Pre-Pottery Neolithic are well recorded, whereas we lack this information for southeast Europe. Although contact between Greece and Turkey must have started during the Pre-Pottery period, around 7000 B.C. or before, western Turkey is little explored and the direct points of contact are not as yet known. The most important Neolithic settlements are in

FIGURE 1–1

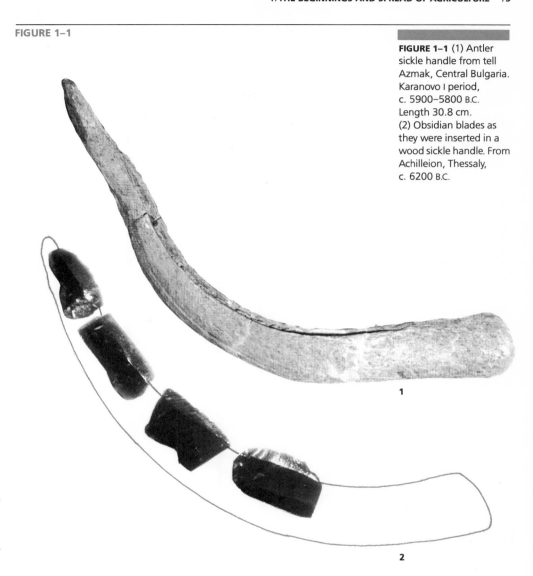

1

2

FIGURE 1–1 (1) Antler sickle handle from tell Azmak, Central Bulgaria. Karanovo I period, c. 5900–5800 B.C. Length 30.8 cm. (2) Obsidian blades as they were inserted in a wood sickle handle. From Achilleion, Thessaly, c. 6200 B.C.

FIGURE 1–2

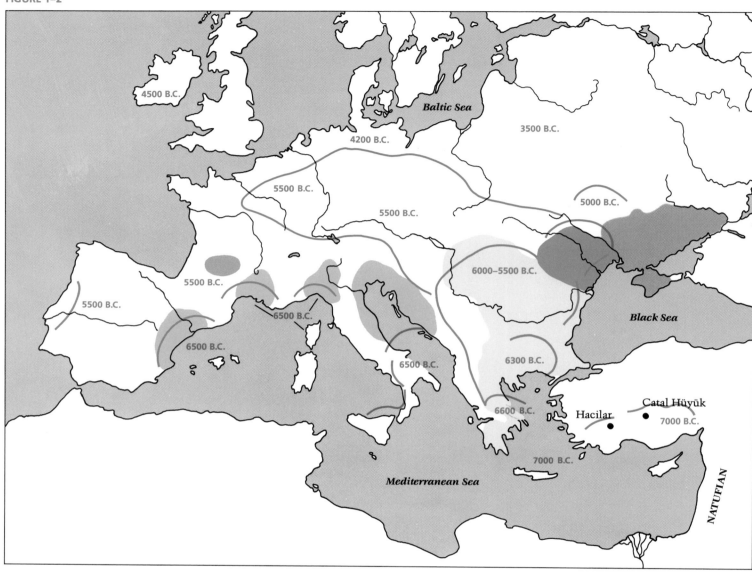

KEY

Upper Mesolithic

Castelnovian Mesolithic with
incipient animal domestication

Mesolithic (Pre-Roucadur) of
central France

Dniester-Bug (Grebeniki)

Kukrek and Crimean Murzak Koba

Neolithic

5500 B.C. Dates marking
spread of agriculture

Extent of Neolithic
with pottery

FIGURE 1–2 Spread of farming in Europe. Dates shown (based on radio-carbon and dendro-chronology) are for full-fledged Neolithic with pottery. In the western Mediterranean zone animal domestication began about a millennium before the transition to fully developed agriculture. In southeastern Europe, the Neolithic started with a full-fledged agricultural complex (with cereals and all domesticated animals except the horse).

central Anatolia, 300 to 600 km from the Aegean Sea. In spite of the distance inland, it is clear that there is a general similarity of culture.

The earliest towns of Anatolia developed an amazingly high cultural level as seen in the two most important: Çatal Hüyük, dating from the end of the 8th to the end of the 7th millennium B.C., and Hacilar, from the end of the 7th to the early 6th millennia B.C.

Çatal Hüyük

The excavation of the 7th millennium B.C. town of Çatal Hüyük by James Mellaart in 1961–63 and 1965 has revolutionized our views on the prehistory of Anatolia and the entire Old World.[13]

Çatal Hüyük consists of two riverside mounds situated on a dry plateau 1000 meters above sea level on the Konya plain in south-central Turkey. The larger mound occupies about 32 acres (16 hectares), one acre of which was excavated. The breathtaking discovery of thirteen building levels with houses, temples, murals, reliefs, sculptures, trade items, and other finds was an eye-opener to the level of Neolithic culture that existed in the 7th millennium B.C. The close cultural similarity of the southeast European Neolithic with that of Anatolia makes it indispensable to look first at Çatal Hüyük, a monument of concentrated information that sheds light on many aspects of Neolithic life: economy, trade, architecture, house and temple furnishings, religion, and art.

The Konya plain was an especially rich part of the Old World, one that abounded in wild cereal grasses and domesticable animals. The town that developed there and continued for more than a thousand years is dated in calibrated chronology to c. 7250–6150 B.C. (in uncalibrated chronology, 6500–5750 b.c.; the latter dates were used in books and articles published by Mellaart and other authors before 1989). Çatal Hüyük did not emerge out of a vacuum. Below it was another mound with twelve levels of an aceramic culture. The bottom levels belonged to the Pre-Pottery Neolithic and Late Natufian which yielded materials related to cultures in Syria and Palestine. The Pre-Pottery Neolithic A level contained a temple model, figurines, loom weights, limestone plaquettes with a rich decoration, and fragments of polychrome wall painting. The late Natufian (bottom level) included wooden plaques with designs, shale plaques, geometric microliths, and other finds.[14] These preceding levels at Çatal Hüyük express the long development of a single culture from the 10th to the 8th millennia B.C. During these early millennia, experiments in local domestication of cereals and animals, especially aurochs, must have been made. The inventive spirit of these early people is reflected by a variety of designs on plaques and the polychrome painting of walls. Religious objects, models of temples, and figurines found here continue throughout the whole Neolithic sequence.

Çatal Hüyük was an orderly settlement that reflects a remarkable stability of social organization throughout many hundreds of years. It is the largest town of the Early Neolithic period in the whole of the Old World, and it is estimated that up to 7,000 inhabitants could have lived there at one time. (The famous Jericho in the Jordan valley, as it is now estimated, could have housed no more than 400–900 inhabitants).[15]

The houses of Çatal Hüyük were densely grouped; many were built against existing structures and open courtyards occurred randomly. (FIGURE 1–3) Houses were timber framed and built of mud brick with flat roofs. There were no doors, and people entered their homes through openings in the roof. Lack of debris or remains of meals inside these houses suggest that the occupants kept their houses scrupulously clean. Interiors were sparsely furnished and raised mud platforms served as seats and beds. From the size of the houses, some 25 square meters, and the number of beds, Mellaart guessed that none of the excavated houses could have accommodated more than eight persons. Kitchens occupied about a third of a house's total floor space and ovens were set low in the walls. Storage rooms contained plaited baskets for grain, tools, and other supplies.

FIGURE 1–3

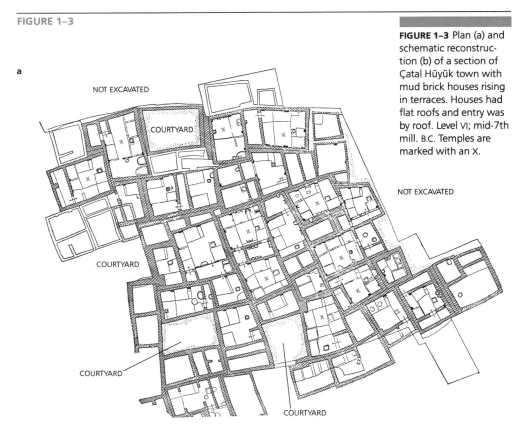

a

NOT EXCAVATED

COURTYARD

NOT EXCAVATED

COURTYARD

COURTYARD

COURTYARD

FIGURE 1–3 Plan (a) and schematic reconstruction (b) of a section of Çatal Hüyük town with mud brick houses rising in terraces. Houses had flat roofs and entry was by roof. Level VI; mid-7th mill. B.C. Temples are marked with an X.

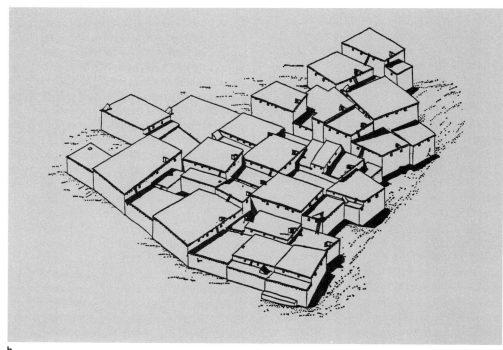

b

The townsfolk cultivated three types of wheat and one of barley, and grew or gathered a wide range of green and root vegetables and fruits. While cattle provided them with most of their meat supply and with dairy products, they also kept goats and hunted deer and wild pigs.

Throughout the existence of the town there was a continuous trading activity in obsidian and flint. Obsidian was obtained from Hasan Dag volcano and other places in central Anatolia. This volcanic glass was used not only for cutting tools, but also for mirrors which they were able to polish without any scratches. Calcite and alabaster (used for jewlery and figurines) probably came from the Kayseri region, and fine white marble from western Anatolia. The western hills beyond Konya, rich in brightly colored iron oxides, may have provided a number of pigments for painting. The copper ores, hematite, limonite, manganese, galena, and lignite were probably from the Taurus Mountains. Shells were imported from the Mediterranean Sea, while rock crystal, carnelian, jasper, chalcedony, and other rocks used for beads whose sources are not clearly known were very likely imported from distant places. Trade must have contributed appreciably to the wealth and prosperity of Çatal Hüyük, and industries flourished with specialized workers in obsidian carving, metallurgy, weaving, wood carving, and other disciplines. Many artifacts display the highest standard of craftsmanship.

It is clearly evident that the practice of religion was integrated into people's daily lives. Temples were found within the area of habitation in houses similar to those in which people lived. From 300 excavated rooms, 88 had painted walls. Each painting was from 12 to 18 m long. (Sketched reconstructions of many of these were published by James Mellaart in *The Goddess of Anatolia*, vol. 1, 1989.) The eastern and northern walls in which platforms were found were painted above with ingenuity and an amazing diversity of designs. These were emphasized with plaster reliefs and bucrania (bull heads or skulls).

The colors used were yellow and brown ochres (from iron oxides), bright blues and greens (from copper ore), deep and bright reds (from mercury oxide and hematite), mauves and purples (from manganese), and lead gray (from galena). Mica dust was used to provide the pigments with a glitter effect. Mellaart observed that these wall paintings had a ritual function and that when a painting had served its purpose, it was covered over with a layer of white plaster. Later, as the need arose, a new picture would be painted on the clean background.

The main theme of these wall paintings and reliefs revolves around the Goddess of Regeneration portrayed as a frog-shaped woman giving birth. She is associated with animals, and around her are both the vulture, representing the death aspect, and the bull head, representing regeneration. There is also a myriad of accompanying symbols rhythmically lined out along the edges, framing the panels. Most of these symbols are abstracted representations of horns, triangles, rhombs or double triangles, or hourglass shapes and butterflies. Symbols are duplicated, triplicated, multiplied, juxtaposed, shown in reverse, and in positive and negative designs. The variety of these combinations of motifs is virtually endless. In addition, there are also some half-naturalistic portrayals of deer hunts, women carrying fish nets, mountains, plants, and water with fish. (We shall return to the temples of Çatal Hüyük in chap. 7; see plates 38 and 39 for examples of wall paintings; for temples with vultures, see fig. 7–26; for bull heads and horns see figs. 7–51, 7–52).

The dead were buried under platforms in the houses after their skeletons had been excarnated (stripped of flesh and internal organs through exposure to birds, probably in open-sided towers). Burials of women painted with ochre were found under the floors of temples and under wall paintings. The rich burial of a woman interred with three tusked lower jaws of wild boars arranged around her head, was found under the largest temple (in E VII, 14). The largest painting which it contained portrayed a town

(presumably Çatal Hüyük itself) with a volcano erupting behind it. The size of both the temple and the wall painting, as well as the unusual symbolic grave items, suggests that this woman had a respected position in the society, perhaps as a queen-priestess. The prominence of older women or girls is similarly distinctive in European burials found under the floors, near the house, under long earthen mounds, or in cemeteries, as discussed in chapter 9. There are no male graves with such extraordinary symbolic items.

The physical anthropological study of nearly 300 skeletons found at Çatal Hüyük as yet is not completed. The preliminary reports divide the peoples into long-headed Eurafricans (54.2 percent), long-headed proto-Mediterraneans (16.9 percent), and short-headed (Brachycephalic) Alpines (22.9 percent). The most numerous group resembles Upper Paleolithic Combe Capelle humans from southern France, described as the Mediterranean version of Cro-Magnon. The point to be emphasized, as Mellaart has remarked, is that the bulk of the population was still close to its Upper Paleolithic ancestry.

Hacilar and After

Hacilar, located 220 km west of Çatal Hüyük, also excavated by Mellaart, was a smaller town of about 50 houses.[16] Its beginning is contemporaneous with the end of Çatal Hüyük and it continued throughout the first half of the 6th millennium B.C. It is contemporary with the rising Neolithic culture in southeastern Europe—Sesklo, Starčevo, and Karanovo groups—while having its own style of pottery and sculptural art.

After Hacilar, Anatolian Neolithic is not well known, whereas the culture of southeastern Europe flourished and reached its climax between 5500 and 4500 B.C. The two areas diverged and local cultural entities were formed in different ecological and geographical zones. In the next chapter we shall describe these areas in some detail beginning with the Aegean area and the Balkans and ending with central Europe.

As it is seen from the temples with their wall paintings and statuary, the Anatolian Neolithic was a Goddess civilization characterized by the dominance of the worship of the Goddess imbued with mysterious generative power, the importance of temples that functioned as social foci and catalysts for creativity in arts and religious expression, and by the balanced matrilineal social structure. From around 6500 B.C., the same features of culture are found in southeastern Europe and later in most of Europe up to the time of the demise of this civilization, between 4500 and 2500 B.C. However, in the Mediterranean islands such as Crete and Thera this civilization flourished until the middle of the 2nd millennium B.C.

Even if we admit the presence of Anatolian influence on southeast Europe during the 7th millennium B.C., we cannot see it as a transplantation like a tree at a certain time, rather this influence affected the European continent as a gradual flow of a river. Furthermore, we cannot equate this matristic and art-loving civilization with a proto-Indo-European culture (a cradle of Indo-European speakers) which is reconstructed by means of comparative Indo-European linguistics and mythology as a patriarchal, patrilineal, warlike, mobile (horse-riding) culture, and having a pantheon of dominant male gods. This equation, as proposed by Colin Renfrew in 1987,[17] is based on a misconception of cultural structures and goes against the evidence of Indo-European studies.

2

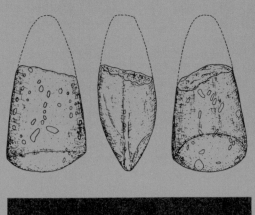

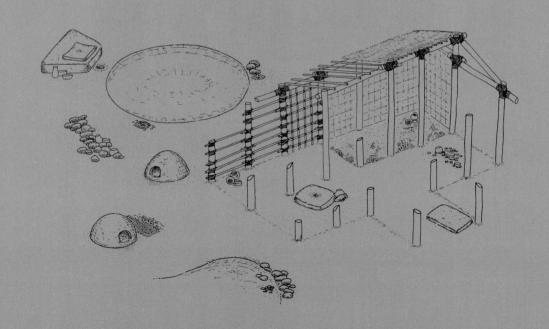

Neolithic Cultures
of Southeastern and
Central Europe

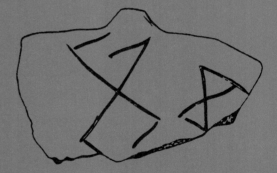

Southeastern and central Europe contains the most outstanding Neolithic cultures of Europe. While many traditions are shared with Anatolia and the East Mediterranean, these cultures are remarkable for their own creativity in art and architecture, and for their ability to explore and adapt to a variety of environmental conditions.

There is a strong cultural interrelationship between the Aegean area (Greece) and Anatolia (Turkey). A strong connection also exists between the southeast and the Danubian plain, and with the region north and west of it. The stream of agriculturation moved up from the southeast to northwest, branching off to the east and west. It flowed like a river, following fertile lands and stopping at or avoiding the mountains. This flow was in stages: It first covered the coastal regions and plains of the Aegean and southern Balkans, c. 6500 B.C.; it spread next along the Lower and Middle Danube plain, c. 6000 B.C.; reaching the Upper Danube and the river valleys north of it, c. 5500 B.C.

The Southeast and Central European Neolithic is known from hundreds of excavated sites—unlike the Anatolian, which is known from only several. It is therefore possible to speak of the distribution of culture groups and to pursue the development of their individual features throughout a millennium or more. It is a true blessing and challenge to the students of European prehistory to explore this great variety of cultural material instead of the monotony of uniformity.

Within this diversity was an expression of the way of life, the belief system, rituals, symbols, and the social structure which was more or less the same during this period between the Aegean and Central Europe. The interrelationship between the various culture groups within this territory is the result of a gradual influx of peoples from the south and their influence on and intermixing with local hunter-fishers who survived in such areas as the Upper Tisza basin, the Iron Gate region, and the Dniester-Bug basins.

Six groups will be introduced, starting with the Aegean area in the south and ending with the Dniester Bug basins in Moldavia and the Ukraine.

1. The Sesklo culture in northern Greece with the fertile region of Thessaly as its bread basket. Excavations began here in the very beginning of the 20th century and continued throughout the second half of this century.

2. The Starčevo (Körös, Criş) culture, distributed over the continental Yugoslavia, southeast Hungary and southern Romania. This culture is still vaguely researched, although information from excavations has markedly increased during the last three decades.

3. The Karanovo culture in central Bulgaria, much related to the Starčevo, discovered in the late fifties and sixties through the intensive excavation of large tells (mounds).

4. The Linearbandkeramik (LBK) culture of central Europe, between France and Romania. This is the most widely distributed culture, which has also been the best explored throughout our century by teams of archeologists from France, Holland, Germany, Czechoslovakia, Poland, and Romania.

5. The Bükk culture in the Upper Tisza basin (northeast Hungary and eastern Slovakia), known by its sacred caves in the Carpathians, from as early as 1876, and from further explorations and publication in the twenties as well as from work in recent decades.

6. The Dniester-Bug culture in the black soil region, discovered in the fifties and sixties. In this area, the domestication of cattle and pigs and the grinding of wild seeds seem to have started independently from the main stream of agriculturation in southeast Europe, before influences from the Starčevo-Criş culture appeared.

FIGURE 2–1 Tells (mounds of habitation debris) from Thessaly. (1) Argisa tell, west of Larisa, Thessaly, with an accumulation of over 12 m of Neolithic and Early Bronze Age debris. (2) Profile of the Sesklo tell, c. 12 m of cultural deposits, with Early Neolithic (Early Ceramic) at the base and classical Sesklo on the top, c. 65th–57th cents. B.C. Sesklo is 14 km west of Volos, Thessaly, N Greece.

The Aegean Neolithic: The Sesklo Culture of Northern Greece

The Thessalian and Macedonian plains are Greece's richest agricultural lands. In modern times as well as for thousands of years these plains have served as the bread baskets of Greece. The large Thessalian Plain is drained by the Penneos River and the Macedonian by the Aliakmon River. Their many tributaries flow down from the mountains before merging and flowing out into the Aegean Sea. The earliest Neolithic settlements were founded on natural elevations near a water source—river or stream. This area is within the Mediterranean climatic zone with dry hot summers and cold wet winters. Eighty-five hundred years ago the climate was moister, with lush vegetation; the river valleys were covered with oak and pistachio groves.

Tells—Mounds of Settlement Debris

The plains of northern Greece are dotted with mounds called *tells*, "magulas" in Greek, which are mound-shaped layers of settlement debris from the Neolithic and Early Bronze Age. Going west from the Bay of Volos and across the plain between the modern towns of Karditsa, Trikala, and Larisa, one can easily count hundreds of them, standing five to fifteen meters high. (FIGURE 2–1) These mounds hold the secrets of people who lived there for many centuries between 8500 and 4500 years ago. Mudbrick and layers of clay daub used for house walls crumbled in time and new houses were built over the old ones causing the tells to grow higher, layer by layer.

These human-made hills are mysterious and archeologists are often intrigued by a desire to unravel their secrets. I was one of them. This irresistible fascination let to the excavation in 1973–74 of one of the early Neolithic tells on the southern edge of the Thessalian Plain. This site, Achilleion, near Farsala, proved to be the key for understanding the chronology, architecture, pottery evolution, and religion of the Neolithic Aegean.[1]

FIGURE 2–1

1

2

FIGURE 2-2

FIGURE 2–2 Distribution of major Early and Middle Neolithic sites in Greece, c. 6500–5500 B.C.

KEY

⌐‿⌐ Large plain of Thessaly

Chronology

From the hundreds of well-preserved tells, only about thirty have been professionally excavated in this century. The first systematic exploration began in 1901 when Chrestos Tsountas launched his extensive investigation of the mound of Sesklo.[2] The name of that site was subsequently given to the culture of Neolithic settlements throughout Thessaly and southern Macedonia. The Early Neolithic of southern Greece, the Peloponnese, and the Aegean Islands is related to the Sesklo of Thessaly and should be regarded as part of that culture. (FIGURE 2–2) In Tsountas' time, the Sesklo culture was believed to have begun about 3000 B.C. Radiocarbon dates now verify the earliest stages with pottery, domestic animals, and cultivation of wheat, barley, lentils, and peas at 6500 B.C. or somewhat earlier.

The stratigraphy of the Achilleion mound in central Thessaly and the forty-two radiocarbon dated samples from this mound have served to determine a chronology of the Sesklo culture with greater accuracy. The gradual succession from one cultural phase to the next is observable from the time habitation began in Achilleion, 6500–6400 B.C. until 5600 B.C.

Only a few of the other excavated sites have been dated by the radiocarbon method. Of these, Sesklo in Thessaly, Elateia in Phocis[3], Nea Nikomedeia in Greek western Macedonia[4], Argisa[5], and the Franchthi Cave in the Peloponnese[6] have yielded more than one date of similar age. (TABLE 1) Early Sesklo corresponds to Early Neolithic (6500–6000 B.C.)[7] and Classical Sesklo to Middle Neolithic (6000–5500 B.C.). Its climax was reached by 6000 B.C.

During the first half of the 7th millennium B.C. there probably existed a prepottery stage, as yet vaguely documented in Thessaly, but evidenced in the Peloponnese by the Franchthi cave, in Crete at Knossos, and on the island of Kythnos.

Architecture

In the Sesklo culture people built their villages of separate houses, a marked departure from settlement patterns of the Near East where communities are clusters of interconnected dwellings with common walls. Sesklo sites of the Middle Neolithic were ringed on the landward side by V-shaped ditches probably for protection against wild animals.

In every phase of Achilleion there is evidence of house building, and the fluctuation of climate from cooler and damper (6500–6000 B.C.) to warmer (6000–5500 B.C.) was reflected in its architecture. The earliest buildings were pit houses in the mid-7th millennium B.C. which were replaced with rectangular houses with pisé walls around 6300 B.C. Timber post houses appeared around 6200 (FIGURE 2–3), and between 6100–6000 there were timber post houses up to six meters long with wattle and daub walls. In the period between 6000–5600 solid rectangular houses of mudbrick were built on stone foundations. (FIGURE 2–4)

FIGURE 2–3

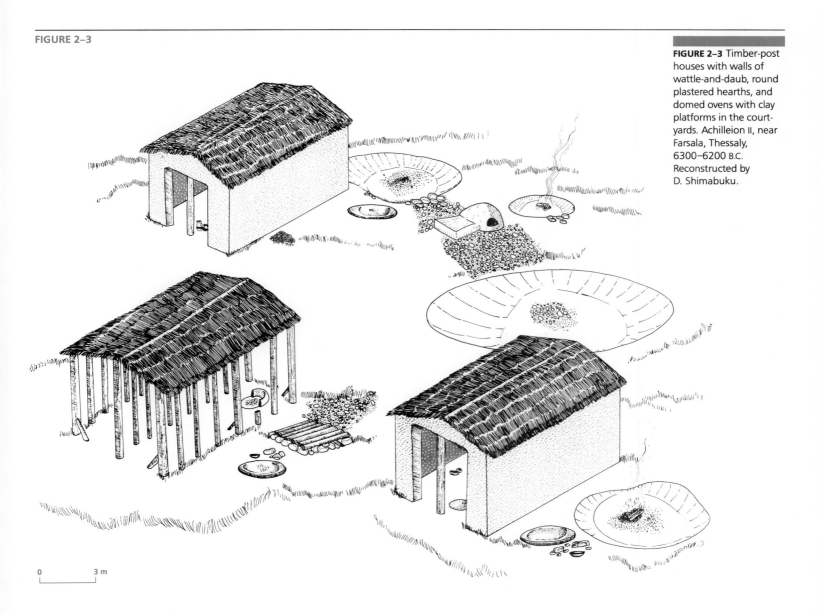

0   3 m

FIGURE 2–3 Timber-post houses with walls of wattle-and-daub, round plastered hearths, and domed ovens with clay platforms in the courtyards. Achilleion II, near Farsala, Thessaly, 6300–6200 B.C. Reconstructed by D. Shimabuku.

FIGURE 2–4

FIGURE 2–4 Stone foundations of Sesklo houses in Thessaly from 5900–5700 B.C., as they can be seen today.

FIGURE 2–5 (1) Artist's reconstuction of the classical Sesklo village. Some 30 houses are surrounded by stone retaining walls including internal stone walls. Based on Tsountas's excavation, 1901. (2) The rest of the settlement extends over adjacent slopes, covering 20–25 acres. 5900–5700 B.C.

FIGURE 2–5

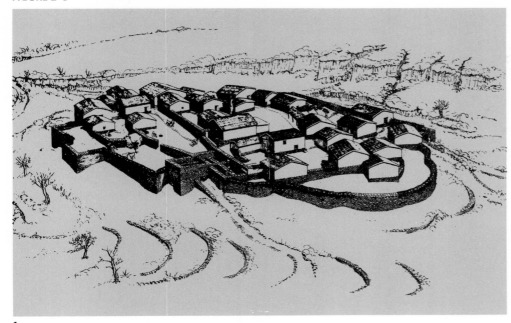

1

2

The settlement of thirty or more houses at Sesklo, on the central knoll, apart from the scattered settlement on adjacent hill slopes, was surrounded by retaining walls of stone (see artist's reconstruction based on Tsountas's excavation, fig. 2-5). Demetrios Theocharis, who continued excavations at Sesklo between 1958 and 1976 has estimated that the entire settlement covered an area of 20 to 25 acres.[8] (For further discussion of Sesklo, see chap. 9.)

The most common houses had only one room, whereas two-room houses, as clarified by excavations at Achilleion, were temples consisting of a temple proper in one room and a workshop in the other (see fig. 7–46). Some houses had two stories or an attic supported by buttresses. Pitched roofs are indicated by miniature temple models of clay. Domed ovens were in the courtyards and had either a rectangular bench attached at one side or a large circular platform in front. (FIGURES 2–6, 1) Figurines of the pregnant-goddess type were found near the ovens or on these platforms (see figs. 7–48 and 7–49), and grinding stones, grain, stone and bone tools, and pots were found nearby. Food preparation and other work was done here, which may account for the conspicuous absence of rubbish on house floors and a tidiness remarkable for this period.

FIGURE 2–6

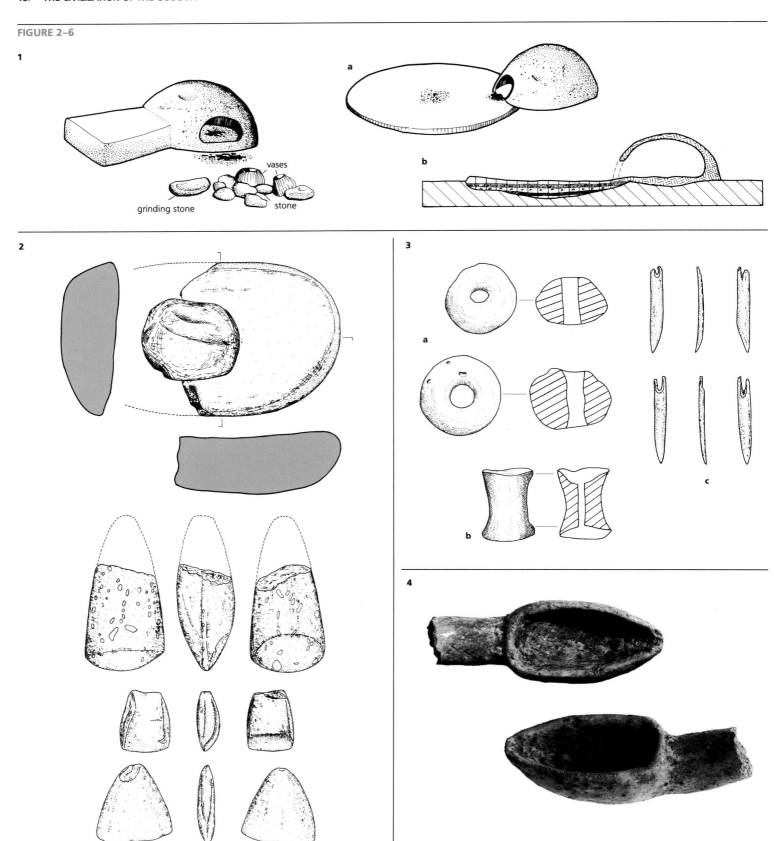

vases

grinding stone

stone

FIGURE 2-6 (1) Domed ovens with a bench or circular platform in courtyards of Sesklo villages. Vases, hand milling stones, pestles, and pounders were found nearby. (a) Achilleion II, c. 6300–6200 B.C., (b) Achilleion IVa, 5900– 5800 B.C. The cross-section shows several layers of plastering interspersed with layers of black earth.

(2) Hand-milling stones and axes used for woodworking from Achilleion IV, Thessaly, c. 5900– 5800 B.C. Small axes were produced of greenstone. Triangular miniature axes were frequently never used and seem to have served as symbols, but their butts display damage, probably from hafting.

(3) Tools used for the textile industry. (a) Clay spindle whorls. (b) Clay spools. (c) Bone needles. (a) and (b), Achilleion III, c. 6100– 5900 B.C.; (c) Achilleion II, c. 6200 B.C.

(4) Clay spoon from Achilleion Ib, c. 6300 B.C.

Economy

Throughout its duration, the Sesklo culture was sustained by a stable economy based on the cultivation of wheat (emmer, einkorn, and club wheat), barley, millet, lentils, vetch, and peas.[9] The earliest levels are characterized by a mixed crop which was a form of subsistence agriculture ensuring that some return was obtained from the land whatever the climate or soil conditions. These annual crops were cultivated to provide a storable surplus of large edible seeds which could supply starch, protein, and vegetable oils for the community throughout the year. The fertility of the soil was replenished by intentionally introducing pulse crops with the cereals which activated nitrogen fixed in the root nodules, thus replacing what was leached from the soil during rainy periods.

At first, sheep and goats were the most numerous domesticated animals, followed by cattle and pigs. The ratio of caprovines gradually declined—from 82 percent at Achilleion I (middle of the 7th millennium B.C.) to 70.6 percent in Phase IV (early 6th millennium B.C.)— as the importance of cattle and pigs correspondingly rose.[10] This change indicates an increasing reliance of animal husbandry on local resources. There were domesticable wild forms of cattle and pigs in Greece, and the occurrence of transitional forms in occupation deposits is indicative of a small-scale practice of local domestication. The climate, damper than at present, produced oak groves and forested mountains sheltering roe, red and fallow deer, aurochs, wild swine, red fox, hare, wild cat, badger, and ibex. Nevertheless, hunting seems to have been minimal, as only three to six percent of animal bones identified at Achilleion and other sites are those of wild animals. Seasonal fruits, acorns, nuts, and berries added variety to the diet. The harvesting and grinding of grass crops is indicated by large quantities of obsidian and chert sickle blades, hand-milling stones, pestles, and pounders. (FIGURE 2–6, 1) Chisels, axes, and adzes speak for woodworking (FIGURE 2–6, 2) while spools,

spindle whorls, loom weights, awls, and very fine bone needles with pierced eyes indicate textile production. (FIGURE 2–6, 3) A variety of clay ladles and spoons have been found (FIGURE 2–6, 4) as well as fishhooks and harpoon points of bone.

Among the products of Early Neolithic craftsmen are marble, porphyry, or greenstone vases and dishes; tiny pendants, beads, and figurines of finely worked blackstone, greenstone, marble, or alabaster; and alabaster and clay seals incised with meanders, spirals, triangles, and zig-zags. A seal or gaming board of alabaster with a meandroid design from Achilleion is a good example of their exquisite craftmanship. (PLATE 2)

Pottery

Pottery is the most conspicuous industry, richly represented in each phase starting with the middle of the 7th millennium B.C. Gradually changing shapes and technology are very helpful for the establishment of chronological phases. The painting of symbols on pottery occurred simultaneously with, or shortly after, the inception of ceramics. By 6400–6300 B.C., several motifs—triangles, zig-zags, chevrons, and net patterns—are recognizably dominant. (FIGURE 2–7; PLATE 3)

FIGURE 2-7

FIGURE 2-8

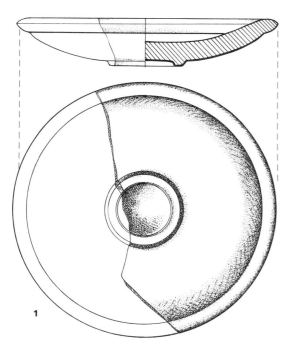

1

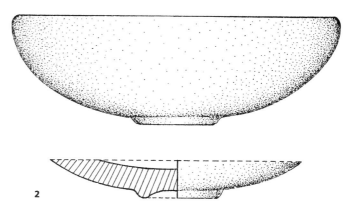

2

FIGURE 2-7 Earliest painted pottery (red on white-slipped background) from Sesklo Ib, c. 6400–6300 B.C. from Argisa, Otzaki, and Sesklo, Thessaly.

FIGURE 2-8 Early pottery shapes imitated stone vessel forms. (1) Greenstone dish and (2) pottery dish, Achilleion Ia, c. 6400 B.C.

FIGURE 2-9 Developmental stages of pottery from the earliest phase, c. 6500–6400 B.C. to the classical Sesklo period, c. 5800–5700 B.C., based on excavation and chronology of Achilleion near Farsala, Thessaly. Phase Ib and II, outflaring rims, small knobs, and pierced lug handles appear. Phase III and IV, a wide assortment of wares in red, brown, and black clays, some very thin walled and well fired. A high percentage exhibit a fine white kaolin slip beneath designs painted in contrasting shades of red iron oxides.

FIGURE 2-10 Red on white painted Sesklo vases from Achilleion with magnificent "flame" designs, c. 6100–5900 B.C. Achilleion, IIIb–IVa, southern Thessaly.

The rounded shapes and ringed bases of the earliest pottery jars and dishes are clearly in imitation of stone vessels that continued to be produced in the Early Pottery period. (FIGURE 2–8) Changes in pottery reflect a progressive technological development from simply shaped globular or semiglobular burnished pots with a blunt lip, some with a ring base, in Early Neolithic I, to a wide assortment of wares in red, brown, and black clays, some very thin walled and well fired, from the Middle Neolithic (Classical Sesklo). (FIGURE 2–9) A high percentage of this later pottery exhibits a fine white kaolin slip beneath designs painted in contrasting shades of red iron oxides. Banded "flames," triangles, zigzags, lozenges, and steps characterize the celebrated Sesklo Style of painted pottery. (FIGURE 2–10; PLATE 4). Ornithomorphic (bird-shaped) and anthropomorphic vases were produced. Goddess masks are frequently found attached to the necks of ritual vases. (PLATE 5)

FIGURE 2–9

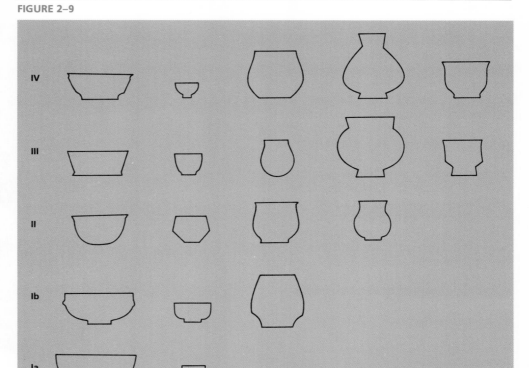

FIGURE 2–10

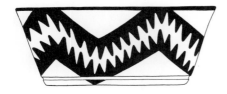

Sculptural Art

The tradition of modeling or carving figurines was inherited from the Upper Paleolithic. In the Aegean area, as in the Near East, their manufacture precedes that of pottery. Clay figurines are known, for instance, from the pre-pottery site at Knossos, Crete. Clay, marble, alabaster, greenstone, and black-stone figurines are documented from the very beginning of the Sesklo series and are evidenced in every phase. In later Sesklo phases about 90 percent of the total number are of clay over pebbles or over cylindrical or round clay cores, while the number of stone figurines decreases. The miniature figurines, some two to six centimeters high, are better preserved than the larger sculptures which are usually found fragmented. At Achilleion, in an excavated area little more than 100 square meters, more than 200 clay figurines came to light. One hundred thirty-two were found within temples, ninety-nine were in the court-yard near a dais or oven, and others were found discarded in pits. It is safe to say that the majority of figurines were kept in groups on altars within temples and in courtyards on a dais and at the bread oven. Almost always they were found in association with fine ware, offering containers, lamps, ladles, and handled seals. This site has revealed that certain types of female figurines (Bird Goddess, Snake Goddess, Nurse) were temple or house goddesses. Others, such as the Pregnant Goddess, were wor-shiped in the courtyard at specially pre-pared platforms, with offering pits near the bread ovens (see figs. 7–46 to 7–49). From the two hundred figurines found at Achilleion, only two fragmented ones were representing a male god, seated on a stool with hands on knees.

Sculptural art was abstract and sym-bolic, produced for religious purposes for the reenactment of seasonal and other rituals, as protective house deities or ancestresses, and as *ex votos*. Although the Sesklo artists did not seem inter-ested in portraying the human body in naturalistic detail, their masterful abil-ity to do so is nevertheless expressed in certain pieces. (FIGURES 2–11, 2–12; PLATE 1)

FIGURE 2–11

1

2

FIGURE 2–11 Seated female figures of clay from the classical Sesklo culture, highly burnished and cream slipped. c. 5800–5600 B.C. (1) Nicea near Larisa. H 5.7 cm. (2) Farsala, S Thessaly. H 7 cm.

FIGURE 2-12

1   2

FIGURE 2-13

FIGURE 2-12 (1) Head (mask) of a large sculpture in clay. Soufli tell at Larisa; early 6th mill. B.C. H. 8 cm. (2) Masked head with an open mouth that served as a spout for a large libation vase. Achilleion, c. 5800 B.C. H 6 cm. Found in temple.

FIGURE 2-13 Dimini vase from Rakhmani, Thessaly. Spirals sweep across a striated background, with a chevron on the handle; painted dark brown on cream. Mid-5th mill. B.C.

Continuity into the Late Neolithic

The Sesklo culture continued into the Late Neolithic and is called Dimini in the 5th millennium B.C. In contrast to the Danubian basin, very few copper and gold items have been found in Greece. The name Dimini derives from the eponymous settlement, four kilometers west of Volos in Thessaly, excavated in the beginning of this century.[11]

Dimini materials, characterized by painted and black wares (FIGURE 2-13), have been recovered in a series of stratified tells in Thessaly overlying Neolithic deposits. Outstanding are the Argisa, Otzaki, Arapi, Soufli, Zarkou, and Rakhmani tells in the area of Larisa.[12] The Dimini period is a long-lasting, continuous cultural development, placed within 5500-4000 B.C., represented by phases I-VII.[13]

In Attica, the excavations of the cave of Kitsos[14] yielded a series of radiocarbon dates which place the incised and matt-painted pottery, obsidian tools, and other finds into the 46th and 42nd centuries B.C. (TABLE 1)

The Cycladic Islands seem to have continued their own Neolithic culture. The excavation at Saliagos near Antiparos (a small island at Paros)[15] in the southern part of the Aegean has revealed a settlement with stone walls and a bastionlike structure. The radiocarbon dates obtained from shells date the Saliagos finds between 5200-4600 B.C. (TABLE 1) The Kephala site on the island of Kea, with analogies in Attica and in the Peloponnese, is placed at the very end of the Aegean Neolithic.[16] Its rhyton and marble vessels resemble those of the Cycladic Early Bronze Age.

FIGURE 2–14

FIGURE 2–14 Neolithic culture groups in the Balkan Peninsula and in east-central Europe, 6300–5300 B.C.

KEY

Starčevo (Körös-Criş) sites

1. Anza, central Macedonia, SE Yugoslavia; stratified settlement with three layers below the Early Vinča stratum.
2. Circea, Lower Danube, SW Romania, settlement.
3. Dévaványa, Körös group, Hungary, settlement.
4. Divostin near Kraguevac, central Yugoslavia. Settlement with Starčevo and Late Vinča deposits.
5. Endröd-Szújósketeszt, district of Békés, E Hungary. Settlement, Körös group.
6. Galabnik, upper Struma, W Bulgaria. Settlement of the Struma group.
7. Gradešnica, near Vraca, NW Bulgaria, settlement with Starčevo and Vinča deposits.
8. Gura Baciului, Transylvania, NW Romania, settlement.
9. Kopancs, settlement of the Körös group, SE Hungary.
10. Kotacpart-Vatatanya, settlement of the Körös group, SE Hungary.
11. Leţ, upper Olt, N Romania, stratified settlement.
12. Obre I, NW of Sarajevo, Bosnia. Late Starčevo (Kakanj) stratified settlement followed by Butmir settlement in nearby Obre II.
13. Perieni on R. Prut, NE Romania, settlement.
14. Porodin near Bitolj, Pelagonia, S Yugoslavia, tell settlement.
15. Röske-Lúdvár, Körös group settlement, SE Hungary.
16. Pernik and Slatino settlements, upper Struma valley, W Bulgaria.
17. Szajol-Felsöföld, Körös group settlement, SE Hungary.
18. Tečić, R. Morava, central Yugoslavia, settlement and graves.
19. Velušina tell near Bitolj and Porodin, Pelagonia, S Yugoslavia.
20. Vršnik near Anza, distr. Štip, SE Yugoslavia. Settlement.
21–23. Mesolithic and Early Neolithic Vlasac, Padina and Lepenski Vir sites in the Iron Gates region, N Yugoslavia (striated area). The local culture continuous from the Upper Paleolithic Gravettian was ultimately absorbed by the Starčevo population.
24. Mehtelek, Proto-Búkk (Szatmar) settlement; obsidian and flint source.

Sites of Karanovo Culture

1. Azmak, Stara Zagora, C Bulgaria; stratified settlement tell.
2. Čevdar, east of Sofia; stratified settlement tell.
3. Karanovo, Nova Zagora, C Bulgaria; stratified settlement tell.
4. Muldava, Plovdiv, C Bulgaria; settlement.

The Starčevo (Körös, Criş) Culture of the Central Balkans and the Lower Danube Basin

The Neolithic of Yugoslavia, not including the Adriatic coast, southern Romania, and southeastern Hungary, is represented by the Starčevo culture (FIGURE 2–14), named for the site excavated near Belgrade in 1932.[17] The northern Starčevo group is called the Körös culture in Hungary,[18] named after the Körös River, and the Criş culture in Romania after the river Criş (same as Körös). Nevertheless, all of these terms refer to branches in somewhat different ecological niches of a single culture, sharing traditions closely related to those of Thessaly and Macedonia.

.The lowlands, inland valleys, and plains of the Balkan Peninsula and the Danube Basin were settled by 6300–6000 B.C., and the Neolithic in this area continued without major changes for a millennium. (TABLE 2) The inhabitants built their villages on river terraces or on sloping land above streams where the soil was conducive to agriculture, with houses arranged in linear rows facing the river. The area of settled territory covered up to ten acres or extended for almost a kilometer along the river. Starčevo deposits rarely yield a layer of material more than one meter thick. Their timber houses have disintegrated into the soil, leaving little debris. This is why there are no Starčevo tells north of Macedonia.

The Spread of Agriculture from Thessaly and Macedonia Across Central Yugoslavia and Western Bulgaria to the Danube Basin

The diffusion of agriculture and stock breeding to the north of Greece is documented by excavations in central Macedonia, particularly at Anza in Ovče Polje, midway between the Aegean area and the Danubian plain.[19] Research at Anza (author's excavation) demonstrates that climatic changes created ecological conditions suitable for the spread of agriculture. When the initial settlement of Anza I was established, about 6300–6200 B.C., climatic conditions were cooler and damper than at present.

Deciduous forests offered a plentiful supply of timber, wild animals, acorns, nuts, cornelian cherries, wild grapes, and berries, while the spectrum of cultivated crops and domesticated animals was generally the same as that of Greece. The people first domesticated sheep and goats, then later cattle and pigs, which altogether account for 96.5 percent of all animal bones at this site. Their principal crop was emmer wheat, supplemented by club and einkorn wheat, hulled six-row barley, peas, and lentils.

In the Vardar-Morava region of central Yugoslavia, no Mesolithic hunter-fisher sites are known at present. The premise that the first agriculturalists in Yugoslavian Macedonia were immigrants from Thessaly is supported by the analysis of human skeletons which shows that the basic population of Anza was a Mediterranean type of the Aegean area. Cultural materials link the colonists of Macedonia with the Sesklo folk of Thessaly: stamp seals, fine burnished wares with white-on-red painted symbolic designs; greenstone carvings, musical pipes, offering vessels, and anthropomorphic and zoomorphic figurines suggesting similarities of ritual and mythical imagery. Throughout the Lower Danube basin, the earliest agricultural settlements demonstrate a surprising uniformity of character. Pottery shapes and designs are remarkably similar between Romania and Macedonia.[20]

At this stage of research, the archeological record suggests that food production technology was carried northward to the Danube basin by migrating populations from Macedonia. Immigrant groups seem to have followed the Vardar and Struma valleys, then up the Morava basin west of the Rhodope and Balkan Mountains to the Danube valley (FIGURE 2–14, *arrows*)

Physical Type of the Population

The physical type of the population of most sites (Tečić, central Serbia; Obre, Bosnia; Deszk, southeastern Hungary) has been shown to be the gracile Mediterranean (small statured; narrow faced). But some sites in the central Balkans (Divostin), in Transylvania (Gura Baciului), the sites of the Tisza Basin, and particularly of the Körös region of southeastern Hungary, have yielded skeletal material that suggests a mixture of dolichocranial Mediterranean with local Cro-Magnon and brachycranial types.[21] This heterogeneity suggests the intermixing of the immigrants with the local Mesolithic populations. As already mentioned in chapter 1, the gracile Mediterraneans continued to move north until they entered the Iron Gate region of the Danube valley in northern Yugoslavia and southern Romania. There they were halted by the local Mesolithic populations. These were hunters and fishermen of the massive Cro-Magnon type,[22] whose culture is called Lepenski Vir, named after the famous site of more than fifty temples and numerous stone sculptures. (See radiocarbon dates, table 2.)

Economy

Although these immigrants brought an economic pattern which was basically the same as that of Neolithic Greece, it was necessary for them to adapt to this subhumid climatic zone of forests in which hunting and fishing were primary food sources. The abundance of antler harpoons, clay net-sinkers, fish bones, and thick layers of river shells recovered from villages is comparable to the high percentage of wild animal bones, including red and roe deer, aurochs, boar, bear, lynx, fox, badger, and birds.

Sheep and goats continued to be the predominant domesticated animals, although proof of experimental cattle breeding comes from a number of southern Hungarian sites where a transitional form, between the local wild *Bos primigenius* and the imported domesticated *Bos taurus*, has been identified.[23] In Bosnia, cattle bones constituted fifty to sixty percent of all domesticated

FIGURE 2–15

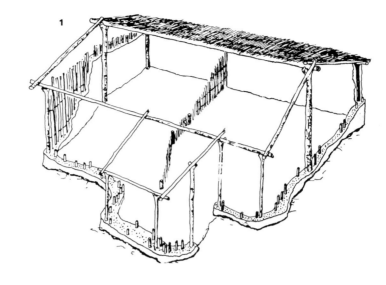

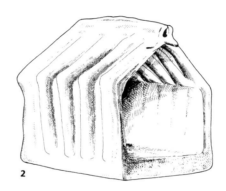

FIGURE 2–15 (1) Starčevo (Körös) house; reconstruction. Tiszajenö, SE Hungary. (2) Clay model of a timber house (or a temple) with a bull's head on the gable. Röszke-Ludvár, SE Hungary.

FIGURE 2–16 During the early 6th millennium B.C. spirals become a major motif in ceramic design, enlivening Old European pottery with their fluid dynamism. These early spiral motifs are painted dark brown on orange. Starčevo 5800–5500 B.C. (1) Starčevo and Vinkovci, N Yugoslavia; (2) Anza II near Štip, SE Yugoslavia.

FIGURE 2–16

FIGURE 2–17

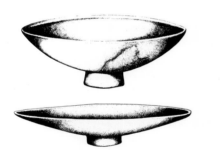

FIGURE 2–17 Footed bowls and dishes, characteristic Late Starčevo ware in Bosnia, W Yugoslavia. Obre I, northwest of Sarajevo; approx. 5300 B.C.

bones as shown by excavations at Obre I, northwest of Sarajevo.[24] Cattle were raised for meat and milk. The number of pigs was minimal.

Architecture

Throughout the Danube basin, the architecture of the later Starčevo period is characterized by timber frame dwellings with wattle-and-daub walls and clay-plastered floors. (FIGURE 2–15) The Late Starčevo settlement at Obre I in Bosnia indicates that by 5500 B.C., the people built houses that were substantial rectangular structures up to nine meters in length and seven meters wide, often built on stone foundations and containing round hearths.[25]

The actual temples were two-room houses, similar to those of the Sesklo culture. Such was the largest house at Obre I out of five houses excavated. This structure differed from the other smaller, one-room residential houses, not only in size but in architectural details. The floor of the main room was carefully covered with stone slabs while floors of other houses were paved only by a compact layer of clay. A horseshoe shaped hearth was in the room's center in front of which were found religious items of exceptional quality—vessels with large ring handles, shallow plates, and footed vessels.[26] These items were most likely used by the townsfolk in their collective rituals.

Trade

The main items of trade continued to be Aegean spondylus shells used for the manufacture of bracelets, rings, and beads, and a variety of hard stones including flint and obsidian used for blades, scrapers, burins, points, axes, and adzes.

Obsidian for use in the making tools was imported from at least two sources: Sardinia via the Adriatic Sea, the Dalmatian coast, and the Neretva pass to Bosnia,[27] and from the Carpathian foothills of northeastern Hungary and eastern Slovakia. The latter supplied the Körös group. The Mehtelek site in the Szamos River valley, more than 150 kilometers northeast of the main area

of Körös distribution, is significant.[28] Eighty percent of the chipped stone industry of this site was based on obsidian which was made into tools at the site as well as traded in a semifinished condition.

Pottery

There is a definite departure from the Sesklo type observable by 5900–5800 B.C. Starčevo pottery is marked by the appearance of brown-on-orange painted curvilinear designs and fingernail-pinched storage vessels, while the most distinctive products of the Starčevo population are its barbotine pottery (decorated with thin clay paste) and the spherical jars, footed bowls, dishes, and bird-shaped vases found even in the northern and western areas of the Starčevo distribution. (FIGURES 2–16 and 2–17) Exquisite anthropomorphic and ornithomorphic vases with intricate symbolic decoration and painting in several colors suggest a highly developed artistic sensibility. (PLATE 6)

FIGURE 2–18

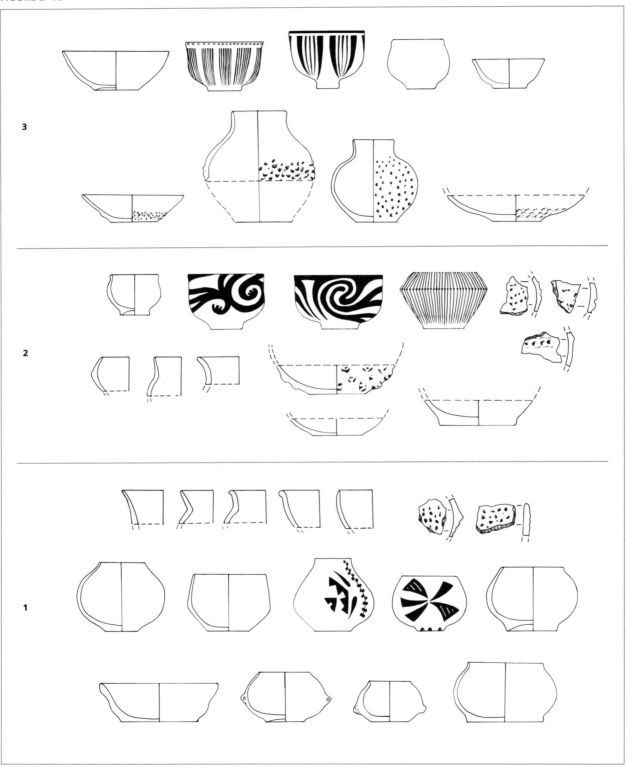

FIGURE 2–18 Ceramic forms from three phases of the Starčevo culture as produced by the stratified site at Anza (Anzabegovo) near Štip, C Macedonia.

(1) 6300–5900 B.C., represented by maroon-slipped and red-burnished thin-walled vases in the earliest (Ia) phase, around 6300–6100 B.C., and white-painted on a ground of red, brown, or black in (Ib) around 6100–6000 B.C.

(2) 5900–5600 B.C., typified by chocolate-brown on orange slip painted vases. Curvilinear design and "barbotine" (appliqué) decoration appear.

(3) 5600–5300 B.C., shapes and utility wares with barbotine and impressed decoration continue. The painted design is more tectonic; converging vertical lines are painted lengthwise from top to foot.

FIGURE 2–19

FIGURE 2–19 Stag with supernatural antlers. A figure in relief on a large vase from Czépa, the Körös group, SE Hungary, c. 5500–5300 B.C.

FIGURE 2–20

FIGURE 2–20 Bird-shaped vases of the Körös group in SE Hungary, c. 5500 B.C. H 11 cm.

FIGURE 2–21 Offering containers. (1) Lepenski Vir; (2) Dudeşti Vechi, Timişoara, W Romania. c. 5700–5500 B.C.

The Anza settlement of the Vardar basin in central Macedonia has yielded a yardstick for the chronology and evolution of ceramic forms based on stratigraphy and radiocarbon dates. (FIGURE 2–18) Exquisitely painted Starčevo pottery—vases decorated with relief figures (FIGURE 2–19), ornithomorphic and anthropomorphic vases (FIGURE 2–20), miniature four-legged offering vessels (FIGURE 2–21), and female figurines—were all produced for ritual purposes. Figurines of clay were more numerous in the south than in the north, where they were probably made of wood and have not survived for posterity.

Influences from Bulgaria and the Adriatic coasts are traceable in the final phases of the Starčevo culture. These stimulated change that resulted in the formation, around 5400–5200 B.C. of the Vinča, Butmir, Tisza, and Lengyel cultures discussed in chapter 3. In the western part of Yugoslavia, Starčevo traditions continued to approximately 5000 B.C.[29]

FIGURE 2–21

1

2

The Karanovo Culture in Central Bulgaria

A veritable land of milk and honey greeted the agricultural-ists who settled in central Bulgaria, probably not later than 6300 B.C. (TABLE 2–3). Massive tells are concentrated in the Marica basin where fertile soils and a mild climate were ideally suited to farming. The long duration of these settlements is demonstrated by great accumulations of habitation material such as the thirteen meter high mound of Karanovo, whose name is applied to the cultural tradition of this area. Owing to the relative isolation of this region created by the Rhodope and Balkan mountains, the Karanovo culture developed a character somewhat different from that of the central Balkan Starčevo complex.

Major Excavations

Decisive information about the Karanovo culture was produced by excavations carried out by V. Mikov and G. I. Georgiev in 1936–37 and 1946–57, and continued in 1984–90 by S. Hiller and V. Nikolov at the Karanovo mound near Nova Zagora.[30] Archeologists distinguished six successive phases, I–VI, which were substantiated and expanded by the excavation by G.I. Georgiev of the Azmak mound at Stara Zagora in 1960–63. New excavations at Karanovo opened one more layer containing houses below Karanovo I (yet unpublished). This will throw new light on the beginning phases of Karanovo I. Subsequent excavations of the Kazanlak tell at Stara Zagora (with eight meters of Neolithic deposit)[31] and other settlements[32] provide a clear picture of the Karanovo lifestyle.

FIGURE 2–22

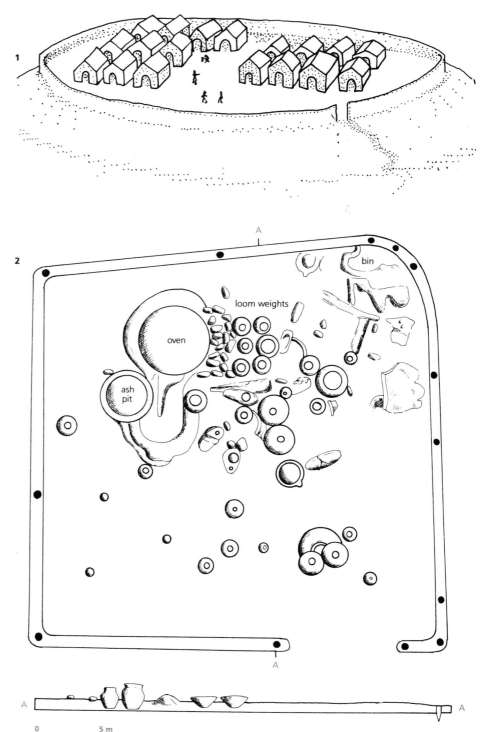

Villages and Houses

Early Karanovo settlements were well-planned communities containing an estimated 300 inhabitants within an area of 3 hectares (a hectare equals 10,000 square meters). Single-room dwellings of six or seven square meters were neatly aligned in parallel rows (FIGURE 2–22, 1), separated by log-paved streets. The people constructed their houses on a framework of thin wooden poles covered by a lattice work of branches and coated with a thick layer of clay. A total of sixty buildings has been estimated for the basal level at Karanovo. Houses contained massive clay ovens as well as large quantities of ceramics and marble vases. (FIGURE 2–22, 2) Ovens were also built in the spaces between the houses. Inside walls in some houses were painted, suggesting that among the village houses, some were probably used as temples. Among the agricultural tools were quern stones, hand-milling stones, pestles, and antler sickle-handles (see fig. 1–1, 1) Bone spoons of exquisite workmanship were also found. (FIGURE 2–23)

Economy

The distribution of sites in the Nova Zagora region demonstrates that settlements were intentionally located on potentially arable soils.[33] A cultivated area surrounded the basal village within a two-kilometer radius, while at larger settlements, more than 760 hectares were tilled.[34] The longevity of these settlements definitely implies that some form of crop rotation was practiced. It is presumed that half the land was left fallow at all times, or planted to restore nitrogen to the soil. Chief crops were einkorn and emmer wheat, barley, peas, and lentils. Only emmer wheat, barley, and pulses seem to have been fully processed, as indicated by large, pure samples. All Neolithic levels contained sickles of deer antler with flint teeth millstones and bone spatulas, perhaps used for scraping flour.

Sheep and goats were the predominant domesticated animals, followed by cattle and pigs. However, the amount of grazing land along the river was too limited for year-round use, and herds were probably moved to hilly regions in the spring and early summer.

FIGURE 2–22 (1) A schematized Karanovo I village plan. (2) Interior of a one-room house from Karanovo I period. Muldava tell near Plovdiv. Left rear, a beehive oven with an ash pit. To the right of it is an accumulation of vases, loom weights, and stone tools. Early 6th mill B.C.

FIGURE 2–23

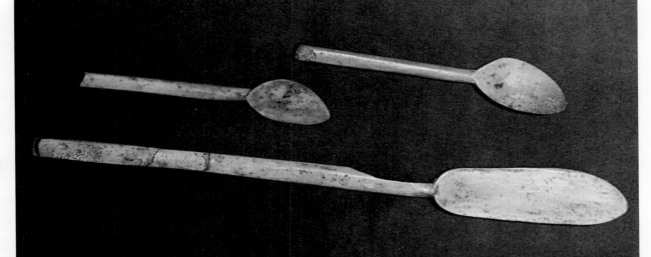

FIGURE 2–23 Bone spoons or spatulas perhaps used for collecting grain, from Karanovo I tell at Azmak, C Bulgaria. Early 6th mill B.C. Stara Zagora Museum. 31.5 cm, 14.4 cm, and 13.2 cm.

FIGURE 2–24

1   2

FIGURE 2–24 Presentative Karanovo I tulip-shaped vases. (1) Painted in white on red in net-patterned hanging triangles and dotted bands. H. 17 cm. (2) White-on-red painted, spiral-decorated, standing on a high conical foot. Early 6th mill. B.C. Azmak tell at Stara Zagora, C Bulgaria. H 28.4 cm.

FIGURE 2–25 Semi-globular jar and dish standing on a ring base with cut-outs. (1) decorated around the body with hanging and inverted triangles filled with a net pattern. (2) decorated with crescents and S-spirals, white-on-red painted. Karanovo I culture, Muldava settlement, C Bulgaria, c. 5800 B.C.

FIGURE 2–25

1   2

Pottery

Remarkably advanced, hard, well-fired pottery without any organic admixture is found in the early levels of all systematically excavated tells. Distinctive tulip-shaped bowls and tall jars with hollow ring bases or cylindrical legs were red slipped and white painted. (FIGURE 2–24) Such pottery is far from "primitive" and is certainly not the earliest to be found in this area. Sophisticated craftsmanship is demonstrated by exquisite footed vases (FIGURE 2–25), and by a series of small triangular or rectangular vessels. New treatments introduced during the Karanovo II phase are channeled or fluted decorations and black colored fabric as a result of a controlled reducing atmosphere. Karanovo III produced an even greater variety of shapes. Typical of this phase are tall vases with zoomorphic, doglike handles. (FIGURE 2–26) The typology of Karanovo I–III pottery is shown in figure 2–27.

FIGURE 2–26 Karanovo III vases with dog-shaped handles (1,2) and an ornithomorphic/anthropomorphic lid handle. (3) Black burnished. Azmak tell at Stara Zagora. Mid-6th mill. B.C. H 14 cm.

FIGURE 2–26

1

2

3

FIGURE 2–27

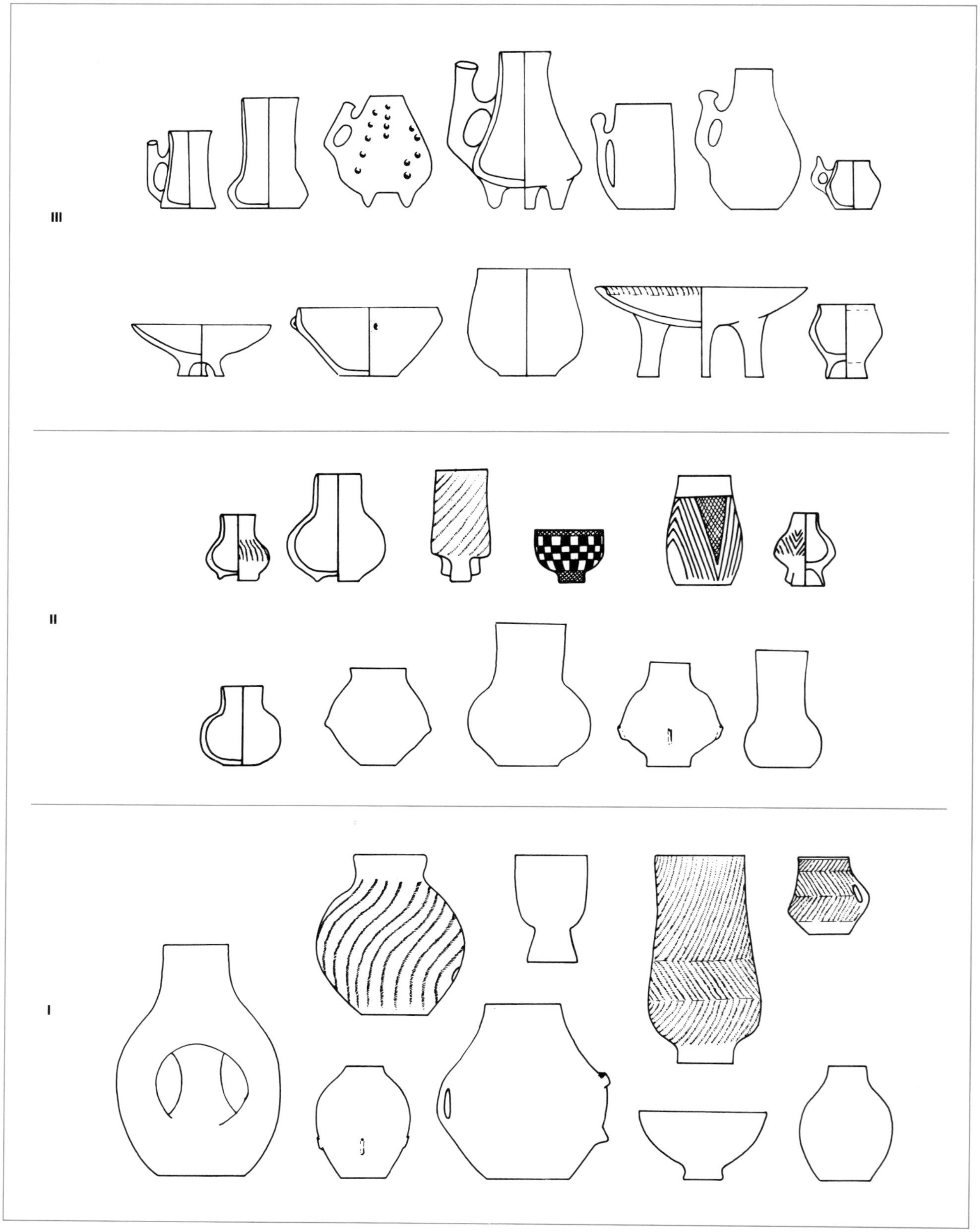

FIGURE 2–27 Typology of pottery from Karanovo I, II, and III, C Bulgaria. I, c. 5900–5800 B.C. II, 5700–5600 B.C. III, c. 5600–5500 B.C.

FIGURE 2–28 Distribution of the Linearbandkeramik culture (LBK) in central Europe. Shaded areas show concentration of sites. Approx. 5500–4900 B.C.

FIGURE 2–28

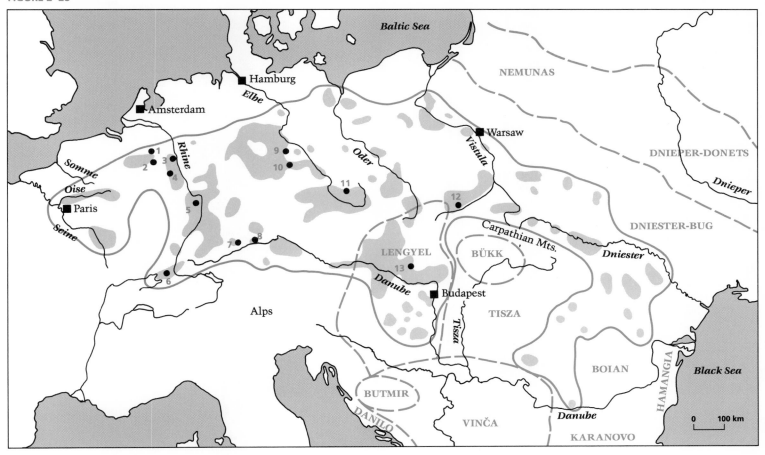

KEY

1. Elsloo
2. Sittard
3. Köln-Lindenthal
4. Aldenhoven
5. Flomborn
6. Rixheim
7. Lautereck
8. Hienheim
9. Rössen
10. Sondershausen
11. Bylany
12. Olszanica
13. Nitra

Figurines

The repertory and style of figurine types from Karanovo villages are much related to those of Sesklo and Starčevo. Well represented are the Bird Goddess terracotta images with beaked noses and protruding, egg-shaped posteriors; the pregnant goddess type holding one hand over her pregnant belly; stiff nudes with a supernatural pubic triangle; as well as zoomorphic figurines. The stiff-nude sculptures were often carved of white marble,[35] an indication that these people traded for marble with the Aegean islands. The predominance of a variety of goddess figurines over an extended geographical area indicates a complex and consistent pattern of religious devotion centered around a multifaceted female deity.

The Neolithic of Central Europe: The Linearbandkeramik (LBK) Culture

This is the best known culture in central Europe and perhaps the most classically Neolithic in the ancient world," said V. Gordon Childe in his *Dawn of European Civilization* of 1925. After seventy years, we can still agree that this culture, between eastern France and Romania (FIGURE 2–28), is best known internationally because of excellent excavations during the last decades by the French, Dutch, German, Czech, Polish, and American archeologists. Childe called it Danubian I culture; however, since it was not distributed over the Lower Danube River system, the term Danubian creates a problem. Archeologists still continue to use *Bandkeramik* and the English Linear Pottery.

FIGURE 2–29

FIGURE 2–29 Characteristic vases of the early LBK decorated with spirals, breasts, bi-lines, horns, and concentric rectangles from the sites in the Znojmo area near Brno, Moravia. 5500–5000 B.C.

The presently used term Linearbandkeramik is abbreviated to LBK. It should be noted that linear bands do not accurately describe this pottery since its design includes spirals, snakes, meanders, rectangles, concentric squares, triangles, V's, chevrons, two lines, three lines, M's, X's, a.o. (FIGURES 2–29 and 2–30) In addition, there are figures in relief expressing anthropomorphic and zoomorphic images, horns, breasts, and other symbols found on ceramics from southeastern Europe. Pottery forms, fabric, and symbolism of LBK culture are similar to late Starčevo (Körös), although there is a general lack of painted ware.

Five hundred years elapsed before the Balkan Neolithic (Starčevo) elements and agriculture were introduced into temperate central Europe. Close affinities between the Starčevo (Körös) culture and the LBK firmly suggest an actual movement of people from the southeast. The oldest phase of LBK groups in the Middle Danube basin developed around 5600–5400 B.C. directly out of the Starčevo (Körös) tradition.[36] Physically, the LBK people are generally related to the small statured gracile Mediterraneans of the Balkans.[37]

FIGURE 2–30

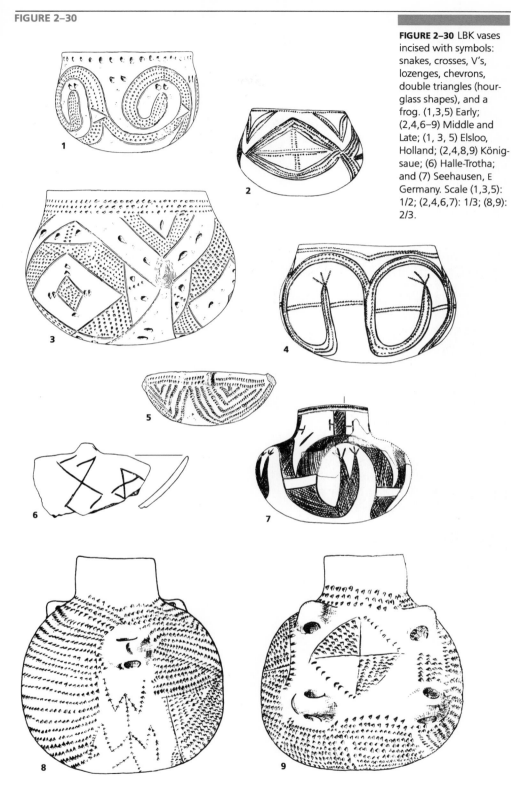

FIGURE 2–30 LBK vases incised with symbols: snakes, crosses, V's, lozenges, chevrons, double triangles (hourglass shapes), and a frog. (1,3,5) Early; (2,4,6–9) Middle and Late; (1, 3, 5) Elsloo, Holland; (2,4,8,9) Königsaue; (6) Halle-Trotha; and (7) Seehausen, E Germany. Scale (1,3,5): 1/2; (2,4,6,7): 1/3; (8,9): 2/3.

Diffusion, Site Location, and Farming

The agriculturalists diffused as far west as eastern France and the Netherlands, and as far north as the lower Oder basin in Germany and Poland. The area from Hungary to Holland is about 1000 kilometers across. The similarity of ceramic style and of lithic equipment within this area suggests that diffusion took place in a relatively short time. The climate of the 6th millennium B.C. was warmer than at present, and central Europe was covered with light mixed-oak forests. LBK groups were moving mostly into an unoccupied ecological niche. Characteristically, LBK agriculturalists settled almost exclusively on the loess (wind deposited silt) plains, which were easy to work once the forest cover had been removed, and were offered very little competition from the local Mesolithic population. In their settlements on valley bottoms and on sunny terraces of rivers and streams (FIGURE 2–31A), the LBK farmers cultivated emmer wheat as the principal crop, as well as einkorn, bread, club, and spelt wheat; barley, rye, millet, oat, peas, lentils, opium poppy, and flax. Since emmer does not extract nutrients from the soil as vigorously as other cereals, it could have been grown on loess soils for indefinite periods, although a rotation system may also have been used.[38]

The LBK people kept domesticated cattle as their prime source of meat, milk, and manure, as well as sheep, goats, pigs, and dogs. Elk, deer, and boar were hunted but hunting was marginal. Some of the villages of this garden type of civilization were occupied for 400–500 years.

FIGURE 2–31A

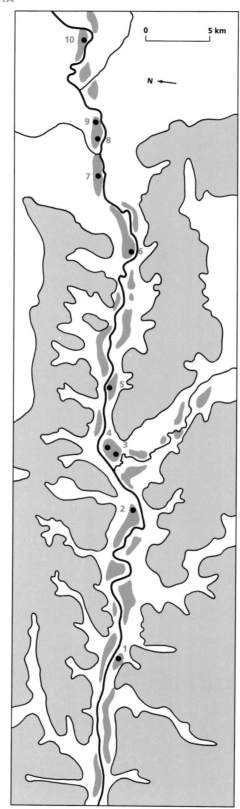

FIGURE 2–31A Distribution of LBK settlements in the valley bottom of R. Aisne, E France.

KEY

▨ Alluvial terraces

▨ Calcarious plateau

Settlements:
1. Pernant
2. Missy-sur-Commune
3. Chassemy
4. Vailly
5. Cys-la-Commune
6. Cuiry-les-Chaudardes
7. Pontavert
8. Berry-au-Bac "Le Chemin de la Pêcherie"
9. Berry-au-Bac "La Croix Maigret"
10. Menneville

FIGURE 2–31B

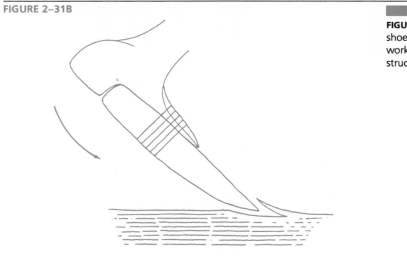

FIGURE 2–31B The use of shoe-last celt for wood-working. (Reconstruction).

FIGURE 2–31C

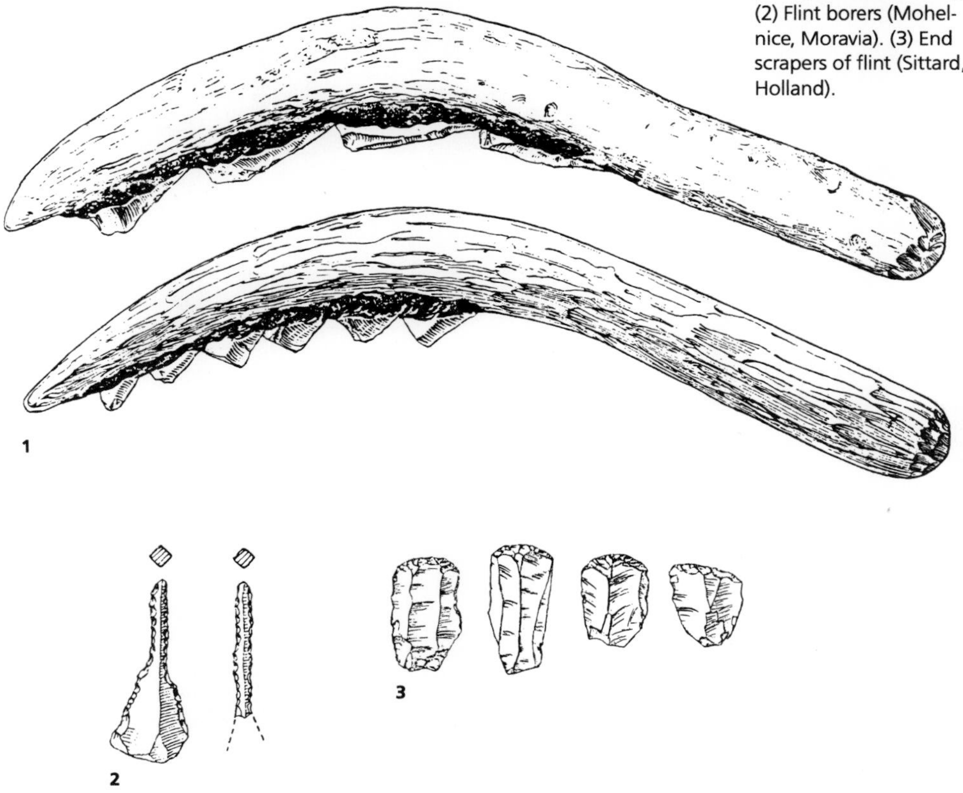

FIGURE 2–31C Typical LBK tools: (1) Wooden sickles with flint blades set in and fastened with pitch (Central Germany). (2) Flint borers (Mohelnice, Moravia). (3) End scrapers of flint (Sittard, Holland).

1

2

3

The basic tool assemblage of the early LBK was composed of ground stone adzes and "shoe-last" celts for wood working (see fig. 2–36). The flint industry continued Starčevo traditions and was composed of microlithic round scrapers, backed knives, sickle blades (for setting into wooden handles), borers, and burins. (FIGURE 2–31B) Local flint sources were explored and some settlements specialized in flint mining and exportation to the neighboring regions. In southern Poland, for instance, a Jurassic flint was mined by the people of the Olszanica settlement located nearby.[39] Obsidian for sickle blades, knives, and other tools was obtained from the Bükk and Tatra Mountains. In later phases of this culture, flint blades were imported from as far as the Dniester region in the southeast for use in the manufacture of tools.

Villages and Houses

LBK settlements are found in clusters of "settlement cells" and are more dense in some regions than in others. Frequently, enclaves consist of eight to ten sites. In southern Poland, according to a survey along the Dlubnia River, the density is twenty sites per 25 square kilometers, although the average density of the entire area northeast of Cracow is one per 32 square kilometers.[40]

Villages range from 125 to more than 500 hectares (about 300 to 1250 acres), the largest supporting perhaps five hundred or more inhabitants. Normally, villages comprised five to eight houses spaced about 20 meters apart. No defensive features such as palisades or ditches are found in the early period of this culture.

FIGURE 2–32

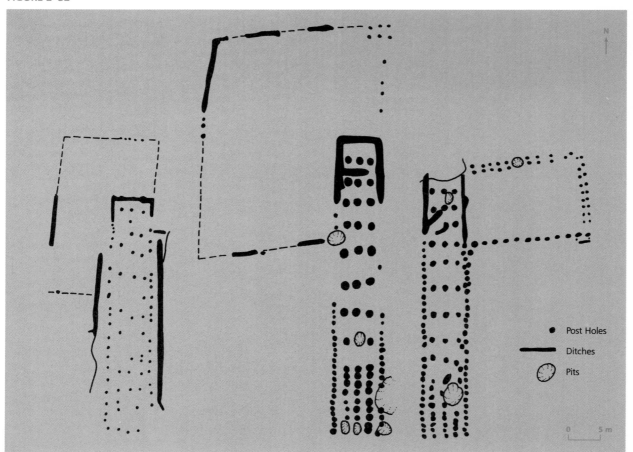

FIGURE 2–32 Plans of LBK long-houses with rectangular enclosures perhaps used as corrals. The outer walls were daubed with clay. Usually the northern end of the house was ditched, apparently for reinforcement. Bylany, east of Prague. Excavation by B. Soudský.

• Post Holes

▬ Ditches

◯ Pits

0   5 m

FIGURE 2–33

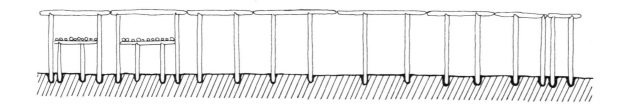

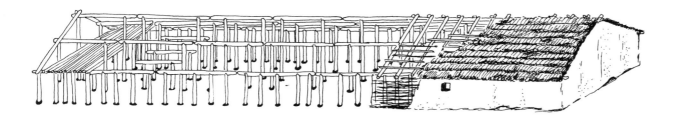

FIGURE 2–33 A longitudinal cross-section and a reconstruction of a large house at Bylany. Excavation by B. Soudský. End 6th mill. B.C. Length c. 45 cm.

The LBK is best known for its long-houses built of upright timber, and many have been excavated in Czechoslovakia, Poland, Germany, Holland, and France.[41] Since prototypes do not exist in the Starčevo culture, a local development is assumed. Timber was abundant, and it is quite normal to find wooden architecture in central Europe.

Dwellings were large, rectangular timber structures, and of the 108 identified as dwellings at Bylany, east of Prague, no more than five to eight were occupied at the same time. Large structures, sometimes 45 meters in length, were surrounded by a fence with a gate, resembling cattle enclosures. (FIGURE 2–32) Houses were generally 5.5 to 7 meters wide and varied in length. Five rows of posts ran the length of each structure; the two outer rows braced wattle-and-daub walls while interior rows supported the roof. (FIGURE 2–33) During later phases (Stroked Pottery and Rössen), houses became trapezoidal in plan.

Cemeteries

The LBK people buried their dead within 100–500 meters from the settlement boundaries, practicing both inhumation and cremation. About two dozen cemeteries have been excavated, some containing more than 100 graves.[42] In inhumation cemeteries, graves were in oval pits with walls covered with clay plaster or stones. The extended or slightly flexed dead were sometimes buried with one or two pots, stone celts, flint arrowheads, stone palettes for coloring materials, and necklaces and arm rings of spondylus shells. (FIGURE 2–34) (We shall return to an analysis of grave goods and how the cemeteries reflect the social structure of the LBK people in chapter 9.)

FIGURE 2–34

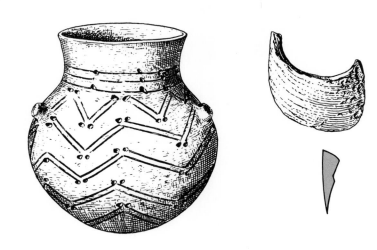
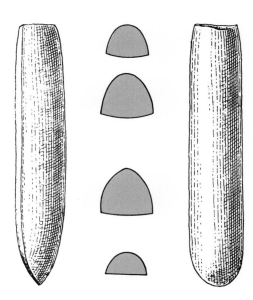

FIGURE 2–34 LBK grave inventory; pot, spondylus arm ring (fragment) and a stone celt (two views). "Musical note" decorated phase. Early 5th mill. B.C. Nitra, Slovakia.

FIGURE 2–35

FIGURE 2–35 Middle and Late LBK pottery. (1) "Musical note" decorated bowl. Early 5th mill. B.C., Bohuslavice, Moravia. (2,3) Stroke-decorated vases from the area of Brno, 47th–46th cents.

Chronology

The LBK has been subdivided into three main periods on the basis of pottery typology: early—second half of the 6th millennium B.C., typified by the spiral-meander-chevron decorated pottery (see figs. 2–29, 2–30); middle—to the end of the 6th and early 5th millennia B.C., characterized by "musical note" decorated vases (FIGURES 2–34, top, and 2–35, 1); and late—to mid-5th millennium B.C., typified by stroked decoration of pottery. (FIGURE 2–35, 2, 3) (See radiocarbon dates: TABLE 4.)

The maximum expansion of the LBK is traced during its middle period. In the east, LBK sites of the middle period are found north of the Carpathian Mountains in the Dniester, Siret, Prut, and Bug valleys of northeastern Romania, and a few sites have been spotted even in the Lower Danube region. The LBK settlers in the east had strongly influenced the further development of culture in Romania and the western Ukraine where the Dniester-Bug culture apparently fused with the LBK. In Moldavia and the western Ukraine, the LBK formed a substratum for the formation of the Cucuteni (Tripolye) culture.

Toward the end of the 5th millennium B.C., (4300–4200) the central areas of LBK culture—the Middle and Upper Danube, Elbe, Oder, and Vistula basins—were colonized by the Lengyel and Tiszapolgár people coming from the south, probably as a chain reaction to the first Kurgan wave in east-central Europe. The western part of this culture continued, but in the period between the end of the 5th millennium B.C. and c. 3500 B.C., profound changes occurred. Settlements are now found outside the ecological niche of valley bottoms, with some defended by palisades built of tree trunks. These changes signal the shift from a peaceful, unfortified lifestyle, to one that required protection against invasion.

Recent research in Holland, Germany, and France has revealed a continuity of village life of LBK descendants in the Rhine area and in eastern France (in the Paris basin and in Hainaut) for almost a millennium, up to the middle of the 4th millennium B.C. In the Rhine basin, the LBK proper was followed by the Hinkelstein, Grossgartach, Rössen, and Epi-Rössen phases. In the Paris basin and Hainaut, the post-LBK culture (in French known as Post-Rubané), distinct in its regional character, is known under a series of names given after the major excavated sites. The sequence in the Paris basin runs as follows: Villeneuve-Saint Germain (with three phases), d'Augy-Sainte-Pallaye, Cerny, Rössen III (with influences from the Rhine area), and Epi-Rössen. In the province of Hainaut, a somewhat different variant parallel to Villeneuve-Saint Germain, is known as the Blicque group. One of the peculiarities of the Final LBK and post-LBK culture in the west is its pottery tempered with crushed calcinated bones.[43]

The Bükk Culture in the Upper Tisza Basin

The name Bükk comes from the Bükk Mountains north of the Hungarian plains, and is used here to identify the culture of the Upper Tisza basin during the 6th millennium B.C., which is also called Eastern Linearbandkeramik.[44] The first finds of this culture were discovered in 1876 in the cave of Aggtelek at the border of northern Hungary with eastern Slovakia. Bükk as a culture name has been in use since 1921 after the publication of Hillebrand's and L. Bella's book, *Der Mensch und die Kultur der Urzeit* (Budapest). Substantial information on this culture appeared in Ferenz Tompa's book, *Die Bandkeramik in Ungarn, Die Bükker und Theiss-Kultur* (Archaeologia Hungarica V–VI, 1929, Budapest). The finds described here were mostly ceramics of several phases. Settlements, workshops, graves, and caves were systematically excavated only after World War II.

Distribution

In the north, the Bükk people reached the mountains and occupied the source area of obsidian in the region of Tokay. A distinctive aggregation of sites is found along the Upper Tisza and its tributaries Sajo, Hernad, Eger, Bodrog, and Szamos. (FIGURE 2–36) Five hundred and fifty sites have been reported in eastern Hungary alone. By combining east Slovakian and northwest Romanian sites, the number is increased to more than seven hundred, indicating that the area was fairly densely settled.

Physical Type of the Population

Most probably, the local Mesolithic hunter-fishers were converted to agriculture by influences from the Starčevo (Körös) culture.[45] This premise of local conversion is supported by studies of skeletal material, indicating that the skeletons from graves in the Miskolc and Borsod areas of northeastern Hungary are of local European (Cro-Magnon) type, which differ markedly from the Mediterranean type found in Starčevo populations.[46] Since settlements from the 8th and 7th millennia B.C. are not investigated in this region, the transition from Mesolithic to Neolithic cannot as yet be shown by actual finds.

Chronology

The earliest Neolithic complex in the Upper Tisza Basin is known as the Szatmar culture.[47] Radiocarbon dates are not available for this phase, but from analogies with the Starčevo ceramic materials, from symbols and religious figurines, and from analogies with other artifacts such as bone spatulae, the acculturation of the Upper Tisza can be judged to have taken place not later than the middle period of the Starčevo culture, that is, before the middle of the 6th millennium B.C. The later phases, Tiszadob and Bükk proper are dated by carbon 14 methods to the second half of the 6th millennium B.C. (TABLE 5)

FIGURE 2–36

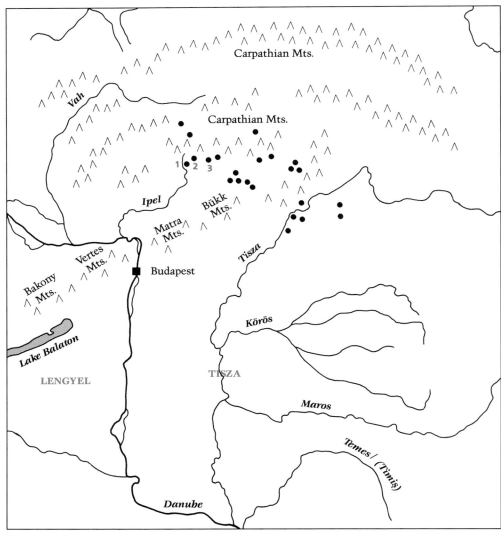

FIGURE 2–36 Distribution of Bükk sites (Tiszadob and Bükk proper phases) in the Upper Tisza basin, c. 5500–5200 B.C.

KEY
1. Domica
2. Ardovo
3. Aggtelek

Trade

Obsidian nuclei, flakes, and blades appear in abundance in workshops, and large vases filled with flint blades of uniform dimensions must have been prepared for export.[48] The presence of spondylus shells in graves of northeastern Hungary and eastern Slovakia is also indicative of exchange. It is obvious that the Bükk people controlled the obsidian and flint-chipping industry.

Farming

Farming is suggested by grain impressions in house rubble (species as yet unidentified), quern stones, antler hoes, and flat dishes assumed to have been used for baking. Domesticated animal bones, predominantly cattle followed by sheep, goats, and pigs, constituted 50 to 78 percent (depending upon ecological conditions) of animal bones found. Aurochs, elk, and hare bones indicate forest hunting.[49]

Open Air and Cave Settlements

Settlements are found in river valleys, usually on first terraces, or on slopes, and occasionally on the tops of small hills and at the bottom of narrow gorges in the Karst region. Remains of wooden structures were discovered at the entrances to caves in the Bükk and Matra Mountains, while traces of habitation and religious worship were found even quite deep in their interiors. In the cave of Domica in eastern Slovakia, such traces were discovered as far as 700 meters from the entrance. Caves were habitable since their temperature of 10–12° C was stable.

Caves such as Domica-Aggtelek on the border of eastern Slovakia and Hungary, Borsod in Hungary, and others were occupied for a very long time. Hearths and traces of wooden posts have been found in some of these caves, from which have come the most attractive Bükk pottery. (FIGURES 2–37, 2–38) There is little doubt that caves were used primarily as sanctuaries. Post holes of light structures, 3 by 4 m with a hearth inside were excavated in the cave of Domica. In this cave outstandingly beautiful Bükk vases appeared in a large

FIGURE 2–37

FIGURE 2–37 An elegant, thin-walled globular vase from the classical Bükk culture. The mirrorlike surface is incised with a coiling snake motif combined with chevrons. Cave of Aggtelek on the border of Hungary and Slovakia, c. 5000 B.C. H 20 cm.

FIGURE 2–38 Extraordinary thin-walled vases decorated by very fine incisions, some with encrustation of white, red, and yellow color from the cave sanctuaries of Domica (1–4,6–10) and Ardovo (5), E Slovakia, c 5000 B.C.

FIGURE 2–38

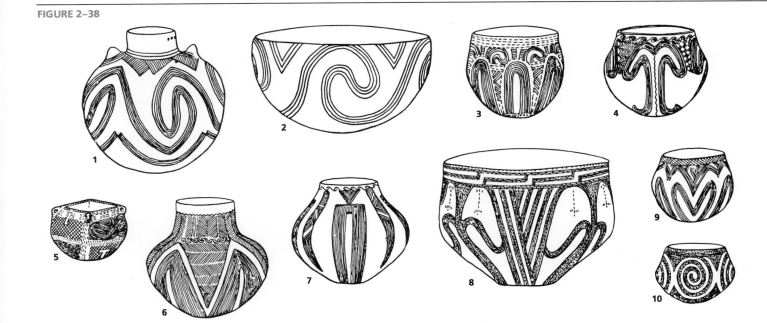

hall at the source of a river. Quality clay for pottery was obtained from the pits nearby.[50] Traces of similar light structures and fine ware were also found in the cave of Aggtelek. An altar of burnt clay 160 cm long was discovered in a niche 200 meters from its entrance which held four sacrificial pits, one large and three small. Fire traces were in the large pit. The small ones probably held containers with offerings. (FIGURE 2–39) There were many potsherds of fine Bükk ware around the altar.

There are only a few totally excavated open air settlements in river valleys or on slopes. The best example of a village from the early phase (Tiszadob) is Oros II which occupied 1000 square meters and consisted of twelve houses. Eight of these formed a semicircular row with four in the middle. Houses were subterranean or semiterranean, about 4.7 by 2 m, and oriented from northeast to southwest. The pit inside the house was 60 cm deep.[51] From the later phase (Bükk proper), a village of five houses was excavated at Boldogkovaralja.[52] These houses were aboveground, c. 4.5 by 2.5 m, oriented from northeast to southwest. No post holes were found. Instead, there were large pieces of house rubble that originally were plastered on wickerwork walls. Next to the houses were workshops consisting of large hearths and pits containing obsidian and flint nuclei and blades. A cashe of 567 quartz blades was in a pit west of house No. 5 indicating that the villagers here clearly specialized in preparation of stone tools for export.

Graves appeared in habitation sites and particularly under the floors of structures located at a cave entrance. The dead were equipped with vases, sometimes as many as four or five.

FIGURE 2–39

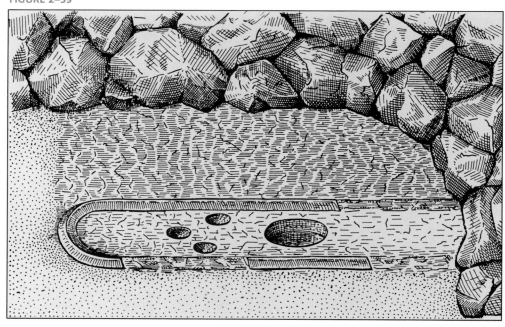

FIGURE 2–40

FIGURE 2–39 An altar from the cave of Aggtelek with one large pit with fire traces and three small pits for the placement of offering containers. Bükk culture, c. 5000 B.C.

FIGURE 2–40 Bükk figurine marked with meanders and other symbols. Vulva is indicated in front. Second half of the 6th mill. B.C. Scale 1:1.

Pottery

Vase shapes originally inspired by southern agriculturalists were continued in the Bükk culture: spherical jars, hemispherical bowls, round dishes, bottle-shaped vases, footed vessels, and tall "fruitstands" with funnel-shaped containers. This fine ware developed into extraordinary thin-walled pottery, decorated by slender incisions, sometimes by encrustations of red, white, and yellow, and by dark brown vertical bands or broad horizontal bands painted around the mouth before firing (see fig. 2–38). Fine ware was frequently slipped or burnished and tempered with sand, while crude ware was tempered with chaff.

Figurines

Bükk figurine art, which is distinct in its rigidly abstract forms, frequently reduced the human body to geometric shapes. Symbols were incised on their flat surfaces. (FIGURE 2–40) Meanders, zig-zags, chevrons, tri-lines, and other typical Old European symbols appear on figurines, anthropomorphic vases, and also on cave walls.

The Dniester-Bug Culture

The Moldavian region of fertile black soil, northwest of the Black Sea between the Dniester and Bug rivers, was conducive to farming.

Local Domestication

The sites in this area that have been systematically excavated indicate that there was an extended period of experiments in animal and plant domestication by hunter and fisher groups who had occupied this area from the Mesolithic. Radiocarbon dates have verified a Neolithic sequence of three pre-pottery and five ceramic phases at Soroki, lasting from 6500–5000 B.C.[53] (TABLE 2–6) The two earliest Neolithic levels lack pottery but contain bones of domesticated cattle and pigs, wild grass-wheat seeds (Aegilop cylindrica), and small grinding querns.[54] Domestication of cattle and pigs was accomplished independently by the Dniester-Bug population, and wild grass-wheat was gathered some 500 years prior to contacts with Starčevo (Criş) agriculturalists. High percentages of fish bones (roach of the carp family, eels, and pike) recovered from the earliest villages indicate that the availability of fish must have provided the initial impetus toward a settled way of life. Throughout the duration of the Dniester-Bug culture, farming was a secondary aspect of an economy based upon fishing and hunting (aurochs, red and roe deer, and boar). The third phase, c. 5800 B.C., contains not only pottery, but einkorn wheat, the most commonly cultivated species in southeastern Europe. Impressions of husks, ears, and grain of emmer and spelt in the ceramics establish the existence also of these species at a number of sites. Further evidence is the use of straw as pottery temper.

Villages, Houses, and Material Equipment

The earliest villages were located on terraces formed by post-glacial floods. In the Atlantic period, damper conditions and increased precipitation apparently influenced the movement of settlements into higher areas. Stone was used in the construction of huts and large long-houses that in earlier phases had been chiefly semi-terranean. Houses above ground were built during the last phase. This period also marks the introduction of elements from the LBK culture of central Europe.

The material equipment of the Dniester-Bug population was notably different from that of Starčevo and Karanovo agriculturalists. Polished stone tools were rarely produced, while antler was employed in a variety of ways, including the manufacture of axes probably used to prepare the ground for planting. A gradual microlithization of flint tools is observed which is opposite to the change in lithics elsewhere. Small trapezoidal chips set in bone or antler handles were used as scrapers and knives. Burins and perforators were also microlithic.

Pottery

The earliest coarse ceramics were large pointed- or flat-based pots, decorated with linear incisions of wavy lines and net-pattern designs, constructed of clays tempered with vegetable matter. (FIGURE 2–41) Later, influence from the Starčevo culture is seen in the appearance of fine, well-fired, plain (gray or buff) and painted wares (see footed vase of Starčevo-Criş type, fig. 2–18, upper row). Starčevo elements were superseded during phase IV by LBK styles from central Europe. At this time, the original character of the Neolithic Dniester-Bug culture had all but disappeared.

The presence of LBK influence indicates a gradual influx of central European people as far as the Dniester valley around 5000 B.C. Their presence in Moldavia later contributed to the formation of the Cucuteni culture c. 4800–4700 B.C.

Overview

In this chapter we have described the process of Neolithization of southeastern and central Europe in the period between 6500 and 5500 B.C. An enormous leap in farming economy, trade, crafts, architecture, and art was made due to the favorable climate of the Atlantic period. The presently arid Mediterranean and Aegean regions were, at that time, lush with vegetation. Central Europe was warmer than in the present and forest and garden trees flourished. Human populations steadily increased in all areas, as expressed by the growth of villages. There is no evidence of territorial aggression, and the total absence of lethal weapons implies a peaceful coexistence between all groups and individuals. Villages have no fortifications except occasional V-shaped ditches and retaining walls where structurally necessary. Villages were usually founded on choice locations near rivers or streams or on lake terraces, and the use of steep hills or other inaccessible terrain for habitation was unknown during this peaceful period.

FIGURE 2–41

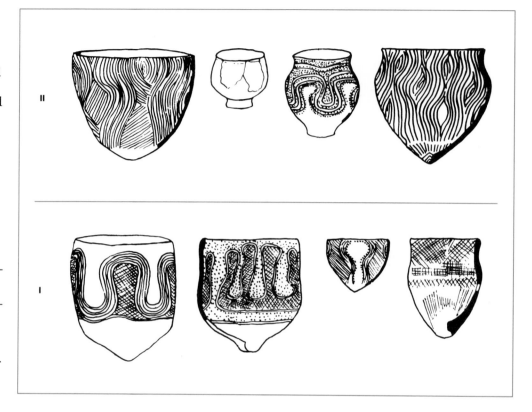

FIGURE 2–41 Earliest pottery of the Dniester-Bug culture (I, Skibinets; II, Sokolets settlement, W Ukraine). End 7th–early 6th mill. B.C.

The achievements that took place during the first thousand years of the Neolithic were not few. Extraordinary progress was made, not only in the domestication of animals and the cultivation of plants but also in the development of pottery and house building and in a series of other crafts. Excavations in Greece have revealed a sequence of architectural changes that were determined by the fluctuations of climate. Dwellings from the middle of the 7th millennium B.C. constructed with pisé de terre (rammed earth) walls were replaced, at the end of this millennium, by timber-post houses with wattle-and-daub walls. Solidly built houses with mudbrick walls on stone foundations followed in the early part of the 6th millennium B.C. The earliest pottery appears in the middle of the 7th millennium B.C. The technological progress in pottery production over the first four to five hundred years, from unfired to well-fired and burnished wares, from very simple rounded shapes to a wide assortment of vases in orange, red, brown, and black clays, some very thin walled, is breathtaking. Pottery painting began c. 6300 B.C. This period was an age for the flowering of ceramics and must not be seen as simply a "Stone Age." Stone vases virtually disappeared after the Early Neolithic, in fact, as pottery gradually replaced stone carving, although the carving of figurines, seals, and jewelry continued.

The emergence of great numbers of figurines—anthropomorphic and zoomorphic, female and male—as well as anthropomorphic, bird-shaped, and animal-shaped vases, miniature replicas of furniture, stools, tables, and thrones, miniature offering tables and containers, libation vases, and lamps, as well as temple models, coincides with the early ceramic period, that is, the second half of the 7th millennium B.C. All of these items, and the great variety of their shapes, speak of an intensive religious ceremonialism. Masked figurines and larger sculptures, some with indications of ritual costumes and headgear or crowns found in a variety of postures and in specific locations associated with their special functions, represent a gamut of divine characters expressing the rich Neolithic pantheon of goddesses and gods. A pattern of worship is established which continues to the end of Old Europe with very few changes. In the southeast, temples are evidenced in the later centuries of the 7th millennium B.C. These are integrated with regular houses and are distinguished by characteristic features: an altar of wood or stones (dais) in the larger room and a workshop for the preparation of ritual objects in the smaller room. This tradition continued during the 6th and 5th millennia throughout most of the Balkans and east-central Europe. At the same time, specific locations of worship are evident, which include not only the temples, but courtyard areas with altars and special offering places. As will be shown in the chapter on religion, temples and other places of worship served a variety of functions and were associated with different categories of divinities.

During this millennium, many basic seeds were planted which must be acknowledged for the subsequent stages of cultural evolution to be fully understood.

3

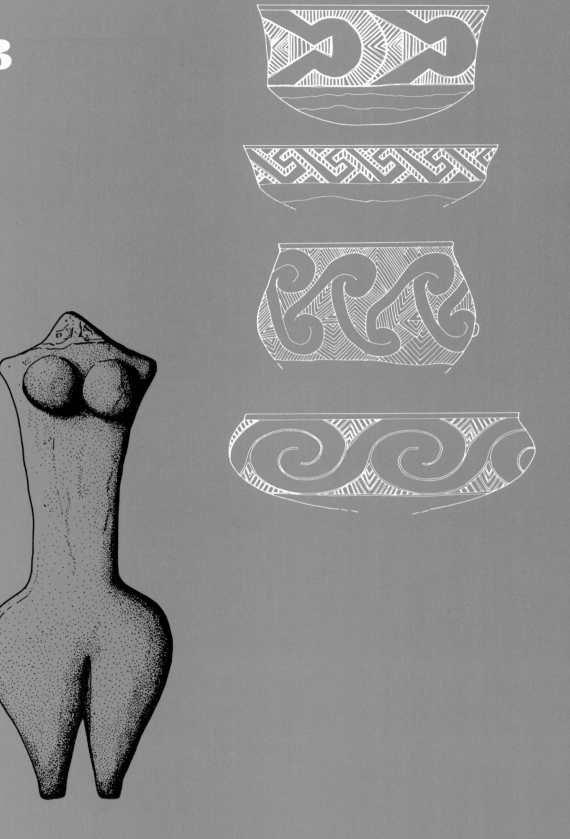
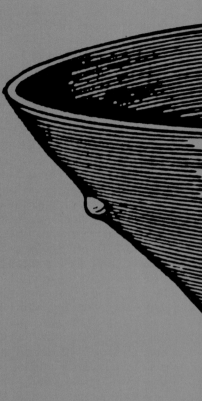

The Climax of European Civilization: East-Central Europe, 5500–3500 B.C.

From a relatively homogeneous Neolithic culture, regional traditions developed that were characterized by diverse art styles as well as increased specialization and development in copper metallurgy and other crafts. Some settlements of this period amounted to townships. The size and number of villages doubled and tripled, reflecting an absolute increase in population, land-use intensification, and a concomitant refinement of social organization.

The appearance of a complex of new traits during this period, particularly of black polished pottery and copper artifacts, has led many scholars in the past to assume that tides of colonization must have burst through the Balkans. They would have come, it was thought, either from Anatolia or from the eastern Mediterranean. This cultural enrichment seems now to have been the product of an essentially local development, since only internal shifts can be observed. An unprecedented diversity and creativity in ceramic art would hardly be the anticipated result of a substantial ethnic movement. From physical anthropological evidence, it appears that the majority of this population must have persisted from earlier times.

Economic patterns of subsistence economy, predicated on the usual crops and domesticates, continued from Neolithic times with a gradual improvement of agricultural and animal-raising techniques. The main innovation in cultivation was a wider use of bread wheat and linseed and a greater specialization in barley production, along with indirect evidence of the use of the plow. A significant increase of cattle and pigs occurred everywhere, while the number of sheep decreased. Between the end of the Neolithic and the end of the Copper Age, the number of cattle in all sites of east-central Europe increased approximately 20 percent.[1]

Local forests abounded in game. In some areas, such as Hungary, Moldavia, the western Ukraine, and northeastern Bulgaria, about 40 percent of the animal bones recovered from settlements are of wild species. Among the hunted animals, the auroch (wild bull) was of prime importance because

of its heavy yield of meat, followed by wild swine, red deer, and roe deer.[2] Fruit, berries, and nuts were also collected where available in the forested uplands. Crab apples, cornelian cherries, strawberries, elderberries, gooseberries, hazelnuts, and acorns have been found at a number of sites.

Numerous barbed harpoons, fishhooks, and spear points of bone and antler in the Tisza, Vinča, Karanovo and other settlements attest to the intensification of river fishing. Large fish such as carp, catfish, and sturgeon must have contributed greatly to subsistence, as did snails and mussels in the coastal regions.

Copper metallurgy began around 5500 B.C. and intensified throughout the course of the 5th millennium B.C. Copper mines are known from central Yugoslavia (Rudna Glava) and central Bulgaria (Ai-Bunar and others). In the midst of this millennium, gold was discovered and was used for the manufacture of religious symbols and jewelry. Craft development and trade reached a climax, while ceramic arts and architecture achieved a true artistic flowering. Vases were produced in a magnificent variety of forms and colors. Decorative techniques included polychrome painting, encrustation, black polishing, channeling, graphite and gold painting. The use of potters' wheels and kilns is a technological surprise in the archeological record, while spacious, multiroom houses and two-story temples are evidence of architectural innovations. The sheer numbers of temples, temple models, articulate anthropomorphic and zoomorphic sculptures and figurines, many marked with symbols and script signs or with an indication of ritual dress, libation and other ritual vases, and the consistent appearance of symbols and script signs on countless sacred objects increase the possibility for the reconstruction of religious beliefs and rituals.

REGIONAL GROUPS AND THEIR CHRONOLOGY

Within the broad geographic region of east-central Europe a multiplicity of cultures developed, each marked by a certain individuality of habitation patterns and ceramic art. (FIGURE 3–1) Eleven cultural areas are briefly described below, starting with the Adriatic and ending with the Black Sea littoral:

1. Danilo-Hvar on the Adriatic Coast
2. Butmir in Bosnia
3. Vinča in the central Balkans
4. Tisza in the River Tisza basin
5. Lengyel in the Middle Danube basin and north-central Europe
6. Boian in the Lower Danube basin
7. Hamangia on the Black Sea coast
8. Karanovo in Thrace and E Macedonia
9. Petreşti in Transylvania
10. Cucuteni in Moldavia and the western Ukraine
11. Dnieper-Donets in the Ukraine

A well-rounded picture of each cultural group is not available since all have not been equally well researched. There is, however, enough material for insight into their chronology, habitation patterns, architecture, art, and religion. Best researched are the Butmir, Vinča, Tisza, and Cucuteni cultures.

The Danilo-Hvar Culture in Dalmatia

The culture that emerged along the Adriatic coast in Dalmatia around 5500 B.C. (FIGURE 3–2) is remarkable for its trade contacts with the west and east. The Danilo people must have been fine navigators. Although no actual remains of boats have been discovered, engravings of sailboats on pottery, such as the one from the Grabak cave on the Adriatic Island of Lesina, offer evidence that sailboats were used. (FIGURE 3–3) They entered into lively contact with Bosnia as well as areas farther inland as distant as Slavonia and Pannonia, thereby influencing the formation of the Butmir and Lengyel cultures. The Danilo people exported spondylus shells, transmitted

FIGURE 3–1

FIGURE 3–1 Culture groups in east-central Europe. 5th mill B.C.

FIGURE 3–2

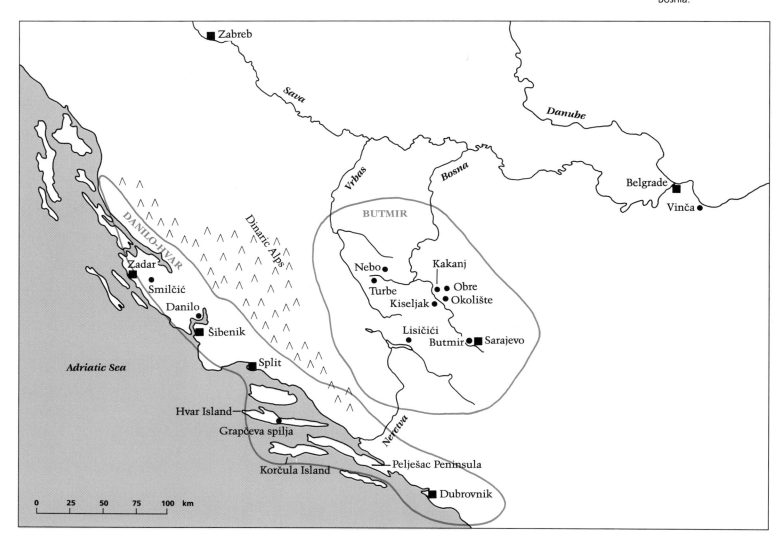

FIGURE 3–2 Danilo-Hvar sites along the Adriatic and Butmir sites in Bosnia.

obsidian from Italy, and spread their own ceramic products into the Bosnian valleys. Some agricultural products were probably imported from more fertile regions in the east and salt from as far as southern Poland.

Settlements

The Danilo people lived in open villages which were surrounded by one or two ditches, 2–3 m wide and approximately 1.5 m deep. These were located in valleys at a water source, some kilometers inland from the sea—conveniently located near adjoining fertile land. Large caves on the islands and along the coast were also occupied, some of which produced quantities of very fine painted pottery from the later period of this culture. I suspect these were used as sanctuaries.

At Smilčić, near Zadar on the Adriatic coast, early Neolithic Impresso layers are succeeded by the sophisticated painted pottery of the Danilo culture,[3] named for the eponymous site near Šibenik in Dalmatia.[4] A soil layer devoid of habitation materials separates the Impresso deposits from the Danilo levels (a total of thirteen habitation horizons).

Pottery

A magnificent variety of shapes and makes of Danilo pottery are present, marking a departure from the Impresso Pottery stage, revealing marked stylistic developments in pottery and chipped stone technology. The fine Danilo ware, which has close parallels across the Adriatic in Italy (Ripoli), has almost no temper and was white slipped and painted with black and red patterns before firing, then burnished. The Danilo type culture may have been introduced by an incoming population from the south via the Albanian coast. Unfortunately, the isolation of Albania for half a century created a visible gap in archeological research; the information available is insufficient.

Another type of Danilo pottery was polished and incised with spirals, chevrons, striated triangles and lozenges, zigzags, nets, herringbone motifs, a.o. (FIGURE 3–4) Rhytons with a massive

FIGURE 3–3

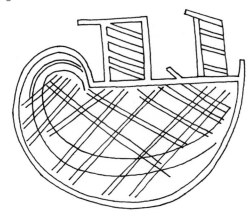

FIGURE 3–3 A sailboat incised on a vase, a symbol of maritime communication throughout Old Europe. Grabak Cave, Lesina Island of the Dalmatian coast, Yugoslavia. 5th mill. B.C.

FIGURE 3–4

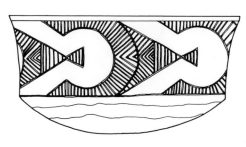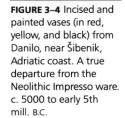

FIGURE 3–4 Incised and painted vases (in red, yellow, and black) from Danilo, near Šibenik, Adriatic coast. A true departure from the Neolithic Impresso ware. c. 5000 to early 5th mill. B.C.

ring handle are also characteristic. (FIGURE 3–5) These have bear legs and are usually solidly decorated with the same patterns as other ceramic vases— striations, meanders, and spirals. They must have been produced locally, although the origin of this particular shape is in Greece, where ring-handled vessels are known from the Sesklo culture of the early 6th millennium B.C. (dated at Achilleion IV from c. 6000–5800 B.C.). Apparently used in certain ritual ceremonies, they (or the idea of the shape) spread widely from Thessaly and central Greece to the west, then along the Adriatic coast as far as Bosnia.

Chronology

Finds from the island of Hvar characterize the final stage of the Danilo culture known as Hvar.[5] There are no radiocarbon dates for the Danilo sequence and the final Hvar stage. However, Italian parallels and typological comparisons with the well-dated Late Starčevo and Butmir materials from Obre permit us to place the Danilo culture within the time-span of 5500–4000 B.C.

The Butmir Culture in Bosnia

Because of its early discovery, the Butmir culture is considerably better known than the Danilo-Hvar culture group. The Butmir settlement in the suburb of modern Sarajevo was excavated by Radimsky and Fiala in 1893–96, and the results were published in 1895 and 1898 in two luxurious, outsized volumes with many colored plates.[6] Butmir vases decorated with running spirals in painting and in relief greatly impressed the scholarly world of the early 20th century. (FIGURES 3–6, 3–7, 3–8; PLATE 7) For decades, Butmir was considered to be "the cradle of the spiral art" of Europe. It seemed almost unreal to discover such highly attractive and advanced ceramics in the valley of the River Bosna, an area culturally remote and modest in our time.

FIGURE 3–5

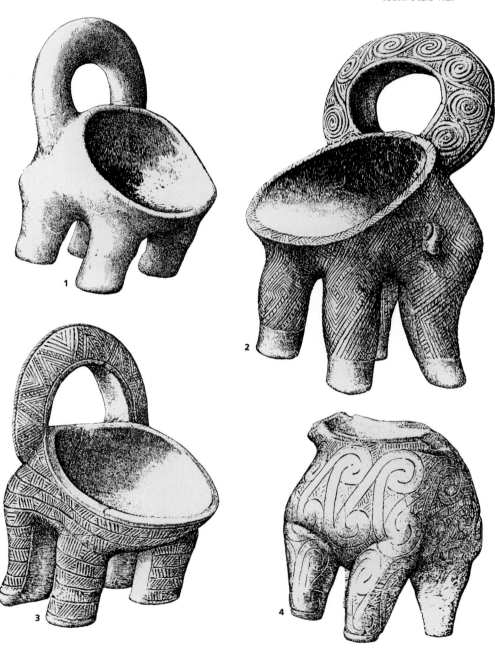

FIGURE 3–5 Bear-legged, ring-handled offering vessels. Danilo culture. (1–3) Smilčić. (4) Bribir near Zadar, Adriatic coast. Scale 1:2.

FIGURE 3–6

FIGURE 3–6 Butmir vase
decorated with running
spiral motif in relief.
Butmir at Sarajevo,
Bosnia. c. 4900–4800
B.C. H. 20.5 cm.

FIGURE 3–7

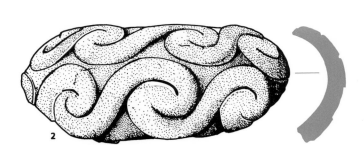
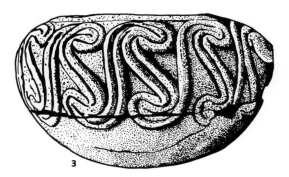

FIGURE 3–7 Spiral-
decorated Butmir vases.
(1,2) Butmir. (3) Nebo,
Bosnia. 49th–48th
cents. B.C. Scale 1:2.

FIGURE 3–8

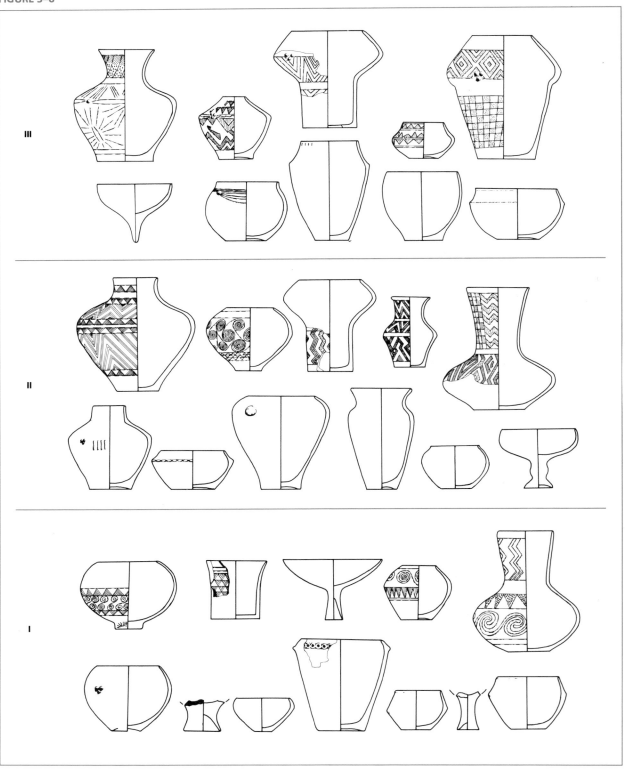

Trade

Seven thousand years ago, however, the lush valleys of the Bosna and Neretva rivers and their tributaries became a highway between the Adriatic and Italy in the west and the Middle Danube basin in the east. The people of this area developed wide-reaching trade relationships which stimulated the rise of the Butmir culture. This is indicated by obsidian, spondylus shells, and painted pottery imports.

The obsidian trade which initiated contacts with the west started around 5500 B.C., before the formation of the Butmir culture. Early Danilo influences on the Late Starčevo culture in Bosnia are traced by the appearance of ring-handled religious vessels. Imports of painted pottery from southern Italy emerged in Bosnia in the early part of the 6th millennium B.C. and communication with the west continued to increase throughout the end of the same millennium.

Chronology

The key site for chronology is Obre II, 65 km northwest of Sarajevo, which was excavated in 1967–68 by Alojz Benac and the author.[7] This site yielded an ideal, uninterrupted four-meter stratigraphy and a series of radiocarbon dates which places the three periods of the Butmir culture (Butmir I, II, III) between 5300 B.C. and the later centuries of the 5th millennium B.C. (TABLE 7) Butmir I is dated c. 5300–4900 B.C.; Butmir II, 4900–4700 B.C. The last period at Obre, Butmir III, was not radiocarbon dated, but typologically runs parallel to Hvar on the Adriatic coast. Its three phases should be placed in the period from c. 4700 to 4300–4200 B.C.

The continuity of culture through three periods can be observed in a very neat sequence of pottery shapes and ornamentation. (FIGURE 3–8) Painted ware banded with red above the black background, with plastic or incised spirals (FIGURE 3–9) is characteristic of Butmir only. The potters' use of the running spiral motif, as well as a series of other geometric motifs—chevrons, lozenges, striated triangles, zigzags,

FIGURE 3–9

FIGURE 3–9 Butmir I vases from Obre II, 5100–4900 B.C.

FIGURE 3–10

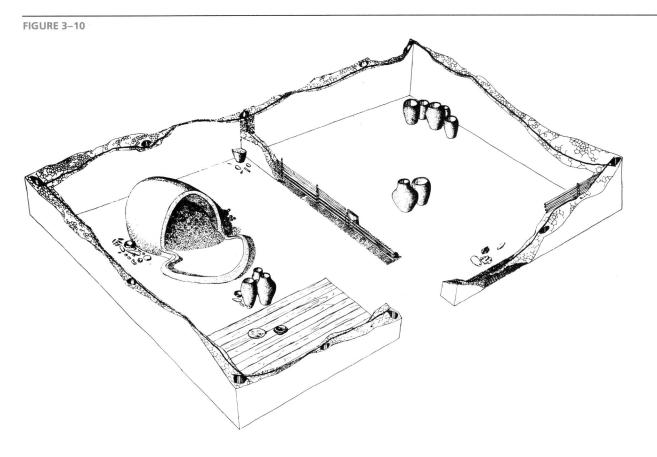

FIGURE 3–10 Butmir house of two rooms with a bread oven in the smaller room from Obre II settlement in Bosnia. Walls are of vertically placed twigs in horizontal lines between timber posts coated with clay 5–8 cm thick on each side. Vases filled with wheat stood on a wood platform in front of the oven. Flint- and bone-working area left of the oven, loom weights (weaving area) is right of the oven. Groups of large storage vessels in both rooms. Butmir II, 4900–4700 B.C.

FIGURE 3–11

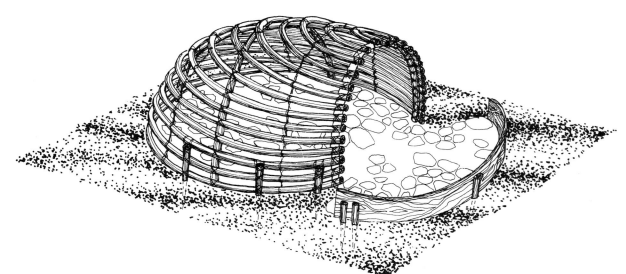

FIGURE 3–11 Frame of an oven built of twigs fastened with bast cord, foundation of flat stones. The frame was preserved in charred form or impression in clay. Obre, Bosnia. Butmir II, c. 4900–4800 B.C.

FIGURE 3–12 (1) Reconstruction of a vertical loom and (2) loom weights. Jasa Tepe, Plovdiv, C Bulgaria, c. 5000 B.C. Similar looms were found in all culture groups described in this chapter.

stylized snake heads—began as an influence from the Danilo culture. These were applied in a peculiar Butmir style on large pear-shaped vases or bulbous vases with long or short cylindrical necks.

Settlement Sites

The Butmir people occupied valley bottoms of fertile soil, settling on the widest terraces of rivers and streams. Their settlements occasionally extended over an area of 500 meters along the river bank,[8] but most of the excavated sites are compact villages delineated by the natural contours of the terrace and river bend. Obre II extended over a surface of 20,000 square meters. Life continued without disruption at this location for nearly a millennium, a pattern we shall see repeated in the Vinča and Tisza territories. Obre II was a village of some sixty dwellings arranged in lines separated by streets from 3 m to 5 m wide between the rows.

Architecture

At Obre II, a number of houses of various habitation levels were exceptionally well preserved. (FIGURE 3–10). The Butmir I village at Obre yielded houses of thin wood construction, stone wall foundations, supporting vertical posts, and compact clay coating on the walls with straw and wood roofs. This building tradition continued from Neolithic Obre I (Starčevo) times. Butmir II houses had thicker vertical posts, and the wood construction of the walls was done in one of three ways: 1) with horizontally arranged twigs bound with bast in several vertical rows between timber uprights; 2) with vertically set twigs bound with bast in horizontal rows; or 3) with vertical, solidly placed split logs. The thickness of the walls depends on the depth of reinforcement. Walls of twig wattle had a clay coating 5 to 8 cm thick on either side, while walls of split-log rows were more heavily coated with clay, 10 to 12 cm thick on either side. Above the timber posts lay thick horizontal beams that carried the roof construction. Floors were coated with clay or were of wooden planks in rooms

FIGURE 3–12

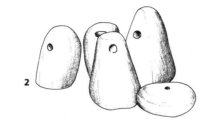

containing the oven. Wall plaster was slipped and decorated with ornaments in relief, such as snake coils. In addition to the regular Obre houses with wattle-and-daub walls supported by wooden posts, there were light structures built only of wood, considered to have been auxiliary farm sheds, among which was one with an apsidal end.[9]

House Furnishings

Within the house, one room always contained a bread oven built of branches, covered by a beehive-shaped roof of clay. (FIGURE 3–11) Its clay floor lay over a foundation of flat stones, forming a platform in front of the oven. In one example, groups of loom weights suggest the presence of a vertical loom standing beside the oven. (FIGURE 3–12) Grinding, spinning, and other tasks were probably also performed in this room since quern stones, spindle whorls, and bone and flint tools were found in concentration at the site of the oven. Opposite, along the wall, was an area covered with wooden boards. Storage jars, groups of vases, and braziers with horizontally pierced holes stood on the floor in this as well as in the adjacent room. Beside every oven was an ash pit in which ash of the best quality was collected. In Benac's opinion, this may have been used as a detergent in washing linen.

An unusual find at Obre houses were large hollow cylindrical ceramic objects found in the walls, which could have served for ventilation.[10] Houses had deep storage pits for food, some of which were two meters deep and about 85 centimeters in diameter. These must have been the refrigerators of their times.

FIGURE 3–13

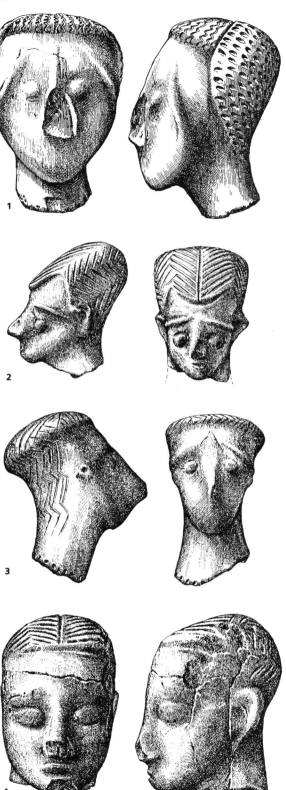

1

2

3

4

Figurines

The excavators of the Butmir site apparently found one or several temples since hundreds of terracotta figurines were unearthed. Some of the preserved heads of female figurines from Butmir have masterfully modeled human heads and hairdos. The majority, however, have outlines of masks with long noses or beaks and no human mouth. (FIGURE 3–13) In my opinion, they were produced for the worship of the protective and life- and wealth-giving Bird Goddess, the main deity of household and temple.

The Vinča Culture in the Central Balkans

In the central Balkans, the continuity of the Neolithic Starčevo complex is traced throughout the middle of the 6th millennium B.C., but around 5400–5300 B.C. innovations occurred that are most clearly reflected in the ceramics, resulting in a cultural configuration called the Vinča complex.

Major Site

The Vinča sequence is best documented at an eponymous (name-giving) site, 14 km east of Belgrade, excavated by Miloje Vasić between 1908 and 1934, which yielded seven meters of stratified Vinča deposits overlying the Starčevo levels.[11] No other site as rich or as well stratified has yet been discovered, and despite the antiquity of the excavation in terms of modern field methodology, this site has remained the backbone for the typology of Vinča assemblages. Other more extensively and recently excavated settlement sites with published results are Anza IV in Macedonia,[12] Banjica northeast of Belgrade,[13] Crnokalačka Bara near Niš,[14] Gradešnica,[15] Rast,[16] Valać,[17] Selevac,[18] Divostin,[19] and Gomolava.[20]

The Vinča complex occupied the central Balkans northward as far as Banat, westward to northeast Bosnia, and eastward to western Bulgaria and southwestern Romania. (FIGURE 3–14) This distribution covers the territory of the Starčevo culture, except for the peripheral areas where other local variants formed.

FIGURE 3–14

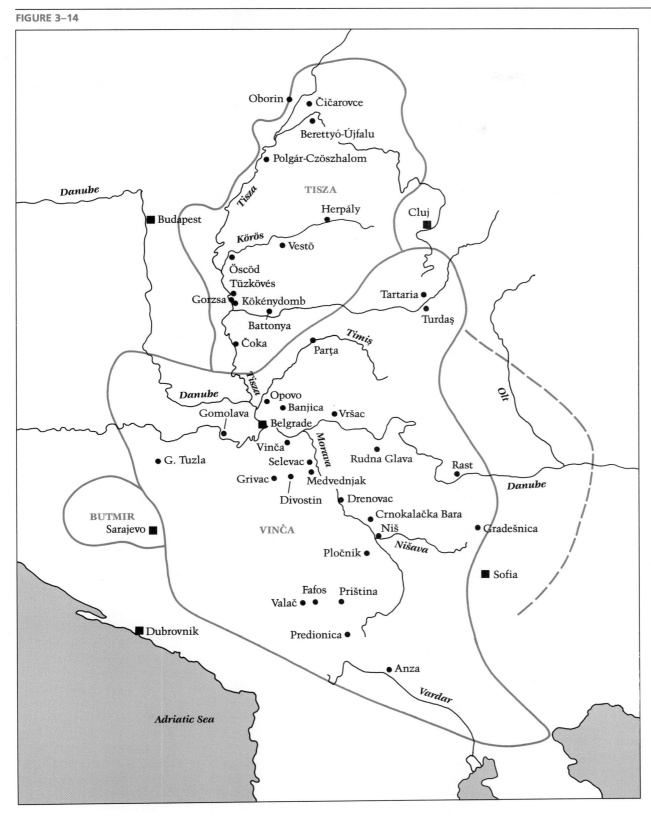

A total of nearly 650 Vinča sites, mostly settlements, are known from excavations and surface collections (listed and placed on the map in a monograph on the Vinča culture by John Chapman, 1981).[21]

Vinča settlements, which are consistently larger than those of the Starčevo, are found unenclosed along rivers. The larger ones occupy a territory of 25–30 hectares and even up to 80 (Selevac) and 100 hectares (Potporanj at Vršac). In areas of high arable potential, villages developed in one location over several generations, in some cases over 500–600 years, forming tells. In Vinča itself, ten habitation horizons were distinguished. These tell settlements are restricted in size and occupy from 2 to 6 hectares, but even they are larger than the Near East Early Dynastic towns.[22]

The varying potential for farming of regional environments became the basis for settlement concentration. Chernozems (black earth), brown forest soils, smonicas, and alluvial (flood deposited) soils were especially sought. The largest concentrations of sites are in the fertile regions of the Morava and Middle Danube basins. Settlements are located either on flat river terraces or on the gently sloping foothills, frequently near streams, brooks, or thermal waters considered holy to this day. The size of villages and towns varied: small settlements held up to 200 persons, medium ones up to 500, while the largest had from 1,000 to 2,500 inhabitants.[23] The research exploring their interrelationship has not yet been done.

Architecture

Vinča villages were carefully planned. The ground was leveled before building began, slopes were terraced, several rows of posts were implanted. Houses stood aligned approximately parallel to one another, and in some villages house rows were separated by streets 2.5 to 3.5 m wide. The Late Vinča settlement at Divostin in central Serbia had four groups of houses arranged in threes or twos within the excavated area.[24] The space between houses ranged from 26 m to 60 m and their courts were bordered with stones.

Early Vinča houses consisted of one large room with an antechamber or of two rooms about 8 m long and 3 to 4 m wide. House size increased greatly during the mid-Vinča period.[25] Houses of three, four, or even five rooms were unearthed along with two-room houses in a number of settlements. (FIGURE 3-15) The largest houses were up to 20 m long.

Houses were built of timber posts or split-plank frame plaited with twigs then plastered with a thick layer of clay or mud. The use of split planks, about 15 cm wide and 2.5 cm thick, was recorded at the Early Vinča site of Anza in central Macedonia, dated to c. 5200 B.C.[26] Floors were finished with smooth lime plaster and had a subfloor of either squared logs or beams, or stones mixed with sherds, or square stone slabs. During the excavation of Anza IV in 1969–70, my own crew members were impressed with the solid architecture and refinement of these houses. In contrast, they lived in little comfort in cow-dung sheds in the nearby village of Anzabegovo. Anza is an excellent example of the high level of Old European civilization seven thousand years ago and the degradation of culture in modern times as a result of incessant wars by patriarchal societies.

The architecture of regular houses and of temples was closely related, as it was also during the Early Neolithic. This fact seems to have obscured the recognition of temples in Vinča settlements, and yet there are multiroomed houses that clearly stand out from the rest. These have painted walls, inside and out, with symbolic designs such as chevrons and meanders painted in red, blue, and white. In at least four Vinča settlements (Vinča, Parţa, Jela, and Kormadin), bucrania were discovered attached to clay columns or walls in the temples. The bucrania consisted of ox skulls coated with a layer of clay, with muzzles painted in blue and a red triangle on their foreheads. (FIGURE 3-16) At Parţa, southwest of Timişoara, several temples, one above the other, were discovered in the 1980s. These yielded altars fenced within clay walls, offering tables, mobile offering hearths, monumental statues, and columns with bucrania attached. Among the most striking discoveries was a double statue of goddesses with two heads and shoulders. A bucranium, with fragments of a bull skull, was found at the statue. The final excavation report on these very important temples has not yet appeared; the information comes from preliminary reports.[27]

Trade and Copper Mining

Vinča culture grew fast economically, not only due to farming and cattle raising, but also due to rising trade activities and mining. Obsidian was obtained for sickles and other precision tools from the Upper Tisza region. Alabaster and marble used for sculptures and spondylus shell for ornaments must have come from the coasts of the Adriatic and the Aegean Seas. Cinabarite for coloring was mined at Šuplja Stena in central Yugoslavia. Copper mining which started no later than 5000 B.C. was one of the greatest achievements. The earliest copper mine has been discovered at Rudna Glava, 140 kilometers east of Belgrade (see discussion below on metallurgy, trade and crafts).

Chronology

When Professor Vasić first reported the results of his excavation of the Vinča mound in the *Illustrated London News* in 1930, he described the site as "a centre of Aegean civilization in the second millennium B.C." He believed that this settlement had been continuously occupied from the beginning of the Aegean Middle Bronze Age until the area was conquered by the Romans. Vasić was quite firm in this belief, and a final statement issued just before his death asserts that Vinča was a Greek colony. Credence in this interpretation still persists in some modern histories of the Balkans where it is cited on his authority. Archeological evidence, however, shows otherwise: Vinča culture formed during the last centuries of the 6th millennium B.C. and continued for a thousand years. Vinča sites demonstrate convincingly that the development of material culture, arts, and religion was integral and uninterrupted. The archeo-

FIGURE 3–15

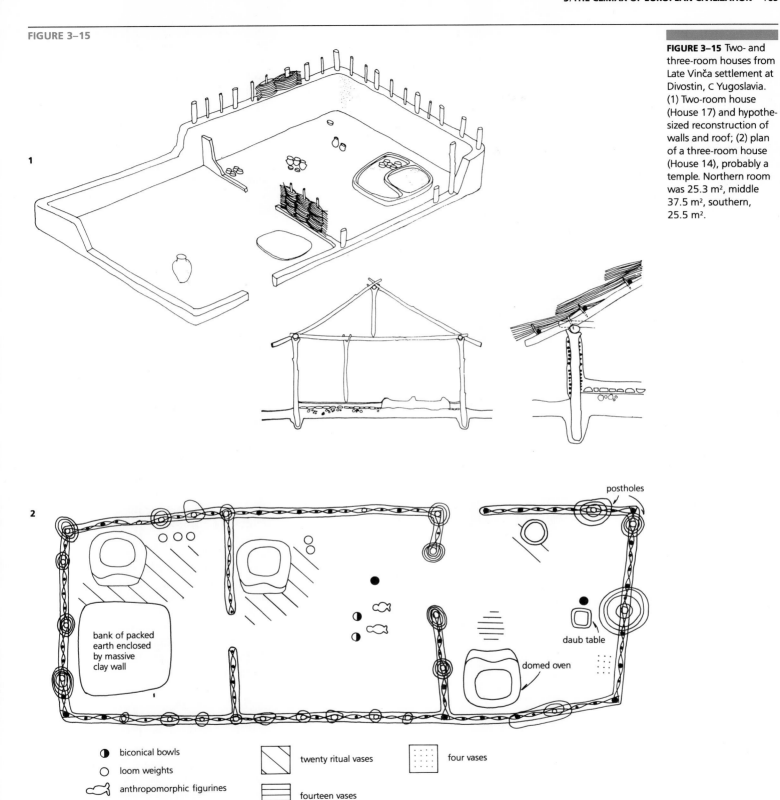

postholes

bank of packed
earth enclosed
by massive
clay wall

daub table

domed oven

biconical bowls

loom weights

anthropomorphic figurines

3-legged container

twenty ritual vases

fourteen vases

four vases

FIGURE 3–16

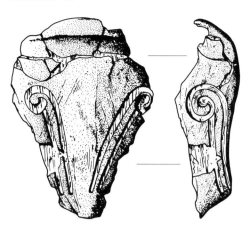

logical consensus today is that Vinča was an indigenous culture, its eventual efflorescence a result of gradual socio-economic change which became more rapid with the emergence of metallurgy and attendant population increase. The size of settlements virtually doubled over the millennium, while the physical type—the gracile Mediterranean—was continuous from Starčevo times.[28]

Radiocarbon dates place the Vinča culture, on the basis of dendrochronological calibration, between 5400–5300 and 4300–4100 B.C. (TABLE 8). The general classification of this culture is suggested as follows: Early Vinča, c. 5400–4900 B.C. and Late or Classical Vinča, c. 4900–4300 B.C. (only in one case is the date later than 4300 B.C.).[29] Both periods have subphases, although there is generally one gradual development for more than 1,000 years.

Pottery

The emergence of a new ceramic style around 5400–5300 B.C., dominated by a black burnished pottery, produced speculations that a new wave of immigrants must have come from western or central Anatolia bringing their tradition of dark-faced pottery. This new style was actually due to influences from the Karanovo culture in Bulgaria where the fashionable black pottery started a few centuries earlier and spread over a large area. By the end of the 6th millennium B.C., dark wares appeared not only in Yugoslavia but also in Thessaly and even in southern Greece.

The transition from Starčevo to Vinča ceramic style can be observed at Anza, Macedonia, which was excavated by the author in 1969–70.[30] The earliest Vinča materials were found above the late Starčevo layer and are radiocarbon dated to c. 5300–5000 B.C. The Vinča horizon is typified by a large percentage of well-made black-burnished wares—gray-black burnished or black slipped and hard fired—and by a much greater variety of shapes and handles than during the previous period. These gradually replaced the orange wares of the Starčevo culture. A variety of biconical vessels, carinated and flat dishes, zoomorphic (animal shaped) and ornithomorphic

(bird shaped) vases, and high-footed vases are now the leading forms in the fine ware category. (FIGURE 3–17) The finest piece is black-burnished to a mirrorlike finish inside and out. The majority of vases were decorated by channeling, produced by burnishing in the pattern. (FIGURE 3–18, 1) This decorative technique as well as biconical shapes (FIGURE 3–18, 2) and a variety of handles and lugs continued throughout the Vinča sequence. Black-topped ware was also introduced during the Early Vinča period. Vessels of this style were slipped with brown, buff, or red and then burnished. The black color of the upper part was intentional and probably produced by inverting the pot and depressing the rim into ashes during firing while the rest of the pot was oxidizing.[31]

Sculptural Art

The art of Vinča developed its own unique identity,[32] which can be easily distinguished from other cultural groups since thousands of miniature and larger clay sculptures have been preserved. In the name-giving site alone, nearly 2,000 figurines and anthropomorphic vases have been unearthed, representing various phases of the culture. Six hundred and thirty were published by Vasić in *Vinča* (vol. 3), and are housed in the Belgrade University and National Museums. Considerable numbers of figurines were found in almost every Vinča settlement. The most remarkable sculptures are from southern Yugoslavia, particularly from the region of Priština in Kosovo Metohije (PLATES 8 and 9), one of the most impoverished regions of our times, inhabited by Albanians.

Vinča figurines, particularly those representing the Bird Goddess, show precious details: a characteristic mask with a large nose or beak with no mouth (FIGURES 3–19 and 3–20); attire such as shoulder straps (FIGURE 3–20), hip belts, or narrow skirt (see figs. 7–87, 7–89 through 7–94); and the incised or painted symbols of the divinity—V's, chevrons, meanders, parallel lines, tri-lines, and bi-lines (see fig. 7–14). Not infrequently, her image appears as a vase with a face shown on the neck (see fig. 7–17), or as a mask attached to the vase's

FIGURE 3–16 A bucranium (an ox skull plastered with a layer of clay) from late Vinča temple (Vinča, at the depth of 2.89 m). Stylized eyes are shown as engraved spirals with lines extending to the muzzle painted in blue. Above the eyes was a red painted triangle, now faded. Horns broken. H 44 cm.

FIGURE 3–17 Early Vinča black burnished pottery: biconical vases decorated by channeling, dishes, handled vases, a footed vessel, and a large vase with Bird Goddess's face on the neck. c. 5200–5000 B.C. Anza IV, Macedonia, SE Yugoslavia.

FIGURE 3–18 (1) A typical Vinča black burnished vase decorated by channeling and by burnishing in the snake coil pattern. Early Classical Vinča, beginning of the 5th mill. B.C. H 14.5 cm. (2) Black polished jug from Crnokolačka Bara near Niš, S Yugoslavia. Early Vinča settlement, c. 5000 B.C. H 37 cm.

FIGURE 3–17

FIGURE 3–18

FIGURE 3–19

1

2

3

FIGURE 3–20

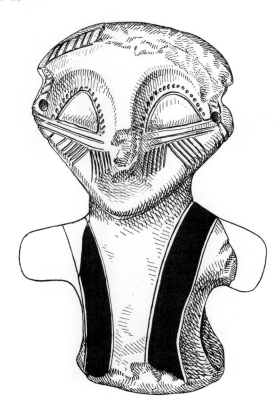

FIGURE 3–19 The Bird Goddess from Vinča wearing a beaked mask. (1) Early 5th mill. B.C. (2,3) Mid-5th mill. B.C.

FIGURE 3–20 Characteristic Vinča figurine with a large pentagonal mask with semicircular eyes marked with horizontal tri-lines and groups of striations under the lines. Black straps bordered with white color over the shoulders. Vitoševac-Lukičski Breg near Niš, SE Yugoslavia. 5000–4500 B.C. H 13 cm.

neck. (FIGURE 3–19, 2) Bird vases with human masks are true masterpieces of this art. The portrayal of masks is universal on all articulately produced sculptures in which divine images are expressed. The Bird Goddess and other divinities of the Classical Vinča period wear pentagonal masks with molded semicircular eyes. (FIGURES 3–19, 3–20) Later Vinča sculptures wear masks with almond-shaped eyes. (FIGURE 3–21) The flat surface of the mask was used for engraving symbols. Monumental life-sized masks have been discovered in southern Yugoslavia. (PLATE 11)

From the predominance of its image, we gather that the primary divinity worshiped in temples of the Vinča site was the Bird Goddess. There are, however, other deities represented, such as Snake Goddesses, Madonnas (mother figures with a bear or bird mask holding a baby (see figs. 7–5 and 7–6). Zoomorphic figurines such as snakes, frogs, hedgehogs, dogs, and fish, and anthropomorphic male figures wearing ram or he-goat masks constitute about 20 percent of the figurines. Of great interest are the centaurs found in southern Yugoslavia, in which a masked human head is grafted onto the body of a bull. (PLATE 22) Typical of earlier Vinča art are owl-faced lids of large biconical vases, most likely used for religious rites as liquid containers. (PLATE 10) Some zoomorphic and anthropomorphic sculptures were carved out of marble, alabaster, and opalite, of which the heads of dogs carved from light green opalite and white marble are particularly fine examples. Offering tables and containers and oil lamps that are frequently found with figurines had anthropomorphic or zoomorphic legs incised with symbols or painted in bright colors. (PLATE 13)

Realistic masterpieces and schematized versions of larger sculptures were present in each phase of Vinča culture as they were one thousand years earlier in the Sesklo culture. The majority of schematized or miniature figurines marked with symbols and inscribed with signs appear in great numbers during the Early Vinča period. Most of these inscribed figurines were probably *ex votos*.

FIGURE 3–21

a

FIGURE 3–21 (a) Vinča Bird Goddess in the shape of a vase with a pentagonal mask shown in relief. Fine light-brown fabric with channelled surface (burnished with pebbles). (b) Three views. Chevron design was executed in front and back in channelling technique. Classical Vinča, early 5th mill. B.C. H 32.5 cm.

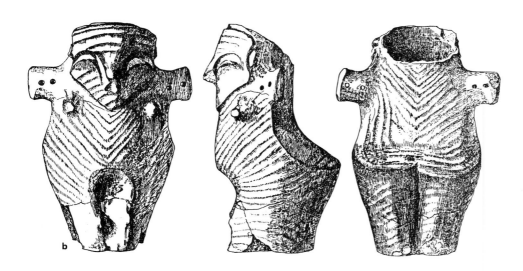

b

I would like to mention here an example from my own excavation of an Early Vinča township at Anza, Macedonia. Alongside the regular small-sized figurines, one of the houses, apparently a destroyed temple, yielded a huge vase, 92 cm tall, decorated with a red triangle and chevrons, with a Bird Goddess face incised on the neck (see fig. 7–17). Another vase of a waterbird was 60 cm long (fig. 7–18) and a life-sized sculpture of a pig was unearthed nearby.[33] The size and detailing of sculptures naturally depended upon the purpose for which they were produced.

The range of aesthetic accomplishment expressed by Vinča ceramics and sculpture inspire a new appreciation of the artistic traditions of Old Europe. Here is an art which is not only infused with mythical values, but is grounded in a technical facility which allowed abstracted, schematized expression as well as finely crafted realism. Certain Vinča torsos, for example, compete with those of Ancient Greece in their perfect rendition of the female body. (FIGURE 3–22)

The Tisza Culture of the River Tisza Basin

The name of this culture derives from the River Tisza which rises in the Carpathian Mountains and flows through eastern Hungary and northern Yugoslavia into the Danube. (see fig. 3–14, *above*). Settlements on alluvial mounds above the flood plain abound along the Tisza, Maros, and Körös rivers. These are clustered in three groups bearing three appelations: the Gorzsa group near Szolnok in southern Hungary, the Herpaly near Debrecen in eastern Hungary, and the Csöszhalom near the town of Nyiregyaza in northern Hungary.

Like the Vinča, the Tisza culture descended from the Starčevo (Körös) culture which is shown by the predominance of the gracile Mediterranean (Starčevo) physical type. Its divergence from the Vinča culture is due to specific ecological conditions in the River Tisza

FIGURE 3–22

FIGURE 3–22 Seated female terracotta figure. Classical Vinča from Čaršija, C Yugoslavia. Approx. 4700–4500 B.C.

FIGURE 3–23 Enthroned goddesses in the shape of anthropomorphic vases decorated in panels bearing chevrons, zigzags, striated triangles, bands of lozenges and X's, and script signs. Bracelets and arm rings are indicated (right, second band). Kökénydomb, SE Hungary. Classical Tisza, early 5th mill. B.C. (1) H 33 cm; (2) H 24 cm; (3) H 23 cm.

basin, and its emergence as a separate unit is correlated with the appearance of tell settlements and tell-based economies.

Discovery and Major Sites

The discovery of the Tisza culture started with the excavation at Čoka (Csoka), now in northern Yugoslavia, by F. Mora from 1907 to 1913.[34] Large scale excavations by J. Banner at the enormously rich tell of Kökénydomb near Hódmezővásárhely in southeastern Hungary from 1928 to 1944 provided a truly scientific basis and impetus for the investigation of this culture.[35] Subsequently, the excavations of Szegvár-Tüzköves at Szentes by J. Czalog between 1955 and 1964, continued in the 1970s by J. Korek, placed the Tisza culture on the map due to the discovery of very impressive ceramic sculptures and anthropomorphic vases. (PLATE 12) Both Kökénydomb and Szegvár-Tüzköves produced outstanding and unique pieces of sculptural art. These included enthroned goddesses in the shape of anthropomorphic vases, richly decorated with symbolic geometric designs in panels (FIGURE 3–23), and male gods, of which the so-called Sickle God from Szegvár-Tüzköves (a male figure holding a sickle-shaped object over his shoulder) is the most famous.[36]

FIGURE 3–23

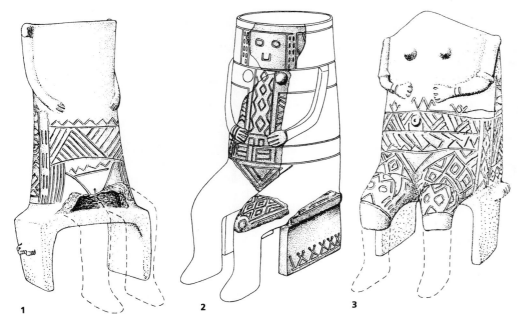

1   2   3

FIGURE 3–24

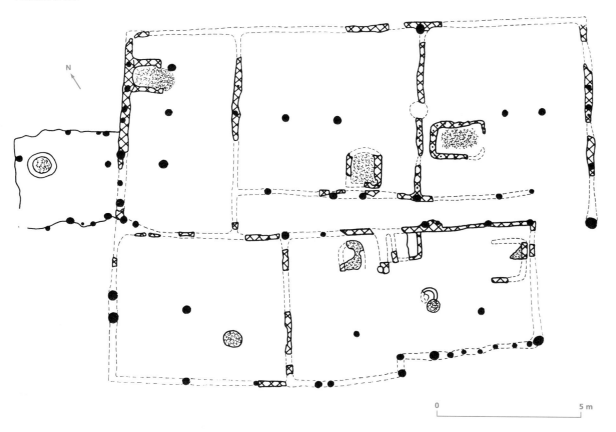

0   5 m

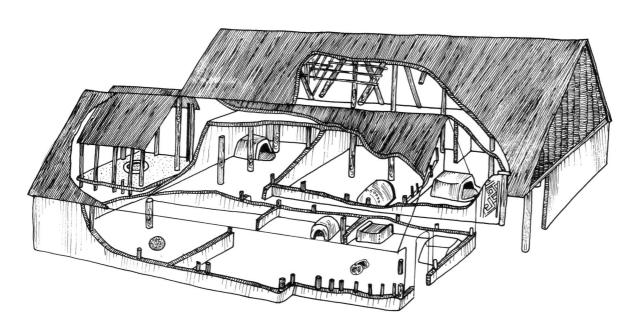

FIGURE 3–24 Groundplan and reconstruction of a house complex. The outer and inner walls of the room with the side entrance and the largest oven (upper, right) were decorated with incised and red-painted meander bands. Gorzsa, SE Hungary. Classical Tisza; c. 4500 B.C.

FIGURE 3–25 Reconstruction of a two-story house (temple?). Herpály, level 8, house 11. E Hungary, 48th–46th centuries B.C. (See radiocarbon dates, table 4.) Three rooms on the first floor were packed with vases. Truncated pyramid shaped ovens were in two rooms on the right, with a round basin in the left room. Two large basins were on the upper floor with vases concentrated on the right.

Chronological Subdivision

The 1970s and 1980s saw further excavations of tell settlements rich with cultural debris from Early and Classical Tisza. Among these sites are Vesztö,[37] Battonya,[38] Herpaly,[39] and Gorzsa.[40] About sixty radiocarbon dates from various tells place this culture between 5400 and 3700 B.C. (TABLE 9) This sequence includes the Early Tisza period called Szakálhát, 5400–5000 B.C.; the Classical Tisza, 5000–4400 B.C., subdivided into three subphases, Tisza I, II, III; and the Tiszapolgár period, 4400–3700 B.C., mainly known from cemeteries, not tells. An excellent survey of very intensive recent excavations has been published in English as the collective work, *The Late Neolithic of the Tisza Region* (1987) edited by Pal Raczky.

Tell Settlement

The precondition for the emergence of tell settlements was an architecture based on the combination of mud and wood. Settlements range from 1.5 hectares (Kökénydomb) to 11 hectares (Szegvár-Tüzköves). The largest northernmost tell is Csöszhalom with five successive occupation levels.[41] All tells lie on elevations rising above flood plains in areas suitable for grain cultivation.

Settlements are classified into three main forms: those which are 3–4 m high, which were densely settled; 1–2.5 m high, which were less densely settled villages which covered a larger horizontal area; and single-layer settlements with loosely scattered houses. These three distinct forms often occur side by side forming one complex of settlements.[42] Houses were closely spaced and formed smaller clusters of four to six or larger clusters of ten to thirteen, usually surrounded by an open area.

Architecture

Tisza architecture is outstanding for its multiroomed and two-story buildings. (FIGURES 3–24, 3–25). The multiroomed houses were up to 18 m long (as at Gorzsa) with tripartite divisions, and were timber framed with pisé (tauf) walls. Timber uprights reinforced the walls and supported the pitched roof. Wattling between posts was of intertwined twigs, branches, and reeds subsequently daubed with clay on both the inside and the outside. Floors were of plastered clay, often covering a raised wooden substructure which preserved the imprints of reed or rushwork matting. The Tisza people decorated the walls with painted or incised designs, and gable ornaments in the form of animal heads modelled from clay have been preserved in a number of settlements (Kökénydomb, Gorzsa, Herpaly). Each room contained an open, domed, or truncated pyramid-shaped clay oven. A characteristic feature of Tisza houses is the large rectangular or rounded clay bins for grain storage. These were either plastered onto the floor or standing on legs. Occasionally, wooden chests and baskets were preserved (at Herpaly).

FIGURE 3–25

FIGURE 3–26

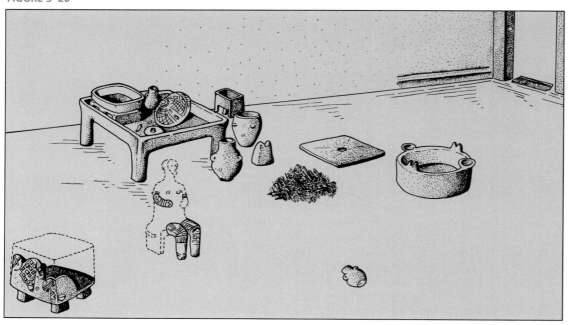

FIGURE 3–26 Tentative reconstruction of the building with ceremonial assemblage: clay table, rectangular containers, a bird headed lid (see fig. 3–27), vases, kernos (right) with horns and small offering containers attached to the rim, and a sculpture in the shape of an enthroned goddess (in hypothetical reconstruction). Vésztö-Mágor, E Hungary. c. 5000 B.C. or earliest centuries of the 5th mill. B.C.

FIGURE 3–27

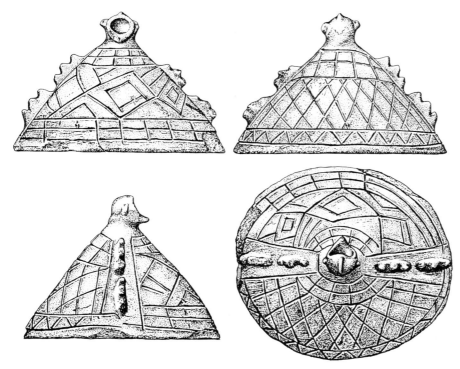

FIGURE 3–27 Bird-headed terracotta lid found on the clay table in the shrine (see fig. 3–26), decorated in panels of incised nets, zigzags and lozenges. Double-notched handles on both sides. Vésztö-Mágor, E Hungary. H 19.7 cm. 5000–4800 B.C.

Clusters of clay loom weights witness the existence of vertical looms near the ovens. Among the internal furnishings of richly equipped rooms, as at Vesztö of the Classical Tisza period, were portable table-like altars, basinlike bowls set on a quadrangular base, a bird-headed lid of a large vase, ornamental bull heads applied onto the walls, offering pits, and kernoi (ceremonial footed dishes consisting of many small containers for various offerings).[43] (FIGURES 3–26, 3–27) These finds speak of ritual activities, and if these rooms were not communal village temples, they were at least domestic shrines.

Temples and Ritual Vases

As elsewhere in southeastern Europe, the temples of the Tisza culture were in the shape of regular houses. The illustrated two-story house from Herpaly (fig. 3–25) was very likely a temple with workshops on the ground floor and a ceremonial room above. One of the rooms of a multi-roomed complex at Gorzsa (see fig. 3–24, room top, right) had decorated walls and a separate entrance, in addition to rich internal furnishings, a large pyramidal oven, and a number of vases. This, too, may have served as a shrine. Tisza houses suggest that worship was intertwined with everyday activities.

Quantities of pedestalled bowls, amphora-shaped biconical vessels, dishes, jars, and rectangular vessels have been found in Tisza houses. They are often decorated with meanders, which are the most frequent image appearing in a multiplicity of variations, as well as chevrons and other motifs. These are elements of a symbolic language associated with the sphere of the Life-giving Goddess. Typically, these motifs incised on vases are framed into aesthetic compartments. (FIGURES 3–28, 3–29, 3–30) Outstanding among the ritual ceramics are small containers or lamps with ram head protomes. (PLATE 13)

FIGURE 3–28

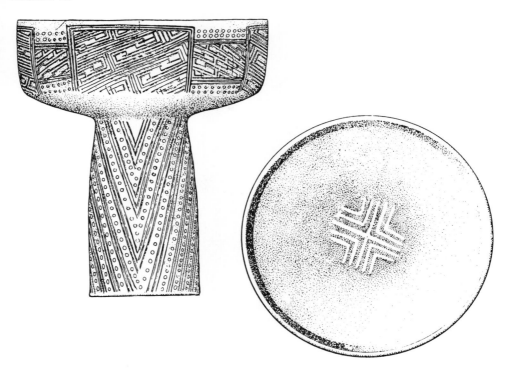

FIGURE 3–29

FIGURE 3–28 Pedestalled bowl decorated with panels of meanders and dotted lines over the bowl, chevrons and dots over the pedestal. In its interior is a fourfold sign painted in white. Classical Tisza culture. Szegvár-Tüzköves, SE Hungary, c. 48–47th cents. B.C. H 29.7 cm.

FIGURE 3–29 Footed vase typically decorated with incised meanders in panels. The front panel has smaller meanders and six dots above and below. Szegvár-Tüzköves, SE Hungary. Classical Tisza, c. 48–47th cents. B.C.

FIGURE 3–30

1

2

FIGURE 3–30 Two anthropomorphic footed vases from Classical Tisza. The Goddess's visage is flanked with chevrons (1) and tri-lines (2). Panels of meander and zigzag designs cover the body. The decoration is engraved and encrusted with white. Szegvár-Tüzköves, SE Hungary. c. 48–47th cents. B.C.

FIGURE 3–31 A coffin burial of the Tisza culture. Vésztö-Mágor, E Hungary. Early 5th mill. B.C.

FIGURE 3–31

In pottery technology, chaff was no longer used for tempering, as during the Neolithic, so differences between coarse and fine wares practically disappeared. A new type of ware appeared, typical of the Classical Tisza period, in which vessels were coated with bitumen into which straw or chaff was embedded, cut into small pieces and arranged into patterns.[44] Another widespread ornamental motif is black painting with wide bands.

Graves

Within the Tisza territory almost four hundred graves have been excavated, both within and outside the settlements. During the Classical Tisza period, wooden coffins were used for burial. The Vesztö site yielded coffins built of wooden planks with protrusions in the upper corners for carrying (FIGURE 3–31), which are the first of their kind found in Europe. Eighteen coffin burials deposited in four layers were found within the limits of habitation.

The Last Phase

The Tiszapolgár complex in eastern Hungary, eastern Slovakia, and adjacent Transylvania marks the end of the Tisza culture and the extension of its eastern and northern limit up to southern Poland. Radiocarbon dates place this stage between the 44th and 39th centuries B.C. (TABLE 9) Its last stage, Lažn'any, is known only from cemeteries of inhumation and cremation graves in eastern Slovakia and represents a dying, isolated culture with diminished copper and obsidian industries and a diminished ceramic style.[45] The most likely explanation of the cause of its demise is the consequence of the First Kurgan Wave described in chapter 10.

The Lengyel Culture of the Middle Danube Basin and Northern Central Europe

The Linearbandkeramik culture of central Europe in the Middle Danube basin was supplanted by the Lengyel culture, a complex with quite different architectural, technological, and artistic traditions. Lengyel settlements, surrounded by wide V-shaped ditches and containing the typical painted piriform vases and fruitstands, have analogies with the Danilo and Butmir complexes. Its formation from a Starčevo core in Slavonia, Syrmia, and Pannonia was due to intensified relations with the west, Bosnia, and the Adriatic coast, a process parallel to the formation of the Butmir group.[46] Obsidian and spondylus shell trade continued, probably in exchange for salt and agricultural products. From the early 5th millennium B.C. the population west and north of the Middle Danube became a clearly distinct cultural group with its own artistic style.

The name-giving Lengyel site and the large settlements of Zengövárkony and Aszód are located in western Hungary. Other Lengyel sites are distributed over a large, low-lying territory of fertile loess plains which include northwestern Yugoslavia, eastern Austria, Moravia, western Slovakia, and southern Poland.[47] (FIGURE 3–32) These sites did not form tells, but were extensive horizontal settlements of wattle-and-daub houses.

FIGURE 3–32

FIGURE 3–32 Distribution
of the Lengyel culture.

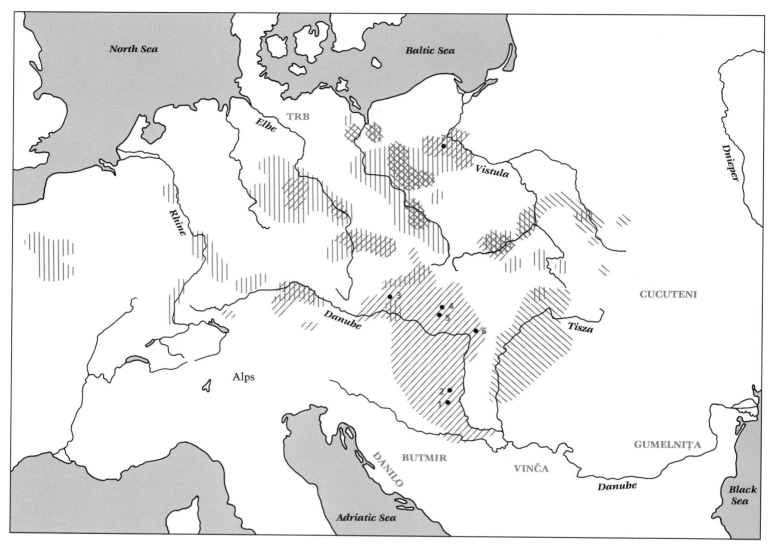

KEY

 Core area, c. 5000–4500 B.C.

Diffusion north and west after the
middle of the 5th mill. B.C.

Tisza culture and its spread to
S Poland during the Tiszapolgár
period, end of the 5th mill. B.C.

Major Lengyel sites:
1. Zengővárkony
2. Lengyel
3. Střelice
4. Svodín
5. Lužianky
6. Aszód
7. Brześć Kujawski

Chronology

Radiocarbon dates from Lengyel sites place the beginning of this culture group around 5000 B.C. (TABLE 10) Stratigraphy and ceramic typology denote five phases, Lengyel I–V.[48] The early Lengyel culture within the first half of the 5th millennium B.C. is characterized by richly painted pottery. As in the Butmir and Danilo groups, spirals, meanders, and other motifs were first incised, then painted in red, yellow, and black. The bright brick-red color of hematite pigments predominates. Warts and buttons on four sides of the belly of biconical vases and fruitstands became characteristic elements of the Lengyel style. (FIGURE 3–33A) Pottery of the next stage, in the middle of the 5th millennium B.C., was mainly white painted and during the end phases of this culture was unpainted. The general typology of Lengyel ceramics is given in figure 3–33B.

FIGURE 3–33A

FIGURE 3–33A Classical Lengyel painted pottery of c. 4900–4600 B.C.: lids, rounded or biconical pots, pedestalled bowls ("fruitstands"), and a vase with a long cylindrical neck. Painted in bright brick-red (the pigment is hematite) on gray background. All vessels are from graves excavated near houses of the settlement at Zengővárkony, county of Barabya, district of Pécs, W Hungary.

FIGURE 3–33B

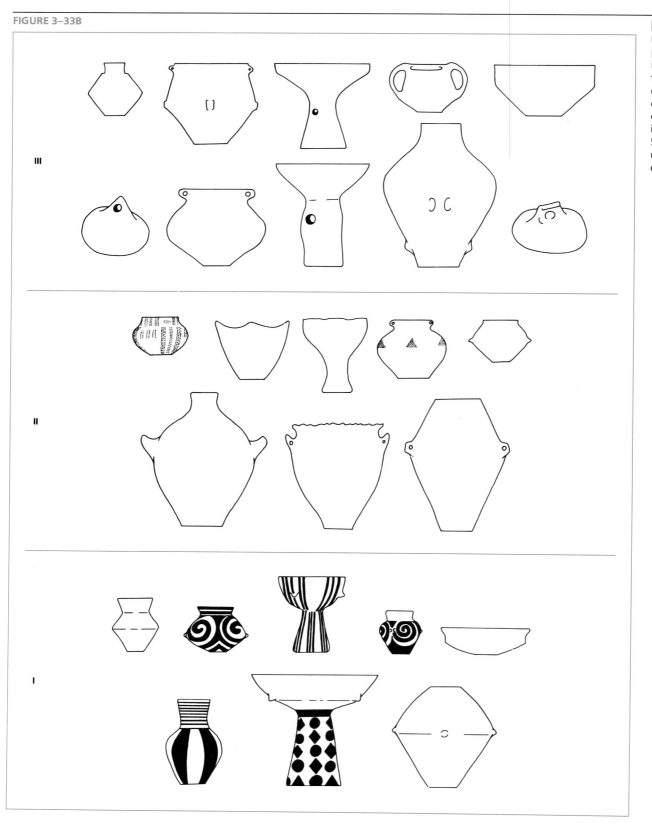

FIGURE 3–33B Lengyel pottery typology. I, Early: including painted pottery (red, yellow, black designs), 49th–46th cents. B.C. II, Middle: less colorful, designs painted in white, middle of the 5th mill. B.C. III, Late: unpainted pottery, c. 43rd–39th cents. B.C.

Lengyel finds do not occur in western Hungary or in western Slovakia after the Lengyel V phase, for this culture is replaced by a Balaton complex from the south. Lengyel V ceramics emerge, however, within the milieu of the west European Cortaillod and Michelsberg, as well as on the Upper Danube, Elbe, and Oder rivers. In Bavaria, central Germany, and western Poland,[49] the Lengyel expansion to northern central Europe was synchronous with the Kurgan I infiltration into the Lower Danube basin. This northward movement may have been caused by a chain reaction to events in east-central Europe which started the disintegration of the Karanovo and Vinča cultures and caused the exodus of their people to the west and north.

Settlements and Architecture

A series of systematically excavated settlement sites with published results in Hungary and Czechoslovakia serve as backbone information for the classical Lengyel culture. Among these are: Zengövárkony in western Hungary,[50] Aszód settlement and cemetery north of Budapest,[51] Lužianky graves and settlement,[52] and Svodin (the largest settlement with over 1,000 houses),[53] both in western Slovakia. Settlements are found on naturally protected, large terraces near a water source. The Aszód settlement occupied 20 to 25 hectares, and its minimum population is guessed to have been 300. How large the villages were at a single time cannot be calculated with accuracy, however, since only small areas have been unearthed. In Aszód, for instance, only five houses were fully excavated, and a final report on Svodin is not yet available.[54] Houses were of timber uprights daubed with clay, about 8 m by 5 m, or 6 m by 4.5 m with pitched roofs. Architectural details can be seen on miniature models of clay. In one example, the wide entrance with a ram or bull head on the gable suggests that it may be a replica of a temple. (FIGURE 3–34)

Systematic investigations of Polish lowlands have shown that the subsistence and settlement patterns of the Lengyel culture differed markedly from those of the LBK. In this area, the Lengyel culture began permanent, year-round village farming. Large settlements are found on patches of rich black earth along lakeshores and meandering streams in Kuyavia, western Poland. The most characteristic aspect of these settlements is their trapezoidal longhouses. At Brześć Kujawski, more than fifty houses have been identified, and many have been excavated over the course of the last fifty years by Polish and American archeologists.[55] (FIGURE 3–35) A number of other sites, such as Krusza Zamkowa, have fewer houses but are similar permanent villages. There is

FIGURE 3–34

FIGURE 3–34 Clay model of a Lengyel house or temple which infers an actual house; walls were timber uprights interspersed with wattle covered with clay daub. An animal head decorates the gable of the pitched roof supported by five massive central and side beams. Střelice near Znojmo, Moravia. Animal figurines from the same site. Early 5th mill. B.C.

FIGURE 3–35

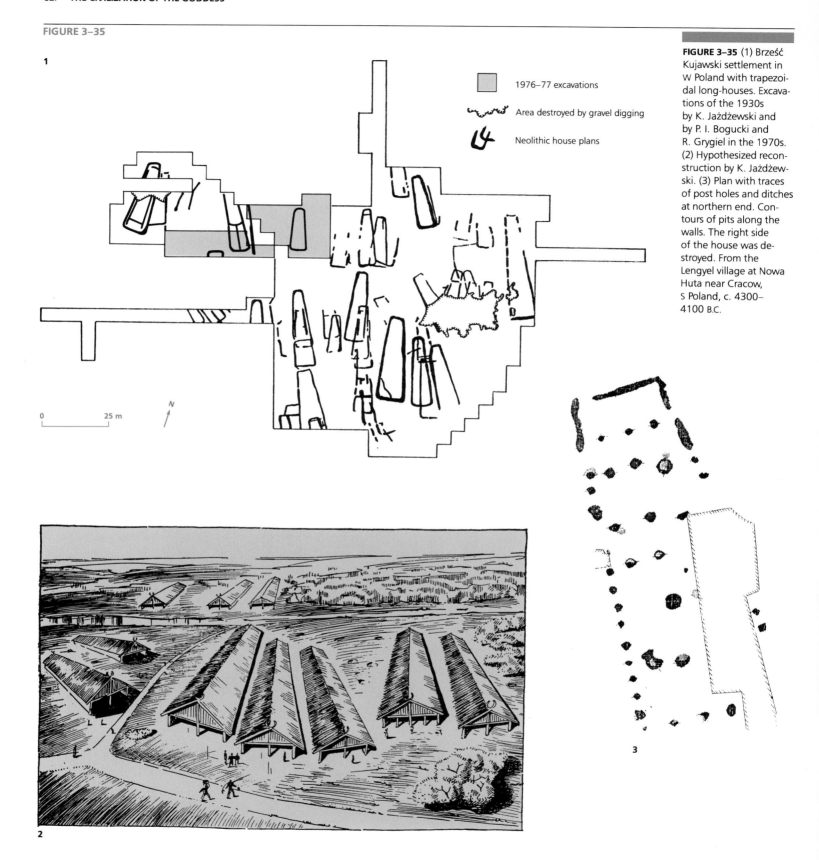

1

1976–77 excavations

Area destroyed by gravel digging

Neolithic house plans

0   25 m

N

2

3

FIGURE 3–35 (1) Brześć Kujawski settlement in W Poland with trapezoidal long-houses. Excavations of the 1930s by K. Jażdżewski and by P. I. Bogucki and R. Grygiel in the 1970s. (2) Hypothesized reconstruction by K. Jażdżewski. (3) Plan with traces of post holes and ditches at northern end. Contours of pits along the walls. The right side of the house was destroyed. From the Lengyel village at Nowa Huta near Cracow, S Poland, c. 4300–4100 B.C.

abundant evidence of grain cultivation and a reliance upon larger numbers of pigs, sheep, goats, and cervids. The exploitation of birds, fish, molluscs, and turtles is also greater than previously found.[56] Lengyel settlements are centralized around multiple long-houses in which trapezoidal buildings 15 to 40 m long (most more than 20) were built using the bedding trench method of construction. Smaller sites occurred within an approximate 5 km radius. Three distinct types of settlements have been distinguished: large, with multiple long-houses, single long-house sites, and temporary sites with no traces of permanent architecture.[57] As in the Tisza area, there was clearly a hierarchy of site sizes.

Art

It was the art, the painted pottery and highly individualistic rendering of female figures, that attracted the attention of interested laymen to this culture in the early decades of the 20th century. One of the early excavators and art lovers was Fr. Vildomec of Znojmo in Moravia who amassed a great amount of classical Lengyel material, mostly from his excavation at Střelice and other sites around Znojmo. Most of it remained in his private collection in a nearby village, and is still there. Other impressive collections of Lengyel art are in the archeological museums of Brno, Prague, Budapest, Vienna, Pecs, and others.

Lengyel sculptural art differs from that of all neighboring groups. As elsewhere, the majority of figurines are schematized, having biconical heads, arm stumps, and large buttocks. Rarely are faces or masks indicated, although some show eyes, eyebrows, pointed noses, and even hairdos and necklaces. The usual type is a standing figurine with weight concentrated in the lower part of the body, while the upper part is reduced, with breasts hardly indicated. (FIGURES 3–36, 3–37) A number of female figures are shown seated on a stool. In addition to the regular type of figurines produced in quantities, there are exceptional pieces of art remarkable for their inventive shapes. Among these are vases

FIGURE 3–36

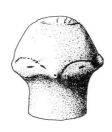
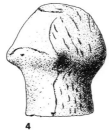

FIGURE 3–36 Typical Lengyel figurines: (1) Figurine with a biconical amorphous head, arm-stumps, small breasts, and a massive lower body. (2–4) Heads with hair, eyes, and nose indicated. Early Lengyel, 49th–47th cents. B.C. Střelice at Boskovštejn near Znojmo, Moravia, C Czechoslovakia.

FIGURE 3–37 Bird Goddess of Lengyel type: pinched nose for beak, arm stumps for wings, small breasts, massive buttocks. Two views. Střelice, district of Znojmo, Moravia. Early Lengyel, 49th–47th cents. B.C.

FIGURE 3–37

FIGURE 3–38

FIGURE 3–40

FIGURE 3–38 Tripartite offering vessel on a human foot. Baked clay. Early Lengyel, c. 49th–47th cents. B.C. Hluboké Mašůrvky at Znojmo, Brno area, Moravia.

FIGURE 3–39 A temple model with a bird head elevated on a massive human leg found at Aszód north of Budapest placed in a grave of a young girl (Grave No. 205). 49th–47th cents. B.C. H 25 cm.

FIGURE 3–40 A particularly beautiful example of the Lengyel figurine art is the ''Lady of Sé'' whose head has unfortunately not been recovered. Early Lengyel (Sé near Vas, Szombately, W Hungary), c. 49th–47th cents. B.C. H 24 cm.

FIGURE 3–39

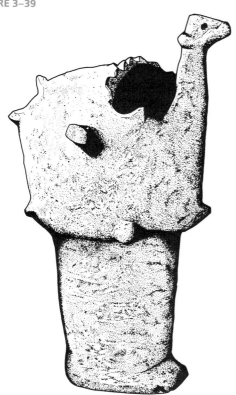

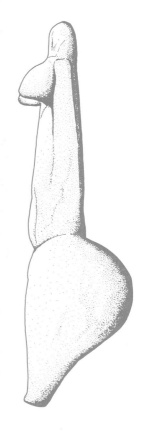

standing on a human leg (FIGURE 3–38) and even a temple model with a bird head on top which is also standing on a single leg. (FIGURE 3–39) The latter was discovered in the grave of a young girl in the cemetery at Aszód. Extraordinary vases came to light in the early Lengyel site at Sé, in the district of Szombately, western Hungary. Among these are a vase in the shape of a woman holding a vase above her head, and the sculpture of a goddess called Lady of Sé with an elongated torso and well-developed breasts. (FIGURE 3–40) Other exquisite Lengyel creations are religious vases in the shape of a bear from the site of Abraham in western Slovakia (FIGURE 3–41), lamps with double-horned animal heads, and wide-open vases with globular or horned protuberances.

FIGURE 3–41

FIGURE 3–41 Vase in the shape of a bear with a cylindrical neck decorated in painted red bands. Abraham near Piešt'any, W Slovakia. Early 5th mill. B.C.

FIGURE 3–42

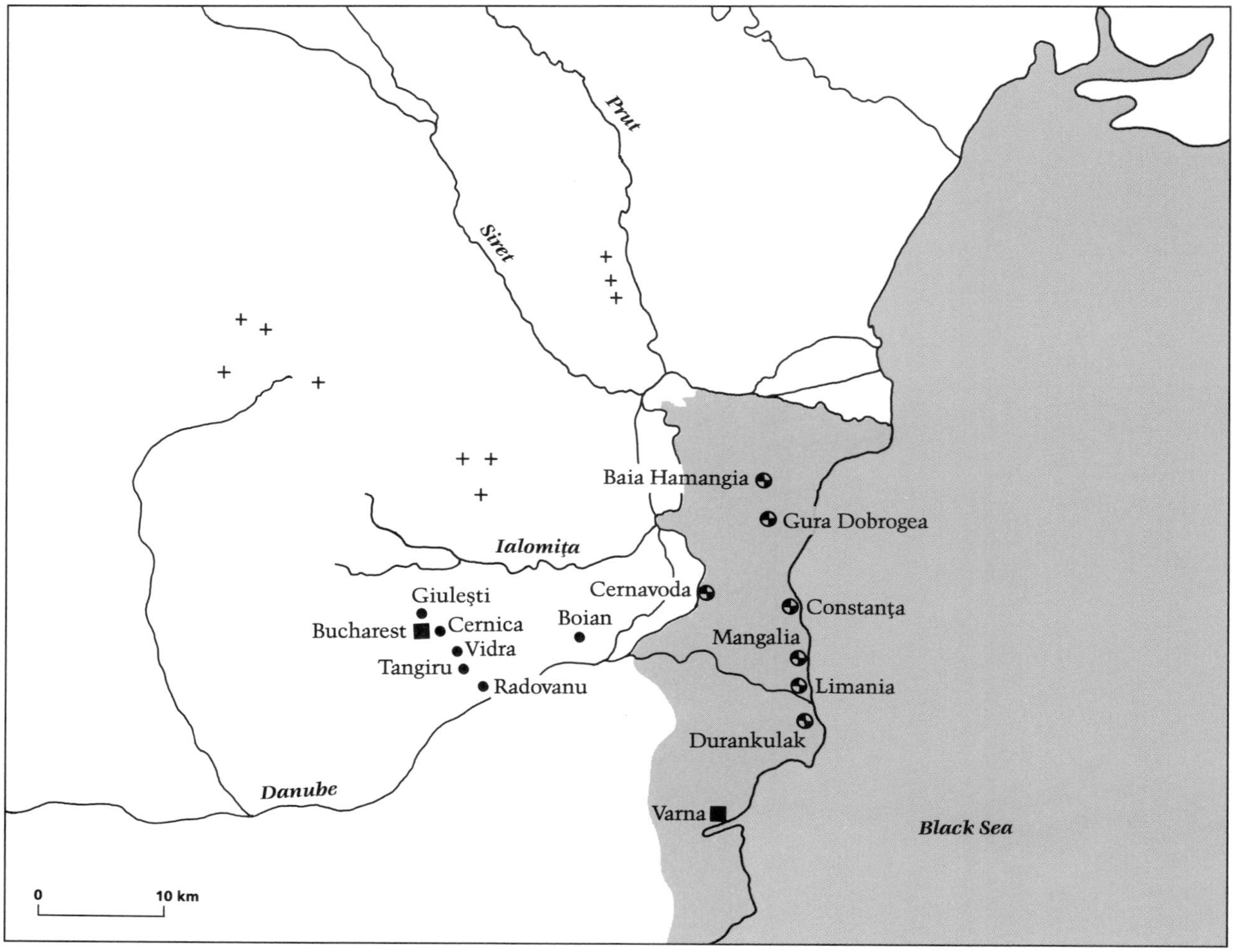

FIGURE 3–42

FIGURE 3–42 Distribution of the Hamangia group (shaded area). Early 5th mill B.C.

FIGURE 3–43 Excavated clay floors of Boian houses from tell at Radovanu near the Danube, S Romania. First habitation horizon. Boian III (Vidra). Houses are arranged in rows. The second habitation horizon yielded two rows of houses; c. 47th–46 cents. B.C.

KEY

Distribution of Hamangia group

● Boian sites

◉ Major cemeteries and settlements

+ LBK settlements

The Boian Culture in the Lower Danube Region

After the middle of the 6th millennium B.C., the Starčevo (Criş) culture, which continued in the lower Danube basin, entered the Early Vinča stage. Around 5000 B.C. the LBK farmers appeared from north of the Carpathian Mountains and settled in Moldavia, Muntenia (the area of Bucharest), and in Transylvania. A symbiosis developed between the Early Vinča and LBK which resulted in the formation of a new culture, called Boian. In Dobruja, on the Black Sea coast, a Hamangia culture emerged with its own art style, which was absorbed by the Boian after 4700 B.C. (FIGURE 3–42) The Boian culture in its second stage exercised a strong influence on Transylvania and Moldavia through shifts of population, stimulating the formation of the great cultures of Petreşti and Cucuteni, described at the end of this chapter.

The name Boian comes from an island site in Lake Boian in southeastern Romania, excavated in 1924.[58]

Tell Settlements

On the whole, about a hundred Boian sites are known, mostly tells, north and south of the Danube down to the Balkan Mountains. However, very few large-scale excavations have been carried out. These cluster north of the Lower Danube, south of Bucharest, and were located on well-chosen elevations, on promontories, higher banks of rivers, and lake shores. Many tells were stratified, indicating a permanent occupation for as many as five hundred years or more. The tell of Tangiru, for instance, yielded twenty-one habitation horizons, twelve of which belong to the Boian culture and the rest to the successive Gumelniţa.[59] On stratigraphical and typological grounds, four Boian phases were distinguished: I, Bolintineanu; II, Giuleşti; III, Vidra; and IV, Şpantov.[60]

FIGURE 3–43

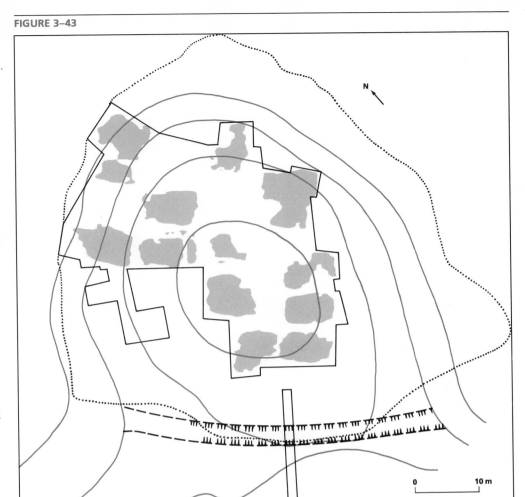

KEY

Clay platforms

Ditch

Excavated area

········· An extension of the village

No long-houses of LBK type are found in Boian settlements. Dwellings were semisubterranean in Boian I; they were above ground in Boian II. Boian III–IV had rectangular timber houses with clay-stamped floors, 7 m by 3.5 m in size, as revealed by an excavation at Radovanu near the Danube in Romania.[61] (FIGURE 3–43)

Pottery

Boian pottery is in a class by itself, characterized by excised and white-encrusted decoration. Most frequently, spiral and rectilinear meander patterns were incised, and rows of small triangles and checkerboard patterns were excised, using a wood carver's technique. After firing, the ornamented surfaces were colored with white or red paint. (FIGURE 3–44) Peg-footed vessels are typical (FIGURE 3–45) as well as biconical bowls and rectangular block vases. The fine ware was of a clean clay, thin walled, often ash-gray or black.

Graves

Three hundred and sixty-two graves were unearthed in the cemetery of Cernica at Bucharest, from the Boian I (Bolintineanu) phase.[62] This is the earliest and largest cemetery known in the area so far. The dead were in pits, in an extended position, oriented from west to east. The skeletons were of a general Mediterranean type, of gracile bones, small or medium statured, but the skulls were not homogeneous. In addition to dolichocephalic, there were also mesocephalic and brachycephalic, even hyper-brachycephalic (Alpine) skulls, and the facial index also varied which suggests that an intermarrying took place with the previous local populations. Vases, stone axes and chisels, bone needles, and awls were laid in the graves. Among the ornaments found were diadems of spondylus shell, bracelets of pectunculus shell (FIGURE 3–46), ring pendants and rings of bone, cylindrical, annular, and profiled beads of shell, greenstone, and copper, as well as perforated elk's teeth. A schematic bone figurine of the Stiff Nude category was also found in one grave.

FIGURE 3–44

FIGURE 3–44 Boian II vase (Giuleşti phase) decorated with excised and white paste encrusted lozenges and checkerboards. 49th–48th cents. B.C. H 11.8 cm.

FIGURE 3–45

FIGURE 3–45 A peg-footed vase with excised and white-encrusted decoration. Boian culture, phase III (Vidra) c. 48th–46th cents. B.C. H 27.9 cm.

FIGURE 3–46

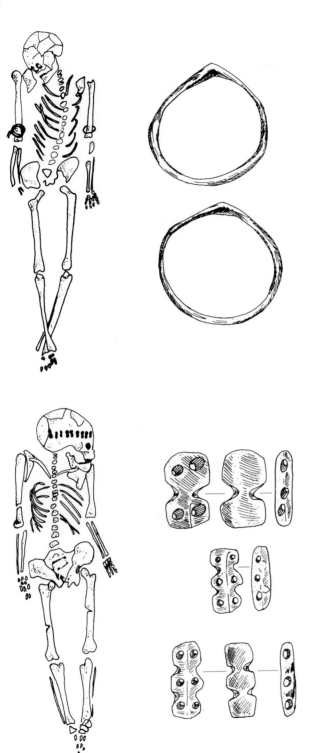

FIGURE 3–46 Skeletons from the cemetery of Cernica at Bucharest showing the position of arm rings of pectunculus shell and a diadem of perforated spondylus shell plates. End of 6th mill. B.C.

The Hamangia Culture on the Black Sea Coast

Hamangian settlements and cemeteries are concentrated along the Black Sea coast (see fig. 3–42), a point of trade where spondylus and dentalium shell and marble were obtained from the south and diffused to the inland areas. D. Berciu, the excavator of the major Hamangian cemeteries between 1952 and 1960,[63] believed, because of the findings of extraordinary sculptures, marble, and spondylus shells, that the Hamangians immigrated from the eastern Mediterranean. It is much more likely that this culture is of local roots, as suggested by the earliest Hamangian pottery which is related to Starčevo (Criş) forms, and a microlithic flint industry known in the same area from earlier times. An analysis of human skeletal material shows a population of a Mediterranean (of several variants) and proto-Europid of gracilized type. In addition, elements considered to be descendant from Upper Paleolithic Předmost type were present.[64] The latter persisted in the Black Sea littoral also in post-Hamangian times.

Sites and Chronology

Semisubterranean dwellings are found on low terraces of lake shores, as at Goloviţa near Baia Hamangia. Five phases of cultural development have been determined on typological grounds which parallel Boian and Karanovo III–IV, between 5500 and 4700 B.C. There is only one radiocarbon date for Hamangia III, which is 5880 BP (from the Groningen laboratory), calibrated within the 49–48th centuries B.C.

The graveyard of Cernavoda located on an elevation near the Danube included no fewer than 600 inhumation graves; 400 were excavated. A vase or two, a polished stone tool, and one or two clay or marble figurines of the Hamangian Stiff Nude type were laid in both female and male graves, but not in all (most finds are from the upper part of the cemetery held to be of a later phase). Pebbles or marbles of a round, semicircular, or

FIGURE 3-47

1

2

3

lozenge shape were frequently found at the head of the dead. In many cases later interments were superimposed on earlier ones or earlier bones were removed and reburied together with the new arrival. Most interesting were ritualistic burials of skulls found in several locations west and north of the main graveyard with remains of feasting. At the graves were deer, pig, cattle, and goat skulls and jaws, very likely as symbols of regeneration. The burial of skulls alone may mean a secondary burial of the dead (other bones were probably considered not as essential as skulls).

The first reports of large-scale excavations at Dourankulak near the Black Sea coast in Bulgaria by H. Todorova and T. Dimov came out as this book was already being finished.[65] As yet, the excavation which commenced in 1978 is not finished. Nevertheless, the discovery of Hamangian semisubterranean pit-dwellings and 846 graves of several phases, as well as a settlement from the succeeding Varna period is of considerable importance. This excavation demonstrates a cultural continuity throughout three-quarters of the 5th millennium B.C. The Hamangia and Varna cultures, which have been considered as separate units, may be shown to be genetically related. The enormously rich cemetery of Varna is treated in this chapter in the section on trade.

Art

The Hamangians developed their own art style expressed as black-burnished pottery decorated with white-encrusted stroked zigzags, meanders, and triangles (FIGURE 3-47), and highly individualistic types of terracotta and marble figurines. Sculptures of the White Goddess of Death have been found on their flat backs in graves. Some figurines are corpulent standing or seated females with columnar heads with no facial features, while others are reduced versions of the same type. (FIGURE 3-48) One grave from the Cernavoda cemetery yielded a pair of terracotta deities, female and male, both nude, masked, and in seated posture. They are about 12 cm high, of well-burnished grayish-brown clay. The male is seated on a stool holding his chin with both hands, while the female sits comfortably with both hands on her right knee (see fig. 7-42). The male, baptized The Thinker after Rodin's sculpture, became one of the most celebrated pieces of art from the European Eneolithic. In addition to the Stiff Nude type of sculpture prominent in cemeteries, a pregnant type is found within the villages. In the settlement of Golovița, in addition to pit houses, one above-ground house of 6 m by 5 m was unearthed which seemed to have been used for worship. Four terracotta female figures were found on the floor, all of a pregnant type, with hands on the belly.

The Karanovo-Gumelniţa Culture in Thrace and Eastern Macedonia

Continuity and Expansion to the North Aegean Area and the Lower Danube Valley

There is a well-documented cultural continuity in Bulgaria and southern Romania throughout the 5th millennium up to 4300–4200 B.C. (TABLE 11)

Many Neolithic tells, such as Karanovo, Azmak, and Kazanlak in central Bulgaria, were occupied for a thousand years without interruption from the middle of the 6th millennium B.C. Neolithic Karanovo I and II were followed by Eneolithic Karanovo III–VI. During the Karanovo III–IV periods, 5500–5000 B.C., this culture influenced cultural change throughout the central Balkans and northeastern Greece. Around 5500 B.C., elements of the Karanovo III assemblage were carried, by ethnic expansion, southward beyond the Rhodope Mountains to the Plains of Drama and Thrace. Outside their homeland in the Marica valley, Karanovo sites yielding phase III materials are found on virgin soil or bedrock. Such are the tells of Sitagroi[66] and Dikili Tash[67] in the Drama Plain north of the Aegean.

FIGURE 3–48

FIGURE 3–47 Black vases with white encrusted zigzags and triangles from the cemetery of Cernavoda, Hamangia culture. 49th–48th cents. B.C. Heights: (1) 11 cm; (2) 15 cm; (3) 13 cm.

FIGURE 3–48 Hamangian Stiff Nude found in graves. Terracotta (1), marble (2). Cernavoda cemetery, at the Black Sea, Romania; c. 49th–48th cents B.C. H (1) 15.7 cm. (2) 9 cm.

1

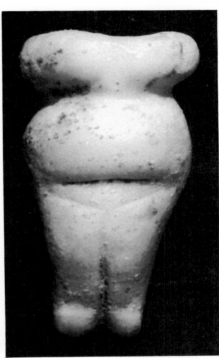

2

FIGURE 3–49

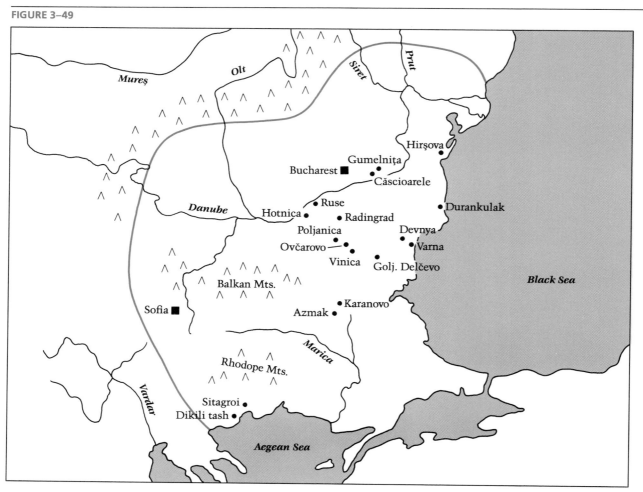

Toward the middle of the 5th millennium B.C., there must have been an influx of population from central to northeastern Bulgaria and across the Lower Danube to southern Romania. Karanovo-type tells began to appear in a much larger area than before. Excavations in the 1970s of Poljanica, Ovčarovo, Goljamo Delčevo, and Vinica in the Turgovište district (by H. Todorova) and Radingrad near Razgrad (by T. Ivanov) revealed a great deal of new information on this culture.[68] Ancient Thrace and Dacia became culturally united during this period (FIGURE 3–49), except for the population of the Black Sea littoral which differed in racial type and architectural tradition.[69] The Karanovo-Gumelniţa population was gracile Mediterranean mixed with gracilized proto-Europid type.

Villages and Houses

The Karanovo villages continued a house to house plan, with paths or very narrow passages in between. (FIGURE 3–50) The Vinica and Ovčarovo tells have accumulations of more than twenty habitation levels in which most of the houses remained in their original places.[70] Excavations at Poljanica have shown that the early village had three parallel palisades, perhaps as protection from wild animals, which are not to be confused with hill-fort fortifications of the Indo-European type. There was an absence of stone work. Houses were built of timber uprights with wickerwork in between, daubed with clay on both sides. Floors were of split logs covered with a layer of clay. (FIGURE 3–51) At Ovčarovo, some houses were plastered as many as forty-seven times, which suggests that they could have lasted fifty years or more, if not burnt down earlier.

FIGURE 3–50

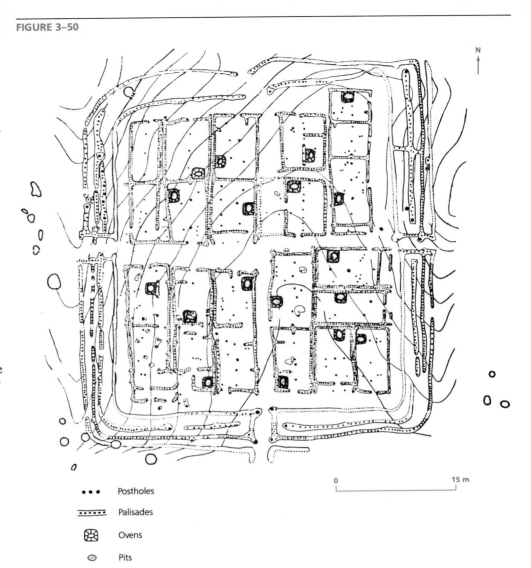

•••	Postholes
······	Palisades
⊞	Ovens
⊚	Pits

0   15 m

Two-story Temples

In every settlement there was a central building adjoined to the other houses (see fig. 3–50, bottom row, *right*) which was often two storied. At Radingrad, it was shown that such two-story buildings were temples with a workshop on the first floor under the worship area. Ceramic models of such temples are replicas of actual buildings. (FIGURE 3–52) Some models have round windows on the ground floor and show traces of painted designs in red, yellow, and white. The largest model, having a very large stereobate with four temples on top, was discovered in the burned temple of Căscioarele on a Danube island in southern Romania (see fig. 7–57). As it is now known from actual temples and their models, the two-story buildings were not houses of chieftains or village elders, as was presumed by excavators, but communal temples and centers of arts and crafts. Open models, such as one from the Ovčarovo tell (FIGURE 3–53), show interior arrangements in the lower level. A large rectangular oven with a pitched roof in imitation of a real house occupied a central position in the middle of the wall to the right of the entrance, while a clay bench and an area fenced with a clay wall was at the rear.

Poljanica, Ovčarovo, and other totally excavated settlement tells are excellent examples of well-organized small towns. According to the excavator H. Todorova, people must have lived there in tightly knit egalitarian communities, their lives revolving around temple activities.

FIGURE 3–51

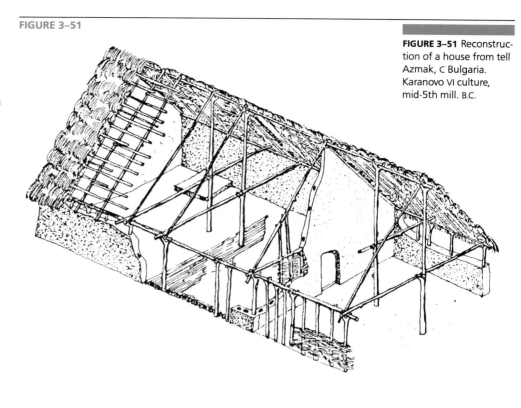

FIGURE 3–51 Reconstruction of a house from tell Azmak, C Bulgaria. Karanovo VI culture, mid-5th mill. B.C.

FIGURE 3–52

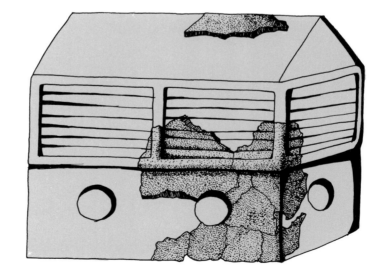

FIGURE 3–52 Reconstruction of a model of a two-story building from Ruse, N Bulgaria. The preserved fragments indicate a stereobate with round windows. The upper story was built of horizontal beams interspersed with vertical. Karanovo VI (Gumelniţa) culture, mid-5th mill. B.C.

Farming

Farming was done around the villages and cattle were fed on what the pastures provided. In all excavated tells, the most significant source of food was cattle, both of meat and milk, while sheep, goats, pigs, and grain were also important.[71] Estimates based on the capacity of the storage pits at Goljamo Delčevo have indicated that the annual requisite of cereals would have been approximately 20,000 to 24,000 kilograms obtained from 16 hectares of cultivated land. Calculations have shown that the workload necessary for the cultivation of this amount of land, divided among twenty families of the village, would have left sufficient labor free for the building of houses, lumbering, cattle breeding, hunting, fishing, gathering, trading, and home and temple crafts.[72] Exquisite ceramics and tools produced in these villages testify to a sufficient amount of leisure time for the refinement of arts and crafts.

Town and Village Interrelationship

Much larger tells found in central Bulgaria which may have had up to five thousand inhabitants have not been fully excavated, so it is too early to speak of their inner organization. These must have been towns central to a district. Since the total number of tells in Bulgaria and Romania from the middle of the 5th millennium B.C. is no less than one thousand (in Bulgaria nearly six hundred and in Romania no fewer than five hundred), the time is not far away when the use of the magnetometer, air photography, and other devices will reveal a new understanding of town and village interrelationships. Cemeteries have not yet been discovered in central Bulgaria near the large mounds, but a considerable number of graves have been unearthed at the northern Bulgarian tells at Vinica, Goljamo Delčevo, Poljanica, and Ovčarovo. These have provided a view of social relationships which are discussed in chapter 9. At this time, changes in social structure occur on the Black Sea coast.

FIGURE 3–53

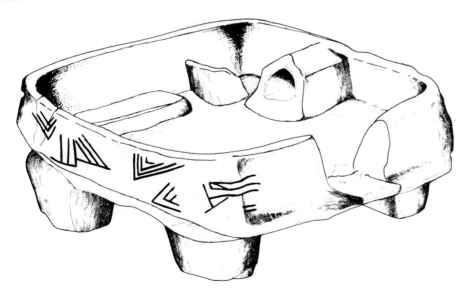

FIGURE 3–53 An open temple model of clay with a house-shaped oven, clay bench (an altar), and a bank enclosed by a massive clay wall. Painted chevrons, tri-lines, and other signs on the exterior wall. Ovčarovo I, NE Bulgaria, Karanovo VI period, mid-5th mill. B.C.

FIGURE 3–54

VI

V

IV

FIGURE 3–54 Shapes and decoration of vases including graphite-painted (black design) ware from Karanovo IV, V, and VI periods, c. 5000–4500 B.C., based on finds from the tell of Azmak at Stara Zagora, C Bulgaria.

FIGURE 3–55 Gold-painted dish: detail, Varna cemetery, Grave No. 1.

Pottery

The production of magnificent ceramics was an essential occupation of the Karanovians, both in larger towns and in villages. The continual aesthetic and technological development of this art demonstrates an enormous investment in time and creative effort. Even if pottery was mainly manufactured for the temple, the sophisticated vases that surrounded families in their everyday life express a cultural enrichment that pervaded all aspects of society.

Vases with gray backgrounds enlivened by white encrustation are characteristic of Karanovo art in the early centuries of the 5th millennium B.C. Tall, hollow pedestalled, tulip-shaped vases of early Karanovo were no longer produced, and the fashion of channelling of the surfaces of vases was, by this time, on the way out. Vases with cylindrical necks, dishes, bowls, and barrel-shaped forms were the leading shapes in the middle 5th millennium B.C. (FIGURE 3–54) Symbolism expressing the familiar ideology of the goddess religion continued to develop, reaching a true sophistication in the masterful integration of symbol and aesthetic expression. Particularly characteristic of the Karanovo VI period are graphite-painted dishes with four-corner designs on the inner side formed of spirals, crescents, and eggs, which are powerfully dynamic. (FIGURE 3–54, *top*) Other frequent motifs are chevrons, rows of triangles, checkerboards, parallel lines, and rows of delicate shell impressions.

The graphite- and gold-painted pottery produced by the Karanovo civilization during the early and mid-5th millennium B.C. was a truly extraordinary technological development. Gold-painted pottery found at the cemetery of Varna (FIGURE 3–55) is eloquent witness of this sophistication. It is presumed that powdered gold was used in post-firing application. Graphite painting began during the Karanovo V phase and became the dominant mode of decoration during Karanovo VI. Black- or dark-brown-burnished pottery was decorated with it in a drawing manner, sometimes in combination with white, buff, or yellow color. Motifs include spirals, meanders, whirls, oblique lines, triangles, circles, and eggs. Before firing, vessels to be treated with graphite were first slipped, burnished when leather-hard, then drawn with graphite when thoroughly dry. A prolonged period of firing in a reduced atmosphere of 850–1000 degrees C in some kind of a kiln was necessary to prevent the graphite from oxidizing. Graphite is present in the metamorphic rocks of the Rhodope and Balkan mountains, and quantities of graphite cones have been found in the mounds around Stara Zagora. It must have been exported from Bulgaria to Yugoslavia and Czechoslovakia, since graphite-decorated pottery also occurs in the Vinča and LBK cultures.

FIGURE 3–55

Sculptural Art

There are a few outstanding examples of Karanovian sculptural art that achieved an excellence equivalent to their fine pottery. As with other cultural groups, however, many of the images were schematic figurines serving as everyday prayer media. Masterpieces were most likely produced for the temple or for important festivities, since their artistic value is more refined. Several pieces of Karanovo-Gumelniţa art have been repeatedly reproduced in art books for more than half a century. Among these is the "Lady of Pazardžik" seated on a throne on her pear-shaped posterior decorated with lozenges. Her vulva is marked with a double spiral, she has a large masked head, and her arms are closed in front.[73] Another celebrity, published more than fifty years ago, is the center piece of the Bucharest City Museum. This is an anthropomorphic goddess vase from Vidra at Bucharest, 42 cm high, decorated with concentric circles and lozenges, holding hands on its belly.[74] From Gumelniţa in southern Romania come remarkable sculptures of women wearing death masks carrying vases above their heads as part of a religious ceremony. (FIGURE 3–56) There are also beautifully rendered offering containers, lids, vases, and lamps in the shape of deer, dogs, bulls, hedgehogs, and birds. (FIGURE 3–57) The tiny clay human figurines, on the other hand, are predominantly schematic, reduced to a sort of sculptural shorthand. Very little effort was focused on molding details of the human body since realism was not their purpose. The emphasis was on marking the figures with symbols. These figurines are solidly incised, encrusted with white or red. From more than 200 anthropomorphic figurines discovered during the excavation at Sitagroi, the majority are of the schematic type.[75] Only about 10 percent are somewhat naturalistically rendered, and even those, except for belly and buttocks, do not show details. Not one can be identified as male. Heads are masked or have a pinched beaked nose and occasionally a coif. (FIGURES 3–58, 3–59) In each site, zoomorphic figurines emerged, either representing whole animals—bulls,

FIGURE 3–56

FIGURE 3–57

FIGURE 3–56 Figure holding a vase above the head, facing front and back. Huge ears have perforations for earrings. Dress is painted in ochre-red bands bordered with white. The figure represents a participant in a religious ritual (possibly connected with death and regeneration rites). Gumelniţa, S Romania, mid-5th mill. B.C. H 22.5 cm.

FIGURE 3–57 Deer head (part of a large vase). The eyes and brows are modelled in relief. Antlers broken. Vidra near Bucharest. Mid-5th mill. B.C. H 9 cm.

FIGURE 3–58

FIGURE 3–58 Schematic figurines marked with symbols: V's, chevrons, zigzags, and three lines between the breasts. Karanovo culture. Sitagroi, Drama Plain, NE Greece. (1) Sitagroi II. (2,3) Sitagroi III, 48th–46th centuries B.C. Scale 1:2.

FIGURE 3–59

FIGURE 3–59 Beaked heads of tiny figurines and a masked head of a larger sculpture marked with two lines and an egg over the cheeks, and with two lines down the chin. Sitagroi III, Karanovo culture, mid-5th mill. B.C. Scale 1:1; head at bottom 1:3.

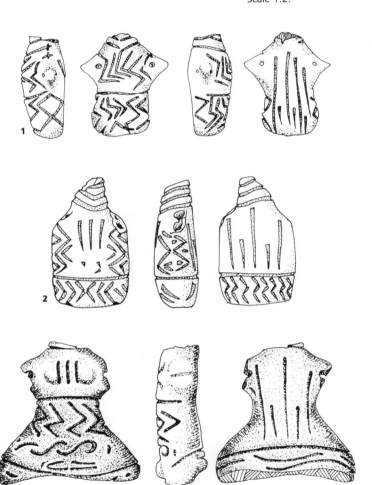

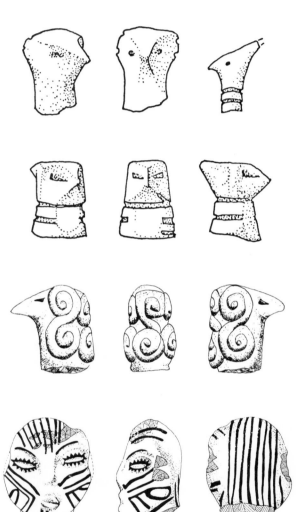

FIGURE 3–60

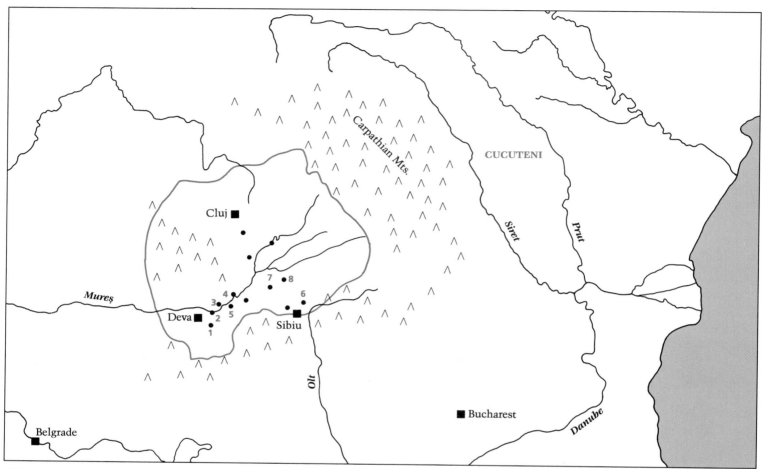

KEY

1. Pianul de Jos
2. Turdaş
3. Tartaria
4. Lumea-Nova
5. Petreşti
6. Casolţ
7. Pauca
8. Seica Mica

rams, pigs, hedgehogs, frogs—or just the heads as protomes of vessels. A distinctive class of Karanovo figurines are Stiff Nude images of flat bone plate or marble which are found in graves and represent images of death (see chapter 7). These have huge pubic triangles and masks with perforations for the attachment of earrings. The masks have the round eyes of a snake and a long mouth with dots underneath it for teeth (see fig. 7–29).

The Petreşti Culture in Transylvania

The Petreşti sites, with their characteristic trichrome painted pottery, are found in the fertile Mures basin of Transylvania. (FIGURE 3–60) They are located on wide terraces on the elevated banks of rivers, reminiscent of the Cucuteni villages described below. This culture was first identified when Petreşti, near Sebeş, was excavated in 1943–47 by D. and I. Berciu.[76] Since then, seven other sites have been excavated, and a total of fifty-two are known from surface collections.[77] As yet no larger synthesis on this culture was published.

Origin

The stratigraphy of a number of Petreşti sites has shown that ceramic finds at the base are of the Boian type which appear in association with Early Vinča materials. At Lumea Noua, Early Vinča deposits are superseded by layers of Petreşti culture. The genesis of this group appears to be connected with the colonization of Transylvania by people who moved in from the south along the Olt River. Vinča elements persist in the earliest Petreşti sites. In later phases, however, an independent Petreşti lifestyle appears. The population is a gracile, small-statured Mediterranean people with dolichocephalic head and narrow face.[78]

Chronology

The Petreşti culture material is classified into phases A, AB, and B, which correspond to the Karanovo VI and Cucuteni A and AB–B. By this correspondence, the Petreşti culture is dated to the middle and second half of the 5th and early part of the 4th millennium B.C.

Architecture

Iuliu Paul, in his study of the Petreşti group of Transylvania, has reconstructed a stilt house from the settlement of Pauca at Sebeş, district of Hunedoara.[79] According to Paul, the baked clay floor rests on heavy posts up to 50 cm in diameter, upon which is raised a frame of logs covered with twigs and leaves. The walls are constructed of timber uprights with wattle-and-daub between. The entrance is slipped and decorated with designs painted and in relief. This "pile house" has close parallels with temple models, such as a Cucuteni (Tripolye) clay model of a two-story building standing on legs, probably a temple, discovered in the area of Kiev (now in the City Museum of Kiev; see fig. 7–58). In broad terms, the Petreşti goup or culture is a cousin of the Cucuteni culture described below.

The Cucuteni Culture in Moldavia and the Western Ukraine

Cucuteni is one of the best explored and richest cultures of Old Europe, a true civilization in the best meaning of the word. A well-deserved celebration took place in 1984 in Iaşi, northeastern Romania, to acknowledge the results achieved by intensive spade work over the hundred years since Cucuteni was first discovered.

It is necessary to clarify the usage of two names for this culture: *Cucuteni* in Romania and *Tripolye* in the Soviet Union. One part of this culture lies in Romania, the other in the Ukrainian SSR. The Tripolye site on the middle Dnieper, 35 km south of Kiev, was excavated at the end of the 19th century by V. V. Khvojko and became famous in

Russia where its name took root.[80] The Cucuteni site on the Prut River near Iaşi in Moldavia, after which the western branch of this culture was named, was discovered in 1884 and excavated in 1901–10 by Hubert Schmidt, and again in 1961–65 by M. Petrescu-Dimboviţa. The site yielded five cultural strata. The fact is, however, that Cucuteni and Tripolye are a homogeneous culture. Since the formation of the culture can be traced to Moldavia, and the Cucuteni site with its superb stratigraphy is one of the most representative and important localities, Cucuteni should serve as the sole designation of this culture. The two names and the differing chronological classification associated with each have created an unnecessary complexity. In the following comparison of terminology, the Romanian Cucuteni and the Russian-Ukrainian Tripolye chronological classifications are compared.

Comparison of Romanian Cucuteni and Russian Tripolye Classification

3500 B.C.	
Cucuteni B 3	Tripolye C I
Cucuteni B 2	Tripolye C I
Cucuteni B 1	Tripolye C I
3750 B.C.	
Cucuteni AB 1&2	Tripolye B Ic
Cucuteni A 3	Tripolye B Ic
Cucuteni A 2	Tripolye B Ib
Cucuteni A 1	Tripolye B Ia
4500 B.C.	
Pre-Cucuteni III	
Pre-Cucuteni II	Tripolye Ab
Pre-Cucuteni I	Tripolye Aa
5000 B.C.	

FIGURE 3–61

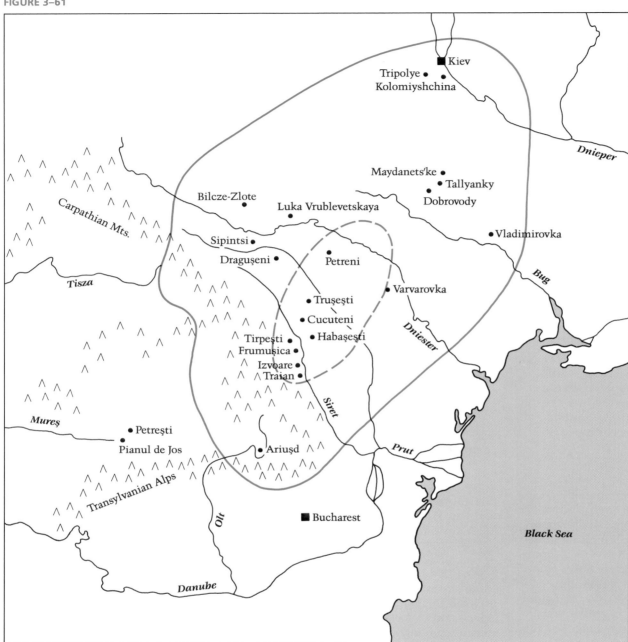

FIGURE 3–61 Distribution of the Cucuteni (Tripolye) culture. Dashed line, area of the formative Early Cucuteni stage; solid line, maximum extension. Sites mentioned in text. 5th and early 4th mill. B.C.

Origin

The colonization of Moldavia from the Lower Danube region by the Boian people modified the Neolithic LBK culture. The resulting amalgam created the beginnings of the Cucuteni culture which spread north of the Carpathian arc in the river valleys of the Siret, Prut, Upper and Middle Dniester, and the Southern Bug which drain into the Black Sea and the Danube. (FIGURE 3–61) The earliest sites appear between the Olt and Siret rivers. During the next phases, the territory was considerably enlarged, extending into the Prut, Dniester, and Southern Bug valleys, reaching the Middle Dnieper around 4000 B.C. The Moldavian-West Ukrainian black soil region was gradually occupied. The earliest Cucuteni sites are contemporary or stratigraphically above the LBK settlements.[81]

Chronology

This culture is subdivided into three main periods: Early, Classical, and Late. Early Cucuteni is still being called "Pre-Cucuteni" because it was discovered after Cucuteni A. Classical Cucuteni is Cucuteni A, divided into three subphases, followed by Cucuteni AB, again subdivided into two phases. Late Cucuteni, or Cucuteni B, is again divided into three subphases. In Russian classification, Tripolye A corresponds to Early Cucuteni, Tripolye B to Classical Cucuteni, and Tripolye C to Late Cucuteni. Early Cucuteni belongs to the 48th–47th centuries B.C., Classical Cucuteni is firmly placed in the second half of the 5th millennium B.C., while Late Cucuteni belongs to the first half of the 4th millennium B.C. (See TABLE 12, chronological classification on the basis of radiocarbon dating, stratigraphy, and typology.)

The Growth of Settlements

The Cucuteni culture lasted for more than a millennium, from c. 4800 to c. 3500 B.C. During that time, the size of settlements and population density grew rapidly, reaching overwhelming proportions. Whereas the average Early Cucuteni village had twenty dwellings,

FIGURE 3–62

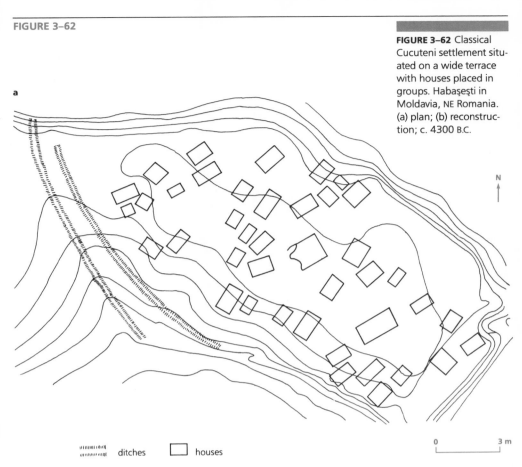

a

ditches   houses

0   3 m

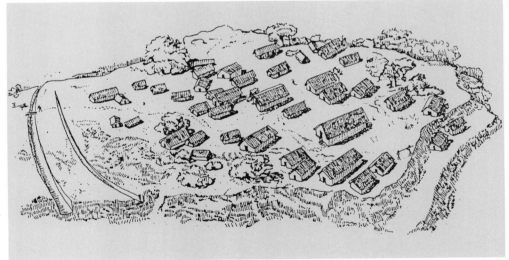

b

FIGURE 3–62 Classical Cucuteni settlement situated on a wide terrace with houses placed in groups. Habaşeşti in Moldavia, NE Romania. (a) plan; (b) reconstruction; c. 4300 B.C.

FIGURE 3–63

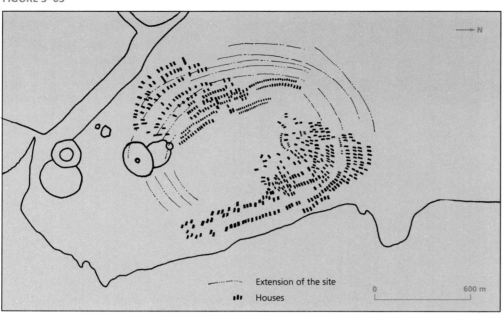

Extension of the site

Houses

FIGURE 3–64

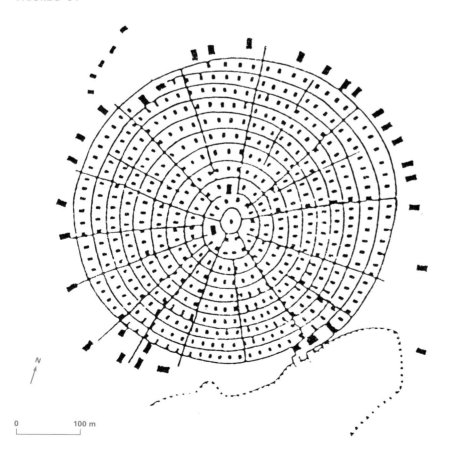

FIGURE 3–63 A Late Cucuteni town at May-dan, district of Uman, W Ukraine. Houses, c. 30 m long in twelve concentric rings, were identified by magnetometer and remains of burned clay house floors. The area of the settlement covers more than 300 hectares. Early 4th mill. B.C.

FIGURE 3–64 The town of Petreni, located between Upper Prut and Upper Dniester, of some 500 houses and c. 4,000 inhabitants arranged in ten concentric rings. Houses measured 8 × 5 m; on the outskirts was a row of larger houses. The settlement was not protected by ditches and ramparts. Late Classical Cucuteni, c. 4000 B.C.

FIGURE 3–65 Cucuteni settlements of various sizes in the Uman region, W Ukraine, based on aerial photography. The largest towns are about equal distances from one another.

this number swelled to one hundred during the Classical period (see the completely excavated village of Habaşeşti, FIGURE 3–62 and Truşeşti, fig. 9–3). The excavated village of Truşeşti consists of ninety-eight dwellings arranged in groups of three or more, as in Vinča settlements, rather than following a preconceived plan. Classical Cucuteni villages were protected inland by funnel-shaped trenches,[82] whereas sites of the late Classical phase are in lower, more open spaces, usually wide terraces, encircled by a deep, wide ditch. The threat of incursions from the steppes may explain their move to more naturally protected areas.[83]

The densification process culminated during the Late Cucuteni period when large towns emerged which are documented in the western Ukraine. By means of magnetometer and aerial photography, Ukrainian archeologists have identified the boundaries of Late Cucuteni sites in the district of Uman, communities planned in ten to twelve concentric ellipses more than two kilometers in length.[84] The largest of these settlements contained as many as 2,000 houses within 300–400 hectares. (FIGURE 3–63)

In the western Ukraine, a large number of these densely populated Late Cucuteni sites have been surveyed by air photography and surface collections. It was observed that large villages are of two types: those occupying 30–70 hectares, and very large towns covering 250–400 hectares. Settlements of both groups were examined in detail. Eight houses of the 498 structures of Petreni, a large village in the Prut-Dniester interfluve, were excavated by von Stern in 1907. In the 1970s, the site was surveyed from the air by K. Šiškin whose work revealed ten concentric rings of houses. Most dwellings measured eight by five meters, although a row of larger buildings were found on the outskirts. An oval platform remained in the center with two large buildings close by. There were no protective ditches or ramparts. (FIGURE 3–64) In 1981, V. Markevič calculated the population of Petreni to have been about four thousand.[85]

Of the group of large towns so far identified, only three have attracted attention and limited excavation. They are: Maydanets'ke, Dobrovody, and Tallyanky. (FIGURE 3–65) Maydanets'ke is located on a wide plateau which rises over a river valley and covers approximately 270 hectares. It is estimated to have consisted of about 1,700 buildings arranged in ten to twelve concentric ellipses. Dobrovody covers 250 hectares and was also arranged in concentric rings. Tallyanky was the largest of all, covering 400 hectares. This settlement was oval in plan and measures 3.5 by 1.5 km. Ten thousand people could have resided there.[86]

The map of the Uman region of the western Ukraine (FIGURE 3–65), based on aerial photography, indicates the location of the largest Cucuteni towns in relation to those of medium size which occupied 30–70 hectares. Not all of the

FIGURE 3–65

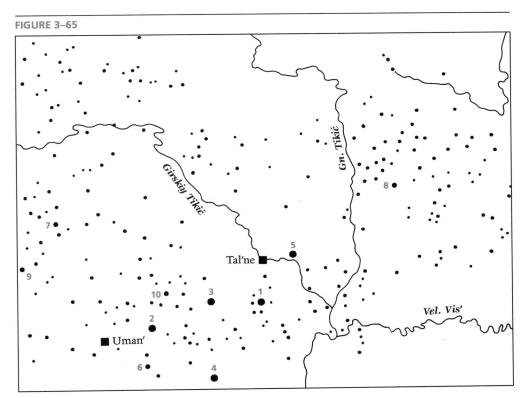

KEY

● Settlements of 250–400 inhabitants
● Settlements of 25–75 inhabitants
• Well-documented settlements
· Poorly documented settlements

1. Maydanets'ke
2. Dobrovody
3. Tallyanky
4. Nebelivka
5. Glyboček
6. Suškivka
7. Krasnostavka
8. Čyčyrkozivka
9. P'yanižkove
10. Kosenivka

FIGURE 3–66

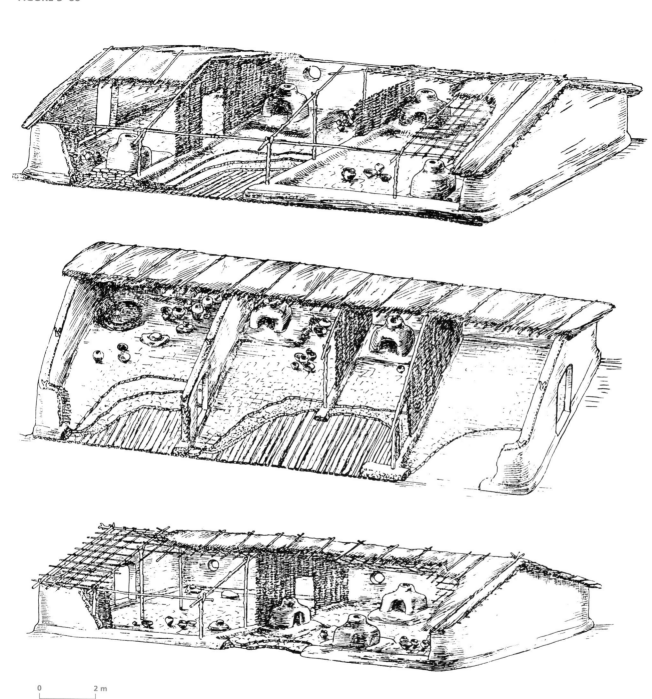

FIGURE 3–66 Cucuteni (Tripolye) houses (reconstruction by T. Passek 1949) from excavations at Kolomiyshchina I near Kiev, W Ukraine. Late Cucuteni, early 4th mill. B.C.

dots marking locations of yet smaller settlements represent the same time frame, although the majority of large towns probably do belong to the same period. It is significant to see that the largest towns are approximately fifteen kilometers from one other. The density of settlement sites is surprising: 253 sites were recorded in an area of 9000 square kilometers.

Houses and Temples

The normal type of house was a rectangular two- or three-room structure, 8–20 m long and 5–6 m wide, with walls of split planks or clay daub on a framework of upright wooden posts. A row of heavy timbers down the center of the interior supported the gabled roof. (FIGURE 3–66) The largest houses reached a length of 30 m and had three to four rooms.

Two-story buildings of the Late Cucuteni period have been discovered in at least six settlements. (FIGURE 3–67), while clay models of two-story buildings are also known from the same area. Markevič, who excavated two-story houses at Varvarovka in Moldavia, gives the details of their construction as follows: The walls, plastered with clay and chaff admixture, were about 30 cm thick. Split beams, placed curved side up, were positioned crosswise on the longitudinal walls over which was spread a 5–12 cm layer of clay with chaff. A second 1–2 cm layer of clay was used as facing. The shorter walls of the second story were then constructed.[87] On smaller sites of fewer than 200 buildings, only one or two of two stories occur, whereas on larger sites such as Petreni, a row of large two-story structures was found.

Excavators believe that these were ceramic workshops. Large ovens and a mass of fine vases were found in three of their ground floor rooms, and it is presumed that pottery was dried on the second stories. In my view, however, these large buildings had a greater significance than being merely workplaces. They were part of a most important temple activity—the preparation of vases and other items of religious significance.

The finest ceramic products were produced in these workshops, created by the best artists in the community, while the upper story of each was very likely a place of worship, as can be deduced from the temple models of both the Cucuteni and Karanovo cultures.

As early as 1907, von Stern, the excavator of Petreni, believed that these large three-room ceramic workshops served some religious significance since he failed to find any hearths, food preparation materials, or workday tools and utensils. What he did find was that these structures were so filled with ceramics that one literally could not move around freely.[88] Vases were packed and stored, and in some cases as many as seven bowls were found one inside the other. They may have been waiting to be used for certain rituals.

FIGURE 3–67

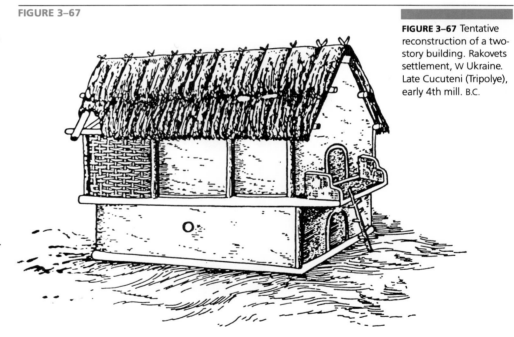

FIGURE 3–67 Tentative reconstruction of a two-story building. Rakovets settlement, W Ukraine. Late Cucuteni (Tripolye), early 4th mill. B.C.

FIGURE 3–68

1

2

FIGURE 3–68 Classical Cucuteni vases, 4400–4200 B.C. Polychrome (white, red, and dark brown) with free-flowing S spirals covering the whole exterior surface. The antithetic spiral or snake heads is the dominant Classical Cucuteni design motif. Note concentric arcs surrounding the spiral heads which seem to symbolize the energy field where two spiral heads meet. (1) Frumuşica; (2) Izvoare near Peatra Neamţ, NE Romania. H (1) 13.5 cm; (2) c. 40 cm.

FIGURE 3–69

FIGURE 3–69 Ceremonial anthropomorphic Cucuteni vase. Bands of V's on the upper register, columns of chevrons in the middle, and snake coils at the base. Painted red on white. Cucuteni A, Drăguşeni, district Peatra Neamţ, NE Romania, 4300–4100 B.C.

FIGURE 3–70 A characteristic classical Cucuteni binocular vase, painted red on white. Drăguşeni, Cucuteni A, 4300–4100 B.C.

FIGURE 3–70

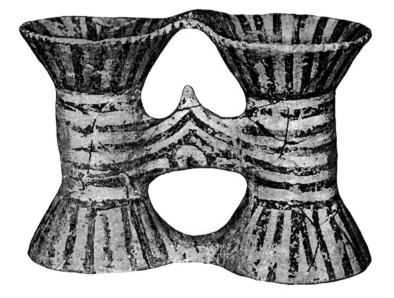

Pottery

The quality of the Cucuteni ceramic production surpassed all contemporary creations of Old Europe. Classical Cucuteni pottery is bichrome and trichrome painted. In trichrome ware white, red, and black mineral-based paints predominate. Free-flowing S-spirals usually cover most of the exterior surface of elegant footed vases or vase supports. (FIGURE 3–68) Other motifs include meanders, chevrons, eggs, splitting eggs, and four-corner designs. (FIGURE 3–69) Typical of Cucuteni are hollow binocular vases which could not have any practical purpose beyond ritual. (FIGURE 3–70) Around 4000 B.C. (Cucuteni AB), changes appeared in vase decoration characterized by the division of space into horizontal panels or friezes. Each was given its own symbolic design, with white on dark brown paint dominating. In Late Cucuteni, friezes with pictorial design, including zoomorphic and anthropomorphic motifs, were typical. Red vases were painted monochrome black. (FIGURE 3–71) The pictorial Late Cucuteni vase painting is a magnificent source for the reconstruction of mythical imagery (which I have profusely used in my previous books on Old European religion).

The study of Cucuteni ceramic technology[89] has shown that Early and Early Classical pottery production was also made at the household level. In the Late Classical and Late Cucuteni periods, there is evidence of the invention and use of a rotational device. (We shall examine this innovation and the use of kilns in the crafts section, beginning on page 122.)

Cucuteni art—in particular the exquisite bichrome and trichrome ceramic vases (some of which are as tall as one meter), anthropomorphic vase supports, large binocular vases, altar screens, ladles, zoomorphic and anthropomorphic figurines—has been appreciated by art historians for some decades. (PLATES 14–16) An extensive treatment of Cucuteni art is to be found in the book *Arta Culturii Cucuteni* by Vladimir Dumitrescu (Bucharest: Editura Meridiane, 1979).

FIGURE 3–71

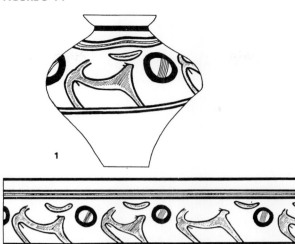

1

2

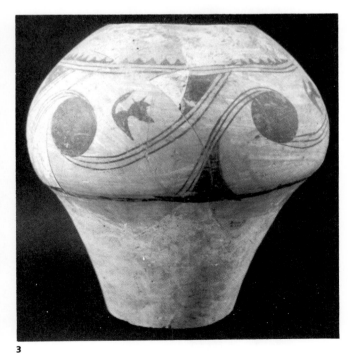

3

FIGURE 3–71 Pictorial design representing mythical themes appears on Late Cucuteni vases. A primary theme is the dog in association with the crescent and full moons. Painted black on red. (1) Truşeşti, 3800–3600 B.C. (2) Ghelaeşti-Nedeia, 3900–3700 B.C. NE Romania. (3) Bilcze Zlote, SE Poland. H (1) 54.2 cm, (2) 36 cm.

FIGURE 3-72

1

FIGURE 3-72 Classical Cucuteni figurines, most likely Bird Goddess images. All-over design of incised chevrons and parallel lines originally encrusted with white paste. (1) Featureless head, wing-stump arms. N Moldavia, Romania, (2) Frumuşica at Peatra Neamţ, NE Romania. H 8.5 cm. Both Cucuteni A2, 45th–44th centuries B.C. H 7 cm (head broken).

2

Figurines

The sculptural art of the Cucutenians is highly schematized. Early Cucuteni figurines are distinguished by huge buttocks, slender trunk, incised lines showing the pubic triangle, with legs usually joined. By the Classical Cucuteni period, the figurines are slenderer and deeply incised with symbols, often with a chevron design and a lozenge area at the midline. (FIGURE 3–72) Late Cucuteni figurines are even more schematic, typically having a round, disk-shaped head with orifices or holes on either side and a beaklike nose. The arms are rounded stumps resembling wings (FIGURE 3–73) often with holes, which could have held feathers or other ornamentation.

The types of divinities represented in sculptural art can only be distinguished by a careful study of incised or painted symbols, postures, the shapes of masks or heads, and their provenance. The primary images are those of the Bird and Snake Goddesses and the Pregnant Goddess (see chapter 7). Images of Stiff Nudes with round masks appeared in graves, sometimes in groups of three. Male figurines are rare, but several types are clearly present: a seated man in a sorrowful posture with head supported by his hands, a bearded man, and a slender, youthful male. The latter can be deduced from finds as the attendant of the Pregnant Goddess, accompanying her in her rituals. As elsewhere, Cucuteni imagery produced significant numbers of zoomorphic figurines and vases (30 percent or more of all images) representing bears, deer, dogs, pigs, bulls, frogs, and birds. The majority of animal sculptures are, however, extremely schematized.

FIGURE 3–73

FIGURE 3–73 Late Cucuteni figurine; a slim nude with a round, flat head, pinched nose, orifices for eyes, and stump arms. Vykhvatintsi cemetery, S Moldavia (Grave No. 29). Mid-4th mill. B.C. H approx. 15 cm.

FIGURE 3–74

FIGURE 3–74 Distribution
of the Dnieper-Donets
culture.

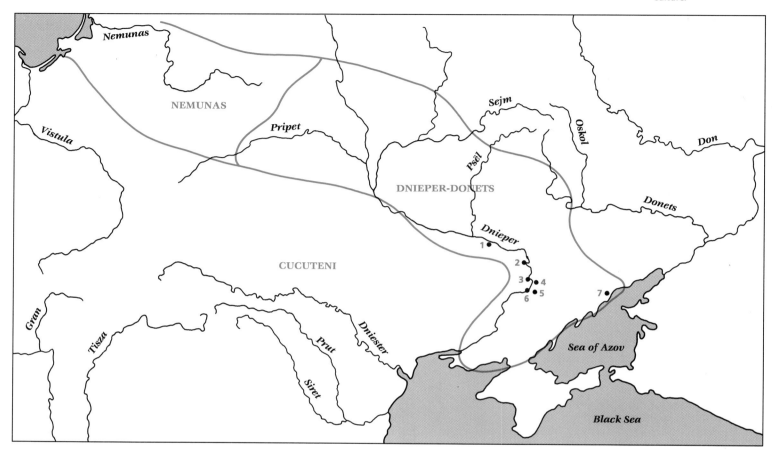

FIGURE 3–74 Distribution of the Dnieper-Donets culture.

KEY

1. Dereivka
2. Nikolskoe
3. Vovnigi
4. Yasinovatka
5. Vilnyanka
6. Sobachki
7. Mariupol

The Dnieper-Donets Culture in the Ukraine

Our present knowledge of this culture is based on finds from about 200 localities including cemeteries, some of which contained more than 100 graves. Settlement sites have been found on low river terraces, although cemeteries are usually located considerably higher up on loess terraces.[90]

North-South Movement of Massive Broadfaced Population

The bearers of the Neolithic culture in the Dnieper basin were massive broadfaced people descended from the Paleolithic Cro-Magnon population. Their direct forerunners lived in the Upper and Middle Dnieper basins.[91] Around 5500 B.C., these people began moving southward into the area of the Lower Dnieper where they dislodged the local inhabitants of the Dnieper rapids region. In the south, they reached the Crimea and the Lower Don where they came in contact with the local Mesoneolithic population, called Surska group (fishermen's culture with pottery). Dnieper-Donets sites are concentrated in the Dnieper rapids area, a region of huge fish resources. (FIGURE 3-74)

Subsistence Economy

Forest hunting was prevalent, indicated by the bones of deer, boar, fox, hare, and roe deer found in the settlement material. During the initial Neolithic phase, subsistence was largely based upon hunting, fishing, and the collection of fresh-water shellfish. The ratio of domesticated animals rose steadily, reaching 87 percent in the second stage of the culture, c. 5000–4500 B.C. By then, all the domesticated animals, cattle, sheep, goats, and pigs, were present.

Not much is known about the architecture or village arrangement. These people must have lived in lightweight, above-ground constructions which have not survived.

FIGURE 3-75

FIGURE 3-75 Large pointed based pots from the middle period of the Dnieper-Donets culture c. 5000 B.C. Habitation site of Grini, located on the bank of River Teterev, Pripyat basin.

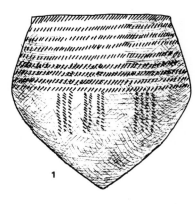

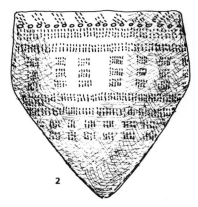

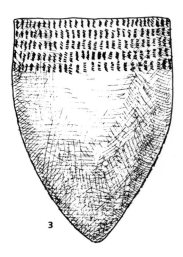

Pottery and Other Finds

Around 5000 B.C. throughout the northern distribution area of this culture, large pointed-base pots with vegetable temper appeared which were stamped or incised with horizontal or vertical lines. (FIGURE 3-75) Later pottery comprised flat-base bulbous vessels with broad rims, decorated by stamping, incision, and wound-cord impressions. (FIGURE 3-76)

Flint was commonly used for axes, arrowheads, knives, borers, and scrapers. Hoes were made of antler while harpoons and fishhooks were of bone. Peculiar plano-convex (loaf-shaped) oval objects with a deep notch in the center appeared in a number of settlements. (FIGURE 3-77) Their symbolic significance is indicated by incised chevrons, parallel lines, pits, and script signs. These suggest the use of the same symbol system seen in the Vinča, Tisza, Cucuteni, and other Old European culture groups.

FIGURE 3–76

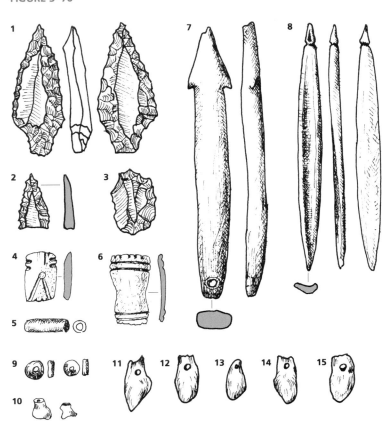
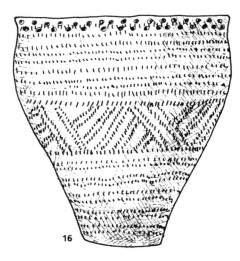
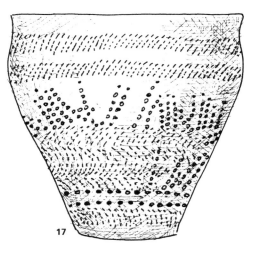

FIGURE 3–76 Grave finds from a late Dnieper-Donets cemetery at Dereivka. (1,2) flint arrowheads; (3) flint scraper; (4, 6) laminae of boar's tusk used for decoration of garments; (5, 9) bone beads; (7) harpoon of bone; (8) netting needle of bone; (10) fish teeth; (11–15) perforated elk teeth used for necklaces; (16–17) pots. 5000–4500 B.C. Scale: c. 1:2.

FIGURE 3–77

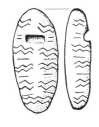
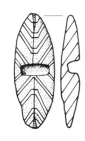

FIGURE 3–77 Plano-convex clay objects inscribed with symbols and with a notch on the outer side from Dnieper-Donets settlements. 5000–4500 B.C. Scale 1:10.

FIGURE 3–78

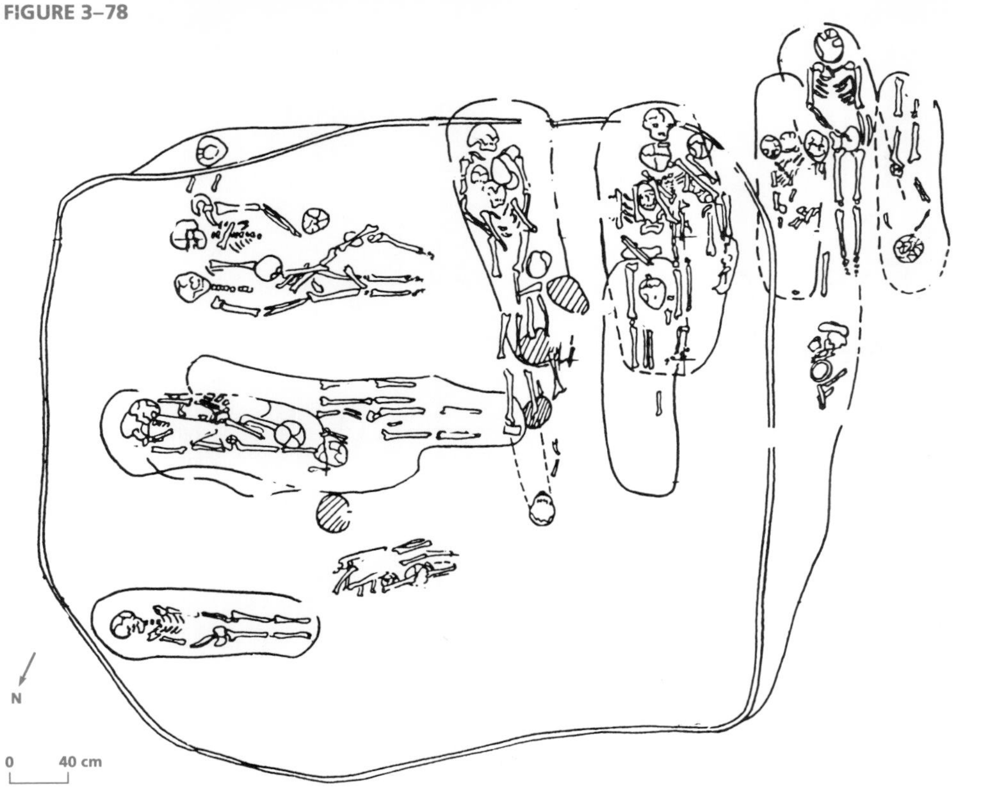

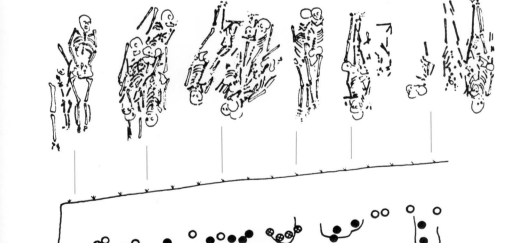

FIGURE 3–79

Collective Burial, Chronology, and Demise

A distinctive feature of the Dnieper-Donets culture is the practice of collective burial in oval or subrectangular pits. (FIGURES 3–78, 3–79) Altogether, more than 800 graves are known from fourteen cemeteries, and based upon these finds the culture is subdivided into three periods: A, B, and C. Period A is characterized by cemeteries of pit hollows and row trenches that contained one to ten or eleven ochre colored skeletons. The dead lay in an extended position on their backs and were covered with powdered red ochre. The legs were pressed together and the arms extended along the body, suggesting that they had been bound in skins or textiles. Microlithic flint tools and beads of elk and fish teeth were usual grave gifts, with a distinct absence of pottery vessels. Annular beads of shell and agate appeared in the A2 subphase which is dated 5500–5000 B.C.

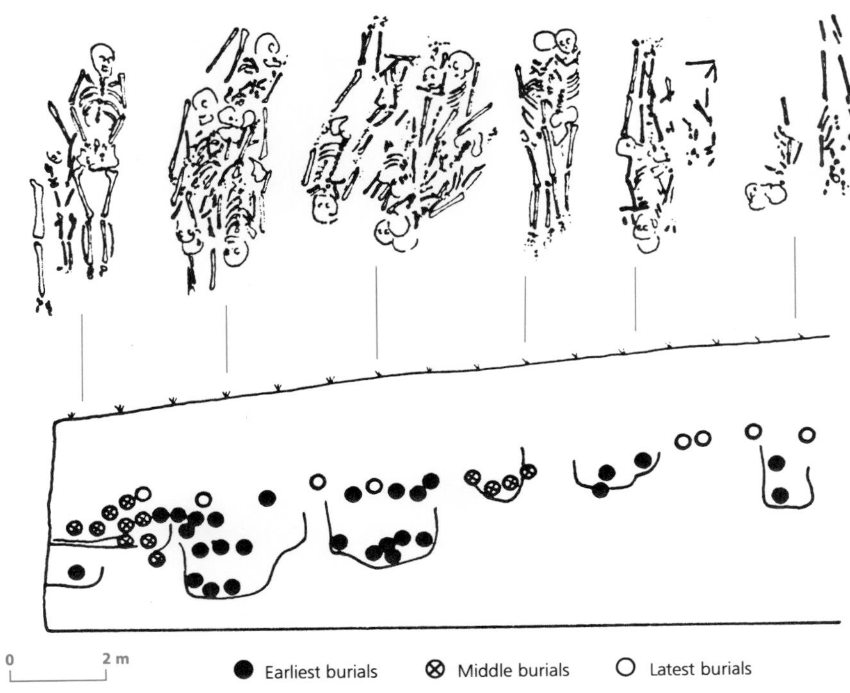

FIGURE 3–78 Collective burials in a large subrectangular pit. Dnieper-Donets culture. Yasino-vatka cemetery near the Dnieper rapids, situated on a high bank of the river. First half of the 5th mill. B.C.

FIGURE 3–79 Plan and cross section of a row of collective graves. Part of the cemetery of Vilnyanka, Dnieper-Donets culture. Mid 5th mill. B.C.

0   2 m

● Earliest burials   ⊗ Middle burials   ○ Latest burials

Period B is characterized by large collective rectangular pits filled up with skeletons, often in several layers, covered with powdered ochre. Since grave pits were used repeatedly, skeletons of the previously buried dead were usually destroyed. The skulls were moved into a distant corner of the pit or were reburied in a separate pit. Fish and deer teeth were not as frequent as in Period A graves, whereas a number of graves contained hundreds of rectangular laminae made of boar tusk enamel, perforated at the ends or center or grooved at the ends. These were presumed to have been sewn on garments in which the dead were buried. (FIGURE 3–80) Bull figurines carved of boar tusk or of bone plate were found in graves (FIGURE 3–80, 3) Unio and pectunculus shells, copper and gold rings, and pieces of rock crystal and pottery vases were also found. Radiocarbon dates from cemeteries in the Dnieper rapids region locate this phase within 5000–4500 B.C. (TABLE 13)

The Lower Dnieper branch of this culture engaged in trade to the west. Spectral analysis of the copper in the rings and pendants shows that it is the same type as that of the Karbuna hoard in Moldavia (see fig. 3–86). This copper very likely came from the Ai-bunar mines in Bulgaria by way of the Cucuteni culture.

Period C, dated approximately 4500–4000 B.C., revealed the disintegration and evident decline of this culture. Collective burials in grave pits vanished and an alien burial practice was introduced. Steppe people of a different physical type (less broad faced) came into this area and the Dnieper-Donets people were either pushed northward or assimilated by the invaders.

The Dnieper-Donets people must have been in close contact with their neighbors in the forest steppe of the Volga basin not later than Period B, 5000–4500 B.C., as the similarity of certain artifacts in both areas indicate (particularly the boar tusk laminae used for dress decoration). This is the Khvalynsk phase of the south Russian Eneolithic culture (see chapter 10). There must have been a gradual infiltration from the Volga basin into the Don and Dnieper

FIGURE 3–80

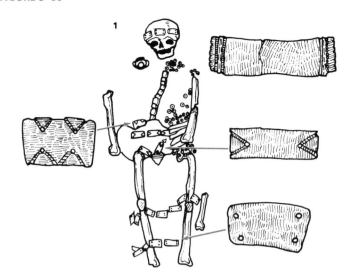

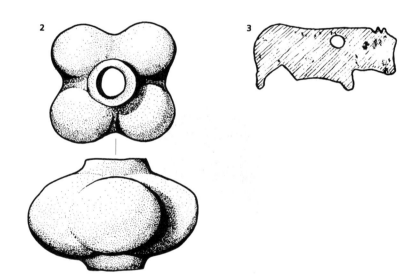

FIGURE 3–80 One of the burials from the Mariupol pit-trench cemetery north of the sea of Azov. Boar tusk laminae (1) were used for decoration of garments and for the diadem. Annular beads of bone were used for necklaces and belts. A mace-head with four breasts was placed at the right shoulder (2). A bull figurine carved out of boar's tusk (3) is from another grave of the same cemetery; c. 4500 B.C.

PLATE 1

PLATE 1 Goddess mask of terracotta on a cylindrical neck, found at Soufli Magula near Larisa, Thessaly. H c. 7 cm. Sesklo culture, early 6th mill. B.C.

PLATE 2

PLATE 3

PLATE 4

PLATE 5

PLATE 6

PLATE 7

PLATE 2 The Sesklo people were excellent carvers of marble, alabaster, porphyry, and greenstone. This is a seal or a gaming board with nine grooves ending in round depressions and outlets. L 5.5 cm. Achilleion IV, Thessaly; 5900–5800 B.C.

PLATE 3 Earliest painted vase (red on white-slipped background) from Early Sesklo ("Protosesklo") culture, c. 6300 B.C. Otzaki, Thessaly.

PLATE 4 Sesklo cup painted red on white slip. The design may be a stylized rendering of ram horns or interconnected bull heads. The handle is decorated with opposed triangles. Narrow triangles or beaks are above the handle and on the interior. Tsani, Thessaly; c. 5900–5800 B.C.

PLATE 5 Goddess masks commonly appear on the necks of ritual vases as this large one from the Sesklo culture; Achilleion IV, 5900–5800 B.C.

PLATE 6 Anthropomorphic Goddess vase from the mid-6th mill. B.C., painted with multiple chevrons, meanders, zigzags, tri-lines, and an M sign. Opposed meanders meet on the forehead, while triple chevrons turn into an M below the beak. Two small meanders mark her breasts and red triangles, as special signs of the Goddess, are at the lower neck. Starčevo culture; Gradešnica, NW of Sofia, Bulgaria.

PLATE 8

PLATE 7 Spherical vase decorated with rows of interconnected S spirals rendered in relief. Nebo, Butmir culture, Bosnia, W Yugoslavia; early 5th mill. B.C.

PLATE 8 A Bird Goddess in terracotta seated on a stool with a round medallion suspended from a V-shaped collar or necklace. Her mask has almond-shaped eyes, an enormous nose representing a bird's beak, and no mouth. Special symbols of the Bird Goddess are indicated by triple lines across the shoulders, a meander over the abdomen, and four lines above it connected by a dash. H. 18.5 cm. Vinča culture, c. 4500 B.C. Predionica near Priština, Kosovo Metohije, S Yugoslavia.

PLATE 9

PLATE 10

PLATE 9 Footed offering vessel of triangular shape painted with a checkerboard motif in red, black, and white. H 15.3 cm. Fafos I near Kosovska Mitrovica, S Yugoslavia. Vinča culture, c. 4500 B.C. or earlier.

PLATE 10 Owl-faced lid with ears as handles, decorated with vertical bands of white-encrusted lattice pattern on a fine black fabric. H 16.5 cm. Vinča culture. Fafos II at Kosovska Mitrovica, Kosovo Metohije, S Yugoslavia, 5000–4500 B.C.

PLATE 11 Life-sized Vinča clay mask with large almond-shaped eyes. H 17.5 cm. Predionica near Priština, Kosovo Metohije, S Yugoslavia, c. 4500 B.C.

PLATE 12 Enthroned Goddess, with head and legs broken, decorated front and back with incised panels of zigzag patterns. H 21.7 cm. Tisza culture, Szegvár-Tüzköves at Szentes, SE Hungary; early 5th mill. B.C.

PLATE 11

PLATE 12

PLATE 13

PLATE 13 Offering container or lamp on four legs with ram head protomes at each corner decorated with spirals, chevrons, and meanders. H 12 cm, L 11.8 cm. Szeged, Tisza culture; early 5th mill. B.C.

PLATE 14 Lidded pear-shaped vase painted with panels of symbolic designs. In front are vulvar forms flanked by floating S spirals which are repeated on the lid. The top band bears chevrons and triangles filled with checkerboard design. Draguşeni, Moldavia, NE Romania. Late Classical Cucuteni culture; c. 4300–4200 B.C.

PLATE 15 ''Binocular'' vase painted black on red with a galloping dog as a central symbol. Late Cucuteni (Cucuteni B); c. 3800–3600 B.C. Bilcze Zlote, Galicia, SE Poland. H c. 15 cm.

PLATE 14

PLATE 15

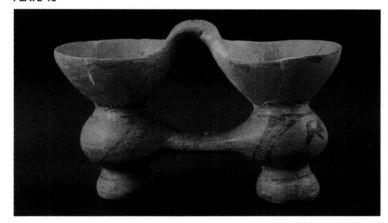

PLATE 16

PLATE 16 Cucuteni dish with interior painted with double-fruit symbol flanking a lozenge in the center. Late Cucuteni (Cucuteni B) from Podei-Targu Ocna, Moldavia, NE Romania; c. 3800–3600 B.C. c. 40 cm. across.

PLATE 17

PLATE 18

PLATE 17 "Serra d'Alto" style vase characterized by fantastic three-dimensional moulding of handles with double-spiral motif. Serra d'Alto period of s Italian Neolithic; Paterno, west of Catania, Sicily; late 5th mill. B.C.

PLATE 18 "Diana" style vase with trumpet handles and brilliantly shining surface lacking decoration. Diana period of s Italian Neolithic; c. 4000 B.C. Paterno, west of Catania, Sicily. H 13.5 cm.

PLATE 19 Animal procession—a ram, a pig, and a goat (three more goats are not shown)—in relief on a stone block near the altar in the Tarxien temple of Malta; c. 3000 B.C.

PLATE 20 Temple of Malta built of globigerina limestone. Ħaġar Qim, SE Malta. A towering menhir that juts out above the temple (right side) may represent the Goddess herself. Second half of the 4th mill. B.C.

PLATE 21 Standing Goddess with ample buttocks and thighs from the temple of Ħaġar Qim, Malta; c. 3500–3000 B.C.

PLATE 19

PLATE 20

PLATE 21

PLATE 22

PLATE 24

PLATE 22 Centaur with a head (mask) of a human and the body of a bull, painted with symbols of regeneration: the egg-shaped forelegs are painted in black with bladder shapes; on top of the mask is an M sign, and across the chest are three lines. Terracotta, H 19.5 cm. Valač near Kosovska Mitrovica, S Yugoslavia. Vinča culture, c. 4500 B.C.

PLATE 23 The Goddess of Lepenski Vir (N Yugoslavia) who comprises features of fish (note the fish mouth), woman (breasts and vulva), and bird of prey (bird's feet instead of human hands). This stone sculpture was found standing at the end of the altar in Temple No. 44, together with another egg-shaped Fish Goddess. H 51 cm. c. 6000 B.C.

PLATE 24 Egg-shaped sandstone sculpture representing the vulva before parturition. Lepenski Vir, Temple 51, found at the end of the altar. The sculpture was solidly painted in red ochre color. Size: 18 × 13.8 cm.

PLATE 23

region much before the Kurgan I pressure began west of the Black Sea after the middle of the 5th millennium B.C. By then, the Dnieper-Donets people were gone from the steppe zone. The last phase of this culture is known only from the territories of the Pripet and Upper Dnieper basins.

METALLURGY, TRADE, AND CRAFTS

Copper and Gold Metallurgy

The earliest copper artifacts in east-central Europe occurred soon after 5500 B.C. Square-sectioned copper awls, beads, and other trinkets shaped by heating and hammering have been found in a series of settlements. The number of copper artifacts increased early in the 5th millennium B.C. Awls, axes, chisels, beads, spirals, coiled wire bracelets, and amulets in the shape of figurines appeared in the Hamangia, Boian, Cucuteni, and Karanovo cultures.

In the early 5th millennium B.C., the exploitation of copper mines became systematic and increased markedly around the middle of the 5th millennium B.C. This period also saw the use of gold, the development of smelting, and the appearance of large copper tools. Shaft-hole axes and axe-adzes were cast in open molds. (FIGURE 3–81) The smelted copper was pure except for insignificant amounts of tin or arsenic occurring as impurities in the original ore. Deliberate alloying of copper with arsenic or tin was not practiced.

Copper ore sources are abundant in the Carpathian, Transylvanian, and Rhodope mountains. One of the earliest copper mines so far discovered, from no later than 5000 B.C., is located at Rudna Glava, 140 km east of Belgrade. Nearly thirty shafts were excavated there between 1968 and 1979 by B. Jovanović.[92] The technology of copper mining was much the same as that of flint mining which was practiced long before the age of metals. Miners got the ore out by digging a horizontal access platform into a slope where a vein reached the surface, then excavating narrow vertical shafts into the vein, in some places to a depth of fifteen to twenty meters. Most of the ore they quarried was malachite and azurite, green and blue carbonates of copper. The basic excavation tool was a stone maul made of a large pebble of gabbro (a granular igneous rock) grooved so that it could be tied with a strap or rope and swung. These mauls were usually 10 to 25 cm long, weighing between 1 and 4 kg (up to 8 or 9 pounds). Antlers found

FIGURE 3–81

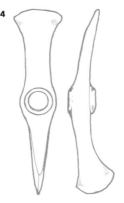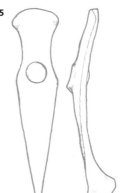

FIGURE 3–81 Shaft-hole copper axes of the middle and end of the 5th mill. B.C. (1) Tibava, W Slovakia, Tiszapolgár group; (2) Pločnik, S Yugoslavia, Late Vinča; (3) Gabarevo, C Bulgaria, Karanovo IV; (4) and (5) Bodrogkeresztúr complex, Hungary. Scale 1:3.

in shafts presumably served as picks. A technique of alternate heating and cooling was used to break up the ore, as evidenced by traces of fire and jugs for carrying water. When the heated rock cracked after being splashed with water, miners widened the cracks with antler tools or wooden wedges, then pried out the loose lumps of ore. The ore was then transported to the nearest village or township in the Morava River basin or farther west.

A chronology of the Rudna Glava mines is based on Vinča pottery found in three different accumulations. Cache No. 3 included black-burnished vases with channeled spiral designs and a lamp standing on four legs with the stylized head of a ram. The lamp is decorated with a triple chevron on its neck and meanders around its body, typical symbols associated with the Bird Goddess. This may suggest that the Copper Age Goddess was the patroness of metallurgical crafts and mining which was one of the many attributes of the Greek Athene. These wares are typical of the end of the Early Vinča and into the middle period. Caches No. 1 and No. 2 yielded pottery of somewhat later type, placed at the start of Late Vinča.

A new insight into the dimensions of copper mining is offered by the discovery of the mines at Ai-bunar, eight kilometers south of Stara Zagora in central Bulgaria, in 1971 and excavated by E. N. Chernykh in 1972.[93] Eleven shafts with a total length of 500 m were uncovered. Some were up to 110 m long and 20 m deep. Such a mine could have produced many tons of copper ore. The Ai-bunar mines are dated to the mid-5th millennium B.C. (Karanovo VI period). Copper tools, including such special mining implements as an axe-adze and a pick-axe, were found in the shafts. An analysis of the copper from Ai-bunar as well as copper found in a number of workshops, graves, and deposits has shown that this site served the entire east Balkan region, Moldavia, the western Ukraine, and southern Russia in the east, and Slovakia and northeastern Hungary in the west.

The discovery of the cemetery at Varna, with hundreds of gold items deposited in graves, has stimulated interest in gold sources.[94] A study by A. Hartmann of 137 gold objects has shown that about one-half contain platinum, others contain none, and twelve have a high content of copper, suggesting that they originated from different sources.[95] The question of where this gold was mined is still open to speculation, although Jovanović suggests that the gold of this period was from native sources.[96] The simultaneous efflorescence of both copper and gold metallurgies speaks in favor of this hypothesis.

It is important to note that copper and gold metallurgy was used for the manufacture of tools, ornaments, jewelry, and ritual equipment, not for weapons of war.

Trade

Trade in shells, marble, obsidian, and copper steadily increased during the period between 5500 and 4500 B.C. Sea and river routes continued to play a vital role. We do not know what was exchanged for these highly valued items, but there must have been some vitally needed commodities such as salt and agricultural products. Salt was mined in southern Poland by the Lengyel people.[97] Varieties of flint and minerals were also widely sought and exchanged with the source areas within a radius of hundreds of kilometers.

Sites along the Adriatic coast and the Black Sea littoral abound in shells, marble, and copper. Hamangian graves along the Black Sea included necklaces of dentalium and spondylus beads, bracelets of spondylus and marble, and marble figurines and dishes. Copper beads and arm rings were also found. From their ports, the shells and marble traveled along the Danube to central Europe. Marble bracelets are found in LBK (Stroked Pottery) graves in Bohemia and central Germany.

A new phase in trade history began with the emergence of copper mining and gold metallurgy. The unprecedented wealth of copper, gold, Aegean spondylus and dentalium shells, and marble, as well as gold- and graphite-decorated vases recovered from the cemetery of Varna, are witness to the success of Varna as an important harbor and trading center during the mid-5th millennium B.C. Around 3,000 gold objects and more than fifty copper tools—hammer-axes, flat axes, chisels, awls, and needles—were uncovered from the graves. Also found were quantities of beads, bracelets, rings, convex round plates with perforations, figurines of bulls, solid gold axes with shafts of gold tubing, diadems, and various religious symbols. (FIGURES 3–82, 3–83, 3–84, 3–85) Outside of Varna, gold bracelets and ring pendants are found distributed in the Lower Danube region, while several gold pendants produced from hammered-sheet gold traveled as far south as the southern Peloponnese.[98] Varna may have functioned as a center where different cultures came to exchange goods from their respective regions in a form of free market. The more than 20,000 spondylus and dentalium shells found in Varna graves had been imported from the Aegean region, probably in exchange for metal tools required by the inhabitants of the Cycladic Islands and Aegean coast. Several hoards were found in the Aegean area containing copper tools with close parallels in the Karanovo culture. Similarly, the marble found at Varna, in the form of beautifully carved conical bowls and rhytons, had probably been traded northward from the Cyclades, whereas transparent, razor sharp obsidian blades had come from the Tokay source in northeastern Hungary. A transparent obsidian blade of outstanding workmanship was also found in a Karanovo VI settlement, thirty kilometers south of Nova Zagora, together with copper beads (Nova Zagora museum). This suggests that central Bulgaria was a link in the obsidian and copper exchange between the Carpathian basin and the Black Sea. Furthermore, central Bulgarian graphite used for painting of pottery was a highly valued commodity and was traded between the Middle Danube region and

FIGURE 3–82

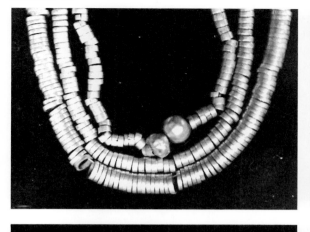
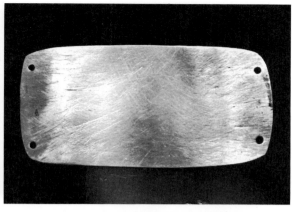

FIGURE 3–82 Gold beads, earrings, bracelet, and plate with perforations in corners, from the cemetery of Varna, E Bulgaria. Grave No. 4. c. 45th–44th cents. B.C.

FIGURE 3–83

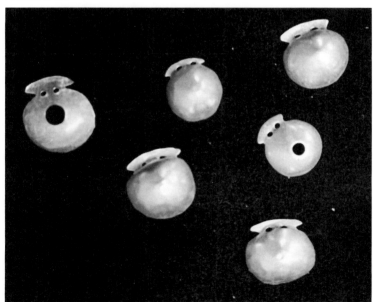

FIGURE 3–83 Round and convex gold pendants "with eyes." Cemetery of Varna, E Bulgaria. Scale: 1:2.

FIGURE 3–84

FIGURE 3–84 (a) Gold from one grave (No. 36, a kenotaph with no skeleton) of the Varna cemetery. Most of it is clearly of ritual significance: bull figurines, bull horns, gold astragalus of a ram, convex plates and rings, pendants with "eyes," a V-shaped object, earrings, beads, gold axe, and a hook. (b) Detail: Solid gold axe with a shaft of gold tubes and bull figurines.

a

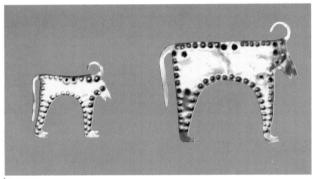

b

FIGURE 3–85

FIGURE 3–85 A mass of dentalium shells, carnelian and stone beads, convex plates of gold, and gold beads. Part of treasure deposited in Grave No. 4 at Varna, Bulgaria. c. 4500–4400 B.C.

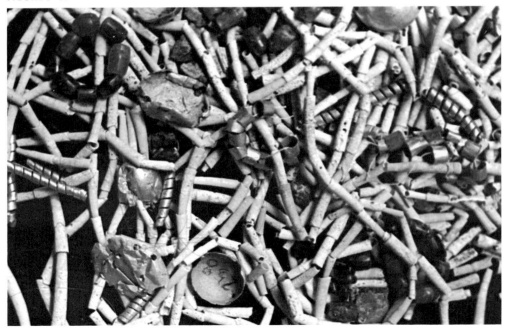

the Black Sea. A graphite cone for the decoration of pottery, deposited in one of the graves of Varna, must have come from the source area, Stara Zagora in central Bulgaria. A hoard of graphite cones was found there in the settlement of Azmak, some perforated and ready for export.

Spectral analysis of copper artifacts indicated trade contacts between the Karanovo and the Cucuteni cultures, and as far east as the Lower Dnieper and Lower Volga basins. A Cucuteni vase filled with more than 400 copper artifacts and more than 400 items of shell and marble, was discovered at Karbuna in Soviet Moldavia, indicating the wide diffusion and quantities of copper used in the Cucuteni territory.[99] Among the copper finds of Karbuna were an axe, a chisel, and spiral bracelets typical of central and eastern Bulgaria, as well as hundreds of flat copper pendant amulets which are seemingly abstract versions of schematic bone figurines. (FIGURE 3–86). In the Ukraine (from the Chapli and Mariupol cemeteries, north of the Black and Azov seas) and in southern Russia (Khvalynsk on the Volga), axes, beads, rings, spiral arm rings, and round-plate pendants have been found which are related to Cucuteni and Karanovo VI forms of copper artifacts. The diffusion of copper over an area of several thousand kilometers must be credited to the horse-riding Kurgan I people of the Lower Dnieper and Lower Volga steppe.

Since accumulations of gold and copper objects are found stored in temples or in vases, we surmise that the distribution of metal artifacts, most of which had a ritual significance, was handled by temple representatives, and that they were very likely owned communally by the temples' participants. This situation, however, was changing in the area of the Black Sea littoral after the middle of the 5th millennium B.C. The cemetery of Varna yielded extraordinarily rich individual graves for both males and females (see chapter 9). As the geographical location indicates, this change could have been stimulated by contact with the Kurgan people for whom private ownership was the norm.

FIGURE 3–86

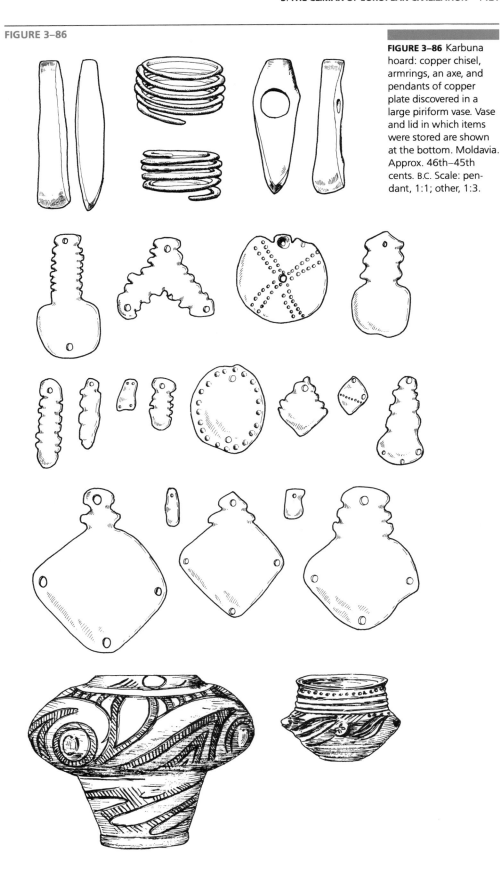

FIGURE 3–86 Karbuna hoard: copper chisel, armrings, an axe, and pendants of copper plate discovered in a large piriform vase. Vase and lid in which items were stored are shown at the bottom. Moldavia. Approx. 46th–45th cents. B.C. Scale: pendant, 1:1; other, 1:3.

Crifts

Workshops and hoards of metal, stone, or shell objects suggest a gradual rise in craft specialization. Smiths' workshops holding copper slag, crucibles, and unfinished copper tools or ornaments are known from a number of Karanovo sites (Sitagroi, Hirşova, Vidra, Ruse, and Karanovo). The mining of flint, minerals, and copper probably also developed into separate professions. The massive amounts of gold objects in Varna graves are surely products of a special class of craftsmen, perhaps artisans from temple workshops, who created true treasures in gold. In the temple of Hotnica in northern Bulgaria, numerous bracelets of similar design and abstract images of the Goddess were found. These were in the form of round plates with eyes and a hole in the middle.[100] Workshops for spondylus and bone ornaments and figurines are known from the Hirşova tell in Dobruja.[101]

The two-story temple at Radingrad, near Razgrad, eastern Bulgaria, built in the early centuries of the 5th millennium B.C., contained a ceramic workshop on the first floor and a temple with an altar on the second. The workshop included a large oven, while on the other side of the room stood finished and unfinished vases, unused clay, and a collection of tools for pottery decoration: polishers of deer bone, flint blades, bird bones, picklike tools, awls, and flat stones for crushing ocher. The Radingrad workshop with the temple on the second floor is a key to understanding the function of other two-story ceramic workshops of the Cucuteni, Karanovo, and Tisza cultures. One of the best examples is the Cucuteni workshop from Varvarovka. (FIGURE 3–87) These were workshops for the temples where the most beautiful vases and other ritual equipment were produced. The possibility is not excluded that household pots needed by individual families could also have been produced in these communal workshops, although only exquisite fine ware has been found.

FIGURE 3–87

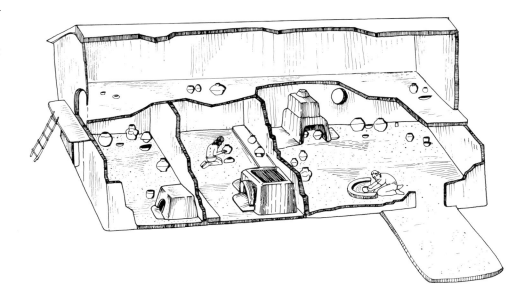

FIGURE 3–88

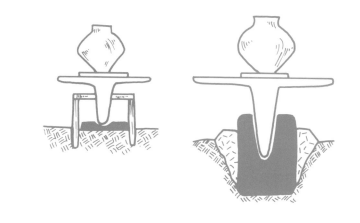

FIGURE 3–87 Reconstruction of pottery workshop from Varvarovka VIII, Moldavia. This is possibly a temple workshop with temple proper on the second floor. Approx. 4000 B.C.

FIGURE 3–88 Variants for reconstructing rotational device for pottery building based on findings at Varvarovka, Moldavia. Approx. 4000 B.C.

FIGURE 3–89 Attempted reconstruction of a kiln. Habaşeşti, Classical Cucuteni, 44th–43rd cents. B.C.

Female members of the family may have supervised this craft, and it is fairly certain that embellishment was also their province. Actual evidence that pottery burnishing and decoration was done by women comes from the cemetery of Basatanya (Bodrogkeresztúr phase) in eastern Hungary, where a tool kit for pottery burnishing, painting, and engraving, consisting of a pebble, a fish bone, a bone polisher, a pyxis, and a dipper, was found in a number of female graves.[102]

Of course, we need many more examples to prove that pottery embellishment was in the hands of women. Men could also have participated in pottery production. However, judging from the temple models, only women are shown producing pottery in temple workshops.

Pottery was hand built using the coil method throughout the Neolithic, but around 4000 B.C. in the Cucuteni culture, a rotational device, in combination with the coil, came into use. Direct evidence of the use of rotary motion was produced by the excavation of the Varvarovka site in Soviet Moldavia.[103] Inside the workshop, a wooden post was found wedged into the ground to a depth of 50–55 cm. It was 36–38 cm in diameter and was packed with clay mixed with chaff. A ring of clay with a rim surrounded the post above the ground. Markevič, the excavator of the workshop, offered several reconstructions of possible methods of rotation, reproduced here in figure 3–88.

Pottery kilns came into use before or around the middle of the 6th millennium B.C. The earliest simple kilns, clay structures in the shape of a truncated cone, are known from the Starčevo culture. By the 5th millennium B.C., kilns were widely used in all culture groups of east-central Europe. In the Cucuteni area alone, they were found in seventeen settlements.[104] The Cucutenians used a complex type of kiln which is cylindrical or rectangular in plan, consisting of two vertically arranged parts: a lower section where the combustion of fuel takes place and an upper section in which the pottery is fired. Both sections are separated by a horizontal grate perforated with holes to allow the hot air from below to rise into the upper cham-

ber. An attempted reconstruction of such a kiln from the village of Habaşeşti of the Classical Cucuteni is given in figure 3–89.

The use of kilns in pottery firing allows greater control over reduction and oxidation conditions. Analysis by X-ray diffraction of the black slips on Cucuteni pottery dating from c. 4000 B.C. have shown that these early potters were able to attain, and probably exceed, firing temperatures of 1,000 degrees C.[105]

The variety of crafts produced at this time—of metal, ceramic, stone, bone, and shell—are evidence of an impressive array of material goods used for personal, ritual and commercial purposes which were distributed locally and traded throughout larger regions.

FIGURE 3–89

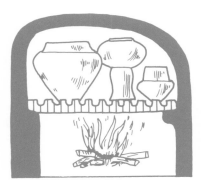

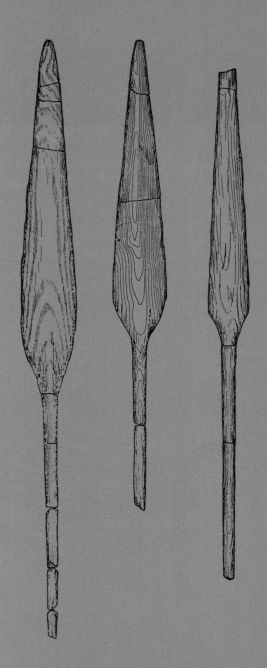

4

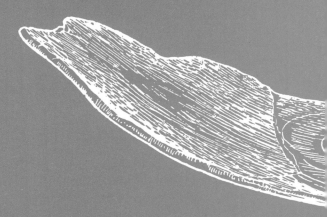

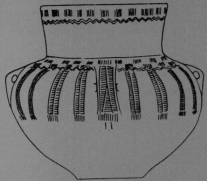

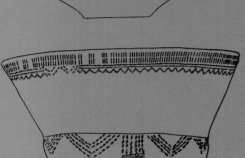

The Neolithic Cultures of Northern Europe

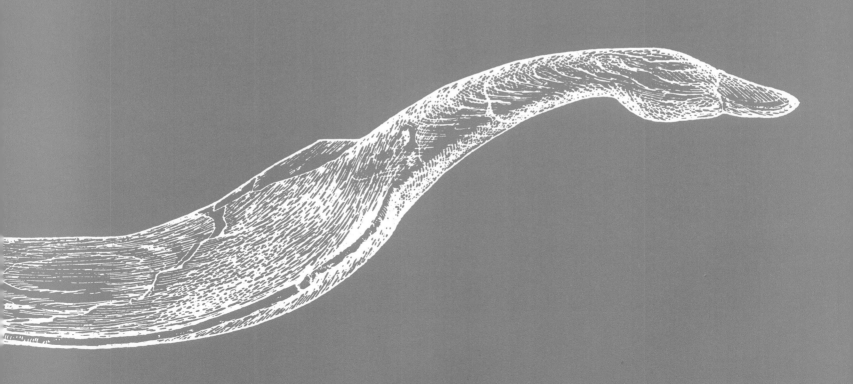

The northern Europeans continued a food-gathering economy for millennia, and were nourished by the bounty of nature. Mixed forests and a network of glacial lakes offered plenty of game animals, water birds, berries, mushrooms, edible roots, nuts, wild plant seeds, and large fish. A food gathering economy continued from Boreal (warm and dry) times, during the 8th and 7th millennia B.C., while fishing was the basic occupation throughout the moister Atlantic period of the 6th and 5th millennia B.C. The central European agriculturalists, however, gradually moved north, entering the territories of the Mesolithic Ellerbeck-Ertebølle food gatherers of northwestern Europe during the last centuries of the 5th millennium B.C.

In the East Baltic area, a gradual evolution took place from the Late Paleolithic to the Mesolithic. People continued to fish and hunt and to produce tools of flint, bone, and antler even into the 4th millennium B.C. when the settled villages of fishermen mark the beginning of the Neolithic period.

Northern central Europe between Holland and Poland was transformed to a food-producing culture through the constant influence and colonization by central European agriculturalists—the late LBK and Lengyel people—during the second half of the 5th millennium B.C. In this region, a fully agricultural society, called Funnel-necked Beaker or TRB, emerged and soon entered into the territory of the Ertebølle culture of southern Scandinavia and the Ellerbek of northwestern Germany. In the later stage of its development, the TRB also expanded to the northeast, colonizing the lower Vistula region of northern Poland and the Nemunas basin up to western Belorussia.

In this chapter we shall first consider the Funnel-necked Beaker agriculturalists and then the local survivals of the Baltic Mesolithic cultures, the Nemunas and Narva.

FIGURE 4–1 Distribution of the Funnel-necked Beaker or TRB (from the German *Trichterbecher*) culture and its regional groups. 4th mill. B.C.

TRB, The Funnel-necked Beaker Culture of Northern Europe

The abbreviation TRB comes from the Danish *Tragtbaegerkultur* and the German *Trichterbecherkultur*, which in English means the Funnel-necked Beaker culture.

These first farmers of northern Europe occupied the Elbe, Oder, and Vistula basins, then spread north to Denmark and southern Sweden. On the west was the Michelsberg culture of the Middle and Upper Rhine basin which was closely related and of intermediate facies between TRB and the western European cultures. On the east was the Cucuteni culture.

Formation

TRB formed at the end of the 5th millennium B.C. and continued throughout the whole of the 4th millennium B.C., lasting to the middle of the 3rd millennium B.C. in its northern fringes. Its beginning coincides in time with the first infiltration of the Kurgan people from the eastern steppes into the Danubian basin. As mentioned in chapter 3, the expansion of the Lengyel people into northern Europe at about 4300 B.C. was most likely the result of a chain reaction of cultural change in the Lower and Middle Danube region. The Lengyel's appearance in central Germany and western Poland was a decisive influence in the formation of the TRB. Another component of the TRB is the Late Linearbandkermik culture which spread in central Europe before the entrance of the Lengyel population.

As agriculturalists moved north into northern Germany and southern Scandinavia, they encountered the local Late Mesolithic populations—the Ellerbeck in northern Germany and Ertebølle in Denmark and southern Sweden—who lived in these regions throughout the 5th millennium B.C. Scholars in the past thought that the TRB culture developed from the Ertebølle culture, but it is now clear that there are no genetic relationships between the two, except for the fusing that must have taken place

FIGURE 4–1

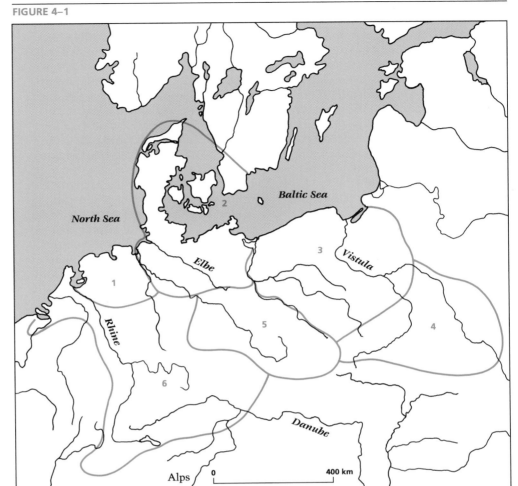

KEY
1. Western
2. Northern
3. Eastern
4. Southeastern
5. Southern
6. Michelsberg

between the TRB and the local Meso-lithic populations. Chronologically, the TRB succeeds the Ertebølle and their site locations markedly differ. While the Ertebølle people occupied the coastal regions of the sea, the TRB population preferred inland areas with light, sandy, clayey soils that could be easily cleared.[1]

In conclusion, the formation of the TRB culture seems to have been the result of the fusion of multiple factors: influences of the Mesolithic Ellerbeck-Ertebølle substratum, continuity of the central European Rössen and Stroked Pottery cultures, and the influx of a Middle Danubian element represented by the Lengyel population.

Natural conditions in the vast forested area that spawned the TRB were varied, and from the beginning, it was a differentiated phenomenon in economic adaptation, settlement strategies, and even in the production of flint tools. On the basis of internal differences, this culture is subdivided into the following regional groups: western (Holland and Hanover), eastern (Oder and Vistula area of Poland), southeastern (southeast Poland and Volhynia), southern or Baalberge (Upper Elbe basin of central Germany, Silesia, Bohemia, and Moravia), and northern (Mecklenburg and southern Scandinavia). (FIGURE 4–1) There are, however, many unifying phenomena: pottery typology, the spread of earthen long-barrows in most of the regional groups and, toward the end of the culture, the diffusion of dolmens and passage graves from the west into the northern territory of the TRB culture.

Chronology

The number of radiocarbon dates is sufficient for an insight into the succession of developmental phases in all regions. (TABLE 14) We shall generalize the chronology using numbers from 1 to 5 for the phases extending from approximately 4200 B.C. to the middle of the 3rd millennium B.C. in calendar years. In addition to radiocarbon dates, this chronology is supported by stratigraphies and pottery typologies. Pottery forms range from simple low-necked beakers and

amphorae from Phases 1 and 2, which were usually undecorated or decorated just around the rim (FIGURES 4–2A, 4–2B), to richly decorated funnel-necked beakers, amphorae, and bowls during Phase 3 (FIGURES 4–2C, 4–3). One of the characteristic vessel types of this culture is the collared flask that appeared in Phase 2. (FIGURES 4–2B,2; 4–2C,2) The pottery forms and decoration of Phase 4, in Poland and in the whole of the southern half of the culture, exhibit some stagnation and influences from the south and east (Baden and North Pontic). In the north, ceramic art continued to flourish during the period of the building of megalithic graves, in which vases were decorated with deep incisions and encrustations with white paste. Hence the name Tiefstich for the pottery of the megaliths. (FIGURE 4–3)

FIGURE 4-2A

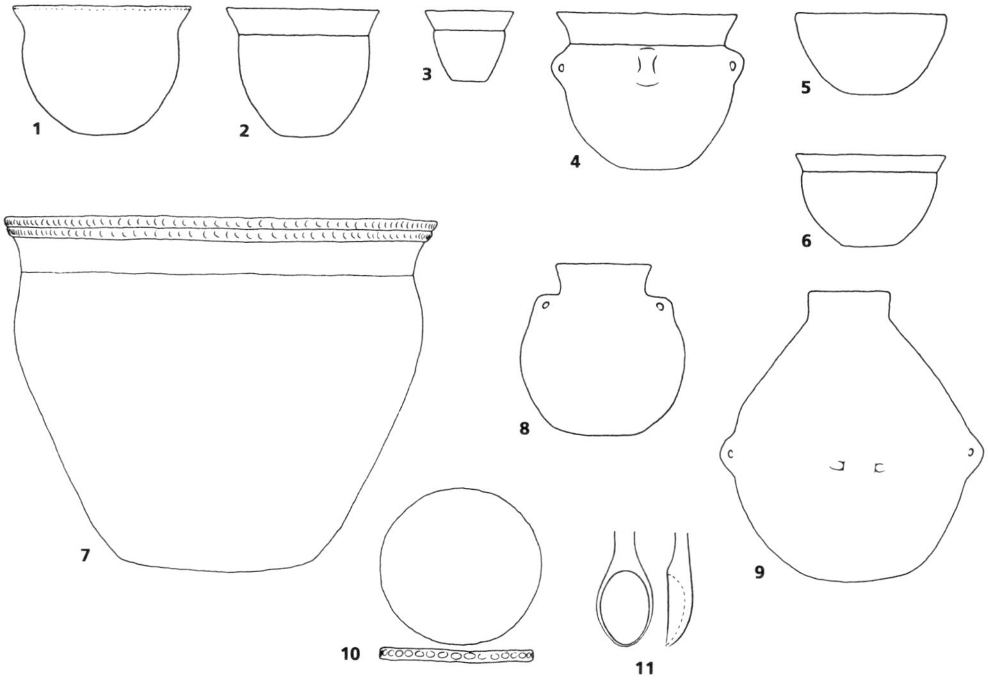

FIGURE 4–2B

FIGURE 4–2A Pottery types of the TRB culture. Phase 1 (or Group A) based on finds from Sigersted, central Zealand, Denmark. c. 4000 B.C.

FIGURE 4–2B Pottery type of the TRB culture. Phase 2 (or Group B) from western Poland. (1, 4, 5) Pikutkowo, distr. of Włocławek; (2) Spławie, distr. of Leszczyn; (3) Obalki, distr. of Konin; (6) Malankowo, distr. of Toruń. Early 4th mill. B.C.

FIGURE 4–2C Pottery types of the TRB culture, Phase 3 (''Wiórek'' group in Poland). (1) Chełmża, distr. of Toruń; (2) Lutynia, distr. of Kalisz; (3) Niedziejewo, distr. of Poznań; (4) Modliborzyce, distr. of Bydgoszcz; (5, 6) Szlachcin, distr. of Poznań; (7) Radziejów Kujawski, distr. Włocławek. Mid-4th mill. B.C.

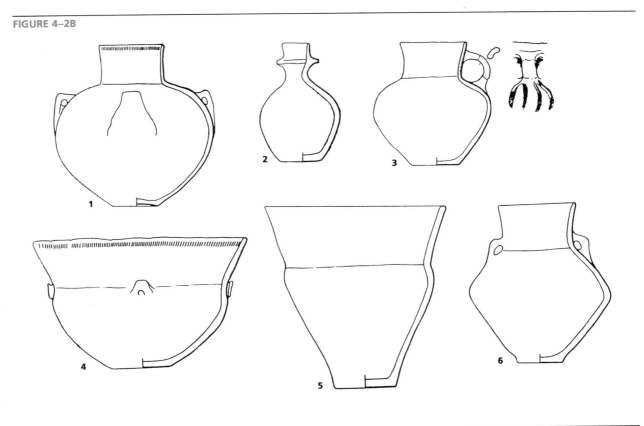

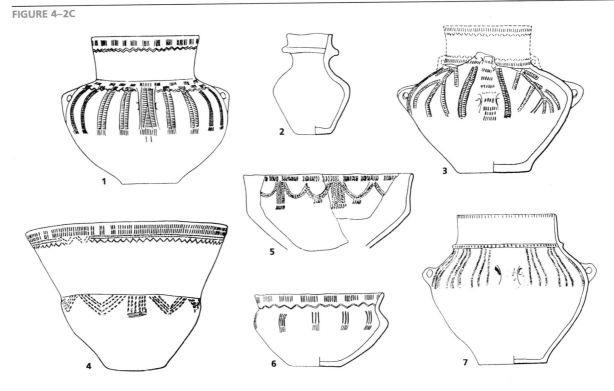

FIGURE 4–2C

FIGURE 4-3

FIGURE 4–3 Examples of the flourishing ceramic art during the megalith grave building period in Denmark. Vases are decorated with deep incisions (''Tiefstich'') and were incrusted with white color. (1) Høbjerg hegn, Kelsinge sogn, Holbo herred; (2) Ebbelnaes; (3) Odder, Hads herred, Århus; (4) Hagebrogård, Haderup sogn, Grinding herred. End 4th mill. B.C. Scale: 1, 1:2; 2–4, 3:4.

FIGURES 4–4, 4–5 Stone and antler mining tools from the mines of Krzemionki Opatowce. S Poland.

Economy

The first agriculturalists of northern Europe inherited the knowledge of domestic plants and animals from central Europe, and the whole range of grains was known: wheat, barley, rye, oats, peas, flax.[2] The dominant species was wheat, (primarily *Triticum dicoccum*, as well as *monococcum*, *vulgare*, *compactum*, and *spelta*), followed by barley. Oats and rye are weakly represented, and millet is reported only from the eastern group (used for porridge). The main agricultural tools were antler hoes and sickles with flint teeth or knifelike blades set in bone or wooden handles. The use of the plow is also presumed since traces of parallel ploughing marks were noticed at the Sarnowo site in western Poland under a long-barrow.[3] A series of settlements revealed an intensive use of wild fruits and berries: apples, plums, cherries, raspberries, nuts, and others. Cattle was predominant among the domesticates (up to 66 percent and more of all the domesticated animals), followed by pigs (in some settlements pigs occupies the second place, up to 40 percent), then by sheep and goats (settlements yielded from 7 to 14 percent of sheep and goat bones), and dog (from 2 to 9 percent of all the bones). The percentage of wild animal bones in settlements is low but varies considerably from site to site (from 2.3 percent to 22 percent of all animal bones).[4]

Flint, which was highly selected from a variety of sources, was the major material for the production of tools, along with wood and bone. In eastern and southern Poland alone at least nine sources of flint were exploited.[5] Chocolate-colored flint was cherished in the early phase of the culture at Sarnowo and was imported from the Upper Tisza region as well as from the source at Radom in central Poland. A gray variety with white dots was also highly valued. In the later phases, starting with Phase 3, other flint sources were intensively exploited, particularly the excellent gray varieties at Swieciechów in southern Poland and from the River Bug basin in Volhynia. Banded flint was obtained from the mines at Krzemionki near Opatów in the upper Vistula region in southern Poland.[6] These mines extend in an arc for four kilometers, and the tunnels discovered there go down from four to ten meters. Chambers from which large quantities of flint were obtained were twelve to eighteen meters in size. In these were found antler, stone, and flint hammers and wedges for mining. (FIGURES 4–4, 4–5) Large nuclei obtained from these and other mines resulted in the macrolithic type of tools typical of this culture. (FIGURE 4–6)

FIGURE 4–4

FIGURE 4–5

FIGURE 4–6

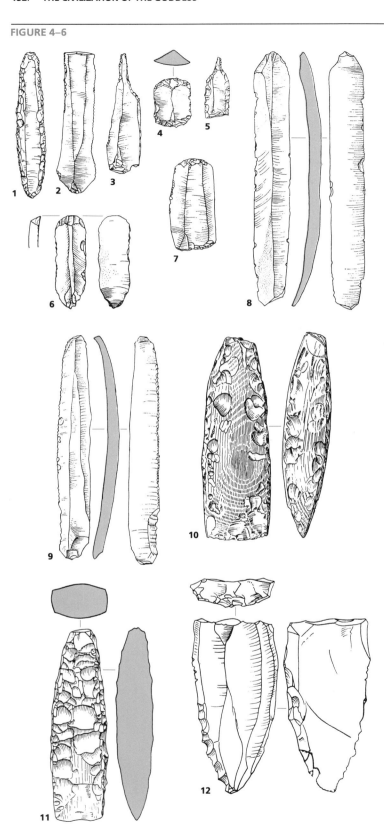

FIGURE 4–7

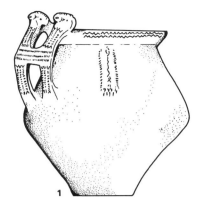

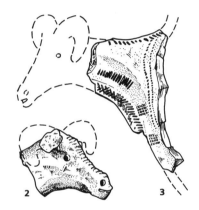

FIGURE 4–6 Typical flint tools of the TRB culture from the habitation sites of southern Poland: (1) knife; (3,5) screws; (2,4,6,7) scrapers; (8,9) sickles; (10–11) axes; (12) nucleus. (1–5,7,10,12) Cmielów; (6) Zawichost; (8,9) Gródek Nadbużny.

FIGURE 4–7 Ram heads appear as handles on ceremonial vases and ram figurines serve as offering vases. Examples are from southern Poland and Silesia. (1) Cmielów, H 33.9 cm.; (2) Nosocice; (3) Krzekotówek; (4) Clay sculpture from Jordanów. Mid-4th mill. B.C. H 13.5 cm.

Settlement Sites

TRB settlements are found in loess and light soil regions, not only in river valleys but also on high elevations. Villages ranged from 100 m to 500 m in length, with the largest villages covering about 10 hectares, with ten to fifteen houses in the southern group (southern Poland). In the north (southern Sweden), only very small villages are known, consisting of a few houses with only some ten inhabitants. There was no single house type, although pit dwellings were frequent, particularly during the earlier phases, and above-ground timber houses with thick clay daub and wickerwork walls were usual during the later phases.

The Ćmielów village in southern Poland consisted of pit dwellings and some above-ground houses, dating from the middle of the 4th millennium B.C. It occupied an area about 500 m long and 200 m wide which included fifteen houses arranged in three groups. A huge pit house was found in the central part of this village in which large vases were stored filled with grain (wheat, peas, and flax). The rich ceramic finds discovered there included beautiful jugs with handles in the shape of ram heads. (FIGURE 4–7) This building, being different in size and centrally located, could have been a temple with a storage area in which grain and fruit were kept for seasonal feasts. Flint and ceramic workshops were located on the outskirts of the village.[7]

Above-ground houses of three or four rooms are known in the preceding central European cultures. Such a house, so far unique for the TRB, was excavated in 1977 at Flögeln, district of Cuxhaven, on the Eekholtjen peninsula at the edge of a TRB settlement.[8] The house was 12.75 m long, 4.80 m wide, and its outline was reconstructed by the discovery of a foundation trench with no postholes. Pairs of timber uprights in the middle axis of the long-house functioned as the holding element. There were a few posts outside the long walls on both sides and the house was subdivided into four rooms by partition walls. (FIGURE 4–8) Radiocarbon dates were obtained from wooden posts and from trenches, suggesting that the date of this house is

FIGURE 4–8

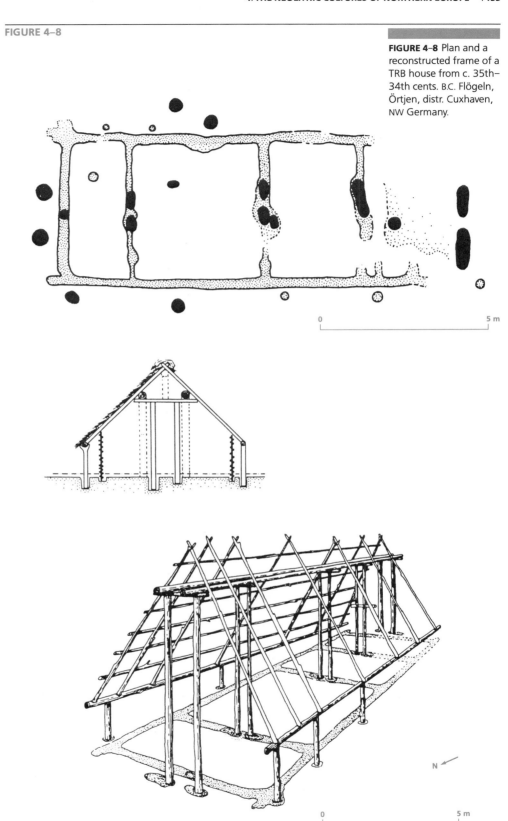

FIGURE 4–8 Plan and a reconstructed frame of a TRB house from c. 35th–34th cents. B.C. Flögeln, Örtjen, distr. Cuxhaven, NW Germany.

0   5 m

FIGURE 4–9

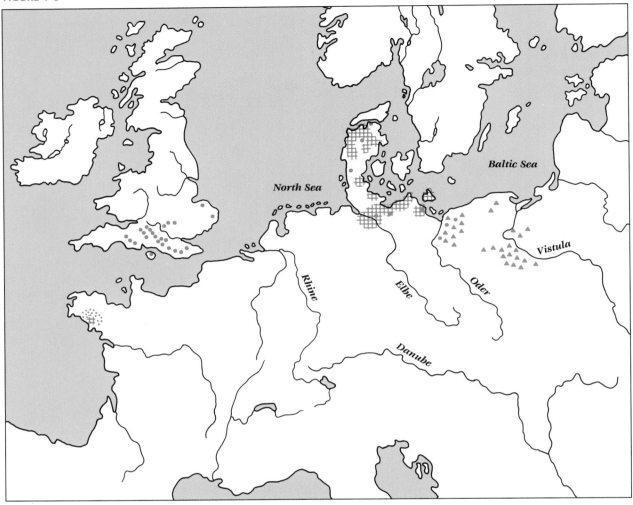

North Sea

Baltic Sea

Vistula

Rhine

Elbe

Oder

Danube

FIGURE 4–9 Distribution of earthen long-barrows in northern Europe. Below: a rectangular long-barrow ("Hünen-bett") from Schleswig-Holstein, NW Germany.

FIGURE 4–10 TRB cemetery of nine triangular long-barrows from Sarnowo, Kujavia, W Poland. Mid-4th mill. B.C.

KEY

⋯ • Barrows of general trapezoid shape

▲ Triangular barrows of Kujavia

▦ Rectangular barrows

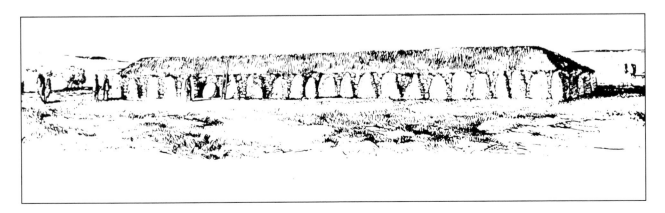

the second half of the 4th millennium B.C. (see table 14, Flögeln dates).

Earthen Long-Barrows

Earthen long-barrows are a northern European phenomenon associated with the TRB population, except for their extension into Brittany and England in the west. (FIGURE 4–9) Long-barrows are found on sandy or clayey morainic soils consistent with the economic exploitation of the mixed forest environment of the TRB people. Considerable numbers of earthen long-barrows have been reported from Denmark, northern Germany (Mecklenburg and Lower Saxony), western and southern Poland. Only a few are known from Bohemia and Moravia. The largest concentration is in the area of Kujavia in western Poland. Detailed information on long-barrows of the TRB culture has been compiled by Magdalena S. Midgley in 1985.[9]

Earthen long-barrows are often found in groups of twos or threes, or occasionally in large clusters, as represented by a cemetery of nine barrows at Sarnowo in western Poland. (FIGURE 4–10) Their dimensions are truly impressive. Although most barrows commonly range from 25 to 45 m in length, about 40 percent of the known barrows are between 60 and 80 m long. The longest ones in Kujavia reach 170 m and are long and narrow. (FIGURE 4–11, 1) Their common width is from 3 m to 11 m, with the wide end considered as the head and the narrow as the tail. Entrance openings have been identified in the middle of the wide end. The principal orientation in about 70 percent of all the barrows investigated is east to west or northeast to southwest, with their entrances opening towards the rising sun. Earthen barrows were retained by stone and occasionally by timber frame enclosures. Stones were abundantly available in these regions in the form of glacially deposited erratic boulders. The builders selected those which had smooth and flat surfaces and used these for the outer sides of each enclosure. Stones were placed according to their size, with larger boulders used for the wider end and smaller for the narrower end, which suggests a good deal of planning.

FIGURE 4–10

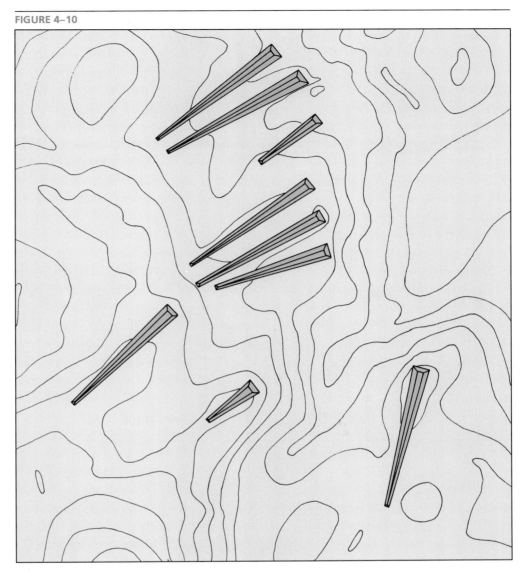

FIGURE 4–11

FIGURE 4–11 Plans of Kujavian long-barrows. (1) Wietrzychowice at Kolsko; (2) Karsko, W Poland.

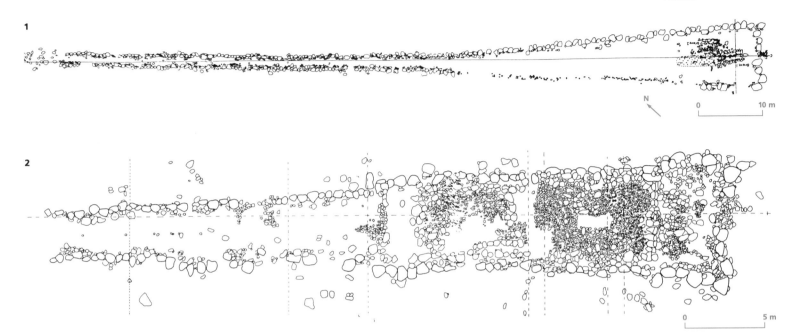

FIGURE 4–12

FIGURE 4–12 Plan of a long-barrow with timber post framing (black dots are post holes). Niedzwiedź, S Poland.

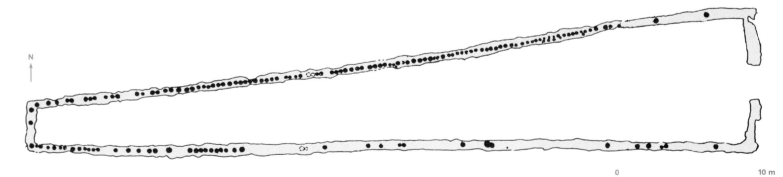

Timber-built enclosures are known from Denmark, Bohemia, and southern Poland in which timber posts were set vertically in a continuous foundation trench. (FIGURE 4–12) Some had solid walls made from split tree trunks. There are also structures surrounded by both stone and timber walls, such as one at Stengade, Denmark.[10] In several cases definite traces of solid timber facades were found.[11] These were rectangular structures built on a frame of small posts of split tree trunks which were packed with stones. The interior of these long-barrows was subdivided into compartments by transverse stone walls or walls built of stone combined with timber. In Danish long-barrows, such as at Barkaer, Djursland, partitioning was done by wooden fences. The two at Barkaer, about 85 m long and 6.5 to 7.5 m wide (earlier regarded to be houses) were subdivided into 26 rooms, each about 3 m long.[12] In addition to such spacial segmentation, there were also timber buildings which represent a typical architectural and ritual element as identified in Kujavia and in Jutland. Rectangular structures were built in the wider end of the Kujavian barrows, which measured approximately 4 m by 4 m, or 3 or 4 m by 5 m. These timber uprights, set in corners, provided a framework for the construction of walls. The roof was probably tentlike. In Denmark, at Bygholm Norremark, an oval building, 12 by 6 m, was built of timber uprights and four central roof-bearing posts[13] with the grave in the center. In Kujavian barrows, however, as at Sarnowo, the structure was above the grave (see fig. 9–13). Charcoal and ashes in the area of these ritual structures speak for deliberate burning, perhaps for purification purposes.

The most common structure within the barrow was a boxlike rectangular chamber built of stone and timber within which single graves in coffins were found. Due to unfavorable soil conditions, however, burial evidence has been obtained in only 20.4 percent of all known barrows, and in only 16 percent of the barrows have skeletal remains been preserved. Graves were in pits or above the ground. All except those in the

Baalberge group of central Germany were extended inhumations and some were clearly buried in wooden coffins. The dead were very modestly equipped, except for some ritual objects, such as decorated vases, boar tusks, and occasional flint tools. The only beads found were amber, worn as necklaces. (FIGURE 4–13) In cases where skeletons were clearly missing bones, it is presumed that after the burial, the chambers remained open for excarnation until the body was reduced to a skeletal state.[14]

Speaking of the long earthen barrows, several points of interest must be stressed. First, their form is mainly triangular or trapezoidal, symbolically inseparable from the regenerative female (or Goddess's) triangle. Triangular stones, about one meter or more high, as symbols of the regenerative triangle of the Goddess herself, were placed at the entrances. Second, the barrows are located in areas of earlier TRB settlement, possibly directly upon the settlement sites themselves, indicating

FIGURE 4–13 Amber necklaces made up of several or more strands of cylindrical beads, sometimes interspersed with axe-shaped spacer beads. TRB culture. Laesten, Viborg, Denmark, c. 3000 B.C.

FIGURE 4–13

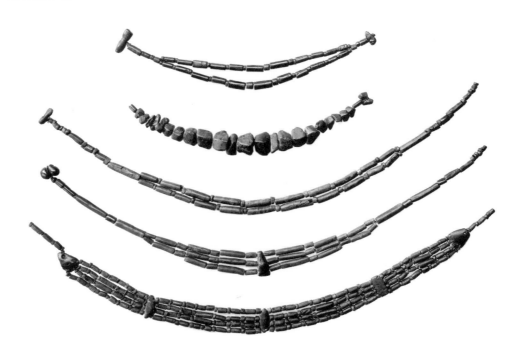

the link with the ancestral land and the ancestors. The triangular-trapezoidal shape recalls the trapezoidal Lengyel houses in western Poland (the Brześć Kujawski type; see fig. 3–35) which preceded the TRB.

The lack of better preserved skeletal materials prohibits us from speaking with certainty about who was buried in these large mounds except in a few clear cases. One example is at Sarnowo Barrow No. 9, where a single woman about 70 years old was buried alone in a coffin with a wooden superstructure above the grave (see fig. 9–13). Other burials were of considerably younger individuals. The physical type appears to be predominantly dolichocephalic, most commonly of the Atlantic type, with an occasional admixture of Cro-Magnon forms.[15] The latter is considered to be continuous from the Late Mesolithic local population.[16]

The Appearance of Megalithic Tombs and Causewayed Enclosures

After the middle of the 4th millennium B.C., dolmens appeared in Holland, Germany, and southern Scandinavia, followed by passage graves around 3200 B.C.[17] Their appearance marks the beginning of a change in burial practices. From this point on, the building of megalithic structures and burial customs in northwestern Europe became closely linked with western Europe. The practice of secondary burial after excarnation and the deposition of the disarticulated bones of many individuals in megaliths, which served as ossuaries, do not differ from the customs in Brittany, Iberia, England, and the Orkney Islands. This tradition must have come from the west, perhaps from Brittany via the coast. It is unlikely that the new customs of dolmens and passage graves were brought by immigrants from the west, however, since other traditions remained intact: there was a continuous pottery and tool making tradition in all regional groups of the TRB culture. Long earthen barrows continued in areas, particularly in Poland, where megaliths are not found. In addition, early dolmens have revealed evidence for the transition

from the burial of the dead singly in an extended position to the practice of deposition of disarticulated bones.

Let us mention one example from the dolmen at Klokkehoj at Bojden, Fünen, Denmark.[18] The dead buried in the primary layer of this dolmen, dating from about the 34th century B.C., were found in an extended position with pottery vessels placed at their feet. The secondary layer contained disarticulated bones of at least 22 individuals, 13 adults and 9 children. The date of this layer is around 3000 B.C.

In all the areas in which megalithic tombs are found, similar construction and burial rituals are recorded: use of large boulders, segmentation of the inner space into compartments (as many as 17 in the passage grave at Rossberga in Västergotland, Sweden),[19] stacking of skulls against chamber walls (FIGURE 4–14), and the practice of scorching the bones with fire. In both dolmens and passage graves, the treatment of burnt and unburnt bones is evident, and in the dolmens of southern Sweden many concentrations of burnt bones have been found. In the Bronsyxan dolmen at Hindby Mosse, 71 concentrations of burnt bones were discovered under the cairn; most were skulls, representing about 10 individuals.[20] In the Trollaster dolmen, concentrations of burnt bones were discovered outside the tomb itself, while at the Gillhog passage grave, such concentrations were found outside the entrance of the tomb.[21] In the Bohuslän region of southern Sweden, passage graves included burnt bones in the chamber and in the passage.

Another common tradition in western Europe is the appearance of so-called causewayed camps (areas enclosed with concentric ditches and banks) in Denmark and southern Sweden during the passage grave period, c. 3200–3000 B.C. (known from Voldbaek, Sarup, and Toftum in Denmark and from Stavie in Scania).[22, 23] The ditches of these camps held potsherds, bovine bones, and in one case (at Sarup) human mandibles. Causewayed enclosures were centrally located in areas where megalithic tombs were concentrated[24] and must have served a ritual function for groups larger

than one village population. Their activities included the cremation of human bodies and the deposition of pottery vessels and other religious objects.

Religious structures were associated with dolmens and passage graves. At Tustrup, Norager district, Djursland, Denmark, three megaliths stood in an arc, and in the middle was a horseshoe shaped ceremonial building, 6 m by 4 to 5 m (FIGURE 4–15) with an opening to the northeast. The building was constructed of stone walls, 1 to 2 m thick, surrounded by a wooden palisade of split tree trunks. In the center was an oval pit filled with sand, and on both sides of it 30 vessels were found including 10 fruit-stands of fine workmanship and 8 disc-shaped spoons, each laid in a fruitstand type vase. (FIGURE 4–16) Several other pits were in the north and northeast part of the building.[25] We shall return to other religious buildings of this culture in chapter 7, particularly to Alvastra, a pile building of wood surrounded by mire from c. 3000 B.C.

FIGURE 4–14

1

0   2 m

FIGURE 4–15

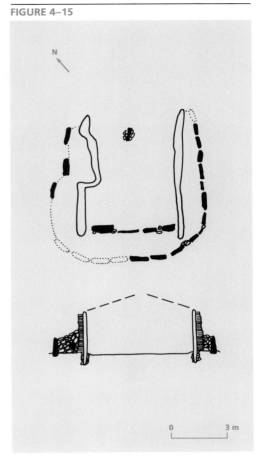

0   3 m

FIGURE 4–14 (1) Dolmen and (2) passage grave with partition walls. Location of skulls and other human bones are indicated. Liepen, district of Rostock, N Germany. End of 4th mill. B.C.

FIGURE 4–15 Plan and cross-section of a cult building at Tustrup, Denmark. Thirty beautiful vases (see fig. 4–16) were found around the offering pit at the entrance. End 4th mill. B.C.

2

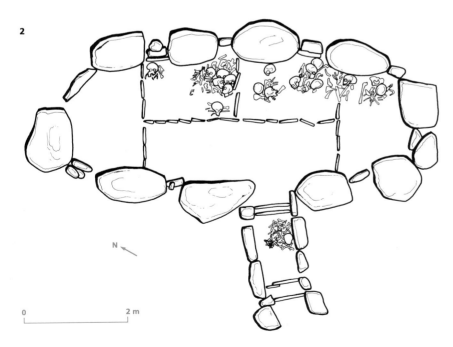

0   2 m

FIGURE 4–16

FIGURE 4–16 Vases and disc-shaped offering spoons (found inside the vases) from the ceremonial building at Tustrup (see fig. 4–15). End 4th mill. B.C.

Disintegration: The Appearance of Patriarchal Pastoralists

The disintegration of the TRB culture began with the spread of the patriarchal Globular Amphora pastoralists into northern central Europe and the movement of the related Baden culture into the southern regions of the TRB. A series of TRB settlements of the southeastern group dating from the end of the 4th millennium B.C. were destroyed by fire, interpreted by archeologists as the result of a violent action. A dramatic decrease in population is recorded.[26] In the north, the TRB culture continued to the early 3rd millennium B.C. when it was gradually replaced by the Corded Ware Single Grave culture. All of these—the Globular Amphora, Baden, and Corded Ware cultures—represent pastoral, seminomadic, and patriarchal societies (see chapter 10).

The Nemunas Culture

The Nemunas culture, distributed between the Lower Vistula in northeastern Poland and southern Lithuania (FIGURE 4–17) had its beginnings in the Epipalaeolithic (Episwiderian) and Mesolithic culture of the same region.[27] The Upper Nemunas basin in southern Lithuania is a very rich source of flint. It is not surprising that Upper Paleolithic and Mesolithic sites are abundant here and continued to be so during the Neolithic. The name Nemunas is most appropriately applied to the Mesolithic and Neolithic periods of this culture. In earlier literature, the culture of the Neolithic stage was known as *Zedmar* in German and *Serowo* in Polish based on excavations at Zedmar (Serowo) in the district of Oziersk, northeastern Poland (formerly East Prussia).[28]

FIGURE 4–17

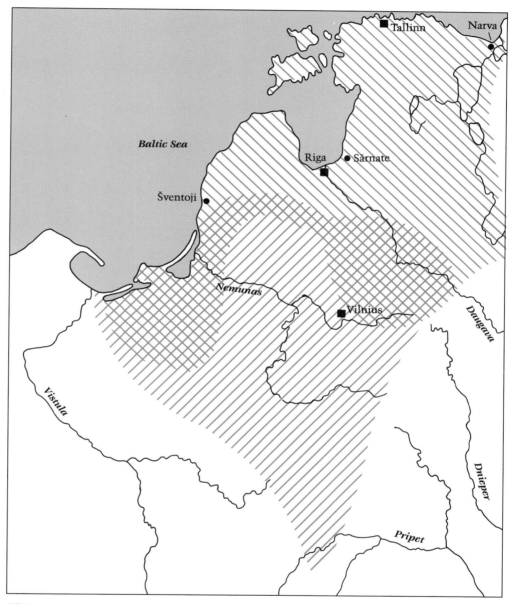

FIGURE 4-17 Distribution of the Mesolithic and Neolithic cultures in the East Baltic area.

KEY

/// Nemunas

\\\ Kunda (Mesolithic) followed by Narva (Neolithic)

FIGURE 4–18

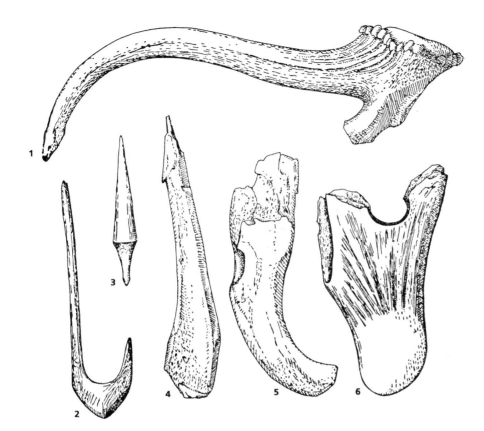

Habitation Sites

A considerable number of sites have been encountered on light soils in the region of end moraines in the Masurian Lake district and on sandy soils of southern Lithuania. These are located on low terraces in the bays or confluences of small rivers or on lake shores. During the period of maximal transgression of the Litorina Sea, sites were located on higher terraces. Only exceptional traces of houses are preserved.[29] From the little that is known, people lived in small agglomerations in light-structured above-ground houses built of timber posts interspersed with wickerworks of branches with a row of posts in the middle supporting the roof. Hearths are found in the central part of the houses.[30] In the majority of cases, these sites yielded only flint artifacts[31] and occasionally bone and antler tools including hoes and axes. (FIGURES 4–18, 1, 6) Fishhooks, harpoons, and conical arrowheads were made of bone. (FIGURE 4–18, 2–4) The flint inventory includes the characteristic Episwiderian type arrowheads, lancette-shaped arrowheads, and trapezoids. (FIGURE 4–19A, Mesolithic; 4–19B, Neolithic) Axes were also made of flint. (FIGURE 4–19B, *bottom right*)

Pottery

Early pots were large with pointed bases, decorated with stick impressions of pits or triangles around the mouth. (FIGURE 4–20, 1, 2) In the late phase, pots became flat based and were more richly decorated with parallel rows of pits, net patterns, and beaded motifs. (FIGURE 4–20, 3, 4). Clay was tempered with vegetal matter and occasionally with crushed shells and in the final phase with ground quartz. The shape, temper, and decoration of the early Nemunas pottery is much related to the pottery of the Dnieper-Donets culture in the Upper Dnieper basin.

FIGURE 4–18 Antler and bone tools from the Nemunas culture in southern Lithuania. (1) Antler hoe (Kašétos). (2) Fishhook (Daukšai). (3) Arrowhead (Alksnénai). (4) Harpoon (Vilkaviškis). (5) Antler axe (Kašétos). (6) Antler hoe (Pašventupys). Early 4th mill. B.C. Scale 1:1.

FIGURE 4–19A

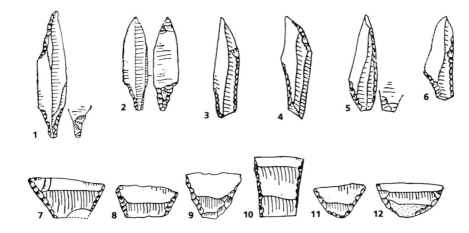

FIGURE 4–19A Typical episwiderian flint artifacts from the Mesolithic sites of the Nemunas culture. (1,2) arrowheads; (3–6) "lancettes" (arrowheads), (7–12) trapezoids, also used as arrowheads. S Lithuania. Scale: (1,2) 1:2; (3–12) 1:10.

FIGURE 4–19B

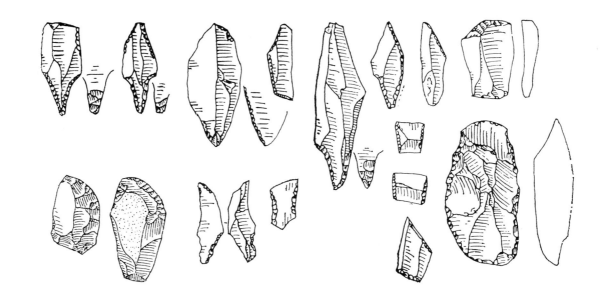

FIGURE 4–19B Neolithic flint artifacts; shapes largely continue as Mesolithic-type arrowheads, scrapers, and trapezes. Flint axes (bottom row, right) appear in Neolithic settlements. Dubičiai and Versminis, S Lithuania. Scale: 1:2

FIGURE 4–20 Pottery types from the Nemunas culture settlements. (1, 2) pointed based and decorated only around the mouth from the early phase (Dubičiai, S Lithuania); (3,4) pointed based and flat based and more richly decorated from the later period (Margiai, S Lithuania). 1, 2, end 5th; 3, 4, early 4th mill. B.C. H c. 30–40 cm.

FIGURE 4–20

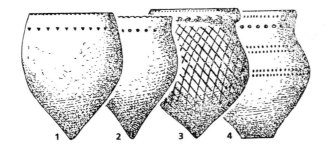

Graves

The dead were buried in an extended position in simple pit graves and were sprinkled with ochre. Among the most frequent grave goods are necklaces of elk, deer, and auroch or bison teeth. Antler hoes also appeared in graves.[31] At Perkunowo, district of Giżycko in northeast Poland, the double grave of a young woman and a three-year-old child was found.[32] Burials of skulls in habitation sites were also practiced as at Serowo where seventeen skulls were found.[33]

There is not enough information available for a clear definition of the physical type of the Nemunas population since the Serowo skulls were too damaged for a fruitful examination. However, brachycephalic skulls of large proportions are known from other locations.[34]

Chronology

The four radiocarbon dates from Serowo (Zedmar) indicate the period between the 43rd and 36th centuries B.C. (TABLE 15) Three out of the four dates suggest that the most likely period for this habitation site was the 37th century B.C. One hopes that a more complete chronology of the Nemunas culture will be solved by future research.

Before or around the middle of the 4th millennium B.C. most of the area occupied by the Nemunas population was infiltrated by the TRB and subsequently by the Globular Amphora people resulting in the hybridization of several traditions and in the final disappearance of the individual features of the Nemunas culture.

The Narva Culture in the East Baltic Area

The East Baltic Narva culture spread between the southern coasts of the Baltic Sea and the Bay of Finland (see fig. 4–17). The name derives from a site in northern Estonia, and radiocarbon dates place this culture in the 5th, 4th, and early part of the 3rd millennia B.C. (TABLE 16)

This was a fisherman's paradise whose culture eventually included the use of pottery. (FIGURE 4–21) The dog was known from the Mesolithic, and there was a gradual selective adoption of cultivated grains and domesticated animals into an essentially Mesolithic way of life.

Physical Type of the Population

The Narva population was a predominantly long-headed, narrow-faced type, Europids as their Mesolithic predecessors of the Kunda culture, although in the northern area a tendency toward mesocran (medium length) skulls and facial flatness is found (presumed to be a mongoloid influence).[35]

Graves

The largest Narva cemetery is found at Zvejnieki in northern Latvia, excavated by F. Zagorskis in the 1960s and early 70s.[36] This site is located over a small hill on the bank of Lake Burtnieki, some 200 meters from the Narva settlement. Three hundred and seventeen Mesolithic and Neolithic graves were unearthed, ranging from the 7th to the 3rd millennium B.C., making this the largest cemetery of its period to be found in all of northern Europe. Solid information was gleaned from this site concerning cultural continuity from the Mesolithic and Neolithic up to the Corded Pottery period of the 3rd millennium B.C. when a totally alien burial appeared with bodies in a contracted posture. Earlier skeletons lay in an extended position, wrapped in animal furs and sprinkled with ochre. Occasionally, the dead were found in collective tombs of two to six together, one above the other, similar to Dnieper-Donets burials. The most com-

mon funerary articles were elk, deer, and boar teeth pendants and necklaces. In later phases dog, wolf, fox, marten, and badger teeth pendants were also found, along with amber pendants and beads and female elk and bird figurines carved of bone. Bird bones found in the graves suggest that fowl were sacrificed with the dead. Burials were also found under the floors of houses, as at Narva where in location No. 1 an adult and a child were buried under the house floor. Skulls were found deposited alone at Šventoji, site 23, near the Baltic Sea in Lithuania. Here, among the crumbled bones of one skull, an amber pendant was discovered.[37]

Peat-bog Settlement Sites

A number of peat-bog settlement sites excavated in the last decades, such as Šventoji in western Lithuania near the Baltic Sea, Sarnate in western Latvia,[38] and a series of settlements around Lake Lubana in eastern Latvia and Lake Kretuonas in eastern Lithuania have provided rich evidence for the reconstruction of the life style of these fishermen.[39] It is fortunate that the waterlogged condition of these areas has preserved many perishable objects such as those made of wood—fishing tools, mallets for crushing nuts, hoes, a variety of household utensils, troughs, and sculptures. Nets, floats, creels, harpoons, spears, forks, dugout canoes, paddles and shove-off stakes, as well as fish bones (mostly of large pike and sturgeon) present splendid information on Narva fishing habits. (FIGURES 4–22 to 4–24) Fishing was done with nets, creels, and bag-shaped baskets, and many fragments show that nets were plaited of linden bast and tied in immobile knots. (FIGURE 4–25)

FIGURE 4–21

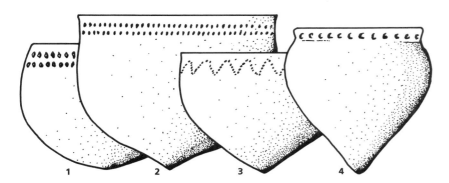
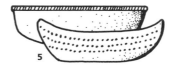

FIGURE 4–21 Narva ceramics; large pots with pointed bases decorated around the mouth (1–4) and boat-shaped lamps; (5) pots were tempered with crushed shells. Šventoji site 1, B, W Lithuania. Late 4th mill. B.C. H. 30–40 cm.

FIGURE 4–22

FIGURE 4–22 (1) Wooden model of a boat, 96 cm long from Šventoji, site 2 B. The broken tip of the prow was decorated, perhaps with a zoomorphic head (not preserved). (2) Lifting up a dugout canoe at Sarnate, W Latvia, end 4th mill. B.C.

FIGURE 4-23

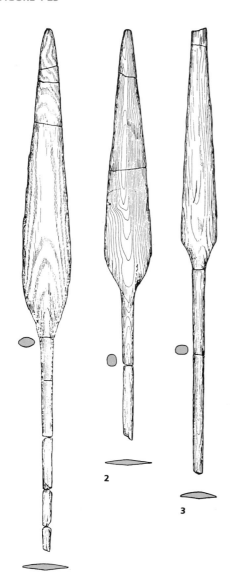

1

2

3

4

FIGURE 4–23 (1–3) Wooden oars and (4) fishing-net weights wrapped in birch bark and fastened with string. Sarnate peat bog settlement, end 4th mill. B.C.

FIGURE 4–24 Bag-shaped fishing net fastened with a wooden frame (reconstruction). Šventoji, W Lithuania, end 4th mill. B.C.

FIGURE 4–25 Remains of fishing nets made of linden bast. Šventoji, end of 4th mill. B.C.

FIGURE 4–24

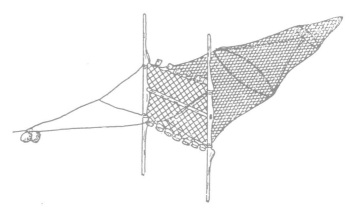

FIGURE 4–25

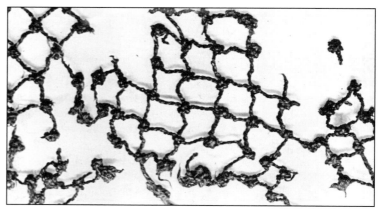

In later Narva settlements, agriculture was practiced, as witnessed by wood, antler, and stone hoes (FIGURE 4–26, 1–3) and the pollen of millet, wheat, and hemp. The latter was used extensively for strings and ropes found in well-preserved quantities. (FIGURE 4–26, 4)

FIGURE 4–26

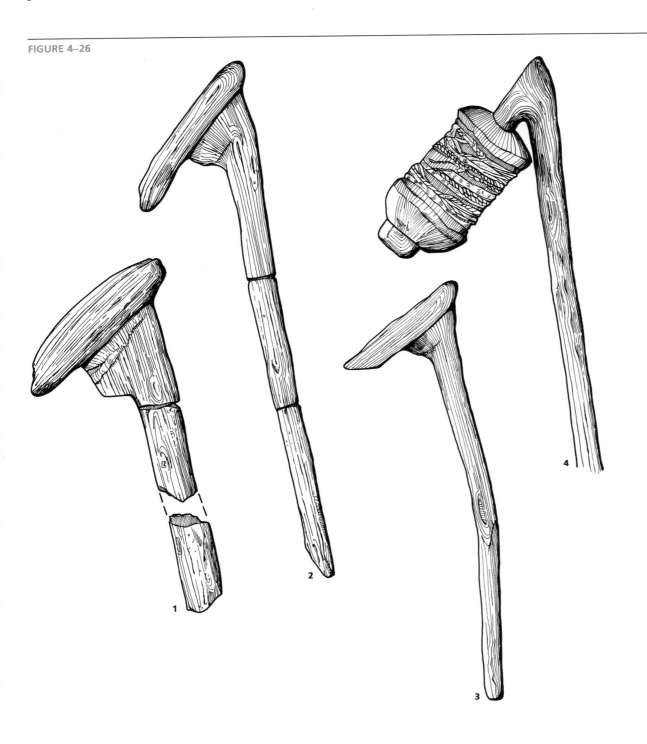

FIGURE 4–26 Wooden hoes and long wooden handle with a stone axe set in a spool-shaped mount with string. (1–3) Sarnate. (4) Šventoji. Narva culture, end 4th mill. B.C.

FIGURE 4–27

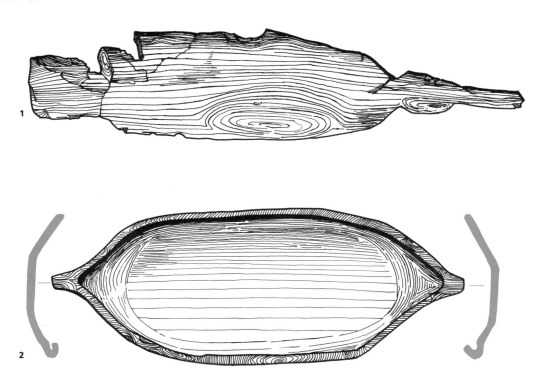

FIGURE 4-27 (1) Wooden distaff; L 43 cm. (2) Small wooden trough. Šventoji, end 4th mill. B.C.; L 75 cm.

FIGURE 4–28

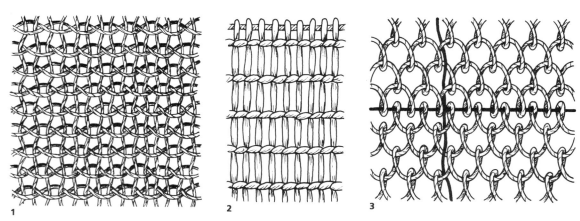

FIGURE 4-28 (1–3) Weaving and plaiting schemes as reconstructed from fragments of textiles; a plaiting instrument. (4) Šventoji. W Lithuania, end 4th mill. B.C.

Wooden distaffs (FIGURE 4-27, 1) and clay spindle whorls speak of spinning, and cloth was plaited or woven of very thin twisted thread made of linden bast. (FIGURE 4-28)

Settlement sites are located on the flat shores of lakes and occupied approximately 1,000 square meters. Villages consisted of four to ten rectangular houses built of timber uprights, not higher than 2.5 m, with a row of posts in the middle supporting the roof. These houses varied from 5 to 11 m in length, with a width of 4 to 5 m. (FIGURE 4-29) Their roofs and floors were covered with spruce and pine bark. Oval, semisubterranean houses of timber uprights, about 6 m across, dug over one meter into the ground, were reported from the 1986 excavations at Kretuonas.[39]

FIGURE 4–29

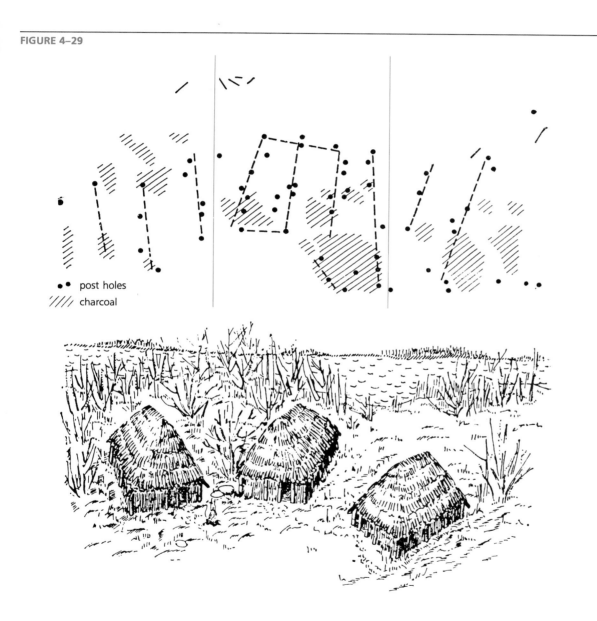

• • post holes

///// charcoal

FIGURE 4-29 Traces of houses (above) and reconstruction. Sarnate, W Latvia, end 4th mill. B.C.

FIGURE 4–30

FIGURE 4–30 (1) Wooden sculpture, about 2 m high, probably portraying an Owl Goddess. (Compare with West European Owl Goddess as stone stelae, fig. 7–27.) Šventoji. W Lithuania. (1a) detail. (2) unfinished idol, 1.68 m high. Sarnate, W Latvia, end 4th mill. B.C.

FIGURE 4–31

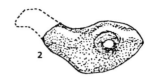

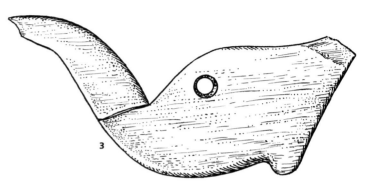

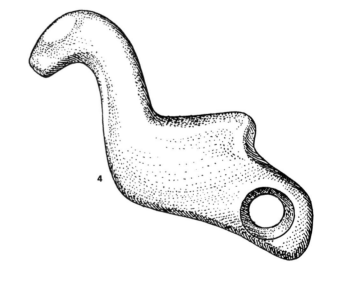

FIGURE 4–31 Water-bird pendants carved of amber and bone. (1,2) amber pendants from Lake Lubana plain (Nainiekste and Zvidzienas Krogs) E Latvia; (3,4) bone pendants from Tamula, Estonia. Late Narva culture. Scale 1:1.

FIGURE 4–32

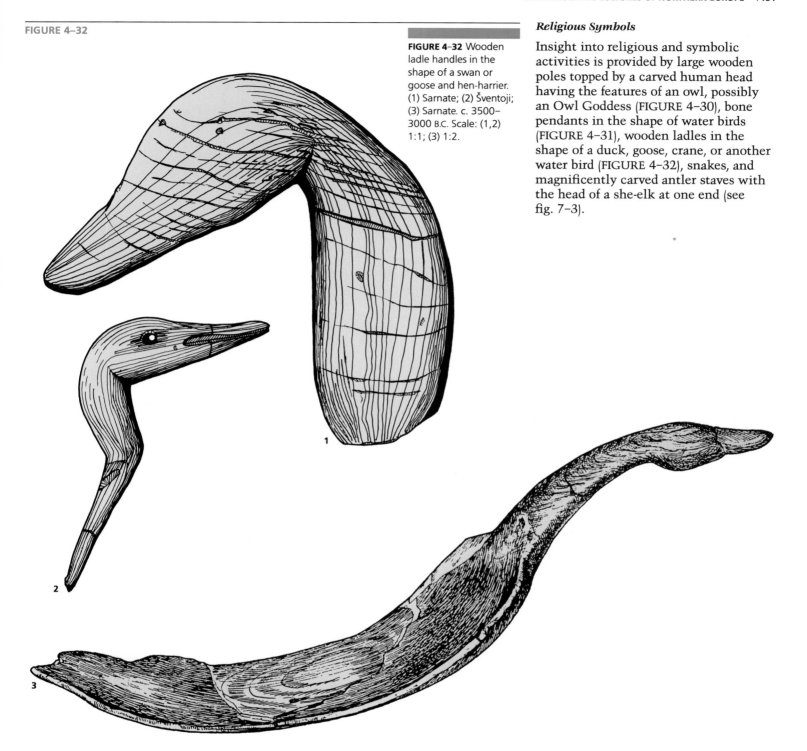

FIGURE 4-32 Wooden ladle handles in the shape of a swan or goose and hen-harrier. (1) Sarnate; (2) Šventoji; (3) Sarnate. c. 3500–3000 B.C. Scale: (1,2) 1:1; (3) 1:2.

Religious Symbols

Insight into religious and symbolic activities is provided by large wooden poles topped by a carved human head having the features of an owl, possibly an Owl Goddess (FIGURE 4–30), bone pendants in the shape of water birds (FIGURE 4–31), wooden ladles in the shape of a duck, goose, crane, or another water bird (FIGURE 4–32), snakes, and magnificently carved antler staves with the head of a she-elk at one end (see fig. 7–3).

Amber Manufacture and Trade

Amber was extensively gathered and manufactured, and a number of amber workshops have been found along the Baltic coast as well as several hundred kilometers inland. Cylindrical beads, round buttons with a V-perforation, anthropomorphic pendants (FIGURE 4–33), and sculptures of water birds, elk, and bears were produced. Amber pendants and buttons were exchanged with people in northwestern Russia for tools and ornaments made of green schist,[40] while some amber products reached Finland and Sweden. Consequently, influences from northwestern Russia increased, signaled by the appearance of comb-and-pit-marked pottery sites in Estonia and eastern and northern Latvia.

Amber was also a catalyst for the development of relationships with the Globular Amphora people in Poland who imported cylindrical beads, buttons, and a variety of pendants, and raw material from the Baltic Coast.[41]

The Appearance of Globular Amphora Patriarchal Pastoralists and the Demise of the Narva Population

Around or before 3000 B.C., Globular Amphora patriarchal pastoralists entered the Narva territory. Their typical ceramics now appeared in the Nemunas culture in the East Prussia area and Belorussia, and also within the Narva settlements.[42] It seems that sheep and goats, horses, and perhaps millet, wheat, and plow agriculture spread into the Narva villages with the first Globular Amphora immigrants from the south, since these appear only in later Narva sites. Three wooden hand plows were excavated at Šventoji, site No. 6. (FIGURE 4–34) The plows could not have been objects of trade, but must have been obtained through personal contacts with the people from the south since the same settlement also yielded Globular Amphora pottery.[43]

FIGURE 4–33

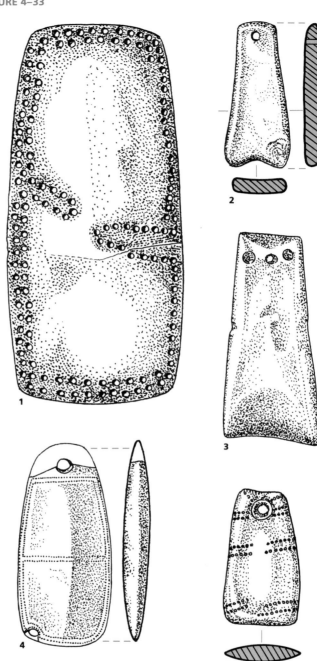

FIGURE 4–33 Schematized anthropomorphic figurines of amber. Narva culture, Lithuania. (1–4) Juodkrantè, (5) Šventoji. End 4th mill. B.C. Scale: 1:1.

FIGURE 4–34

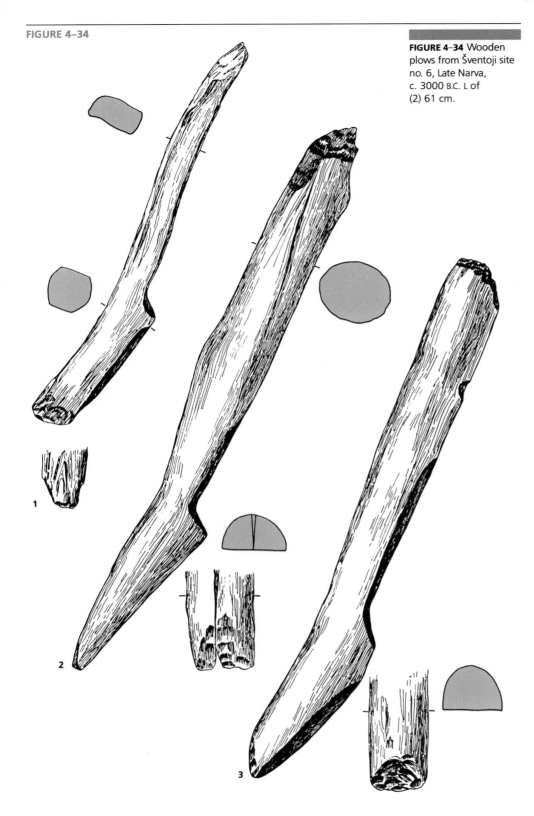

FIGURE 4–34 Wooden plows from Šventoji site no. 6, Late Narva, c. 3000 B.C. L of (2) 61 cm.

1

2

3

The transformation of the Narva culture and a gradual fusion with the Central Europeans continued throughout the first half of the 3rd millennium B.C. Narva traditions such as the building of above-ground timber houses and religious symbols continued. The importance of snakes, water birds, frogs, elks, and other elements of religious symbolism did not diminish. The persistence of Old European goddesses in Baltic mythology to this day is due to the survival of the local population, evidenced by the continued presence of a specific physical anthropological type.[44]

5

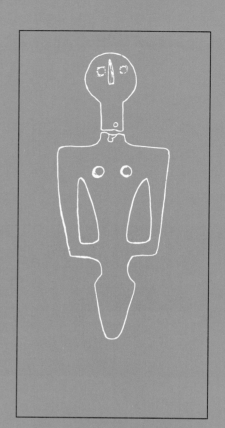

Neolithic Cultures
of the Adriatic
and Central
Mediterranean

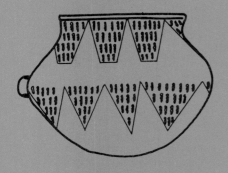

The early inhabitants of the coasts and islands of the Adriatic subsisted on small game hunting until sometime before 7000 B.C. when a transition took place to a shellfish gathering economy.[1] As their navigational skills improved, intercommunication increased between the Adriatic islands and the coastal regions of southeastern Italy, western Greece, Albania, and Yugoslavia.

Three open settlements found at Sidari on the northwestern tip of the island of Corfu, west of Greece, are excellent examples of influences from various areas. Each settlement, found in stratigraphic sequence, belonged to "mariners" of different origins.[2] The earliest Mesolithic layer, radiocarbon dated to the early 7th millennium B.C., is characterized by a thick deposition of cardium edule shells and microlithic flint tools made of a flint foreign to the island. The closest parallels are found in a series of coastal sites in southern Italy and Sicily, the coastal strip of the Adriatic in Yugoslavia, and in the northwestern Peloponnese.

The next layer, described as Aegean Early Pottery Neolithic, indicates a break with the past in which the manufacture of microliths ceased and pottery and domesticated sheep and goats appeared. The radical contrast between these two cultures suggests the arrival of a different group of people, probably from southern Greece before 6500 B.C. This site was soon abandoned, followed by a period of alluviation.

Around the 64th–63rd centuries B.C., the area was occupied by people making Impresso (i.e., cardial shell impressed) pottery which was much better fired than that of the preceding occupation. The pinkish clay was tempered with grit and crushed flint, while the outer surfaces of these ceramics were smoothed and decorated with fingernail impressions or were stamped with a blunt instrument. Perforated lugs appeared and bases were made round or flat.

The shapes, technology, and decoration of this pottery compare closely with those of the early Impresso Ware from western Yugoslavia. Along its entire length, the east Adriatic coast of Yugoslavia is strung with a series of Impresso sites, found also on coastal islands, which are dated within the time sequence of 6500–5500 B.C. (TABLE 17) Rock shelters on the Adriatic coast of Yugoslavia have yielded cultural deposits ranging from the Paleolithic to the Neolithic, the latter included pottery impressed by shells, toothed stamps, or fingernails.[3]

A second stage of development is documented by advanced Impresso layers at Smilčić near Zadar in Dalmatia.[4] Smilčić was an open settlement of above-ground houses of wattle-and-daub construction showing evidence of domesticated sheep, goats, and cattle. Grinding stones found there may indicate the cultivation of plants. Large amounts of bone, antler, and chipped-stone tools were also found, as well as cardium, spondylus, and other shells. The pottery was decorated with cardium shell impressions, organized in banded panels or rocker-stamp patterns. Vessels are semiglobular and oval, while dishes are conical, all with flat or ring bases. They were generously tempered with sand and decorated before firing.

Southern Italy (Tavoliere, Materano, and Sicily)

The Tavoliere of Apulia is a low plain, hemmed in by the Gargano and Murge mountain massifs, opening to the Adriatic on one eastern location near the town of Manfredonia. The first farmers are believed to have arrived here transporting Impresso pottery and sheep from across the Adriatic. This area contains the highest concentration of Neolithic sites in Italy (FIGURES 5–1, 5–2) which are found in caves, on lake shores, along coastal areas, and on slight rises of the plain.[5] There are hundreds of open-air sites which consisted of houses located beside compounds surrounded by C-shaped ditches. (FIGURES 5–3, 5–4) Larger sites, which

FIGURE 5–1

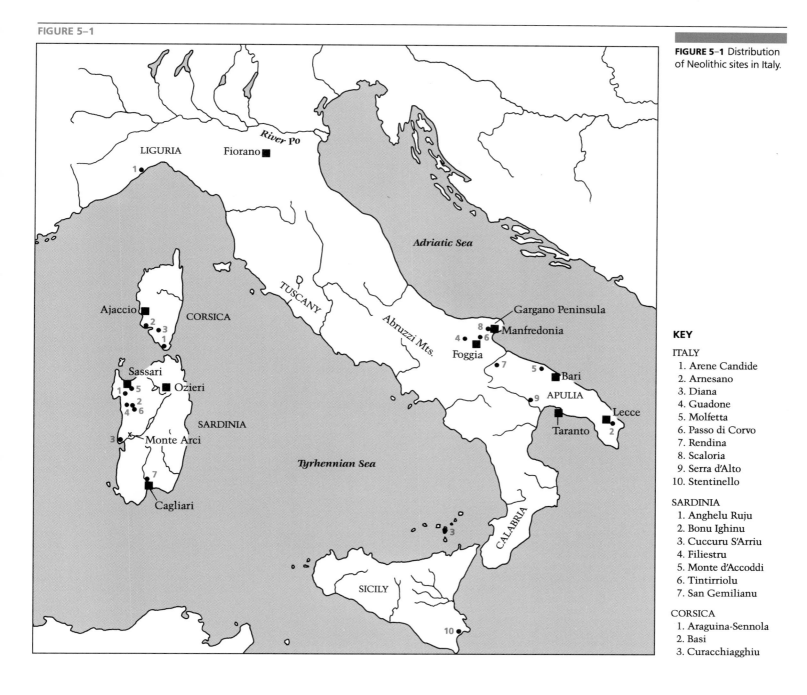

FIGURE 5–1 Distribution of Neolithic sites in Italy.

KEY

ITALY
 1. Arene Candide
 2. Arnesano
 3. Diana
 4. Guadone
 5. Molfetta
 6. Passo di Corvo
 7. Rendina
 8. Scaloria
 9. Serra d'Alto
10. Stentinello

SARDINIA
 1. Anghelu Ruju
 2. Bonu Ighinu
 3. Cuccuru S'Arriu
 4. Filiestru
 5. Monte d'Accoddi
 6. Tintirriolu
 7. San Gemilianu

CORSICA
 1. Araguina-Sennola
 2. Basi
 3. Curacchiagghiu

FIGURE 5-2

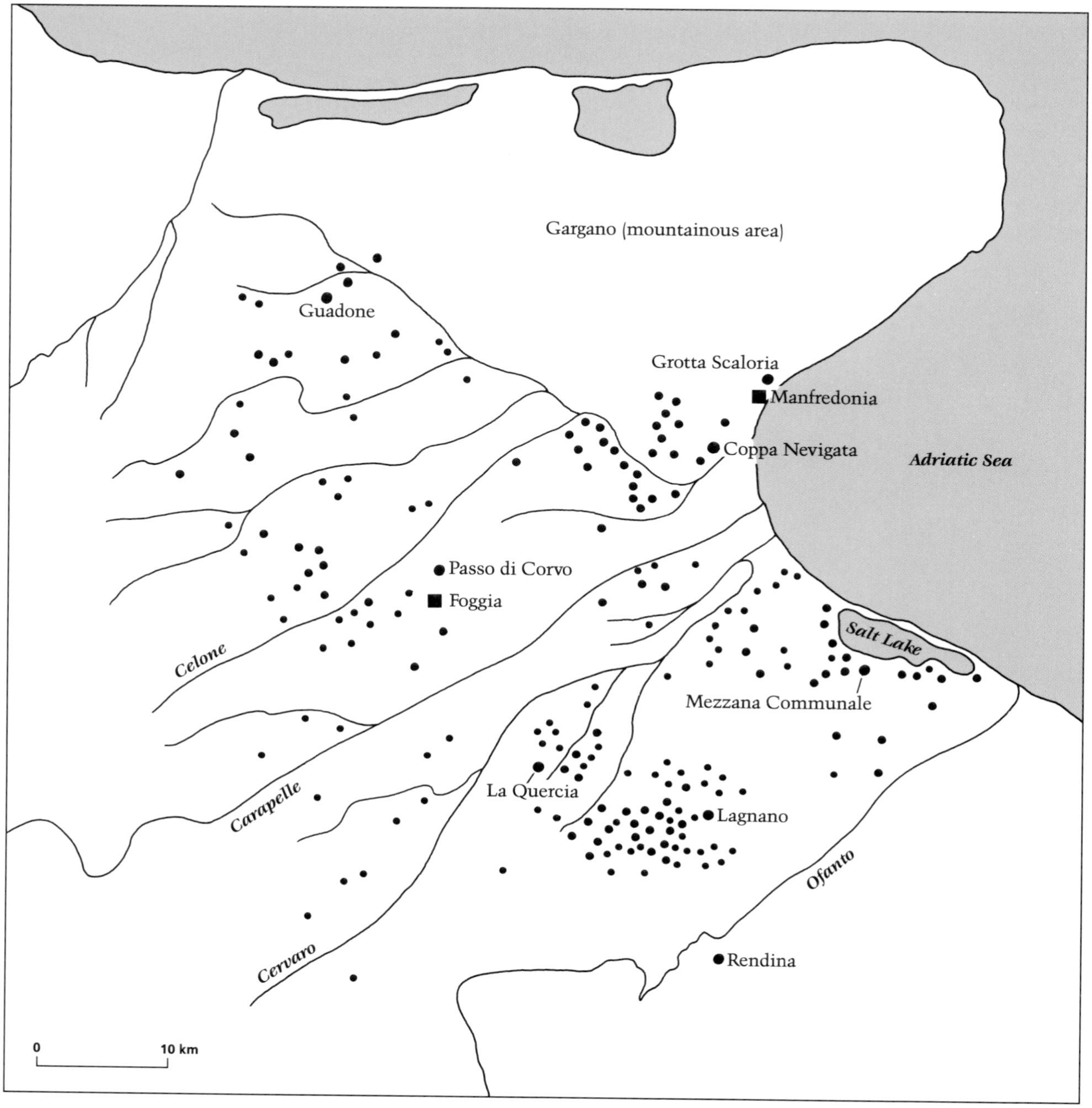

FIGURE 5-2 Distribution of Neolithic sites in Tavoliere based on aerial photography, surface collections, test trenches, and magnetometer.

KEY

● More important excavated sites

● Known from aerial photos, surface collections, test trenches, and magnetometer readings

FIGURE 5–3

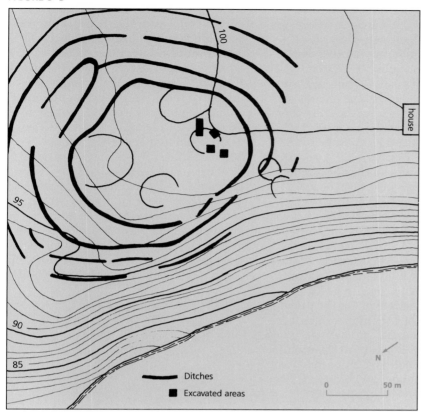

Ditches

■ Excavated areas

0   50 m

N

are few, date from the Middle Neolithic (2nd half of the 6th millennium B.C.) and contain several to a hundred or more compounds. These unusual concentrations were first noticed in 1943 by British army officer John Bradford when the Royal Air Force flew many photographic sorties. He noted the discovery of "one of the densest concentrations of prehistoric settlements yet known in Europe."[6] Approximately one thousand sites on the Tavoliere were identified from the air.

In 1978–79, I personally witnessed this incredible density of ditched villages when I worked with a magnetometer and a UCLA team in the area between the Cervaro and Ofanto rivers. In several weeks we identified 75 ditched settlements. The magnetometer recorded the ditches since almost all that once belonged to farmsteads— pottery, stone and bone tools, and animal bones—was washed down into them. Unfortunately we cannot reconstruct the houses, temples, and their furniture, as in east-central Europe and the Balkans, since very little remained *in situ.*

FIGURE 5–4

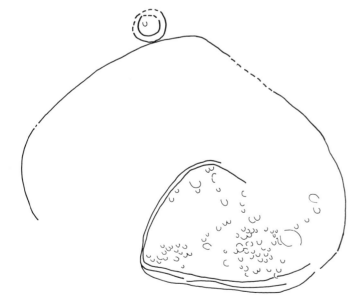

FIGURE 5–3 Plan of Lagnano I settlement with four ditches around and four C-shaped ditches within the area. Tavoliere, SE Italy. Early 6th mill B.C.

FIGURE 5–4 Passo di Corvo town near Foggia surrounded by a ditch. C shapes are outlines of ditches of the homesteads. The outer ditch is approximately 1 km across. (The plan is based on aerial photography).

Ditched Villages

Radiocarbon dates for the early Impresso settlements established near the coast are from approximately the middle of the 7th millennium B.C.[7] (TABLE 17) It is possible that these earliest communities were not practicing farming and only gradually ventured inland to explore the possibilities of agriculture. A distinctive farming culture of ditched villages was eventually developed.

The Tavoliere and Materano plains near the town of Matera were occupied during the second Impresso stage. These sites are generally found near areas of *crosta* soil, with access to animal pasturage. The calcarious stratum called *crosta*[8] is resistant to water penetration and is usually found on slight rises or hillocks. It is light to work and relatively fertile. In contrast, alluvial soils are found in valley bottoms and in coastal areas.

The large Neolithic village of Passo di Corvo, composed of one hundred hut compounds surrounded by triple ditches, is on the crest of a low Tavoliere ridge, overlooking the Celone valley.[9] This site and the one kilometer territory around it are nearly 100 percent *crosta*, and further territory within a five kilometer radius includes 65 percent heavy alluvium, conducive to pastoral exploitation.

Crop species identified at Impresso pottery sites, such as Rendina in the Ofanto valley, include einkorn, emmer, free threshing wheat, spelt wheat, six-row barley, broad beans, and lentils. The Middle Neolithic Passo di Corvo site yielded similar species including wild oats.[10] An analysis of animal bones has shown the overwhelming majority of domestic animals in comparison to wild ones. Five domestic species have been found: sheep, goats, cattle, pigs, and dogs, with the caprovines as the dominant group.[11]

The occurrence of so many ditches around the hamlets and C-shaped ditches within the compounds remains a puzzle. Until recently, these ditches were believed to have protected dwellings or enclosed animals. Neither explanation seems to fit, however, since dwellings were outside the ditches and the compounds were too small to serve as corrals. Rendina, dating from the early centuries of the 6th millennium B.C. (TABLE 17, southern Italy), revealed two dwellings next to the C-shaped ditches.[12] It is possible that these ditches, which are sometimes three to four meters deep, could have served to drain and collect water in the rainy winter months and in May just before the summer drought. The Atlantic climate of that period was about 1° C warmer than at present, accompanied by increased precipitation. On the other hand, wells about six meters deep are found in settlements, indicating that the water table was not beyond the reach of Neolithic technology.[13] It appears that a C-ditch did not enclose individual farmsteads but served other purposes.

Houses can only be vaguely reconstructed. At Rendina, post holes were found around a sunken oval area having fragments of clay daub. The excavator, Cipolloni Sampo, has reconstructed two houses, one 8 m long and the other 12 m long and approximately 4 m wide. The larger house had two rooms with an entrance on the lateral side. Excavations at Passo di Corvo by Santo Tinè yielded a house with a stone foundation up to 45 cm high. This house had an apsidal end which was separated by a partition wall from the rest of the house. (FIGURE 5–5, tentative reconstruction) Since nothing was found within, the function of the end room is not clear, and we do not know if this arrangement was the norm. In the same Passo di Corvo settlement, circular or oval platforms of about 2 m in diameter were found which could have served as floors for small huts. At Molfetta, a settlement west of Bari, forty oval beaten-clay floors, 2–4 m in diameter, were found in an area of one-quarter hectare during excavations by Mosso in 1908–9.[14] Small hut floors are reported from several other settlements,

so it seems that they were floors of regular dwellings. The two-roomed houses could have served ritual purposes as in the Sesklo culture in Greece.

Communities were composed of hamlets of up to ten or more dwellings. Large villages are not found before the middle of the 6th millennium B.C., after which, there was a marked increase in population. Large villages such as Passo di Corvo housed at one time about 200 inhabitants.[15] The digging of deep ditches must have involved well-organized communal labor. At Passo di Corvo, the external ditches, which served for protection against wild animals, run for 5 km and are 5 m wide and 4 m deep. Tinè has calculated that their excavation involved the removal of some 100,000 cubic meters of material.

FIGURE 5–5

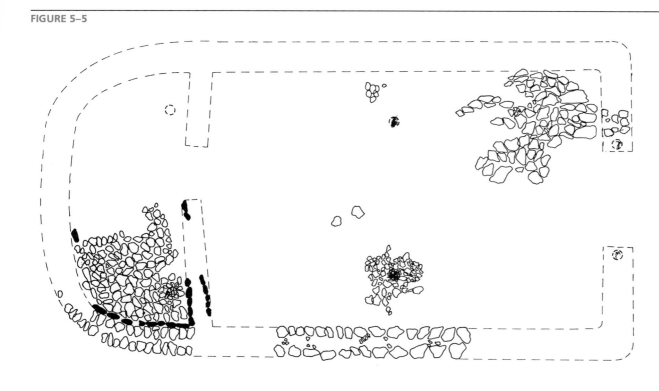

FIGURE 5–5 Two-room structure with an apsidal end, from Passo di Corvo settlement near Foggia. Plan with remains of cobbled stone pavement and stretches of drystone walling. Attempted reconstruction by S. Tinè, 1983. c. 5500–5300 B.C.

FIGURE 5–6

FIGURE 5–6 Pottery typology of Tavoliere, SE Italy. Four periods within 6500–5000 B.C. (1) Early Impresso, cardium shell and nail or stick impressed; (2) Second stage of Impresso with organized design, impressed, incised, and white or red encrusted; (3) Incised and painted in red, dark brown, or black; (4) Great variety of shapes, red band or red edged with black painted; (1–4) from Passo di Corvo, (4a) from Scaloria cave.

Chronology and Pottery Sequence

Pottery that survives from ditched villages is our prime means for chronological classification of settlements, especially if combined with radiocarbon dates. Four periods have been distinguished between 6500 and 5000 B.C. which mirror a constant development of ceramic art and technology within the Neolithic of southern Italy.

The earliest examples of impressed ware from around the middle of the 7th millennium B.C. are large bag-shaped vessels and spherical and semispherical jars and bowls. These were decorated before firing with the edges of shells, the ends of sticks, or by pinching with the fingertips. (FIGURE 5–6, 1)

The next stage, which coincides with the spread of ditched villages in Tavoliere, Materano, and Sicily at the end of the 7th and early 6th millennium B.C., is Late Impresso, in which shapes became more varied and elements of design and symbols appeared. (FIGURE 5–6, 2) Fine ware was medium thick and brown-burnished, decorated by incision, incrustation, and rocker stamps. Motifs expressed on this fine ware include triangles, chevrons, lozenges, frogs, vulvas, vertical and horizontal zigzag bands, and bands formed by groups of striations. Anthropomorphic vases, handled stamps, and female anthropomorphic and zoomorphic figurines were also created at this time. (FIGURE 5–7)

A considerable enrichment of the repertoire of shapes and decoration on ceramics took place during the third phase of this development which included the introduction of painting in red and dark brown or black-on-buff. Triangles, chevrons, striated and net-patterned triangles, bands, lozenges and discs, and bands of parallel lines that appeared (FIGURE 5–6, 3) are generally related to the design patterns and symbols of the Sesklo and Starčevo cultures of c. 5800–5500 B.C.

The fourth phase is distinguished by the introduction of red-band painting, black- and brown-burnishing of fine ware, and by the introduction of carinated and square-mouthed pots. These peculiar pots suggest contacts with northern Italy and France. During this phase, red bands became edged in black on a background of buff or white. (FIGURE 5–6, 4) The most numerous examples of this type are from the cave of Scaloria at Manfredonia, south of the Gargano Peninsula. Here, fragments of 1,500 vases were recovered, decorated with symbols of regeneration: triangles, butterflies, plant shoots, suns, and snakes (see fig. 7–114). Radiocarbon dates place this period in the second half of the 6th millennium B.C. (TABLE 17, *bottom left*) To this Scaloria period belongs the large ditched village of Passo di Corvo.

Tavoliere was nearly abandoned after the Scaloria period, but life continued to flourish in Materano, Calabria, Apulia, Sicily, and north of the Gargano Peninsula in the Abruzzi. North of Matera is the Late Neolithic village of Serra d'Alto, famous for its *figulina* pottery.[16] *Figulina* is an unusually delicate pottery made of compact clay of an orange buff or creamy color which is smoothly polished, either left plain or painted in dark brown or red. It is unlikely that its refinement could have been achieved without fine kiln firing.

FIGURE 5–7

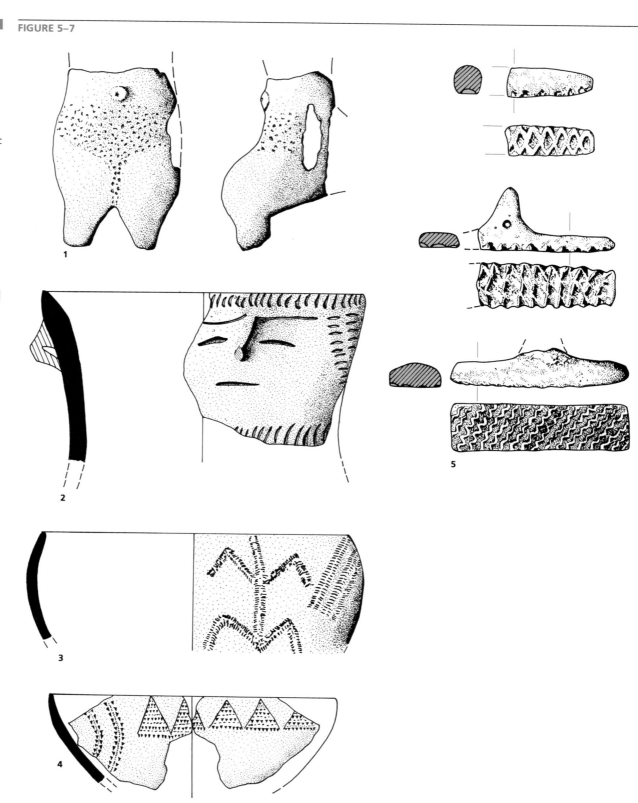

FIGURE 5–7 Characteristic finds from Late Impresso stage of the Early Neolithic in SE Italy. (1) Fragment of a sculpture of a seated Goddess. (2) Goddess, face on the neck of a vase. (3, 4) Impressed symbolic designs (frog, tri-lines, triangles) on bowls, and (5) handled seals. Rendina, near Melfi, Ofanto valley, c. 6100–5800 B.C. (Illustrated objects are from several phases of the settlement). Scale: (1) 1:4; (2) 1:1; (3, 4) 1:2; (5) 2:3.

FIGURE 5–8 Serra d'Alto (*figulina*) cups with fantastic zoomorphic handles. Painting dark brown on buff. Matera, S Italy. Mid-5th mill. B.C.

FIGURE 5–9 (1) Egg-shaped rock-cut tomb with a crouched skeleton; (2) An owl-masked figurine of calcareous rock and (3–4) rounded vases with red-slipped surface were placed in the grave. Arnesano near Lecce, Apulia. End 5th–early 4th mill. B.C.

The Serra d'Alto *figulina* pottery of the middle of the 5th millennium B.C. (TABLE 17, *middle left*) is the most attractive Neolithic pottery of Italy. Zones of triangles, meanders, zigzags, and other geometric motifs decorate the bulbous part of the vases, but the most distinctive feature is the surprisingly inventive three dimensional moulding of the handles, in which a ram, bull, or other fantastic animal head or spirals are found attached to the handle top. (FIGURE 5–8, PLATE 17) *Figulina* vases were exported to Liguria, the River Po valley, across the Adriatic to the Butmir culture in Bosnia, and to the south as far as Malta. These vases must have been prized for their quality and aesthetic perfection, but it is also possible that some liquid substance such as wine or oil was traded in them since the predominant vessel shapes are narrow necked jars.[17] Their proliferation could have been linked with the trade in obsidian from the island of Lipari north of Sicily and from Sardinia.[18] Jade axes from the north Alpine region are found in southern Italy and Sicily, while jade and steatite rings are found in Sardinia, testifying to the wide range of trade circulation during that time.

The final Neolithic pottery of southern Italy, widely spread over Apulia, Calabria, and Sicily, is unpainted, red slipped, with cylindrical or trumpet-shaped handles labeled "Diana ware" after a find place on the island of Lipari. It is also called "Bellavista type" after a site northwest of Taranto. The fantastic Serra d'Alto type handles and rich geometric designs disappeared. The emphasis was focused, instead, on the roundness of the vessels and their brilliantly shining surfaces. (PLATE 18) Shining red vases were placed in egg-shaped rock-cut tombs next to schematically rendered figurines representing the Death Goddess. At Arnesano near Lecce in Apulia, a figurine of calcareous rock with an owl mask and triple chevron, with the lower body reduced to a cone, was placed in a tomb in front of a crouched skeleton. (FIGURE 5–9) The Diana period is within the end of the 5th and early part of the 4th millennium B.C. (TABLE 17, 17–20)

FIGURE 5–8

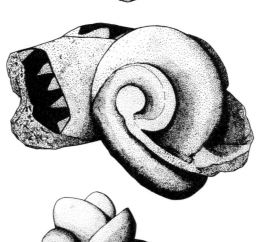

FIGURE 5–9

Sardinia and Corsica

From prehistoric times, Sardinia and Corsica have been stepping stones between the central and western Mediterranean world. Much of the traffic between southern and northern Italy and southern France was through these islands, continually bringing elements from the mainland, preventing the culture of these islands from becoming insular. During the 5th and 4th millennia B.C., their culture, particularly that of Sardinia, was astonishingly rich and distinctive, with their own ceramic and sculptural art and truly amazing tomb architecture.

As in southern and central Italy, the agricultural life on the islands began toward the end of the 7th millennium B.C. during the Impresso Pottery period. The earliest radiocarbon dated materials in stratified caves, such as Basi and others in southern Corsica,[19] and Filiestru, Mara, in northern Sardinia,[20] are characterized by the advanced Impresso pottery. Mariners who settled these islands are presumed to have come from Tuscany across the Tyrrhenian Sea, where sites with similar pottery are known. Although acquainted with emmer and einkorn wheat and domesticated animals, the first settlers lived in cave shelters and were more hunters, fishermen, and shell collectors than pure farmers. Their economy was largely based on shellfish, fish, hunted animals, and the raising of domestic animals.

Obsidian Source in Sardinia

Sardinia had flourished on its obsidian. Obsidian tools are found on both islands from the earliest Neolithic settlements and throughout all later periods. Obsidian was the main trade item with southern France, Liguria, the Alpine region, and even across the Adriatic with Bosnia. The source area is Monte Arci near Oristano in west-central Sardinia. This obsidian-rich mountain was researched more than thirty years ago by Puxeddu who located four quarries on the mountainside, ten collecting centers, a number of workshops, and 162 sites

which yielded obsidian tools and nuclei.[21] Monte Arci produces translucent (type A) and opaque (type B) obsidian. The translucent type was used in the Early Neolithic of the islands, although this gradually diminished in later periods and was supplanted by the opaque variety.

Chronology and Cultural Sequence

An unbroken cultural sequence on these islands is subdivided into Early, Middle, and Late Neolithic. The key site for understanding this cultural succession is the stratified and radiocarbon dated Filiestru rock shelter excavated by David Trump in 1980. This site revealed six superimposed cultural layers from approximately 6000 to 3000 B.C. Another cave in the same Bonu Ighinu valley at Sa Ucca de Su Tintirriolu, also excavated by Trump, yielded stratified deposits of Middle (Bonu Ighinu) and Late (Ozieri) Neolithic.[22] Both the Impresso and the following Filiestru layer which continued Impresso traditions are considered Early Neolithic, covering the 6th millennium B.C. (FIGURE 5–10; TABLE 17, Sardinia)

In the middle part of the 5th millennium B.C., during the Middle Neolithic, caves were abandoned as permanent habitations and villages were established. Increased farming activities are indicated by carbonized barley and wheat grains. Bonu Ighinu pottery was well burnished and of more varied forms than during the Early Neolithic. In addition to globular shapes, vases and cups appeared with elaborated handles, sometimes zoomorphic, reminiscent of the fantastic Serra d'Alto style. Impressed, dotted, and incised designs include symbols such as horns and vulvas, as well as mythical figures. (FIGURE 5–11)

Oven or egg-shaped rock-cut tombs are distinctive of this period. In the tombs, Stiff Nude figurines of a particularly Sardinian style, have been found placed in front of the dead. Sculptures of this type, made of alabaster, soft stone, or clay, display an amazing sculptural harmony and are found in all parts of Sardinia. (FIGURE 5–12) They are usually from 10 to 20 cm in height. One sculp-

FIGURE 5–10 Sardinian Early Neolithic vases. (1) Globular vase with shell impressed neck and handles with a Bird Goddess's face on each handle. Grotta Verde de Alghero, NW Sardinia, c. 6000 B.C. H 24.5 cm. (2) Plain rounded vases with perforated lugs from the Filiestru rock shelter (second Neolithic stratum). Scale, 1:3

FIGURE 5–11 Middle Neolithic (Bonu Ighinu) vase and handle decoration. (1) Snake heads with a long mouth shown in relief on top of the handle. Filiestru cave. (2) Vase decorated with triangles and horns and with zoomorphic handles. The central motif in dotted technique probably represents a bucranium or vulva and bull horns, a typical symbol of regeneration. Grotta Rifugio di Oliena. Scale, c. 1:2.

FIGURE 5–10

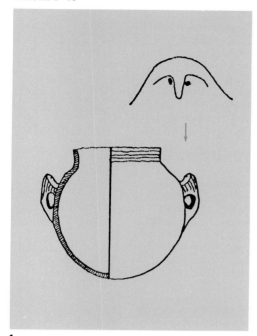

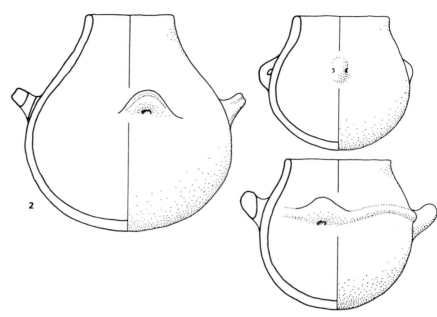

FIGURE 5–11

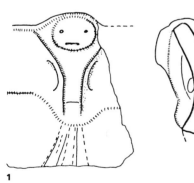

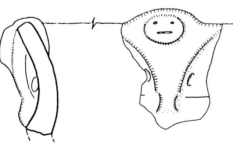

FIGURE 5–12

FIGURE 5–13

FIGURE 5–12 The rotund Sardinian seated nude of alabaster shown with folded arms and wearing a hairdress. Middle Neolithic period, Bonu Ighinu, Su Cungiau de Marcu (Decimoputzu), Cagliari, Sardinia; mid-5th mill. B.C. H 18.5 cm.

FIGURE 5–13 Stone sculpture with Bird Goddess mask (typically with long nose, eyebrows, and no mouth), and a zigzag band around the neck. Middle Neolithic, Bonu Ighinu culture, mid-5th mill. B.C. Sa Màndara, Cagliari.

FIGURE 5–14 Late Neolithic Ozieri vases with richly decorated exterior and interior; c. 4000 B.C. (1) Cuccuru Arrius, (2) Pauli Fenu-Riola, (3) Conca Illonis, (4) Grotta di sa Uca de Su Tintirriolu di Mara, (5) Puisteris, C Sardinia.

ture of the same Bonu Ighinu style was found holding a baby (her provenance unfortunately is unknown). To the same period, but not to the graves, belong large stone sculptures with faces or masks of the Bird Goddess, identified by her large nose, eyebrows, and no mouth. (FIGURE 5-13)

The late Neolithic Ozieri culture of the end of the 5th and early 4th millennium B.C. is the burgeoning period. (TABLE 17, Ozieri) The first Ozieri sites were discovered in the 19th century (Grotta di Bartolomeo near Cagliari in 1878) and early 20th century. The famous necropolis of underground tombs at Anghelu Ruju, Alghero, was excavated in 1904–1908, and the name-giving site, Grotta di San Michele at Ozieri in the central part of northwest Sardinia, was discovered in 1914.[23] The almost triple number of Ozieri sites, compared to those of the Middle Neolithic, speak of a rapid growth of population with large concentrations of settlements and tombs in the Cagliari area, the southwestern part of the island, Oristano, and Sassari. Large villages occur for the first time. At San Gemilianu di Sestu, 14 kilometers north of Cagliari, rescue excavations came across more than eighty lowered house floors, oval or rectangular, about 8–10 m in length, scattered on an alluvial terrace 220 by 200 m in size.[24] This large village dates from the Ozieri and several later phases. The actual size of a single period village remains unknown.

The Ozieri culture is characterized by an extraordinary richness of vase shapes—amphorae, jars, canisters, bowls, dishes, vase supports, tripods, tetrapods, vessels with animal protomes—decorated by incision and impression with a great variety of symbols—oculi, suns, ram horns, snakes, chevrons, triangles—ritual scenes (FIGURES 5-14, 5-15) The pictorial representations on Ozieri vases are a rich and eloquent source for the reconstruction of religious rituals, similar in value to Late Cucuteni pictorial painting of the same period.

FIGURE 5-14

FIGURE 5–15

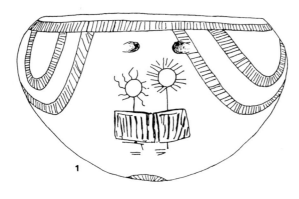

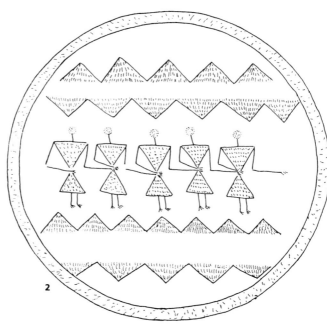

FIGURE 5–15 Mythical images and ritual scenes incised on Ozieri vases. (1) Two figures with radiating suns for heads and striated squares as bodies. Serra Is Araus, San Vero Milis. Found in a subterranean tomb. (2) A scene of a ritual dance. Five hourglass-shaped maidens holding hands incised on the interior of a dish. Monte d'Accoddi sanctuary, Sassari. Scale, c. 1:3; c. 4000 B.C.

FIGURE 5–16

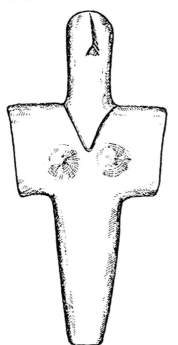

FIGURE 5–16 Marble sculpture from Senorbi, north of Cagliari, Sardinia. An abstracted image of the Goddess of Death and Regeneration with folded arms. A V sign is engraved above her breasts. Her abstracted face is represented by the nose (or beak) alone. Ozieri culture. Tentative date, c. 4000 B.C. H 42.2 cm.

FIGURE 5–17 Marble statues of Porto Ferro type representing The Goddess of Death and Regeneration. Early 4th mill. B.C. found in a subterranean tomb. (1) Porto Ferro. H 30 cm; (2) Monte d'Accoddi sanctuary; Sassari, N Sardinia. H 23 cm.

FIGURE 5–17

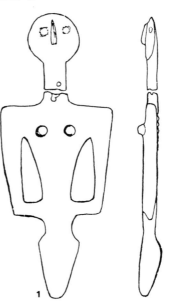

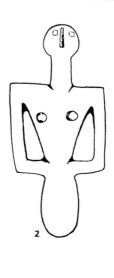

The celebrated Ozieri marble and alabaster sculptures found in tombs are White Death Goddesses with the lower part reduced to a cone, while the arms are folded in the upper part forming a rectangle. (FIGURES 5–16, 5–17) The head is schematized showing only the nose, or is round, representing a mask. The abstract Sardinian Nudes described in earlier literature were thought to be imported from or influenced by the Cycladic art of the early or mid-3rd millennium B.C., but these Sardinian Nudes predate the Cycladic by more than a millennium and must have been a local innovation. The image of the White Death Goddess in each region has deep local roots and its own stylistic evolution.

The Ozieri culture's most remarkable creations are the subterranean tombs, locally called *Domus de Janas*, "witches houses," hundreds of which can be visited in northern Sardinia. (FIGURE 5–18) The simplest are single oval (egg-shaped) rooms, while others are elaborate complexes of halls and chambers. (FIGURE 5–19) The roofs are supported by pillars, and bull heads or horns are frequently shown in relief above the entrances (see fig. 7–109). Red, purple, and yellow ochre were used for painting outer and inner walls and ceilings, while the interiors are decorated with symbols of regeneration: vulvas, bucrania, triple vulvas, hourglass shapes (double triangles), ram horns, and oculi. These elaborate underground structures are temple tombs (i.e., as sacred as temples) not just graves, rightly termed so by Atzeni in 1981.[25] We shall return to these in the section on burials at the end of chapter 7.

FIGURE 5–18

FIGURE 5–18 Plan of Anghelu Ruju cemetery of subterranean tombs. Alghero, NW Sardinia. Ozieri period, c. 4000 B.C.

FIGURE 5–19

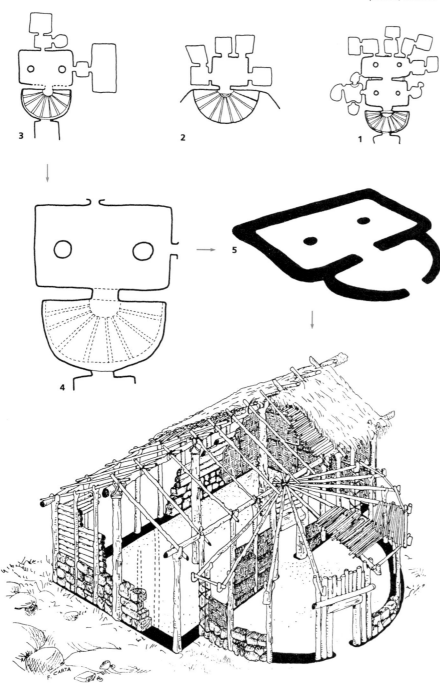

FIGURE 5–19 Outlines and reconstruction of multichambered tombs of northern Sardinia. (1) S. Andrea Priu; Bonorva; (2) M. Petrusu-Ploaghe; (3–5) Coro-neddu, Bosa. Ozieri period, around 4000 B.C.

Malta

The Maltese archipelago, composed of the larger islands of Malta and Gozo and three tiny islets of Camino, Cominotto, and Filfla, lies some 80 km south of Sicily. (FIGURE 5–20) On a clear day, Sicily is visible from Malta, so it is obvious that the experienced navigators of the Impresso Ware culture had no difficulty discovering these islands. The first farmers settled in Malta in the 6th millennium B.C. during the advanced stage of the Impresso period, around the time they settled in Sicily. These were mixed farmers living in villages, rearing sheep, goats, cattle, and pigs, and cultivating wheat, barley, and lentils. The islands were not as barren 8,000 years ago as they are today and agriculture was possible. These first pioneers were drawn to these islands by the abundance of workable stone—specifically coralline and soft globigerina limestone. The use of this durable stone played an essential and decisive role in the formation of the Maltese culture, famous for its monumental temples built without metal tools. The stone architecture of Malta continues to astonish investigators after several centuries.

Discovery

There are 43 temples recorded, 9 on Gozo and 34 on Malta, all built of either coralline or globigerina limestone of unhewn blocks weighing up to 30 tons, including blocks of ashler masonry, and orthostats. Some of these remarkable monuments were noticed as early as the 17th century with no idea of what they represented. Even in the 19th century there was not much understanding of their significance. Ggantija, the first temple to be excavated in 1827, was described by C. Mazzara in Paris as a "Temple ante-Diluvien des Géants" (Ante-diluvian Temple of Giants). When two more temples, Hagar Qim and Mnajdra, were unearthed in 1839 and 1840, they were considered to be Phoenician monuments.

Only in 1901 were the Maltese temples assessed for the first time to be prehistoric monuments in the work by Albert Mayr "Die vorgeschichtlichen Denkmäler von Malta" (The Prehistoric Monuments of Malta), a shorter version of which was translated into English, appearing in 1908. More professional work started with Themistocles Zammit, Director of the Malta Museum, and under his direction the excavation of the famous Hypogeum of Hal Saflieni, accidently discovered in 1902, was completed and published in 1911. In 1914–19, Zammit excavated Tarxien, the largest and richest temple of Malta. This was followed by a number of other significant excavations in the 1920s by Zammit and British archeologist Margaret Murray and others.

The first general account of the prehistoric cultures of Malta was written by J. D. Evans in 1959,[26] and an extensive survey by the same author appeared in 1971.[27] In the postwar period, the only major discovery was the temple and settlement at Skorba by D. Trump.[28] Coincidental with this excavation was the radiocarbon dating of a series of samples from Skorba and other sites that provided the possibility of revising the long and nebulous chronology of these monuments.

FIGURE 5–20

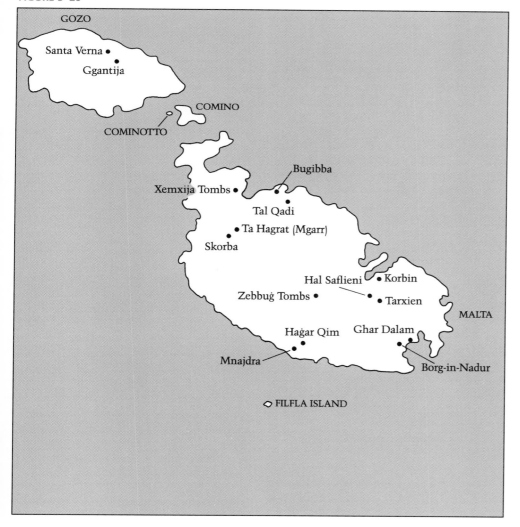

FIGURE 5–20 Map of Malta and Gozo.

Chronological Chart for Malta

Calibrated Dates B.C.	Phase	Monuments
c. 2500	Tarxien cemetery	Tarxien Cemetery
c. 3000	Tarxien	Temples: Tarxien, Borg in-Nadur, Hağar Qim, Mnajdra S., Hal Saflieni Hypogeum
c. 3500	Ġgantija	Temples: Ġgantija, Mnajdra E., Skorba W., Korbin, Bugibba, Santa Verna. Hal Saflieni Hypogeum.
c. 4000	Mgarr Zebbuġ	Xemxija and Zebbuġ tombs
c. 4500	Skorba	Red Skorba temple Gray Skorba site
c. 5000	Ghar Dalam	Ghar Dalam cave sanctuary
c. 6000		Impressed Ware

Chronology

At present, the Neolithic caves, tombs, and temples of Malta, from the 6th to the 3rd millennia B.C., are roughly classified into seven phases. The temples of Malta belong to the 5th, 4th, and early 3rd millennia B.C. This chronological sequence is given in the chart below, while radiocarbon dates are listed in Table 17, right column.

Cave Sanctuaries

The first ritual centers on Malta were its caves. By the time the first immigrants came to these islands, the Old European expression of human spirituality was in full flower, and the equation of cave to temple was already established. It is probable that the doming and vaulting of some of the natural caves (as at Ghajn Abul on western Gozo and Mixta on central Gozo) reflects this attitude.

The cave at Ghar Dalam on southeastern Malta represents one of the earliest temples. Brown, grey, or buff roundbased bowls and globular jars have been found there decorated with impressions and linear patterns: bands formed by two to four parallel lines, diagonally hatched or crosshatched, and by hatched triangles with plain chevrons. Many pots were encrusted with white gypsum. Numerous phallic shaped stalagmites and stalactites are found there, apparently considered sacred as symbols of mysterious energy. Very likely, regeneration rites were performed in the cave.

Rock-cut Tombs and Hypogea

The earliest Maltese rock-cut tombs are egg- or kidney-shaped, found at Zebbuġ and Xemxija. The Zebbuġ tombs are small, about 1.9 m in diameter, whereas the Xemxija tombs are larger, averaging about 3.5 m in width. (FIGURE 5-21) These Maltese rock-cut tombs are generally related to those of Sardinia and southern Italy. The presence of lobed or egg-shaped tombs in Malta has a special significance since they are considered to prefigure the temples with their lobed interiors.

Among the grave goods, which included lumps of red ochre, shells, and buttons, a limestone head was found at Zebbuġ with a mask engraved in low relief. (FIGURE 5-22) This is an early portrayal of a divinity associated with the tomb, a Goddess of Death and Regeneration, which in a later period of Sardinia and the Cyclades, became the slim, stiff nude. Her mask bears characteristics of a bird of prey. Fragments of pottery were also found incised with anthropomorphic stick figures having large triangular heads. (FIGURE 5-23) Skeletons were found in fetal positions with large amounts of red ochre on and around them.

The largest accumulation of egg-shaped underground tombs is the famous hypogeum at Hal Saflieni in eastern Malta near the temple of Tarxien (see fig. 7-104) in which the dead were buried from the 4th millennium B.C. until the end of the Maltese culture around 2500 B.C. (A discussion of the symbols of regeneration found in the hypogea of Malta will be discussed in the Burial section of chapter 7.)

The Temples of Malta

J.D. Evans was the first to recognize the relationship between tombs and temples, an observation that is crucial for the understanding of their meaning and functions.

The lobes of the tombs became apses in temple architecture. Several earlier temples, such as Ta Hagrat, are trefoil, while the majority are four- or five-apse temples which have an anthropomorphic shape similar to that of the fat Maltese Goddess sculptures. This formal relationship is not accidental. Originally, however, the shape of the temple resembled an egg as the Goddess's womb, while the human shape was a secondary development during the 4th millennium B.C.

Like the egg-shaped, rock-cut tombs (as in Xemxija) from which they derive, the Maltese temples symbolize the Goddess's body itself, emphasizing her regenerative buttocks. Their entrances have a primarily southeastern alignment which, given the half-degree shift per hundred years of the precession of the earth's axis, probably indicate an original north-south alignment. Forecourts formed circular or elliptical shapes, with the concave temple facade and its trilithon entry at the focal point. Although most of the surrounding walls have now disappeared, there is plenty of evidence

FIGURE 5–21

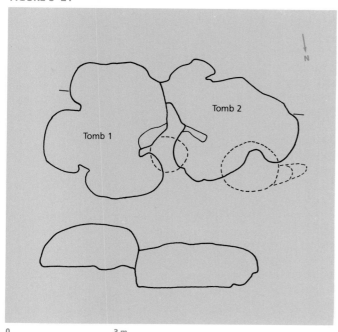
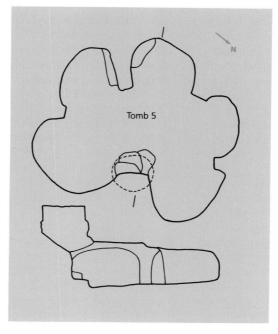

0   3 m

FIGURE 5–21 Kidney-shaped rock-cut tombs. Xemxija, Malta. Plans and cross-sections. End 5th mill. B.C.

FIGURE 5–22

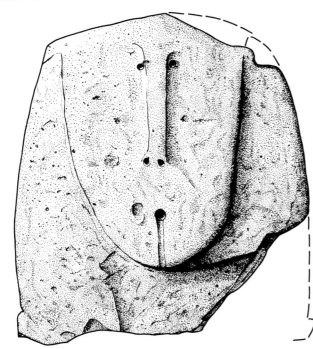

FIGURE 5–23

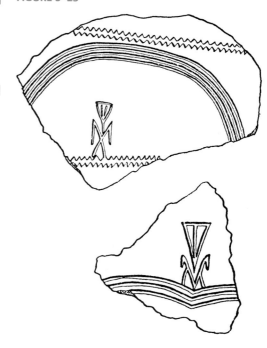

FIGURE 5–22 Limestone sculpture found in a rock-cut tomb. Zebbuġ, tomb 5. End 5th mill. B.C. H 18.5 cm.

FIGURE 5–23 Stick figures with large triangular heads incised and white encrusted on vases deposited in rock-cut tombs. Zebbuġ, tomb 4. End 5th mill. B.C.

that they were a regular feature, deliberately conceived for times of public assembly. It seems reasonable to suppose that these activities would have included offerings, religious ceremonies, and festive activities including music and dancing. Many forecourts, including those at Tarxien, Ħaġar Qim, and Mnajdra, have a huge perforated stone near the temple entry, interpreted as a tethering block. If such stones were used in this way, their scale implies the sacrifice of cattle.

Typically, the temples occur in pairs, with one significantly larger than the other. The alignment here is significant, and we may suppose the larger temple to be the mother and the smaller the daughter of the divine family, or we may see them as a pair of sisters, perhaps like the two-headed goddesses from Çatal Hüyük (c. 6500 B.C.) and the two-headed Bird Goddess from Gomolava (Vinča, c. 4800 B.C.). Still another possibility is that the representation is of two different aspects of the same Goddess, symbolizing youth and maturity, or death and regeneration.

Since the east symbolized the beginning of life and the west its end, this later interpretation is very appealing. More religious material and furniture is found in the larger, western temples, and we may suppose that most rituals having to do with death and regeneration took place there. These were stuccoed or painted in red, which has long disappeared, and are built of darker brownish-red limestone. Ceremonies celebrating birth may have been divided between the smaller temples, while spring rituals of regeneration may have taken place there and in the tombs. These eastern temples tend to feel more open spatially and are built of the lighter colored limestone.

The main temples of Malta are introduced below.

Each temple seems to have had its own emphasis. One of the oldest, from the 5th millennium B.C., is Red Skorba, but it is too ruined to offer much architectural information. Of interest are clay and stone figurines found in this shrine wearing triangular masks with a nose indicated and a dot for a mouth. They have long necks, large breasts, the shelflike posteriors of a bird and a large pubic triangle, and wear a cinch belt and necklaces. (FIGURE 5–24) These features clearly portray the Bird Goddess, while the posture and attributes of these sculptures have close analogies to Early Vinča culture.

The quintessential double temple is the complex at Ġgantija on central Gozo. (FIGURE 5–25) An outer wall of rough, undressed coralline limestone blocks encircles both temples, rising to a height of 6 meters. Some blocks weigh 50 tons and are among the largest used for temple building in Malta. The internal walls and doorways are of dressed globigerina limestone.

The larger temple was found with elaborate furniture. Some of the characteristic details: Apse 2, the first chamber to the right inside the shrine, contained a red-painted niche of slabs, probably important for ritual practice or storage of sacred goods. Toward the back of the room are several blocks decorated with interconnected spirals in low relief. Apse 5, the eastern arm, has in it a shallow stone basin, 1 meter in diameter, which appears to have been a ritual hearth. Against the southeast end of this apse is a pillar on which is carved a snake in low relief (see fig. 7–61). Apse 6 served as an interior triple shrine (see fig. 5–25, 2). It contained three table altars and a trapezoidal slab set upright like a pillar. Apse 7, with tall limestone slabs, has the main altar in front decorated with pit marks.

Other temples on Gozo also belong to the Ġgantija phase. The amount of territory available per temple was 7.4 square kilometers.

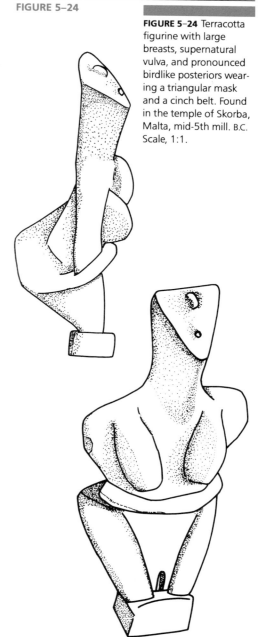

FIGURE 5–24

FIGURE 5–24 Terracotta figurine with large breasts, supernatural vulva, and pronounced birdlike posteriors wearing a triangular mask and a cinch belt. Found in the temple of Skorba, Malta, mid-5th mill. B.C. Scale, 1:1.

FIGURE 5–25

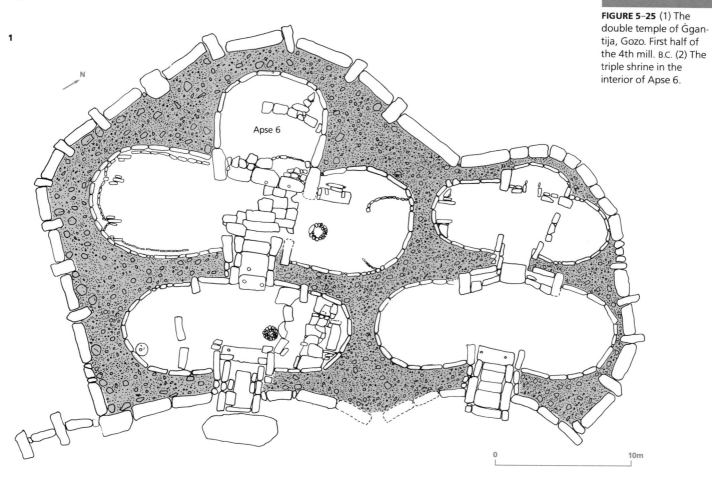

1

N

Apse 6

0   10m

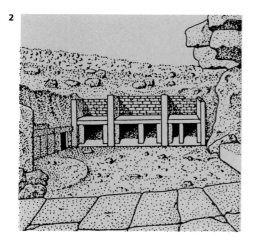

2

FIGURE 5–25 (1) The double temple of Ġgantija, Gozo. First half of the 4th mill. B.C. (2) The triple shrine in the interior of Apse 6.

Ḣaġar Qim is one of the most impressive temples of the Tarxien period, located on the southern coast of Malta. (FIGURE 5–26, PLATE 20) It has a well-preserved surrounding wall of globigerina limestone, a facade of vertical slabs, ten apses, inner slabs with rectangular windowlike openings, and stone altars. It also has the best known Maltese stone sculptures of seated, squatting, and standing fat ladies. These show remains of ochre paint, and stand about 20 cm high. (PLATE 21) This temple is situated on a knoll overlooking the sea just above the Mnajdra temple.

In its shape, Ḣaġar Qim differs from Ġgantija and Mnajdra since it may have been a complex of three double-apsed shrines. The main entrance was on the southeast, but the western and northern shrines also had their own entrances. There was a small semicircular niche of vertical slabs built into the thickness of the eastern wall of vertical slabs, also entered from the outside. This housed a triangular altar stone, a pubic triangle symbolizing regeneration. North of this holy site and north of Apse 5 is a very tall upright stone that juts out above all the other temple construction, a towering menhir very likely representing the Goddess herself. On the left of the main (southern) entrance to the back, stood a sacrificial tablelike altar topped with a container and decorated in front with a tree of life growing from a pot. Its surface had a pitted decoration, characteristic of Maltese temples. Next to it, a

FIGURE 5–26

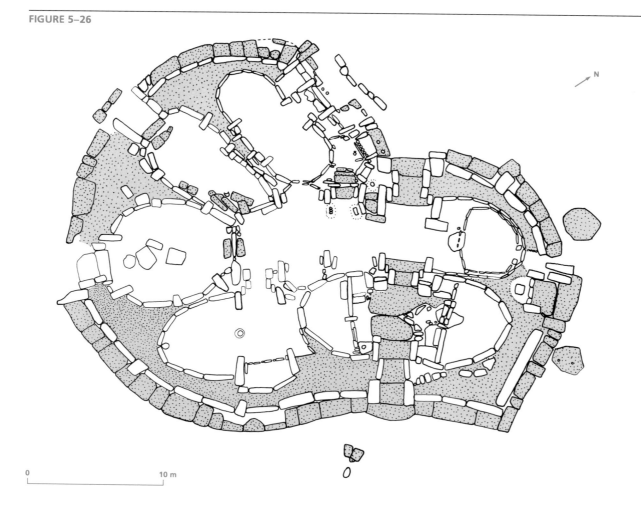

FIGURE 5–26 Plan of Ḣaġar Qim temple. Southern coast of Malta. End of 4th mill. B.C.

0   10 m

standing slab with a double spiral or "oculi" design was found. Two niches in the central courtyard contained mushroom shaped limestone altars with concave tops. Two further rooms in this central area housed pitted table altars and a stone pillar. Another pillar stood at the end of the apse of room 10, the southwestern shrine.

A typical double temple with semi-circular forecourt of coralline limestone of the Tarxien period is found at Mnajdra on the southern coast of Malta, 60 m below the Ḥaġar Qim temple, close to the sea. It is oriented now to the east and southeast, but was probably originally oriented southeast and south. (FIGURE 5–27) (The east trefoil temple is from the earlier Ġgantija period.) Both

temples are closer in size to each other than temples elsewhere on Malta, although the western temple is much more elaborate, with many niches and the remains of a hard torba floor in the main room. One of the most elaborate entrances flanked by triangular and phallic stones was found in this section (see fig. 7–60).

Left of the entrance doorway stands a conical stone phallus, 75 cm high. In Apse 4, the second "eastern" apse, many strange clay objects and twists of clay were found which look a great deal like human embryos. Figurines in birth-giving posture suggest that some of the rituals here at Mnajdra had to do with healing and childbirth (see fig. 7–64).

FIGURE 5–27

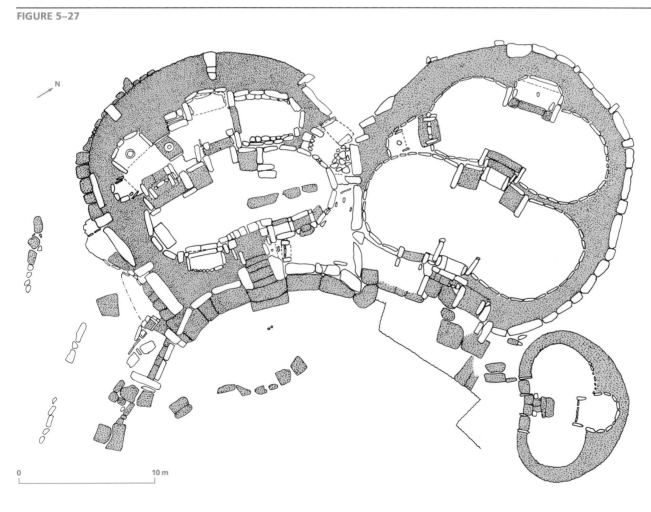

FIGURE 5–27 The double temple of Mnajdra, southern coast of Malta. End of the 4th-early 3rd mill. B.C. The small three-apse temple to the east is of the Ġgantija period.

0   10 m

FIGURE 5–28

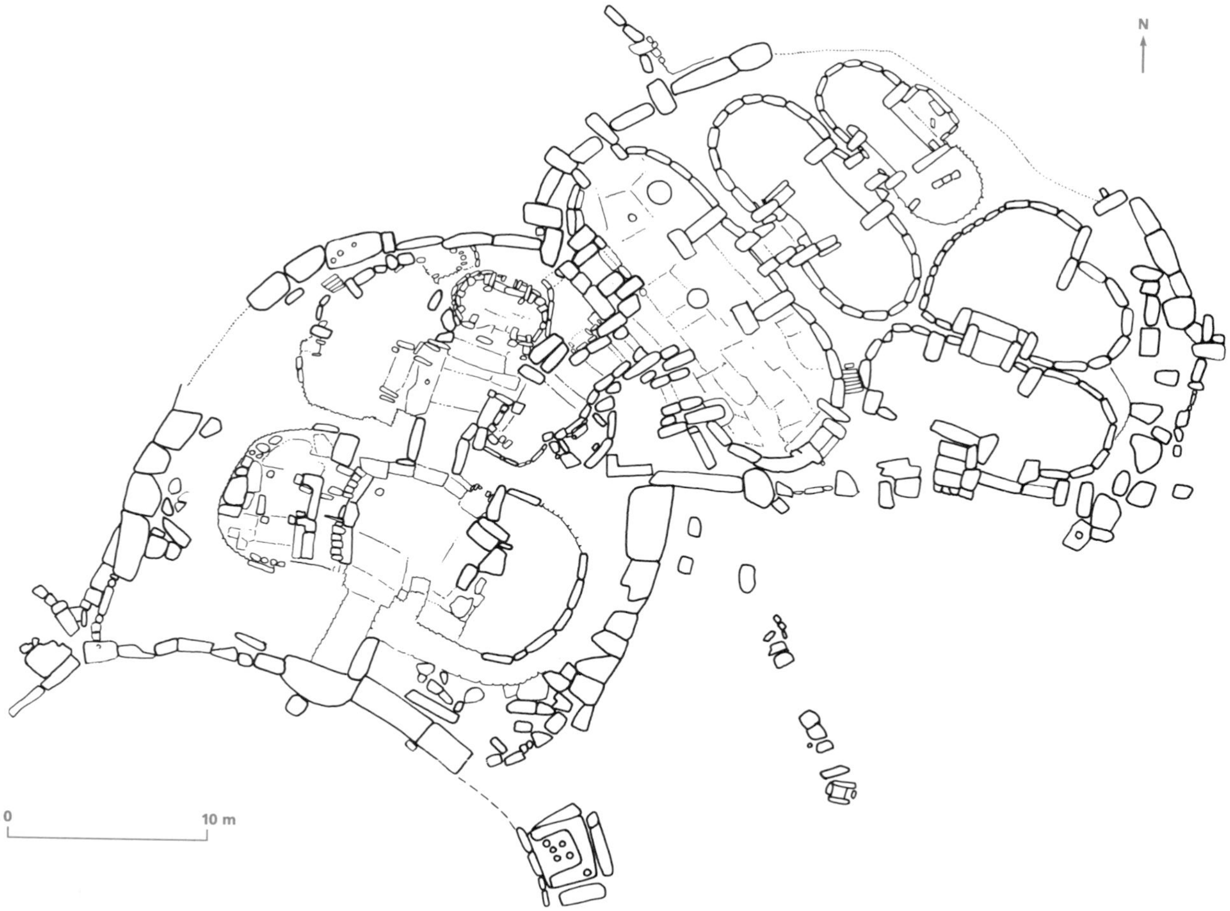

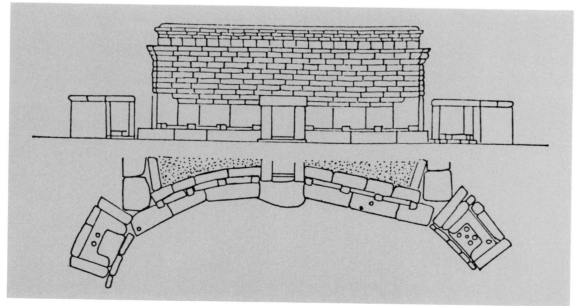

N

0   10 m

FIGURE 5–28 Tarxien temples. Early 3rd mill. B.C.

FIGURE 5–29

FIGURE 5–29 Conjectural reconstruction of the facade of Tarxien.

The three temples at Tarxien on eastern Malta near the hypogeum at Hal Saflieni were modified many times, making interpretation difficult. Like Ġgantija, Tarxien has a large central court. (FIGURES 5–28, 5–29) Fortunately, the Tarxien temples are decorated with highly sophisticated, articulate symbolic images. Numerous spiral and plant-spiral motifs are carved in relief on stone blocks. These energy signs are associated with the rising plant and serpent forces, harkening to the principle of the cyclic regeneration of life.

Pottery, animal horns, stone and clay basins, and altars are numerous. In the first western Apse 3, the remains of a very elaborate altar, the top of which shows signs of burning, testify to its use in ceremony. Along the side of the altar, a ram, a pig, and four goats move in procession. (PLATE 19) The ram is an animal sacred to the Goddess, its curled horns are seen elsewhere as snake spirals carved on pillars and slabs throughout the monument. Apse 5, the second western apse, was found filled with bones and horns of cattle and sheep or goats. Room 13, between the first and second temples, contained a heap of animal bones. Along the east wall were bulls facing left and right, beneath which was a relief representing a bitch with thirteen suckling pups (see fig. 7–62, 3). The great number of altars and animal bones suggest that sacrifices, perhaps for divination, were common at Tarxien. In a small area east of the second temple, fifty stone cups, perhaps for ritual celebration or libations were found, and further to the east, thirteen cups were found set upside down.

Domestic animals were offered in sacrifice to a figure of the Goddess. Tarxien West, Court 2, houses what is probably the world's earliest known monumental statue. This figure, Our Lady of Tarxien, is cut from limestone and stands on a carved plinth. Her upper half was unfortunately quarried away long ago, although her original height was around 2.5 to 3 m (see fig. 7–64).

With the great temple of Tarxien, the temple building period of Malta came to an end. It is not known what happened to the temple builders, but perhaps they abandoned the islands because of deforestation or crop failure, followed by famine, plague, or other calamities. Foreign people with different traditions settled in the islands. The Tarxien cemetery of cremation graves, dated to the post-temple building period after 2500 B.C., belongs to an alien culture group, but clearly Old European, having the same religion. Vases found in these graves have relatives in Sicily and as far away as western Yugoslavia.

6

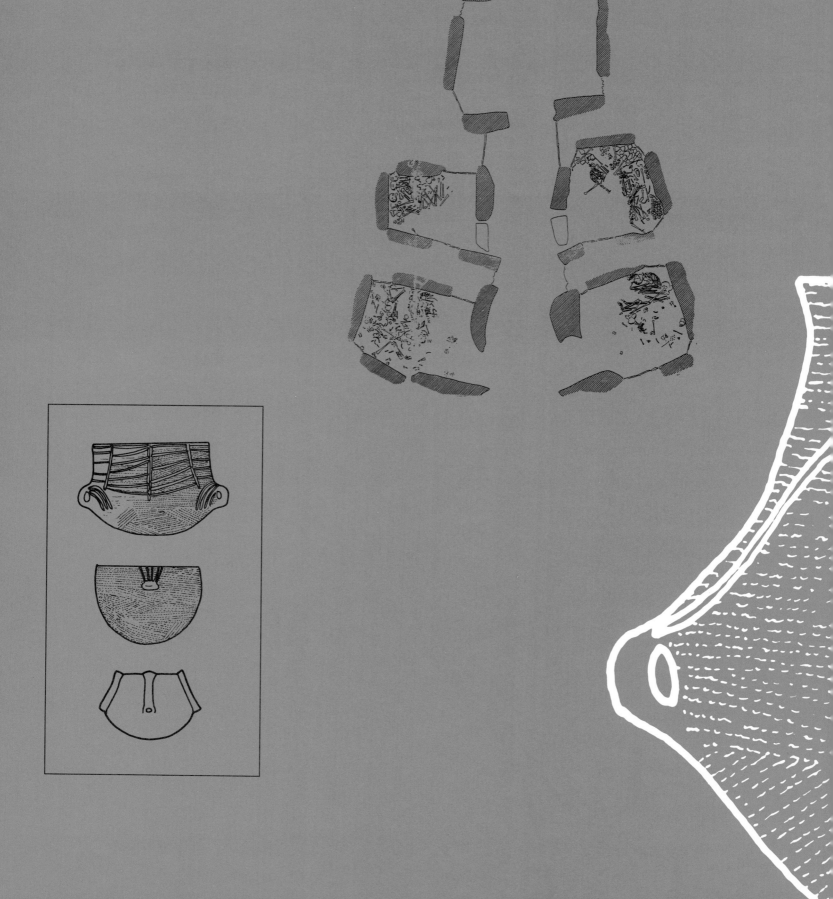

The Neolithic of
Western Europe

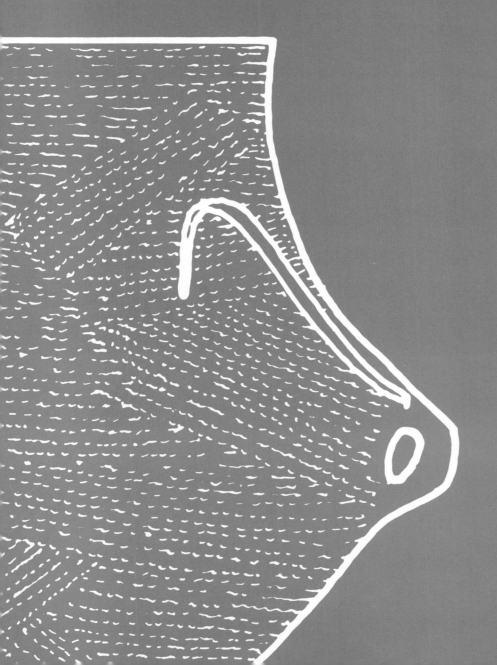

The Neolithic of Western Europe was decidedly a local development by the indigenous Epipaleolithic-Mesolithic inhabitants of Iberia (Portugal, Spain), France, and northern Italy (of the Sauveterrian-Tardenoisian and Castelnovian cultural traditions). It is not possible, however, to deny the influence of ideas circulated through navigation and local trading activities along the coastal regions of the western Mediterranean and Atlantic. The spirit of creativity visible in the emergence of pottery and religious expression was, to a certain extent, the result of communication with the inhabitants living in these regions. Neither Iberian nor French Mesolithic culture was isolated, and the increase of coastal communication during the Middle Neolithic is demonstrated by the diffusion of the unique idea of the megaliths that developed during this period. Whoever has been to Brittany or Portugal will believe that the appearance of the first megalithic structures was conditioned by the great abundance of stone. Their dating in the 5th millennium B.C. dismisses the antiquated notion that the dolmens and passage graves were inspired by the Egyptian pyramids or the tholos tombs of Crete and the eastern Mediterranean.

The British islands were converted to agriculture around the middle of the 5th millennium B.C. by colonists arriving from the continent, probably first from the direction of central Europe during the period of the late Linearbandkeramik culture, since the longbarrows and causewayed camps of the islands have parallels in central Europe. The passage-grave builders arrived next during the 4th millennium B.C., either from Brittany or Iberia, bringing their religious practices with them. By the second half of the 4th millennium B.C., Ireland and England were covered by many tomb-building traditions, all manifesting one belief system.

Although the western European Neolithic populations have not left temple models and religious paraphernalia associated with worship, or the thousands of clay figurines and painted vases as in southeastern Europe, they have left for us the virtually indestructible stone and earthen monuments, which were associated with elaborate funeral rites. These great monuments, some with courts in front and engraved with symbols, were not only ossuaries but were also sanctuaries where entire communities gathered to enact a variety of rituals. The megalithic tombs, in which communal burials took place, as well as gigantic enclosures continue to speak of the permanent association of the kin groups with their ancestral land and ancestors. These monuments were central symbols of Neolithic communities.

FIGURE 6-1 West Mediterranean Europe with the indication of major Early Neolithic sites.

The Early Neolithic of the Western Mediterranean

The last decades have seen a change in thinking about the Neolithization of the entire west Mediterranean area from northern Italy to Spain and Portugal. (FIGURE 6-1) It was previously assumed that this process came about due to diffusion from the eastern part of the Mediterranean, but it has become evident that the Neolithic began in the West not much later than it was established in the East.

Acculturation of a Mesolithic Population

For more than half a century the appearance of shell-impressed pottery known as Cardial or Impresso was held to be an important sign for the beginning of the Neolithic. Evidence from animal husbandry, stone tools, and ornaments now suggest that the process of Neolithization in this area was not a diffusion of pottery makers and sheep breeders from the East, but an adaptation by the indigenous Mesolithic population. Archeologically, there is no perceptible

FIGURE 6-1

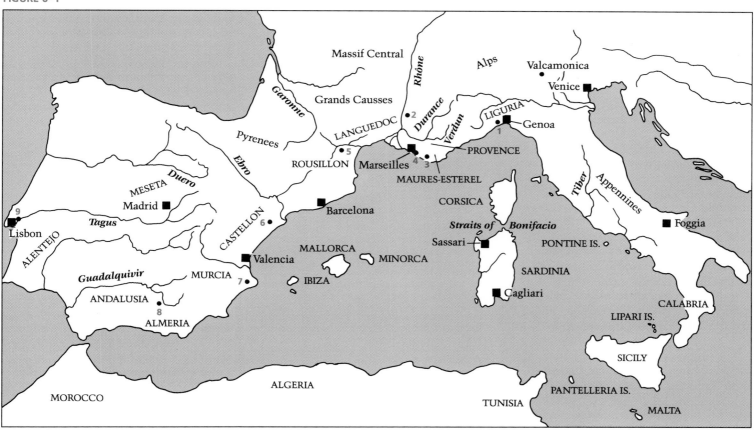

KEY

1. Arene Candide
2. Le Baratin
3. Cap Ragnon and Île Riou
4. Châteauneuf-les-Martigues
5. Gazel
6. Cova Fosca
7. Cova del Or
8. Murcielagos de Zuheros
9. Moita

cultural break between the final Paleolithic, Mesolithic, and the earliest Neolithic flint industries. For instance, under the primary ceramic level at the cave at Gazel (Sallèles-Cabardes, Aude) in southwestern France, in the level designated by tools as Mesolithic, the inhabitants were apparently breeding caprines (ovis/capra, sheep/goat).[1] Sheep bones were also found in the Mesolithic strata of Châteauneuf-les-Martigues, northwest of Marseilles, and in Moita, Muge, Portugal. There is very little difference between the Mesolithic tools and the ones associated with the Cardial pottery; this is also true of ornaments. One example is stone bracelets which are found with Mesolithic as well as Neolithic associations.[2]

Chronology and Cultural Sequence

Radiocarbon dates from at least three sites near Marseilles in Provence have indicated that a Neolithic economy was already developing before or about the middle of the 7th millennium B.C. These sites are the cave of Cap Ragnon, the open settlement of Île Riou in the Bay of Marseilles, and the cave of Châteauneuf-les-Martigues northwest of Marseilles. The lowest radiocarbon dates for these stratified sites are: Cap Ragnon (MC500A) 7970 ± 150 B.P., Île Riou (MC440) 7600 ± 150 B.P., and Châteauneuf (Köln date) 7420 ± 240 B.P. (TABLE 18) Calibrated, these dates would be placed in the middle of the 7th millennium B.C. These sites continued a Mesolithic type of economy with an emphasis on fish and molluscs, although sheep and Cardial pottery were already present.[3]

The process of acculturation of a Mesolithic population adopting Neolithic ideas and cultural items also seems to have taken place in the area of the Pyrenees. Here, Neolithic artifacts arrived piecemeal, not in a single stroke as one would expect if the people had brought them.[4]

Excavations of the Cova Fosca in Castellon near Alto Maestrazgo on the eastern coast of Spain, by Carme Olària and F. Gusi in the 1970s, have shown that the transition from a food-gathering to a food-producing economy started even earlier and was a long process.[5] The lowest levels of this stratified cave were aceramic and the lithic industry was Mesolithic, but sheep, assumed to have been tamed, were already present. Two radiocarbon dates, 9460 ± 160 and 8880 ± 200 B.P., indicate the 8th millennium B.C. Olària calls this period "Mesoneolithic" since it combines features of both; it can clearly be seen that there was no break between the two. People, without giving up hunting and gathering, were the protagonists of an economic change.

The next period represented by the Cova Fosca stratigraphy (Strata II and I), dated between c. 6500 and 6000 B.C. (TABLE 18, left), contained pottery, mostly deep egg-shaped bowls, which were not shell impressed as would be normal for the early pottery, but were engraved, fluted, or decorated with cordons. In this period, permanent occupation began as indicated by the remains of floors. The inhabitants cultivated grain and raised sheep, goats, and pigs.

A stratified site, Cova de l'Or at Beniarres in Alicante, southeastern Spain, excavated in 1955 and 1958, followed Cova Fosca by some 500 years.[6] Its five radiocarbon dates place it within the second half of the 6th millennium B.C. (TABLE 18, upper left) This site yielded emmer wheat, naked barley, bread wheat, and einkorn wheat;[7] the domesticated fauna was represented by sheep, goats, pigs, and dogs. Its lowest levels are typified by cardium-impressed deep jars decorated with wave patterns and chevrons. Other levels contained incised and plastic-decorated vessels in addition to shell-impressed pottery. The uppermost layer included square-mouthed pots of the Middle Neolithic.

A further cultural continuum is represented by the stratified cave Murcielagos de Zuheros in the district of Córdoba. Its sequence is confirmed by twelve radiocarbon dates which range between 6250 ± 35 and 5930 ± 130 B.P. The calibration of these dates places it at the end of the 6th and beginning of the 5th millennium B.C. (TABLE 18, upper left) All domesticated animals were present at this site: sheep, goats, cattle, pigs, and dogs. In one of the layers (IV), a pit filled with cereals was found. Acorns also had been part of the diet. This site yielded formidable red-slipped bowls which were present in three levels. Other vases had handles and were decorated with incised designs and vertical cordons. Among the ornaments were stone bracelets, some very thin, incised with from one to four ochre-filled concentric rings.[8]

The date for the base level with pottery at the site of Abrigo de Verdelpino in Cuenca, Meseta, central Spain is quite beyond expectations—7950 ± 150 B.P., that is, before the middle of the 7th millennium B.C. The pottery is plain. The lithics of the same level are considered to be Magdalenian, continuing Upper Paleolithic traditions.[9] This dubious date will have to be confirmed in the future by similar finds in other sites. Upper layers of Verdelpino date from several millennia later.

In coastal Portugal, sea- and freshwater oriented economies continued from the Mesolithic well into the 7th and 6th millennia B.C. Cardial pottery reached central Portugal around the middle of the 6th millennium B.C., and the stratified caves indicate a long-lasting Epicardial (late Cardial) period.[10]

So far we have mentioned stratified cave sites in which excellent sequences of cultural development are evidenced through the Mesolithic, the "Mesoneolithic," and the Neolithic. There are also a few open-air sites, but the village size, plan, and architecture are insufficiently known. Some of the open-air sites contain circular huts with cobblestone floors and hearths in association with Cardial pottery. Unfortunately, some sites have been covered by the rise of sea level.[11] The earliest of the known submerged villages are at Île Corrège (6772 B.P.) and Le Baratin, Vaucluse (6600 B.P., i.e., early to middle 6th millennium B.C.). On present evidence it appears that at least a thousand years separated the first larger agricultural villages from Mesoneolithic activities, suggesting that this was a slow process of acculturation by the local Mesolithic people.

The revelation of this long process of development between the Epipaleolithic and the Neolithic has inspired new insights into the chronology of the

Levantine rock art of southeastern Spain (spread from Catalonia to Murcia). This art has no firm chronology. The possibility now arises of connecting this so-called "dynamic stylized style," in which animals—cattle, red deer, fallow deer, ibex, boar—and hunting scenes dominate, with the Mesolithic and Mesoneolithic periods.[12] (FIGURE 6–2) A second stage, characterized by a schematic style of a more symbolic nature, should belong to the Neolithic. (FIGURE 6–3) Schematic paintings actually are known from a Neolithic inland cave site at Cariguela del Piñar (Granada).[13]

FIGURE 6–2

1

2

3

4

FIGURE 6–2 Examples of the dynamic style of rock art in southeastern Spain. (1) Hunting scene and (2–4) hunters equipped with bows and arrows. Probably Mesoneolithic, c. 8th–7th mill. B.C. (1) Racó de Nando (Els Covarjos), Benasal, Castellón; (2, 3) Cueva Saltadora, Valltorta; (4) Mas d'en Josep, Valltorta.

FIGURE 6–3

FIGURE 6–3 A ritual scene with groups of dancing females and males. On the left, an image that appears to be an exaggerated phallus. "Barranco" de Los Grajos, Cieza, Murcia, SE Spain. Probably Early Neolithic, 6th mill. B.C.

Pottery Typology

For the Early Neolithic of the west Mediterranean, pottery is the most diagnostic fossil for insight into chronological sequences, in contrast to stone tools which changed more slowly. The earliest pottery at Cova Fosca from the second half of the 7th millennium B.C. was egg shaped and not shell impressed. The succeeding fully agricultural society of the 6th millennium B.C. is characterized by Cardial and Epicardial (late Cardial) pottery. (FIGURE 6–4) A stratigraphy of cave sites in southern France and eastern Spain has revealed a long and gradual evolution throughout most of the 6th millennium B.C. It should be noted, however, that what is understood as Cardial and Epicardial pottery includes not only the shell-impressed but also that decorated by other methods: applied cordons, channelling, punctuations, incisions, beaded decoration, and other techniques. Archeologists have observed three stages: 1. *Ancient*—within the first half of the 6th millennium B.C.—when cardium impressions dominated but plastic decoration was also used. 2. *Middle*—in the middle of the 6th millennium B.C.—when shell impressions diminished and pots were variously decorated by incisions, channelling, plastic-impressed cordons, punctuate ornament, and dot designs; pot forms are spherical, but necked vases also appear. 3. *Late*—at the end of the 6th millennium B.C.—when shell impressions are very rare. Typical decorations are combinations of vertical and horizontal cordons bordered by impressions. White incrustation is used and spherical forms continue to be dominant. Necked vases with parallels in the Fiorano type in northern Italy are known. During the succeeding phase, regarded as transitional to the Middle Neolithic, ornament entirely disappeared.[14] (FIGURE 6–5A) This plain pottery with characteristic vertical tunnelled handles, called the Montbolo type, centered in the Mediterranean Pyrenees and in Catalonia, provides an obvious transitional link between the Cardial Neolithic and the Middle Neolithic Chassean culture.

FIGURE 6–4

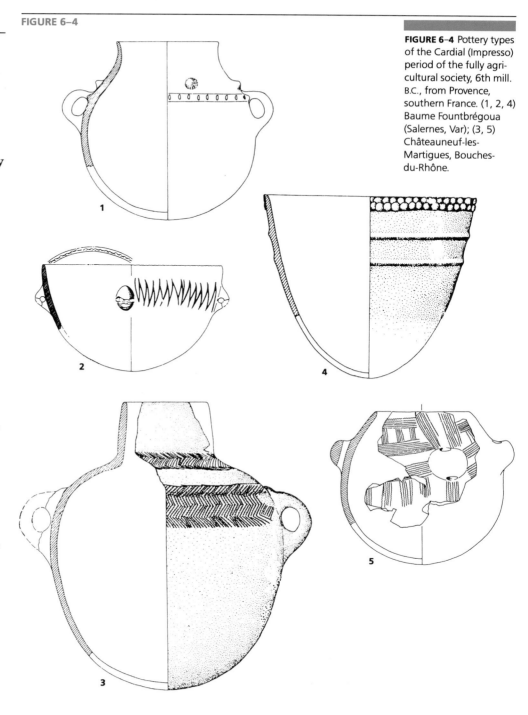

FIGURE 6–4 Pottery types of the Cardial (Impresso) period of the fully agricultural society, 6th mill. B.C., from Provence, southern France. (1, 2, 4) Baume Fountbrégoua (Salernes, Var); (3, 5) Châteauneuf-les-Martigues, Bouches-du-Rhône.

FIGURE 6–5A

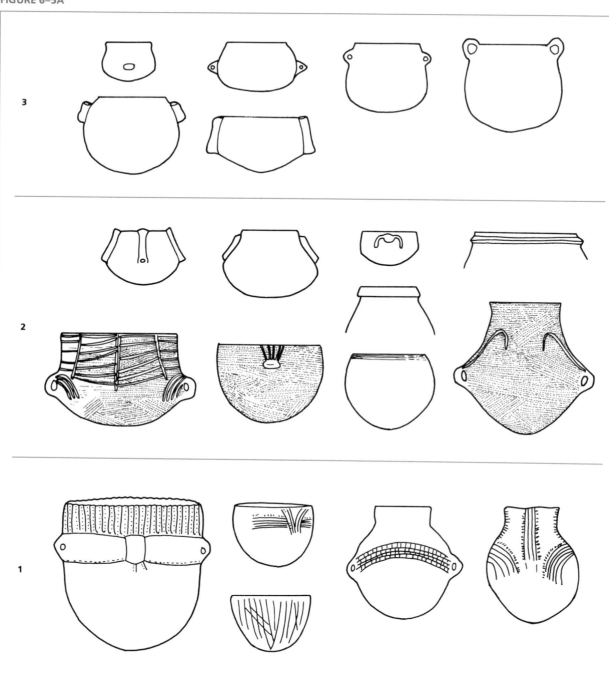

FIGURE 6–5A Pottery sequence from early Neolithic Epicardial stages (1, 2) to early Middle Neolithic period and (3) to Montbolo phase in Catalonia, northeastern Spain. Late 6th to early 5th mill. B.C. (1) Examples from caves Reclau Viver, El Toll, des Lladres, and Puig Mascaro site; (2) cave Pénédes and d'El Toll; (3) Montbolo.

FIGURE 6–5B In Liguria and S France the Epicardial pottery layers were overlain with Middle Neolithic layers typified by square-mouth pots. The illustrated examples are from the stratified cave of Arene Candide, Liguria; end 5th and early 4th mill. B.C.

The above typology cannot be applied to the inland regions of France (Pyrenees, Aude, Causses, and Aquitaine) where regional variations of ceramic types are contemporary with Cardial wares elsewhere. A good example is the pottery from the lowest level of one of the major sites, Roucadour, near the Lot River, with the date of 6650 B.P. (i.e., within the first half of the 6th millennium B.C.). This pottery is coarse, coil built, badly fired, with pointed bottoms. The same type was also found in a number of other sites.[15]

Early Agriculture in Northern France

Research in the area of Brittany has been focused on the megalithic monuments that dominate the area, and as a result our knowledge of other factors regarding the Neolithic in Brittany is not very complete. It appears that in addition to the gathering of shell fish, around the mid- to late 6th millennium B.C., people of northwestern France may have domesticated some animals. The remains of domesticated dogs, sheep, and goats were found in the levels of Teviec and cattle at Hoedic (Morbihan).[16] Moreover it appears that land clearance took place below the megalithic monuments at Dissignac (Loire-Atlantique), Île Carn (Finistère), and Les Fouaillages (Guernsey, Channel Islands), since cereal pollens have been detected.

Much of eastern and northern France as far as Normandy and the Channel Islands is the westernmost extension of the Linearbandkeramik (LBK) culture discussed in chapter 2.

The Middle and Late Neolithic

The development of a post-Cardial culture in France is represented by the Chassée culture; in Switzerland by Cortaillod; in northern Italy by Square-mouthed Pottery period, followed by Lagozza; and in the Barcelona area of Spain by pit graves in stone cists. The megalithic tombs of these cultures, described in the next section, are spread along the Atlantic coast. All of these culture groups in a broad sense are interrelated; in fact archeologists often consider Chassée-Lagozza-Cortaillod as one culture. This is an advanced stage of Neolithic culture in which people's lifestyle is increasingly settled and more intensively horticultural. Their ceramics and lithics are technologically advanced.

The cultural continuum can best be observed in a series of stratified caves which contain Cardial, Epicardial, early and advanced Chassée (in France) or Square-mouthed Pottery and Lagozza materials (in Liguria). (FIGURE 6–5B) Radiocarbon dating places this stage in the 5th and early 4th millennia B.C. (TABLES 19, 20)

The Chassée Culture in France

Almost all of France was occupied in the 5th and 4th millennia B.C. by the Chassée, a very homogenous culture showing little variation over time and geographical regions. (TABLE 19) The name is after the Camp de Chassée, a late Chassée hilltop site in the French department of Saône-et-Loire.

Earliest Chassée

The earliest Chassée sites, termed "proto-Chassée," are found west of the Rhône. It is assumed that this culture spread up the Rhône, colonized Grands Causes, and eventually reached the Paris basin and Jura-Burgundy. The population and number of habitation sites constantly increased. A more intensive agriculture is indicated by finds of emmer wheat, bread wheat, barley, beans, and vetch as well as by stone querns, grinding stones, and flint blades with silica sheen. An increase of stone

FIGURE 6–5B

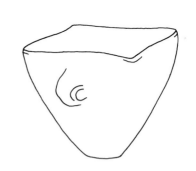
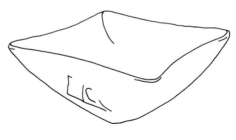
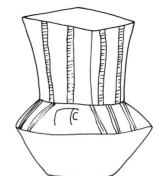

axes suggests increased felling activity for fields. However, people did not abandon hunting, fishing, and collecting of molluscs.

Stone Artifacts and Trade

Flint arrowheads used for hunting (transverse, lozenge, and leaf shaped) appear in almost all Chassée sites. The fine quality blond flint used abundantly for tools is presumed to have come from local sources in the Lower Rhône basin. Hard stone from the Pyrenees was used for the production of massive stone tools, and a variety of colored stones such as greenstone, metalasite, eclosite, and pyroxenite was imported from the Alpine foothills via Liguria. The variscite (callais) used extensively for the production of beads was mined near Barcelona at Can Tintorè à Gavà. Obsidian was imported from Monte Arci in Sardinia and also from Lipari.[17] Excavations at Plussulien in the center of Brittany, a source of dolerite used for stone axes, have revealed several phases of exploitation throughout the 4th millennium B.C. Axes made of dolerite have been traced over much of France and into southwest Britain.

Aside from the production of obsidian tools and stone axes, Chasseans excelled in carving highly polished balls, possibly of ritual value, and bracelets of limestone, which are found in a significant number of sites in southern France.

Pottery

Chassean pottery is a well burnished or even glossy ware, usually of dark brownish slate color or a beige tending toward yellow or brick red. The main shapes are low bowls, carinated bowls, and baggy jars with rounded bases. The addition of ground calcite or quartz as temper to the paste gave it a distinctive texture. More evolved pottery forms included a great variety of new silhouettes achieved through the use of shoulders and carinations, globular pots with cylindrical necks, and dishes with large flat horizontal rims. The latter had the appearance of a shallow soup bowl, and the wide rims were usually beautifully decorated in geometric design.

These were more abundant in southern France. Hollow stands or supports for the round based pottery were a feature of Chassée culture. They were either round or square and were decorated very elaborately in geometric designs. The technique of fine incision was used to create geometric patterns filled with lines or dots, bands of triangles, zigzags, rhombs, and checkerboard motifs. Sometimes red or white color was rubbed in to give an encrusted effect. The decoration was applied after firing. Lugs and handles on Chassée ware gave it a distinct flavor. Characteristic lugs on early pottery were perforated so that half of the perforation was in the lug and half penetrated into the belly of the pot. Handles resembling pan pipes, and so named for this reason, made a timid appearance in early Chassée times and burgeoned in the later period. Another type of handle resembling a series of cartridge-like vertical hollow tubes became very popular. These two types can be regarded as diagnostic of Chassée culture. They were found mainly on collared bowls and bottles and were typical of later phases of the culture. (FIGURE 6–6)

Villages and Houses

Open-air settlements on the edge of lagoons, former marshes, or terraces vary in size. Some of them occupy four to five hectares, others extend over a territory of 20 or even 30 hectares. One of the largest excavated sites is Saint Michel-du-Touch, located on a promontory of the Garonne River, district of Toulouse. The rectangular houses were about 12 meters long and 2.5 meters wide and had cobbled floors. In Saint Michel-du-Touch more than 300 cobbled floors were discovered which belong to various periods of the site's duration (radiocarbon dates, 5500–4500 B.P., indicate a period of 1,000 years). (TABLE 19) Their walls may have been of pisé or wattle and daub.[18] Two parallel palisades, 50 meters apart have been discovered cutting off the tip of the promontory. This large village could have been a regional center. Other villages revealed small semisubterranean round structures.

Huts with cobbled floors continued to be built in the Later Neolithic. A village of nine huts has been excavated at Dorio, Felines-Minervois, in southern France, which belongs to the Ferrières culture group spread in the departments of Herault, Gard, and Ardèche. The huts were small, rectangular in shape, with large posts at their corners, ranging in size from 5 × 2.40 m to 5.8 × 2.80 m.[19]

Stone-cist Graves

The stone-cist graves in pits, *sepulcros de fosa*, dated to the 4th and early 3rd millennia B.C., great numbers of which were excavated in the Barcelona area of Catalonia, contained plain jars and bowls, some with tubular handles and buttons. Their shapes have close parallels in the Chassée and Lagozza groups. There were the usual grave goods: bone and shell beads, flint and obsidian nuclei, polished axes, and trapezoidal flint arrowheads.

In southern France, the dead were buried either in a crouched or extended position in oval pits which were sometimes lined with cobbles. Grave goods were few, mostly vases and items of symbolic significance. In one woman's grave from St. Michel-du-Touch, four hedgehog jaws were found next to a vase with a tiny cup inside it. Another grave yielded a pierced boar incisor.

Clay figurines and larger sculptures from the Chassée layers are few; they do not appear by the hundreds as in southeastern Europe. There may have been a woodcarving tradition of statuettes which have not survived. Occasionally, large stone statues are found. One of the most impressive, 50 cm high, was carved of arkose, a local rock, from Capdenacle-Haut in the province of Lot, dated to c. 4000 B.C. The figure has large breasts, a V sign above her breasts, a round mouth and round eyes. Her enormous hands are tri-fingered. These features allow us to classify her as a Bird Goddess with life-giving, nourishing, regenerating functions (this sculpture is reproduced in my book, *The Language of the Goddess* (1989), fig. 50). Such excellent statues and the engraved symbols on vases and on vaguely anthropomorphic figurines of limestone speak for the existence of religious symbolism in the Chassée culture which is identical with much of the rest of Old Europe. Although the Chassée culture is pre-megalithic, such a figure as the Goddess from Capdenac-le-Haut has relatives in later stone statues standing at the entrances to the megalithic tombs of southern France of c. 3000 B.C.

Lake Shore Villages of Northern Italy and Switzerland: the Square-mouthed Pottery and Cortaillod Cultures

Villages with Square-mouth and Lagozza Pottery in the River Po Region

A number of lake shore villages have been excavated in the region of the Po River. One of the earliest is Molino Casarotto near Vicenza (Veneto) of the Square-mouthed Pottery period, dated before and around the middle of the 5th millennium B.C.[20] (TABLE 20, *bottom left*) The excavation revealed timber platforms with hearths on top. The inhabitants of this village hunted red deer and boar, fished pike and turtle, collected mussels, raised sheep and cattle, grew wheat and grapes. Another lake shore village, farther west in the Po valley, was excavated on the little island Isolino Virginia in Lake Varese, Lombardy. Here earth platforms reinforced with beams and piles were discovered. This settlement also belongs to the Square-mouthed Pottery period.[21] Modest lake shore villages continued into the middle and late 4th millennium B.C., known as the Lagozza period, named after a village discovered in 1875 situated in a small, now dry lake near Besnate in the province of Varese. This site is a roughly rectangular area of wooden piles, about 100 × 300 m in size. Barley, lentils, flax, and four types of wheat, as well as wild nuts, berries like the Cornel cherry, beech mast, and acorns were used by the inhabitants.[22] Pottery, whose fine ware was black burnished, was generally related to Chassean. (TABLE 20, *upper right*: Lagozza chronology)

FIGURE 6–6

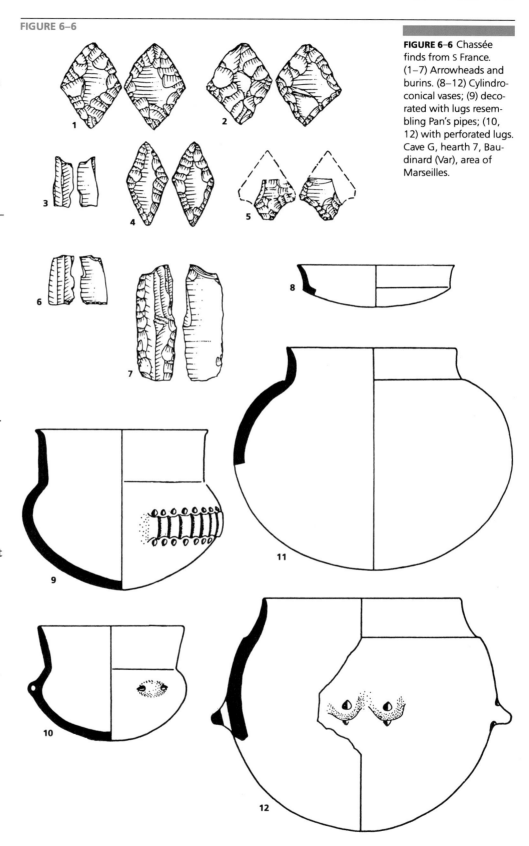

FIGURE 6–6 Chassée finds from S France. (1–7) Arrowheads and burins. (8–12) Cylindro-conical vases; (9) decorated with lugs resembling Pan's pipes; (10, 12) with perforated lugs. Cave G, hearth 7, Baudinard (Var), area of Marseilles.

FIGURE 6–7

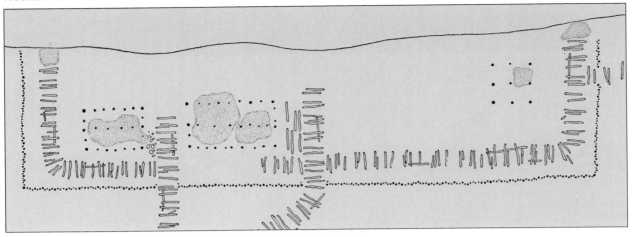

a

b

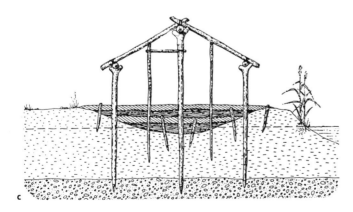

c

FIGURE 6–7 Small lake shore village of pile dwellings in Switzerland. Seeberg-Burgäschi South, 37th–36th cents. B.C. (a) Plan of houses, log roads, and fence. Dots indicate vertical piles; strips, corduroy log roads; and irregular shapes in the house areas, mounds of loam and rubble; (b) reconstruction; (c) cross-section of a house showing how piles were driven into the ground.

FIGURE 6–8 Cortaillod pots with ornamental patterns cut out of birch bark and stuck on with pitch. St. Aubin (Tivoli), Lake Neuchâtel, Switzerland.

The Cortaillod Culture in Switzerland

One of the best researched groups of lake shore dwellers is Cortaillod (named after the locality on the Lake Neuchâtel) in western and central Switzerland and eastern France. It belongs to the Alpine forested foothill region, a naturally bounded geographical province. On both sides of the Alps, small groups of people settled glacial lake shores and river valleys. Before a Neolithic economy appeared here, the Alpine foothills were occupied by Tardenoisian hunters and fishers also living in a wooded environment. These local Mesolithic peoples probably adapted a Neolithic way of life during the 4th millennium B.C., but the Chassean influences should also be accounted for. Stone-cist graves with contracted skeletons excavated at Lake Geneva (cemetery of Chamblandes), and in the province of Valais (Colombey Barmaz cemeteries I and II), as well as in the Rhône valley have revealed a small statured Mediterranean population.[23]

The first synthesis of Cortaillod site materials was attempted by Victorine von Gonzenbach in 1949.[24] The most important sites were excavated, however, in the 1950s: Egolzwil near Zurich, central Switzerland, by Emil Vogt in 1950–51 and by René Wyss in 1956,[25] and Lake Seeberg-Burgäschi South in the Swiss midlands between Bern and Zurich by Hansjürgen Müller-Beck of the Bern Historical Museum (1950–63). The Burgäschi materials are published in nine volumes by the Bern Historical Museum with the participation of many specialists, 1965–69.[26]

The Problem of "Pile Dwellings"

In older archeological works, the Swiss lake dwellers were among the most important Neolithic peoples of Europe. The idea that they lived in pile dwellings goes back to the work of Ferdinand Keller 150 years ago (1854) who put forth the view that their houses were built on piles in shallow water. This idea persisted until E. Vogt published a study on the pile dwellings in 1955.[27] His work shows that the idea has no basis in fact. The settlements were shore villages of small rectangular houses and were over dry or swampy ground. Those that are now in the water, accessible only in very dry summers, were made when the level of the lakes was lower. House floors are often logs laid parallel and are sometimes in more than one stratum, perhaps due to sinking into swampy soil. Hearths are also sometimes stratified. If these house floors and hearths had once stood above the water on platforms and had later fallen down, they would not be found intact by the excavators. The best explanation for the piles that were supposed to hold up the platforms is that they were driven down to the hard layer of clay to give stability in the rather soft ground. The fact that some villages were abandoned and covered by a layer of peat merely means that the water level rose enough to make the site too damp to live in.

The Seeberg-Burgäschi South site is located on the south shore of Burgäschi Lake, which is a third of a mile in diameter. The distribution of 3,000 piles of alder, ash, and oak defined a settlement measured approximately 50 × 10 yards wide. Three structures were indicated with loam floors which were enclosed by a palisade fence. Log roads connected each of the structures to the outside of the enclosure. (FIGURE 6–7) Seven and eleven houses were discovered in Egolzwil settlements.

Pottery

The basic types of Cortaillod ceramics were bag-shaped pots, round-based bowls or beakers, and dishes. There was almost no ornamentation. In the later phase, however, some pots had ornamental patterns cut out of birch bark and stuck on with pitch. (FIGURE 6–8) Birch pitch had many different uses: to fix flint blades in their handles, to secure arrowheads to their shafts, and to mend broken pots whose cracks were sealed over by strips of birch bark. Pieces of baskets and wooden vessels were also preserved. These wet sites ideally preserved many perishable objects.

FIGURE 6–8

Agriculture and Tools

Agriculture is attested to by wheat, barley, millet, peas, and lentils as well as carbonized apples (found cut in half for drying), pears, and plums. In several lake-dwelling sites, such as Wangen, Bodman, and Mondsee, apples have been found that are much larger than the crab, and it is agreed that they do not represent a wild type. (The Mondsee type was found to contain an anthocyanin that is present in cultivated apples only.) In Sipplingen (Lake Constance), three sizes of plums occurred, the largest of which is suggestive of a cultivated form. Another important cultivated plant was flax. Opium poppy (*papaver somniferum*) was found in Robenhausen, Sipplingen, Federsee, and other sites, and it must have been of great significance judging from its frequency. Field cabbage (*brassica campestris*) was identified in Burgäschi.

Querns, sickle flints, and even wooden sickles with the flints set into them, as well as many wooden tools and utensils, were found. (FIGURES 6–9 to 6–13) The Burgäschi-South settlement alone yielded approximately 200 wooden objects from 26 tool categories which represent most of the techniques and activities possible in the European Neolithic. Woodworking is represented by axes, adzes, chisels, and wedges, accompanied by mallets and hammers, which are not used solely to work wood. Quite numerous also are the agricultural tools, not only simple hoes but also more refined wooden spades, plough-like furrow sticks ("hand ards") and harvesting knives with stalk catchers. Independent categories are formed by unspecialized knives with hafting in long and short handles or awls that could be used for working leather or fabrics. Quite numerous also are throwing sticks, bows, arrows, lances, javelins, and short wooden projectile points. The percentage of household items such as vessels of different shapes, bowls, mugs, cups, ladles, spoons, and fire drills is comparatively large.

FIGURE 6–9

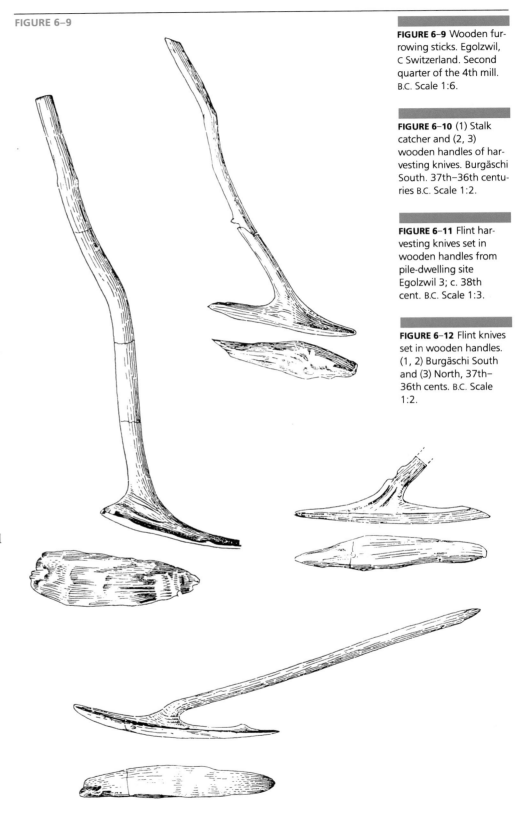

FIGURE 6–9 Wooden furrowing sticks. Egolzwil, C Switzerland. Second quarter of the 4th mill. B.C. Scale 1:6.

FIGURE 6–10 (1) Stalk catcher and (2, 3) wooden handles of harvesting knives. Burgäschi South. 37th–36th centuries B.C. Scale 1:2.

FIGURE 6–11 Flint harvesting knives set in wooden handles from pile-dwelling site Egolzwil 3; c. 38th cent. B.C. Scale 1:3.

FIGURE 6–12 Flint knives set in wooden handles. (1, 2) Burgäschi South and (3) North, 37th–36th cents. B.C. Scale 1:2.

FIGURE 6–10

FIGURE 6–11

FIGURE 6–12

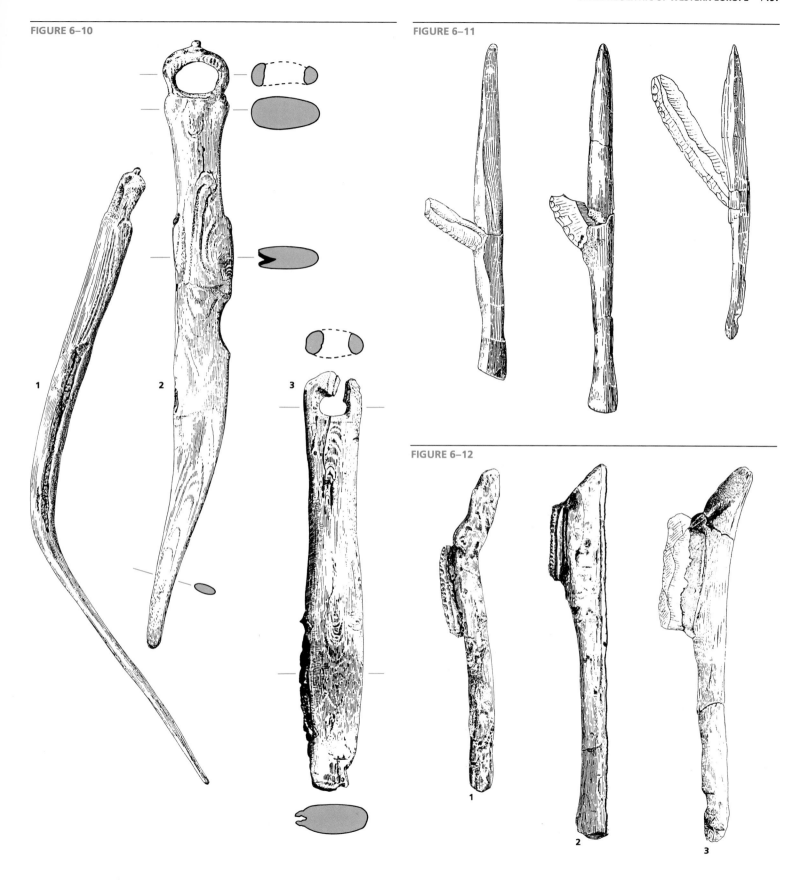

FIGURE 6–13

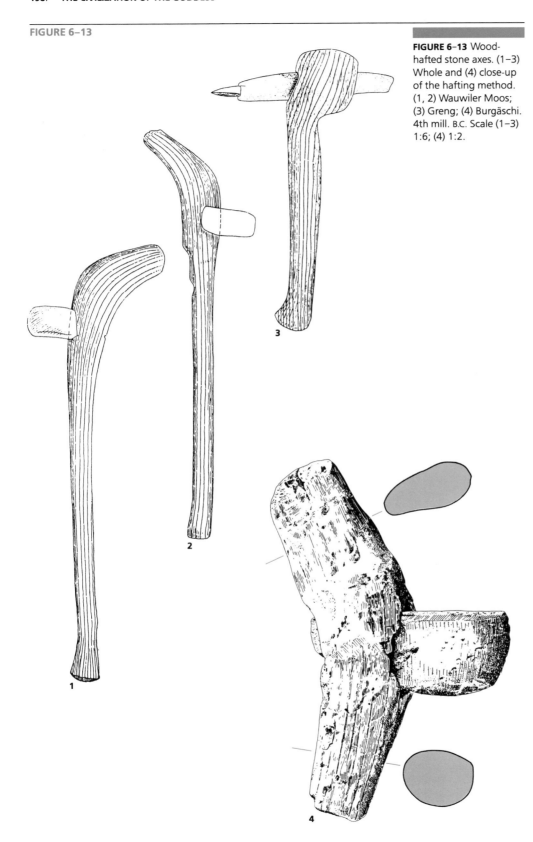

FIGURE 6–13 Wood-hafted stone axes. (1–3) Whole and (4) close-up of the hafting method. (1, 2) Wauwiler Moos; (3) Greng; (4) Burgäschi. 4th mill. B.C. Scale (1–3) 1:6; (4) 1:2.

The relative high standard of technological development documented in the wooden tools from Burgäschi-South is most impressive. A fine example is offered by the highly stressed axe handles which show good construction attained with a relatively small amount of work based on a very skillful selection of available tree materials. The same is true for the large clubs, the throwing sticks, the hand-ards, and the harvesting knives. In general, it may be stated that in all kinds of working, skill and lightness of execution was much more important than sheer force, which would have endangered the tools.

In a number of Cortaillod villages, bastmats, baskets braided in coil, strings, spools of flax yarn, clay spindle whorls, and loom weights were found.

Cattle are the predominant feature in the economy, followed by pigs, and then by sheep and goats.[28] All domestic animals were much smaller than those of settlements north and east in middle Europe. At Burgäschi, pig bones could not be identified as wild or domestic, which may indicate a process of local domestication. Animals fed on tree leaves and forest meadows in the summer, while in the winter they were kept in stalls.

From the evidence at Burgäschi, Müller-Beck deduced that the entire community consisted of no more than two or three families, perhaps three generations in lineal descent with 20 to 40 people.[29] The rather surprising discovery of a string of copper annular beads of various sizes indicates that even these culturally modest people living in small communities in the Alpine region were not isolated from European trade routes.

In Burgäschi, pollen analyses have shown that the clearing of woodland for cultivation in the vicinity of the settlement was only occasionally undertaken. This suggests that the agricultural fields may have been at some distance from the settlement; the natural vegetation was only slightly affected by the activities of the Burgäschi Lake people.

At most sites, hunting was still a valuable part of the economy. Red deer was by far the most frequent animal, with roe deer, elk, chamois, aurochs, bison, pig, horse, wolf, fox, and other forest animals also represented. Beaver, badger, bear, water birds, and fish were eaten.

Chronology

Swiss lake shore villages belong to the 4th millennium B.C. The best dated settlements are Egolzwil, Seeberg-Burgäschi, and several others.[30] (TABLE 21) Because of the existence of well-preserved oak timbers, an ideal situation was created here for the comparison of the carbon 14 contents of the samples with those dated by the application of tree-ring chronology.[31] The difference between conventional radiocarbon dates and the age value determined by dendro-chronology amounts to about 800 years. Thus, 2796 b.c. is a radiocarbon date from Burgäschi in absolute chronology which, by tree ring counting, is 3595 B.C. Burgäschi dwellings were constructed before the middle of the 4th millennium B.C. and continued for 100 to 150 years.

Megalithic Tombs of France and Iberia

The greatest concentrations are found in Portugal, in Brittany in the northwest of France, and in the Department Aveyron in the Central Massif area. (FIGURE 6–14)

Passage Graves

There are now about 50 radiocarbon dates for these monuments, both in Iberia and France, that indicate an early appearance and a duration of at least 2000 years, during the 5th, 4th, and early 3rd millennia B.C. Most of the research and dating has been done in Brittany[32] (TABLE 22), and the passage grave of Kercado near Carnac (FIGURE 6–15) has one of the earliest radiocarbon date of all megaliths, c. 4700 B.C. There are, however, a number of others that date nearly as early: Dissignac, Guennoc, Bougon (TABLE 22, distribution of dates). Kercado is particularly interesting as it not only has a menhir on top but is decorated inside with geometric designs, a hafted axe, and an anthropomorphic female

FIGURE 6–14

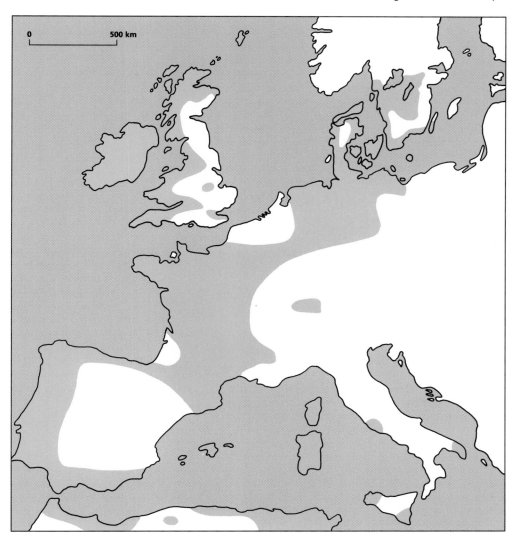

FIGURE 6–14 The distribution of megalithic graves in western Europe.

0   500 km

FIGURE 6–15

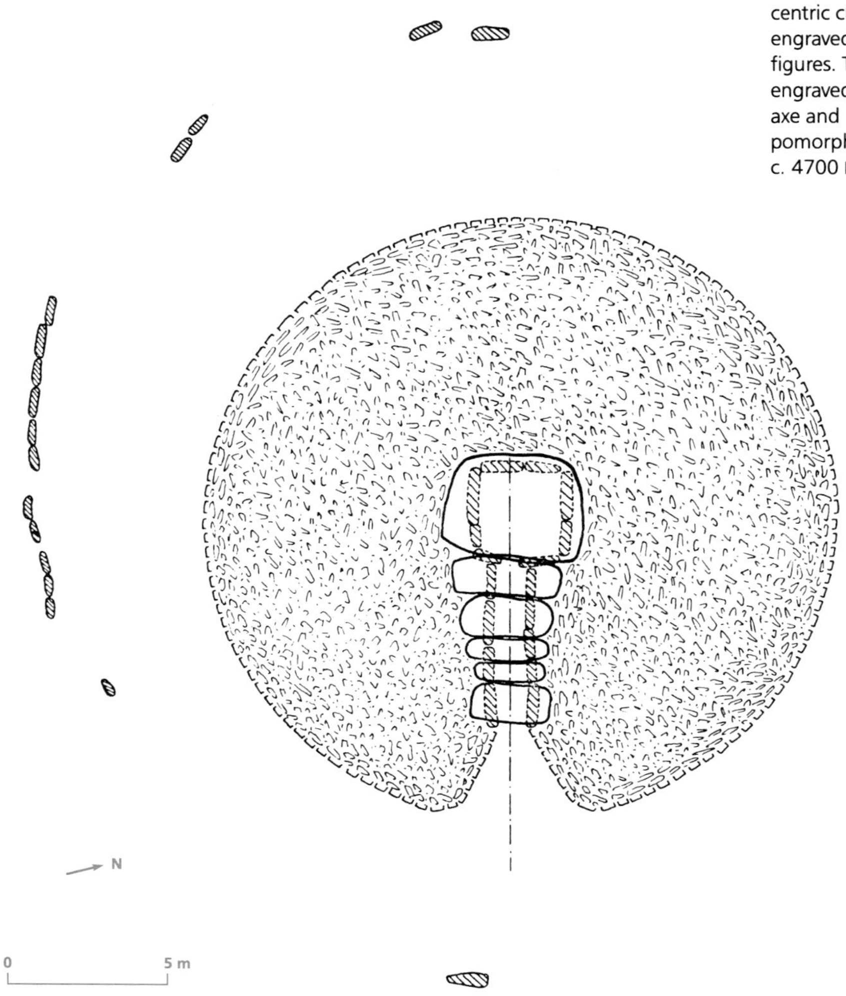

FIGURE 6–15 Passage grave built of large stones, covered with a round cairn and surrounded by a stone ring, Kercado, Carnac, Brittany. Stone slabs of the chamber and corridor were decorated with cupmarks, circles, concentric circles, and over-engraved with larger figures. The capstone is engraved with a hafted axe and roughly anthropomorphic images; c. 4700 B.C.

0   5 m

N

figure. This indicates that art work began very early in the development of these tombs.

Architecturally, passage graves are quite simple, consisting of a passage which ends in a chamber. (FIGURES 6–15, 6–16) The entire structure is covered by a mound of soil or a stone cairn. There is, however, a great deal of variation. First, a number of tombs can be found within one mound. Perhaps the best known is at Barnenez in Finistère. Here in a long cairn placed on a summit of a small promontory, eleven tombs open out to the side. (FIGURE 6–17) Barnenez was excavated from 1955 to 1968, and it was shown to have been built in two stages. The primary cairn, which is trapezoidal in shape, contained five small passage graves with entrances facing southeast. These tombs show a variety in plan with most of the chambers being corbelled, except for the central tomb, which has a huge capstone. The floors are all leveled and covered with stones. The secondary cairn contained six tombs, five of which are built of dry stone walls with the sixth built of large orthostats.[33] The primary cairn and the core of the secondary cairn are made of local dolerite found naturally within a few hundred meters. The surface of the secondary cairn, however, is of granite, the closest source being about a kilometer away. The entire cairn at Barnenez resembles a stepped pyramid and is one of the largest monuments in Brittany. (FIGURE 6–17, *bottom*)

Although Brittany has a number of mounds that contain multiple passage graves, one of particular interest, just south of Brittany, is at Dissignac near the mouth of the Loire. Built on the site of Mesolithic/Neolithic occupation, two tombs sit side by side under a single mound, Passage B aligned to the midwinter sunrise. The art work includes a multitude of hafted axes.[34]

FIGURE 6-16

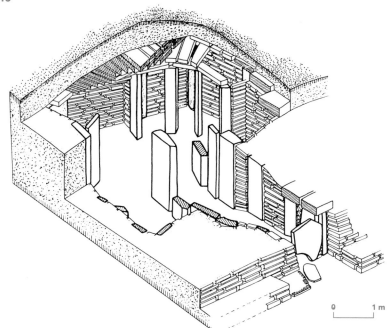

FIGURE 6-16 Isometric projection of a sub-divided chamber and a short corridor showing the interior walls and corbelled roof. La Forêt-Fouesnant near Kerléven, S Finistère, Brittany. Mid-4th mill. B.C.

FIGURE 6-17

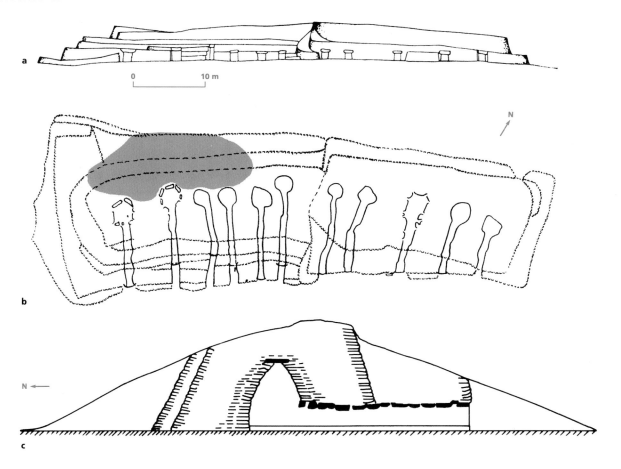

FIGURE 6-17 Cross-section (a) and plan (b) of the stepped pyramid-like mound of Barnenez including eleven passage graves (five on the right side are earlier than six on the left side). Gray-shaded area shows disturbance by quarrying. (c) Cross-section of one of the tombs indicating the corbelled roof with a large slab on the top. Barnenez, Plouézoch, NW of Morlaix, Brittany; used from the middle to the end of the 5th mill.B.C.

The earliest passage graves of the 5th millennium B.C. have circular chambers, but over time they took on a variety of shapes, with rectangular chambers appearing later than circular[35] (see fig. 6-16). Other shapes include transeptal chambers, angled (FIGURE 6-18), with lateral chambers (FIGURE 6-19), and V-shaped.

The finest example of a passage grave in France, Gavrinis, has quite simple tomb architecture with a nearly square chamber under a complex cairn, but with the most elaborate art work of any megalithic tomb in Europe (see figs. 7-128 and 7-129). Recent excavations at Gavrinis have shown that this tomb had a huge facade, 6 meters high. The adjoining rectangular edifice was covered by a circular cairn.[36] Another celebrated tomb with art work is Petit-Mont, Arzon, Morbihan, with a rectangular chamber (FIGURE 6-20), and a magnificent entrance with two juxtaposed stone pillars. Its mound was a vast trapezoid, 50 × 42 m and 10 m high.[37] Edifices in front of tombs at a number of passage graves of Brittany must have been used for funeral rituals.

Grave goods were rare since many tombs were robbed in antiquity. Exceptions are the Portugese passage graves which yielded numbers of symbolic items: Goddess's amulets made of slate plaques decorated with rows of triangles which had triangular heads with eyes (see fig. 7-120, 1, 2) cylindrical images of stone and bone with owl eyes geometrically decorated with striations, net patterns, arcs, and other motifs (see fig. 7-120, 3-6). Stone hooks (croziers) were richly decorated with similar geometric motifs (FIGURE 6-21) and so-called "pine cones" which were possibly related symbolically to phalli. (FIGURE 6-22) Both hooks and pine cones as well as Goddess's effigies must have served in graves as symbols of regeneration and life energy. They certainly were not items of prestige or rank as some archeologists continue to think.

FIGURE 6-18

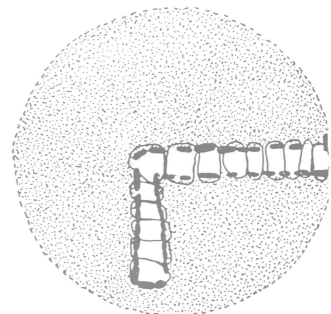

FIGURE 6-18 Plan of angled passage grave. Le Bono, Morbihan, Brittany. End 5th mill. B.C.

FIGURE 6-19

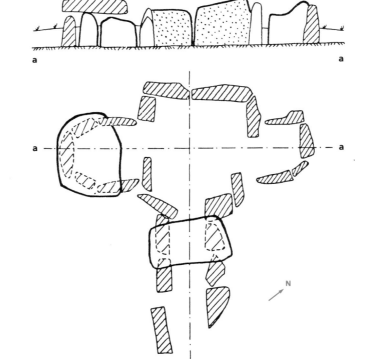

FIGURE 6-19 Cross-section and plan of passage grave with lateral chambers. Locoal-Mendor, Locqueltas, Brittany, c. 4000 B.C.

FIGURE 6–20

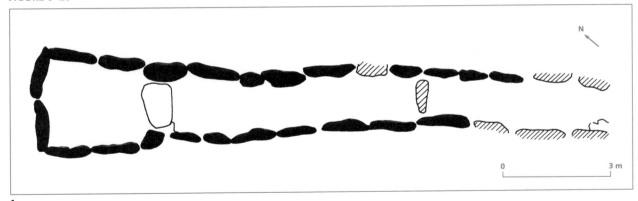

1

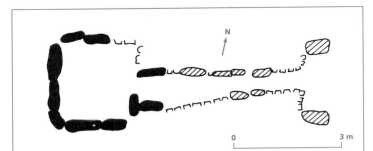

2

FIGURE **6–20** Plans of passage graves famous for their carvings on the inner walls of the corridor and chamber. Stone slabs shown in black have art work (see figs. 7–128 to 7–130). (1) Gavrinis, Larmor-Baden, Morbihan; (2) Petit-Mont, Arzon, Morbihan, Brittany. No radiocarbon dating available; possible chronology: 4000–3500 B.C.

FIGURE 6–21

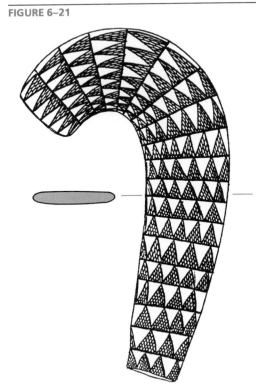

FIGURE 6–22

FIGURE **6–21** One of the many hooks made of schist plate as attributes of the Goddess and as symbols of regenerating energy, found in Portugese passage graves. They are decorated with net-patterned triangles and striated parallel lines.

FIGURE **6–22** So-called pine-cones, possibly related symbolically to phalli, decorated with a net design from passage graves of Portugal. (1) and (2) Martinho de Sintra; (3) Carenque-Baútas. Early 3rd mill. B.C.

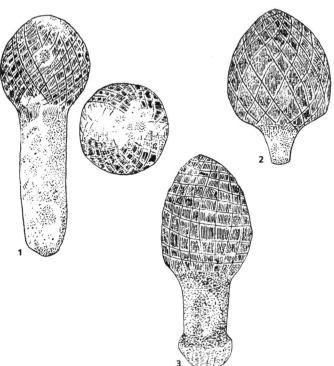

FIGURE 6–23

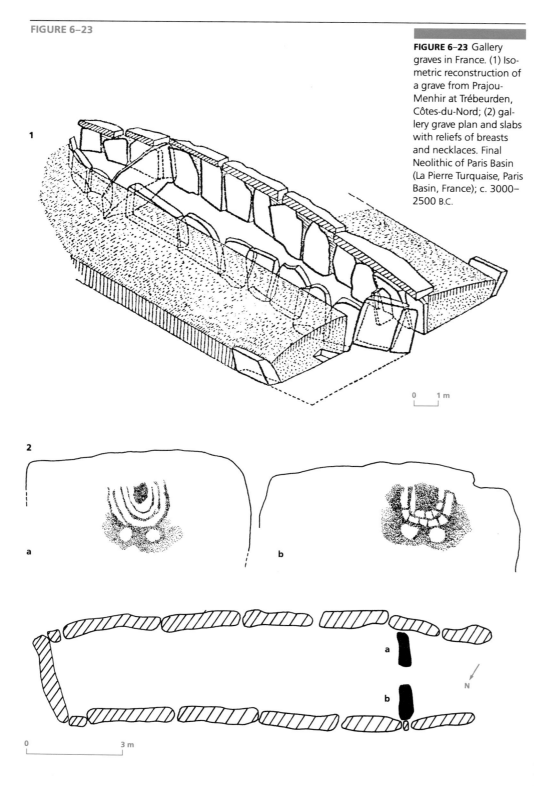

FIGURE 6–23 Gallery graves in France. (1) Isometric reconstruction of a grave from Prajou-Menhir at Trébeurden, Côtes-du-Nord; (2) gallery grave plan and slabs with reliefs of breasts and necklaces. Final Neolithic of Paris Basin (La Pierre Turquaise, Paris Basin, France); c. 3000–2500 B.C.

Gallery Graves and Menhirs

The "gallery graves" or *allées couvertes* are a later development of the megalithic tomb type, dating to the late 4th and early 3rd millennia B.C. These have an elongated room built of massive boulders and no chambers. (FIGURE 6–23)

Menhirs that stand alone are another type of megalithic monument. They are not tombs but are often found in conjunction with tombs. For example, a menhir still stands just outside the entrance of the angled passage grave Les Pierres Plates. Evidence throughout Old Europe indicates that menhirs, mostly in the guise of owls, were statues representing the Goddess of Death and Regeneration.

The largest known menhir is Le Grand Menhir Brisé at Locmariaquer in Brittany. This enormous stone would have stood about 17 m when erect and weighs nearly 350 tons. Moreover, it is not of local stone; the nearest source is almost 4 kilometers away. Like many other menhirs, it is smoothed and shaped. A. Thom and A. S. Thom have claimed it to be a foresight for long distance astronomical alignments.[38] Like many other menhirs, it is clearly associated with a now nearly destroyed mound and chamber, but it is also only a few yards from the extant passage grave of La Table des Marchands.

Los Millares Passage Tombs of Southeastern Spain

Circular chambers with a short corridor covered with a round earthen mound surrounded by stone rings are found in Almeria, southeastern Spain, which continued throughout the 4th and early 3rd millennia B.C. They are known as the Los Millares type, named after the largest cemetery at Los Millares where at least 80 passage tombs were found near a long-lived settlement.[39] (FIGURE 6–24) Deep, red-polished bowls and jars found in some chambers are characteristically decorated with symbols of regeneration. Outstanding is the oculi motif representing the numinous regenerating eyes of the Goddess. (FIGURE 6–25)

FIGURE 6–24

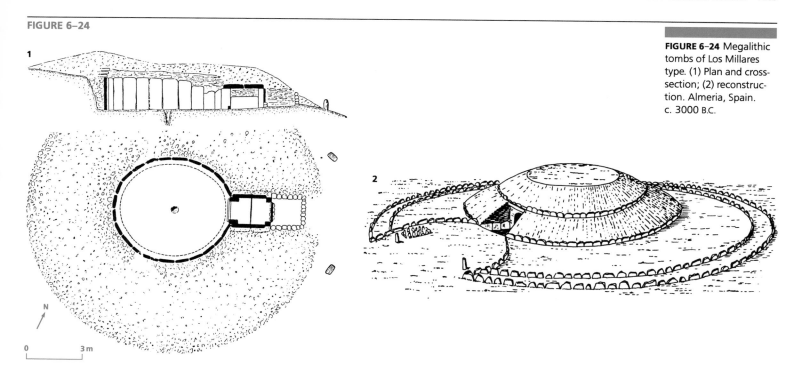

FIGURE 6–24 Megalithic tombs of Los Millares type. (1) Plan and cross-section; (2) reconstruction. Almeria, Spain. c. 3000 B.C.

FIGURE 6–25

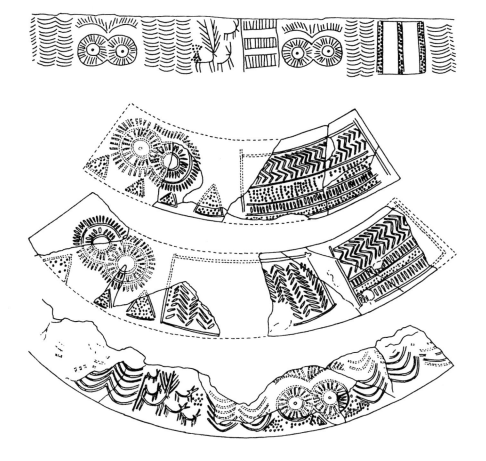

FIGURE 6–25 Symbolic design on vases from Los Millares megalithic tombs (shown extended). The oculi motif (Owl Goddess's eyes) are associated with antlered stags and other horned animals, triangles, hourglass, and rows of parallel lines, curved lines, zigzags, and dots.

The Neolithic in England and Ireland

By 4500–4000 B.C. a Neolithic economy was firmly established in England and Ireland although the actual process of change from the Mesolithic is not well known. Alasdair Whittle has argued that the central European Linearbandkeramik culture played a major role in the Neolithic colonization.[40] There can be little question that some aspects of it had to be imported from the continent as there were no wild cereal indigenes on the islands, nor wild sheep. Wild cattle were present on the British mainland but not in Ireland, which did, however, have wild pigs. The early domestic animals were smaller than their wild cousins, suggesting the importation of already domesticated animals and not the domestication of wild ones. There is no clear evidence of Neolithic sites overlaying Mesolithic ones as in Spain and France, which leads to the assumption that incoming people brought the new way of life.

Settlements

The earliest Neolithic dates for these islands come from Ireland at Ballynagilly, County Tyrone, from a hearth associated with pottery, around 4500 B.C. The earliest date for the British mainland is c. 4350 B.C. which comes from Broome Heath, Ditchingham, Norfolk.

Ballynagilly, which has been the subject of long term excavation,[41] provides good evidence for the earliest type of Neolithic houses. A small rectangular house was found here with split plank walls, the earliest found in these islands.[42] Within Britain, similar houses built of planks or timber have been found at a number of sites.[43]

By around 4000 B.C., isolated farmsteads existed in parts of both England and Ireland. Larger areas were being settled. The area around Lough Gur, County Limerick, provides very good evidence for settlement, and at the Knockadoon site, the remains of at least ten houses, both rectangular and round, which appear to be contemporary, have come to sight. The radiocarbon dates for

FIGURE 6–26A

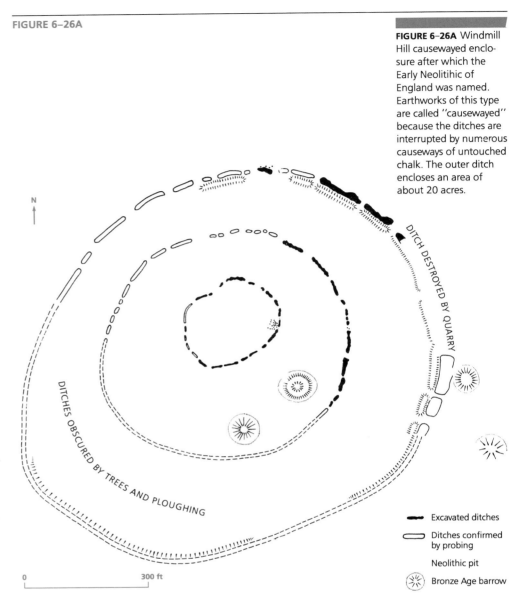

Excavated ditches

Ditches confirmed by probing

Neolithic pit

Bronze Age barrow

FIGURE 6–26A Windmill Hill causewayed enclosure after which the Early Neolithic of England was named. Earthworks of this type are called "causewayed" because the ditches are interrupted by numerous causeways of untouched chalk. The outer ditch encloses an area of about 20 acres.

Knockadoon are: 4690 ±240 B.P., calibrated to be 3980–2710 B.C. (D-41); and 4410 ±240 B.P. calibrated at 3690–2460 B.C. (D-40).[44] Further indication of settlement and land distribution in Ireland comes from work being done in the surveying and excavation of field walls that were built prior to the growth of peat.[45]

Quite a different situation is found in the Orkneys in Scotland later in the Neolithic where several settlements of connecting houses have been found. Skara Brae is the best example. Here, seven stone houses built into the midden are connected by passageways. An additional house (No. 8) stands alone, and although it contains a hearth and built-in cupboards, it lacks the beds and dressers typical of all other houses. Because of the amount of flint and chert flakes, it was suggested by V. Gordon Childe that this was a workshop.[46] The Links of Noltland is another example of this type of village in the Orkneys and it, too, has one separate house, probably a religious structure. Here, remodeling had occurred, and this house was carefully filled with a number of artifacts including "numerous skulls, a completely articulated skeleton of an otter and large wedges of compacted fish and rodent bones with no midden admixture. Lying on the rubble infill of the main chamber were two cattle skulls and an apparently articulated eagle skeleton."[47]

Causewayed Enclosures—Henges, Rings, Cursuses

The field monuments with the early dates are causewayed enclosures which are roughly oval and surrounded by one to four or more concentric but not continuous ditches. It is from the enclosure at Windmill Hill (FIGURE 6–26A) which produced a great deal of early Neolithic material, that the Early Neolithic of England was named. These enclosures are concentrated on the chalklands of central southern England and have recently been found also in Ireland. The ditches are certainly not fortifications of settlements. The few banks that survive are more continuous than the ditches, indicating that they may have

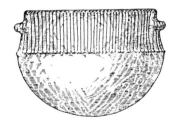
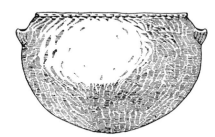
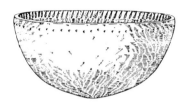
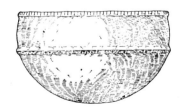
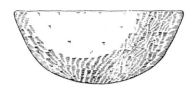
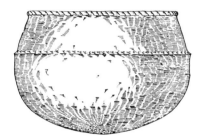

FIGURE 6–26B

FIGURE 6–26B Pottery types from Windmill Hill.

been the more important feature, while the ditches were only quarries for the banks.[48] The ditches have almost vertical sides and U-shaped bottoms with banks on the inside. These enclosures range in size from three to four acres, as at Coombe Hill, Sussex, to 19 to 20 acres at Hambledon Hill, Dorset, or 20 to 21 acres at Windmill Hill itself.[49] Timber constructions have been found within a number of enclosures. A timber gate was found only at Whitehawk, but at Hembury and Orsett, Essex, posts were set into the bank. At Orsett there was evidence of an impressive timber entrance.[50]

Within the ditches human and animal bones, pottery, large quantities of food remains, and flint and bone tools have been found. Most of the bones are of cattle, then pigs, sheep, goats, and dogs. (FIGURE 6–26B) There are also a few bones of red and roe deer. Large quantities of bones, many split for marrow extractions, were pushed into ditches. There is also evidence of careful burial of caches of animal bones as well as whole animals. Most human bones are disarticulated, but in some whole skeletons were found.[51] At Staines, two burials of presumably Neolithic date were found. The first was an inhumation of a woman in her mid-thirties, and the second was a cremation, also possibly a female in her thirties.[52]

Various theories have been advanced for the use of the causewayed enclosures. The most widely accepted put forward by Smith[53] is that they were some kind of meeting place, perhaps for ritual and trade purposes. Drewett makes a strong case for the causewayed enclosures being places where the dead were exposed, and through erosion bones and grave offerings were pushed into the ditches. Animal bones speak for rituals including sacrifices.[54] Most causewayed enclosures date to the 4th millennium B.C. Continental enclosures from the Lengyel and Linearbandkeramik cultures date from the 5th millennium B.C. and from the Funnel-necked Beaker culture, from the 4th millennium B.C. (FIGURE 6–27)

Ancient Britain, particularly southern England and Wales, is exceptionally rich in enclosures—henges with standing stones made from natural boulders or quarried stones, or with timber rings. Altogether, no fewer than one thousand of them are known. Some are truly prodigious masterpieces, such as the now famous Stonehenge, Avebury, Woodhenge. Some fifty of these circular or elliptical monuments have, alongside,

mysterious gigantic cursus earthworks. These are linear features, composed of two parallel ditches and banks of very great length, often of one or two kilometers, and sometimes of up to four kilometers or more.

The near-perfect circles, ellipses, or egg shapes of these enclosures have intrigued scholars for decades. Alexander Thom argued that the Neolithic planners must have understood the principle of the Pythagorean triangle two thousand years before Pythagoras, otherwise the perfect flattened circles and perfect ellipses could not have been prepared.[55] Lunar and solar observances have also been accorded a significant role in the building of these monuments. Other solutions to the origin of perfect shapes have also been proposed. As explained by Terrence Meaden in his just-published work, their geometries could also be linked to the realm of meteorology in which circles are created in grass and crops by vortices of whirling wind. Circles, ellipses, and cursuses were then observed and marked by Neolithic farmers, and were held sacred as manifestations of the Goddess's power.[56]

FIGURE 6–27

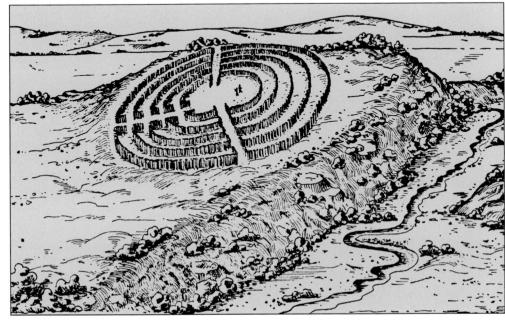

FIGURE 6–27 Close parallels to Windmill Hill and other enclosures are known from the continent. The illustrated example with five concentric rings of timber palisades is from Quenstedt, central Germany, of the TRB culture; 4th mill. B.C. Reconstruction.

Flint Mining

Flint mining was an important industry. By 4200 B.C., mining is in evidence at Church Hill, Findon, Sussex. Despite the fact that flint is ubiquitous south of the Wash in eastern England, the superior flint lies below the chalk surface. Sometimes it is only about a meter deep, as at Harrow Hill, Sussex, but at Grimes Grave in Norfolk, shafts were dug to a depth of 15 meters.[57] Evidence of ladders has been found at Cissbury, Sussex, and Grimes Grave in addition to steps cut into the shafts. Intricate tunnelling went on at both Grimes Grave and Harrow Hill. Flint nodules were chipped at the mine site and sent on to their ultimate destination. Flint tools were homogeneous from Cornwall to East Anglia.[58]

In Ireland, the only good flint, as well as porcellanite, is on the Antrim coast where it is plentiful in the cliffs and along the shore. In other areas of Ireland, there is some low-grade flint from glacial drift. When flint was unavailable, chert and quartz were used for tools.

Grimes Grave gives us a glimpse of Neolithic religion in the form of a female figurine beside a chalk phallus. These items were found along with a pile of flint amassed in the form of a triangle with a chalk cup in the base of the triangle opposite the figurine. These were all placed in a spent shaft and are clearly a religious feature that must be accepted even by the most intransigent doubters. What is remarkable is the parallel found in east-central European copper mines where, for example at Rudna Glava in Yugoslavia, exceptionally beautiful pottery and a container with a ram head, sacred animal of the Bird Goddess, were found in spent shafts of the Vinča culture c. 5000–4500 B.C. The Goddess very likely was patroness of crafts including metallurgy and flint tool making (see Metallurgy, Trade, and Crafts in chap. 3).

Axe Factories and Axe Symbolism

In addition to flint mining there were numerous stone-axe factories, that is, places where axes were roughed out and then sent elsewhere for polishing.

Hoards of polished stone axes have been found along with what are clearly ritual axes made of chalk. Although axes did find their way to distant areas, there seem to be local areas which were serviced by an individual factory. Despite this, Welsh and Cornish factories seem to be the greatest exporters. Those in north and central England, Wales, and southern England produced far more than were needed locally, and it appears they were traded in bulk.[59] Porcellanite seems to have been a particularly prized stone, although clay, slate, mudstone, greenstone, dolorite, diorite, epidiorite, and pick granite were also used.

Many of the polished axes that have been found—those of chalk, clay, jadeite, and serpentine, for example—were clearly never used nor intended for use except for ritual purposes. Individual axes have been found carefully buried at the entrance of Creevykeel court tomb in Ireland and some were imported from the Continent. In Brittany, axes hafted and unhafted are common motifs in the megalithic tombs. The axe, as well as the Goddess's pubic triangle, served as a symbol of regeneration. The same symbolism is encountered throughout the Neolithic in all of Old Europe between Greece, Scandinavia, and Ireland.

Trackways

About 4000 B.C. trackways began to be built in southern England, particularly in the area of Somerset[60] which are broadly contemporary with the causewayed enclosure at Hembury, the long-barrows at Windmill Hill and Fussell's Lodge, and the flint mines in Sussex. The earliest is Sweet Track, dating between 4200 and 3700 B.C. These trackways were built of wood as walkways over wet marshy areas and were subsequently buried in the peat that formed.

Pottery

The pottery known as Grimston/Lyles Hill pottery (after Grimston, Yorkshire, and Lyles Hill, County Antrim, Ireland) has both the widest distribution and the earliest date. The salient features are the limited forms, round bottoms, S profile,

and carinated bowls. Grimston/Lyles Hill pottery is usually undecorated, but there may be fluting or rippling on the rim and on the inside of the neck. There are no lugs or handles.[61]

Hembury ware is found mostly in southwest Britain. It is completely lacking in decoration but has horizontal and tubular handles that expand outward much like a trumpet and have thus come to be known as "trumpet lugs." The finer vessels of this style of pottery have been found in Cornwall, Devon, Dorset, and Wiltshire, and in contexts that date to c. 4200–3200 B.C. It is made of gabbroic clay which is only found at the Lizard Head in Cornwall. There is a true homogeneity amongst these vessels which suggests that they were manufactured in one place, providing evidence of long-distance trade.[62] In the later Neolithic, domestic pottery falls under the term Peterborough ware and appears to have evolved from the earlier Grimston/Lyles Hill pottery.

In Ireland, localization of pottery is not as apparent. With the exception of the Limerick style which is concentrated in the Lough Gur area, other styles appear throughout the island. Carrowkeel ware is found in association with passage tombs and settlements and can be placed at least as early as the mid-4th millennium B.C. It is thick, coarse, round bottomed, and decorated with stab-and-drag linear designs. Another category is the decorated Linkardstown pottery associated with single burials.[63]

The most prevalent types of pottery in Scotland and the northern islands are Unstan ware and Grooved ware. Unstan is a round-based, fine ware found both in burial monuments and in domestic sites; it appears to be a local version of an early Neolithic tradition. Grooved ware is flat based with plastic rather than grooved decoration. It was widely distributed throughout Britain and is termed Rinyo-Clacton in the south of England. There seems little question that Grooved ware extended into the later Neolithic.[64]

Burial Monuments in Ireland

The megalithic burial monuments of Ireland have been carefully surveyed during the past 30 years and the results compiled and published by de Valera in four large volumes in the 1960s.[65] This has provided a great deal of information previously unavailable or scattered through many publications. This survey places the vast majority of megalithic tombs into four categories: court, portal, passage, and wedge tombs. The latter belong to the Bronze Age and will not be discussed here.

Court Tombs

The nearly 300 court tombs, also called "horned tombs," are found almost exclusively in the northern part of Ireland with large concentrations in the coastal areas of Counties Mayo, Sligo, and Donegal in the west, and Counties Louth and Down and around the Carlingford Lough in the east. There is wide diversity in the architecture of these tombs, but the basic features include a large court area flanked by standing stones and a burial chamber or chambers covered by a triangular, trapezoidal, or roughly rectangular stone cairn which is now mostly denuded. (FIGURE 6–28)

Both cremation and inhumation have been found in these tombs although cremation seems to be more prevalent. Males, females, and children were buried in court tombs, but no tomb has produced a great number of individuals. Audleystown, County Down, produced 34 individuals and almost all of these were unburnt. The grave goods from court tombs include decorated and undecorated pottery, arrowheads, scrapers, and knives.

The few radiocarbon dates from these tombs suggest the first half of the 4th millennium B.C.

FIGURE 6–28

a

N

0   2 m

⊗ post holes

▮ stones

b

Portal Tombs

Classically, these tombs have a single chamber made of six stones—a pair of portal stones, two side stones, a back stone, and a capstone which is often a dramatic site on the landscape. (FIGURE 6–29) The capstone usually rests on the portals and backstone, slanting backwards; the sidestones frequently bear no weight at all and often do not even sit in sockets. These tombs are now usually found without any covering mound.

Their distribution is much like the court tombs although less restrictive. There are also some in Leinster on the southeast portion of the island and a few in Counties Clare and Galway. These tombs are generally on lowlands, often near streams. It has been suggested that portal tombs derive from court tombs, but until better radiocarbon dates are available this point must remain moot.

Until the recent excavation of Poulnabrone, County Clare, cremation had been the only known burial rite for these tombs. But at this site, the remains of 22 unburnt individuals were found. The grave goods from portal tombs usually include arrowheads, scrapers, pottery, polished stone axes, and beads, but Poulnabrone also produced a bone pendant, two quartz crystals, and a fragment of a mushroom-headed bone pin.[66]

FIGURE 6–28 A court tomb of Ireland. (a) Plan and (b) reconstruction. Note the large court and paved area in front. A large triangular stone stands to the right of the entrance. The stone cairn was enclosed by wooden posts as post-holes suggest. Shanballyedmond, Co. Tipperary.

FIGURE 6–29 A portal tomb built of large stones from Ireland, Drumanone, Co. Sligo, east of Blyle, located on a low ridge in a rolling pasture land. This tomb consists of a polygonal chamber covered by one enormous roofstone.

FIGURE 6–29

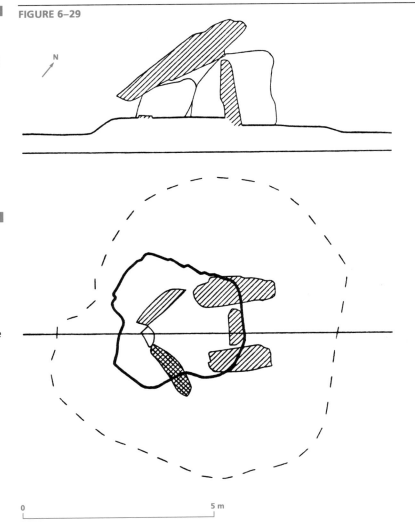

0 _____ 5 m

FIGURE 6–30

a

b

FIGURE 6–30 Great mound with burial chamber of the mega-lithic tradition is New-grange in County Meath, Ireland, shown in reconstruction (a). The corbelled vault of the chamber (b) is 20 feet high. c. 3300–3200 B.C.

Passage Tombs

Of all the megalithic tomb types in Ireland, by far the greatest amount of attention, particularly in the past two decades, has been focused on the passage tombs. During this time, two of the largest tombs, Newgrange and Knowth (FIGURES 6–30, 6–31) have been excavated and published, providing unforeseen information.

Unlike the other types, passage tombs are found in cemetery settings usually with one dominant tomb and a number of satellite tombs. This is perhaps best seen at Knowth where the great tomb, Site 1, is surrounded by at least sixteen smaller tombs.[67] (FIGURE 6–32) The range of sizes within a cemetery can be staggering. Site 1 is approximately 85 m in diameter while Site 16 is a little over 4 m in diameter.

Unlike the triangular, trapezoidal, or oval mounds of the other tomb types, the mounds of passage tombs are circular. Another difference is that they are placed on elevated areas. There is a generally easterly orientation of the tombs, and there can be no question that the great tomb at Newgrange is oriented to the midwinter sunrise.

The passage tombs have grave goods that are nonutilitarian. Flint tools are extremely rare in the tombs and only one type of pottery, Carrowkeel ware, has ever been found in a primary context. The large mound at Newgrange presented an extreme example in that not a single sherd was found.[68] The passage tombs have produced bone and antler pins, marbles, pendants, and beads. The marbles are made of a variety of materials such as chalk, baked clay, and various kinds of stone including ironstone, limestone, marble, quartzite, serpentine, and basalt. Knowth 1 has produced two "maceheads," one of which is a magnificent piece of art, beautifully carved. (FIGURE 6–33) It represents an anthropomorphic head with a wide open mouth, spiral eyes with snake spirals on both sides, and a fluted design along the forehead and chin. This is possibly a highly stylized rendering of the head of the tomb goddess, the Goddess of Death and Regeneration. Passage tombs, particularly those in the Boyne Valley, are

FIGURE 6–31

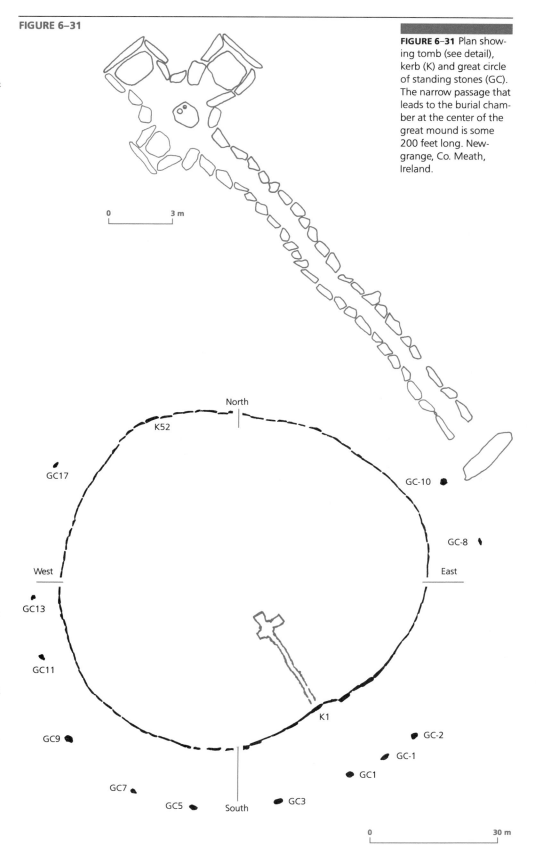

0   3 m

North
K52
GC17
GC-10
GC-8
West   East
GC13
GC11
K1
GC9   GC-2
GC-1
GC1
GC7   GC3
GC5   South

0   30 m

FIGURE 6-31 Plan showing tomb (see detail), kerb (K) and great circle of standing stones (GC). The narrow passage that leads to the burial chamber at the center of the great mound is some 200 feet long. Newgrange, Co. Meath, Ireland.

FIGURE 6–32

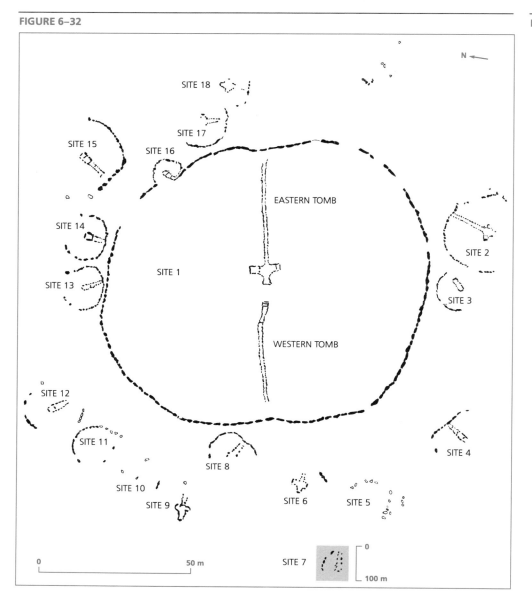

FIGURE 6–33

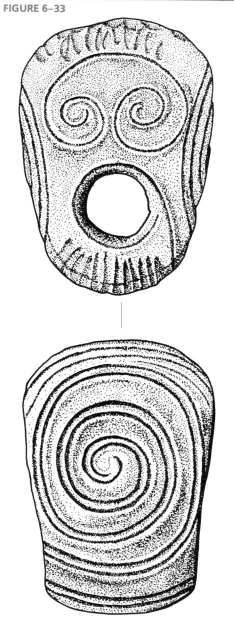

FIGURE 6–32 Plan of the Knowth complex showing the main tumulus including the eastern and western tombs with long corridors and the small satellite tombs. Co. Meath, Ireland. Mid-4th mill. B.C.

FIGURE 6–33 A magnificent art piece from Knowth: an anthropomorphic head of flint with a wide open mouth, spiral eyes, snake spirals on both sides, and fluted design along the forehead and chin. Possibly a stylized rendering of the head of the Goddess of Death and Regeneration.

FIGURE 6–34 Stone basin with engravings from the right recess of Knowth, East.

noted for their art work which is carved (technically pecked) on the surfaces of the stones in and out of the tombs. There can be little question that these carvings had a ritual purpose (see discussion in chap. 7). Both in Newgrange and Knowth, stone basins of fine workmanship were found. (FIGURE 6–34)

Radiocarbon dates from both Newgrange and Knowth firmly place these great tombs in the mid- to late 4th millennium B.C. (TABLE 24).

FIGURE 6–34

Linkardstown Barrows with Single Graves

The Linkardstown tombs of eastern-central Ireland are a totally different type. These are found in stone cists under round mounds, but unlike all of the megalithic tombs they are not receptacles for communal burials but are for single burials only. The eight that are considered in the Linkardstown group, and an additional twenty-two which are considered related, all contained the unburnt remains of an adult male. These burials are indications of the primacy of males within this culture. A few contained additional remains, usually a child or a younger person, and one site contained a cremation along with the inhumation. Although there may be more than one person in the tomb, the burial rite was performed only once and then the tomb was permanently closed. There is no evidence of ongoing ritual as is present in the megalithic tombs.

The major grave good of these burials is a highly decorated round-bottomed clay bowl with horizontal neck. The decoration covered the entire vessel and on all but one, a cruciform or rayed pattern covered the bottom.

Radiocarbon dates show that at least three of these tombs date to the mid-4th millennium B.C., making them roughly contemporary with the great passage tombs of the Boyne Valley.

These Linkardstown tombs are extremely important because they show the earliest evidence of single burial in Ireland and a completely different approach to burial than that provided by the megalithic tradition. They represent the Kurgan (Indo-European) tradition as convincingly demonstrated by Karlene Jones-Bley in her dissertation of 1989.[69] Solar patterns on pottery belong to an alien ideology brought by the people who buried their dead in single graves under round mounds. Analogies are known across the Channel in the Rhine and Upper Danube region where the earliest solar patterns emerged in the Rössen and Aichbühl-Schwieberdingen groups dated to the period of 4300–3900 B.C. (see chap. 10). The intrusive element in eastern Ireland coexisted with the Passage-grave people, but thereafter were either amalgamated with them or were pushed out.

Burial Monuments in England

In the west, stone monuments are more common and are related to Irish monuments, while in the eastern areas, the earliest burial monuments were built of wood covered with long earthen barrows.

Portal Tombs

In Wales and Cornwall the portal tombs, much like the ones found in Ireland, are perhaps one of the earliest types owing to the evidence of pottery found at Dyffryn Ardudwy which is associated with the mid-5th millennium B.C. causewayed enclosure at Hembury.

Chambered Mounds

Chambered mounds, related to the court tombs of Ireland, are built of stone and are subdivided into the Cotswold-Severn group of southern Wales and west England (along the Severn River and in the Cotswolds), and the Clyde tombs of the Clyde-Carlingford, group which straddles the Irish sea.[70] The Clyde group is in the west and southwest of Scotland while Carlingford is the name for what are now called court tombs in Ireland. Although these terms are still useful because they denote various forms and geographical placement, it is becoming apparent that they are just that—variations.

Earthen Long-Barrows

The earthen long-barrows have the earliest radiocarbon dates, several to the 5th millennium B.C. (TABLE 23, *left column*). They range from southern England primarily up the eastern part of the island to southern Scotland, covering the area of the "lowland zone" and its northern extension. Most of the earthen long-barrows are on the chalk, as opposed to the long cairns which concentrate on the more acid clays and boulder clays.[71]

From the time of John Aubrey, the great 17th century antiquarian, these impressive, very long mounds (FIGURES 6–35, 6–36, 6–37) have been thought of

FIGURE 6–35 (a) West Kennet long-barrow, England, 100 m long. In front, at the broad end, is a forecourt leading to the megalithic burial chambers in which disarticulated skeletons were deposited. (b) Detail of primary burials. Second half of the 5th mill. B.C.

FIGURE 6–36 Plans of a double barrow at Wayland's Smithy near Ashbury, Berkshire, England. (a) Plan shown with side ditches used as quarries for the second long-barrow; (b) shows more details of the primary barrow. The first tumulus was 16.5 m long and encircled by large orthostats. Inside was a wooden chamber with a trapezoidal forecourt. Bean-shaped ditches flank the barrow. Disarticulated skeletons of at least 13 individuals and one crouched skeleton lay on the stone floor of the chamber. The second trapezoid barrow built above the first, 54 m long, was also encircled by large orthostats. The burial chamber was covered with white chalk and had two side niches at the broad (facade) end in which bones of eight individuals were found.

FIGURE 6–35

FIGURE 6–36

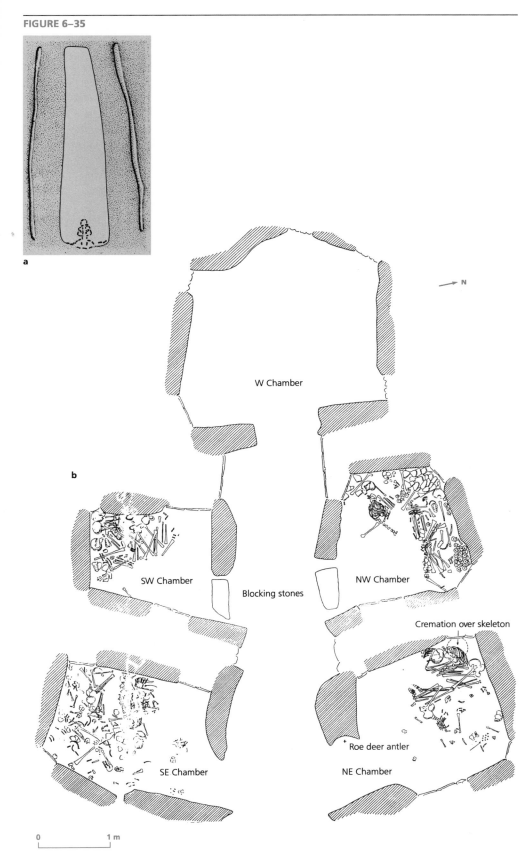

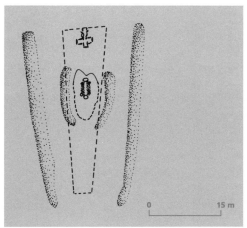

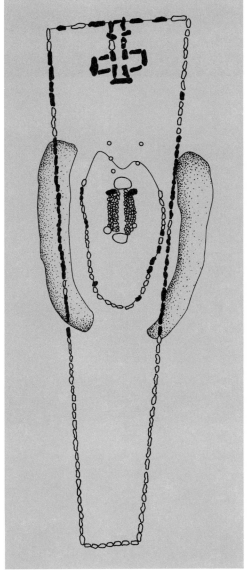

FIGURE 6–37

FIGURE 6–37 Conjectural reconstruction of a long-barrow at Fussell's Lodge, Wessex, England. c. 3900–3800 B.C. L 51.5 m.

as funerary in nature and indeed many have yielded human remains. Others, however, have had no skeletal material and in some cases, such as Fussell's Lodge, an earthen long-barrow was built over a wooden mortuary house. Recent work has shown that this practice of a mortuary house under a long-barrow was not infrequent. At Wayland's Smithy we have an example of a timber mortuary house covered by an earthen long-barrow covered by a chambered tomb.[72] Many of the tombs also contain a great amount of debris from funerary feasts and rituals. This debris is dramatically attested at West Kennet where pottery representing 250 vessels, animal bones, flints, and other objects in a matrix of chalk rubble filled the passage of the chambers.[73]

Chambered Tombs and Passage Graves in the Orkney Islands

The chambered tombs and long mounds of Scotland and the Orkneys have been thoroughly reviewed by Audrey Henshall,[74] who divided the chambered tombs into Clyde tombs and passage graves. Clyde tombs, found in Argyll and Arron, the Hebrides, Perthshire, and the southwest of Scotland, are similar to the court tombs of Ireland. Passage graves are subdivided into four major types: 1) The Orkney-Cromarty-Hebridean (O-C-H) are the basic passage tombs, although the chambers are sometimes extended to such a degree that the mounds are no longer round, but long. These are mostly found in the Orkneys. Good examples are Midhowe on the island of Rousay and Isbister on South Ronaldsay (see fig. 7–115). 2) The Bargrennan type is described as a small group of tombs showing local hybridization between early Clyde tombs and O-C-H passage graves. Their distribution falls within the Clyde group. 3) The Clava type chambers are found around Inverness and adjoining counties. There are only about twelve of these tombs which differ from other passage tombs by generally facing southwest as opposed to the usual easterly orientation. This group is also surrounded by a circle of stones.[75] 4) The Maes Howe group is confined to the Orkneys and is most closely comparable to the Irish passage tombs. The chambered tombs of the Orkney islands are placed by radiocarbon dates between the end of the 4th and the middle of the 3rd millennia B.C. (TABLE 23, right).

The long mounds are usually stone cairns in Scotland as opposed to earthen barrows but are similar to the long mounds found in England. Two completely excavated mounds are Lochhill, Kirkcudbrightshire[76] and the Dalladies, Kincardineshire.[77] Both of these mounds produced evidence for an internal mortuary structure. A plank from Lochhill gave a radiocarbon date of c. 3900 B.C.

Emergence of Single Burials, Under Round Barrows

Toward the middle of the 4th millennium B.C. a number of changes began appearing in both Britain and Ireland. Perhaps of most significance was the rite that emphasized individual burial, first seen in the mid-4th millennium B.C. in Ireland's Linkardstown burials. The evidence for this is not as apparent in Britain but does exist with such burials as Liff's Low, Derbyshire, and Duggleby Howe. Perhaps the most dramatic evidence of the change of burial rite comes from Whitegrounds Barrow, Burythorpe. Here a large round mound with a central male inhumation completely covered an earlier oval mound which contained the remains of eight people. The earlier mound had a radiocarbon date of c. 3700 B.C., while the later mound produced a date of c. 3340–3120 B.C.[78] These mounds represent two entirely different social systems, religious practices and burial rites. One emphasizes communal return to the realm of the ancestors for regeneration within the tomb/womb of the Goddess, whereas the other celebrates the personal importance of individual males (see chaps. 7 and 10).

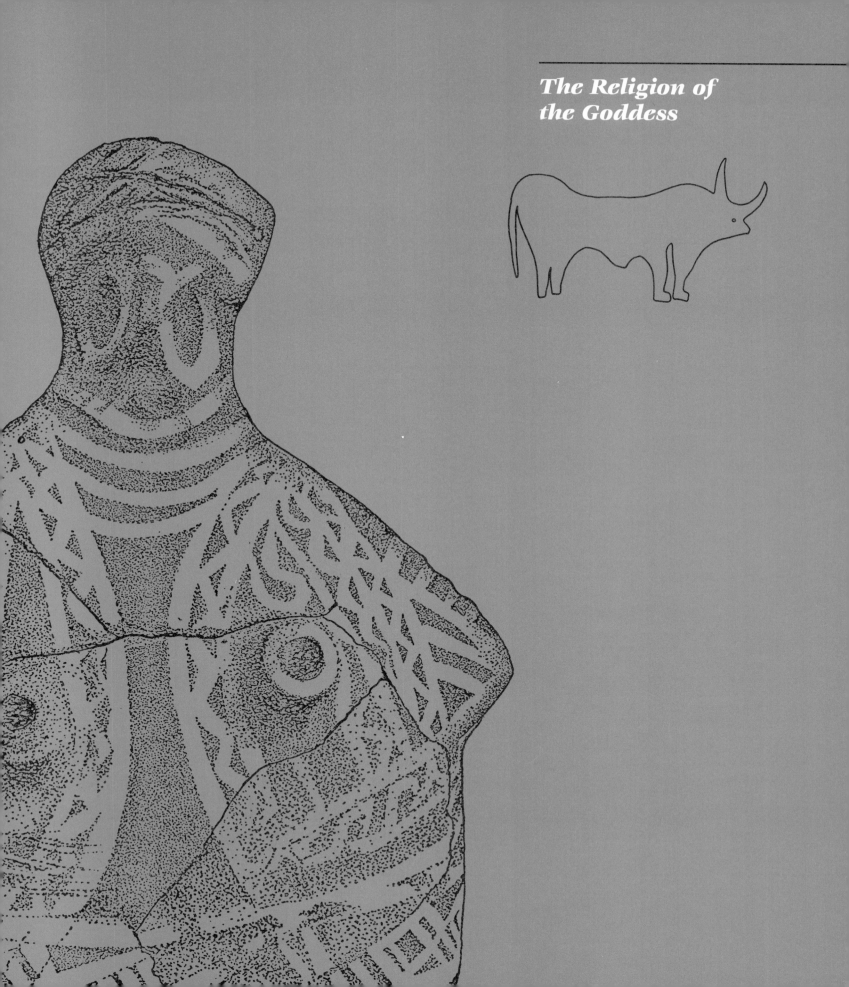

The Religion of
the Goddess

According to myriad images that have survived from the great span of human prehistory on the Eurasian continents, it was the sovereign mystery and creative power of the female as the source of life that developed into the earliest religious experiences. The Great Mother Goddess who gives birth to all creation out of the holy darkness of her womb became a metaphor for Nature herself, the cosmic giver and taker of life, ever able to renew Herself within the eternal cycle of life, death, and rebirth.

Flint sculptures of female figures and animals have been found that date as far back as the Acheulian period of the Lower Paleolithic, more than 500,000 years ago.[1] From the Middle Paleolithic-Mousterian epoch, 100,000 to 40,000 years ago, triangular stones were deliberately placed above burials and cupmarks were engraved into stones. This very early religious symbolism has yet to be systematically studied; most research has been done on the Upper Paleolithic period, 40,000 to 10,000 years before our present time.

A veritable explosion of art took place during the Upper Paleolithic, expressed by innumerable cave paintings, rock carvings, and sculptures. The caves in which we find exquisite animal drawings and engravings were sanctuaries for the enactment of seasonal rites, initiation rituals, and other ceremonies related to a participation in the sacred cycles of life.[2] Miniature sculptures in stone, horn, or bone, representing a variety of deities, appeared between 27,000 and 25,000 B.C. About three thousand sculptures have been found in the area between southern France and central Siberia.[3] From such an abundant sample, we may approximate their figurative significance. The various shapes, gestures, and attributes portrayed on these sculptures, in addition to their provenance, lend themselves to a classification of types representing various aspects and functions of the Goddess.

The very earliest symbols engraved on rocks and articles of bone or horn reflect a profound belief in a life-generating Goddess who represents One Source while pictured in many forms. From as early as 25,000 B.C., She is depicted with exaggerated breasts, vulva, and buttocks, indicating the centers of emanation of her procreative powers. A study of symbols in Paleolithic art demonstrates that the female, rather than the male, was the deity of creation. In fact, there are no traces in Paleolithic art of a father figure. The bearing and nourishing of offspring—plant, animal, and human—was the primary model for the development of the image of the Goddess as the all-generating deity.

Miniature sculptures of female figures carved from ivory or soft stone were not "Venuses," as they tend to be identified in literature, nor were they "fertility charms" designed to arouse male sexuality. Their functions were considerably more important: the giving and protection of life, as well as death and regeneration. The Goddess personifies the eternally renewing cycle of life in all of its forms and manifestations. An interpretation of these functions follows from careful study of particular attributes of these early sculptures: their postures, gestures, headgear, and associated religious symbols. Numerous expressions of the divine female which persisted for many thousands of years can be clearly seen from extant artifacts from the Upper Paleolithic.

We find at this time an iconography of the Goddess comprised of several kinds of abstract or hieroglyphic symbols: X's, V's, triangles, meanders, and the like; representational images such as vulvas, breasts, and birds' feet; and animal symbols representing various aspects of the Goddess, embodying her power. Essentially the same iconography attended the religion of the Goddess well into the agricultural era, although evolved, reflecting changing economic conditions.

During the Neolithic there was a renewed flowering of artistic expression. The invention of ceramics, c. 6500 B.C., marked the appearance of thousands of figurines and vases, temples and their miniature models, wall paintings, reliefs, and countless ritual articles. The number of religious symbols multiplied a hundredfold, providing abundant data for deciphering the Goddess's iconography. Moreover, the symbolism of Old Europe, 6500–3500 B.C., provides an essential key to understanding Paleolithic religion, since many of the images are continuous. The reconstruction of this symbolic system is described by this author in The Language of the Goddess.[4]

The figurines represent various images of the Goddess, portrayed articulately with details of attire and headdress, or reduced to bare outlines. The latter, very likely, were ex votos, or amulets in her image. Figurines have been recovered in temples on altars, on oven platforms, in specially prepared offering places, and in caves and graves. They have frequently been found in caches stored in vases, or as miniature tableaux representing certain religious activities. Obviously, groups of figurines were used for the reenactment of rituals. The incessant production of figurines witnesses an energetic process shared by all participants.

There are at least twenty female and five male anthropomorphic and half-human, half-animal figurine types that differ in posture, facial features, masks, headgear, and associated symbols. These identifiable images are also portrayed in reliefs and paintings on temple or cave walls and on vases.

Categories, Functions, and Symbolism of Deities

The multiple categories, functions, and symbols used by prehistoric peoples to express the Great Mystery are all aspects of the unbroken unity of one deity, a Goddess who is ultimately Nature herself.

For the purpose of this study, these deities will be arranged in four main groups. First, the Goddess who personifies the generative forces of nature. To this category belong the various life propagating, birth-giving, life-maintaining, and life-stimulating aspects of the Goddess. Second, the Goddess who personifies the destructive forces of nature —the Death Goddess, rendered as a stiff nude, a poisonous snake, or bird of prey: vulture, owl, raven, or crow. Third, the Goddess of Regeneration; it is she who controls the life cycles of the entire natural world. Her manifestations are the various symbols of the uterus, pubic triangle, or fetus: toad, frog, hedgehog, bull head, triangle and double triangle. She also appears as an insect: bee, butterfly, moth. Death and regeneration are inseparably connected within the normal cycle of nature; therefore the Goddess of Death and Regeneration is depicted as one deity, in acknowledgment of the simultaneous function and cyclic continuum of these aspects. The fourth category focuses on the prehistoric male deities who make up only three to five percent of the corpus of Neolithic sculpture.

The Generative Goddess: Life Giver and Mistress of Animals and Plants

The Goddess of the Paleolithic and Neolithic is parthenogenetic, creating life out of herself. She is the primeval, self-fertilizing "Virgin Goddess" who has survived in numerous culture forms to the present day. The Christian Virgin Mary is a demoted version of this original deity. If the role of the father was understood in ancient times, there is no archeological evidence that this was given any importance. From the artifacts it seems clear that woman's ability to give birth and nourish children from her body was deemed sacred, and revered as the ultimate metaphor for the divine Creator.

It was not always necessary for the Goddess's entire figure to be carved, for it was typical in prehistoric periods to depict only those body parts that emitted her generative powers: vulva, pubic triangle, buttocks, and breasts. It was sufficient to carve her vulva into rock, to find a stone shaped like a triangle, or to make a bone amulet shaped like breasts or buttocks. Such symbols represented the potency of her generative powers.

Attempts to explain the representation of vulvas, breasts, and buttocks have resulted in fantastic hypotheses. For the most part, these images have been viewed through the lens of 20th century bias. One explanation of the "beginning of art" is that manual love play—the touching of vulvas, buttocks, and breasts—stimulated art creations some 30,000 years ago.[5] To conclude that these Paleolithic symbols were objects created for the erotic stimulation of males completely ignores their religious and social context. Attention must be paid to how they are rendered, with what other symbols they are associated, and whether their depiction extends over long ages.

The symbol of the vulva does not end with the Aurignacian period, but can be traced from the Upper Paleolithic, through the whole of the Neolithic, Copper, and Bronze ages, up to historical times. It is pictured as a supernatural triangle, lozenge, or oval, often together with aquatic signs—meanders, zigzags, wavy parallel lines—or as seeds depicted as a dot in the center of an enclosure. Sometimes the branch of a plant is shown as a substitute (some Neolithic figurines have a little branch or budding tree in place of a vulva).

In all prehistoric art, the vulva is never to be seen as a passive object but as a symbol of the source of life itself. It is the cosmic womb, analogous to the blossoming of a bud, from which all birth and new vitality unfolds. Figurines representing the generative forces of the Goddess are always depicted with large vulvas or pubic triangles. The Birth-giving Goddess, shown in birthing posture, has an enlarged, swollen vulva. (FIGURE 7–1) She is well evidenced in Paleolithic and Old European art, including examples in Malta. (FIGURE 7–2) Vulva and seed patterns depicted alone may have represented her, or had an amuletic quality, especially when portrayed as pendants.

The life- and birth-giving mother was anthropomorphic and zoomorphic. Her main epiphanies were the deer, elk, and bear witnessed by numerous sculptures of pregnant deer (FIGURE 7–3), bear-mothers holding cubs, ritual vases and reliefs in the shape of these animals, as well as by a strong presence of their role in myths. The earliest evidence of a veneration of the deer is seen in the Upper Paleolithic and Mesolithic. In El Juyo, in northern Spain east of Altamira, a deer was buried fourteen thousand years ago in a hole shaped like an egg, covered with red ochre and violet, orange, or reddish pieces of clay, deer horns, and other objects.[6] Deer horns found with part of a skull, fashioned to be worn on the head for ritualistic dances, were found in Star Carr, England, dating from 8000–7500 B.C.[7] Dances with deer or elk horns have survived into modern times. Red-deer horns, skulls, and shoulder blades found at the altars and burials of Lepenski Vir from the 7th millennium B.C. were apparently for the increase of life forces and regeneration (see sec. 6, Burial Practices). Canes carved of horn with artfully fashioned she-elk heads, more than five thousand years old, have been found at Šventoji near the Baltic Sea in Lithuania (FIGURE 7–4) and in a cave at Gaban in northern Italy from the 5th millennium B.C.[8] These canes were probably used in rituals dedicated to the worship of the Elk-Mother. The "Sitting Goddess with Horns" is known from Minoan seals and from the Bronze and Iron Ages in western Europe.

FIGURE 7-1

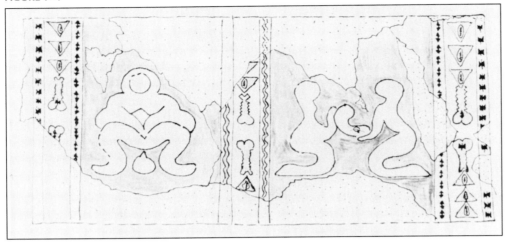

1

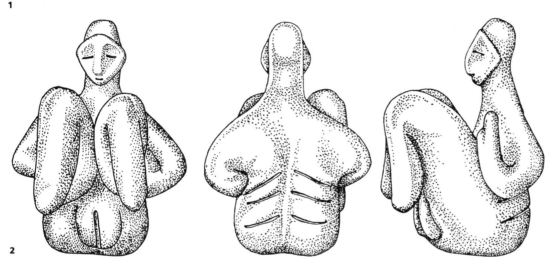

2

FIGURE 7-1 Birth-giving representations in paintings and sculpture. (1) Wall painting from Çatal Hüyük temple. 7th mill. B.C. (2) The Birth-Giving Goddess is portrayed in a seated, birth-giving posture. Her mask is anthropomorphic, and is marked with three lines on the back. Early Sesklo from Achilleion II, Thessaly, Greece; c. 6300–6200 B.C. H 6.4 cm.

FIGURE 7-2

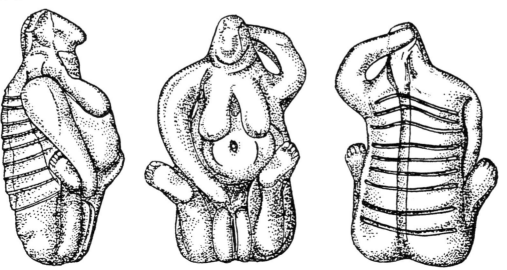

FIGURE 7-2 The Birth Goddess of Malta. With upraised legs, pregnant belly, and hand on her swollen vulva, she is ready to give birth. The nine lines across her back may represent the nine months of gestation. Maltese temple period. From Ħaġar Qim, end of 4th mill. B.C. Drawn in reconstruction (found with right leg and face damaged). H 7 cm.

FIGURE 7–3

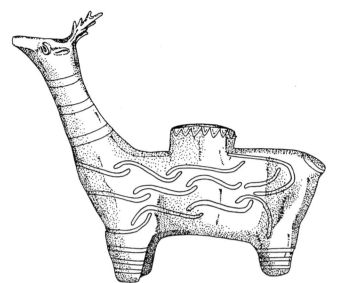

Belief in the Deer-Mother who created life was very strong for many thousands of years. In European folklore, especially of the Irish and Scots, we can still find many references to supernatural deer and deer-goddesses. In northern Asia it is believed to this day that the pregnant deer is the birthing Mother Goddess. The Evenks imagined the World Mother as a deer or reindeer doe. Greek Artemis appears as both deer and bear.

The bear as a symbol of motherhood is well illustrated by sculptures from the Vinča culture of the 5th millennium B.C. in the forms of a madonna with a bear mask holding a cub (FIGURE 7–5) and a nurse with a bear mask carrying a pouch on her back to hold a baby (FIGURE 7–6).

FIGURE 7–4

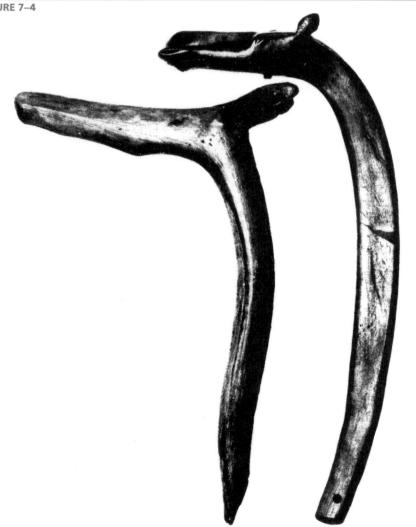

FIGURE 7–3 The sacred animal of the Goddess in birth-giving aspect was the deer, and her portrayals are frequent and exquisite. This zoomorphic vase used as a lamp in birth rituals is testimony to the symbolic connection between the deer and crescents or snakes, and triple bands. Painted white on red. Karanovo I. Muldava, C Bulgaria; early 6th mill. B.C. H c. 50 cm (from feet to antlers).

FIGURE 7–4 Ritual staffs carved of antler portraying she-elk heads. Šventoji, waterlogged settlement, site 3B, near the Baltic Sea, Lithuania; end 4th mill. B.C. H 42.5 cm and 40 cm.

FIGURE 7–5

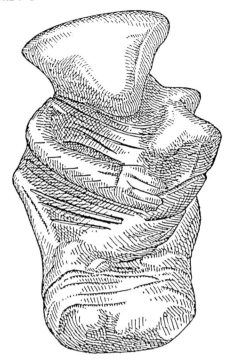

FIGURE 7–5 Bear-masked Mother or Nurse holding a baby. Terracotta from the Vinča culture, c. 4500 B.C. Fafos at Kosovska Mitrovica, S Yugoslavia. H 5.7 cm.

FIGURE 7–6 The "Divine Nurse" is shown carrying a pouch. Her massive pentagonal mask is either of a bear or a bird (since it has no mouth). Late Vinča culture from Čuprija, C Yugoslavia, 4500–4000 B.C. H 9.2 cm.

References in folklore have preserved much information about an earlier bear-descendant and bear-mother giving new life. To this day in Lithuania, a woman in childbirth is called a bear. A custom has survived into the 20th century in eastern Slavic lands in which the grandmother places the newborn child on a bear skin. This same custom is known from a description by Porphyry in the third century A.D.[9] The Celts worshipped *Dea Artio*, another example of the Bear Goddess existing into historical times. Mary, Mother of God, is also linked with the bear. In western Crete, for example, February 2nd is celebrated as the festival in honor of Panagia Arkoudiotissa, "Mother of God of the Bear."[10] Here, Artemis Bear has been transformed into the Christian Mother of God in the shape of a bear.

This ancient Goddess is also shown among male animals, as in the Çatal Hüyük images of the Goddess between two leopards (FIGURE 7–7), dogs, and other animals. Here she is the same *Potnia Theron* (Mistress of Animals) as known later in Minoan and Mycenaean cultures and in Classical Greece. The wall paintings of Çatal Hüyük and Minoan frescoes of the 16th century B.C., especially those found on the island of Thera, show that she was not only the Birth Goddess but was also the incarnation of the primordial fertility of nature. In frescoes and Minoan seals she is shown standing, surrounded by dogs and lions. In a fresco from Thera, this Goddess is sitting on a throne on a triple platform flanked by a winged griffin and a monkey. Around her are blossoming hills where girls are gathering crocuses and bringing them in baskets as offerings. (FIGURE 7–8) Similar landscapes in the frescoes of Knossos—with river and hills and a profusion of wild plants and animals, bursting with the energy of life—are certainly connected to a profound veneration of the natural world. On vases from the 7th and 6th centuries B.C. in Archaic Greece, Artemis is still depicted among animals and birds as well as with energy-stimulating symbols—whorls, swastikas, upward-rising snakes—while in her womb is a fish.

FIGURE 7–6

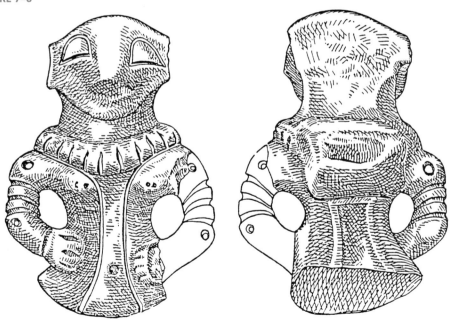

FIGURE 7–7

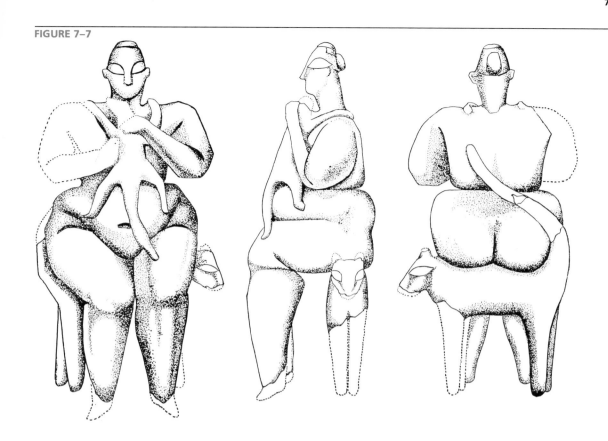

FIGURE 7–7 "Mistress of Animals" seated on a leopard and holding a leopard cub. Terracotta from Hacilar, Neolithic Anatolia, House Q, VI, early 6th mill. B.C. H 13.5 cm.

FIGURE 7–8

FIGURE 7–8 Tentative reconstruction of the entire room of a temple in Akrotiri, at Thera. The wall painting on the upper level shows the "Mistress of Animals," while the lower possibly depicts an initiation rite. 16th cent. B.C.

The Agricultural Pregnant Goddess: Mother Earth

From the Upper Paleolithic, symbols appear representing the Goddess's fertility. She is portrayed as a naturalistic nude with hands placed on her enlarged belly, her pregnant form apparently likened to the fecundity of the seeded earth and all its creatures. (An excellent example is the relief of a naked woman found at the entrance to the cave in Laussel, southern France.) Her womb is associated with caves and the curving contours of the land. The abundance which flows from her body represented a harvest to the gatherers of the Paleolithic. Before she was mother to domesticated grains, she was mother to the wild plants.

At the beginning of the Neolithic, this already ancient deity was transformed into an agricultural goddess, the progenitor and protectress of all fruits of the harvest, but especially grain and bread. (FIGURE 7–9) Knowing the sacred earth as Mother, pregnant in spring, ripening into the birth of harvest, her fruited vines cut like umbilical cords and celebrated in autumn are beliefs that are thousands of years old. The belief that the earth's forces are concentrated in mounds, hills, rocks, and trees; a gratitude and profound respect toward the earth for providing continuing nourishment for all of life; and the necessity for ritually participating in the holy round of nature continued with great intensity from prehistoric times into the historical era. From the Neolithic, special altars were built for her next to the bread baking ovens, and she was worshiped wherever grain was ground and bread was being prepared and baked (see illustration from Achilleion, figs. 7–48, 7–49).

From surviving folk motifs and prehistoric symbols, we may surmise that the pregnancy of earth and woman was held in great esteem. It was strongly believed in the Slavic lands until the 20th century that one must not strike the earth or spit upon her, for this would make her weep. The pregnant earth must be honored and assisted in various ways for the growth of new life to be encouraged. Neolithic sculptures of the Pregnant Goddess were decorated with symbols of vital energy: spirals, snakes, two lines, and four-corner signs. Especially characteristic was the sign of the four corners, which is akin to the cus-

FIGURE 7–9

tom of sowing grain to the four corners of the earth.

For at least eight thousand years, the sacred animal of Mother Earth was the pig, perhaps because it is a rapidly growing and fattening animal and highly prolific. Its growth and fecundity were compared to the abundance of the harvest. Clay sculptures of pigs have been found dating from the beginning of the Neolithic. (FIGURE 7–10) The Vinča and Karanovo cultures from the 5th millennium B.C. produced masks of pigs and ceremonial vases whose lids were in the form of a pig's head. Most of them had earrings. Ceremonial vases and anthropomorphic pigs' heads show that the forces of Mother Earth were incarnate in the pig. From the 3rd millennium B.C., in Syria, a small sculpture of the Goddess with a pig's head was found nicely seated on a throne (she is presently housed in the Louvre Museum, Paris). A very graceful marble vase shaped like a pig has been found in the Cyclades from the same period. Masks and ceremonial vases indicate that there were holidays, probably in celebration of sowing and reaping, at which times offerings were made to the Goddess while dancing with pigs' masks. Similar festivities in honor of Demeter took place in Classical and Hellenistic Greece at which time suckling pigs were sacrificed to Demeter and her daughter Persephone.[11] In October, during the fall harvest holiday of Thesmophoria, women would bring the remains of suckling pigs that had been buried and rotting in the earth and place them on altars. These were later mixed with seed to be sown in the fields, thus helping to evoke an abundant harvest of crops. Two thousand years later a very similar custom was described in writings of 18th century Lithuania in which a black suckling pig was ritually sacrificed to the Earth Mother at the time of blessing the seed in the fall.[12] Such customs show the influence of the pig on the fertility of the fields. An intimate connection between suckling pigs and grain is seen in the clay sculptures studded with grain from the Linearbandkeramic (LBK) and Cucuteni cultures, 5th millennium B.C. (FIGURE 7–11, 1, 2)

FIGURE 7–10

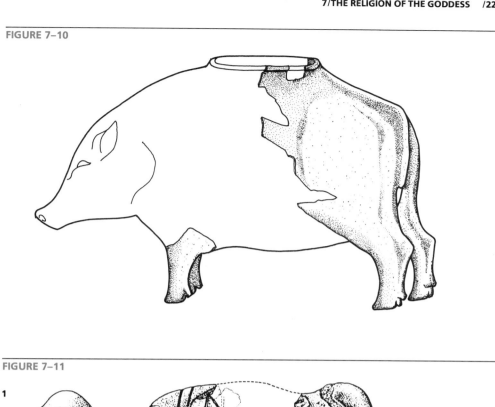

FIGURE 7–11

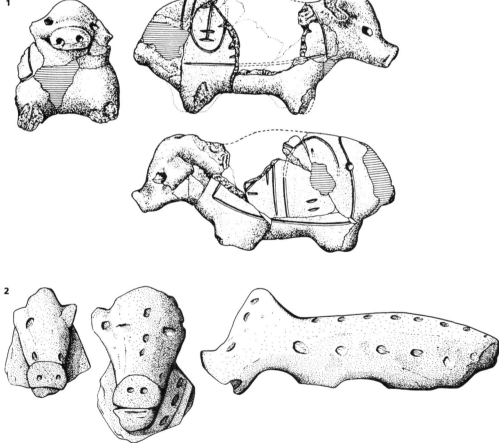

1

2

There is no doubt that the prehistoric veneration of Mother Earth survived intact up to the time of the worship of Demeter and Persephone in Greece, Ops Consiua in Rome, Nerthus in Germanic lands, Žemyna or Zemes Mate in the Baltic area, Mother Moist Earth in Slavic lands, and elsewhere. Her power was too ancient and deep to be altogether destroyed by succeeding patriarchal religions, including Christianity. She was therefore absorbed, and became known in western Europe as various saints: Radegund, Macrine, Walpurga, Milburga, among others.[13] In many other lands, especially eastern Europe, she fused with the Mother of God, Marija.

The Black Madonna is this same Earth Mother, whose blackness represents the color of earth's fertility. The yearly renewal of her fecundity is her fundamental miracle. Ancient mysteries, enacted throughout prehistoric and historic millennia—in caves, cemeteries, temples, and in the open fields—were for the purpose of expressing gratitude to the source of all life and nourishment, and to ritually participate in the secret of the earth's abundance.

The Bird Goddess and Her Symbols

The Bird Goddess appears as a bird with a beak or a pinched nose, a long neck, female breasts that are sometimes exaggerated, wings or winglike projections, and protruding female buttocks outlined in the shape of a duck or swan or an egg. She often has no mouth, sometimes has a hairdo or crown, and is usually sitting in an erect posture, although her upper body may be bent forward like that of a bird. Meanders and chevrons are her symbols, and can be found decorating her body as well as on objects that are associated with her. Multiple chevrons and "beak and eyes" symbols are typical decorative designs on vases dedicated to her.

The Bird Goddess had a dual nature. She was a giver of life, well-being, and nourishment. On the other hand, she appears as Death in the guise of a vulture, owl, or other bird of prey or carrion eater. Red bird's feet are painted on the walls of Paleolithic caves as well as on

Neolithic red-painted ceramics (the Hacilar vases from central Anatolia are a good example). This motif also occurs alternately with triangles. The anthropomorphic hourglass symbol sometimes has bird's feet instead of hands and is repeated from Portugal to Romania and Bulgaria in cave drawings and ceramic decoration.

The breasts of the Goddess's body were considered numinous, demonstrated by their exceptional rendering over not less than twenty thousand years. From the beginning of the Upper Paleolithic, breast ornaments were marked with symbols of the Goddess: V's, X's, parallel lines, or two or three lines. Such ornaments were probably worn as magical beads for life stimulation and protection. Paleolithic sculptures are sometimes fashioned in such a way that only the breasts are emphasized. Such a bone figurine, shaped like a flat board with breasts, was found at Dolní Věstonice, Moravia, with incised horizontal lines, from about 24,000 B.C. An ivory sculpture from Lespugue, southern

FIGURE 7–12

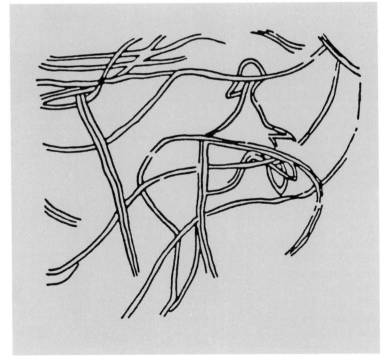

FIGURE 7–12 Upper Paleolithic female nude with pendulous breasts, wings for arms, and bird-head mask overpainted with "macaronis." Pech-Merle (Cabrerets), Lot, S France. H c. 70 cm. Painted with fingers; probably Magdalenian. She predates by some 10,000 years the Neolithic Bird Goddess, with bird heads or masks and with large breasts.

FIGURE 7-13

FIGURE 7-13 Two views of the Bird Goddess's head with a massive nose, coffee bean eyes, neatly combed hair with a bun. Sesklo culture, from Achilleion near Farsala. Found in temple dated to 5900–5800 B.C. Terracotta torso restored; see fig. 7–47. H c. 15 cm.

France, from c. 23,000 B.C., a true masterpiece of Paleolithic art, has neatly rounded breasts, almost the same size as the buttocks. All focus is on the breasts and buttocks, while other parts having no importance for this goddess are neglected.[14] Drawings from the Upper Paleolithic show that magical breasts were associated with the Bird Goddess. Black coal drawings from Peche Merle, Magdalenian culture, show naked women with pendulous breasts, little wings, and bird masks. On the women and around them were many parallel lines, the so-called "macaroni" motif, related to the symbol of flowing life or the water of life. (FIGURE 7–12)

Sculptures of the Neolithic Bird Goddess either have large breasts or are specially decorated with her symbols: chevrons, meanders, parallel or zigzag lines, and the number three. She often has a collar and diagonal lines or bands across her cheeks. These same designs and attributes are repeated over thousands of years. If the figurine is not too schematically rendered, we can notice her lovely hairdo, and a turban or ribbon on her head. From the Sesklo culture in Greece, wonderfully fashioned Bird Goddesses survive with nicely developed breasts, long cylindrical necks, a birdlike head (long, large nose without an anthropomorphic mouth), with neatly combed hair or a bun. (FIGURE 7–13) The

FIGURE 7–14

FIGURE 7–15

FIGURE 7–14 Duck-masked and crowned Bird Goddess from the Late Vinča culture. She sits on a throne incised with three lines and wears a bolero jacket; her pelvis or apron is marked with chevrons, her knees with spirals, and her limbs with coiling lines. From Svetozarevo, C Yugoslavia; c. 4500 B.C. H 16 cm.

FIGURE 7–15 This duck vase from Vinča wears a mask with a pointed nose (beak) and large human semicircular eyes and ears. Constructed of terracotta with very thin walls, light brown fabric, rippled, and painted with black bands of bituminous material. It is hollow inside, with an opening at the tail. Classical Vinča; discovered 7.05 m deep in Vinča mound, east of Belgrade. Early part of the 5th mill. B.C. L 36 cm, H 20.8 cm.

FIGURE 7–16

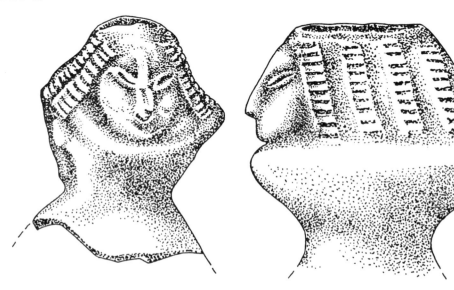

FIGURE 7–16 Bird with human mask and "braids." Top and base are broken; this probably served as an attachment to a large vase. Sesklo culture from Magoula at Lake Boebeis in the region of Stephanovikion, NW of Volos, Thessaly; probable date, end of the 7th mill. B.C. Scale 1:1.

FIGURE 7-17

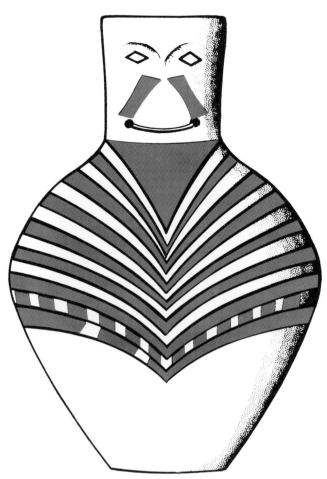

FIGURE 7-17 Large pithos with the face of a Bird Goddess on the neck (beak in relief, eyes executed by incision). Two red bands painted diagonally below the beak. The necklace is shown in relief. The body is incised and painted with red bands which merge in front forming a triangle. Early Vinča; Anza, Macedonia; 5200–5000 B.C. H 92 cm.

Bird Goddess sculptures of the Vinča culture are usually decorated with symbolic signs and depicted with characteristic pentagonal masks with a sharp nose, accentuated eyebrows, with no mouthd (see figs. 3–20, 3–21). Sometimes the mask is clearly of a duck. (FIGURE 7–14) Some exceptional sculptures of birds with goddess masks have survived from this culture. One, especially well crafted, was found in Vinča itself, near Belgrade. It is a hollow vase, 36 cm long, shaped like a duck, whose surface is decorated with a channelling technique. (FIGURE 7–15) Sculptures of birds with human masks, a mythical image well known in ancient Greece and later times, go back to c. 6000 B.C. (FIGURE 7–16)

The Bird Goddess was also represented in the shape of vases painted with chevrons, meanders, or other symbols, with her face or mask on the neck. Such a huge goddess vase, 92 cm high, painted with red chevrons, was found during my excavation in Anza, Macedonia, in an early Vinča culture sanctuary from 5300–5000 B.C. (FIGURE 7–17) Her face was on the neck of the vase with a collar and bands diagonally across her cheeks. In the same place, a vase 60 cm long was also found in the shape of a water bird. (FIGURE 7–18)

FIGURE 7-18

FIGURE 7–18 Vase in the shape of a water bird. Anza IV, Macedonia. Early Vinča culture, c. 5200–5000 B.C. L 60 cm.

Goddess vases frequently have breasts that can have holes in the centers as spouts. An example from the sanctuary of Mallia in Crete, 3rd millennium B.C., shows the whole goddess with wings, a bird's beak, large round eyes, a turban, and holes in her breasts. (FIGURE 7–19) The entire vase was painted white with zig-zag lines and striated bands, with as many as four collars on her neck. Such a vase was probably used for libations in honor of the Bird Goddess.

The breast motif in the ceramic art of Old Europe survived for thousands of years. Some very finely crafted pitchers with breasts have been found in western Turkey, in the Cyclades—especially on the island of Thera—and in Crete from the first half of the 2nd millennium B.C. In central Europe, the breast motif is found almost throughout the entire 2nd millennium B.C., even though the Goddess was not, at that time, universally worshiped. Vases with breasts and symbols of the Bird Goddess that are related to water, the fountain of life, make it clear that this Goddess was the Nourisher, who maintained life and brought good fortune.

The representation of water birds—geese, cranes, swans, and others—appears in Upper Paleolithic art in bone carvings and cave drawings. The water bird was an important source of food and, consequently, a symbol of well-being. Water birds in fairy stories remain as magical birds, increasing or decreasing wealth and fortune. Water nymphs of European folklore who magically perform various kinds of women's work, especially spinning and weaving, appear as mortal women, naked with very long breasts. Sometimes they appear dressed, but one can notice their bird's feet and if their clothing is parted, there would be the body of a hen, a goose, or a duck. They work very quickly, without a moment's respite, but if angered, they can destroy everything. (Such nymphs are the amazingly archaic Baltic Laumes.) Through them the influence of the Goddess is multiplied and spread among the people.

FIGURE 7–19

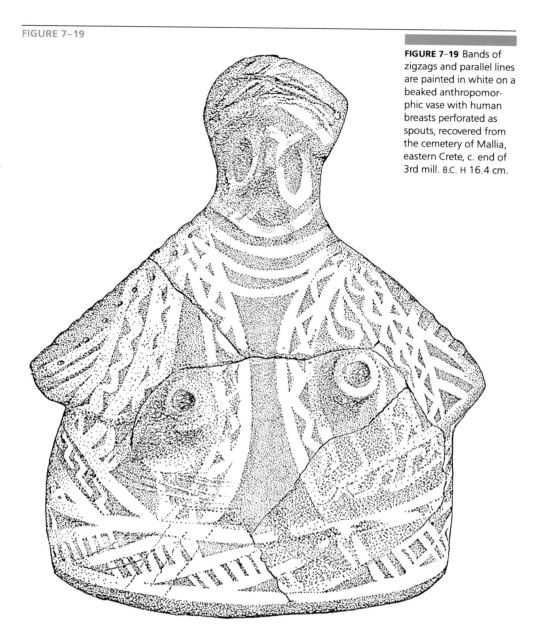

FIGURE 7–19 Bands of zigzags and parallel lines are painted in white on a beaked anthropomorphic vase with human breasts perforated as spouts, recovered from the cemetery of Mallia, eastern Crete, c. end of 3rd mill. B.C. H 16.4 cm.

The sacred animal of the Bird Goddess was the ram, which gained symbolic importance during the Early Neolithic when sheep became an important source of food and rams were needed for reproduction. Many figurines of rams have been found masked and marked with the symbols of this goddess. The ram motif is frequently found on ritual earthenware and lamps. (PLATE 13) Its head decorates the facades or roofs of temples. Ram horns and snake spirals are depicted alternately with the Goddess's eyes in graves and funerary ceramics. To this day, the meaning of the ram in folklore is similar to the water bird as a magical animal which brings abundance. In the vases of Classical Greece, the ram is shown being offered to Athena as her sacred animal. Athena, the descendant of the prehistoric Bird Goddess, is frequently associated with birds: the sea hawk, sea-gull, duck, diver bird, swallow, dove, owl, and vulture.

Buttocks and breasts share the magical power of being double, while also being symbols of life proliferation. Two has more life-giving power than one, and in the art of Old Europe, from the Neolithic to the end of the Minoan culture, the motif of doubleness is frequent. In addition to breasts and buttocks, there are often two spirals, two snakes, two phalli, two caterpillars, two seeds, or two fruits.

What we see in the rock carvings of the Magdalenian culture from Gönnersdorf in the German Rhineland, from La Roche at Lalinde and Fontales in southern France (FIGURE 7–20), in the little sculptures from Pekarna, Moravia, and Petersfels in southern Germany, and in the figurines from the Starčevo and Sesklo cultures (FIGURE 7–21), is none other than the hybridization of bird and female forms. This is the identification of female buttocks with the long body of a bird or bird carrying an egg. Buttocks, like eggs, have special powers of generation. On buttocks we frequently find carved or painted snakes, spirals, concentric circles, crosses, or whirling signs, as well as the motif of two C's in opposition—life-stimulating symbols. We must note that these peculiar hybrids of female

FIGURE 7–20

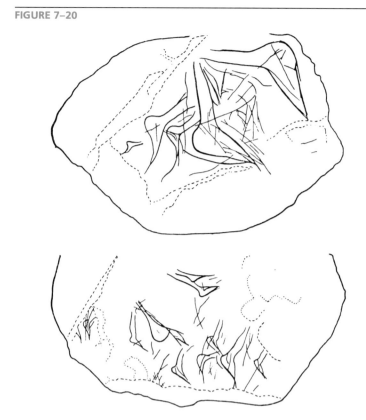

FIGURE 7–20 Engravings on rocks of schematic figures with egg-shaped buttocks, usually headless (if there is a head it is of a bird), marked with one, two, or more lines. Magdalenian IV, c. 10,000 B.C. La Roche at Lalinde, Dordogne, S France.

FIGURE 7–21

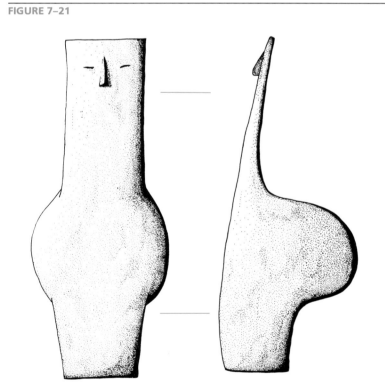

FIGURE 7–21 4,500 years later, egg-shaped buttocks appear on Neolithic terracotta sculpture. This figurine reveals the emphasis on exaggerated egg-shaped buttocks to the exclusion of all other body parts. Starčevo/Körös (Röszke-Ludvár, SE Hungary; c. 5500 B.C.). H 11.5 cm.

and bird are most frequently depicted without breasts, indicating that the buttocks were especially important. In this case, generation was more important than nourishment.

The Snake and the Snake Goddess

The snake is a main image of the vitality and continuity of life, the guarantor of life energy in the home, and the symbol of family and animal life. We can recreate the snake's symbolism, not only from prehistoric depictions of the Snake Goddess and her worship as a household deity, but also from archaic folk beliefs in the power of snakes, both female and male. For example, the belief that killing a green snake kept in the house would result in the death of a family member still survives in 20th century Lithuania.[15] Until recently, Russians and other Slavs believed in a "Domovoi," a protector of home life and well-being, which was sometimes a snake and sometimes a (male) human being, and in whom resided the soul of a family ancestor. Hundreds of Greek and Roman reliefs and drawings witness the existence of house-guardian green snakes, who are the *Zeus Ktesios* in Greece and *penates dii* in Rome. The image of the snake is intimately connected with the cycles of death and rebirth in nature. Its hibernation is analogous to death, while the shedding of old skin represents a kind of immortality, a continuum of life. The return of the snake in springtime signifies the rebirth of the natural world.

In Lithuania, on the "Day of the Snakes" around the first of February, people prepared various dishes for the snakes and invited them into the homes. If the snakes tasted the food, the year would be prosperous; their choice determined the course of the whole year.[16] In Ireland, during the holiday of Brigit on February 1st, it was believed that "the queen was returning from the hills."[17] The queen was a Snake Goddess to whom all other snakes belong. A belief in the magical crown of the snake queen still survives in European folklore: whoever catches hold of the crown will know all the secrets of the world, find enchanted treasures, and understand the speech of animals. In prehistoric times,

FIGURE 7–22

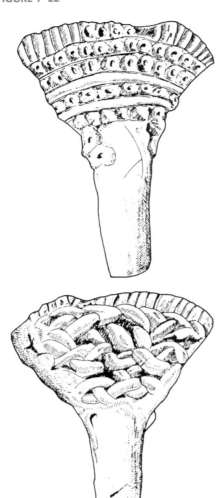

sculptures of the crowned Snake Goddess are found starting with the 7th and 6th millennia B.C. in Crete, the Aegean area, and in the Balkans. On her crown is sometimes found a whole nest of snakes. (FIGURE 7–22)

The anthropomorphic Neolithic Snake Goddess has been found in a yogic pose, usually with snakelike hands and feet (FIGURE 7–23, 1, 2). If the head is anthropomorphic, it has eyes and a wide mouth, but never a birdlike nose. She is also known by the snakelike shape of her head or the wavy lines painted over her body. (FIGURE 7–24) A snake with horns or a moon crescent appears in Paleolithic cave drawings, and from the Neolithic, snakes with crescents or horns are found represented in relief on vases. (FIGURE 7–25) These must have signified her regenerative powers.

The most widely known sculptures of the Snake Goddess or her sacred attendants are the 16th century B.C. faience or ivory figurines from the temple of Knossos in Crete. These are the most elegant of all, with exposed breasts and snakes encircling their waists and arms. Their clothes are also of snakelike design with curving spirals and checkerboard or rhombic stripes. In western Europe, depictions of the Snake Goddess continued up to the Celtic La Tène culture in France, 4th to 3rd centuries B.C. In Crete, the feet of the Goddess are sometimes snakelike, in weavings and drawings, well into modern times.

Influenced by Christian, Semitic, and Indo-European religions, we are accustomed to think of the snake as an incarnation of evil. The snake of Old Europe, however, represents the antithesis of Christian, Semitic, and Indo-European religions. She assures the well-being and continuity of life through intimate identification and harmony with the cycles of nature. Through seasonal renewal of vital energy, the snake assures and protects the life of humans and animals. There are hundreds of beliefs in the snake's magical plants and flowers which can heal the sick and even raise the dead. Even the snake's body was used as medicine. The snake is also present in her poisonous aspect, appearing as the Goddess of Death.

FIGURE 7–22 During the Minoan Bronze Age, the crown of the Snake Goddess was sometimes enormous, as this five-tiered example shows. The back reveals a mass of writhing snakes. Middle Minoan I from Kophina, c. 2000 B.C. H 7 cm.

FIGURE 7–23 The Snake Goddess of the Neolithic (1) in a yogic type posture with snakelike limbs. This example is of clay burnished dark gray and encrusted with white lines. Early Cretan Neolithic; Kato Ierapetra; probably around 6000 B.C. H 14.2 cm. (2) Marble figurine of the Snake Goddess from an Aegean island. H 20.3 cm.

FIGURE 7–24 The Snake Goddess identity is made known through the snakelike shape of her head or the wavy (snake) lines painted over her body, representing the life current (''Kundalini''). Red painted on cream. Anatolian Neolithic, provenance unknown; probably 6000–5500 B.C. H 10 cm.

FIGURE 7–25 A horned snake with large, round eyes. Relief on the shoulder of a vase. Dibel near Bitolj, S Yugoslavia. Early 5th mill. B.C.

FIGURE 7–23

FIGURE 7–24

FIGURE 7–25

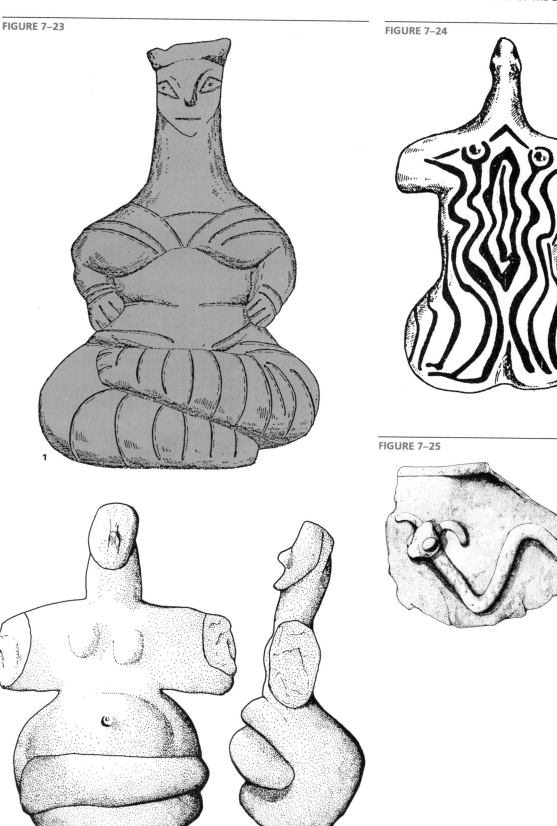

1

2

The Goddess of Death: Announcer of Death as Bird of Prey and Poisonous Snake

The Goddess of Death often appears as a woman dressed in white (the color of bones) or even as three white women, often with a white dog as her companion. Frequently, when she is prophesying death, this Goddess manifests as an owl or crow—birds of prey. European folklore is full of the same kinds of warnings from birds of prey to this day: owls, crows, ravens, jays, hawks, and sea-gulls are dreaded birds; their sounds, prophesying misfortune or death, make us shiver. White dogs, especially grey-hounds, are considered supernatural. Another animal associated with the Death Goddess who creates destruction is the boar, its bristles considered poisonous as snakes.

Skeletons of birds of prey, especially their wings, are found buried in Paleolithic and Neolithic sites. It is not surprising, then, that the main manifestations of the Neolithic Death Goddess became the vulture and the owl, found in temples and graveyards. The custom of excarnation, leaving dead bodies to be devoured by birds, existed in western Europe until the Bronze Age.

The most impressive Vulture Goddesses are those from the wall paintings of Çatal Hüyük where they are visualized attacking headless bodies. (FIGURE 7–26, 1) The head, as the primary dwelling place of the soul, was removed after death and placed near the head of a bull (a symbol of regeneration). The appearance of the Vulture Goddess in the motherly act of gathering the remains of the dead into herself undoubtedly goes back to very ancient times. (FIGURE 7–26, 2) A number of stunning wall paintings reconstructed from Çatal Hüyük by James Mellaart show variations of a Goddess/vulture motif, as seen in FIGURE 26, 3. These designs, further abstracted, can be seen even today in Turkish kilims.

FIGURE 7–26

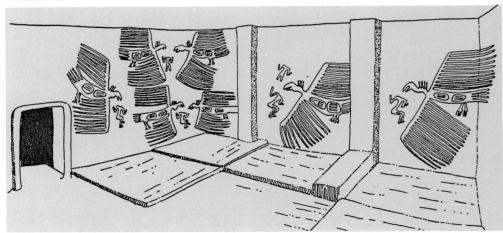

1

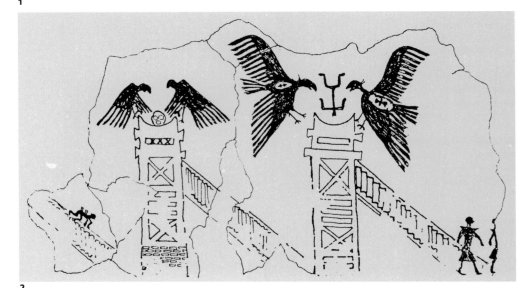

2

3

FIGURE 7–26 (1) Vultures with tremendous broomlike wings descending upon headless corpses. Wall painting from temple in Level VII,8 at Çatal Hüyük, C Anatolia. End mid-7th mill B.C. (2) Sketched reconstruction of a wall painting from Çatal Hüyük showing a human head and a headless body on towers, surrounded by vultures. From Shrine E.VIB/3. (3) Sketched reconstruction of a wall painting from Çatal Hüyük, Shrine E.V/9 showing red and black vultures with goddesses.

FIGURE 7–27 The Owl Goddess (half owl, half woman) as statue menhirs from Portugal, Spain, and southern France. Frequently only her eyes and nose (beak) and occasionally breasts are shown. A hook is sometimes shown in relief (4,6). Late Neolithic, 4th to early 3rd mill. B.C. (1) Asquerosa, Granada, Spain. (2) C Portugal. (3) Crato, Alentejo, C Portugal. (4) Mas de L'Aveugle, Collorgues, Gard, S France. (5) Trigueros, Huelva, S Spain. (6) Aven Meunier, I, S France. Scale: (1) 60.2 cm; (2) 50.9 cm; (3) 50.3 cm; (4) 163 cm; (5) 2 m.; (6) 164.1 cm.

FIGURE 7–27

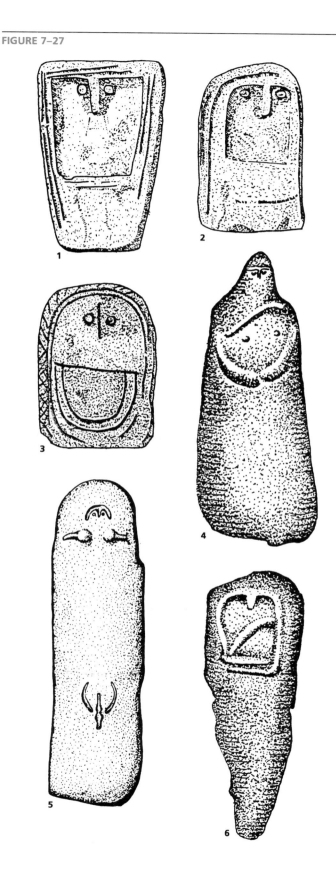

Vultures in Europe exist only in the area of the Mediterranean Sea, between Spain and Turkey. There are no Vulture Goddesses to the north; there are, instead, goddesses representing the owl and other birds of prey. In western Europe the Owl Goddess is found engraved on menhirs that stood at the entrances of megalithic graves or even within the graves themselves. (FIGURE 7–27) The round eyes of this goddess, and sometimes the eyes and beak joined with eyebrows, are found in megalithic temples such as Newgrange, Knowth, and others, while the Owl Goddess of southeastern Europe appears in the form of an urn. Wherever the Owl Goddess is found she is associated with spirals, snakes, bucrania, triangles, triangle-shaped axes, and hooks. The latter two are frequent attributes of the Owl Goddess menhirs in Britain, France, and Portugal as powerful symbols of regeneration.

The Vulture Goddess is known from the Minoan culture of Crete portrayed on seals and vases. She is shown with one arm or wing up, the other down (FIGURE 7–28, 3, 4), perhaps a gesture of power or verdict. The same gesture begins to appear on incised or relief figures of early Neolithic ceramics. (FIGURE 7–28, 1, 2)

In historical times, Vulture and Owl Goddesses continued in the forms of Athena in Greece, and the Morrígan in Ireland who turns into a crow or raven. Under the influence of Indo-European culture, both of these were militarized, granting victory or defeat to armies at the time of battle.

The White Goddess of Death:
The Stiff Nude of the Graves

The main characteristics of this Goddess—stiff pose, nude, usually without breasts, hands either on chest or extended along her sides (or even without arms), having a large pubic triangle—occur for thousands of years from the Upper Paleolithic through the Bronze Age in every culture of Europe. Whereas the Neolithic stiff nudes are rotund, Copper and Early Bronze Age images of the 4th and 3rd millennia B.C. are slim and abstracted. Their legs are usually reduced to cones and their folded arms become rectangles. Others are even more schematized, lacking arms and legs, with amorphous elongated necks. (FIGURE 7–29) Found at grave sites, singly or in groups of three, she is the White Goddess because death was envisioned as a white bonelike form. Almost without exception she is carved of bone, marble, or alabaster, and if these materials were not available, her images were molded from light-colored clay or sculpted from light-colored stone. Some of the most well known in the history of art are the marble White Goddesses of the Cyclades, some of which reach 1.5 m in height. These are appreciated for their elegant rendering and well-proportioned bodies. The figurines found in rock-cut tombs of Sardinia from the 6th and 5th millennia B.C., as well as in Greece and elsewhere, are no less noteworthy. (FIGURE 7–30) Their body parts harmonize

FIGURE 7–28

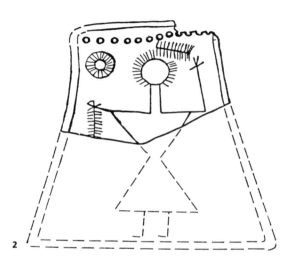

FIGURE 7–28 Neolithic and Minoan Goddesses with one arm raised and one pointing down. (1) Incision on a vase from Karanovo I culture, early 6th mill. B.C. (2) Incision of an hourglass figure with sun-head, upraised bird's foot, associated with branches from the Ozieri culture (Conca Illonis), Sardinia, end 5th mill. B.C. (3) Bird Goddess design with snake crest on painted pottery from Phaistos, Crete, early 2nd mill. B.C. (4) Design on steatite prism from Mallia, Crete, mid-2nd mill. B.C.

FIGURE 7–29

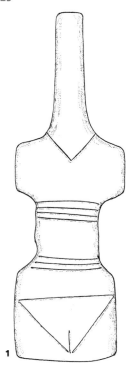

1

2

FIGURE 7–30

FIGURE 7–29 Cycladic schematic abstract marble figurines with large vulvas and cylindrical neck or large mask, V signs and groups of parallel horizontal lines around the body. Early Cycladic I. (1) from LOS (Norwich·University of East Anglia Collection). (2) Delos island. H 11 cm.

FIGURE 7–30 (1) Egg-shaped rock-cut tomb with a crouched skeleton. Figurine representing the White Goddess of Death and Regeneration (see 2) was placed near the chest. A dish with an open shell filled with red paste, and other vases were nearby. Cuccuru S'Arriu, Oristano, central W Sardinia; mid-5th mill. B.C. (2) Rotund Sardinian Stiff Nude with a headgear found in an oven-shaped tomb. Gray stone. Cemetery of Cuccuru S'Arriu, Oristano, C Sardinia; mid-fifth mill. B.C. H 17.2 cm.

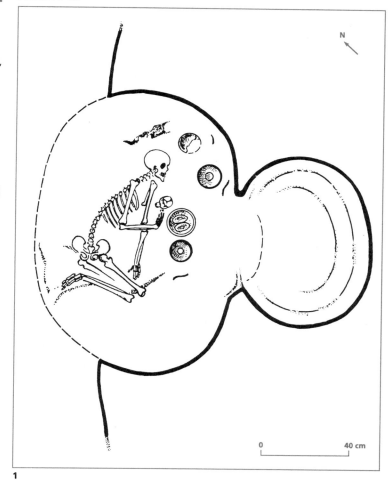

1

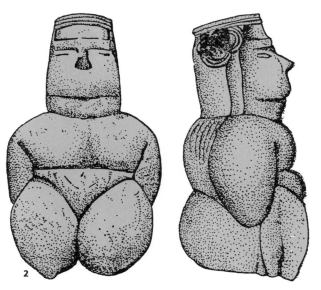

2

with the triangle which is almost in the center of their form, while their hands are lowered and the face (or mask) is very serene.

The White Death Goddesses of Karanovo in Bulgaria and Romania, made of clay or bone, are rendered with terrifying masks: round eyes, a long mouth, and teeth. (FIGURE 7–31) In the Aegean and Mediterranean regions, however, her masks usually do not have a mouth, only a large nose, which is the mask of the Bird Goddess.

In the cemetery of Varna on the coast of the Black Sea in Bulgaria, life-sized clay masks were buried separately. All had the same attributes as the masks of the Karanovo figurines, although these were made of gold, having round eyes and a long mouth with teeth. Each wore a diadem, and near the chin were hung round ornaments with a hole in the center and two eyes at the top (FIGURE 7–32). In graveyards of the Late Cucuteni culture, bone figurines of the White Death Goddess were found in sets of three without arms, with round, hollow eyes.

In European folklore, the White Goddess of Death is also expressed in these two forms, bird of prey and poisonous snake. In Ireland the foretellers of death are always birds that make horrifying wailing sounds, while in Lithuania death is felt as the creeping of a poisonous snake. The name of the Lithuanian Death Goddess expresses a great deal: she is *Giltinė, gilti* meaning "sting." The words *galas* ("end") and *geltonas* ("yellow"—the color of bone) are also in the same family group of words. In folk stories she is called the sister of the goddess Laima, who apportions life.

It is profoundly significant that every stiff nude is represented with an enlarged pubic triangle in the center of her body. Even in death she holds the promise of regeneration, for indeed her womb is eternally the pivotal center between nonlife and new life.

FIGURE 7–31

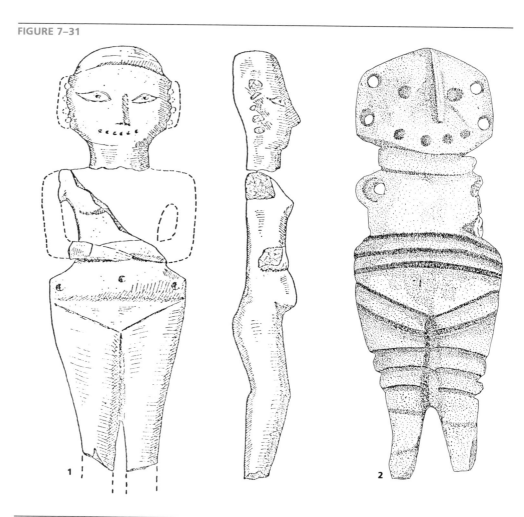

FIGURE 7–32

FIGURE 7–31 Marble and bone figurines portraying the White Goddess of Death and Regeneration from the middle of the 5th mill. B.C. Note the teethlike depressions at the mouth. The broad masks have holes in the ears for copper earrings. Karanovo VI culture. (1) Blagoevo at Razgrad, NE Bulgaria. (2) Căscioarele, island site, Lower Danube, S Romania. H (1) 33 cm (originally); (2) c. 20 cm.

FIGURE 7–32 Life-size mask moulded of clay from Grave No. 2 of the Varna cemetery. Decorated with a gold crown, mouth, teeth, earrings, and two ring-shaped pendants with eyes and projections attached to the chin. Such masks were placed in symbolic graves (kenotaphs) showered with gifts. This grave also included additional gold earrings and plates, a mass of Aegean shell beads, a copper needle, a bone spindle whorl, a fragment of a bone figurine, a small lidded vase, and a large dish with graphite painting of a fourfold whorl design. Mid-5th mill. B.C.

The Goddess of Death and Regeneration

All life in nature proceeds from death, as death from life. This is most obvious in the vegetable world, in which the mulch from once living plants is essential for new growth. The acknowledgment of this interdependence and continuum between life and death is expressed in prehistoric mythologies as the Mystery at the core of all being. It is no wonder that the lives of ancient peoples seem to have pivoted around seasonal observations of death and regeneration.

In the religion of Old Europe, death and regeneration are expressed as two interdependent, contiguous aspects of one deity. Although death and birth are seen as polar opposites in our linear, dualistic culture, the Great Goddess of the Stone Age embodies both simultaneously, representing the unbroken continuity of the one ever-repeating cycle that underlies all manifestations. It is she who holds dominion over death; the cold darkness of winter, caves, graves, and tombs in the earth are her dominion, but she is also the one who receives the fertile seed, the light of midwinter, the fertilized egg, which transforms the tomb into a womb for the gestation of new life. This explains the fact that many graves have been found in the shape of an egg, sometimes covered with a triangular stone or cairn. Megalithic graves in Western Europe are often in the form of a vagina and uterus, or in the shape of the anthropomorphic body of the Goddess (see figs. 6–15 to 6–20).

There are a number of images of the Death Goddess surviving into our modern age that are important to mention. Memories of her live on in fairy tales, rituals, customs, and in language. Collections of tales, such as the German *Märchen*, are rich in prehistoric motifs describing the Goddess of winter and death. She is the ugly Old Hag with a long nose, large teeth, and disheveled hair known as Frau Holla (or Hell, Holda, Perchta, among other names). Her strength lingers in her teeth and hair and she controls the making of snow, the appearance of the sun, and the regeneration of nature. Once a year she

appears as a dove, a blessing which ensures fertility. As a frog, she is Holla who brings the red apple, the symbol of life, back to the earth from the well into which it fell at harvest. Her realm is the inner depths of mounds and caves (*Holla*, the name of the Goddess, and *Höhle*, the word for "cave" are certainly related). For Holla as the Mother of the Dead, bread was baked at Christmas time called *Hollenzopf*, meaning "Holla's braid." The elder tree, called *Holler* or *Holunder*, was the sacred tree of the Goddess. Under this tree, which had healing powers, lived the dead.[18] This powerful goddess was not erased from the mythical world but lives on throughout Europe as the Baltic Ragana, the Polish Jędza, Mora and Morava from Serbia, the Basque Mari, the Irish Morrígan, and the Russian Baba Yaga.

Baba Yaga, whose main changes of form are into bird and snake, is described as tall, lean, with a long hooked nose and a bone leg, who lives in a little house standing on bird's feet. Analysis of her name reveals characteristics of the prehistoric Goddess. In Old Russian and Serbo-Croatian languages, *baba* refers to "woman," "old woman," and "pelican"— and *yaga* from *yęga* means "sickness," "fear," and "wrath," hence a survival of the Death Goddess. In the Proto-Samoyed language, the word *nga* means "Goddess of Death" or "God."[19] In western Europe, the Death Goddess in Breton was called *Ankou*, and in Old Irish *Anu*, meaning "the guardian of the dead" or "mother of gods."[20]

In language there is a connection between the Goddess Death who causes nightmarish feelings and the short-lived moth or butterfly. Both the Irish *Maro* and the Lithuanian *More* mean "The Goddess Death" or "Old Hag"; the Greek, Slavic, and Germanic *mora*, *mara*, and *morava* mean "terror," "nightmare," and "night butterfly" or "moth." The Germanic *Mahr* and the French *cauchemar* are also related. The dreaded Death becomes the butterfly of regeneration.

The degradation of the Goddess in all of her forms, which began during the period of Indo-Europeanization of Old Europe in the 4th and 3rd millennia B.C., continued throughout the historical period, with great intensification by the entire array of Hebraic-Christian traditions. In spite of extreme attempts to eradicate her during historic times, especially by the European Inquisition of the Middle Ages in which virtually every woman of wisdom and influence was burned, her importance in life and storytelling did not disappear. The Goddess of Death and Regeneration was demonized and degraded into the familiar and highly publicized image of the witch. She came to represent all that was denied and considered evil within this relatively recent mythology of dualism. This was a complete reversal of the religion of Old Europe which conceived of life and death and all cyclic polarities as sacred and inseparable. No longer was the earth considered our Divine Mother, from whom we are born and to whom we return in death. Deity was removed into the heavens and earth became a place of exile.

The witch-Goddess in folklore still controls, or at least influences, death and rebirth, the cycles of the moon, and the energies of sun, storms, and lightning. She is skilled in the use of medicinal herbs and is the balancer of human, animal, and plant vitality, so that bounds will not be overstepped or life energy needlessly wasted. For this reason she controls human sexuality, which intensifies men's fear of her. The witch kills infants, because both the newborn and the dark womb remain in her domain for forty days. Disposal of the placenta after birth survives as a custom to insure that the newborn will be freed from her influence. In Malta it is said, "I am burying not you, placenta, but the Zagas (witch)."[21] The mythology of witches that has come down to us contains traditions of the ancient goddess intermingled with the demonized Judaic and Christian versions.

The identification of the womb as the Goddess is a central motif and an important key in understanding an entire series of prehistoric symbols. It is no coincidence that the principal incarnations of the witch are identical with those of the prehistoric Goddess: toad, frog, hedgehog, and fish.

Symbols of Regeneration

The Goddess who represents regeneration appears in forms related to female generative organs: the pubic triangle, expressed as triangles and hourglass shapes (double triangles); the vulva, rendered as an oval with a dot and line in the center, as seed and bud shapes and related images; the uterus, expressed as fish or hedgehog; as well as fetuses shown as frogs or hares. The female womb with its fallopian tubes resembles the shape of a bull's head with horns, which may well account for the prevailing use of this motif to represent regeneration. This Goddess is also rendered in art as a bee, butterfly, moth, or other insect, sometimes having the anthropomorphic head of the Goddess. Insects may represent the Goddess herself, or souls that leave the body at death or during dreams. These associations are recorded in history as well as in archeological data and continue throughout European folklore.

In the large stone sculptures of Lepenski Vir, described later (see below, Burial Practices), we find a typical hybridization of fish and Goddess, and sometimes fish, woman, and bird of prey. These were found at the head of the altar in triangular/trapezoid temples. Here, and in other temples of the Iron Gate region of the Danube, fish, dogs, roe-deer, and boars were sacrificed to the Goddess Regeneratrix at the time of burials. In the temples of Malta and in underground egg-shaped graves, sculptures of fish were found respectfully lying on couches (see fig. 7–107). The couch, whether underground or at night, suggests a transition to rebirth.

The Goddess in the form of a frog or toad predominates in the temples, and her icons or amulets of marble, alabaster, green stone, ivory, or clay are found throughout the Neolithic, Bronze Age, and even throughout historical times. (FIGURE 7–33) Beliefs in the body's "traveling womb" in the form of a frog occur widely from Egypt, Greece, and Rome, to northern Europe during the historical period and, in some places, to this day. The very ancient character of this image is confirmed by bone carvings from the Upper Paleolithic in the form of half woman, half frog. In the Neolithic and later periods, frogs are pictured frequently with anthropomorphic features, with a vulva or human head. Sometimes the head is replaced by a bud.

The hedgehog occurs in European iconography from the 5th millennium B.C. There are vases in the form of hedgehogs found in the Karanovo culture in Romania and Bulgaria whose lids have the anthropomorphic features of the Goddess. (FIGURE 7–34) In later times, hedgehog-shaped vases and figurines were found in the Mycenaean culture from the 14 to 13th centuries B.C., and in Greek and Etruscan graves from the 9th to 6th centuries B.C. Large jars (pithoi) shaped like hedgehogs were also found enclosing the skeletons of infants. Here we have a synthesis of three related symbols: the grave, the womb, and the hedgehog. Until the 20th century in Alpine countries there was a custom of placing red-painted spiky balls inside graves. These balls had been offered to the Virgin Mary in church for help with uterine problems. In Lithuanian folklore collected in the mid-20th century, there is mention of an old woman who turns into a hedgehog in the cow barn.

An even more esoteric symbol of the womb of regeneration is the bull's head or skull (bucranium). The similarity of the bucranium with the shape of a woman's uterus and fallopian tubes was noticed by artist Dorothy Cameron while working with James Mellaart at Çatal Hüyük. (FIGURE 7–35) This is a plausible if esoteric explanation for the importance of this motif in the symbolism of Old Europe, Anatolia, and the Near East. Ox heads can be seen depicted on anthropomorphic vases in place of the uterus. (FIGURE 7–36) A great deal of information on the symbolic role of the bull's head is revealed by the wall paintings from Çatal Hüyük. In many, the bucranium is either shown in place of the uterus in the body of the Goddess, or is shown below the frog-shaped Goddess.

FIGURE 7–33

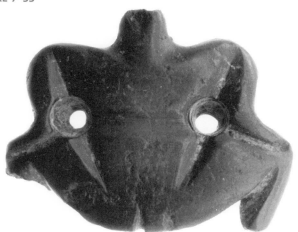

FIGURE 7–35

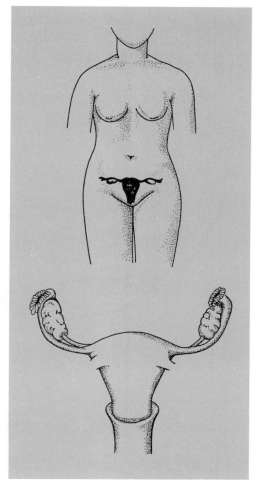

FIGURE 7–33 Stone amulet in the shape of a frog-woman. Achilleion I, c. 6300–6200 B.C. Black stone. H 3.2 cm.

FIGURE 7–34

FIGURE 7–34 Hedgehog Goddess portrayed on the lid of a large vase. Karanovo-Gumelnița culture. Căscioarele on the Lower Danube island, S Romania, c. 4500–4300 B.C.

FIGURE 7–35 Female reproductive organs from a medical textbook. The similarity with the bull head is striking.

FIGURE 7–36

FIGURE 7–36 Bull head with large horns, shown in relief on an anthropomorphic marble vase, representing a woman's uterus. Early Cycladic, c. end of 4th mill. B.C. H 10.5 cm.

FIGURE 7–37

FIGURE 7–37 Vase with a bull head protome. Painted snake spirals and eggs suggest regeneration symbolism. Poienești, Classical Cucuteni culture, c. 4200–4100 B.C. H 19 cm.

In ceramic art from the beginning of the Neolithic to the end of the Minoan culture, bucrania are associated consistently with symbols of regeneration and energy. The motif of the bull's head occurs on painted ceramics of Cucuteni. (FIGURE 7–37), and little ones are frequently found in relief on the ceramics of Butmir. Bucrania coated with a layer of clay are found in Vinča temples (see fig. 3–16).

The bull head motif in the underground tombs of Sardinia is predominant as a sign of regeneration. Bull heads, that is, uteri, were pictured above or near the entrance, and in some caves the entrance itself was an oxhead, while above it were large horns (see figs. 7–112, 7–113). To enter this underground temple, one must symbolically pass through the sacred womb. The close relationship of a cow, bull, or ox head with the womb is confirmed also by the intimate connection of the ox with waters, the fountain of life. In Lithuanian legends, the ox comes from water, while clouds and lakes are formed from oxen. Sculptures of cattle from the Neolithic and Minoan or Mycenaean cultures were decorated with nets or eggs covered with a net design. The net motif symbolizes the water of life or amniotic fluid. The "horns of consecration" we find from the 3rd and 2nd millennia B.C., which are especially characteristic of the Minoan culture of Crete, continue the symbolism of the womb and regeneration.

From antiquity, flowers and plants—life trees—have been shown growing between the "sacred horns." Bees and butterflies, sometimes having anthropomorphic heads, arise from bull heads, as painted on Minoan vases and temple walls. (FIGURE 7–38) From the Roman authors Ovid, Virgil, and Porphyry we know that moths and bees were thought to be the souls of humans born from an ox. From the Cucuteni culture of the beginning of the 4th millennium B.C., an ox head was found carved out of a bone plate on which an hourglass-shaped goddess is depicted with arms upraised. (FIGURE 7–39) Here she is not death but rebirth. A cave painting from Spain shows an hourglass-shaped goddess with bird's feet and hands, bee's eyes and

FIGURE 7–38 The Goddess arising from a bull head. Painting (detail) on a late Minoan I vase from Pseira, eastern Crete, depicting the resurrection of new life as the butterfly rising from between the horns of a bull, which symbolizes a uterus. (2) Crowned Goddess with butterfly wings rises from between the horns. Seal impression from Zakros, E Crete, Middle Minoan III.

FIGURE 7–39 A punctate silhouette of the Goddess in her hourglass form is rendered on a bull's head carved of bone plate. Cucuteni culture, from Bilcze Zlote, Upper Seret valley, W Ukraine; c. 3700–3500 B.C. H 17 cm.

FIGURE 7–40 The hourglass-shaped Goddess with bird's feet, bee's eyes and antennae. The three lines are the Bird Goddess's identifying marks. Late Neolithic, S Spain. H 11.2 cm.

FIGURE 7–38

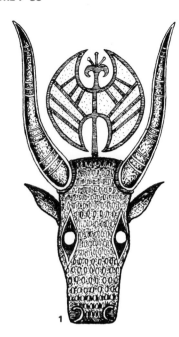

FIGURE 7–39

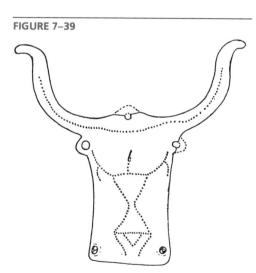

FIGURE 7–40

antennae, and three lines which mark the Bird Goddess. (FIGURE 7–40) She is at once a bird of prey, a woman, and a bee—a manifestation of death and regeneration.

The Bird Goddess also takes part in the process of regeneration. Her image or her breasts and necklaces show up in megalithic graves. (FIGURE 7–41) Here, the breasts of the Bird Goddess have the function of regeneration out of death, not of nourishment to the living and providing worldly goods. The same function of breasts can be seen 3,000 years earlier in the shrine of Çatal Hüyük where breasts covering the skulls of vultures were carved in relief on the walls, the necrotic character (death symbol) of the Goddess covered by a symbol of life. Her life-giving aspect triumphs while

the death aspect, in the form of a bird of prey, is unavoidable but is only a temporary, passing phase.

The ubiquitous Snake Goddess functions not only in the realm of the living, in both benevolent and poisonous aspects, but also in the realm of regeneration. She is a symbol of resurrection and immortality, inspired by the ability of snakes to awaken from the hibernation of winter and to shed their old skins. Snakes are often rendered in coils which sometimes reverse direction from the center, suggesting the ebb and flow of life, death, and rebirth and the cyclic eternity of time. They are the undulating creatures of the dark, moist earth, messengers of the mysteries of the underworld, whose secret is the ultimate paradox: from death comes life.

FIGURE 7–41

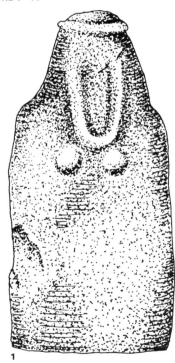

1

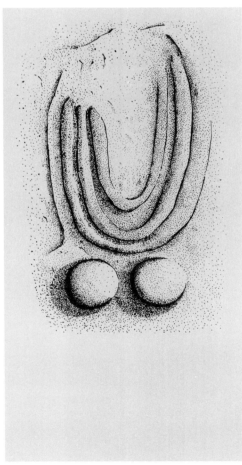

2

FIGURE 7–41 The Goddess's presence in megalithic gallery graves is often symbolized by representations of her breasts and identifying necklace. (1) This granite statue-menhir belongs to a megalithic gallery grave. Catel, Guernsey, Great Britain; c. 3000–2500 B.C. H 1.53 m. (2) Necklaces and breasts of the Goddess in a megalithic tomb. Bellée at Boury, Oise, France. Approx. 3000 B.C.

Male Deities

The very small numbers of sculptures representing male figurines from Neolithic settlements and cemeteries do not mean that male images were less divine or that they were representing mortal men. I do not use the term "hero" for male gods as it is used by Heide Göttner-Abendroth in her important work *Goddess and Her Hero*, 1983. I see male gods as partners, consorts, and brothers of goddesses. Although man is not the life-giving force and fatherhood was unknown in the early times, man's sexual and physical power was esteemed as magically enhancing female life-giving powers. Female and male sexes were not dichotomized in the Neolithic; on the contrary, it was believed that their fusing created potency necessary to charge nature with life powers. Goddesses of regeneration were sometimes protrayed with male genitals or with phallic necks.

At least five categories of male divinities can be distinguished which repeat in the same posture through time. Some are seated on a stool or throne and their importance cannot be disputed. However, they are not birth givers or generative deities in the sense of the female goddess who creates life from her womb, nor are they house or temple gods—except the phallic god who alternates with the snake or Snake Goddess. Their absence from temples and houses can be explained by recognizing that male deities are associated with wild nature and vegetation. Worship of the male gods must have taken place in nature which has left little record.

Strong and Dying Gods of Vegetation

Best represented in Neolithic southeast Europe is "The Sorrowful Ancient," a figure sitting quietly on a chair with hands on knees or supporting his chin. Sculptures of this type representing the quiet, mature, or aged god, have been found in various cultural groups between the 7th and 4th millennia B.C. Such a sculpture of a male god was found together with a female figurine in the Cernavoda cemetery of the Hamangia culture in Romania near the Black Sea.

Both are seated, wearing masks. The male sits in a chair, elbows resting on his knees, head supported with his hands, reminiscent of Rodin's "Thinker." Since he was buried together with a female goddess who probably represented the old Earth Mother, we may guess that this sorrowful male god represents dying vegetation. (FIGURE 7–42) This is analogous to the historically known flax god Linos, who spends winter as a seed, is born in spring, dies in summer, and returns to earth again.

Young males in ithyphallic posture (FIGURE 7–43) most likely express the potency of springtime fertilizing powers. This Strong God must have been the consort of the Goddess. Various goddesses had their consorts as we know from historical mythology: Demeter had

FIGURE 7–42 The masked female and male gods in thoughtful posture, found in a grave. They are perhaps forerunners of the Dying Gods of Vegetation known from historical mythology. Hamangia culture from Cernavoda, Black Sea, Romania, c. 48th–47th centuries B.C. H 12 cm.

FIGURE 7–42

FIGURE 7–43

FIGURE 7–45

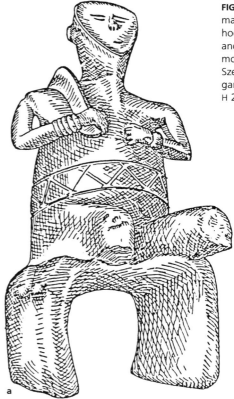

FIGURE 7–45 (a) Seated masked god holding a hook. Note arm rings and belt with zigzag motif. Tisza culture from Szegvár-Tüzköves, Hungary, early 5th mill. B.C. H 25.6 cm. (b) Detail.

FIGURE 7–44

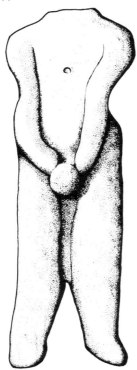

FIGURE 7–43 Strong youthful god in ithyphallic posture seated on a stool. Porodin, S Yugoslavia, c. 6000 B.C. H 5.25 cm.

FIGURE 7–44 Youthful ithyphallic figure, a likely forerunner of pre-Hellenic Hermes. Terracotta. Sesklo culture, Sesklo, Thessaly. H 9 cm.

b

Dionysos, Artemis-Actaeon, Hera-Heracles, Athena-Erechtheus, Cybele-Attis. Five thousand years before ancient Greece, goddesses very likely had their consorts or partners also. Sacred marriage is evidenced from the early Neolithic by couples of females and males embracing.

Phallic God or Snake

Phalli and standing ithyphallic men (FIGURE 7–44) are perhaps prototypes of the Greek herms and god Hermes, originally a phallus or snake. As a snake, this god assures fertility, increase, and health. Greek Hermes was a god of luck who gave wealth and increased flocks and herds. The importance of phallic men, phallic stands, and snakes seem to have been intertwined from prehistory, through Greek and Roman history and into modern folklore.

Centaurs

Centaurs with the body of a bull and the head of a man (PLATE 22) were stimulators of life powers. We know these images from ancient Greek vases where they are shown next to the tree of life. In Cyprus, centaurs were laid in graves of the Chalcolithic period, c. 3500–3000 B.C. to stimulate the regeneration of the dead.

Guardians of Wild Nature

Another role of the male gods could have been as guardians of forests and wild animals, since this motif has survived in folklore and in the customs of northern Eurasia. This is the Master of Animals figure or "the one of the forest," still alive in folklore between Ireland and Russia. This type is more difficult to identify from archeological remains because his cult must have taken place in the wild, not in homes or temples. His prototype, in my understanding, is the Paleolithic half-human, half-animal creature known from cave drawings, shown with animal herds. In one of the Çatal Hüyük wall paintings, a male stick figure holding vultures, considered to be a Master of Animals, alternates with a female figure holding vultures, as Mistress of Animals. This suggests that they were parallel figures.

There is a single sculpture from the Tisza culture in Hungary, referred to as "The Mature Male Holding a Hook," which is perhaps ancestral to the historically known Silvanus, Faunus, and Pan. (FIGURE 7–45) These are forest spirits and protectors of animals, and hunters who are also shown holding hooks.

Sacred Images and Their Provenance

Temples can be classified into two main categories regarding the type of goddess worshiped: the goddess-protectress of life energy and health; guardians of the family (Bird Goddess, Snake Goddess, Birth-giver, Nurse, or Madonna); and those in which death and regeneration rituals were performed. In the latter, the Goddess appears in several aspects: the Vulture Goddess; the Fish- and Frog-shaped Goddess of Regeneration; and the regenerating uterus in the shape of the bull's head, triangle, or double triangle (hourglass or butterfly shape). The early Neolithic Pregnant Goddess was worshiped at the bread oven in the courtyard.

We shall take several excavated early Neolithic sites as examples that have yielded evidence for the various types and functions of deities worshiped in temples or courtyards. Essential information comes from the temples of Achilleion in Thessaly, from 6400–5600 B.C. and from the town of Çatal Hüyük in central Anatolia, with numerous temples dating from the 7th millennium B.C.

Achilleion

This settlement near Farsala in southern Thessaly (excavated by this author with Shan Winn and Daniel Shimabuku in 1973 and 1974) belongs to the Neolithic Sesklo culture in Greece.[22] Its chronology, between the mid-7th and mid-6th millennia B.C., is determined on the basis of forty-two radiocarbon dates in addition to comprehensive data from stratigraphy and typology. The several temples discovered in Achilleion, the two hundred miniature sculptures and the ceremonial platforms with fire pits used for offerings in the courtyard, are significant for religious studies. Moreover, the research at Achilleion has demonstrated that worship was localized in special areas designated for particular goddesses. This research broke new ground by distinguishing between goddesses represented iconically in temples and those worshiped outside—in the courtyard, by the bread oven, and on specially prepared platforms or altars.

The temples in Achilleion were designed in the form of two-room dwellings. Two temples, one above the other, were uncovered from the latest Achilleion period dated, respectively, 6000–5900 B.C. and 5900–5800 B.C. (FIGURE 7–46) The larger chamber with an altar constituted the temple proper, while the smaller was a workroom suited to preparations for religious ritual: the sculpting of figurines, the decoration of pottery, and so forth. Figurines portraying Bird Goddesses, Snake Goddesses, Birth and Nurse Goddesses, were placed on the temple altar. Each temple yielded as many as thirty sculptures, including those that had been discarded in a dump adjacent to the sanctuary. The finest ceramics were found next to the altar. These included huge libation vases with funnels at the top, miniature libation cups, ladles, and ceramic discs (probably loom weights). From the same area we have the masterpiece of the Achilleion excavations: a remarkable ceramic human head with open mouth, no doubt the spout of a libation vase (see fig. 2–12, 2).

Ceramic figurines, particularly the larger ones, are rarely found intact. These were sculpted eight thousand years ago around pebbles or clay nuclei molded separately for the head and neck, stomach and thighs. The heads found in the temples of Achilleion are mainly cylindrical, with beaks (protruding noses), and without anthropomorphic mouths (see figs. 7–16, 7–47). A few sculptures of better quality, reconstructed or partially reconstructed, are presented here. (FIGURE 7–47, lower)

FIGURE 7–46

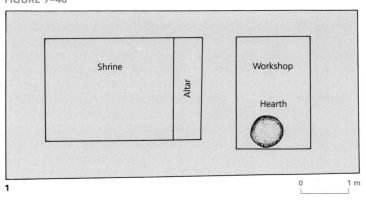

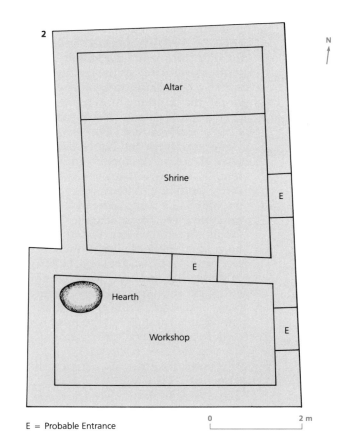

E = Probable Entrance

FIGURE 7–47

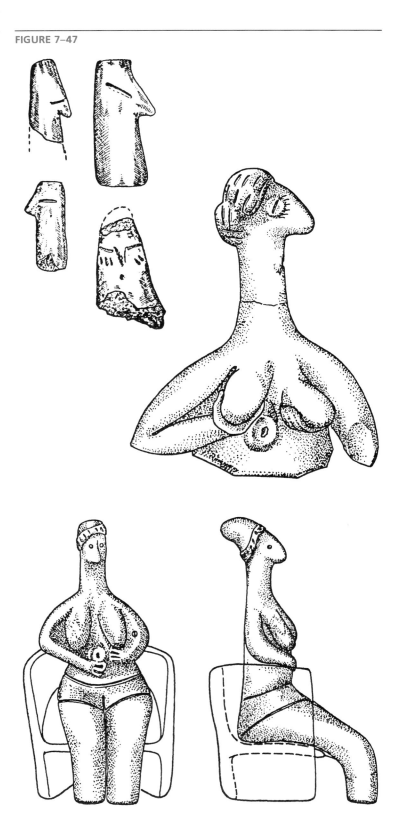

FIGURE 7–48

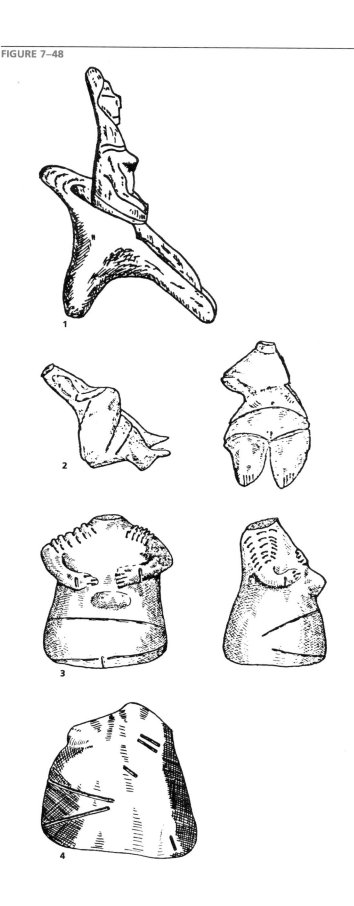

FIGURE 7–46 The temples of Achilleion, Thessaly, consisting of two rooms: the larger is the temple proper, the smaller is a workshop. Sesklo culture. (1) 6000–5900 B.C., Achilleion IV, early; (2) 5900–5800 B.C., Achilleion IVa, middle.

FIGURE 7–47 Beaked heads (fragments of broken figurines) and figurines with beaked noses, elaborate hairdoes, and headgear, with large breasts. Unearthed on and near the altar in Achilleion temples (see fig. 7–46). Sesklo culture, Achilleion IV, 6000–5800 B.C.

FIGURE 7–46 The Pregnant Goddess of Achilleion holding her belly; enthroned, reclining, and standing on a flat base. Found in courtyards, at bread ovens, or at special platforms with offering pits. (1,4) Achilleion II, c. 6200 B.C. (2,3) Achilleion IV, c. 6000–5800 B.C. Scale 1:10.

The Pregnant Goddess was worshiped at the bread oven in the courtyard. Indeed, a hundred of her figurines were discovered in diverse phases of Achilleion. Several portrayed the Goddess seated on a throne, others stood leaning back on their strikingly oversize buttocks, and some were founded on a plane base. (FIGURE 7–48) Bread ovens were equipped in front or on the side with a platform resembling a bench which held the sculptures. From Achilleion III, 6100–6000 B.C., we have a sloping clay platform with pits in the corners, paved with pebbles and consolidated with clay. Traces of coal betray their use for offering fires, perhaps on the occasion of sowing or harvest. (FIGURE 7–49) The excavation of this ceremonial site, found between the oven, stone bench, and platform with fire pits, yielded remarkable objects: large, stout vases with raised anthromorphic handles and a mass of fragmented painted pottery. These findings included phallic necks with masks (characterized by human rather than bird's nose and mouth) probably belonging to larger sculptures of the Pregnant Goddess. Separately crafted ceramic masks, attachable to cylindrical necks, were also found and dated from two periods, Achilleion II and III, 6300–6100 B.C. (FIGURE 7–50) These are the earliest objects of their kind in European prehistory.

FIGURE 7–49

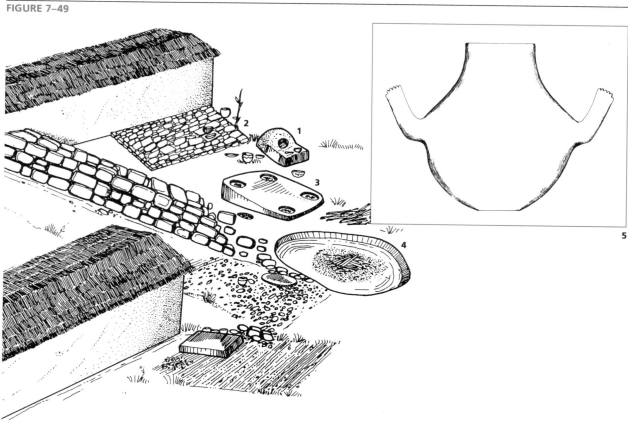

FIGURE 7–50

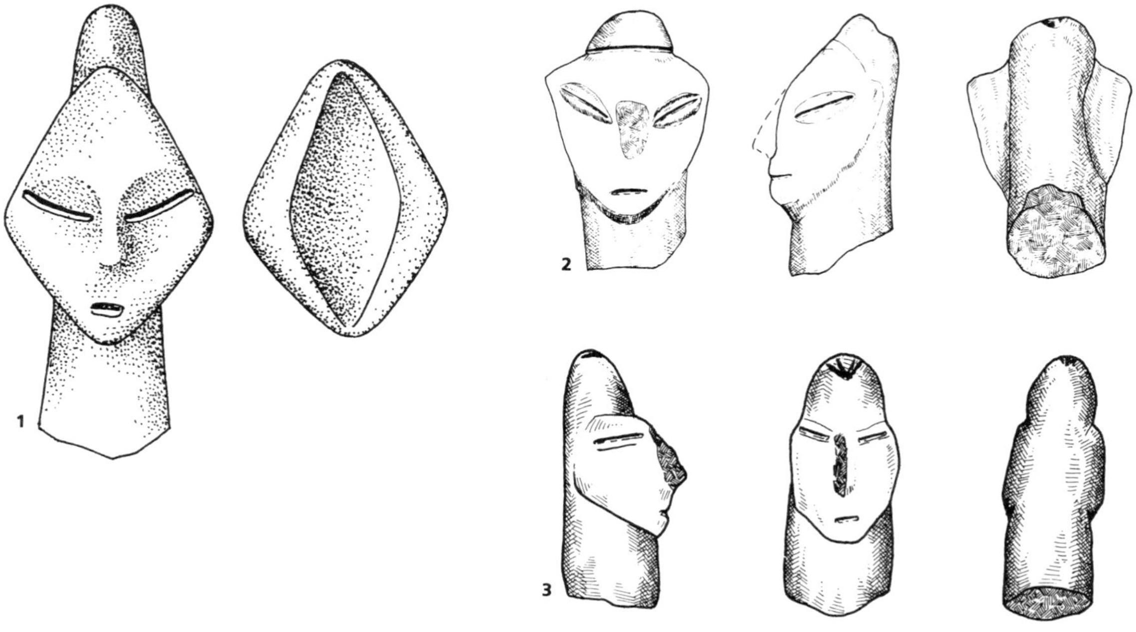

FIGURE 7–49 Courtyard area arranged for the worship of the Pregnant Goddess, the Bread Mother. (1) Bread oven; (2) stone altar; (3) sloping clay platform with four offering pits lined with pebbles in corners. A fifth pit is at the side. (4) hearth; (5) anthropomorphic red-burnished vase with upraised arms found at the altar. H 31 cm. Achilleion IIIb, c. 6000 B.C.

FIGURE 7–50 Masks on phallic necks of figurines. Some masks were removable, with concave backs which fit onto conical necks. (1) At Achilleion, removable masks date from the period between 6300 and 5700 B.C. (2,3) These masks with slit eyes, nose, and mouth are from Achilleion IIIb, 6100–6000 B.C., found in an area dedicated to the worship of the Pregnant Goddess.

FIGURE 7–51 Çatal Hüyük temple with a Frog Goddess in the center (H 1.2 m). Immediately below her is a large bull's head with spreading horns; another is at her side. A row of bull horns are mounted along the opposite wall. Shrine VI 13.8, late 7th mill. B.C.

FIGURE 7–52 In this temple of Çatal Hüyük human breasts were found above the heads of bulls. The breasts covered skulls of vultures or the lower jaws of boars, symbols of death. North and east walls of shrine VII 35, end of 7th mill. B.C.

Of the two hundred figurines excavated in Achilleion, two represent male gods. One of these was situated by the fireplace in a courtyard, a location connecting the icon with the realm of the Pregnant rather than the Bird Goddess or other goddesses worshiped in the temples. This male deity is represented on a chair, arms on knees, in a calm manner. The provenance of the other highly damaged male figurine was not clear.

Çatal Hüyük

Only a segment of this very ancient city has been excavated, yet the findings are overwhelmingly significant for a reconstruction of Neolithic religion.[23] The many structures excavated here are not ordinary dwellings but temples appropriated to the themes of death and regeneration. Wall paintings and reliefs on the interior walls which were above the burials under the floor represent the Goddess in two aspects: Death in the form of vultures, and Regeneration in the shape of frogs, which alternates with a birth-giving posture. Vulture Goddesses with anthropomorphic attributes and large broom-shaped wings have been identified in several wall paintings attacking decapitated corpses (see fig. 7–26). The human head may have been considered the abode of the soul and was removed after death; skulls were found separately in the temples, set beneath the sculptured heads of bulls. These wall paintings indicate not only the practice of excarnation (the intentional removal of flesh from the bones) but the belief that to be consumed in this way was to be absorbed, after death, by the Goddess. Rites of regeneration were followed in the temples, indicated by the reliefs and paintings of Birth-giving Goddesses and bull heads. (FIGURE 7–51)

It is interesting to note that James Mellaart uncovered a layer of reliefs at Çatal Hüyük featuring female breasts while investigating vulture heads on the surface of temple walls. (FIGURE 7–52) These breasts, symbols of nourishment and regeneration, covered the skulls of vultures and the lower jaws of boars, symbols of death. Such contrasting images may well indicate the inevitable

FIGURE 7–51

FIGURE 7–52

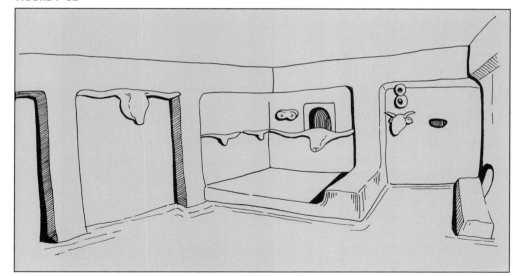

cycle of being "eaten back" into that primordial source which gives birth and nourishment to all life.

Sculptures of bull heads and wall paintings of large bulls and of bucrania were discovered in most of the temples in Çatal Hüyük. We may pause to inquire how this relates to regeneration, and why human skulls were found beneath the heads of bulls. As already mentioned, the symbolism of the bucranium was deciphered by the artist Dorothy Cameron who identified the bull head with the uterus and the horns with fallopian tubes (see fig. 7–35). An association of the bull with the Goddess of Regeneration was then evident. As a symbol of regeneration, the bull head or skull is also found in the Near East and extensively in the art of Old Europe. This symbol might actually originate in the Paleolithic when human excarnation was customary. The exposition of human organs would have offered the occasion to notice such a similarity of images. All other symbols associated with the Goddess and bull heads in the temples of Çatal Hüyük are symbols of life stimulation and regeneration: triangles, double triangles, honeycombs, chrysalises and butterflies, vulvas and phalluses, brushes and handprints, plants and animals, and life-giving water or amniotic fluid. The multitude of temples and their paintings and reliefs witness a constant concern for the continuity of life.

The shrines of Lepenski Vir on the Danube in Yugoslavia, from 6500–5500 B.C. (see sec. 6, Burial Practices), offer strong evidence of the association of burials with temples dedicated to the Goddess of Death and Regeneration. The main goddess of Lepenski Vir, portrayed as a fish woman or as a hybrid of fish, woman, and bird of prey (see fig. 7–102), was placed at the head of the altar. The temples, which date from later periods, represent functions similar to either the Achilleion or Çatal Hüyük types.

Graves

Figurines and sculptures of stiff nudes represent tomb goddesses. Starting with the 5th millennium B.C. and continuing through the 4th and 3rd millennia in the Aegean and Mediterranean region, they are found in rock-cut tombs, hypogea, and collective or single earth graves and cemeteries (see figs. 7–29 through 7–32). They were laid in graves singly or in threes or more. In the megalithic tombs of western Europe, the tomb goddess as the Owl appears as menhirs (standing stones) or as stelae, and her abstracted image, or just her eyes or breasts, reappear engraved on stone walls, bones, cylindrical stones, or flat schist plates.

Temples

The term *temple* is used here instead of *shrine* since it designates an edifice or place dedicated to the service or worship of a deity or deities. This is what the Old European and Anatolian temples of the Neolithic and Copper Age were. The term shrine is narrower, understood to mean a receptacle for sacred relics or just an altar or chapel consecrated to some saint or deity. The Neolithic and Copper Age temples, first of all, were places of worship and rituals, not merely receptacles of sacred relics.

Temples and Their Models, 7th to 5th Millennia B.C.

Clay Models of Temples

The earliest clay models conveying significant information about the architecture and purpose of temples appeared c. 6000 B.C. These models, about 25–50 cm long, offer a full view of temple structure. These miniatures are often extensively decorated with symbols, and adorned, above the entrance or roof, with the bust and mask of a goddess, her sacred animal, or horns. Hundreds of these models, variously preserved, have been excavated. Perhaps they were votive offerings to the goddess of a particular temple; or if the temple symbolized a

certain goddess, the production of models might be equated with the sculpting of goddess figurines. Some models were located near altars or buried beneath the foundations of a temple, and some were found in graves (see fig. 3–39, found in a girl's grave).

Archeologists have considered these models to be "replicas of dwellings." Such interpretation expresses the prevailing tendency among archeologists to avoid matters relating to religion in their investigation of cultural monuments. In my view, all of these models are replicas of temples which provide an invaluable source for the reconstruction of Neolithic religion.[24]

These models are predominantly related to worship of the Bird Goddess. Some are structured in imitation of a bird's features, with its head looming over the roof, while others have round entrance holes, indicating their use as bird houses. Particularly interesting models of this kind were found in the settlement of Porodin in Pelagonia, near Bitolj in southern Yugoslavia, excavated by M. Grbić et al. in 1952 from the end of the 7th millennium B.C. or c. 6000 B.C.[25] Here numerous replicas of house-shaped temples were found with "chimneys," that is, hollow cylinders bearing masks of the Bird Goddess at the top. Reliefs sculpted around the chimney depicted the Goddess's collar or necklace. (FIGURE 7–53) Several Porodin temple miniatures exhibited inverted T-shaped entrances, and one contained an altar with a triangular aperture. Another temple model from southern Yugoslavia depicts the bust of the Goddess above a rectangular structure with two rounded openings. The head features T-shaped browridges, eyes, a large nose (beak), and no mouth. Breasts and naval are indicated, and on her downward bent arms are two arm rings. (FIGURE 7–54) The rectangular structure may portray a temple workshop (compare with fig. 7–57 in the model of Căscioarele from southern Romania which has a large substructure with round openings). While Porodin dates from the end of the 7th millennium B.C., temple models belonging to the Vinča culture c. 5300–5000 B.C. also feature attributes of the Bird Goddess.

FIGURE 7–53

FIGURE 7–53 (1) Clay temple model as the body of the Goddess from Porodin, western Macedonia near Bitolj. It has wide inverted T-shaped entrances on wall sides and a Goddess mask on a cylindrical chimney, with her necklace on the roof. H c. 35 cm. (2) A cylindrical "chimney" of another temple model with a Goddess's mask. H 20.8 cm. Porodin, c. 6000 B.C. H 20.8 cm.

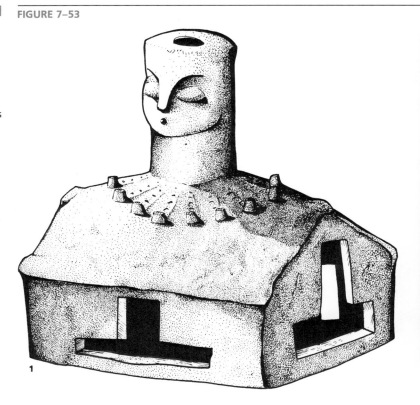

1

2

FIGURE 7–54

FIGURE 7–54 Temple model with a bust of the Goddess on top of a stereobate (or workshop) with rounded windows. Nose and horn-shaped brows probably indicate a bucranium, symbol of regeneration. Macedonia, S Yugoslavia. Approx. 5500 B.C. H c. 30 cm.

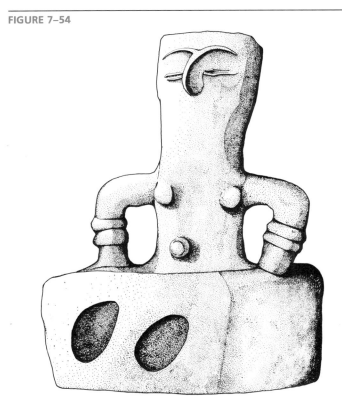

FIGURE 7–55

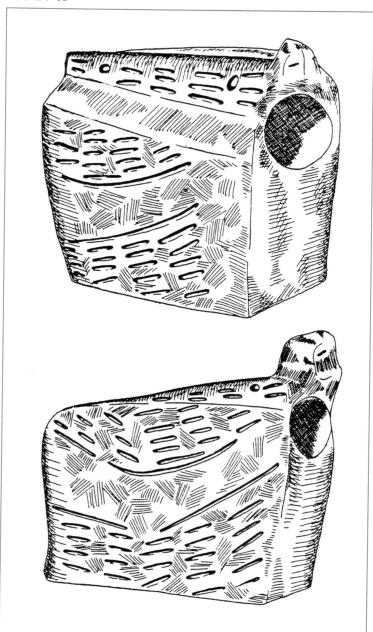

FIGURE 7–55 Clay model of a shrine with decoration in imitation of a bird's plummage, a schematic head and a round opening below, perhaps for the Goddess to enter in the shape of a bird. Early Vinča from Turdaş near Cluj, W Transylvania; c. 5200–5000 B.C. H 20 cm.

A miniature from the settlement of Turdaş in western Romania was decorated with the motif of bird feathers. (FIGURE 7–55) A model from the Vinča culture found in Vădăstra, southwestern Romania, was ornamented throughout by large meanders, inlaid with a white paste, a motif which connects the Goddess with the water sphere. The roof of this model supported a sculpture of the Goddess's head, complete with collars around her neck, while the back included a round hole, likely a doorway designed for the Goddess's epiphany in bird form. (FIGURE 7–56, 1) The roofless model of a rectangular temple from a Vinča site at Gradešnica in northwest Bulgaria, richly decorated with white-encrusted meanders, lozenges, and parallel lines on all four sides, had divine figures on each corner. The main divinity was portrayed with wings and marked with three lines in the center. (FIGURE 7–56, 2)

One of the largest models from the mid-5th millennium B.C. was found in the excavation of a village in Căscioarele, southern Romania, on an island in the Danube. It is 51 cm in length and 24.2 cm in width, rendered in two stories. The first level has several rows of round windows, while the top level displays a row of four shrines with wide open entrances. Each of these shrines was decorated with either a horn or an animal head motif. (FIGURE 7–57) This model belongs to the very zenith of the culture of Old Europe, a time when perfection and sophistication had been reached in both architecture and ceramics. This model is a replica not of a single sanctuary but of a whole complex. These shrines could have belonged to four families or kin groups. The lower level was a huge workshop in which ceremonial vases and hundreds of other objects needed in rituals must have been produced.

The existence of two-story temples in the 5th millennium B.C. is witnessed by many miniatures found in various cultural groups. A model was found near Kiev, at Rozsochuvatka, which belongs to the Cucuteni culture. The lower level was a workshop while the main shrine, consisting of two rooms, was on the top

FIGURE 7–56

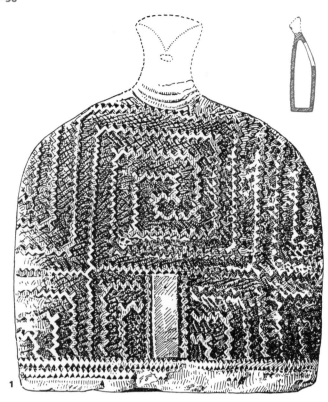

1

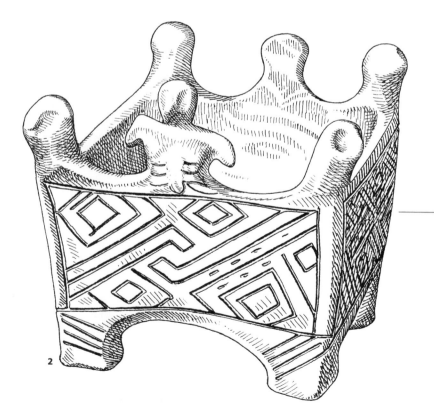

2

FIGURE 7–56 (1) This clay temple model depicts the Goddess's sphere as the watery realm symbolized by meanders, to which an entrance (at the bottom) has been provided. Three necklaces are preserved on top. Head is reconstructed. On the back, this model has a round aperture (for the Goddess to depart in the epiphany of a bird?). The surface is excised and white-encrusted. Vădăstra group of the early Vinča culture from Vădăstra, SW Romania; 5200–5000 B.C. (2) A roofless model with heads of divine figures on each corner and what is probably the main divinity portrayed with wings, beaked head, and three lines on both sides of the body in the center. All four sides are decorated with white-encrusted meanders and lozenges. Vinča culture, Gradešnica, NW Bulgaria; c. 5000–4500 B.C. H 14.5 cm

FIGURE 7-57

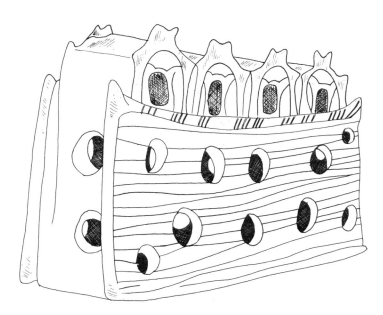

FIGURE 7-57 Clay model of an edifice from Căscioarele, an island settlement west of Oltenița in southern Romania. The model portrays a large substructure with round openings supporting four temples. The substructure apparently served as a huge workshop for the temples. This mid-5th mill. B.C. artifact was burned along with the temple in which it was found. H 24.2 cm.; L 51 cm.

FIGURE 7-58

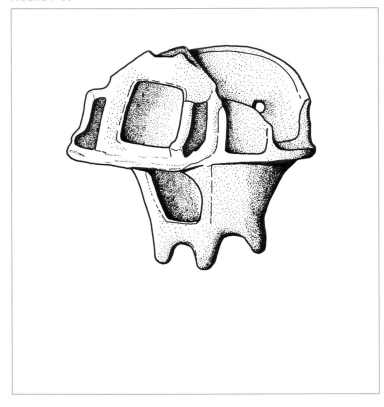

FIGURE 7-58 Clay model of a two-story temple found south of Kiev at Rozsokhuvatka. On both floors there are wide entrances, and in front of the large portal and around the second-floor temple is a balcony. A small round window was in the rear wall. H c. 30 cm. Cucuteni (Tripolye) culture; c. 4300-4000 B.C. Actual two-story temples were excavated in Cucuteni, Petrești, and Karanovo cultures and they resemble this model.

level. Surrounding the temple was a terrace for the congregation to walk around, similar to the Căscioarele model, which had a terrace connecting the four shrines. (FIGURE 7-58)

Actual Temples

A full scale two-story temple from about 5000 B.C. was excavated in Radingrad near Razgrad, northeast Bulgaria.[26] This temple proved that the models were true replicas. Here in the lower level were found all the implements of a ceramics workshop: tools for decorating ceramics placed on a platform, small dishes for grinding ochre, and palettes for paints, as well as a big oven. In the upper level was an altar with a loom beside it for weaving ceremonial clothing, indicating that the process of weaving itself must have had a sacred meaning. The practice of weaving sacred attire within the temple continued well into Classical times, while the earliest evidence goes back to the 7th millennium B.C., evidenced by loom counterweights, shaped like disks, found in the temples of Achilleion.

Some temples were dedicated to the Snake Goddess, as witnessed by a well-preserved example from Sabatinivka in Soviet Moldavia from the Cucuteni culture c. 4800-4600 B.C. This structure was in the form of a house, about 70 sq m. At one end was an altar shaped like a bench, on which sixteen snake-headed sculptures were found seated on horn-back chairs. Only one of these figures has arms, and she holds a snake-like infant or a phallus (FIGURE 7-59). Next to the altar stood a life-sized chair, its back decorated with horns, which probably belonged to the priestess who directed the ceremonies. Nearby was a bread oven with pots at its side, one of which held bones of burnt animals. Other sculptures were found near the oven and on the flagstone pavement near the entrance. Altogether, thirty-two sculptures were found in this one temple, all replicas of the Snake Goddess.

Temples dedicated to regeneration ceremonies had a different character. In the settlement of Căscioarele, from a level earlier than previously mentioned,

FIGURE 7–59

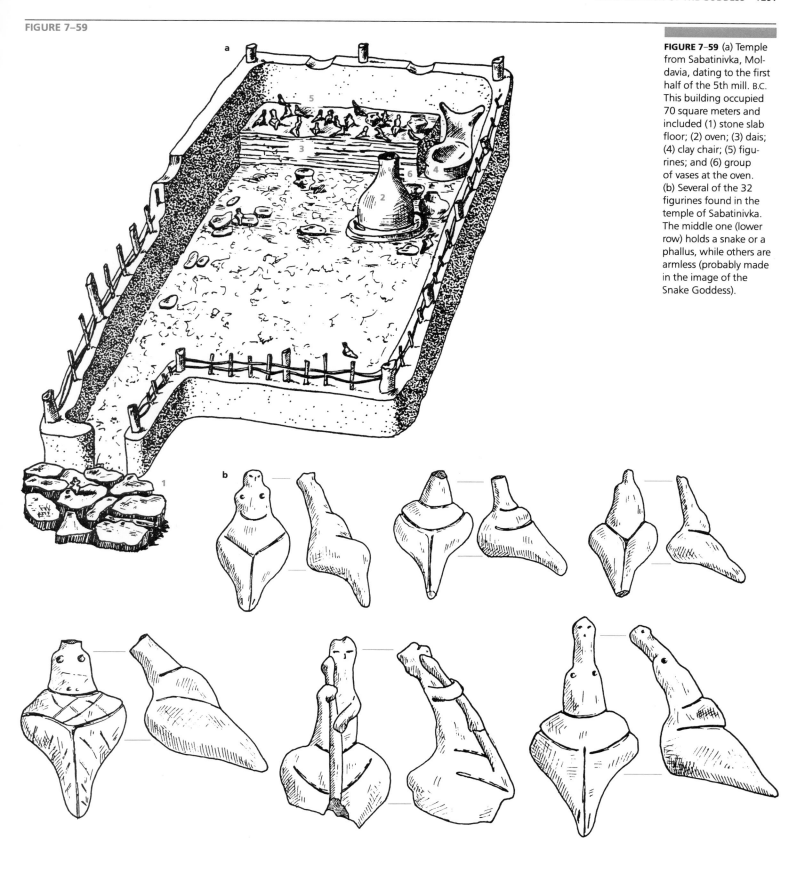

FIGURE 7–59 (a) Temple from Sabatinivka, Moldavia, dating to the first half of the 5th mill. B.C. This building occupied 70 square meters and included (1) stone slab floor; (2) oven; (3) dais; (4) clay chair; (5) figurines; and (6) group of vases at the oven. (b) Several of the 32 figurines found in the temple of Sabatinivka. The middle one (lower row) holds a snake or a phallus, while others are armless (probably made in the image of the Snake Goddess).

a temple was found with two columns, dated c. 5000 B.C. These were wooden, plastered with clay, and painted with a symbolic angular spiral pattern. The walls were decorated with red eggs, concentric circles, and spirals.[27] All of these motifs are linked with regeneration.

The presence of these columns is of particular interest, since they must have symbolized trees of life. A life column can be a plant, a tree, or a tree turned into a column, such as those in the Căscioarele temple, an upward-rising snake or phallus, and similarly a stalagmite growing mysteriously in a cave. Many stalagmite caves on the shores of Greece, Yugoslavia, and Italy became temples where for ages regeneration ceremonies and mysteries were held. Such cave-temples in these countries were in use from the Neolithic, and in Crete, even from the Bronze Age.

Other temples with columns of wood and clay, life-sized sculptures, and bull heads associated with them from around 5000 B.C. have been excavated in 1980–85 by G. Lazarovici at Parţa, 15 km southwest of Timişoara in western Romania.[28] The final excavation report is not yet published. Two consecutive temples which belong to a complex of houses within the center of the settlement were built of timber uprights interspersed with wickerwork and covered with clay daub. Inside were found table-like altars of earth and clay, mobile hearths on three or four feet, and monumental sculptures enclosed by low partitions within interior corners. The earlier temple measured 12.5 by 7 m, and the second was 11.6 by 6 m in size. The columns stood spaced out in twos or threes in the western and eastern sides of the temples. The clay podium (base) for a large sculpture in the earlier temple was 60 cm across. The statue itself was burnt, but in the temple of the second phase a female statue of clay with two heads and two shoulders survived. It stood on a podium built of earth and sand, covered with a layer of clay. Next to one of the shoulders was a bull head, and two others were in front of the statue. On the side of the statue stood a pan-shaped container for offerings. On one of the three altars, more than 5 m

long, stood mobile hearths, chalices, and vases with a face of the Goddess incised on the neck, filled with animal bones. On another altar stood a clay sculpture with grain impressed in the head. In the partition wall dividing the temple into west and east rooms was a round opening. At the side of it, a crescent moon was moulded in relief, and a chalice was placed below it. At the north wall stood a verticle loom (only clay plates for its support and loom weights survived). There was also a pit with potsherds of twelve to fourteen vases and a couple of quern stones for grinding arranged in a bed of clay.

There are many more settlements, especially in northern Greece, Pelagonia, and Macedonia, that yielded floor areas with altars, fenced receptacles for offerings, temple models, miniature tables, tripods, kernoi, anthropomorphic and zoomorphic figurines, and vases. Many of them are either unrecognized temples or come from small-scale excavations, too small for reconstructions of any kind. Their finding places are usually described as "a cult place" or "an offering place."[29]

From what is already known, the existence of temples in all of southeast and central Europe throughout the 6th and 5th millennia is unquestionable. In them, offerings and rituals took place at birth, at death, and on many other occasions.

Temples of Malta, 4th to 3rd Millennia B.C.

The origin of the temples of Malta are egg-shaped underground tombs. Even during their apogee in the 4th millennium B.C., and during the beginning of the 3rd millennium, these temples were not formed like houses, as were those in southeastern Europe, but were actually expressions of the regenerating body of the Goddess with enormous egg-shaped buttocks (see figs. 5–25 to 5–29). This image is repeated in numerous stone sculptures of the Goddess.

Symbols found on ceramics, reliefs and wall engravings, stone blocks and altars, speak without exception the same language of regeneration. The pubic triangle of the Goddess is repeated in vari-

ous places, carved from large stones and erected with the narrow end downward in the apse or niche of the shrine, like altars. (FIGURE 7–60)

Triangles, altars, columns, and stone blocks were almost always pitted. Perhaps these were not considered decoration but had a symbolic meaning, like the cupmarks on menhirs and megalithic graves in western Europe and elsewhere. These little marks were, indeed, a penetration into her element.

To the sphere of regeneration also belong upward-rising snakes, lizards, and related images. A relief of such a snake was found in the temple of Ġgantija. In the temple of Tarxien, sculptures of a lizard and phalli were found which had been placed in niches in groups of twos and threes. (FIGURE 7–61) In the temple of Ħaġar Qim, near the entrance, stood an altar in the shape of a small table, decorated in front with a tree rising from a vase. This stood near a large table-shaped altar above which were carved two reliefs of double snake spirals joined at the top by a triangle. The same motif is found on a stone block in the Tarxien temple, which is famous for its spiral motifs. From these spirals emerge budding and branching plant shoots, indicating a deeper significance than mere geometric decoration. Here we see the celebration of plant energy and the springtime renewal of life.

FIGURE 7-60

1

FIGURE 7-60 Altars in the shape of pubic triangles in Maltese temples. (1) Pitted triangle stone in a niche of the temple of Ħaġar Qim (east, exterior). (2) Large pitted triangle in the temple of Mnajdra, Room 1; 3500–3000 B.C. H 1.60 m.

FIGURE 7-61 Snake, lizard, and triple phalli as symbols of regeneration in Maltese temples. (1) Upward rising snake in relief. Ġgantija temple; c. 3600 B.C. (2) Figurine of a lizard. (3) Phalli from Tarxien. c. 3000 B.C.

FIGURE 7-61

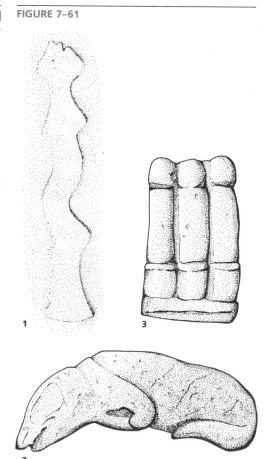

1

3

2

2

FIGURE 7–62

FIGURE 7–62 (1, 2) Two bulls and, (3) a bitch with thirteen puppies carved in relief on a slab of limestone. Symbols of regeneration from the Tarxien temples. Bulls, H 27 cm; bitch, H18 cm.

FIGURE 7–63

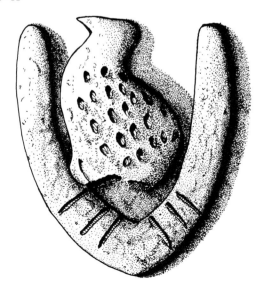

FIGURE 7–63 A bird emerging from between the horns portrayed in relief on a vase. Tarxien temple.

In the Tarxien temple were found two bulls with big horns carved as reliefs on stone slabs (FIGURE 7–62, 1, 2), and next to these a bitch with thirteen newborns (FIGURE 7–62, 3). On a vase fragment were horns expressed in relief, with a bird in between. (FIGURE 7–63) An animal procession of sheep, pigs, and goats was skillfully carved on a single block of stone. Although these have been interpreted as sacrificial animals, they could also be read as a celebration of the renewal of life within the animal world.

More than thirty impressive stone sculptures were found in Malta, ranging from 5 cm to 3 m in height.[30] The main group were nudes with egg-shaped buttocks, one hand extended downward with the other held over her chest. These were found in the Hal Saflieni hypogeum and in the Ḥaġar Qim temple. Some are standing, some are sitting easily with legs turned to the right or left. (PLATE 21) Several were clothed in long dresses with collars. The double-egg motif—purposely enlarged buttocks—links these sculptures with the theme of regeneration. At Hal Saflieni were found buttocks-shaped pendants as well as completely schematic statuettes with cylindrical or phallic heads, carved from bone.

The largest stone sculpture, whose original height must have been almost three meters, found in the Tarxien sanctuary, undoubtedly depicted the most important deity of that sacred place. Only its bottom part has survived, which is one meter in height, showing egg-shaped legs up to the knees with a skirt to mid-calf. (FIGURE 7–64) A smaller fragment has survived of another similar sculpture in a seated pose, also from the Tarxien temple. Below the skirt, near the feet of the Goddess, are seated four heavy female figures represented in relief. Such gigantic sculptures are unique examples of prehistoric art since other large figures made of clay or wood have not survived to our time.

FIGURE 7–64

FIGURE 7-64 The largest stone sculpture (bottom part is 1 m high) of Malta from the Tarxien cemetery. It has typical egg-shaped calves and the design on the pedestal are eggs alternated by columns. Approx. 3000 B.C.

Who is this large Goddess? The remaining leg fragments show that she is similar to the goddess depicted in the Ħaġar Qim sculptures. Her calves are unnaturally thick but her feet are tiny. There may be a symbolic meaning in this depiction—perhaps they are eggs. If so, this would be one more element in understanding the functions of this Goddess. She is not simply a fertility goddess, as she has been depicted until now, for her obesity has a deeper meaning—that of regeneration. She is, in fact, a specifically Maltese expression of the Goddess of Regeneration.

The temples of Malta, which were built in pairs, are best expressed by the temples of Ġgantija and Mnajdra (see figs. 5–25, 5–27). We may surmise that each represented different aspects of the Goddess in which various rituals could have been held: in the larger western sanctuary, rites of death and regeneration; in the eastern, celebrations of birth and regeneration of humans as well as nature. The apses of the western temples were built of darker, reddish-brown globigerina limestone, painted red, while the eastern sanctuaries were built of a somewhat lighter stone. Double temples were, perhaps, expressions of a double goddess, mother and daughter or two sisters, pictured as Siamese twins, found widely both in Europe and Anatolia between the 7th and 3rd millennia B.C.

FIGURE 7–65

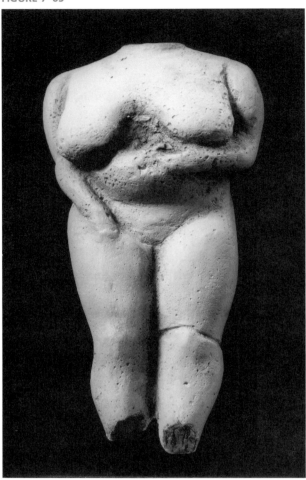

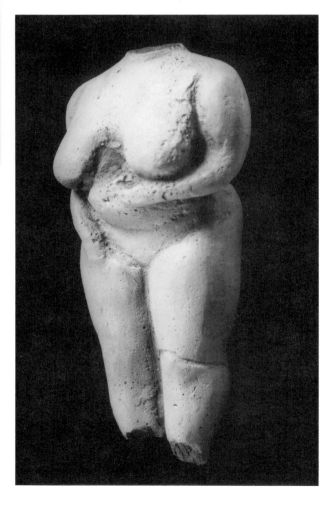

FIGURE 7–65 The "Venus of Malta," a naturalistically portrayed female body with left hand on her abdomen and large breasts. Terracotta. Found at Ḥaġar Qim temple. End 4th mill B.C. H 12.5 cm.

FIGURE 7–66

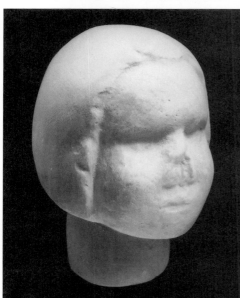

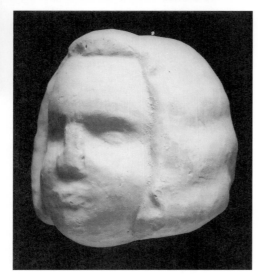

FIGURE 7–66 Limestone heads with youthful faces and neatly combed hair. Hal Saflieni hypogeum, Malta; approx. end of 4th mill. B.C. H. taller head: 11.5 cm.

In the temples of Mnajdra and Tarxien were found clay figurines of pregnant women with enlarged breasts and swollen vulvas, 5–6 cm in height, which may be miniature replicas of the Birth Goddess (see fig. 7–2). Although to our eyes they are not particularly beautiful (J.D. Evans called them "deformed" and "pathological"),[31] it is important to view these figures as symbolic. To dismiss any prehistoric art as falling short of contemporary expectations of beauty is to miss its deeper significance. It is interesting to note that on the backs of both figurines are incised nine horizontal lines which could mean the nine months of pregnancy. Such images could have been *ex votos*, prayer offerings to the Birth Goddess in hopes of a successful delivery. We may surmise that birthing took place in the eastern sanctuary where figurines of this type have been found.

An exceptionally beautiful clay torso of a naked woman with large breasts, 12.5 cm in height, has been found near the Hagar Qim temple. (FIGURE 7–65) Because of its beauty, closer to the 20th century ideal, this sculpture attracted the attention of archeologists and was named "The Maltese Venus." Another, smaller nude in a relaxed, seated pose was found in the Tarxien temple. Unfortunately, the heads of both sculptures were lost. There are other masterpieces of Maltese art still hiding the secret of their function and meaning. Among them are the limestone heads portraying youthful faces found in the hypogeum of Hal Saflieni. (FIGURE 7–66)

Sanctuaries of Northern Europe, 4th to 3rd Millennia B.C.

Temples or sanctuaries of the Funnel-necked Beaker (TRB) culture have been discovered in Denmark and Sweden. The horseshoe shaped building in which a great many outstanding vases and ladles were found has already been mentioned (see figs. 4–15, 4–16). A unique type of sanctuary, dated to c. 3000 B.C., was found in Alvastra, southern Sweden, at the foot of Omberg Mountain in a rich agricultural area. This large structure on piles, which had no walls, occupied about 1000 sq m. It was described by its excavator Mats Malmer[32] as having more than 1000 vertical piles of oak, elm, lime, hazel, apple, and other deciduous trees. These form two rectangular areas, each surrounded by a rather widely spaced oak palisade. Dendrochronological research has shown that the history of this building spanned 42 years. During this time, a number of reconstructions took place with several long intervals of no activity. The site was uninhabitable during the winter season. The floor foundation was made of parallel logs covered with limestone slabs. There were over a hundred fireplaces, surrounded by great numbers of wild and domestic animal bones and the bones of birds and fish, the remains of burnt offerings. In addition, forty double-edged stone axes and miniature axes of amber and bone were found. Another unusual discovery was a collection of implements for making fire—sharpened pieces of quartz and pyrite balls—which seem to have been left behind as offerings. Human bones appeared in the last phase of the sanctuary. Since they were not in anatomical order, it is assumed that the dead were placed on platforms erected especially for excarnation purposes.

Alvastra is situated in a spring mire where the groundwater, which is under pressure, pours forth like a small fountain. Judging from the structure's location at the water fountain and at the foot of a mountain, the deposition of double axes, symbolic amber and bone axes, as well as instruments for making fire, offerings of animals, grains and fruit, and disarticulated human bones,

FIGURE 7–67

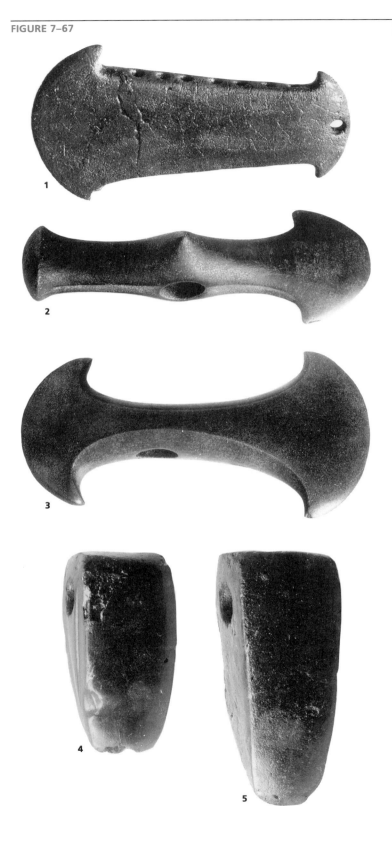

FIGURE 7–67 Double-axes and triangle-axes of northwestern Europe were symbols of regeneration, as they also were in other parts of Old Europe and in Minoan Crete. Ritual axes of amber and stone from megalithic tombs. (1) Skovager at Viborg. This amber axe has seven perforations across for seven strands of an amber bead necklace. (2,3) Føllenslev. (4,5) Triangular amber axes from Hørdum, Thy, Denmark. Scale c. 2:3.

it seems plausible to assume that the sanctuary of Alvastra was used for spring regeneration rites and was associated with funeral rituals. The axe and double axe, found throughout Old Europe and in Minoan Crete, was associated with the Goddess in her function of regeneration. Their symbolic role explains their extraordinary rendering in amber and stone. (FIGURE 7–67)

Although sacred buildings of this northern European zone of deciduous trees differed from the southern European solid temples of stone or clay, their functions may well have been related. Regeneration rituals were performed in both locations.

Hairstyles, Headdresses, and Ritual Attire

It is fortunate that many figurines from the 6th to the 4th millennium B.C. are incised or painted with costume details. In many sculptures, hairstyles are also shown. Whether these costumes were popularly worn or were the attire of deities or participants in rituals is conjectural. The latter is probably the case, since figurines are masked and seem to capture the postures of actors in ceremonies or those seated on thrones. Even so, we can presume that these costumes, headdresses, and hairstyles reflect some semblance of the clothing worn 8,000 to 6,000 years ago. Special treatments preserved on clay figurines by deep incisions and encrustations clearly indicate hairstyles, turbans, crowns, caps, jewelry, hip belts, narrow ankle-length skirts, aprons, fringes, blouses, and footgear. Signs and symbols also appear incised or painted on sculptures, but they are distinct from details of dress.

Coiffures

Special attention was rendered to hairstyles and headgear, especially for Bird and Snake Goddesses or priestesses portrayed in her likeness. The classic Bird Goddess figurine from Achilleion, with her hair carefully parted and pulled into a chignon, is probably the best

example of how women of the Sesklo culture wore their hair some 8,000 years ago (see figs. 7–13, 7–47). A neat chignon would be the most suitable hairdo for a busy mother, but it could be transformed into an elegant coiffure when she participated in rituals. This could be achieved, with some assistance from others, by twisting tresses into coils. Elaborate coils are depicted on Sesklo figurines from the early 6th millennium B.C. (FIGURE 7–68) A hair net or hair covering is suggested by the head of a Sesklo figurine from Tsani Magoula, dated c. 5900–5700 B.C. (FIGURE 7–69) At Sitagroi, a beaked figurine is shown with her hair pulled austerely back and then looped into elegant snake spirals on the side and back of the head (see fig. 3–59).

FIGURE 7–68 Sixth millennium B.C. figurine with elaborate curls falling on either side of a center part. Sesklo culture. Magoula Panagou near Larisa, Thessaly, c. 5900–5700 B.C.

FIGURE 7–68

FIGURE 7–69

FIGURE 7–70

FIGURE 7–71

FIGURE 7–72

FIGURE 7–73

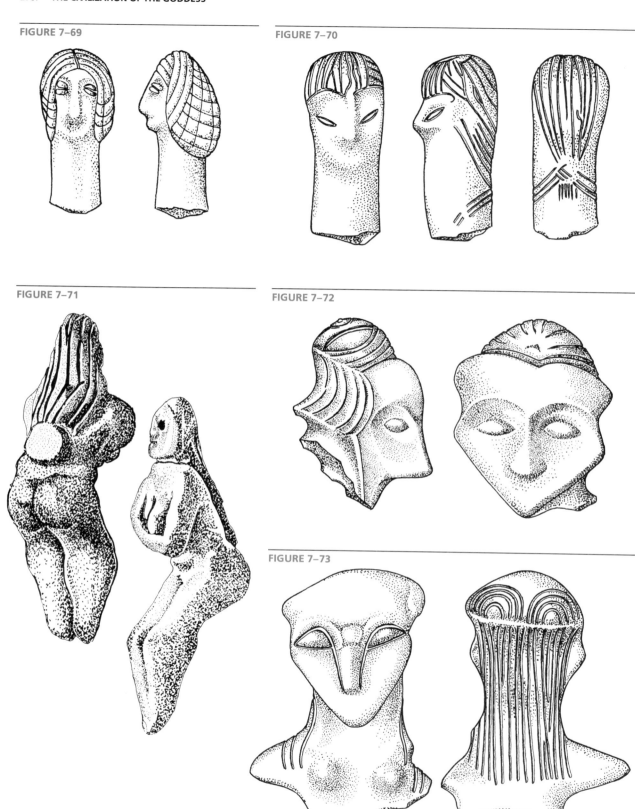

FIGURE 7–69 Head from Tsani Magoula depicts hair falling from a center part, perhaps covered with a net or scarf. Sesklo culture, c. 6000–5800 B.C.

FIGURE 7–70 This figurine illustrates a hairdo with tresses pulled tightly off the face, perhaps caught by a thong at the nape of the neck. Starčevo culture, from Vinča near Belgrade, c. 5600–5400 B.C.

FIGURE 7–71 A natural free-falling hairstyle is depicted on this figurine. The "knob" on her back represents a ceremonial adornment. Late Cucuteni culture, Krinichka, district of Odessa, W Ukraine, c. 3700–3500 B.C.

FIGURE 7–72 This masked Vinča head wears a classic chignon. The hair is pulled back from the forehead and is twisted in swirls at the top of her head. Classical Vinča culture, Crnokalačka Bara near Niš, S Yugoslavia, c. 5000–4500 B.C.

FIGURE 7–73 The back of this Vinča figurine clearly indicates an elaborate coiffure in which the hair is coiled in two chignons and then falls freely down the back. Note the tresses falling across the shoulders of this masked woman. Classical Vinča, from Vinča near Belgrade, c. 5000–4500 B.C.

We also have examples of long, free-falling tresses which permit us to conjecture that young girls spent time combing and dressing their hair. Long hair streaming down the back and caught by a thong at the nape of the neck is rendered on a 6th millennium Starčevo sculpture from the Vinča mound. (FIGURE 7-70) Examples from the Late Cucuteni culture portray participants in a ritual dance in which they toss their hair, which is fastened by a knob at the back. (FIGURE 7-71) Elaborate coiffures are seen on Vinča figurines from 5000–4500 B.C. (FIGURES 7-72, 7-73, 7-74) Perhaps the most intriguing prospect is the notion that Neolithic women actually devised methods of dressing their hair in long curls. At times of ceremonies, did they use oils and thongs to twist and dry their hair into corkscrew curls? One Sesklo artist produced a woman's head with hair falling from either side of a center part into luxuriant sausage curls. A beaked Bird Goddess also is shown with curls. This suggests that when the occasion called for it, a considerable amount of time was devoted to creating elaborate coiffures.

FIGURE 7-74

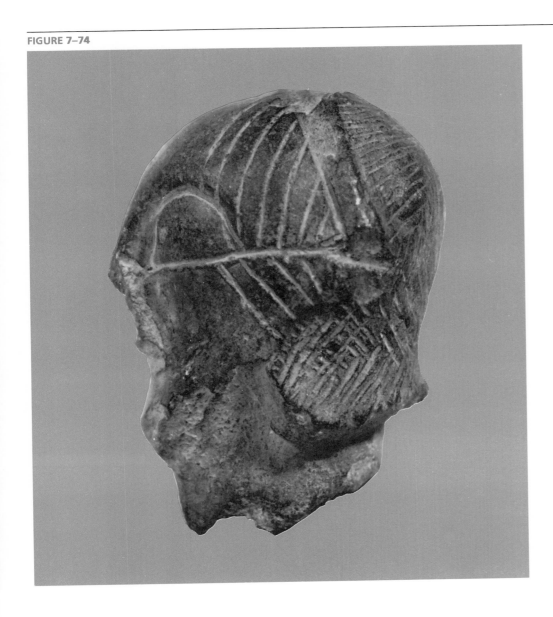

FIGURE 7-74 Terracotta head with neatly combed coiffure, from Vinča culture. Pavlovac near Vranje, S Yugoslavia, c. 5000–4500 B.C.

FIGURE 7–75

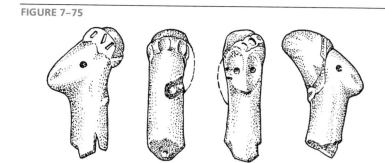

FIGURE 7–76

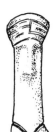

FIGURE 7–77

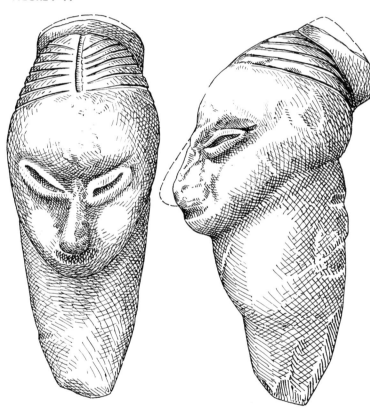

FIGURE 7–75 Meticulous detail is frequently given to headgear of the Bird Goddess no matter how small the figurine. This minute head recovered from Achilleion portrays a beaked goddess crowned with a turban. A band of fabric encircles the head, and is looped at the side and clasped at the nape of the neck by a disk. Achilleion IV, Thessaly, Sesklo culture, c. 5800 B.C.

FIGURE 7–76 A crown-like turban is worn by this cylindrical-necked Bird Goddess. Coils of clay replicate folds of fabric wound around the head. The intentional indentation on the back is a further indication of an elaborate turban much like village women of the Middle East wear today. Achilleion IV.

FIGURE 7–77 A neatly parted hairdo swept into a chignon is crowned by a loop or tiara on this damaged Sesklo figurine dated to c. 6000–5800 B.C., Karaikia near Larisa, Thessaly.

FIGURE 7–78 The chignon on this figurine is reminiscent of African hairstyles. Bands seem to cross the top of the head. The exaggerated bun would have required some stiffening agent to achieve this unnatural effect. Sitohoron tell near Farsala, c. 6000–5800 B.C.

FIGURE 7–78

Headdresses

Minute Sesklo figurine heads, scarcely larger than a fingertip, are depicted with ornate headdresses that resemble turbans. (FIGURES 7–75, 7–76) Such headgear could have been easily prepared by wrapping fabric around the head and securing it in place by looping it beneath the folds. Another figurine has neatly parted hair, pushed to the back of the head and covered by a cap or a band of cloth or leather. (FIGURE 7–77; see also fig. 7–13) Still another Sesklo figurine is shown with an exaggerated chignon at the nape of the neck. (FIGURE 7–78)

Aghios Petros, a Neolithic settlement on a tiny island at Pelagos, Sporadhes, in the northern Aegean, yielded figurines wearing tall, sophisticated hats decorated with groups of parallel lines. (FIGURE 7–79) Several heads from the Sesklo and Vinča cultures are shown wearing conical caps. (FIGURE 7–80) The actual hat was most likely fashioned of felt to achieve its pointed shape.

FIGURE 7–79

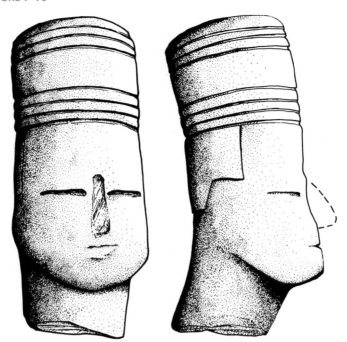

FIGURE 7–79 Figurine wearing a sophisticated tall hat. Hair cut steplike is shown on the sides. Aghios Petros, Pelagos island, Sporadhes, N Aegean. Approx. mid-6th mill. B.C.

FIGURE 7–80 Conical caps. (1) Head of a Sesklo figurine wearing a conical cap as in Hacilar, Anatolia. Her eyes are like coffee beans, characteristic of the early 6th millennium B.C. Three lines incised on each cheek are typical markings on Bird Goddess masks. (2) This masked Vinča figurine is wearing a pointed, conical cap. Vinča site, c. 5000–4500 B.C.

FIGURE 7–80

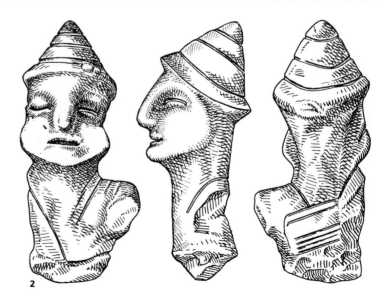

2

FIGURE 7–81

FIGURE 7–82

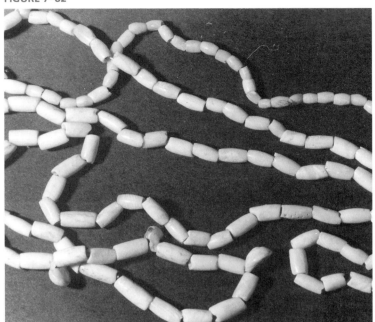

1

2

FIGURE 7–81 We see on this Late Cucuteni terra-cotta figurine a double-stranded necklace and a three-stranded hip belt indicated by punctate lines. Punctations around the ankle area suggest that the long, narrow skirt may have been caught at the bottom by strands of beads. The necklace was looped twice, one strand falls at the throat region, the other drops to the navel. Bilcze Zlote, W Ukraine.

FIGURE 7–82 Shells and clay beads were meticulously perforated to create a necklace that would have enhanced the appearance of any bare shouldered maiden or priestess; (1) Vršnik, C Macedonia, c. 5500 B.C. This necklace of spondylus beads was found deposited in a ritual buttocks-shaped vase. (2) Vinča culture, Vinča site, c. 4500 B.C.

The symbolism of the crown may have its roots in the Neolithic, for we have many examples of figurine heads wearing a tiara-like object. Such headdresses could have been produced by knotting hemp or twisting branches into garlands. Spondylus shells were used in the manufacture of diadems. Graves from the cemetery of Cernica yielded diadems made of spondylus plates with triple perforations (see fig. 3–46). Regardless of the medium, it is important to realize how early the imagery of a sacred headdress began.

Jewelry

More than half the figurines of Old Europe appear to be nude above the hips, hence we presume they represent goddesses or priestesses as they enact rituals. The climate of Old Europe would rarely have been warm enough (except in summer) to make seminudity a common or comfortable practice as it is in equatorial regions. During religious ceremonies, however, a bare-torsoed young woman adorned with necklaces would have made an appealing vision to deities and spectators alike.

Punctate dots frequently indicate strands of beads. A Late Cucuteni figurine from Bilcze Zlote is portrayed with a strand of beads falling below the throat; a second strand is suspended to the hips, which are also encircled with beads. (FIGURE 7–81) Clay pendants or disks were probably hung from leather thongs, and shells were collected and strung into elaborate necklaces. (FIGURE 7–82)

Shell and stone beads were popularly worn and do not belong to the attire of deities only. Many were found in graves and settlements. The majority of shells—spondylus, dentalium, pectunculus—were imported from great distances and must have been highly valued. Spondylus was cut locally and worked into various shapes. The most popular configurations were cylindrical, biconical, and barrel-shaped forms with the larger beads strung intentionally in front. It is truly amazing that prodigious quantities of spondylus beads have been found in Germany, France, Hungary, and Czecho-slovakia, more than 1,500 kilometers from their source. A cache recovered from one grave in the Lužianky cemetery of western Slovakia contained 610 spondylus beads. If strung, this would have produced a necklace 450 centimeters long. Fragile dentalium shells are found in great numbers not only in the coastal regions of the Varna culture, but far inland in the Vinča and Lengyel areas. Green or black semiprecious stone beads are also found. Greenstone and marble beads are common in the earliest Neolithic layers of the 7th millennium B.C. and continued to be fashionable throughout the Sesklo culture. Necklaces depicted on Sesklo figurines probably represent those made of stone beads. (FIGURE 7–83) Copper and gold beads were more frequent in the mid-5th millennium B.C.

FIGURE 7–83 A necklace painted on a figurine neck depicting stone beads from the Sesklo culture. Masked figurine head (three views) is from Achilleion IV, c. 5800–5700 B.C. (Greenstone and marble beads were found at the same site, from the period c. 6000–5700 B.C.)

FIGURE 7–83

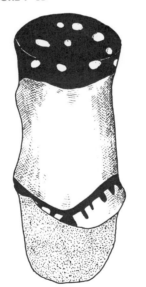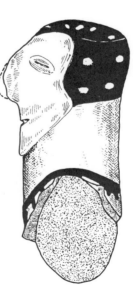

From 6000 B.C. onward, figurines wearing a large circular pendant or medallion are associated with temples. (FIGURES 7–84, 7–85)

Hip Belts

The hip belt of beads or string with fringes is typical of nude figurines from the 6th to the 4th millennium B.C. What could be more pleasing to the eye than an ornate hip belt to offset the natural beauty of a bare-bosomed woman?

One example from the Starčevo culture depicts an ample nude torso adorned with a hip belt fashioned of graduated stone beads, shells or clay disks strung on a leather thong (FIGURE 7–86). Clay "medallions" appear on the hips of another Starčevo figurine from the site of Vinča. Fringes, probably created from leather thongs knotted with beads at the end, fall from the front, sides, and back of a hip belt. The presence of a fringed or multistranded hip belt is known from the Vinča, Karanovo, and Cucuteni cultures. (FIGURES 7–87, 7–88)

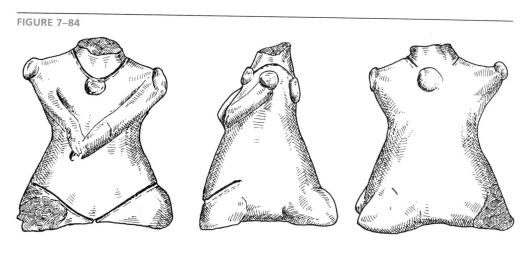

FIGURE 7–84

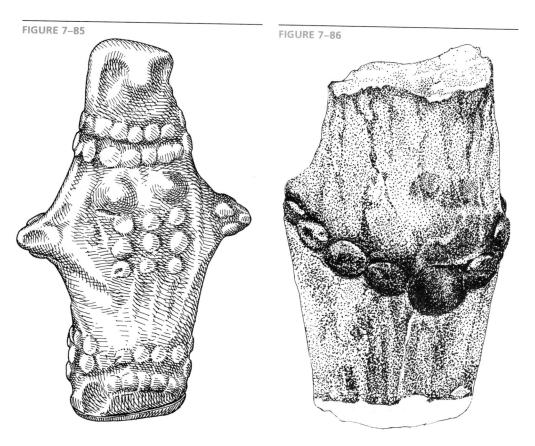

FIGURE 7–85

FIGURE 7–86

FIGURE 7-87

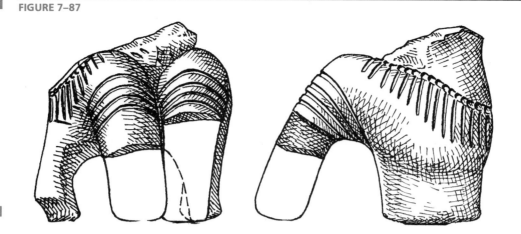

FIGURE 7-84 Tetrapodal figure from a Sesklo temple; her only adornment is a necklace with pendants or knobs front and back (probably clay disks suspended from a leather thong.) Note disks on the shoulders and a V indicating the pubic area. Achilleion IV, from a shrine of the early 6th mill., c. 5800–5700 B.C. H 6 cm.

FIGURE 7-85 The Bird Goddess is adorned with a necklace and hipbelt of two strands of pendants (clay disks?) which are repeated below the breasts in three times three (3x3). Vinča culture, Vinča site, c. 5000–4500.

FIGURE 7-86 Old European figurine art reveals a marked respect for the hipline demonstrated by a carefully detailed belt of the Starčevo culture, c. 5800–5500 B.C. Graduated disks are portrayed on this fragmented figurine, perhaps replicating perforated clay disks strung on a leather thong. Vinča mound near Belgrade.

FIGURE 7-87 A hip belt is indicated by fringe suspended from the belt on the lower half of an enthroned statuette of the Vinča culture. Vinča, c. 5000–400 B.C.

FIGURE 7-88

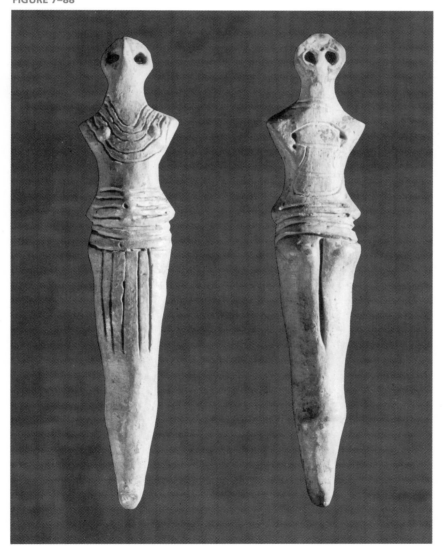

FIGURE 7-88 Hip belts also appear in the Late Cucuteni culture. Here, a figurine is adorned with numerous thongs from waist to hip with a fringed ritual "apron" in front. Sipenitsi, W Ukraine, c. 3700–3500 B.C.

Narrow Skirts

Figurine art offers visual testimony for the dressmaking skills of Old Europeans. Over the centuries, Vinča artists depicted their sculptures in beautifully designed narrow ankle-length skirts that fall from the hips. These skirts tend to invert below the knees, which suggest a draping fabric which is gathered and pulled up from the ankles by thongs suspended from the hip belt. The narrowness of the skirts gives the impression of constrained movement conducive to ceremonial steps but not to the performance of household chores. (FIGURES 7–89 to 7–92)

Aprons

Another feature of costume seems to be ritualistic aprons. These are depicted by punctate dots and incisions representing draped, rectangular, looped, or V-shaped aprons covering the lap area. In all instances, these aprons bear snake spirals, V's, chevrons, or other designs frequently found on goddess figurines. (FIGURE 7–93)

FIGURE 7–89

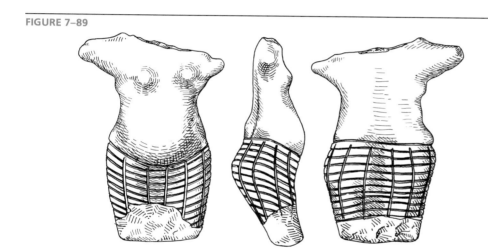

FIGURE 7–89 This bird-winged figurine was depicted with a nude torso and a hipline skirt or girdle. Intentional lines on the garment suggest either a ''plaid'' fabric or a tightly wound cloth with horizontal stripes with vertical fringe hanging from the hips. Gradac, classical Vinča site, early 5th mill. B.C.

FIGURE 7–90

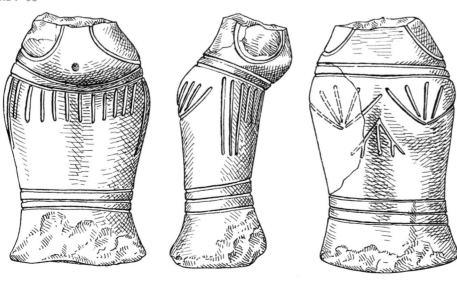

FIGURE 7–90 This figurine fragment from the Vinča culture has a narrow ankle-length skirt caught at the hipline and lower legs by bindings, possibly of leather, and a fringed ''apron.'' The fringe is suspended from the hip belt in the front only. Vinča site, c. 4500 B.C.

FIGURE 7–91

FIGURE 7–91 Draping, so common in classical Greece, is found on this fragment of legs of a large figurine from the Vinča culture of Yugoslavia. Fabric has been gathered and pulled from the ankles at the front and possibly caught by a hip belt. The feet are bare as we can discern from the carefully modeled, red-painted toes. Vinča site, c. 5000 B.C.

FIGURE 7–92 In this Vinča figurine the skirt has been wound tightly around a full figure, then pulled up from the back and caught by a hip belt. C Yugoslavia, c. 5000–4500 B.C.

FIGURE 7–93 A long, narrow skirt topped by a second decorative garment or "apron" is displayed on this headless, armless Vinča figurine. A leather thong is on the front of the torso and an apron is indicated by punctate marks. Drapery is again implied in the chevron treatment at the lower part of the body. Snake spirals are on the sides and on each buttock. The three lines and dots on the back may represent thongs knotted with beads. Classical Vinča culture from Beletinci at Obrež, N Yugoslavia, c. 48th–45th cents. B.C.

FIGURE 7–92

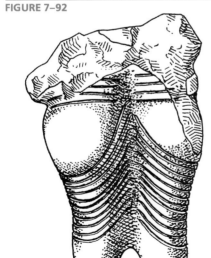

FIGURE 7–93

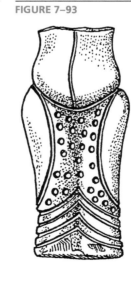

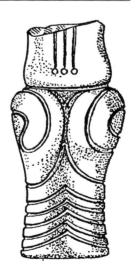

FIGURE 7–94

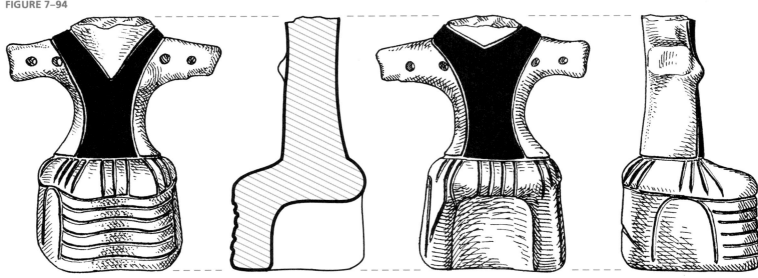

FIGURE 7–95

FIGURE 7–96

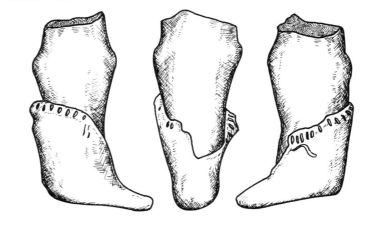

FIGURE 7–94 The torso of this enthroned Vinča fig-urine is covered with a V-necked front and back panel. The arms are per-forated twice on each side, indicating that some material was inserted for decoration. Note the fringe on the hip belt and the horizon-tal lines suggesting a ritual "apron." Banjica near Belgrade, early 5th mill. B.C.

FIGURE 7–95 Many examples from complete and partial figurines leave no doubt that mocassin-type footwear was worn by the Old Europeans. They were most likely made of leather, secured by thongs, or cut for the foot to slip into and then tied at the ankle. A speci-men from the Cucuteni A–B settlement of Koshi-lovce with perforations for laces. c. 4000 B.C.; about 3 x 9 cm.

FIGURE 7–96 In this terra-cotta foot fragment, leather appears to have been cut for an ankle-high boot; perforations probably indicate how leather thongs were laced and then tied. Late Cucuteni culture (Ghelaieşti), 3900–3700 B.C.

FIGURE 7–97

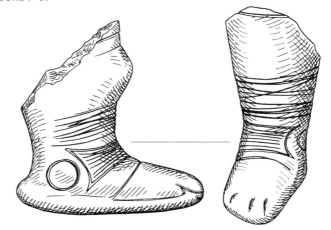

FIGURE 7–97 This foot fragment seems to represent a leather boot with padding on the sole and painted or beaded designs. Gumelniţa-Karanovo VI culture. From Vidra, Bucharest, 4700–4500 B.C.

Blouses or Bodice Panels

Certain figurines appear to be wearing blouses consisting of front and back panels which leave the sides of the body bare. (FIGURE 7-94) If this design corresponds to an actual costume, we can only guess at its composition. If it was not made of cloth, perhaps it was constructed of leather. Bodice panels which are worn by figurines wearing masks indicate a ceremonial purpose rather than everyday wear.

Footgear

Figurine fragments indicate that the Old Europeans fashioned boots of leather that were cut to fit the foot, then gathered around the ankle with thongs. (FIGURES 7-95, 7-96) One Gumelniţa-Karanovo VI specimen from Vidra offers the suggestion that some soles were padded, and shoes were painted with symbols; in this case, the designs also appear on other parts of the sculpture. (FIGURE 7-97) The footgear that appears on goddess figurines may reflect a semblance of everyday wear.

From what we can see from our discussion and illustrations of hairstyles, headdresses, and ritual attire, it can be concluded that ceremonial clothing was elaborate and tasteful. Its preparation required a great deal of time and skill, perhaps as a collective creation in temple workshops.

Burial Practices

The Old European burials are entirely distinct from the Indo-European burials that supplanted them. These dissimilar practices represent different ideologies. The Old Europeans emphasized cyclic regeneration from the body of the Great Mother, whereas the Indo-Europeans emphasized a lineal continuity of the importance of powerful males. The Indo-Europeans buried their dead in mortuary houses or tents in order to continue their individual lives. Personal belongings—tools, weapons, horses, even wives and servants or slaves—went into the grave. The more socially prominent an individual was, the more lavishly his grave was equipped. An incredible amount of grave goods and sacrificed horses and people are found in royal tombs of the Bronze and Iron Ages.

In contrast, the burials of Old Europe clearly indicate a respect for the community of ancestors rather than particular individuals. Individual grave goods hardly exist except for a few ornaments or tools that are mostly symbolic, associated with the Goddess or with regeneration rites. These include antlers and bones of red deer, jawbones of boars and pigs, skeletons of dogs, ox skulls or horns, and the bones or wings of birds of prey. For the Old Europeans, the tomb was a womb.

Symbols of regeneration—the egg and the regenerative organs of the Goddess (pubic triangle, vulva, uterus, belly, buttocks)—are the basis of Old European tomb shapes. These are manifested in the architectural forms of western European megalithic graves and earthen long-barrows which are triangular or trapezoidal. The inner tombs have passages into chambers, symbolic of a vagina and uterus, or the tombs have "courts" in the form of open legs leading to the inner chambers. Occasionally, these tombs are anthropomorphic, in the shape of the body of the Goddess. Long-barrows are also bone shaped, symbolizing death: the Old Hag's bone.

Elsewhere in Old Europe, the egg is the dominant shape of graves, often expressed as a simple egg-shaped pit or a rock-cut tomb in which the dead were placed in a contracted fetal position and sprinkled with ochre. (FIGURE 7-98) The dead were also buried in egg-shaped pots, especially newborn babies or separated skulls. (FIGURE 7-99)

The egg-shaped halls and niches of subterranean tombs are frequently painted in red. The placing of ochre in graves was an almost universal feature; it was extensively sprinkled on the skull or scattered all over the body. This red was the color of life, of blood, which was necessary to secure regeneration.

Individual and Collective Burial

In all of Neolithic Europe, both individual and communal burials are encountered. In northern and central Europe, individual burials prevailed. In the 5th millennium B.C. in the Dnieper-Donets culture, collective family burials were practiced, and in western and Mediterranean Europe, communal collective burials in megalithic graves and hypogea (underground burial chambers) were the rule. Collective burials of members of extended families continued in Crete throughout the 3rd and early 2nd millennia B.C.

In Brittany, the transition from individual to "family vault" burial is evidenced around 5000 B.C. Here, Late Mesolithic stone-lined pit graves contained both single and collective inhumations. Such were found in two cemeteries, Teviec and Hoedic, located on islets in the Gulf of Morbihan.[33] The latter has been radiocarbon dated to 4625 ±350 B.C. The ten Teviec graves contained twenty-three burials, up to six skeletons to a grave. At Hoedic, the remains of fourteen individuals of all sexes and ages were buried in nine graves. These graves were covered with slabs on which fires were lit and ritual deposits of deer and boar jawbones were placed and which were then sealed with stone cairns. Some graves were covered by a beehive of large red-deer antlers. The larger collective graves had been used successively; the previously buried skeletons had been disturbed to make room for each new burial. The continu-

FIGURE 7–98

FIGURE 7–98 Egg-shaped tombs of the Linear-bandkeramik cemetery at Nitra, Slovakia. c. 5000 B.C.

FIGURE 7–99 Skull in an egg-shaped pot supported by stones. Funnel-necked Beaker culture. Metzendorf, distr. Harburg, Nieder-sachsen. 4th mill B.C. H 42.5 cm.

FIGURE 7–99

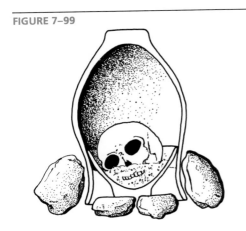

ous deposition of human remains of a family or of one community into one grave in the 4th millennium B.C. was continued by the megalithic tomb builders. Communal burial is the predominant rite in rock-cut tombs in the Tagus River basin of Portugal and in Granada, Spain. Although not radio-carbon dated, these tombs most probably belong in the 5th millennium B.C., followed in the late 5th and early 4th millennia by the megalithic passage graves which included collective multi-stage burials. In the early megalithic tombs in Iberia, France, and Britain, collective burials of crouched bodies are found. New burials often dispersed the bones of the first occupants. Selective treatment of skulls is seen from the very beginning of the use of megaliths. If the earlier burials were disturbed, their skulls were respected—they are frequently found stacked along the tomb walls.

Two-stage Burial: Excarnation and Reburial

A two-stage burial prevailed for many centuries in Europe and Anatolia. This term is used to describe a deposit of disarticulated bones, particularly skulls, that were buried after the flesh had decayed or had been removed from the body. Decaying flesh is transitional between life and death, not the end of the cycle; only a clean bone symbolizes death. All flesh was removed from the dead body by excarnation (usually through exposure to birds of prey) or by cremation before being returned to the community of ancestors. Purified bones were then placed in graves of the kin group to which the dead belonged.

During the Early Neolithic, between the 8th and the mid-6th millennium B.C. in the Near East and in Europe, formal disposal areas of the dead outside habitation areas are not known. Babies, youngsters, and women were buried beneath the floors of houses, although complete skeletons are found only of newborns who were buried in a fetal position. Skulls were usually buried separately, and the disarticulated skeletons often had missing parts. Male burials are

clearly missing,[34] and it is very likely that their bodies were exposed for the vultures and their disarticulated bones were later buried somewhere in or out of the village. In Greece, such graves containing disarticulated skeletons have been found.[35] Bull horns, deer antlers, dog skulls, and stone axes are also found under the floors or in post holes. Although formal disposal areas emerged in southeast and Danubian Europe after 5500 B.C., the two-stage burial must have continued for some time since skeletons in many cases were found missing skulls, hands, or feet. In some cases, the skulls were buried in a separate area of the cemetery, accompanied by skulls and jaws of deer, goat, pig, and ox (as in the Hamangia culture).

The best visual documentation of the existence of excarnation is on the walls of temples at Çatal Hüyük where the Goddess is depicted in the guise of a vulture descending on headless corpses (see fig. 7–26). This motif indicates that the skull, as the most important part of the human body, must have been removed before excarnation. In the temples of Çatal Hüyük we see them placed under bucrania, symbols of the uterus. In Pre-pottery Neolithic Jericho in the Jordan Valley, skulls found beneath the floors had facial parts modelled in gypsum, their eyes marked with shells.[36] In northern Europe of the 6th and 5th millennia B.C., skulls of the dead in the cemetery of Zvejnieki in Latvia were covered with a layer of blue clay and their eye sockets filled with amber discs.[37]

The disarticulated bones in the communal burials of western European megaliths are further evidence of the two-stage burial. Complete skeletons, with rare exceptions, are not found in megalithic graves. Where cremation was practiced, as in Newgrange, it was observed that unburnt bones were broken into small bits and scattered throughout the passage, chamber, and recesses. Such practices may indicate the desire to promote a faster disintegration into the realm of the ancestors.

FIGURE 7–100

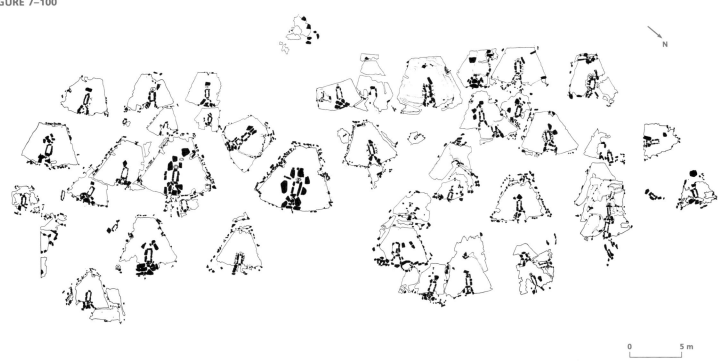

0   5 m

We shall now look in some detail at several outstanding burial places and tombs from various parts of Europe in which excarnation and two-stage burial were practiced and the symbolism of regeneration is richly expressed: Lepenski Vir in northern Yugoslavia, the hypogea of Malta and Sardinia, the Scaloria cave in southeast Italy, and the Isbister barrow in the Orkneys, Scotland. We will conclude with the symbolism of the megalithic tombs of western Europe.

Lepenski Vir

Lepenski Vir is a burial site and locus of semisubterranean sanctuaries on the Danube near the Iron Gate in northern Yugoslavia, excavated by D. Srejović and Z. Letica from 1965 to 1968.[38] This site is impressive with respect to its natural surroundings since the temples on the shore of the Danube confront a gigantic whirlpool (in Serbo-Croatian *vir* means "whirlpool") with bare cliffs on the opposite bank. Triangular/trapezoid shaped structures of diminutive size (triangular with one squared angle) form a semicir-

FIGURE 7–101

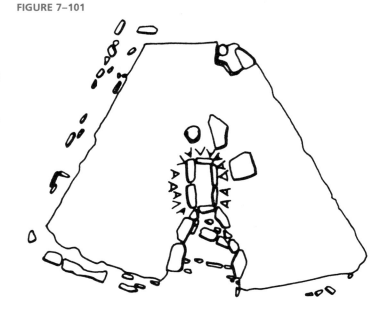

FIGURE 7–100 Triangular-trapezoidal plans of semisubterranean shrines at Lepenski Vir, including lime-plastered floors and rectangular altars, c. 6500–5500 B.C. Iron Gate region, N Yugoslavia.

FIGURE 7–101 Interior features of a Lepenski Vir shrine. The floor is of reddish lime plaster. In the center is a rectangular sacrificial altar lined with stones set on edge. The altar is outlined with thin slabs of stone set vertically in a pattern of continuous triangles. A sculpture is placed behind the altar. Lepenski Vir Id, shrine No. 19, c. 6000 B.C. Diameter c. 7 m across at the wide end.

cle on the shore of the Danube with entrances facing the river. (FIGURE 7-100). These temples span almost a millennium, from 6500 to 5500 B.C. (TABLE 2), and their sacred location was probably the site of ritualistic exposure of the dead to birds for excarnation. The bones were gathered and buried beneath temple altars, accompanied by rites of regeneration.

Lepenski Vir was not a regular village of a certain time. Sacred structures were built continually, one by one, for about one thousand years.

More than fifty temples have been excavated, all of similar form and structure. Their floors were constructed from a mixture of red limestone and clay, so hard that they withstood millennia of Danubian flood waters. At the center of each temple's floor were the remains of a rectangular stone altar surrounded by V-shaped flat stones set on edge in a pattern of continuous triangles. (FIGURE 7-101) At the head of the altar were one or two statues of red limestone, egg-shaped boulders or receptacles for offerings up to 50 or 60 cm high. One was an egg-shaped sandstone sculpture, painted in red ochre, representing a vulva before parturition. (PLATE 24) Altogether, fifty-four round, oval, or elliptical sculptures were found, fifteen of which exhibited anthropomorphic features—faces and breasts—or fishes' mouths and eyes. There are also representations of three-fingered hands, considered to be birds' feet. Several sculptures appear to be comprised of three manifestations of the Goddess of Death and Regeneration: those of woman, fish, and predatory bird. (FIGURE 7-102; PLATE 23) Many were carved with labyrinth motifs and painted, completely or in part, with red ochre. Symbols of regeneration are dominant: the egg, the fish, the labyrinth, and the red color.

FIGURE 7-102

1

2

FIGURE 7-102 Egg-shaped Fish Goddess sculptures of sandstone from Lepenski Vir found at the head of stone altar. Lepenski Vir II, c. 6000 B.C. H (1) 38 cm, (2) 51 cm.

The floor plan of these temples is in the shape of the female pubic triangle. The altar in the center is joined by two rows of stones, which seem to outline a passage to the uterus of the Goddess. The sculpture at the head of the altar represented either the Goddess herself or her regenerative womb. These were symbolically interchangeable, and almost every object found within these temples was marked with symbols of regeneration—labyrinths, spirals, nets, and fish.

The bones of fish, red deer, dogs, and wild boars were found within the rectangular altars.[39] According to the research of prehistoric and historic symbolism, dogs and boars are attendants and epiphanies of the Goddess of Death, while red deer and fish represent her aspects of birth and regeneration. The sacrifice of these particular animals suggests that Lepenski Vir was not an ordinary inhabited settlement subsisting on hunted game, but a field for the selection of certain animals appropriate for the Goddess. Several altars sheltered entire canine skeletons, indicating that the dogs were not eaten but were most likely sacrificial offerings. The fish bones were those of large fish—sturgeon, carp, pike, catfish—and the remains of red deer were, for the most part, skulls and shoulder blades, apparently endowed with special powers.

Sacred sites resembling Lepenski Vir, though less abundant in archeological finds, were excavated in fourteen locations along both shores of the Danube, and designated as branches of Lepenski Vir culture. Some precede it chronologically. For example, Vlasac, 3 km southeast of Lepenski Vir, dates to the 9th millennium B.C., and Cuina Turcului, on the Romanian side, to the 12th or 11th millennium B.C. Lepenski Vir culture is thought to be a direct continuation of Paleolithic Gravettian culture.[40]

Similar burial and sacrificial traditions were continuous over millennia. Human bones were found mainly in arbitrary arrangements, not always in accord with anatomical hierarchy. Skulls were buried with exceptional care, however, by enclosure or covering with stones, severally or individually. Newborn infants, of five or six days, were buried under the temple floor. Bones were lined with red ochre and occasionally the teeth of large fish were juxtaposed with the jawbones of dogs and wild boars, as well as the horns, skulls, and shoulder blades of red deer. In Vlasac, cremated bones were discovered. The remains of predatory birds in front of the rows of sanctuaries—eagles, owls, pelicans, ravens, and magpies—attest to the practice of excarnation in these locations. Skeletal material, neglected by the birds, was gathered and interred beneath or beside the temples.

The Hypogea of Malta and Sardinia

The hypogeum at Hal Saflieni on eastern Malta is one of the most impressive shrines in all of Old Europe.[41] Its Main Hall, like the thirty-three other chambers, was carved out of globigerina limestone with an exquisite temple facade and three lintels leading up to a corbelled vault. (FIGURE 7–103) It took many centuries to build the hypogeum. Its first levels were begun c. 3600 B.C. with the Mgarr phase and finished in the Tarxien phase c. 2500 B.C. The entire complex is cut into a hill encompassing an area of 480 sq m on three levels which have been excavated; there are more beneath which have been left unexcavated. The eight rooms of the first level are roughly egg shaped, irregular and roughly finished like the subterranean tombs of Xemxija on northwestern Malta. The middle level has nineteen major rooms and about fourteen smaller niches. The halls here are larger and are decorated both with temple architecture carved into the limestone and with red spirals and discs like trees of life painted on the ceilings and walls. (FIGURE 7–104) The lowest level has six main rooms and six more niches which are high and narrow. Some of the excavated graves held pottery, figurines, and food offerings, and in nearly every case the bones were in complete disorder, perhaps because they were brought to the mausoleum after the defleshment stage.

Some tombs held the bones of young calves, kids, lambs, and rabbits, as well as what appear to be hedgehogs, frogs, and pigs—animals known to be sacred to the Goddess of Regeneration. The presence of roe deer skulls with antlers intact indicate that tomb rituals took place in spring, since deer shed their antlers in October of each year and grow a new set that mature in March. Also found were a schematic bone figurine portraying a stiff nude representing the Death-White Goddess and two buttocks-shaped pendants as well as figurines with egg-shaped buttocks of alabaster and globigerina limestone.

The lower two levels were decorated freely with red ochre, a symbol of the blood of life. Symbols of the cyclic renewal of life such as trees or vines, snakes and spirals are most evident in the Oracle Room and the Main Hall.

The hypogeum, with its rooms painted liberally with red ochre wash, represents the Goddess's regenerative womb. This image of the tomb as womb, combined with symbols of regeneration, add further testimony that the hypogea and burial tombs of Malta were sacred ceremonial sites for ritual participation in the great round of death and rebirth. Those skeptical of ancient "womb symbolism" are reminded here that Delphi, which is the most famous of the Greek oracular sites, derives its name from the Greek word *delphys* meaning "womb."

FIGURE 7–103

FIGURE 7–104

FIGURE 7–103 The floor plans of the three underground stories of interconnected tombs at Hal Saflieni, Malta. Large halls and side niches are egg shaped. This hypogeum was used during the 4th and early 3rd mill. B.C.

FIGURE 7–104 Hal Saflieni hypogeum, the so-called oracle room showing the ceiling painted in red ochre with spirals or vines and discs.

FIGURE 7–105

FIGURE 7–105 "The Sleeping Lady" of Malta. Woman (goddess or priestess) lying on a dish-shaped couch with her head resting on a pillow. Her buttocks are double-egg shaped suggesting the symbol of regeneration. The hypogeum of Hal Saflieni, Malta, found in an egg-shaped chamber. Terracotta; traces of red coloring still visible. End of the 4th mill. B.C. L 12 cm.

FIGURE 7–106

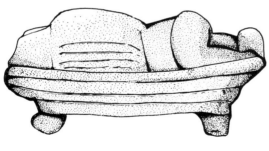

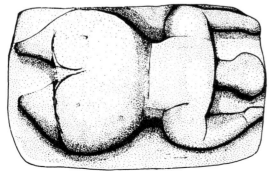

FIGURE 7–106 Another Maltese "Sleeping Lady" lying face down on a couch is portrayed with an emphasis on the symbolic importance of egg-shaped buttocks, symbolic of regeneration. Hal Saflieni hypogeum, found in a subterranean egg-shaped room painted with red snake spiral design. End of the 4th mill. B.C. L 6 cm.

FIGURE 7–107

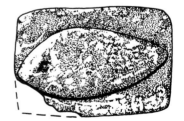

FIGURE 7–107 Clay fish on a bed from the hypogeum. Malta. H 5.5 cm; L 8 cm.

An indication of the religious use of these womb-shaped chambers are the figurines of Sleeping Ladies lying stretched out on low couches, associated with two cubicles opening into the Main Hall. (FIGURES 7–105, 7–106) The more articulate one, known as "The Sleeping Lady of the Hypogeum," is a true masterpiece. This generously rounded lady with egg-shaped buttocks lies on her side, asleep, almost visibly dreaming. Why is she sleeping in the tomb? One explanation is that this represents a rite of initiation or incubation. To sleep within the Goddess's womb was to die and come to life anew. The Sleeping Lady could also be a votive offering from one who successfully passed through the rite of incubation in the hypogeum. This could also represent a healing practice. In the classical world, incubation was closely associated with rituals of healing, best known as taking place in the temple of Asklepios at Epidauros. The treatment consisted of an initial purification of the patient by washing and fasting, followed by a night spent in the temple. In another representation, a fish lies on a couch. (FIGURE 7–107) Since the fish in Old European symbolism is an incarnation of the Goddess or her uterus, it can be surmised that the Goddess herself in the function of regeneration was represented in this image. Lying on couches, both fish and women could have symbolized incubation, regeneration, or both.

There are still other symbols of regeneration on vases found in the mausoleum, especially bulls, bucrania, and eggs. On the inner side of one plate nine bulls with huge horns are incised and white encrusted, while on the outer side eggs interconnect with parallel lines. (FIGURE 7–108) The combination of bulls or bull horns with eggs is a typical Old European symbol of regeneration which lasted for millennia. The best representations of this symbol are from the Cucuteni and Minoan cultures. In general, the Maltese symbolism of regeneration conforms very well with that of the rest of Old Europe.

In Sardinia there are hundreds of impressive subterranean tombs, most of them dating from the Ozieri period of

FIGURE 7–108

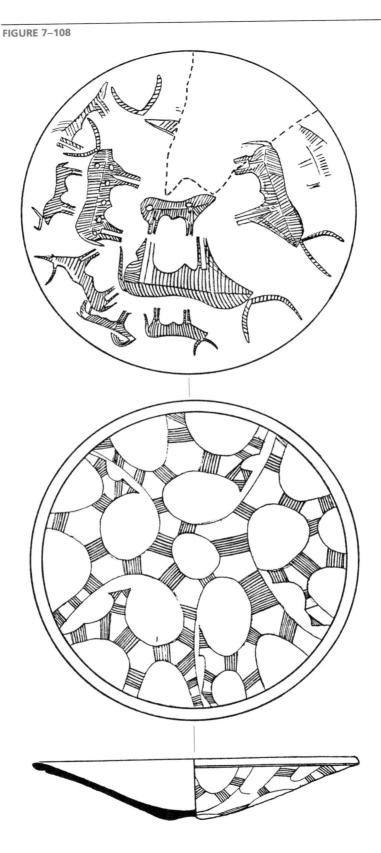

FIGURE 7–108 Egg and bull, two main symbols of regeneration, combine on this Maltese dish. Note striations which probably are symbolic of water or lines of energy. Hal Saflieni, Malta, end 4th mill. c. 3000 B.C. Diameter 27 cm.

the end of the 5th and early 4th millennia B.C. (FIGURE 7–109) These must have developed from the preceding rock-cut tombs with egg-shaped cells.

The Ozieri hypogea represent a true explosion in tomb building. Some are small with one, two, or three egg-shaped cells while others have multiple cells and a hall with pilasters in the center. Such is the S. Andrea Priu hypogeum in Bonorva, northern Sardinia (see fig. 5–19). These large tombs are easily accessible and have been robbed in antiquity leaving only the paintings, incisions, and bas-reliefs which decorate the tomb walls.

Only in very exceptional cases have human bones been found in these tombs, as in San Benedetto, Iglesias, southwestern Sardinia. Here, the skeletal remains show that a two-stage burial was practiced in Sardinia as it was in Malta and elsewhere. Thirty-five skulls and disarticulated bones were placed in the main and side cells. (FIGURE 7–110; small circles within the tomb indicate the location of skulls and bones.)

Not much is known of how the dead were exposed, but there is one puzzling monument in northern Sardinia that was probably used for funeral rituals. This is Monte d'Accoddi near Alghero, a huge rectangular platform raised high on a stone foundation with a ramp leading to it. (FIGURE 7–111) A dish was found on this monument with the representation of a dance scene in which maidens, rendered in hourglass shapes, hold hands in a circle, apparently dancing (see fig. 5–15.2). This platform must have been perfectly suited for ritual celebrations. If the dead were exposed on it for birds, we do not know.

Huge horns or bull heads in relief were placed above entrances to the hypogea, suggesting that to enter these chambers, one must pass through a bucranium or symbolic womb. (FIGURE 7–112) Large bull heads or horns were also painted or portrayed in relief on walls inside the chambers, usually in red. (FIGURE 7–113) In addition to this prominent symbol, decorations are found which include vulva triangles (single, triple, or multiple), ram horns or snake coils, and concentric circles. The most richly decorated pottery of Sardinia and the

FIGURE 7–109
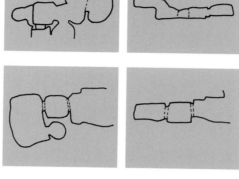

FIGURE 7–109 Plans and sections of Sardinian subterranean tombs in the area of Ozieri, N Sard. Ozieri period, end 5th–early 4th mill. B.C.

FIGURE 7–110
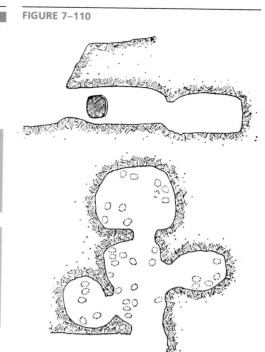

FIGURE 7–111
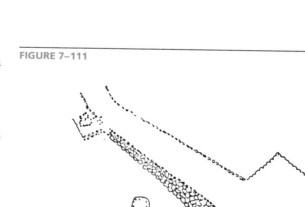
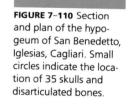

FIGURE 7–110 Section and plan of the hypogeum of San Benedetto, Iglesias, Cagliari. Small circles indicate the location of 35 skulls and disarticulated bones.

FIGURE 7–111 Sketch of the Monte d'Accoddi monument northwest of Sassari. The rectangular platform measures 37.5 by 30.5 m. Funeral rituals with music and dancing may have taken place here during the Ozieri period of Sardinia, end of the 5th mill. B.C. A dish with a portrayal of dancing girls holding hands was found here (see fig. 5–15, 2).

FIGURE 7–112

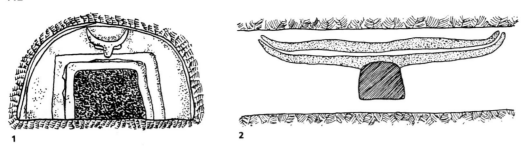

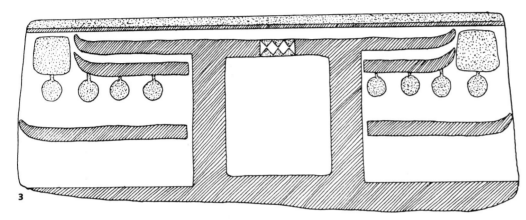

3

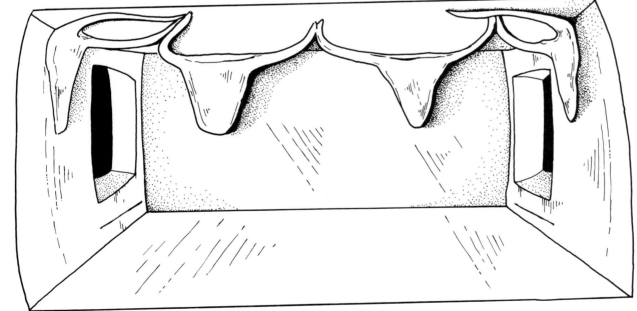

FIGURE 7–112 Bull-head shaped entrances and bull head above the entrance to Sardinian underground tombs. (1) and (2) Sos Furrighesos, Anela. (3) Mandra Antine o Turri, prov. of Sassari. c. 5th mill. B.C.

FIGURE 7–113

FIGURE 7–113 Uterus-shaped bull heads in relief on the interior walls of a subterranean tomb. S. Lesei, Bonnanaro, Sardinia; c. 4000 B.C.

FIGURE 7–114A

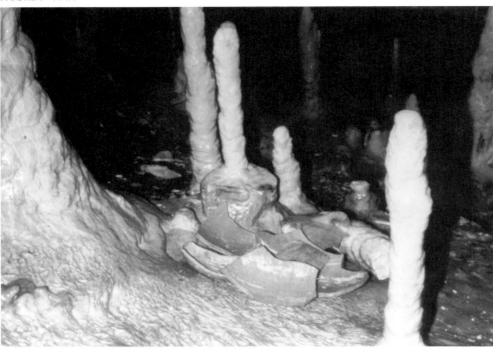

FIGURE 7–114B

celebrated alabaster, marble, and bone figurines of the nude White Death Goddess come from what local inhabitants call "witches houses" (*domus de Janas*).

Scaloria Cave in Southeast Italy

The Scaloria Cave in southeastern Italy near the city of Manfredonia consists of two separate parts: the top cave is a wide hall, suitable for habitation where ceramic and stone tools were found, dating from the end of the 7th to the end of the 6th millennium B.C.; the lower cave is long and narrow like a sleeve, with stalagmites and a live spring near the bottom. Near this spring many painted ceramic objects were found indicating, through radiocarbon dates, that ceremonies occurred there during the mid-6th millennium (c. 5600–5300 B.C.). (FIGURE 7–114A)

Local archeologists as well as amateurs found the cave in the beginning of this century and large quantities of ceramics were taken out. Fortunately, there are well-preserved vases which solidified next to stalagmites which could not be removed. During my expedition in 1979 and 1980, pottery sherds were collected from upper and lower cave levels which belonged to 1,500 vases. These were decorated systematically with symbols of regeneration: eggs, triangles, snakes, plant and sun designs, and symbols of the Goddess of Regeneration herself—V's, triangles, hourglass shapes, and butterfly motifs. (FIGURE 7–114B) Ceremonies which took place at this mysterious depth near the "water of life" must have been related to regeneration.

At the entrance to the narrow cave, as many as 137 persons were buried on top of each other without any order. Most of the skeletons belonged to young individuals, particularly to women 20 to 22 years old who probably died at childbirth, and to children. Some skulls had been removed before the rest of the bodies were deposited, and some had cut marks.[42] This discovery can now be understood within the context of ancient and widespread burial practices in which the heads of the dead were removed to receive special ritual attention before being buried separately. This does not indicate human sacrifice.

FIGURE 7–114A The life columns are represented by phallus-shaped stalagmites in cave sanctuaries. At Scaloria cave near Manfredonia, SE Italy, decorated vases were found standing around stalagmites and near the sacred water at the bottom of the cave; c. 5600–5300 B.C.

FIGURE 7–114B Vases recovered in Scaloria cave at Manfredonia, SE Italy, are decorated with symbols of regeneration: eggs, suns, plants, and Goddess's signs—V's and triangles; red on white painted. Dated by radiocarbon to 5600–5300 B.C.

Isbister Megalithic Tomb of Orkney, Scotland

The Isbister Tomb, located on one of the Orkney Islands off the northeastern tip of Scotland, is one of the very rare megalithic ossuaries in which hundreds of disarticulated human skeletons, carcasses of sea eagles and other birds of prey, hundreds of fish skeletons, animal bones, grains, and other finds were preserved. In the majority of megalithic graves, nothing has been found inside, since most were robbed in antiquity or destroyed by diggers.

Isbister is one of seventy-six megalithic monuments known in the Orkney Islands. These tombs were built of local stone and were covered by a round or oval cairn. The entrance is through a corridor leading to a chamber in the center which had either multiple cells or tripartite or multiple stalls. On the outside, the tombs had forecourts and were surrounded by platforms of stone. Some were surrounded by a bank of earth.

Isbister, located on the southern tip of an island in the south of Orkney, was covered by a cairn dome 3 to 3.50 m high, measuring 10 by 8 m. It had an inner chamber about 8 m long with side cells and end stalls. (FIGURE 7–115) The main excavation of the tomb by R. Simison took place in 1976. Its construction, according to radiocarbon dating, began around 3150 ±80 B.C. It was in use for eight hundred years.

Because of the discovery of bones and carcasses of sea eagles, the Isbister tomb became singled out as "Tomb of the Eagles" which is the title of the book on Isbister by John W. Hedges.[43] This tomb was not, however, an ossuary for birds alone. It was, like other megalithic graves, a sacred place to which human bones were returned after excarnation. Some 90 percent of the birds of prey that

FIGURE 7–115

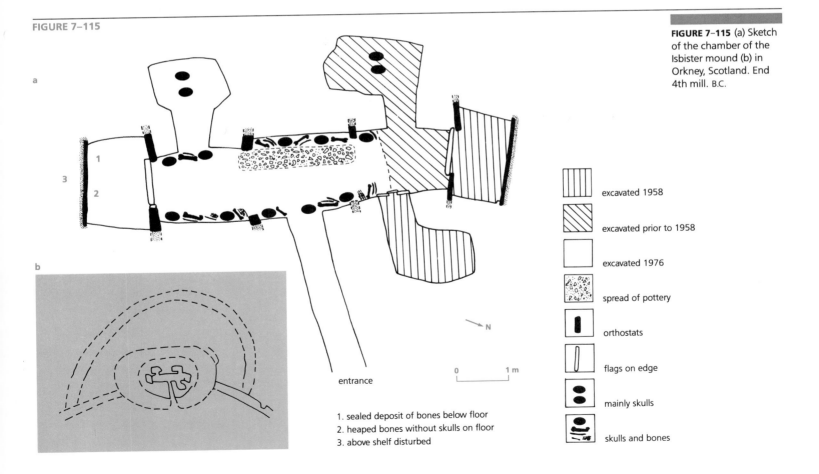

a

b

FIGURE 7–115 (a) Sketch of the chamber of the Isbister mound (b) in Orkney, Scotland. End 4th mill. B.C.

excavated 1958

excavated prior to 1958

excavated 1976

spread of pottery

orthostats

flags on edge

mainly skulls

skulls and bones

entrance

0   1 m

N

1. sealed deposit of bones below floor
2. heaped bones without skulls on floor
3. above shelf disturbed

would have defleshed the corpses were white-tailed sea eagles. Thirty-five of their carcasses were counted alongside those of gulls, owls, crows, ravens, and other birds found in the chamber and scattered around the tomb. The burial or sacrifice of eagles within the chamber speaks for their extraordinary importance as birds of the Goddess of Death and Regeneration.

The excavation at Isbister revealed the strongest evidence for the practice of excarnation since none of the human bones were deposited while still articulated. The bodies were defleshed outside the tomb before a selection of the skeletal remnants were transferred to the chamber. These bones were bleached and weathered and must have been exposed for a considerable length of time. The disarticulated bones were placed in piles along the sides of the main chamber, skulls in the side cells and residual bones under and on the shelves of the end stalls. It is believed that excarnation took place near the tomb, perhaps on specially prepared platforms. On the basis of the number of corpses represented by the thousands of bones in the chamber and the known span of its use, Hedges suggests that there would have been an average of two excarnations per year. The process of exposure lasted long enough for the bones to become bleached and weathered. Judson T. Chesterman analyzed the bones of another Orkney tomb, Quanterness, and noticed that some bones in the chamber were in prime condition while others were so weathered and broken as to be almost unidentifiable.[44] This indicates that the bones were not brought into the chamber when a specific stage of excarnation was reached but perhaps were gathered on a specific ritual occasion.[45] It can be imagined that the bodies of those who died early in this term would have been reduced to bones while the very recent dead would still be corpse-like. In another tomb, at Midhowe, several burials are stated to have been found in a crouched position which could be the products of incomplete excarnation.[46] The vast majority of bones, both in Quanterness and Isbister, showed evidence of burning. Moderate heat by fire was applied to the broken bones, which is not considered cremation since bones were not reduced to ashes. Remains of burnt areas in tombs indicate that fires were lit within the tomb. This custom may have been for a final purification of the bones, especially if there were traces of ligaments or flesh.

Special days for the return of the bones to the ancestors were joyously celebrated. Remains of feasting are abundant: bones of sheep, goats, cattle, and pigs were found within the chamber. The meat animals were killed young, mostly in their first year, and there was a preference for joints, particularly for the legs of lamb. More than three hundred seeds of barley have been recovered as well as the bones of red deer and otters and hundreds if not thousands of fish carcasses. Why were there so many fish? If they had been consumed, only fragments and single bones would have been found. I assume that the fish found at Isbister, as well as the sea eagles, were incarnations of the powers of the Goddess and were buried in the tomb as essential symbols of regeneration. The role of the fish in regeneration rites is known to us from the Hal Saflieni hypogeum in Malta where a fish was sculptured and deposited in the tomb lying on a couch (see fig. 7-107). At Lepenski Vir, the fish was a main sacrificial animal along with the dog and deer, and the Fish Goddess was depicted as a hybrid Fish/Woman/Bird of Prey, magnificently represented in stone sculpture. (See fig. 7-102 and plate 41.)

In other megalithic tombs of the Orkney islands, not fish but dogs were buried as sacred animals of the Goddess: at Cuween, twenty-four dog skulls were found, and at Burray, dog skulls and skeletons were discovered in each compartment of the grave.[47] At Holm of Papa Westray North, a dozen pairs of deer antlers were found, as symbols of regeneration or as remnants of headdresses for deer dances. The latter has been evidenced from early postglacial times to the present.[48] Around the New Year, men still dress as women with antler headdresses to perform the famous stag dance to promote regeneration and secure happiness for the coming year.

The burial of fish, dogs, and deer speaks for more extensive celebrations than the simple eating of meat. Music and dances were certainly involved. There are, unfortunately, no pictorial representations on pottery found in the megalithic tombs in Orkney, but we do know that dance was associated with funeral rites of the Sardinian hypogea and other monuments (see figs. 7-111, 7-112, 7-113). Funerary ceramics from the Hallstatt period in Hungary of the 6th century B.C. continue to portray dances and lyre players alongside the hunt and funerary games, as seen on a vase from Sopron.[49] Dancing figures are triangular or hourglass shaped, as is the Goddess riding in a four-wheeled vehicle. (FIGURE 7-116) The muscians, hunters, and those involved in games are men. The panel decoration in a band below the main funerary celebrations on the Sopron vase are either rows of triangles, hourglass figures, or a combination of triangles and lozenges. The same motifs, as we shall see in the next section, appear on the walls of megalithic tombs. A continuity of imagery over three thousand years is strong evidence for the symbolic role of these figures in association with funeral rites.

Ethnographic Parallels

Isbister is a perfect example of a Neolithic ossuary, the most sacred place on the land of a kin-group. The imposing megalithic structures symbolized the Center and were the link with the ancestral land, the ancestors, and the members of the kin-group. To call the megalithic tombs "territorial markers" as Colin Renfrew has done[50] is somewhat denigrating to the culture itself. We do not call the village churches of our times "territorial markers" although they are visible, highly revered religious centers, as were the megalithic shrines.

There are ethnographic parallels with the practice of two-stage burial and the construction of large megalithic edifices. Close analogies are found among the Merina of central Madagascar.[51] The Merina are endogamous people who live in kin-groups on ancestral land (which M. Bloch calls *demes*). These people stress their unity in terms of the permanent association of their group with the irrigated lands which they hold in common. Every deme has its own tomb, an extremely solid megalithic building, which is a central symbol for the group. The Merina practice a two-stage burial in which the corpse is first buried without any particular sepulcher near the locality where the death took place. The second stage, called *famadihana*, involves exhumation of the decomposed corpse and reburial in the communal tomb in the ancestral land of the deceased. The return of the bones is a joyous event, celebrated with music and dances, even dancing with bones. Individuality is what decomposes, whereas the bones belong to the world of the ancestors. *Famadihana* emphasizes the importance of the group rather than the individual dead. This grinding together of the corpses in the tomb is the supreme act which leads to the blessing of the ancestors. The building of permanent megalithic structures by the

Merina, which serve as ossuaries of a single kin-group, and the enactment of the *famadihana* ritual is a Neolithic tradition continuous to modern times; it mirrors the tradition of two-stage burial in the megalithic culture of Western Europe.

Despite Christian influence, the continuity of Neolithic burial traditions can still be traced among the modern day Basques of Spain.[52] In their country, the primary unit of social organization is the rural farmstead, called *basseria*, which cannot be dismembered by sale or inheritance. Each *basseria* is associated with a *sepulturie* on the floor of the local church, which is a symbolic burial plot where rites to the dead take place. On Sundays the women surround it with candles. Masses said are for the collective dead and for all former owners of the farmstead which, until the late 18th century, was the real burial site. Today, corpses are buried outside the church in plots allocated by household. The individual grave is of little importance.

FIGURE 7–116

FIGURE 7–116 Scenes from funeral rites depicted on Hallstatt vases. Sopron, Hungary. 6th cent. B.C.

Whenever there is a death, the grave diggers exhume a previously buried corpse, deposit the bones in the ossuary, and then bury the newly deceased. There is, of course, no excarnation, but the role of the church as an ossuary is an obvious link with the Neolithic megaliths.

The ritual of collecting the bones years after the person's death and placing them in ossuaries is still practiced in southern Europe (Italy), in eastern Europe (Slavic countries), and in south-eastern Europe (Greece). The reburial of the dead after five years is recorded in Thessaly, northern Greece, as late as the early 1980s. The burial soon after death is considered here to be temporary, but elaborate memorial services take place on the third, ninth, and fortieth days after death, and again six months and one year after death. The female relatives of the deceased gather at the grave for an hour of crying and singing, and a ritual food called *koliva*, a mixture of boiled wheat, sugar, cinnamon, nuts and raisins, is distributed. This marks the start of a long transitional period, during which the person is considered neither fully alive nor fully dead. The decaying flesh must disappear, purified by the powers of destruction. Only then can it begin the journey to the ancestors. Five years is regarded as about right, but even in five years, the hair and other parts of the body are sometimes not fully decomposed. The exhumation of the body is women's work. I shall cite here a moving description by Loring Danforth[53] of an exhumation of Eleni, a twenty-year-old woman, who died in an accident in Thessaloniki and was buried in Potamia, a small village in northern Greece.[54]

"As Eleni's two brothers begin to dig through the sandy soil, a crowd of village women sings a loud, haunting lament that fails to drown out the increasingly hysterical cries of Eleni's mother, Irini. The lamenting grows more intense and Eleni's brothers, overcome with emotion, pass their shovels to two young women who continue digging. The brothers stand awkwardly outside the circle of wailing mourners, out of place in the women's world of death.

"Eventually, the young women with shovels are replaced by an old widow who, after striking something solid, begins to dig with her hands. Crossing herself, she bends to retrieve Eleni's skull, and greets it by saying, 'Welcome, my dear child.' As mourners toss flowers into the grave, the screaming and wailing reach a new peak. The widow wraps the skull in a white kerchief, places some paper money on it, kisses it and hands it to Irini saying, 'You have received her well.' Sobbing hysterically, Irini cradles her daughter's skull in her arms. Three times she kisses the skull and touches it to her forehead, then she passes the skull across the grave to be greeted by Eleni's father and the rest of the family.

"A few women sift through the earth, recovering the rest of Eleni's darkened bones and placing them in a metal box. The women count the bones and discuss the best way to arrange them. Irini is finally persuaded to relinquish her daughter's skull and place it in the box on top of the other bones.

"The village priest arrives and chants a portion of the Greek Orthodox funeral service. The box containing Eleni's remains is placed in the village ossuary, a small cement building in a corner of the graveyard. While the immediate family goes home to prepare for an elaborate reception, everyone else gathers in the church courtyard for the traditional distribution of *koliva*."

Through exhumation, the spirit of the deceased returns for a final time to the world of the living. After being checked to see if it is ready and fit for the society of the ancestors, it departs and leaves the living in peace.

Relics of a related custom of returning the bones to the ancestors are found among the Slavs. Exhumed bones are cleaned, wrapped in a towel called *ubrus*, brought into the house and placed in the sacred corner where the icons are kept. This is the place of communication with the ancestors. The *ubrus*, through contact with the skull, is sanctified.[55]

Symbolism of Regeneration in Megalithic Graves of Western Europe

As we have seen, the megalithic tombs of Western Europe were not graves as we understand them today, but sacred monuments in which community rituals took place relating to regeneration and the worship of ancestors. Engravings on tomb walls reveal images symbolic of regeneration.

Entrance stones, orthostats, roof stones, and kerbstones were pecked, incised, and occasionally painted with symbols. For almost a hundred years, however, megalithic art has been treated mainly as ornament with no acknowledgment of religious significance. The symbols on megaliths are of no less importance in deciphering the religion of their builders than are the sculptures and paintings in Christian churches.

Elizabeth Twohig has done a great service for the study of megalithic art by collecting, in one large volume, almost every symbol engraved or painted on stones between Portugal and Ireland.[56] Although she has made no attempt at interpretation, this study has made the sources of megalithic art accessible.

A clue to the deciphering of megalithic art was given by M. Brennan, who saw the alignments of monuments and their symbols as connected to solstices, equinoxes, solar and lunar risings, and lunar cycles.[57] The importance of this observation cannot be denied. However, their symbolism must not be interpreted as an expression of astronomical and mathematical knowledge with no relation to religion. All megalithic monuments must be viewed within a ritual context. We do not learn much by knowing that Gavrinis, Newgrange, Maes Howe, and other tomb shrines were oriented to the rising sun at winter solstice. The issue is why they were so oriented. The answer to such a question can come only from an analysis of megalithic symbolism.

There is a definite symbolic language represented by the signs engraved or painted in every region where megalithic art appears. These designs, whether single or in groups, are not accidental doodles or graffiti but belong to an ancient system of religious expression. The contents of this system can be divided into the following categories:

Schematized images of the Goddess: Hill shapes with or without a protrusion for her head (sometimes shown with hair), owl-shaped menhirs or stelae, and images of eyes or breasts. Her generative vulva is expressed by triangles or double triangles as well as lozenges and hourglass shapes.

Aquatic signs: Zigzags, wavy lines, multiple arcs, and cupmarks.

Serpents: Coiled or winding. Single snake coils are interchangeable with suns, double snake coils with eyes or with ram's horns.

Suns with rays and *sundials* with a cupmark in the center as symbols of life energy.

Trees of life or *life-columns:* Vertically piled arcs, vertically winding snakes, and similar images.

Spirals, hooks, horns, axes, and *"combs"* as stimulators of life energy.

Bulls or *bull heads* as homonyms of the womb of the Goddess.

Ships as bridges to the underworld and catalysts of rebirth.

The meaning of these images can only be deciphered within the context of the entire Neolithic symbolism of Old Europe. However, the study of motifs and their consistent associations on richly decorated single monuments, such as Gavrinis in Brittany or Newgrange and Knowth in Ireland, is particularly illuminating.

It is important to ask why only certain symbols appear on megaliths. Why triangles, vulvas, cupmarks, concentric arcs, eyes, snake coils, suns? Why trees of life and columns of life on funerary monuments? The association of certain signs with each other is significant. There is a consistent link between aquatic signs, serpents, and female images. The cupmark and triangle are interchangeable and are associated with or surrounded by aquatic symbols, concentric arcs or circles, and water waves. Further interrelationships are found between snake coils and suns, and snake coils and eyes.

Spirals, crescents, horns, hooks, and axes accompany symbols of the source of life as stimulators of life energy. All are "symbols of becoming."

First, let us look at symbols that can be defined as conventional abstractions of the Goddess. Her human form hardly exists except in anthropomorphic menhirs, schematized human shapes (FIGURES 7–117, 7–118), and woman-bird hybrids. These are more owl shaped than anthropomorphic, as depicted on a stela found in the passage of Knowth West (FIGURE 7–119), and on schist plaques

FIGURE 7–117

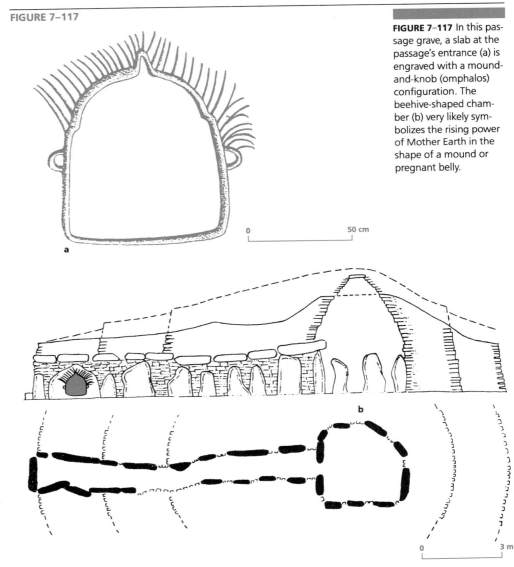

0   50 cm

a

b

0   3 m

FIGURE 7–117 In this passage grave, a slab at the passage's entrance (a) is engraved with a mound-and-knob (omphalos) configuration. The beehive-shaped chamber (b) very likely symbolizes the rising power of Mother Earth in the shape of a mound or pregnant belly.

FIGURE 7–118

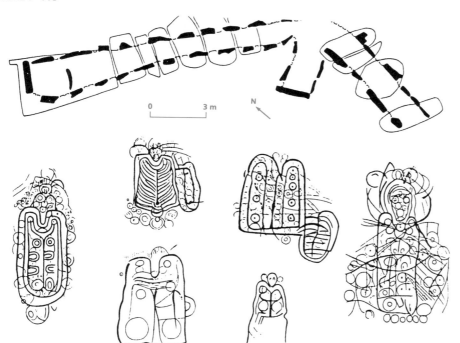

FIGURE 7–119

FIGURE 7–120

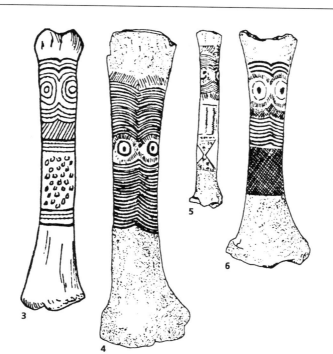

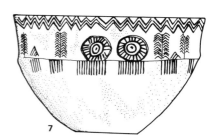

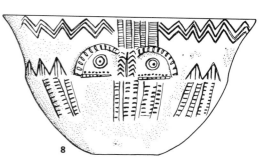

FIGURE 7–121

FIGURE 7–118 The plan of an angular passage grave of Les Pierres-Plates, Locmariaquer, Brittany (top) and schematically engraved figures of a probable Owl Goddess on the inner faces of stones in the passage (below). Figures have a central vertical line and three or four circles or arcs are on each side. Note that all of these images have a multitude of incised circles, carved at different times. Probably early 4th mill. B.C.

FIGURE 7–119 The Goddess in the shape of an owl engraved on a standing stone to the right of the chamber in the western passage of Knowth, Ireland. Rotund eyes of an owl are seen on top, but the body dissolves into a labyrinthine-aquatic design. At the center is a vulva, clearly the focal point. c. 3500 B.C. H 48.1 cm.

FIGURE 7–120 The eyes of the Owl Goddess on a trapezoidal plaque of schist, on cow bones from the passage graves of Portugal and Spain, and on vases from northern European passage graves. The rest of the surface is decorated by rows of zigzags, triangles, arcs, striations, and net-patterned areas. (1) Quinta Farinheira. (2) Los Millares, S Spain. (3–6) Almizaraque, Spain. (7) Kyndeløse, Kirke-Hyllinge. (8) Hyldehøj, Denmark. c. 3000 B.C.

and bones from Portugal, Spain, and southern France. More frequent symbols of the Goddess are just her eyes, beaks, and brows (FIGURE 7–120, 7, 8), eyes as snake coils or suns, breasts, and necklace (see fig. 7–41), as well as her geometric forms—triangle, lozenge, and hourglass. At the entrances to megalithic tombs, huge triangular stones are sometimes found which may represent the Goddess herself. (FIGURE 7–121)

The intimate link between the Goddess and her signs can be seen on trapezoidal schist plaques and cow bones and on vases found in passage graves. Some have abstracted faces or just eyes, while also engraved with rows of triangles, zigzags, lozenges, arcs, cup marks, and occasionally with X's or hourglass shapes (see fig. 120).

Now let us look at some of the most significant megalithic tomb shrines.

FIGURE 7–121 Large triangular stone at the entrance to the grave chamber. Wildeshausen, district of Oldenburg, Schleswig-Holstein. H c. 1.3 m.

FIGURE 7–122

FIGURE 7–122 Symbols on the entrance stone at Newgrange, outstanding in the virtuosity of its design. Triple and double snake coils interspersed with lozenges and adjoined by chevrons (right) and multiple lozenges (left). The two larger coils are connected forming an oculi, and its outer six windings encircle a triangle (bottom, center). c. 3200 B.C.

FIGURE 7–123

FIGURE 7–123 Symbols on Kerbstone 52 at Newgrange, divided by a vertical channel into two parts. Left: a large oculi motif of two double snake coils with a third smaller coil and a multiple arc attached to it, associated with a triangle-lozenge-zigzag area below. Right: three cartouches with three cupmarks. Others are triangles (vulvas) or cupmarks within concentric circles. c. 3200 B.C.

Newgrange

At Newgrange, aggregations of symbols are found either in the most visible places or in areas important for worship.[58] Such areas are the entrance kerbstone, the roof stone in the east recess, and kerbstone No. 52. These are outstanding in the virtuosity of their design and excellence of technical execution.

Kerbstone No. 1 exhibits one of the most characteristic groupings of Newgrange symbols. (FIGURE 7–122) Single, double, or triple snake coils cover most of the surface. The two upper coils form an eye motif, typical of Irish passage graves. These two are connected to a third, making a triple spiral, also repetitious in Newgrange and other monuments. She is one, She is two, She is three—the totality. If the snake coil symbolizes the source of life energy, then the triple spiral is the most potent. The outer windings of the third, lower coil extend beyond the triple spiral and, turning in the other direction, form a figure of a multiple arc with a triangle in the center. The spaces between the snake coils are filled with lozenges, and the area to the left of the triple coil is marked with lozenges protected with concentric arcs.

Kerbstone No. 52 is divided into two registers by a vertical band. (FIGURE 7–123) The dominant figures on the left side are the snake coil oculi. Multiple coils meet in the center to form the beak and browridge motif. There is a smaller snake coil attached at the right, and on top of it are two cupmarks and concentric arcs. Below, the area is covered with triangles, lozenges, and zigzags. The right register consists of three cartouches enclosing three round cupmark depressions with triangle and hourglass shapes in between. Associated with the cartouches are concentric arcs with a triangle in the center. Multiple arcs with a triangle inside must stand here for the enhancement of the generative vulva of the Goddess. The emphasis on triple depressions may be significant as symbols of a triple life source, while the meaning of the triple cupmarks may be related to the triple snake coil in the left register.

The web of symbols on the underside of the roof-stone in the east recess at Newgrange consists of round owl eyes and a triple or multiple beak and a browridge motif which is quadrupled. This forms a rosette pattern with a rectangle in the center, large snake coils, and a concentric oval pattern with two opposed semicircles in its center. The large snake coil in the center is connected with the triple eye-and-beak image. These main symbols are flanked with a zigzag area and are interspersed with V's, chevrons, lozenges, zigzags, and winding serpents. (FIGURE 7–124)

It can be seen that the main purpose of these symbols was to indicate the presence of the deity in her guise of owl and snake. This is made obvious by the outstandingly positioned owl oculi and their interrelationship with snake coils, both powerful symbols of regeneration.

FIGURE 7–124 A group of intertwined symbols on the underside of the roof-stone in the east recess of Newgrange: quadrupled oculi, triple eye and arc motifs, large snake coils, and a concentric oval with two opposed semicircles at the center interspersed with V's, chevrons, circles, lozenges, and winding serpents. Partially reconstructed.

FIGURE 7–124

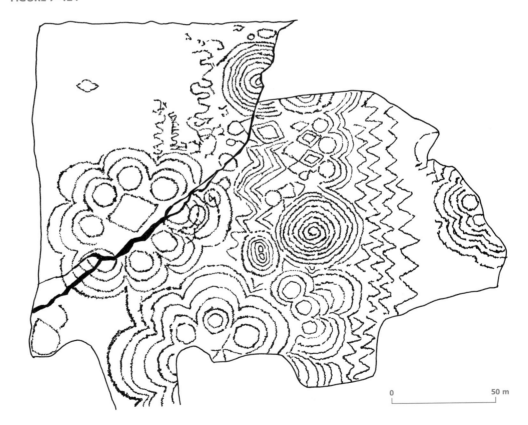

0   50 m

Further relations exist between these images and the cupmark, triangle, double triangle or lozenge, and the number three.

Knowth

A number of kerbstones at Knowth are engraved with snakes and lunar cycles. According to Brennan, winding snake motifs may have also functioned for time reckoning, since many serpentiforms have fourteen to seventeen turnings, the number of days the moon is waxing. A snake coil flanked with C-shaped arcs on Kerbstone No. 5 of Knowth, Site 1,[59] could be an example of a lunar cycle from crescent to full moon and back to crescent. (FIGURE 7–125) It is certainly possible to view the snake coil as a polyvalent symbol, being at once the full moon, a symbol of the source of energy, the spiral of eternity within the field of time, as well as the Goddess herself.

The prominent and repetitive snake and coil motif at Newgrange, frequently accompanied by rows of lozenges or zigzags, appears on stones in the west recess of Knowth, in the main chamber, on four orthostats, and on several kerbstones. The angular motifs are not for decoration alone, as stated above, but are elaborations on the theme of the Goddess's generative triangle. The hourglass shape, made of two triangles, represents the Goddess herself, and is emphasized in importance when framed in a cartouche, as found on Orthostat No. 48 at Knowth East, at the side of the central chamber. (FIGURE 7–126)

The motifs on corbels and lintels above orthostats are always "angular," lozenges flanked with zigzags or rows of zigzags. (FIGURE 7–127) This is repeated on all major tombs: Newgrange, Knowth, and Fourknocks. Carvings on the forward-facing narrow side of stones shows that they were meant to be viewed edge-on. These designs were carved in advance, then put in particular locations. Although decorative, they are not independent of the symbolism of regeneration. Here, motifs have been expressed in abstract, geometric repetitions to create a kind of chant, a litany, or visual incantation.

FIGURE 7–125

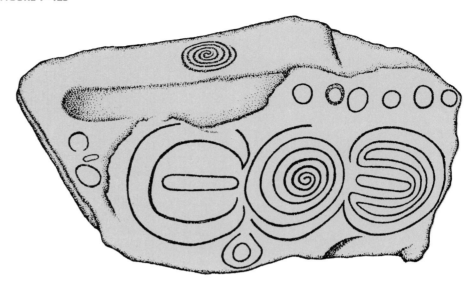

FIGURE 7–126

FIGURE 7–125 A snake coil flanked by circular arcs with a dash in the center, perhaps representing a moon cycle. Knowth, NE 6. 3500–3200 B.C.

FIGURE 7–126 The hourglass as a special sign for the Goddess, made of two triangles joined at the tips, is shown three times within frames at the center of this orthostat. Above are accompanying rows of zigzags and lozenges. Knowth East, orthostat No. 48.

FIGURE 7–127

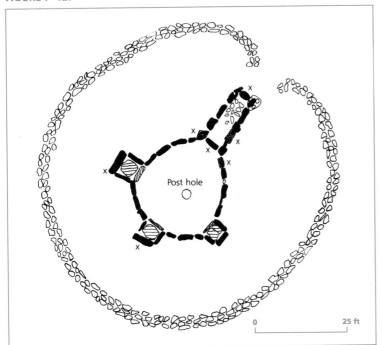

1

Post hole

0   25 ft

FIGURE 7–127 (1) Plans of the Fourknocks I tomb-shrine indicating (x) the location of decorated orthostats, corbels, and lintels. 3500–3000 B.C. (2) Detail of the entrance lintel decorated with zigzags.

2

FIGURE 7–128

FIGURE 7–129

FIGURE 7–128 Engraved orthostats from the tomb-shrine of Gavrinis. The leading, repetitive motif is the vulva sign enclosed by concentric arcs, wavy lines, and serpentine forms. Late Neolithic, Brittany, 4th mill. B.C.

FIGURE 7–129 Concentric arcs radiating from a central vulvar opening with omphali protruding from the tops. Engraved orthostat from Gavrinis, Brittany, early 4th mill. B.C.

Circles, dot-in-circles, suns, and cupmarks are often found on surfaces hidden in the ground or at the bottom of orthostats. These carvings were not made for human view, but as ritual actions for communication with the divine, an evocation of the Goddess's regenerative powers hidden in stone. These are the symbols of the center, the source or focal point where life begins and flows out, increasing in concentric circles and arcs. If it were possible to count all cupmarks (artificial and natural), circles (concentric and open), and dot-in-circle motifs, it would become clear that these symbols are the most numerous of all, and therefore germinal.

Gavrinis

The evocation of the Goddess's regenerative powers through carving of symbols is best expressed at Gavrinis. Gavrinis is one of the richest megalithic monuments in Brittany, remarkable for the excellence of its relief engravings. (FIGURES 7–128, 7–129) It is placed within the period of late Neolithic passage graves, about the end of the 4th millennium B.C.; its closing date of use was c. 2500 B.C.[60] Surrounded by water, the primordial life source, it occupies the southern end of a small island in the gulf of Morbihan (originally a peninsula connected to the continent on its northern side). It is aligned to the rising sun at winter solstice, whereas the main orientation of the passage is toward an extreme rising position of the moon.

Engravings within the sanctuary completely cover the surface of twenty-three orthostats, giving an overall impression of symbolic unity. Extensive use of wavy and concentric arc motifs is suggestive of the surrounding watery element. The dominant symbol is a concentric circle with a dot or vertical line in the center, that is, the vulva. This is interconnected with, or surrounded by, multiple wavy lines and serpentine arcs piled one on top of the other in vertical columns. (FIGURE 7–129) These life columns seem to say that the generative force of the Goddess is inexhaustible, rising and flowing like waves. This rising life force is manifest, as well, in the form of wiggly lines, possibly representing serpents. Several bulls and an axe are found engraved on the outer stone slab at Gavrinis, adding weight to the womb/generation symbolism. (FIGURE 7–130)

The art of the megaliths is a symbolic acknowledgment and celebration of the cycles of life and death on a cosmic scale. The tomb as the body of the Goddess, aligned with solar and lunar risings, decorated with images of regeneration, is an elegant metaphor for the inevitable cycles of the universe. The universe *is* the body of the Goddess, within whom all death and rebirth takes place. The light that enters the megalithic tombs on winter solstice, illuminating their inner chambers, is also metaphoric. This is the sign of quickening—the womb of Death made fertile for new life.

The Identity of the Goddess as Tomb and Womb

As we have seen, the shape and symbols of the megalithic graves are unquestionably linked with the formidable Goddess of Death and Regeneration. Her symbols range from bare bones to eggs and uteri, from stiff nudes and vultures, boars and dogs, to regenerating eyes and snake coils. Some megalithic tombs to this day are regarded as "caves" of the Goddess. The passage grave at Knockmary, County Tyrone, Ireland, is called "Annia's Cave." Is this Her name? For this we should turn to folklore and historic sources. In folktales She appears as an Old Hag or a Giantess, but She is also identified as *Ana, Annia, Anu,* and *Ankou.* From early literary sources it is known that the Breton *Ankou* or *Maro* is "Death." The Irish *Morrígan* is identified with *Ana* who is regarded as "Guardian of the Dead" or "Mother of the Gods." We can guess that these names are inherited from the megalith builders.

The Goddess of Death and Regeneration is goddess of winter and darkness. In folklore throughout Europe she appears as a bony-legged hag, a white woman, or a snow woman. Her activities and power unfold in the winter season, more specifically in the last part of December and the beginning of January.

In Scandinavia, this period is called *jol,* or Yule, with no relation to the Christian belief in the birth of Christ. We may surmise that in prehistoric times most of the rituals necessary for the awakening of nature and the appeasement of the Winter Goddess took place at this time. At the very beginning of spring, the frightening Winter Goddess, or Hag, turns into a beautiful nude maiden. In brooks, creeks, lakes, and rivers she appears combing her golden hair or swinging in willow branches. Her sexual beauty is the expression of the transformation of winter into a time of regeneration. This motif is still extant in European folklore, and its symbolic imagery parallels the expression of death and regeneration found on Neolithic funeral monuments.

FIGURE 7–130

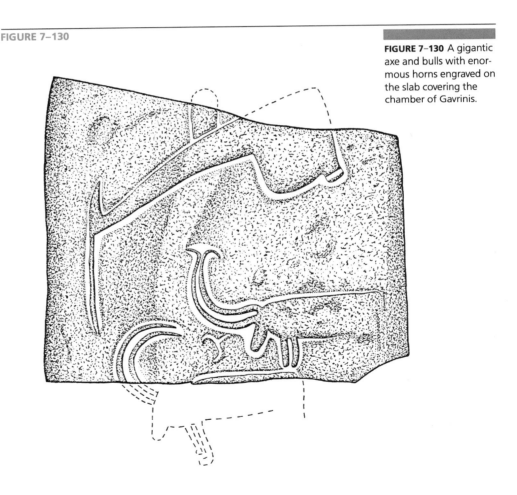

FIGURE **7–130** A gigantic axe and bulls with enormous horns engraved on the slab covering the chamber of Gavrinis.

8

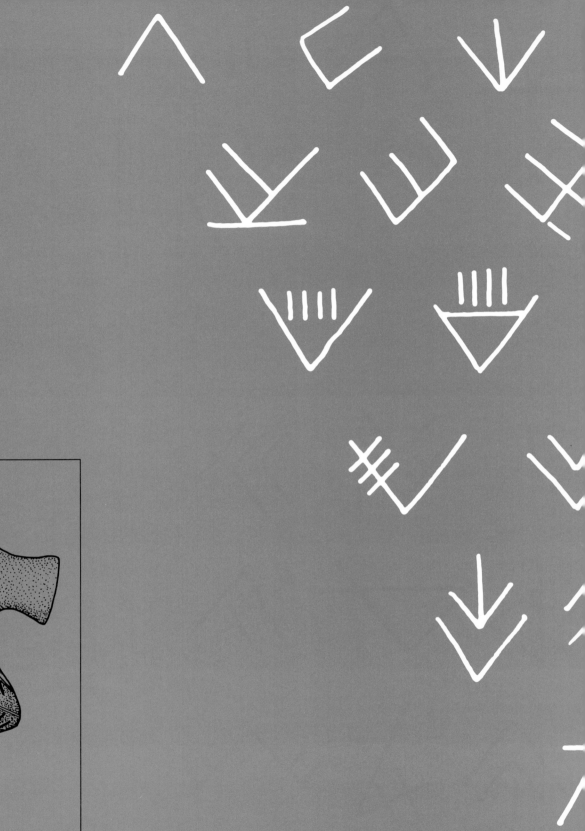

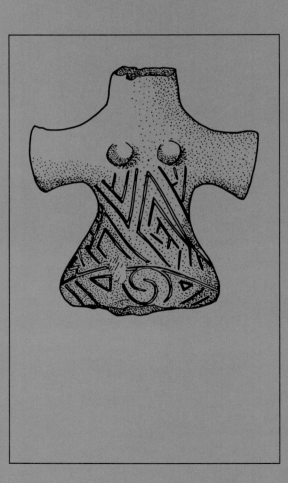

Votive offerings—gifts to the divinity in accordance with a vow, a wish, or desire—inscribed on religious objects usually found in clusters or rows, are characteristic finds of the Neolithic and Copper Ages, particularly in east-central Europe. The invention of a script some eight thousand years ago has seemed so unthinkable that to this day the possibility is ignored and its evidence given very little attention. I am not going to attempt to give a detailed analysis of script signs, or attempt to "read the script" as a number of amateurs are trying to do with the help of Indo-European languages. This Old European script was, undoubtedly, non-Indo-European, as are the Cretan Hieroglyphic, Linear A, and Cypro-Minoan scripts that still remain unde-ciphered for the same reason. The only hope is to wait for the happy discovery of a multilingual Rosetta Stone that will translate its message into an Indo-European language, which should not be an impossibility. Let us now exam-ine this extraordinary Old European achievement.

Although the Sumerians are generally thought to be the inventors of written language, a script in east-central Europe appeared some two thousand years earlier than any other that has yet been found. Unlike Sumerian script, the writing of the Old Europeans was not devised for economic, legal, or admin-istrative purposes. It was developed, instead, from a long use of graphic symbolic signs found only within the context of an increasingly sophisticated worship of the Goddess. Inscriptions appear on religious items only, indi-cating that these signs were intended to be read as sacred hieroglyphs.

FIGURE 8–1

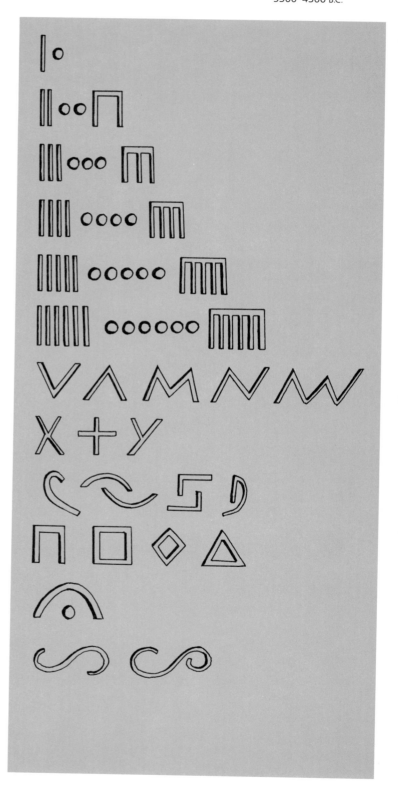

FIGURE 8–1 Core signs of the Old European script. 5300–4300 B.C.

History

The first archeological finds bearing these signs were excavated in 1874 at Turdaş (Tordos), an early Vinča site in Transylvania. It was only much later, in 1961, when the Tartaria plaques were unearthed from an early Vinča sacrificial pit near Cluj, also in Transylvania, that these inscriptions excited much interest. Assuming that they were derived from known Sumerian script, the Tartaria plaques were thus judged by M.S.F. Hood and other scholars to have been "an uncomprehending imitation of more civilized people's written records. . . ."[1] Although hundreds of other inscribed sacred objects have since been found, their importance has remained ignored regardless of their well-documented stratigraphy.

Calibrated radiocarbon chronology demonstrated that this script appeared during the first half of the 6th millennium B.C. and was used continuously for about two millennia. It is certain that the Old European script is considerably older than the Sumerian from Mesopotamia, as well as the Indus script of the Harappa civilization, and predates the Cretan Hieroglyphic and Cypro-Minoan by several thousand years. The idea that this script was imported from Mesopotamia must be entirely ruled out, for it is clearly contradicted by chronological evidence.

The presence of a sacred script in Old European cultures is consonant with their stage of development. At the time in which this script was in use, east-central Europeans enjoyed metallurgic industry, a high degree of architectural sophistication, extensive trade relations, a remarkable sophistication and specialization in the craftsmanship of goods, and an increasingly elaborate and articulated system of religious thought and practice.

Distribution

This earliest writing was not the ephemeral occurrence of a single locality but a widespread phenomenon. At present, nearly one hundred sites are known to have yielded inscribed objects. Most are from the Vinča and Tisza culture groups in the Morava, Danube, and Tisza basins of Yugoslavia, eastern Hungary, northwestern Bulgaria, and western Romania, and of the Karanovo culture in central Bulgaria and southern Romania. Inscribed or painted signs, unnoticed earlier, are now being recognized on Dimini, Cucuteni, Petreşti, Lengyel, Butmir, Bükk, and Linear Pottery ceramics. Therefore, it is no longer proper to speak of the "Vinča script" as the sole example of this phenomenon. Instead, this script was a universal feature of the most advanced cultures of Old Europe during the 6th and 5th millennia B.C. Signs of this script are occasionally found on pottery and bone objects from Neolithic southern Italy as well as from the megalithic culture of western Europe.

Internal Analysis

An internal analysis of inscriptions from 29 Vinča sites was presented in a dissertation by Shan M. M. Winn, "The Signs of the Vinča Culture" (1973), later published in 1981 as "Pre-writing in Southeastern Europe: The Sign System of the Vinča Culture."[2] Winn catalogued 210 recognizable signs, including symbols, modified symbols, lines, dots, and curves. He assumed their derivation from five core elements: 1) a straight line; 2) two straight lines intersected at the center; 3) two lines joined at one end; 4) a dot; and 5) a curved line. It was not Winn's objective to distinguish between symbols and script signs. His classification presents, instead, a hypothetical process of graphic development from simple to complex.

From the corpus of 210 Vinča signs, about one-third are symbols, universally used throughout Europe. These appear in isolation, not in rows of inscriptions, with the exception of V, M, X (or +), and two to four vertical strokes or dots which are incorporated in the script. There are about 30 core signs (FIGURE 8-1), while the rest of the script is made of core signs with one, two, or three lines added, or two core signs combined (duplicated, inverted, opposed). (FIGURE 8-2)

Core signs are disparate and complete very early. I do not believe that the V, for example, could have developed from a single diagonal, since it was in use as a V since the Upper Paleolithic. Likewise, the M sign does not seem to have developed from a multiplication of inverted V's, since it appears as a zigzag from the very beginning. As with the Egyptian hieroglyph for water 〰〰〰, *mu*, M as an ideogram for water may have had a phonetic value from very early times. In the classical Cypriot syllabary, ∧∧ represents the syllable *mi*. These same signs existed in the 6th millennium B.C. Since there is a continuity of certain signs from as early as the Upper Paleolithic, it is not improbable that they may have represented phonetic values that were also continuous.

FIGURE 8–2

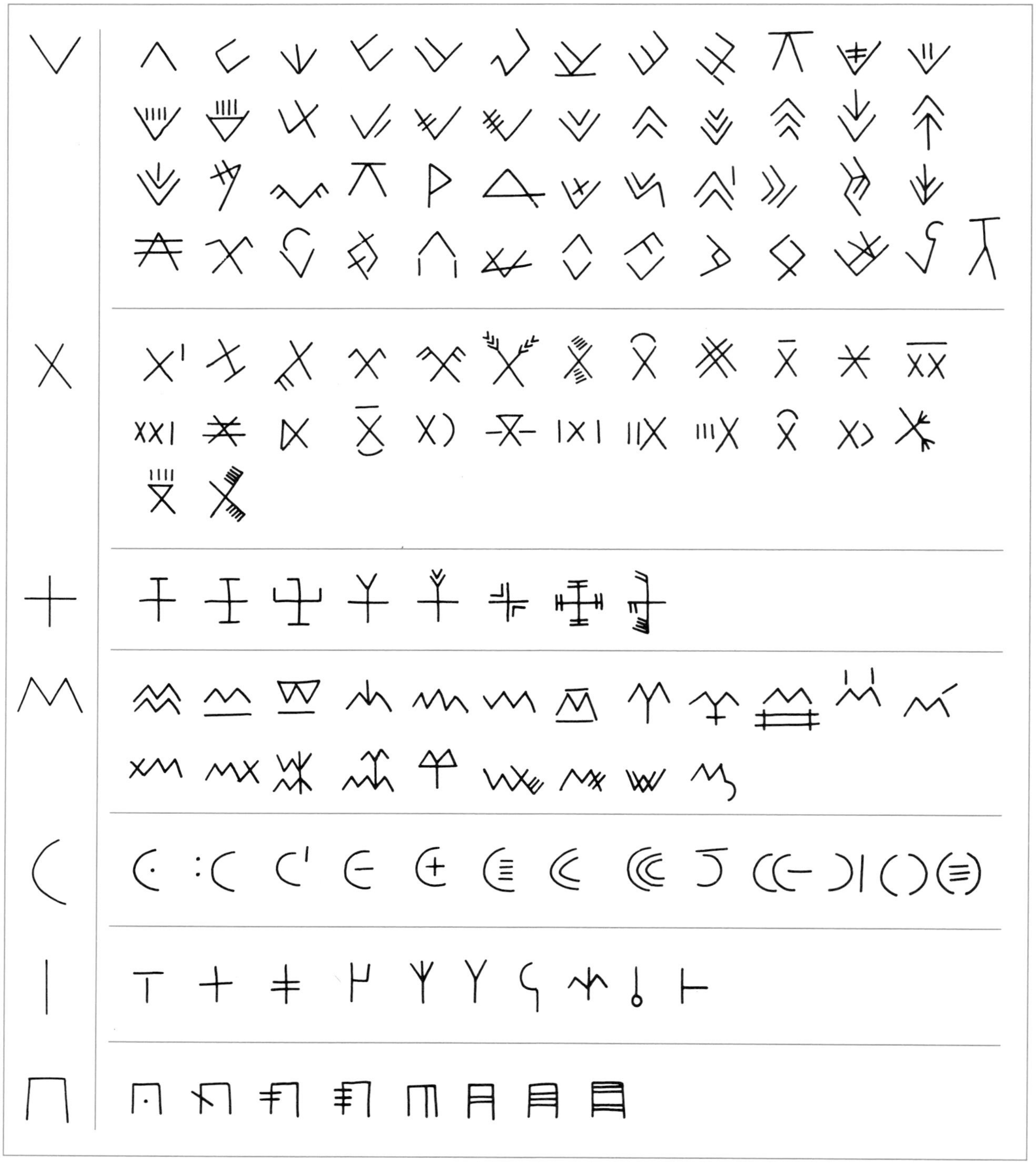

FIGURE 8–2 Core signs (left) and derivatives (right) formed by means of additions of a line or two, a dot, a curve, or by duplication or inversion of core signs.

FIGURE 8–3 Madonna from Rast, W Romania, inscribed over the back and sides. On the back is a clear band with script signs. The child was also inscribed. Vinča culture, early 5th mill. B.C. H 12 cm.

FIGURE 8–4 Terracotta figurine from the mound of Tangiru, Lower Danube basin, Romania, inscribed with signs in bands in front and back (see drawings below figurines). Boian culture group, IIa phase, end 6th mill. B.C. H 9 cm.

The script that emerged after the middle of the 6th millennium B.C. was created by symbols modified by lines, curves, and dots. Symbols combined with linear signs are clustered in groups or rows on figurines, anthropomorphic vases, spindle whorls and loom weights, temple models, libation and other ceremonial vases, offering receptacles, and other religious objects. The V sign, for example, appears with the following combinations: with the addition of a dash or line at the side, across, or above; connected to an inverted V; filled with one, two, or three lines; amplified by two or three parallel lines; joined with an M; and extended by a curved line. The most frequent combinations are of one or two lines with a V, X (or +), and M. Some inscriptions demonstrate a maze of repetitive V's, or V's and M's, or V's and Y's. This suggests that the meaning of such inscriptions should be related to the meaning of the repeated symbol.

Inscriptions appear in horizontal or vertical rows, in circles, or in randomly placed groups. On figurines there are bands of signs front and back, across the chest, or under the abdomen. (FIGURES 8-3, 8-4) Inscriptions also occur on figurine masks (FIGURE 8-5) and around the legs (FIGURE 8-6). On vessels, bands of inscriptions occur on the wall near the base or rim, on the base or bottom of a dish, around the central portion, or in panels. (FIGURE 8-7) They also occur in panels on temple models—on both sides, or above the entrance (FIGURE 8-8), and on stands supporting a phallus (FIGURE 8-9). On spindle whorls, inscriptions occur in a circle around the hole (FIGURE 8-10), whereas on miniature bread loaves made of clay, they encircle the entire form (FIGURE 8-11). Occasionally, inscriptions appear in four horizontal rows, as in the shallow vessel from Gradešnica, an early Vinča site. (FIGURE 8-12)

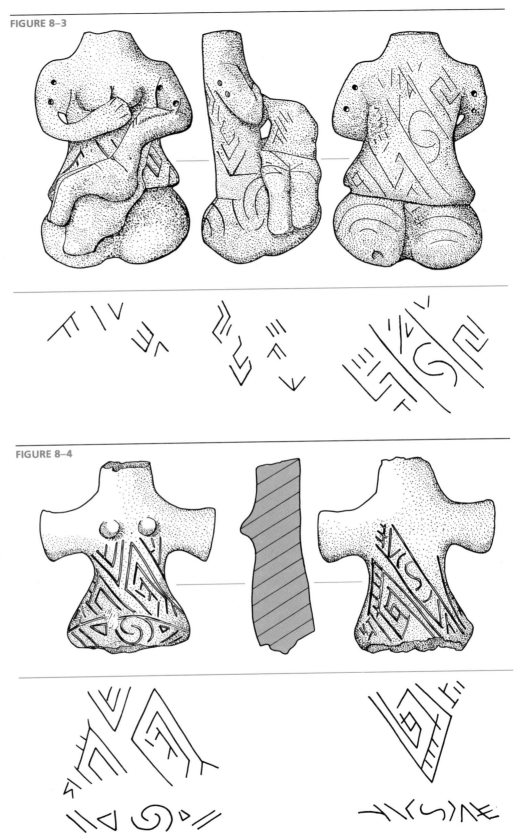

FIGURE 8-3

FIGURE 8-4

FIGURE 8–5

FIGURE 8–6

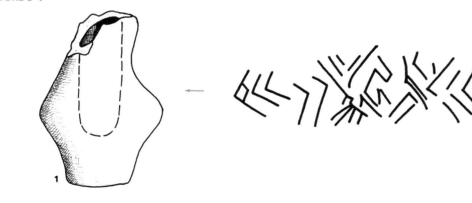

FIGURE 8–5 Clay figurine wearing an incised mask; from the Vinča settlement. H 5 cm.

FIGURE 8–6 Bands of inscriptions around the legs of an anthropomorphic vase of the Tisza culture, c. 5300–5000 B.C. Kökénydomb near Szeged, SE Hungary.

FIGURE 8–7

FIGURE 8–7 Horizontal and vertical rows of inscriptions on miniature vases, probably *ex votos*. (1) Vinča, from the mid-Vinča period. (2) Szegvár-Tűzköves near Szentes, Hungary, Tisza Culture. (3) Daia Romana (Dallendorf), distr. of Alba, W Romania, 5000–4500 B.C. (1) H 5 cm; (2) H 8 cm; (3) W 6.4 cm.

FIGURE 8–8

FIGURE 8–11

FIGURE 8–11 Oval terracotta plaque (symbol of a sacred loaf of bread?) with a meander incised in the center, surrounded by an inscription. Two views. Early Vinča, c. 5200–5000 B.C. from Banjica near Belgrade. L 15 cm.

FIGURE 8–9

FIGURE 8–8 Clay model of a temple from Gradešnica. Facade, walls, and roof are decorated with symbolic designs. The front columns at either side of the entrance are vertically inscribed with script signs. Vinča culture, early 5th mill. B.C. H 14.5 cm.

FIGURE 8–9 Clay phallus on an inscribed pedestal. Ocna Sibiului, distr. of Sibiu, C Romania, Starčevo-Criş culture, c. 5500 B.C. H 10 cm.

FIGURE 8–12

FIGURE 8–12 Shallow vessel from Gradešnica near Vraca, a Vinča settlement in NW Bulgaria, bearing inscriptions on both sides. (1) Outer side with signs around the symbolic figure. (2) Inner side with four lines of signs. Early 5th mill. B.C. L 12.5 cm.

FIGURE 8–10

FIGURE 8–10 Inscribed spindle whorl and extended inscription (below). Fafos, a Vinča site at Kosovska Mitrovica, S Yugoslavia, c. 5000–4500 B.C. L 8.2 cm.

Groups of signs seem to have communicated statements. Inscribed objects—figurines, spindle whorls, loom weights, pendants, libation vases, miniature vessels, and temple models—seem to have been *ex votos*. The inscribed statements could have been dedicatory formulas, or the name or epithet of the Goddess. Similar groupings of signs are repetitive on figurines and on temple models (see figs. 8–3 and 8–8). Inscriptions around the hole of a spindle whorl could have been associated with a function of the Goddess as the "spinner of the thread of life," and as the determiner of the quality and length of life itself; or with her role as Goddess of crafts.

In later times, inscribed figurines, spindle whorls, loom weights, pots, and even tablets were votive offerings to Minoan, early Greek, Etruscan, Venetic, and Roman goddesses. Among votive offerings to Venetic Rehtia, the Birth-giver, related to Artemis of the 6th to 4th centuries B.C., loom weights and alphabetic tablets of lead were inscribed. Inscribed spindle whorls were among Greek Athena's gifts, also. If the Old European signs do indeed have hieroglyphic meaning, this tradition of *ex voto* offerings with inscriptions may have had its beginnings five thousand years before Rehtia, Artemis, or Athena.

Abstract Signs as Symbols From Which the Script Developed

Were these inscriptions, from the very beginning, purely graphic, consisting of bare lines and their combinations, or did they develop from already extant, religiously significant glyphs? In my view the latter is true, and it is revealing to examine symbolic signs that were in consistent use prior to the script's emergence.

Independent abstract signs, not pictographs, such as V, X, and Y, originated during the Upper Paleolithic. A number of them, engraved on stone, bone, and antler, continued through the Mesolithic into the early phases of the Neolithic. In Old Europe and Anatolia they consistently recur on ceramics in various arrangements: duplicated, triplicated, multiplied, inverted, opposed, and associated with meanders and parallel lines.

Some signs are continuous from the Upper Paleolithic Gravettian and Magdalenian cultures into the Neolithic, Copper Age, and even early Bronze Age of Europe and Anatolia, a span of 15,000 years. An excellent example is the V sign that derives from the vulva or pubic triangle, one of the earliest symbols known from prehistoric art. A comparison of the inscriptions on Upper Paleolithic Mezin figurines (FIGURE 8–13) with those on Vinča figurines of the 5th millennium B.C. (FIGURE 8–14) reveals striking similarities in the appearance of this inscription. Its repetitiveness in homologous contexts speaks of its central role in the symbolism surrounding certain aspects of the Goddess.

The V glyph may be shown on a figurine singly, or it may be repeated several times. Frequently it is tripled, or is endlessly incised, forming a multiple chevron. The size of V's and chevrons varies. On some figurines, the X's, chevrons, or interconnected chevrons are shown in compartments as they also are on vases. (FIGURE 8–15) V's, multiple V's or chevrons appear consistently on both articulate and schematic effigies of the Bird Goddess, and on objects associated with her veneration, such as ornithomorphic vases and ram figurines or miniature offering tables or receptacles. (FIGURE 8–16) The V or chevron sign is

FIGURE 8–13

FIGURE 8–13 Upper Paleolithic ivory figurines of anthropomorphized waterbirds incised with V's, chevrons (multiple V's, X's), and two lines. Mezin, Upper Desna basin, Ukraine; c. 17,000–14,000 B.C. H (1) 30 cm; (2) 7.2 cm.

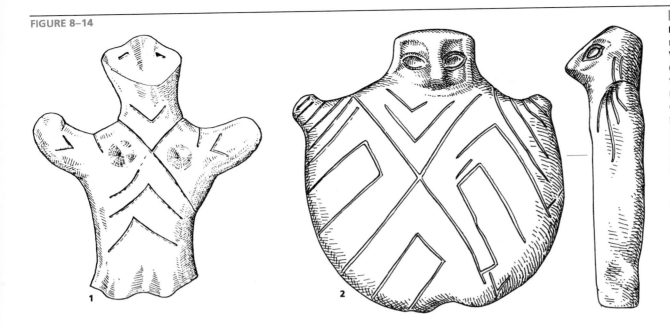

FIGURE 8–14

FIGURE 8–14 Vinča figurines marked with X's, V's and meanders. (1) Masked and winged figurine from Turdaş near Cluj, W Romania; c. 5200 B.C. (2) Disc-shaped figurine with a beaked (Bird Goddess) head and stumps for arms or wings. The whole flat area is for the depiction of symbols and is divided by a large X into four compartments; at the top is a chevron below the neck; in the three others, the ends of meanders are seen. Parallel lines adorn the shoulder areas. Vinča site, c. 5000 B.C. H (1) 9 cm; (2) 12 cm.

FIGURE 8–15

FIGURE 8–15 The body of this figurine is divided into four panels, each with multiple and interconnected chevron designs of various proportions and directions. Gomolava, mid-Vinča period. Early 5th mill. B.C. H 8.5 cm.

FIGURE 8–16 A zoomorphic offering vessel marked with a cartouche comprising chevrons, single V's, and a lozenge (two V's joined together). Triple chevrons are repeated on the neck of each animal (stylized rams). Vinča culture, Priština, S Yugoslavia, c. 5300–5000 B.C. H 6.7 cm.

FIGURE 8–16

FIGURE 8-17

FIGURE 8-17 Symbolic designs of meandroid, spiraloid, and net patterns organized in panels cover the surface of a large vase from Vădăstra II, c. 5200–5000 B.C. SW Romania. Incised design with white encrustation. Gray background. H 55 cm.

commonly associated with two, three, four, or multiple parallel lines. The meander also appears as a single or multiple image or in panels interspersed with other panels of spirals or snakes. (FIGURE 8-17)

Examination of the repertory of symbols on figurines leads to several observations. Signs surrounding the image of the Bird Goddess, for example (such as V's and chevrons combined with X) identify her, while V's associated or connected with meanders, zigzags, or parallel lines emphasize her intimacy with the aquatic life-giving sphere, suggesting her function as a giver of moisture and life waters.

Duplication and multiplication had, perhaps, invocational or magical intent. Nevertheless, we can see in the combination of two signs, such as V and ⧟ , forming ⧠ , the devising of a more complicated meaning which is a requirement for the development of any formal script per se. This juxtaposition of images goes beyond simple repetitive magic to become an abstraction capable of expressing subtle distinctions. It is for this reason I believe that the Old European sign system developed into a script from extensive use of very ancient symbolism. It is possible that certain symbols could have a phonetic sound much earlier than the 6th millennium B.C.

The fact that abstract signs are not merely ornamental motifs is best seen from excised or incised motifs on clay seals, from stamped marks on vases, and from symbols painted or incised on figurines, as well as within bands, circles, or rectangular compartments on pottery. Handled stamp seals with conventional signs from the 7th and 6th millennia B.C. were used to mark ceramic objects, and probably other more perishable religious objects as well. Marks occurring on clay or stone seals consist of the following signs: chevron, multiple chevrons, X's with V's between the arms, zigzags, M's, N's, whirls, crosses, filled crosses, concentric circles and squares, triangles with a dot, parallel lines, double and triple lines, tri-lines joined by a horizontal bar, brushes, and quadruple and more multiple lines, alone or joined by a line. (FIGURE 8-18)

FIGURE 8–18

FIGURE 8–18 Seals bearing symbols from c. 6000–5500 B.C. (1–3) Sesklo, Greece; (4) Anza II, Starčevo culture, central Macedonia, Yugoslavia; (5,6) Nea Nikomedeia, Sesklo site, northern Greece; (7,8) Čevdar, Karanovo site, east of Sofia, Bulgaria; (9,10) Kopancs and Kotacpart, Starčevo (Körös) sites, SE Hungary; (11) Pyrasos, Thessaly, Sesklo site; (12) Perieni, NE Romania, a Starčevo site; (13,14) Tsani and Nessonis, Sesklo culture, Thessaly, Greece.

FIGURE 8–19

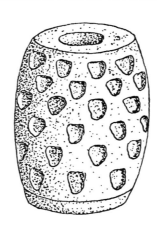

FIGURE 8–19 Cylindrical seals bearing symbols: meanders, antithetic spirals, zigzags, dots. Malik IIa, Albania, c. 5000–4500 B.C. H c. 5 cm.

FIGURE 8–20

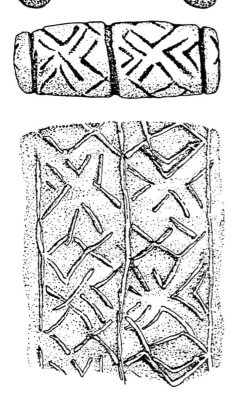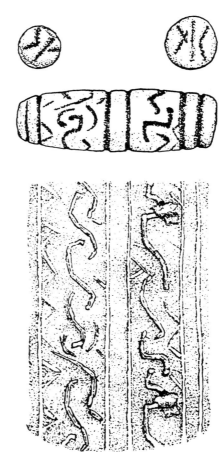

FIGURE 8–20 Cylindrical clay seals from Sitagroi, Drama Plain in Macedonia, NE Greece. The seals are divided into two zones (see extended design). The first on the left comprises rather careless incisions of V's forming X patterns. There are several additional lines in between and each end is marked with an X. The second, right, bears S and Z signs accompanied by V's along the sides and at the ends. Sitagroi II, 5200–4600 B.C. L (1) 3.8 cm; (2) 3.9 cm.

Also found are meanders, snake coils, spirals and double spirals, nets and checkerboards, and snakeskin symbols (dotted bands with interconnected lozenges). When cylindrical seals came into use around 5000 B.C., they continued to be engraved with such single symbols. (FIGURE 8–19) However, on cylindrical seals from Sitagroi in Macedonia in the middle of the 5th millennium B.C. in addition to single signs, clusters of V's, S-spirals, and dashes appeared. (FIGURE 8–20)

The earliest handled seals which bear more than one sign date from the first half of the 6th millennium B.C. from the Starčevo (Körös) and Karanovo cultures. (FIGURE 8–21) The same can be observed on Hacilar seals of central Anatolia. This combination of signs represents the incipient phase of early writing. The real explosion in the development of Old European script occurred at the end of the 6th millennium B.C. Thus, we can classify this development as follows: Early Phase, c. 6000–5300 B.C.; Climactic Phase, c. 5300–4000 B.C. The latter was not a "pre-writing" but a script of its own kind.

Survival

The Old European script virtually disappeared at the time of the disintegration of the Karanovo, Vinča, and other Old European cultures around 4300–4000 B.C., following the infiltration of horse-riding pastoralists from the southern Russian steppes, presumed to be Indo-European speakers. It survived, however, in the Aegean area where the Old European civilization endured for more than two millennia longer than in the Danubian areas of Europe. It is not surprising, therefore, to perceive similarities between Old European script with script signs of the early Bronze Age Aegean, Minoan, and Cypriot scripts. Analogies between Old European characters and those of the Cretan hieroglyphs and Linear A of the 3rd and 2nd millennia B.C. are intriguing. These suggest that the Old European script, devised some four

FIGURE 8–21

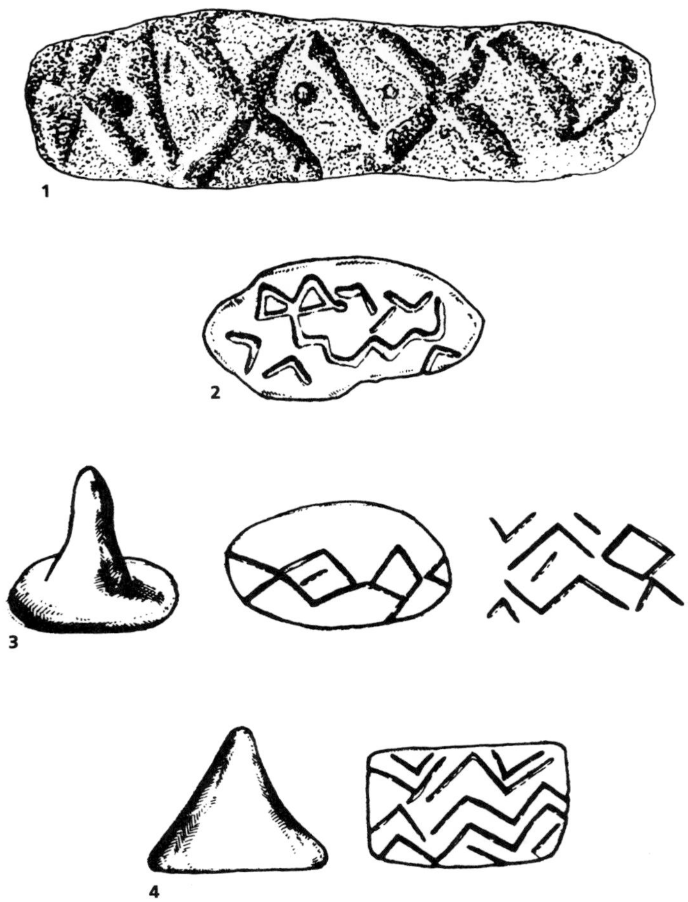

FIGURE 8–21 Clay handled seals incised with more than one sign emerge in the first half of the 6th mill. B.C. in Starčevo (Körös) and Karanovo cultures. The illustrated examples comprise V's, X's, zigzags, straight lines, and dots. (1) Kopancs; (2) Kotacpart, both Körös sites from SE Hungary, c. 5600–5400 B.C.; (3,4) Azmak I at Stara Zagora, Karanovo I culture, c. 5800 B.C. Scale 1:1.

thousand years before Minoan hieroglyphic and Linear A on Crete, was a
related script developed by ancestral
non-Indo-European speakers.

The hieroglyphic script of Crete had a
sacral function in ritual ceremonies and
represents a direct continuity in tradition from Old European script. Linear A,
a more evolved writing, was also associated with religious practices but not
exclusively with ritual ceremonies.
However, the relationship in terms of a
dependency on the original Old European script can be substantiated by a
comparison of the sign inventory of the
two writing systems. Harold Haarmann
(1990) has arrived at a set of not less
than fifty sign parallels.[3] (FIGURE 8–22)

The Cypro-Minoan script dates from
the middle and later centuries of the 2nd
millennium B.C., while the classical
Cypriot was used from the 7th to the
2nd centuries. The Cypro-Minoan,
although related to the Minoan Linear
A, probably is descended from another,
more archaic common ancestor. Like
Linear A, it is not yet deciphered,
whereas the classical Cypriot was deciphered in the 1870s by means of a key
provided by bilingual inscriptions in
Cypriot and Phoenician. It was used to
write Greek and Eteocypriot, a language
as yet unidentified and very likely of the
same family as Minoan and Old European. Each sign of the classical Cypriot
script represents a whole syllable, not a
single letter; a consonant plus vowel; or
a plain vowel. Such a system is incon-
venient for Greek, and it is therefore
believed to have been adapted for the use
of Greek from an earlier non-Indo-European language.

For our amusement, a list of signs of
the classical Cypriot script is provided.
(FIGURE 8–23) Note the characters of
*ma, me, mi, mu, sa, se, si, so, ra, re, ri,
ro, ta, te, ti, to, tu, pa, pe, pi* in the series
and compare with Old European glyphs
shown in the next columns. The similarities suggest that Old European script
could have been syllabic and a distant
relative of Cypriotic script. Phonetic
values within a linguistic family could
have existed for many millennia, in this
case for more than 5000 years.

FIGURE 8–22

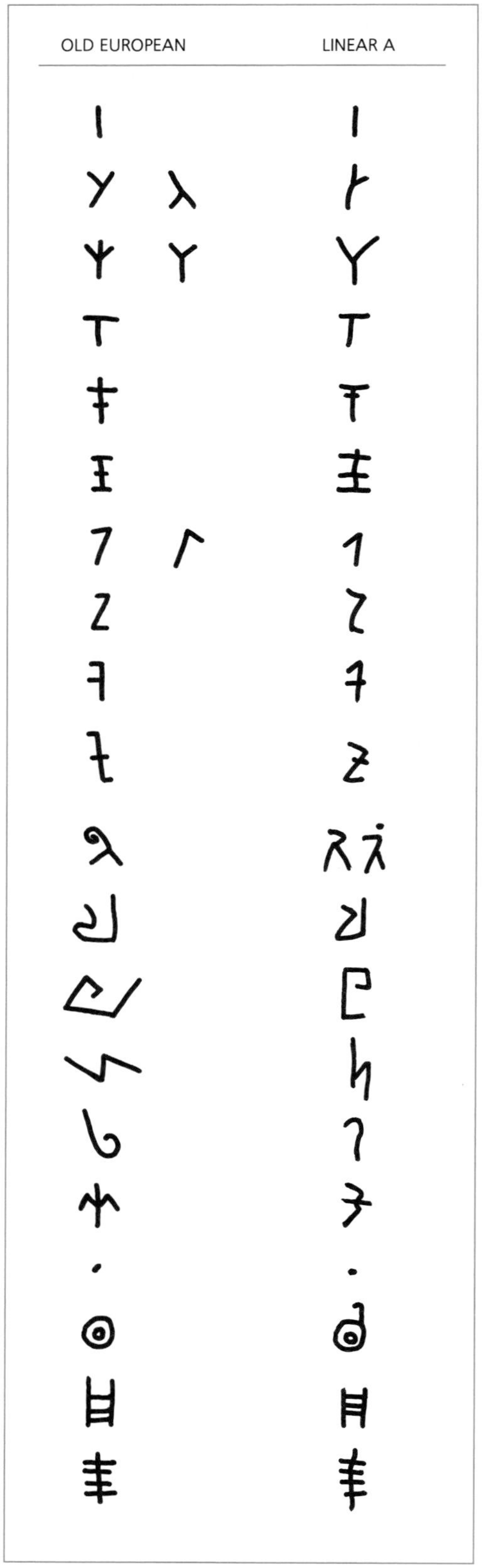

OLD EUROPEAN   LINEAR A

Conclusion

The Old European script which
was in common use between
c. 5300–4300 B.C. was a form of
sacred writing that is found inscribed
on religious objects: figurines, thrones,
temple models, offering receptacles,
altars, libation vases, sacred bread models, pendants, plaques, and spindle
whorls. Its purpose was the communication between individuals and deities; it
has nothing to do with the much later
commercial-administrative scripts of
Mesopotamia or Mycenaean Linear B.
This script developed during the Neolithic period from the extensive use of
a variety of symbolic signs, some of
which were continuous from very
ancient times and could have a phonetic
sound. Around 6000–5300 B.C. the first
compounds appear: symbols with additional linear signs. It is guessed that
hieroglyphic linear signs entered Old
European script as phonetic values from
which other phonetic values, syllables
or words, were devised. This was accomplished by the modification of the
original signs by the addition of straight
or curved lines and dots, duplication,
inversion, or juxtaposition, finally
becoming a complex script. Within this
script there are about thirty core signs
and more than 100 modified signs, if
variations are not counted.

From the end of the 6th millennium
B.C., isolated symbols and compounds
seem to have coalesced into morphemo-
graphic (logo-syllabic) script with widespread use in the Vinča, Tisza, Karanovo,
and other culture groups throughout
Old Europe. Its disappearance during
the end of the 5th millennium B.C. coincides with the beginning of the Indo-
Europeanization of central Europe. Its
descendants survived for more than
several millennia in Crete and Cyprus.

FIGURE 8–22 Old European script signs compared with Linear A signs of Crete (after Haarmann, 1990).

FIGURE 8–23 Surprising formal similarities between the classical Cypriot syllabary and Old European script signs.

FIGURE 8–23

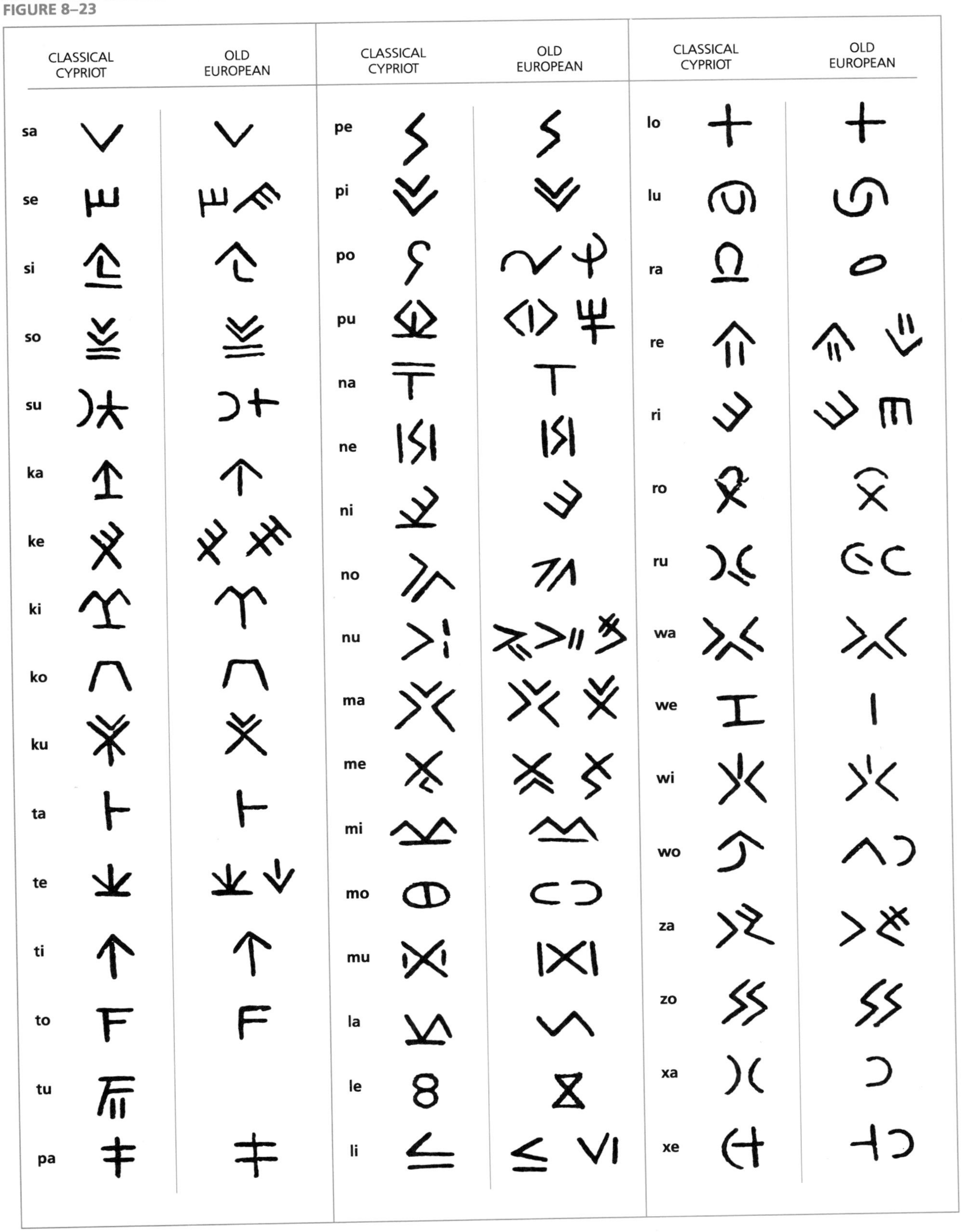

9

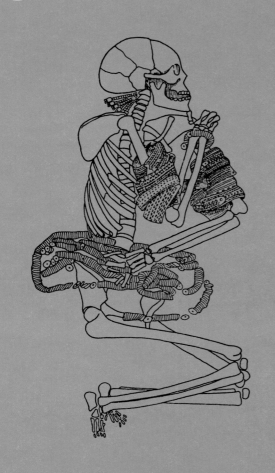

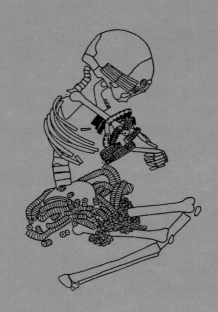

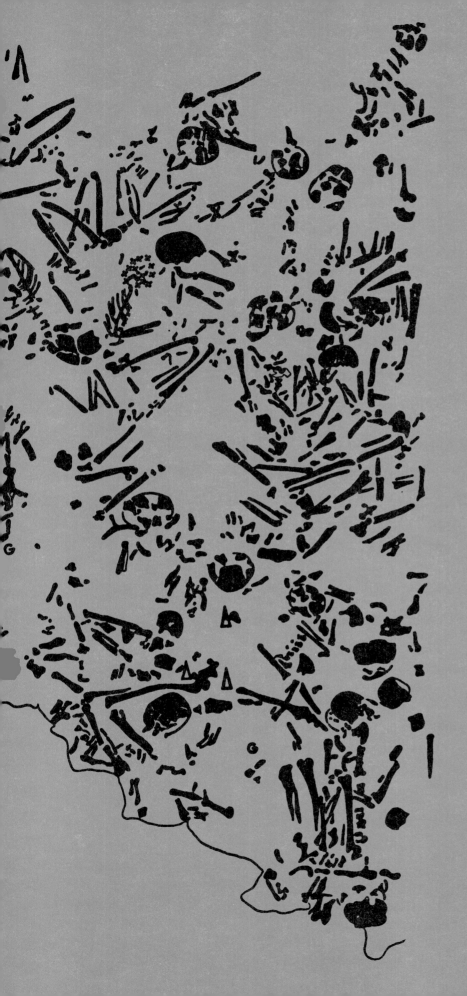

The earliest civilizations of the world—in China, Tibet, Egypt, the Near East, and Europe—were, in all probability, matristic "Goddess civilizations." Since agriculture was developed by women, the Neolithic period created optimum conditions for the survival of matrilineal, endogamous systems inherited from Paleolithic times. During the early agricultural period women reached the apex of their influence in farming, arts and crafts, and social functions. The matriclan with collectivist principles continued.

There is no evidence in all of Old Europe of a patriarchal chieftainate of the Indo-European type. There are no male royal tombs and no residences in megarons on hill forts. The burial rites and settlement patterns reflect a matrilineal structure, whereas the distribution of wealth in graves speaks for an economic egalitarianism.

Early research on the societies of the ancient world, as represented by the work of J. J. Bachofen (1815–87) and R. Briffault (1873–1948), was based on a study of early historical records, archeology, myth, and ethnographic parallels.[1] These men concluded that ancient European society was matrilineal (the structure in which inheritance takes place through the female line) and matriarchal. In the 20th century no large scale interdisciplinary work has been done beyond George Thomson's The Prehistoric Aegean: Studies in Ancient Greek Society, 1949.[2] Recent studies focus on separate geographic regions, mainly western Europe[3] or central Europe.[4]

A serious and continuous obstacle in the study of ancient societies is the indolent assumption that they must have resembled our own. Bachofen warned in 1859 that "the scholar must be able to renounce the ideas of his own time and transfer himself to the midpoint of a completely different world of thought,"[5] but the existence of "a different world" is the hardest thing to admit. The difficulty with the term matriarchy in 20th century anthropological scholarship is that it is assumed to represent a complete mirror image of patriarchy or androcracy—that is to say, a hierarchical structure with women ruling by force in the place of men. This is far from the reality of Old Europe. Indeed, we do not find in Old Europe, nor in all of the Old World, a system of autocratic rule by women with an equivalent suppression of men. Rather, we find a structure in which the sexes are more or less on equal footing, a society that could be termed a gylany. This is a term coined by Riane Eisler (from gyne, referring to woman, and andros, man, linked by the letter l for lyein, to resolve, or lyo, to set free). Gylany implies that the sexes are "linked" rather than hierarchically "ranked."[6] I use the term matristic simply to avoid the term matriarchy, with the understanding that it incorporates matriliny.

Settlement Evidence

In this section we shall use information from southeastern and central Europe where evidence on village and house structures is more complete than elsewhere in Europe.

Sesklo Culture, c. 6500–5500 B.C.: Core Tells, Clusters of Houses Associated with Temples

We do not know much, as yet, of political and economic entities of the earliest Neolithic. It is presumed that each rural community had to control its own productive resources to secure an adequate yield through agriculture, stock breeding, and other means of survival. However, we should not think of earliest farmers in southeastern Europe as primitive farmers. They were more: not only food producers, but traders, builders of houses and temples, carvers of stone, bone and wood and ceramicists (from the middle of the 7th millennium B.C.), and above all they were able to express their religious ideas in sculptural art and painting using a complex symbolism. We should also not forget that they were in constant contact with the people along the Aegean and Mediterranean coasts who were navigators, and that not far to the east, Çatal Hüyük flourished with beautifully sophisticated art.

From 6500 to 6000 B.C., core tells are evidenced that perhaps functioned as district and religious centers. These remained inhabited for hundreds and even thousands of years while parts split off to start other settlements five to twenty kilometers away.

Some authors have interpreted certain features of the Classical Sesklo culture in Thessaly during the early part of the 6th millennium B.C. as signs of hierarchy.[7] The term *acropolis* has been applied to the permanent tell settlement at Sesklo located on a knoll near a gorge (see figs. 2–4, 2–5) and *city* to the settlement established across the gorge. The city is believed by Demetrios Theocharis to have covered from twenty to twenty-five acres and to have housed about 3,000 people. In 1973 he wrote, "We are now almost certain that the highest part of the settlement was in fact the acropolis of the small middle neolithic 'city.'"[8]

The use of the term acropolis seems to be a misunderstanding. Furthermore, the excavators (Tsountas in the beginning of the 20th century and Theocharis in the 1970s) speak of "megaron" buildings in the center of the village where some thirty houses were uncovered. The absence of outstanding central buildings which could suggest a hierarchy was noted in all other excavated Sesklo settlements. In my view, the Sesklo megarons were certainly not central buildings of the Early Bronze Age type which housed the rulers. The stone wall around the Sesklo tell was obviously necessary since the knoll had rather steep slopes.

Houses of two rooms, one larger than the other, assumed to be megarons by the excavators of Sesklo, were actually temples as shown by my own excavation at Achilleion (see fig. 7–46), dating from c. 6000–5800 B.C., the same period as the Sesklo "megarons." The architecture of these temples, which has been identified in large and small villages, did not differ much from regular houses except that they were usually of two rooms (temple proper and workshop). At Sesklo, the richest ceramic finds, including extraordinarily beautiful vases, were found in a two-room temple. (FIGURE 9–1) The temple proper (left room) contained a stone dais (altar) and traces of two wooden columns in the middle.

FIGURE 9–1

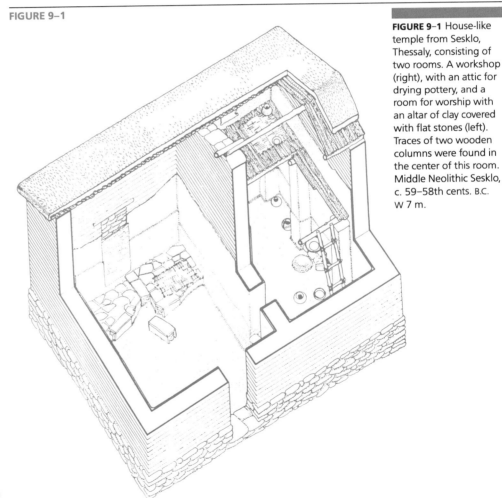

FIGURE 9-1 House-like temple from Sesklo, Thessaly, consisting of two rooms. A workshop (right), with an attic for drying pottery, and a room for worship with an altar of clay covered with flat stones (left). Traces of two wooden columns were found in the center of this room. Middle Neolithic Sesklo, c. 59–58th cents. B.C. W 7 m.

Temples were close to other houses. In the early Neolithic village of Nea Nikomedeia in Macedonia of c. 6300–6100 B.C. a larger temple about twelve meters wide was found surrounded by six houses about eight meters wide clustered within two to five meters of each other.[9] (FIGURE 9–2) Inside were sculptures of the Bird Goddess, askoi (bird-shaped vases), a vase with a goddess face on the neck, outsized and unused greenstone axes (Goddess symbols), and other sacred items.

The tradition of building churches next to regular houses, usually of inconspicuous architecture, is continuous to this day in villages and small towns on the Aegean islands. One family or a cluster of interrelated families in four to six houses will own a little church which is cared for by the women. Male priests of the modern Orthodox church appear as guests to serve only on special occasions. I have observed this tradition on the islands of Skyros, Paros, Naxos, Kythnos, Melos, Mykonos and others within the last few decades.

The interrelationship between the larger tell settlements and surrounding villages, and between regular houses of the village and the temples, is not always known in detail because settlements are rarely completely excavated. Nevertheless, there is a significant pattern which repeats throughout the millennia in which there are no acropolises, no heavy fortifications, and no outstanding central buildings. The temples are always integrated with the everyday village life.

East-Central Europe, 5500–3500 B.C.: Large Tells as Religious Centers, Clusters of Houses with Integrated Temples, Large and Solid Houses of Matrilineal Stem Families

In the period between 5300 and 4300 B.C., permanent central villages which continued for centuries are well attested in the Vinča, Butmir, Tisza, and Karanovo cultures. These central settlements occupy from two to five hectares, even up to eleven hectares in the Tisza culture (the largest being Szegvár-Tüzköves in southeastern Hungary). Next to tell settlements, single-layer settlements are known which probably housed the overflow populations extending over an area of twenty-five to thirty hectares. The large tell settlements were religious centers analogous to the Minoan temple-palaces, which can explain their permanence. Vast numbers of ceremonial objects have been recovered from them, as from the Vinča tell where no fewer than 2,000 figurines, zoomorphic and ornithomorphic vases, offering tables and containers, and other items were found. The huge Tisza tells, such as Szegvár-Tüzköves and Kökenydomb, yielded large anthropomorphic vases, sculptures, and altars. Temples were usually two-room or two-story buildings whose interior and exterior walls were painted with symbols, while interior walls and gables were sometimes decorated with bucrania. Inside they housed basins, altars, kernoi (offering dishes), huge rectangular vases, and ovens.

Houses having two to five rooms stood in clusters. In the Vinča culture, two or three houses stood close together; and in the Tisza culture, there were clusters of four to six houses, the largest of ten or more. In the Tisza and Karanovo cultures, one of the buildings in a cluster of houses would certainly be a temple (see figs. 3–24, 3–50). Such clusters were very likely occupied by people related by kin.

As we have already discussed in chapter 3, the Cucuteni settlements in the period from c. 4800 to 3500 B.C. grew from villages of twenty dwellings in the Early Cucuteni to villages or small towns of up to two hundred dwellings in the Classical Cucuteni (see fig. 3–62),

becoming large towns covering 250–400 hectares in the Late Cucuteni, in the first half of the 4th millennium B.C. (see figs. 3–63, 3–64). The largest towns, which housed up to 10,000 people, were located approximately ten to fifteen kilometers from one another and, by this period, had clearly become centers of a district. In between, there were considerably smaller towns and villages (see fig. 6–65). This is the only area of Europe where settlements grew to such extensive proportions, their continuous growth of population sustained by the most fertile region of the Ukraine and Moldavia.

Many Classical Cucuteni villages, several of which were fully excavated, consisted of 100 to 200 houses. These did not follow a preconceived plan as did the Late Cucuteni towns, which were arranged in concentric rings. Houses of various proportions—large, medium, and small—stood in clusters or in irregular rows and may have housed extended, kin-related families (descending from a common ancestor).

Let us have a look at the completely excavated large village of Truşeşti in the Prut valley of northern Moldavia (FIGURE 9–3) excavated by Petrescu-Dimboviţa in the 1950s. This site could have held up to nine hundred people. Nearly a hundred houses were excavated, the majority of which belong to the Cucuteni A2 phase, c. 4400–4300 B.C., only five belong to Cucuteni B of the early 4th millennium B.C. The floor plans of excavated houses reveal groups or rows consisting of five to eight dwellings of various sizes: large (12 to 20 m long), medium (8 to 12 m), and small (5 to 8 m). Large houses were not separated from the rest, there was no clear distinction between large and medium-sized dwellings, and there were no central buildings in the village.

FIGURE 9–2

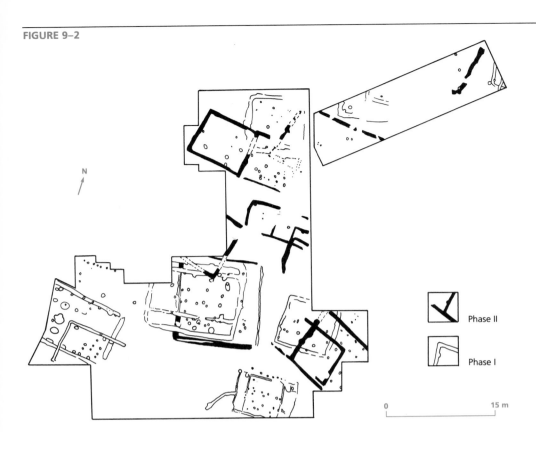

Phase II

Phase I

0   15 m

FIGURE 9–2 Early Neolithic village of Nea Nikomedia, Macedonia; plan of the dwellings and the temple (the large building in the center). c. 6300–6100 B.C.

FIGURE 9–3 Simplified plan of the Cucuteni settlement at Truşeşti, Prut valley, N Moldavia, Romania. 4400–4300 B.C.

FIGURE 9–3

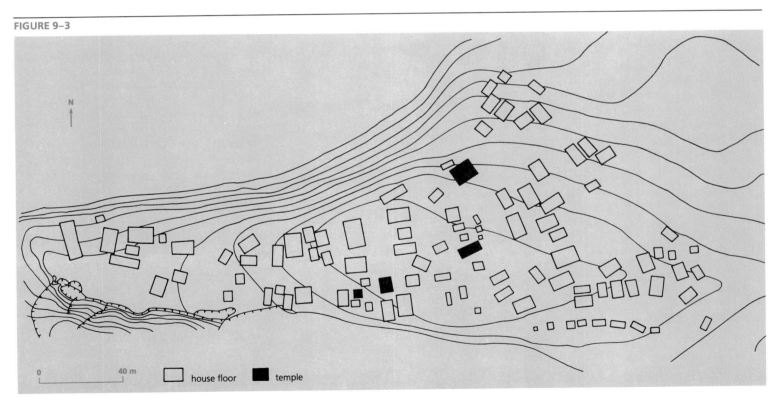

0   40 m   ☐ house floor   ■ temple

FIGURE 9–4

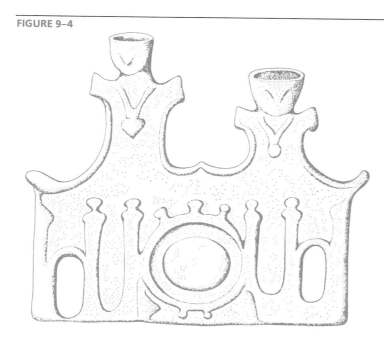

FIGURE 9–4 Altar piece (ceramic) or replica of a temple facade with a round entrance and two anthropomorphic figurines on top. Truşeşti, NE Romania (House No. 24). Cucuteni A2, c. 4400–4300 B.C. c. 150 cm.

FIGURE 9–5

FIGURE 9–5 Altar piece portraying the Goddess with upraised arms. Truşeşti, NE Romania (House No. 27) 4400–4300 B.C. Size: 73 x 70 cm.

The temples were identified by the presence of altars, huge altar pieces, altar screens (FIGURE 9–4) and, in one instance, a large sculpture of the Goddess with upraised arms made of a layer of clay which was probably attached to the temple wall. (FIGURE 9–5) Huge decorated vases, some with reliefs of goddess figures and other outstanding anthropomorphic images, were found in temples (see fig. 9–3, buildings marked with black).

In Truşeşti, Habaşeşti, and other Classical Cucuteni villages, dwellings that would indicate hierarchical "big man's" rank cannot be seen. The larger houses probably belonged to the core families while the smaller could be interpreted as accommodating the growth of their extended families or as men's quarters, analogous to the growth patterns of the villages themselves.

When village and town plans developed into concentric rings in the Late Cucuteni, dwellings continued to be grouped in clusters and were of various proportions. One of these entirely excavated settlements is Kolomiyshchina in the Middle Dnieper basin near Kiev, excavated in 1934–39 by Tatyana Passek. (FIGURE 9–6) Due to its early date of excavation and an artist's reconstruction of the complete village, Kolomiyshchina was reproduced many times in general books on European prehistory as an example of a Neolithic village. Unfortunately its structure was inaccurately interpreted, based on the artist's drawing, not on the excavator's report. For instance, Kolomiyshchina was interpreted by B. Brentjes as follows: "The two larger houses in the inner circle are chief's quarters, the inner ring of smaller houses—his retinue's accommodation, the outer ring of houses represents the free peasantry."[10] This interpretation has also been repeated in a recent book on European social evolution.[11] According to Tatyana Passek, the village community consisted of thirty-one houses in the outer ring and eight houses in the inner. The center was left open, perhaps for rituals and feasts or for keeping stock. Houses differed in size: ten large (16–23 m long), thirteen medium (10–15 m long), and five small with

FIGURE 9–6

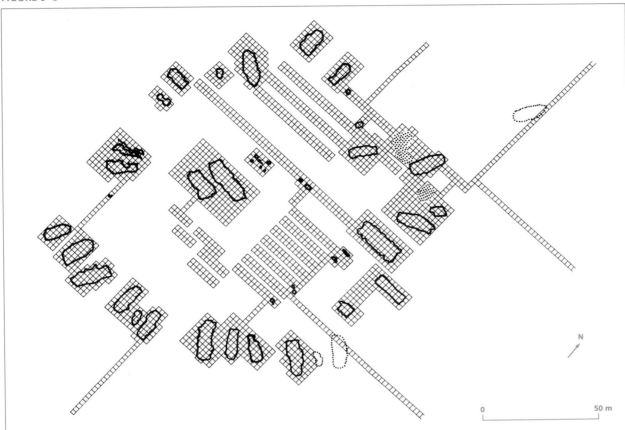

a

b

FIGURE 9–6 Plan (a) and reconstruction (b) of Kolomiyshchina village arranged in concentric circles. Houses were of three sizes: small, up to 8 m long; medium, up to 15 m; larger, up to 20–22 m. Early 4th mill. B.C.

single rooms (4–8 m long). The large houses, considered to be core houses, had floors of several layers of clay bricks superimposed on a wooden platform; in some rooms the floor elevations varied. These had three or four rooms with ovens in each (see fig. 3–66). They clearly indicate a stability of occupation through several generations, whereas the small dwellings do not. The medium-sized houses imitated the larger ones, except that they were less elaborate and had a lesser number of floor layers. The small houses had only single layers of floor and a small oven. According to Passek, the small houses in the inner circle are indicative of the growth of the village community in which a branch from a large matrilineal family would split off to occupy other houses. She thinks that the outer ring is primary, the inner secondary, with the population expanding into the center. Finds in the two larger houses within the inner circle were inconspicuous (they contained only kitchen ware), and there is no shred of evidence that they were the dwellings of chiefs, rendering such characterization arbitrary and unsupported. Twenty to thirty people of an extended family could have lived in these large houses, and the total number of inhabitants at Kolomyshchina may have been about 500.[12]

LBK Culture of Central Europe: Solid Long-Houses of the Matrilineal Stem Family

We shall turn now to the Linearband-keramik (LBK) culture of central Europe where entire hamlets were excavated and settlement systems analyzed. Villages here were considerably smaller, showing two to six houses within the farmstead area. Individual houses were used for an average of thirty years.[13] An analysis of house structures has revealed distinctions in both size and function with large, medium, and small houses as in the Cucuteni villages. One to several very long houses appeared in a number of settlements (for example, Bylany near Prague; Olszanica in southern Poland; Aldenhoven Plateau, near Cologne).

These are distinct, not only in their great length but also in their solid construction: postholes were large and deep, and the walls of the northwestern section were constructed of split logs, while other houses had wattle and daub walls. (FIGURE 9–7) Thus, the northwestern end of a long-house seems to have been the most distinguished area, while the middle part is considered to have been used for living and working, with the front of the house used as a granary and for storage.[14] The study of finds within the long-houses has shown that their contents, especially the decorated pottery, were richer than in other houses. The privileged long-house has been interpreted as a "clubhouse" where district gatherings took place[15] or as the residence of a district "big man," chief or priest.[16]

Since the LBK culture spread to central Europe from the Balkano-Danubian region, we should expect to find here a related social structure and similar house function. This system is, in fact, very much related to that of the Starčevo-Vinča and to the just-described Cucuteni village system, except that in the LBK culture no large accumulations of people are found. There is no evidence for chiefs or big man's houses in this culture as there is none in the entire region of Neolithic Old Europe. The cemetery analysis that follows speaks for prominent men in crafts and trade, not in chieftainship. The long-house could have been the seat of a core family which directed the religious, social, and economic life of the village or of several related hamlets located nearby.

Interesting results were achieved by van de Velde's study of pottery found in individual LBK houses. Since there is evidence that women were the potters, it was expected that an extended family in a stem system would yield a homogeneous pottery assemblage. Indeed, individual houses have shown consistent assemblage composition over the estimated thirty years of occupation, arguing for the prevalence of the matrilineal stem family.[17] Analogous research has been done in the Verdon valley in southern France by Patricia Phillips.[18] Here, the presence of pottery-making families

FIGURE 9–7

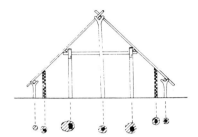

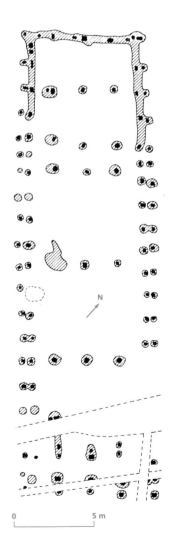

FIGURE 9–7 Long-house from Linearbandkeramik culture. The north-western end was more solidly constructed than the rest of the house. Bochum-Hiltrop, W Germany, end of 6th mill. B.C. L 28 m.

0   5 m

or lineages has been shown through analysis of pottery and stratigraphic sequences. The indirect results indicate an endogamous, matrilocal residence. In fact, in many other areas of Old Europe where habitation from several hundred to a thousand years or more is indicated by stratigraphic sequences, the persistence of pottery-making traditions is striking. This is particularly seen in the large tells of the Sesklo, Karanovo, Vinča, and Butmir groups (see fig. 2–9).

Conclusion

In conclusion, the settlement evidence of southeast and central Europe speaks for the existence of focal houses, large and better built than the rest, which we surmise were occupied by stem families of matrilineal lineage. Such houses may also have been the loci of gatherings or decision making councils who organized the surrounding houses, the whole village, or even several villages or districts. Extended families lived in large and medium-sized houses, all on equal footing. Small houses perhaps belonged to offshoots from extended families, or to adult men or craftsmen. Houses of various sizes were grouped in clusters or rows that may represent the residences of kinsfolk. Temples were integrated within these groups and are distinguished by wall paintings and reliefs and by outstanding ritual ceramics.

The absence of weapons of war and hill forts over two millennia, from c. 6500–4500 B.C. argues for an absence of territorial aggression.

Cemetery Evidence

Southeast and Central Europe, 6500–3500 B.C.: Distinct Grave Categories of Prominent Women and Male Traders and Craftsmen

During the 7th and 6th millennia B.C. the southeastern European Neolithic cultures of Sesklo, Starčevo, and Karanovo practiced intramural burials in which children, young individuals, and females were interred under the floors of houses. This indicates the status bestowed on females and their children and their strong ties with their homes. As mentioned in chapter 7, burial sites for adult males are conspicuously lacking.

In the second half of the 6th millennium B.C., in some areas of the Balkans, children were buried near the houses in courtyards and in specially stone-paved areas (as shown by the excavation at Obre I, a late Starčevo site in Bosnia.)[19] Adult burials have not been found and their location remains a mystery. A deposition of ten adults has been discovered in the lowest layer of the Vinča site east of Belgrade dated to c. 5400–5300 B.C., which is the only example of its kind throughout all of east-central Europe. These adults were found irregularly placed in a deep pit covered with a wooden superstructure, and of the ten individuals, eight were male and two were female.[20]

Of the seventeen early and middle Neolithic pit burials found in caves and open-air settlements at Franchthi, Peloponnese, only female adults appear to have received offerings. The largest concentration of grave goods, eleven items in all (pots, bone and obsidian tools), was found with the tightly flexed burial of an older woman[21] which indicates her revered social status.

When cemeteries appeared around 5000 B.C., infants continued to be buried under the house floors or in courtyards. Intramural burials of adults are found to the end of the 5th millennium B.C. although at the same time formal disposal in cemeteries was also being practiced. From the early 5th millen-

nium B.C. in most culture groups of central Europe and the Balkans (LBK, Butmir, Tisza, and Boian),[22] clusters of five to ten graves in variously sized cemeteries began to appear. In larger cemeteries, such as in Aszód north of Budapest, graves appeared in three groups, about thirty each. (FIGURE 9–8) In the Dnieper basin, burial was in collective pits containing different ages and sexes, with from two or three to eight, ten, or more in each. Such pits often adjoined each other in a row forming a long trench (see figs. 3–79, 3–80) which may represent burial trenches of kin-related individuals. In larger cemeteries of the Dnieper-Donets culture, two or three parallel trenches of graves were also found, perhaps representing groupings of individuals belonging to one stem or lineage. Groupings of twenty to thirty individuals were also observed within collective burials in megalithic tombs. This pattern was repeated in Old Europe until the collective burial was replaced by individual burials in the second half of the 4th and early 3rd millennia B.C. Physical anthropological studies by Hubert Ullrich of skeletons buried collectively within chambers from the TRB culture in central Germany (of the Walternienburg group of the second half of the 4th millennium B.C.) have shown that each tomb contained two or three groups of twenty to thirty skeletons that were genetically interrelated.[23] (FIGURES 9–9, 9–10)

Regarding grave analysis, one of the best researched area is the Linearbandkeramik (LBK) culture of central Europe around 5000 B.C. About twenty well-excavated cemeteries are known from eastern France, Holland, Germany, Poland, and Czechoslovakia.[24] These cemeteries are located within 100 to 500 meters from settlement boundaries and consist of inhumation and cremation burials. Cemeteries range from around 20 to more than 200 graves. The largest are Elsloo at Limburg in Holland with 113 inhumation and cremation burials; Flomborn, district of Alzey-Worms in West Germany, with 85 inhumation burials; Aiterhofen in Bavaria with 160 skeletal and 69 cremated graves; and Nitra in Slovakia with 72 inhumation

FIGURE 9–8

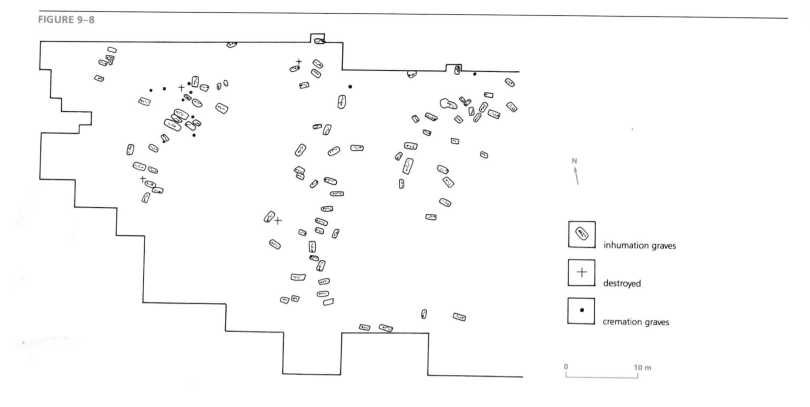

inhumation graves

destroyed

cremation graves

0   10 m

FIGURE 9–9

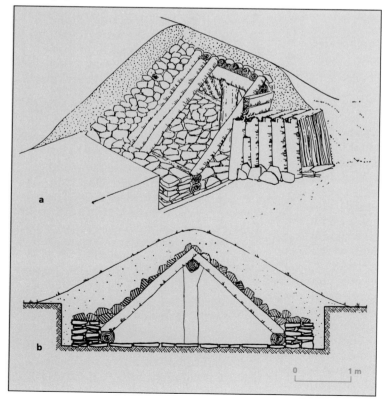

FIGURE 9-8 Three groups of graves, very likely of kin-related people, in the cemetery of Aszód north of Budapest. Lengyel culture, early 5th mill. B.C.

FIGURE 9-9 Reconstruction (a) and (b) and plan (c) of a collective burial in the chamber of the tomb at Nordhausen, district of Sonderhausen, Thüringen, C Germany.

FIGURE 9-10 (1) Three groupings of deposited skeletons, studied on the basis of their physical relationship in the chamber of the tomb at Nordhausen. (2) This drawing shows physical interrelationships between the buried individuals in a tomb at Niederbösa, district of Sonderhausen, Germany. There were two groups of about 30 individuals according to the study of H. Ullrich.

graves. In a few cemeteries, the clustering of graves was clear, as in Nitra where 10 groups of 5 to 10 graves were identified.[25] Another is at Aiterhofen where many clusters among the 160 skeletal graves are considered to represent family or kin-related groups.[26] Cremated burials in this cemetery were arranged in semicircular formations in one part of the cemetery. In several other cemeteries, a tendency to bury one sex together was observed, and groups of two or three men or women were frequent. Nowhere was there a spacial hierarchy in which rich and poor graves appeared in separate areas.

Interesting results were obtained from the analysis of grave goods. Not more than 30 percent of the graves were equipped with gifts. Some contained a vase or two, spondylus beads, arm rings, or some stone tools such as stone celts (adzes of shoe-block type), scrapers, arrowheads, grinding stones, or palettes for mixing colors. The correlation of grave goods with gender has shown that in the majority of cemeteries, men's graves were associated with stone celts, spondylus jewelry, and occasionally with flint scrapers and arrowheads. In a number of cemeteries, about 20 percent of the graves included stone celts; these graves were often found in pairs or threes. In the Danube region of Bavaria, not stone celts but spondylus jewelry dominated the equipment of male graves. This indicates that the best handworkers, especially wood craftsmen and house builders as well as spondylus traders, were specially honored. At Nitra it was observed that flint tools for woodworking were found in the graves of older men[27] who had probably excelled in their craft as house builders. The division of grave goods between males and females was not a rule everywhere. For instance, quernstones for grinding grain appeared in male as well as in female graves, and stone celts were found in female graves, or these were found together in the graves of both sexes. In general, women's graves included decorated pottery, ochre, quernstones, palettes, jewelry, and a variety of symbolic items. Spondylus jewelry in male graves seems to symbolize trading

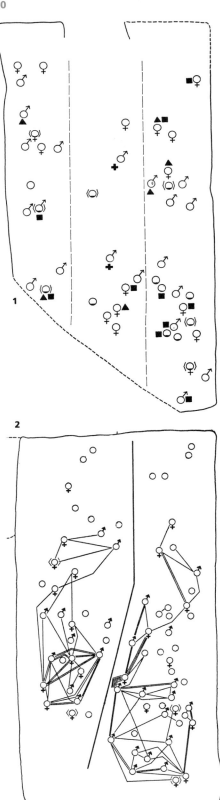

FIGURE 9-10

activities in spondylus shell and respect for this occupation. In the cemetery of Rixheim in eastern France, the distribution of jewelry was heavily biased in favor of the women where four out of five graves displayed either necklaces, arm rings, finger rings, or head decorations.[28]

The graves of older women were honored with symbolic items, often with richly decorated vases. There is an example of a 50- to 60-year-old woman from the Samborzec cemetery in Poland who held a pot filled to the brim with red ochre placed in her right hand near her face.[29]

In conclusion, the analysis of grave goods of the LBK cemeteries indicates two distinct categories of graves: those of male traders and craftsmen, and those of prominent women in religious life. The evidence, as stated, indicates some men of status but not of ruling rank, and some elder women who were obviously honored. Not a single male grave included insignia of rank as one would expect from a ruling aristocracy. Evidence reveals that elder women, the great clan mothers, received the highest social respect.

Similar customs were practiced in other culture groups. In Lengyel cemeteries, men were equipped with stone axes and antler hammer-axes, females with quantities of spondylus shell or bone arm rings, necklaces of animal teeth, spondylus and copper beads, and hip belts of dentalium shell and stone beads. In the cemetery of Aszód, the most outstanding grave was that of a teen-age girl which contained a large temple model of clay with a bird's head on top, standing on a human foot[30] (see fig. 3–39). The girl was apparently connected to the core family and to the temple. Female graves in this and other Lengyel cemeteries often contained an assortment of vases painted with spirals and meanders.

An analysis of graves from the Lengyel cemeteries of Moragy-Tüzködomb and Zengővárkony in western Hungary by István Zalai-Gaál have shown that in addition to the great numbers of vases in female graves, the most exceptional graves that were rich with ornaments

FIGURE 9–11

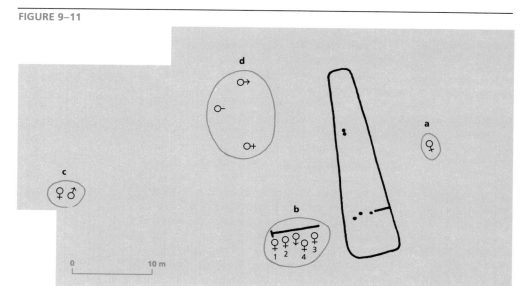

FIGURE 9–12A

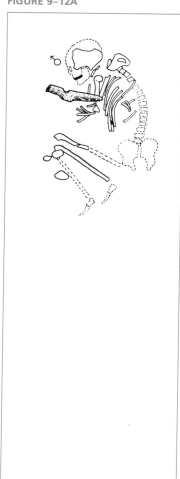

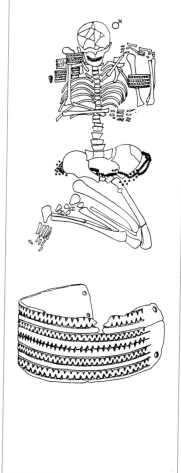

1

2

FIGURE 9–11 Clusters of graves near the trapezoidal house at Brześć Kujawski village, Kujavia, W Poland, site 4, House 56, Lengyel culture. c. 4300 B.C. (a) Woman c. 45 years old. (b) Four women, ages 1) 55–60, 2) 50–55, 3) 65–70, 4) 45–50; and one man age 50–55. (c) Woman c. 35–40 years old, man 40–45. (d) Two women (one may be a man) and a man.

FIGURE 9–12A Male and female graves (Group C) at Brześć Kujawski, House 56; c. 4000 B.C. (1) Male grave equipped with an antler hammer-axe. (2) Female with arm rings of bone incised with zigzag patterns (see detail: arm ring), hip belt of shell beads, and beads in the neck and chest area.

and symbolic objects were those of girls and female infants. Boys' graves were poor and adult and mature male graves were equipped rarely with more than one or several tools. The importance of girls is explained by their hereditary status in a matrilineal society.[31] The serogenetic study done by Imre Lengyel in 1986 has also proven the same. A series of grave goods was found with blood-related females and children, and an analysis of ABO blood groups has shown a high degree of endogamy (marrying inside the lineage) in this society.[32] Males were not related, and in burial customs some male graves were distinct in foreign features, indicating that they may have been buried according to customs of their original homeland.

At Brześć Kujawski, a Lengyel settlement in western Poland from the late 5th millennium B.C., burials of individuals of advanced age were discovered near trapezoidal houses.[33] At one such house, several groups of burial pits were found (FIGURE 9–11) in which the skeletal remains were very well preserved and an anthropological analysis was possible. The first person buried east of one house was a woman of 40 to 45 years old (FIGURE 9–11, a) with copper beads at her skull. To the west of the house five individuals were buried: four women and one man, all of advanced age, 50 to 70 years old. The oldest was a woman 65 to 70 years old; the man was 50 to 55. (FIGURE 9–11, b). The female graves included copper beads, a necklace of animal teeth, a belt of shell beads, and a vase, while no grave goods were in the man's grave. There were two more groups some distance from the house. (FIGURE 9–11, c, d) Burials of a woman and a middle-aged man were found, as indicated in figure 9–11, c. The man was equipped with an antler hammer-axe, while the woman, 30 to 35 years old, was showered with beads and wore three arm rings of bone with minute geometric decoration and a hip belt of shell beads. (FIGURES 9–12A, 9–12B) These clusters of graves, found so near the houses, suggest that old age was revered. The graves of older women, as heads of the family, were equipped with jewelry,

FIGURE 9–12B

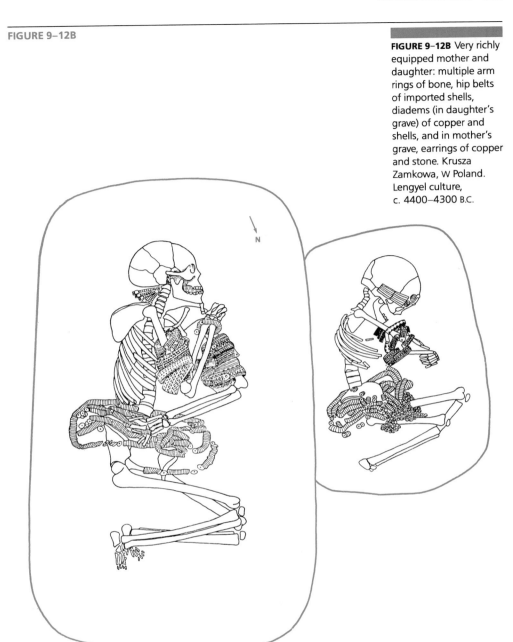

FIGURE 9–12B Very richly equipped mother and daughter: multiple arm rings of bone, hip belts of imported shells, diadems (in daughter's grave) of copper and shells, and in mother's grave, earrings of copper and stone. Krusza Zamkowa, W Poland. Lengyel culture, c. 4400–4300 B.C.

indicating their honored status and primacy within the family kinship system.

In northeastern Hungary, the sexual dichotomy in grave goods was studied in the cemetery of Basatanya, located between the Tisza River and Polgár town, excavated by Ida Bognár-Kutzián, and later analyzed by Susan Skomal in 1983 and Marita Meisenheimer in 1989.[34] This cemetery belongs to the Tiszapolgár phase, with fifty-seven graves, and was followed by the Bodrogkeresztúr phase, with eighty-seven graves. This location was immediately accessible to obsidian, flint, and copper sources in the Carpathians. Obsidian and flint nuclei were found only in male graves which suggests that males were involved in trade and manufacture of obsidian and flint tools. Not much can be said from grave evidence for copper trade since copper arm rings appeared in both male and female graves, and copper finger rings and beads as well as a copper ingot were found in female graves. The analysis of Basatanya grave finds has convincingly shown that the manufacture and decoration of pottery was in women's hands. Pebbles for burnishing and polishing pottery, coloring materials, and stone palettes were found exclusively in female graves.

During the early Tiszapolgár phase five male graves were found equipped with more than one tool. In addition to obsidian or flint nuclei and a flint blade, several graves included a stone or antler axe, an adze, a mace, and an arrowhead. As in other areas, the richest male graves seem to represent their prominence in crafts, hunting, and trade. Female graves were distinct in having many more vases and ritual objects than those of males. An exceptional example in this cemetery was Grave No. 4, in which a young girl was buried with a copper arm ring, the skull of a goat, and a mandible of a pig. Here too, as in the Lengyel cemeteries, the girl may have belonged to an important hereditary line of a matrilineal society, perhaps a lineage of priestesses.

The same pattern repeats in a number of culture groups where cemeteries are known. Most frequently teen-age girls were either richly equipped with jewelry or included in their graves items of exceptional ritual value. In the cemetery of Cernica at Bucharest (mentioned in chap. 3), the richest grave out of 362 graves was of a girl about sixteen years old. She was buried with eight arm-rings on one arm and two on the other, a bone ring on her left hand, and a mass of shell beads. In the Late Cucuteni cemetery at Vykhvatintsi in Moldavia, two exceptional burials of girls of nine to ten years old appeared, each buried in a central position in two sections of the cemetery. They were equipped with five exquisite vases, shell beads, a spindle whorl (in one of them), and even with three figurines of the stiff nude type representing the Goddess of Death and Regeneration. No other graves of this cemetery contained three figurines.[35]

The highly honored status of women is demonstrated by burials in the Funnel-necked Beaker (TRB) culture. Here, huge long-barrows were raised for a single woman. At Sarnowo in Kujavia, western Poland, a triangular barrow thirty meters long covered a central grave pit in which the bones of a woman about 70 years old were found. She was buried in a wooden coffin and under her skeleton was a thin layer of white limestone dust. Above the grave, traces of a rectangular structure 300 by 240 m built of wooden planks came to light. This apparently was a sacral structure where rituals were performed. Quantities of potsherds were found scattered in and around the grave (FIGURE 9–13) and the grave fill contained a clay spoon and an antler point.[36]

We do not know with certainty that all of the triangular/trapezoidal barrows of huge proportions were built for prominent women, since many of the skeletons in primary graves for which the barrow was built unfortunately were not preserved. This is likely, however, on the basis of the prominence of female burials in Old European society. Some of the gigantic TRB graves included secondary burials of disarticulated individuals buried behind the primary burial. Osteological inspection showed breakages and incisions in the long bones reaching far into the marrow cavities.[37] This speaks for secondary burials with bones cleaned of tissues and marrow (not for cannibalism, as was originally thought by the excavators). The old woman who was honored by the construction of a triangular barrow was perhaps a queen-priestess or was considered an ancestress of the clan, a Great Mother.

Old European cemeteries cannot be divided into rich and poor grave categories, as in Indo-European times, since grave goods do not represent the wealth of an individual; they are essentially symbolic, expressing either religious symbols or personal qualities. Burials having more or fewer grave goods intermingle and are not set off physically from the rest of the cemetery. The types of symbolic and trade objects found in graves are repeated in hoards found deposited in temples or at house foundations, sometimes stored in beautifully decorated vases. A number of such temple hoards consist of pristine stone axes made of greenstone, blackstone, marble, or also of clay or amber and never used for work. Their appearance in graves had a symbolic value and they were not considered as tools to be used in the afterlife. Rather, these were placed in female and male graves as symbols of regeneration, their triangular forms being associated with the Goddess's generative vulva.[38] The symbolic role of the axe throughout the Neolithic of western Europe is indicated by its engraving on menhirs and tomb walls. It is of interest to note that more axes were found in hoards and cemeteries than in settlements. Also, it is a peculiarly Old European phenomenon to find many more ornaments in houses than in graves. As J. C. Chapman has observed, without a comparison of house and grave finds, the burial data could have been interpreted as reflecting a poor community with a weak ornamental tradition. In this regard, the cemetery evidence is an illusion[39] if we look for treasures and personal possessions accumulated in graves as evidence of the community's material wealth.

FIGURE 9–13

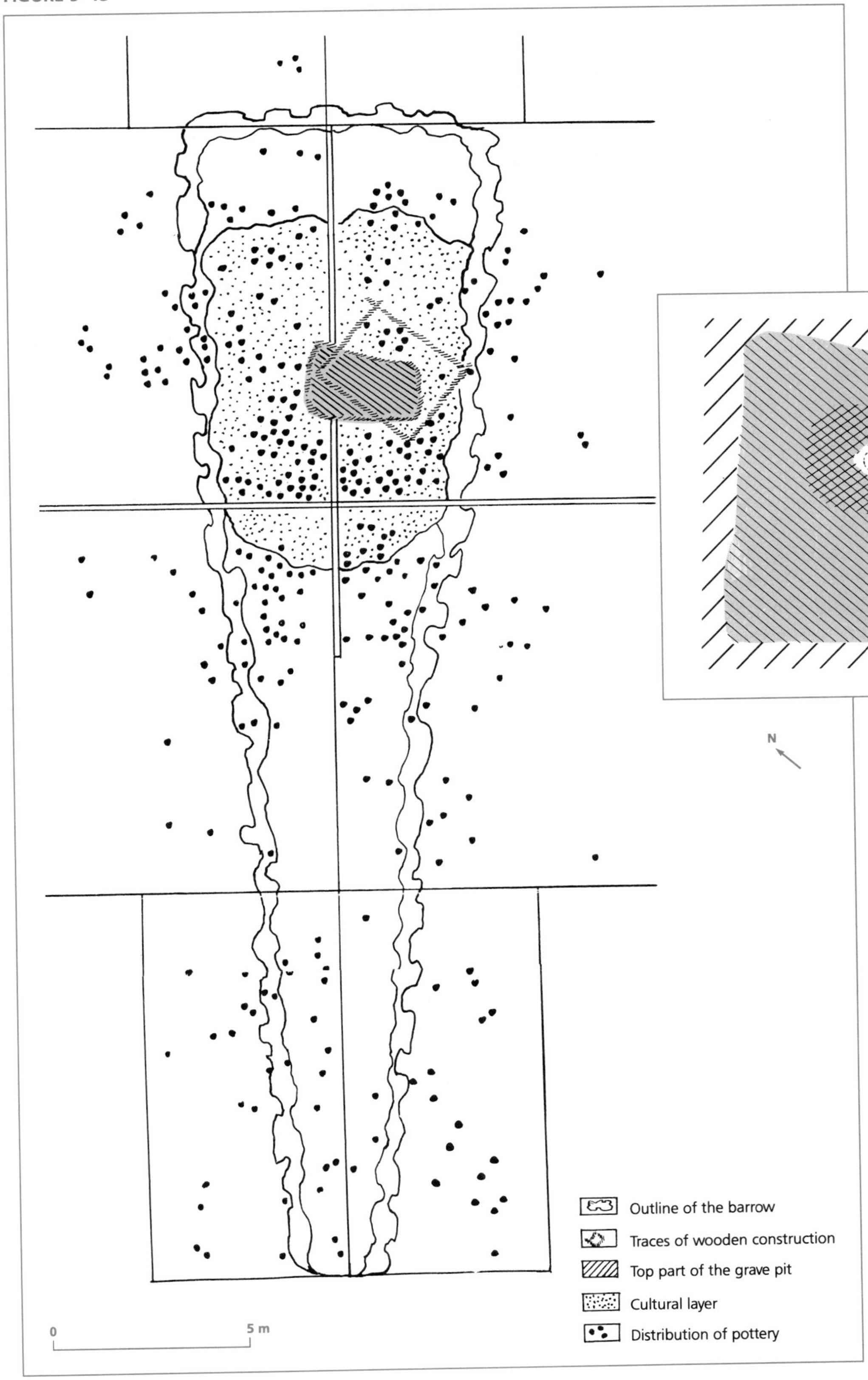

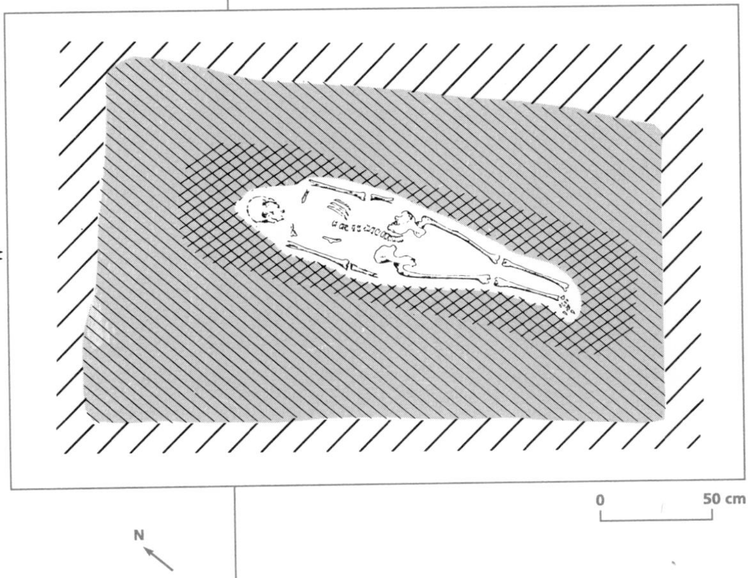

FIGURE 9–13 The long-barrow (No. 9) of Sarnowo, district of Włocławek, Poland, constructed for the burial of a woman about 70 years old, buried in a grave pit in the center and covered with a wooden construction (see detail, *right*). Length of barrow, 30 m. Early TRB.

N

0   50 cm

Outline of the barrow

Traces of wooden construction

Top part of the grave pit

Cultural layer

Distribution of pottery

0   5 m

Conclusion

In summary, the cemetery evidence in central and east-central Europe during the 5th millennium B.C. speaks for the existence of kinship based societies. Graves were arranged in rows or in groups of twenty to thirty-five people, which may reflect kin-related units. The most honored members of the Old European society were elder females, perhaps heads of the stem or queens, and girls who were very likely members of a hereditary line or priestesses. Their graves do not indicate the accumulation of personal possessions but are marked by symbolic items, sometimes of exceptional quality, and by the erection of gigantic mounds and consecrated structures. The graves of girls and female infants were consistently equipped with exceptional ritual objects not found in other graves. Analysis of blood groups testify to a pronounced endogamous society which may suggest that these girls were important heiresses in a hereditary female line.

Black Sea Coast: Several Cemeteries in East Bulgaria After 4500 B.C. with Very Rich Male Graves

The only area where marked changes in social structure has been observed is along the Black Sea coast in Bulgaria. Here, in several cemeteries, the dominance of adult males in the burial domain does seem more overt than in any other part of east-central Europe. Researchers see "incipient patriarchal tendencies."[40] I consider this change a result of rapidly rising trade activities of the inhabitants of the Black Sea coast with the Dnieper-Volga steppe population who were wedging their way into territories west of the Black Sea.

There are three cemeteries near the Black Sea coast—Varna, Durankulak, and Devnja—which exhibit a deviation from the Old European norm of female-prominent social structure. In each cemetery at least three male adult graves were distinct because of their extraordinary richness. Although next to these, female and symbolic graves at Varna (with no skeletal remains) were also very rich, it cannot be denied that the male

graves surpassed them, for the amount of gold jewelry amassed in them is unprecedented. The male skeleton in grave No. 43 at Varna was showered by three gold necklaces, three massive gold arm rings on each arm, two gold earrings for each ear, six gold hair rings, three large double-perforated gold discs, two oblong gold plates, several other plates apparently sewn on a garment, and a large gold disc and biconical beads. Gold nails and gold plate mountings were also present. In addition, a copper spear, a flint spearhead, a 55 cm flint knife, large copper shaft-hole axes, a stone shaft-hole axe with golden tube mountings, a stone axe, and a heavy copper chisel were found in this grave, totalling twenty-eight categories of finds. Gold objects amounted to 1,011. The buried man was 40 to 50 years old. The inventories of two other graves of males in this cemetery of 190 graves were also extensive, befitting leading members of the community.[41] The less rich cemetery of Devnja also included three adult male graves equipped with copper and gold, while female graves had no gold items.[42]

It is obvious that a transformation in burial rites coupled with major social changes had taken place. The numbers of tools, weapons, and ornaments in these male graves express a level of personal status and power that was entirely unknown in all other Old European societies. The accumulation of such wealth among a few individual males, indicating the rise of male power in relation to female power in these towns along the Black Sea coast, is exceptional. These men do not seem to be invaders from the East, since all finds from these cemeteries represent local manufacture.

In the interior of northern Bulgaria cemeteries continued to demonstrate a gylanic society. For instance, in the fifty-three graves at Vinica, little difference in wealth was discernible between male and female. Two of the richest were of females and two of males, and all four were people over 50 years of age. One female, about 55, was endowed with five beautiful vases of superior workmanship, a copper chisel, and a dish in which a necklace of spondylus beads was placed. One of the males, about 65, was

equipped, in addition to a dish and lidded vase, with a stone shaft-hole axe, a copper chisel, cylindrical spondylus beads, and gold earrings.[43]

The prominent males in the Varna society were not chieftains of the Indo-European type and were not buried separately with pomp and human or animal sacrifices. The Old European wealthy men were probably overseers of commerce by which they achieved their wealth. This richness, however, does not necessarily imply a dominant or auto-cratic political role.

Evidence from Megalithic Tombs, Long-Barrows, and Henges of Western Europe

There are more than 10,000 megalithic tombs and long-barrows known in western Europe. Nevertheless, the essential evidence of social structure is either hidden by the nature of the burial rites themselves, or the tombs were robbed in antiquity. Megaliths, as already discussed, were ossuaries and ritual centers, focal points of one or several villages. Bones of the dead which had been defleshed during excarnation were placed in these tombs. Those which were exposed to birds and sun for a longer time were fragmental, and in many cases only single bones, such as skulls or long bones, were collected. Cremation also was practiced. Therefore it is nearly impossible to count the number of individuals in a particular tomb and calculate the approximate number and sex of individuals in the territory during the time of its use.

The association of megalithic tombs and long-barrows with habitation sites is rarely known since the houses have long since disappeared. The solid structures of stone barrows and gigantic henges still stand in their majesty today, and it is from their location and architecture that most information on the society that built them can be extracted. Most work on the reconstruction of Neolithic society has been done in the British Isles, particularly in the Orkneys, north of Scotland.

In 1976, Colin Renfrew described megalithic culture as composed of small-scale segmentary societies lacking the centralized, hierarchical structure of a chiefdom or state, consisting of cellular and modular autonomous units,[44] but he assumes that population stress and greater pressure on critical resources stimulated an emphasis on territoriality.[45] Evidence of a hierarchical structure of the Indo-European chiefdom type cannot be found during the entire duration of the building of megaliths, in spite of their imposing architecture and the enormous time and energy expended in building them.

The theory of the existence of cellular and autonomous village communities consisting of about the same number of inhabitants can be applied to the early stage, before the middle of the 4th millennium B.C. From about 3500 B.C. onward, with the increase of population, clusters of sites emerged having a certain formal arrangement (spatial stratification) composed of large megalithic structures, chambered cairns, and large henges which indicate an expanded composite of social units.

Some clarity on the spacial distribution of larger and smaller tombs was obtained on the Orkney Islands, an area of intensive archeological research in recent decades. Ten chambered cairns (stone-covered tombs) with volumes in excess of 340 cubic meters were plotted on the islands. (FIGURE 9–14) These have a dispersed distribution in which two large cairns are never found in close proximity. It was noted that each large cairn is associated with a single group of islands or a tract of land that makes a natural topographic unit.[46] Small cairns were located near habitation sites, and it is assumed that they served as community centers for single villages. A large cairn would be built and used by the inhabitants of a local collection of communities, whereas large henge monuments served as centers for the entire population of Orkney. A reconstruction of a large composite social unit is offered in a drawing by David Fraser. (FIGURE 9–15) In his interpretation, the small cairns close to the houses were an essential part of village daily life, whereas the large cairns were not subject to the same locational constraints.

FIGURE 9–14

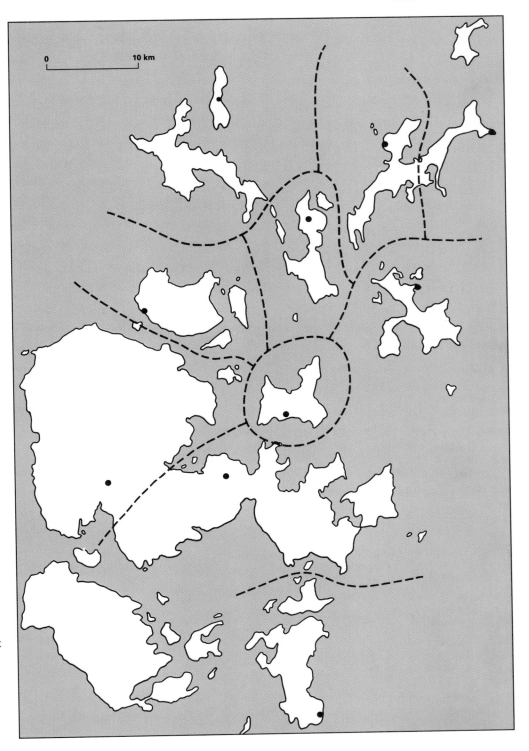

FIGURE 9–14 Distribution of chambered cairns in the Orkney with volumes in excess of 340 m³ as mapped by D. Fraser 1983.

0   10 km

FIGURE 9–15

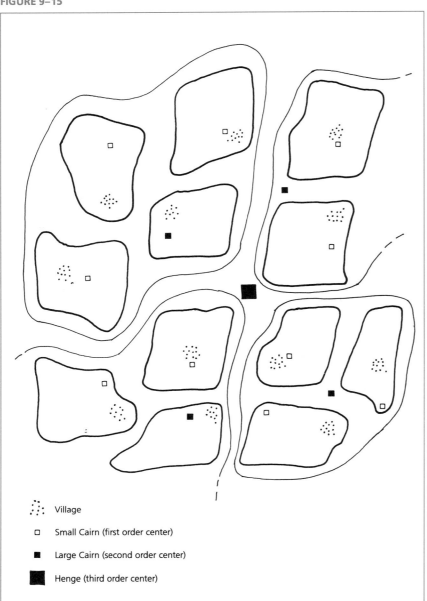

Village

□ Small Cairn (first order center)

■ Large Cairn (second order center)

▪ Henge (third order center)

FIGURE 9–15 Spacial stratification in Neolithic Orkney. (Simplified reconstruction by D. Fraser.)

The henge monuments would serve as meeting places at intervals of a year or more and would be built and maintained by representatives of every village at Orkney. Henges, truly gigantic works of construction, served a vital purpose and are products of the communal effort of large groups of people. Clearly such large scale work had to be based on a society's social and religious system. The ability to organize communal work on a grand scale is one of the chief characteristics of the culture of megalith builders. According to Fraser, however, there is no evidence on the Orkney Islands that power resided in the hands of a single individual.[47] This system, judged from radiocarbon dates, existed on the islands for more than a millennium, from the end of the 4th and throughout the 3rd millennium B.C.

An analogous situation can be seen in southern England where monuments from long-barrows to causewayed camps and henges exist. The human effort expended in the construction of these camps is an order of magnitude greater than required for large megalithic tombs, and henge monuments required even more. The Windmill Hill causewayed camp, for instance, is calculated to have required 120,000 work hours, the Avebury monument 1.5 million, and Durrington Walls 0.9 million. On the basis of such calculations, Renfrew has assumed the existence of chiefdoms in Neolithic Wessex.[48] This statement is in contradiction to information concerning the composite social units of the Orkney Islands since in both areas the spacial stratification is similar. The megalithic culture of all of Britain and western Europe is interrelated, and it is questionable that Wessex diverged from the pattern to become a patriarchal chiefdom society. It should not be forgotten that the superordinate monuments of southern England and Ireland—Avebury, Silbury, Durrington Walls, Newgrange, Knowth—*are religious monuments and communal property, the products of collective work, dedication, and love.* They are far from being royal tombs or administrative structures ordered to be built by a king or chief for his own glory. The latter do not belong within the context

of the belief system of Old Europe. When secularization of life began in Britain with the Indo-European chieftains, religious monuments of this kind vanished.

Henges consisting of two to six concentric ring ditches and palisades of upright wooden posts are not a phenomenon of Wessex or Britain alone. They have been discovered in the Linearbandkeramik (LBK) culture of central Europe, in the Lengyel culture in Moravia, and in the Funnel-necked Beaker (TRB) culture in eastern Germany[49] (see fig. 6–27). It can be expected that henges will also be discovered in other culture groups of Old Europe.[50] The Lengyel and LBK henges belong to the 5th millennium B.C. Hence, it can be seen that the tradition of henge monuments in Old Europe was continuous for at least several millennia. They were not built for the protection of people and their property, as it was believed earlier, but as festival centers and meeting places for funerary rituals, including music and dances, perhaps also as grounds and courses for sports and games.[51] Woodhenge and Durrington Walls contained timber buildings inside their enclosures made of concentric circles of wooden posts supporting a cone-shaped roof.[52] Such a circular building may have stood at the center of Stonehenge I.[53] Cremation deposits found there in Aubrey Holes indicate that the central building was very likely a temple associated with death and regeneration rituals.

Let us return now to the burial evidence and see what is known about the individuals whose bones were placed to rest in megalithic tombs and trapezoidal long-barrows. Bones have been found and analyzed from only a very few of the early tombs; most information comes from recent excavations. The sexing of individuals from the ancient tombs of Brittany, Normandy, southern England, and in the Orkneys has shown equal numbers of males and females. In the early passage graves of Normandy, at La Hoguette, eighteen men, nineteen women, and eighteen children were found.[54] In the trapezoidal barrow at Ascott-under-Wychwood between Oxford and Cheltenham, which is 50 m long, with two chambers each with three

compartments, 4,311 bones and 236 teeth were recovered. Of this number, 49 individuals were identified with virtually an equal number of males and females. The study of bones by Chesterman has shown that an excarnation rite was practiced in which bones were exposed to the sun. Most were in a fragmented state, not all bones were transferred to the tomb, and only some were in an articulated condition.[55] From the 76 megalithic tombs on the Orkney Islands, human bones were found in 26 (in 28 percent of the known tombs). The reliable bone reports that throw some light on the society come from Quanterness[56] and Isbister.[57] In the first, 157 individuals were identified, in the second, 341. The general results of the study from both cairns revealed that both sexes were present in roughly equal numbers, infant mortality was high (although in Quanterness infants under eight months were not found), the burials could represent all the dead of an entire community, and the average age at death was low. Interesting results were obtained on paleopathology. Chesterman was able to identify a large number of healed fractures and ruptured spinal discs. Evidence was found of osteoarthritis of the costo-transverse rib joints attributed to the carrying of a weight on the back by means of a rope sling. A rare congenital abnormality was found in skeletons of both cairns, which implies that these individuals were related to each other. There was no indication at either site that any individual had died a violent death,[58] indicating an absence of interpersonal violence.

Old European Social Structure As Mirrored by Religious Imagery and Myth

The emergence of the Goddess religion in the Paleolithic must have coincided with the model provided by preexisting human social structure. The worship of female deities is connected to a mother-kinship system and ancestor worship in which the sexual identity of the head of the family and kin formulated the sexual identity of the supreme deity. In the mother-kinship system, woman as mother is the social center. She is duly venerated and petitioned, with prayer and thank-offerings, as the progenitor of the family and stem.

Prehistoric religion is one of the main sources for the reconstruction of the social organization of the Upper Paleolithic and the Neolithic. In fact, the study of the types and functions of goddesses, their costumes, their worship in temples, courtyards, or tombs, their appearance surrounded by attendants, and their relations with male gods reveal not less, and in some aspects appreciably more, than settlement patterns and cemeteries. Furthermore, the survival of goddess worship in historical times and in myth is another rich source that fills the gap of an incomplete archeological record.

An interdisciplinary approach has been lacking in standard archeological consideration, whereas a cross-pollination of disciplines has the potential to further illuminate and expand our understanding of the past. This integrated approach, which is the way I choose to work, is a new discipline of knowledge which I call Archeomythology.

A great deal of information is found not only in ancient Greek and Roman religions and mythologies, but also in Basque, Old Irish, Welsh, Gaulish, Norse and German, Lithuanian, Latvian, and all Slavic mythologies and folklore. It is remarkable that beneath the intertwined layers of Christian and Indo-European influences, many elements of the Old European layer are still richly preserved.

The Goddess as Macrocosm and Life Giver

The Paleolithic Goddess was typically a macrocosmic extension of a woman's body. Her essential parts—vulva, breasts, buttocks, belly—were endowed with the miraculous power of procreation. These symbols continued into the Neolithic and can later be explained as a reflection or memory of a matrilineal system in which paternity was considered unimportant or difficult to establish. The Goddess was a cosmic Creatrix, Life- and Birth-giver, while the father image is not known to Paleolithic or Neolithic art.

There follows a resume of the three main aspects of the Goddess.

Mistress of Nature

This goddess is a manifestation of life-giving and life-destroying energies of nature. Her pattern is cosmic—the endlessly repeated cycle of birth, death, and rebirth, corresponding to the phases of the moon and to spring, summer, and winter. She was worshiped in nature—on mountain tops, in caves, at wells, brooks, and streams—and in tombs and temples as a Regeneratrix.

Goddess of Fertility

The Pregnant Goddess, rising and dying with vegetation, is a metaphor of the death and renewal of plant life. She was worshiped at bread ovens in courtyards or in houses as bread giver.

Goddesses as Symbols of Perpetual Life

The Bird and Snake Goddesses are incarnations of life energy and a link between the ancestors and living members of the family. These house and temple goddesses developed from the beginning of agriculture and settled life into protectresses of the family and hearth.

Male Deities as Partners of Goddesses

There are no sculptures of male gods in the Paleolithic, and there are no male gods associated with life and birth giving or death wielding throughout the Neolithic period. The half-human, half-animal figure that appears in cave art, usually interpreted as a shaman, may

have been a "Master of Animals and Forests" since the existence of such a mythical image is well documented in European mythologies. As a complementary figure to Mistress of Nature, Master of Animals appears in Çatal Hüyük wall paintings. The rising and dying Earth Fertility Goddess had a male partner, a year god, a fructifying consort, who appeared in the spring, matured in the summer, and died in autumn with the vegetation. This god cannot be traced in the Paleolithic and is associated only with the cultivation of agriculture. In Neolithic art, as already discussed in chapter 7, he is portrayed as strong and youthful in an ithyphallic posture and as an old sorrowful god seated on a stool or throne with hands on knees or supporting his chin. The extraordinary Hamangia couple (see fig. 7–42) found in one grave, may represent female and male vegetation gods—not necessarily a married couple but more likely sister and brother. In European mythologies, Earth Mother has a brother. The Lithuanian Žemyna has a brother Žemininkas, while in Norse mythology, Freya has a brother Freyr. The Greek Poseidon, whose name is mentioned in Linear B script as Posei-das ("Lord of the Earth" or "Husband to the Earth Mother"), was the consort of the Goddess in her spring aspect.

The representation of copulation in Neolithic imagery may be connected with Sacred Marriage. Such a sculpture of a female embracing a male was found at Çatal Hüyük in central Anatolia from the 7th millennium B.C.,[59] while a similar sculpture from the 5th millennium B.C. was found in Gumelnița, Romania. In the Near East, an "erotique" statuette from the Natufian culture was discovered at Ain Sakhri, which sets the beginning of this imagery at nearly 10,000 B.C. The hieros gamos was celebrated in erotic hymns at Sumer (Inanna's stories and hymns were published by Diane Wolkstein and Samuel Noah Kramer, 1983). A strong continuity of hieros gamos persists in myth and ritual throughout history and well into the 20th century. A ritual mating with the local goddess has been the basis of inauguration of each of the 150 tribal kings reigning in Ireland in the first centuries A.D. The earliest traditions about Medb identify her as the Goddess whose wedding periodically created a king at Tara.[60] A similar tradition of kings mating with the Goddess is known in Scandinavia prior to the late 5th century A.D. There is also the celebration of Beltane in the British Isles and the marriage of a May Day Queen and King in rituals practiced in Germany in the 19th and early 20th centuries.

The Enthroned Goddess of Nature and Community

All major goddesses are called "Mistress," "Lady," "Queen." From the Early Neolithic, the Snake Goddess wears a crown, a symbol of her omnipotence and omniscience which still exists in 20th century folklore. Other goddesses of the Neolithic, particularly the Bird Goddess, have beautiful hairdos, turbans, or ribbons around their heads. The Bird Goddess wears a necklace and sometimes a crown (see fig. 7-14), while her assistants or attendants are more modestly portrayed.

The Goddess exemplifies the infinite powers and patterns of nature expressed through plant, animal, and human life. Greek and all other European mythologies describe the Goddess as lawgiver, who insured a high standard of moral conduct among her followers. She condemned lying, the breaking of promises, and lack of proper respect for sacred things and for people. One cannot deceive the Goddess. In Baltic mythology, the Earth Mother actually punishes people by devouring them or not accepting them after death. In the Basque area, the Goddess acted as a guardian of the law codes, investing established custom with an inviolable sacredness. As lawgiver, she presided over communal life and watched to see that her commandments were kept.[61]

In the archeological record and in myth, the Goddess is portrayed surrounded by a council or attendants. In temples and temple models in which many figurines are found, one is often shown to be the most important, incised or painted with insignia and symbols representing the Goddess herself, while others are smaller in size and are less carefully rendered (see fig. 7-9). At Poduri in northeastern Romania, in a vase from around 4800–4600 B.C., twenty-one figurines were discovered, probably ready to be placed on an altar. Their lack of arms, their snake-shaped heads, and the snakes coiling over their abdomens suggest that they represent the Snake Goddess and her attendants; only one of them has an arm raised to her face, a gesture of power. The twenty other figurines are large, medium, and small, indicating a gradation of age or perhaps of function within the council. This pattern repeats throughout the Neolithic, Copper Age, and Minoan Bronze Age, suggesting the existence of a permanent council or college of priestesses within the realm of a certain goddess. The Goddess has a number of priestesses in Minoan art, in Greece and Rome, and in existing folklore. The Basque Vulture Goddess does not appear alone but is surrounded by other vultures, and the Baltic Ragana flies as a crow in a large group of Raganas of lesser importance. The huge white and crowned Snake Goddess appears in tales surrounded by hundreds of other snakes.

The continuous tradition of the Goddess's association with a group of priestesses implies that in secular life the queen and kin-mother also had a council of advisers. At Knossos in Crete, the throne room was adjoined by a smaller room with a series of low benches around the walls which would seat nine people. In view of the sanctity attached to the number nine, it is quite possible that this was where the council of women conferred, where decisions were made. This tradition survived in historical Athens where functions connected with agriculture were exercised exclusively by women, where the chief civic female functionary, the "queen archon," was assisted by a council of matrons.[62] Even into the early 20th century the Basque priestess, *serora*, and her female helpers inhabited caves and grottos where they were consulted as oracles and prophetesses. Their status was higher than that of the Catholic priest. The structural linkages between the *serora* and her helpers and the Goddess and her helpers is evident.[63]

Early historic records speak of sisterhoods of virgins or enchantresses who could exercise great power through incantation, singing, and dancing. Two recently discovered Gaulish inscriptions are of great interest. One mentions the power of women through the incantation, *brixtia anderon*; the other represents a statement about an indigenous sisterhood of enchantresses.[64] Assemblies of nine muses or priestesses are well known in ancient Greece, such as the Nine Wild Muses of Mount Parnassus, Mount Helicon, and Mount Olympus. They were representations of the Goddess worshiped on these mountains.[65] Pomponius Mela in the 1st century A.D. describes a community of nine virgins living on the island of Sena (Sein) off the coast of Brittany to whom he attributed magical prophetic powers, such as arousing the waves of the sea by their singing, changing animals into whatever they wished, curing incurable sicknesses, and predicting the future. Strabo in the early 1st century A.D., citing Posidonius, refers to a college of priestesses living on an island in the territory of Samnitae who, like the Greek maenads, participated in the ecstatic worship of a god akin to Dionysos. No mortal men were allowed on the island.[66] A community of priestesses or enchantresses reappears in medieval literature as the nine witches of Gloucester in the Welsh tale of Peredur, and the thrice nine women who welcome the voyager in the Irish Immram Brain.[67] Groups of fairies, it is believed to this day, dance in circles or around stone rings creating tremendous energy. Men are not allowed in these circles, and if they happen to stumble into a ring dance, they are punished by instant death. Vestiges of the existence through history of the collective power of priestesses and fairies unquestionably stem from prehistoric traditions.

Women's rituals inherited from matristic cultures in which men are not allowed are not only expressed in fairy dances, but also in essential birth and agricultural rituals performed in historic times as well as in our own times in patriarchal societies. The examples are many. It will suffice here to mention one of the most characteristic rituals from ancient Greece: the festival of Demeter Thesmophoria, a birth and earth fertility ritual known to us from epigraphic evidence and from an account by Aristophanes. Every year in the administrative districts called the *demes*, women choose from among themselves those who will preside over the ceremonies and exercise power in the Thesmophoria. The chosen ones preside over the assembly held on the days established by tradition and see to it that what is sanctioned by custom is carried out. The citizen-women form a council and decisions are voted by majority rule. They vote alone, without men. At the Thesmophoria, no male eyes are tolerated.[68]

The following can be said of how religion and myth mirrors the social structure of Old Europe: prehistoric and historic evidence strongly supports the existence of a matrilineal structure. The image of a Goddess and her council who guided the life of a community reflects the role of an honored elder, the great clan mother, who was assisted by a council of women. Although these sisterhoods or communities of women were endowed with great power, they seem to have functioned as collective entities, not as autocracies.

Judging from mythologies and surviving kinship terminology, the brother of the queen (or priestess, as representative of the Goddess), rather than her consort, played a major role. In Neolithic times, the queen-priestess presided over agriculture and religious life. Her brother may have assumed leadership responsibilities (but not dominating control) over public works, craft organization, and trade.

Survival of Old European Matriliny in the Bronze Age and in Historic Times

A strong indication for the existence of matriliny in Old Europe is the historic continuity of matrilineal succession in the non-Indo-European societies of Europe and Asia Minor such as the Minoan, Etruscan, Pelasgian, Lydian, Lykian, Carian in western Turkey, Basque in northern Spain and southwest France, and the Picts in Britain before the Celts. This influence is also found in Indo-European-speaking societies—Celts, Teutons, Slavs, and Balts—who absorbed matricentric and matrilineal traditions from the rich substratum of Old European populations.

Traces of matrilineal practices have been found in recent centuries in peripheral areas of the west and north of Europe, and in the Aegean islands. In a number of islands, including Lesbos, Lemnos, Naxos, and Kos, matrilineal succession to real property was the rule at the end of the 18th century A.D. The facts were reported by an English traveller, John Hawkins, who wrote: "In the large number of the islands, the eldest daughter takes as her inheritance a portion of the family house, together with its furniture, and one third of the share of the maternal property, which in reality in most of these cases constitutes the chief means of subsistence; the other daughters, when they marry off in succession, are likewise entitled to (a portion of) the family house and the same share of whatever property remains. These observations were applicable to the islands of Mytilin (Lesbos), Lemnos, Scopelo, Skyros, Syra, Zea Ipsera, Myconi, Paros, Naxia, Siphno, Santorini and Cos, where I have either collected my information in person or had obtained it through others."[69]

The matrilineal system in the 18th century, and in some islands up to the 20th century, certainly did not emerge in these late centuries but must have continued unbroken from prehistory. Its persistence is found in areas not touched by the Indo-Europeans, where the process of Indo-Europeanization was weak,

or where the Old European substratum was very strong, as in Greece and Etruria. In the same areas where matrilineality survived, a non-Indo-European language persisted into historic times. A non-Greek language, for example, was still spoken in parts of Crete and the Aegean islands as late as the 4th century B.C.

We shall proceed with the Minoan culture of Crete, then move to western Asia Minor and the Aegean islands, then to the Etruscans and Rome, and across the Mediterranean to western and northern Europe.

Minoan Crete

Old European culture continued on the island of Crete for several millennia longer than on the mainland and reached a magnificent flowering in the first half of the 2nd millennium B.C. The Minoan culture was described by Sir Leonard Wooley as "the enchantment of the fairy world," and "the most complete acceptance of the grace of life the world has ever known."[70]

The Minoan communities were generally small scale, although by the end of the 3rd millennium B.C. the population at Knossos approximated 18,000. The country was governed by a theacracy (rule of the Goddess). This culture declined after the middle of the 2nd millennium B.C., not from internal strife, but as a result of natural catastrophy in combination with the gradual incursions onto the island of patriarchal, Indo-European-speaking Mycenaeans.

Cretan burial rites of the Early Minoan period (3rd millennium B.C.) were not unlike those of the western European megalithic culture. Communal burials, usually in a circular tomb called *tholos*, were practiced, and from the provision of ceremonial space in front of the elaborate entrances to the tombs, it seems that funerary rites with feasting in both areas may have been similar. The study by K. Branigan has shown that these tombs are identified as burial places of extended families with a living membership of about twenty persons. The extended family was an important social unit in this society, and at many sites, two or three tombs are built immediately alongside one another. Since these are contemporary with each other, they seem to represent adjacent burial places of two or three extended families. The tombs are linked with settlements and are no more than ten to fifteen meters away. It was noticed that one tomb is architecturally superior to the others, which suggests that one extended family claimed primacy or pre-eminence and that communities already knew a degree of social ranking.[71]

Although this culture is called Minoan, its flowering in the early 2nd millennium B.C. had nothing to do with king Minos, whose legendary appearance actually came during the demise of this great culture. The palaces were not built by kings and were not administrative centers for a ruler, but were palace temples where elaborate religious rituals took place within a theacratic system. Contrary to the subsequent Mycenaean influence, Minoan culture was primarily feminine inspired.

From the first discovery of this culture at Knossos in the beginning of the 20th century, the self-possessed independence and confidence of women was noticed. Frescoes, to the great astonishment of the scholarly world, revealed beautiful, elegant women dressed in exquisite costumes, frequently bare breasted. They are shown mixing freely with men in festivals, riding in chariots driven by female charioteers, and participating as athletes during the ritual bull games. Frescoes from Thera (sixty kilometers north of Crete) show women presiding at large naval festivals, standing on balconies overseeing processions of young men who are carrying an animal for sacrifice. (FIGURE 9–16) There are great numbers of outstanding women portrayed as priestesses and goddesses, and it cannot be doubted that women maintained a centrality in religion until Mycenaean times. The seat of honor in the throne room at Knossos was most likely the seat of the highest representa-

FIGURE 9–16

FIGURE 9–16 Detail of a wall painting from Akrotiri, Thera. A prominent woman, perhaps a queen, stands on a balcony with her right arm upraised, overseeing and blessing a naval festival. She is shown larger than the male figures; a boy is behind her. Thera (West House, room 5, southern wall frieze). 16th cent. B.C.

tive of the Goddess. The throne was decorated with a circle and a crescent, and griffins were painted on the wall at each side. The griffin acted as guardian to the Goddess, as shown on a fresco from Thera (see fig. 7–8).

Men also appear in Minoan art but never as priests or kings, and only a very few images have been interpreted as depicting a god. Men are usually shown engaged in a variety of occupations such as cup bearers, pages, musicians, harvesters, craftsmen, and sailors. In the naval festival portrayed in the miniature fresco from Thera, sailors can be distinguished as representing at least several categories: simple oarsmen, captain, assistants to a captain, and important males in long cloaks sitting in the cabin of the boat. (FIGURE 9–17) The miniature fresco also reveals rustic people wearing fur or skin coats, while young men participating in rituals are shown in the nude or with hip belts. Men's long robes seem to denote advanced age and social status. The important women and priestesses of adult age in Thera, as in Crete, always wore long, flounced skirts.

Marriage in Crete was matrilocal and this custom continued late into the historical period. Matrilocal marriage is described by Strabo in the 1st century B.C. and is witnessed by the laws inscribed on the walls of the temple of Gortyna. From these we learn that a woman, on marriage, retained full control of her property and had the right of divorce at her pleasure. Also, the mother's brother occupied an important position and was responsible for bringing up her children.

Sparta

At Sparta, in the center of the Peloponnese, where the inhabitants were a mixture of Indo-European warrior clans with the indigenous prepatriarchal peoples, women's position was similar to that in Crete. As Briffault remarked, "Spartan women were entirely unrestricted in their social and sexual relations. Virginity was not demanded of a bride. Children born out of wedlock were called 'virgin born' and were regarded as equal to those born in wedlock. The

FIGURE 9–17

FIGURE 9–17 Thera: Drawing of the best preserved ship of the fleet from the S. frieze, room 5, West House. 16th cent. B.C. Note various categories of represented men: captain, assistants to a captain, males in long cloaks in the cabin, and oarsmen.

Spartans practiced fraternal polyandry, and their marriage was matrilocal."[72] The clan in the area of Corinth, according to Herodotus, observed the custom of "marrying and giving in marriage among themselves," a clearly endogamous system. The name of the clan is Bakchidai, i.e., a matrilineal clan.[73] The typical Greek clan name has the patronymic termination -idas, -ides, based on the element id-, which in Greek is feminine. It follows that in early times the women and not the men had been regarded as delineators of the clan.

The survival of a matrilineal system can be traced in the very structure of Greek speech and legal customs. In Homer, a sharp distinction was drawn between a brother from the same mother, and a brother with the same father but not the same mother. The ordinary appellation for brother continued to be adelphos, which means "from the womb," and is therefore a relic of the time when the relationship of a brother was reckoned on the mother's side only.[74] The Greek adelphos and adelphe, "brother" and "sister," are without parallel in the other Indo-European languages.[75]

Western Asia Minor and the Aegean Islands

Herodotus described the Lycians of western Turkey as having practiced matrilineal descent. He further wrote: "Their customs are in part Cretan and in part Carian. But they have one which is their own and shared by no other men; they take their names not from their fathers but from their mothers; and when one is asked by his neighbor who he is, he will say that he is the son of such a mother, and recount the mother of his mother."[76] When Plutarch mentioned the Lycian clan, he called them Ioxidai or Ioxides, implying that the feminine form (Ioxidai) was the proper one by giving it first.[77] Succession too was matrilineal since daughters inherited in preference to sons. The basic unit of society, attested by sepulchral inscriptions, was the matrilineal household. Some of these inscriptions contain a formula of the familiar matrilineal type: "Neiketes son

of Parthena . . . Neiketes son of Lalla . . . Euteches, father unknown. . . ."[78]

The Carians and Leleges both belonged to the Anatolian seaboard and the distinction between them is somewhat indefinite. We learn from Herodotus that at the time of the Persian War his native Halikarnassos was under a Carian queen, Artemisia. Her mother was a Cretan, and though she had a grown-up son she retained the royal power. Her domain extended to the adjacent islands of Kos, Kalymnos, and Nisyros, and when Xerxes of Persia invaded Greece, she furnished him with a contingent of five warships, commanded by herself. At the battle of Salamis when the Persian threat had begun, her flagship was hotly pursued by the Athenians, but she saved herself by adroitly turning about and ramming a Persian vessel.[79]

The Ionian conquerors of Miletos took Carian wives who, resenting the slaughter of their menfolk, refused to eat with their new husbands or call them by their names.[80] At Teos, another Ionian settlement, a list of annual magistrates was discovered. In eleven cases out of twenty-five, the clan and village had the same name. This means that the identity of the two units was still largely intact and, therefore, their native institutions must have been preserved.

The Pelasgoi survived still speaking their own language at several places in the north Aegean—Akte on the Macedonian coast, Kreston somewhere in the same region, and Lemnos on the Propontis. They are also recorded in Samotraike, the Troad, Lydia, Lesbos, and Chios.[81] The Pelasgoi of Lemnos figure in one of the Greek legends. After setting sail from Thessaly in quest of the Golden Fleece, the Argonauts put in at Lemnos which was then "ruled by women" under Queen Hipsipyle.

Matrilineal Succession of the Etruscans and the Roman Monarchy

The Etruscans are known to have been matrilineal. In bilingual inscriptions, the father's name is inserted in the Latin version only, while the mother's name, always given in Etruscan, is sometimes omitted in the Latin. It was Bachofen in the mid-19th century A.D. who first noticed that the status of Etruscan women, in the archaic period at least—7th to 5th centuries B.C.—was surprisingly high in comparision to that of Greek and Roman women.[82]

Tomb paintings and inscriptions have told us more of the Etruscans' luxurious style of life and the considerable role played by women.[83] Accounts of Greek and Roman writers give further evidence of these facts and, more importantly, they indicate how the high status of women frightened them. Their writings express the view that the relations between men and women and their differing attitudes toward sex create a conflict, since strong women were seen as a threat to the power of the state. Historian Larissa Bonfante suggests that Rome's first "cultural shock" was that she was becoming too much like the Etruscan city that confronted her across the Tiber and from whom she took so much external culture—letters, the arts, and symbols of royalty. For the Romans, the Etruscans would always represent "the others."[84]

What we know best about the Etruscans is from their art and literature which express the freedom and power of women in their society. Theopompus, the Greek historian of the 4th century B.C., was startled by this. According to his report, Etruscan women took great care of their bodies, often exercising in the nude with men and with each other, which was not considered shameful. They were very beautiful, and it was not uncommon for them to recline publicly at dinner with men other than their husbands. These women liked to drink, and they even took part in the toasting traditionally reserved for men at Greek symposia. Most shocking of all, they raised all their children, according to Theopompus, whether or not they knew who the fathers were. The fact of raising their children without their husbands' formal recognition was probably connected with their right to own property.

In dress, too, there was less distinction between men and women. An outsider could easily think that Etruscan women dressed like men. In the late 6th century, for example, they wore mantles and high shoes, symbols of citizenship and rank. All these marks of equality shocked the Greeks, who took them as signs of immorality.

Each of the last three Etruscan kings of Rome owed his throne to an Etruscan woman. The individual names of Etruscan women indicated their different and legal social status. In contrast, a Roman woman bore no name of her own. She was known first as her father's daughter and later as her husband's wife. Succession from father-in-law to son-in-law in Roman society was a recognized mode of matrilineal inheritance in which queenship passed from mother to daughter. Furthermore, we hear from Greek historians that the Etruscans and prehistoric Athenians had "wives in common" and "their children did not know their own fathers." In such a system, the woman is free to marry the man of her choice, or as many as she pleases, and she retains control of her children without regard to their paternity. On this basis, George Thomson in his work on ancient Greek society made the assumption that group marriage was combined with common ownership in prehistoric Aegean societies.[85]

Western and Northern Europe

In western Europe, several cultural islands, like strongholds, have continued Old European traditions throughout the millennia: the Basques in the western Pyrenees of northern Spain and southwestern France, the Iberians in southeast and eastern Spain, and the Picts in the Scottish Highlands. The Celts, Teutons, and Balts also inherited a great deal of Old European features in their social structure.

The Basque language is a relic of the ancient western European languages, and is not only pre-Latin but is also pre-Indo-European. It is the only indigenous language to survive the invasions and cultural influences of the last 3,000 years.[86] The Basque people have shown a remarkable ability to integrate influences without losing their cultural identity. Indeed, they are the great exception to all the laws of European political and cultural history.[87] There is no doubt that the Basques are living Old Europeans and their roots are sought even in earlier times. Proponents of the Upper Paleolithic origins of the Basques point to the persistence of the racial characteristics of the Cro-Magnon type and to the persistent traditions of mythological themes.[88] The religion of the Goddess, the usage of a lunar calendar, matrilineal laws of inheritance, and agricultural work performed by women continued here into the early 20th century.[89] The high status attributed to the Basque woman in law codes, as well as to her place as inheritor, judge, and arbitrator in pre-Roman, medieval, and modern times has been widely discussed for over a century.[90] The codes of the French Basque region reflect a system of laws governing succession in which there was total equality between the sexes. Exceptions to this norm were found only among the tiny noble class of Labourd and to a limited extent among some of the nonrural houses of Soule. In the indigenous Basque system, no preference was given to the male over the female. Up until the eve of the French Revolution, the Basque woman was truly "the Mistress of the House," hereditary guardian, and head of the lineage.[91] "Among the Iberians," according to Strabo in the 1st century B.C., "the men bring dowries to the women. With them the daughters alone inherit property. Brothers are given away in marriage by their sisters. In all their usages, their social condition is one of gynaecocracy."[92]

The Picts are another Old European group surrounded by Indo-European speakers who preserved the matrilineal laws, Goddess's religion, and Her symbols. Among the Picts, the transmission of property was exclusively matrilineal; an inherited estate passed to the children of the daughter, in the case of siblings. Matrilineal kinship of the Picts lasted until A.D. 842. Women did not leave home on marriage, a practice that survived in the Scottish Highlands even into the early 20th century.[93]

Archeological finds have revealed incredibly rich graves of Celtic princesses from the Hallstatt and La Tène periods, 7th to 4th century B.C., in southern France and the Rhineland. This has roots in earlier local traditions, together with the preservation of the worship of the Goddess and matrilineal succession in all Celtic territories. Early historians have also left ample remarks on the high status of Gaulish women. The historian Diodorus Siculus, writing in the 1st century B.C., gives us a description of Gaulish women which states that they were "not only equal to their husbands in stature, but they rival with them in strength as well."[94] We also know that the Britons of the 1st century A.D. had powerful queens. One of the most impressive figures described by Dio Cassius is Boudicca, widow of Prasutagus, who resisted the Romans and launched a revolt for the seizing of her inheritance: "She was huge of frame, terrifying of aspect.... A great mass of bright red hair fell to her knees: she wore a great twisted golden torc, and a tunic of many colors, over which was a thick mantle, fastened by a brooch."[95] Later evidence from Britain and Ireland supports the view that Gaulish noblewomen had personal prestige and the right to possess property, despite the patriarchal Indo-European legal system. From the legendary account of the founding of Marseilles, it can be seen that Gaulish women could choose their own spouses.[96]

Irish traditional narratives show that marriage was essentially matrilocal in which the wife or mistress retained superiority. In the literature of the Irish and British Celts, heroes are represented, as in the archaic Greek sagas, as leaving their homes to seek an heiress in some foreign tribe whom they could marry and with whom they would share dominion over her estates. Ancient laws of Ireland and Wales reveal an important role of the mother's brother who represented the maternal kin.[97] There can be no doubt that matrilineal succession was the immemorial rule with Celtic speaking peoples.

The Old European survival of matriliny is equally well attested in Scandinavian and German regions. The account given by Tacitus in *Germania* in the 1st century B.C. says that "the sons of a sister have the same position as regards their uncle as with their father." Researchers agree that Germanic matrilineal social organization inherited from the Old European substratum survived until the historical period.[98] The Chauci have been characterized as a free peasant society enjoying, until the first century A.D., a balanced social structure, reflected in the equality of property ownership.[99] For millennia, the maternal relationship was regarded as more important than the paternal. According to the laws of the Thuringians, if a man died without children, his property passed to his sister or his mother; similarly in Burgundy. Ample evidence confirms that property and titles in royal houses were transmitted through the women. Saxon aspirants to the throne did not consider that they had fully established their claim until they had married the queen. Briffault's *The Mothers* gives us a number of examples from various Germanic tribes of matrilineal succession. It was usual for the kingdom to be inherited by marrying the queen or a royal princess. Among the Scandinavians the kingdom passed to the daughters and to their husbands as late as the 8th century. In the oldest Nordic and Germanic documents men are often referred to by the names of their mother without mention of the father as in the non-Indo-European tribes of the Aegean area. The use of the word *Geschwister* for "sibling," suggests the emphasis on female offspring.

The culture of the Baltic speakers, Prussians, Lithuanians, and Latvians farther east along the Baltic Sea coast is a true blend of Old European and Indo-European social systems and religions. The Indo-European patriarchy is diluted here by Old European elements of matriliny, matrilocality, matricentrality. The Old Prussian term for grandmother was *ane* (compare with the Old Irish *anu* or *ana* for "old hag" and "guardian of the dead"). The important role of the moth-

er's and wife's brother, as well as traces of endogamy and trial marriage, are well attested in Latvian and Lithuanian folklore.[100] The matricentric pantheon of goddesses among the Balts is as strongly preserved as among the Basques. The Slavic culture is equally replete with matricentric elements, with goddesses preserved in Slavic folklore and folk art as they are in the Baltic and Basque cultures.[101]

In conclusion, the sources from Herodotus in the 5th century B.C. to Strabo in the 1st century A.D. speak of: 1) matrilineal structure, inheritance in the female line, successor of the throne in the female line (queenship passed from mother to daughter); 2) endogamy, matrilocal marriage and group marriage combined with common ownership; 3) metronymy (naming through the mother, father not recognized); 4) importance of the queen's brother, no husband (only a consort); 5) the general high status of women, particularly in Minoan and Etruscan societies.

Conclusion

Summing archeological, historical, linguistic, and religious evidence, we visualize Old European society organized around a theacratic, communal temple community, and a higher female status in religious life. This was an endogamous society guided by a highly respected elder—Great Mother of the clan and her brother or uncle, with a council of women as a governing body. The structure was matrilineal, with succession to leadership and inheritance within the female line.

10

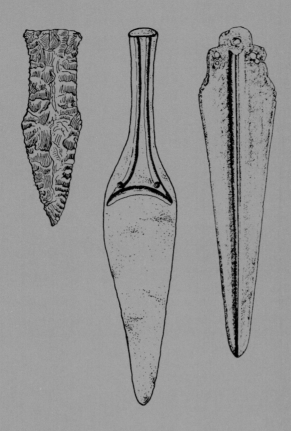

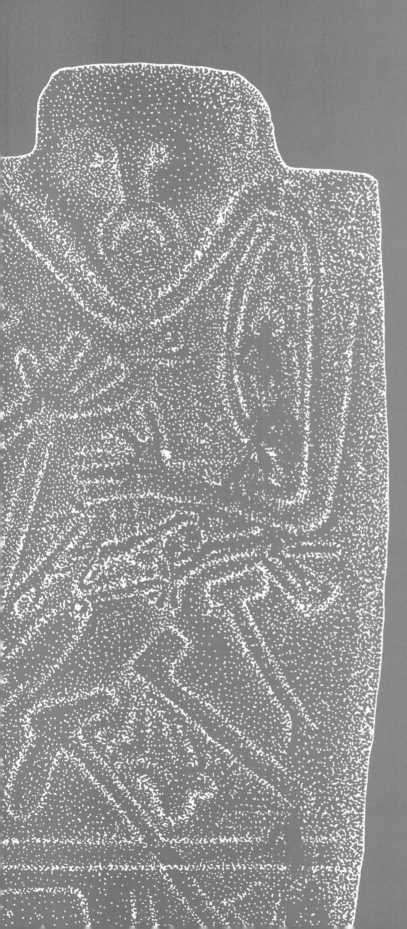

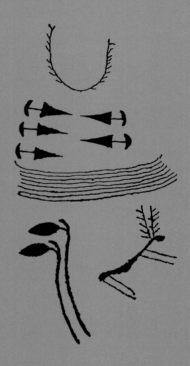

The collapse of Old Europe coincides with the process of Indo-Europeanization of Europe, a complicated transformative process leading to a drastic cultural change reminiscent of the conquest of the American continent. Archeological evidence, supported by comparative Indo-European linguistics and mythology, suggests a clash of two ideologies, social structures and economies perpetrated by trauma-inducing institutions. The Proto- or Early Indo-Europeans, whom I have labeled "Kurgan" people, arrived from the east, from southern Russia, on horseback. Their first contact with the borderland territories of Old Europe in the Lower Dnieper region and west of the Black Sea began around the middle of the 5th millennium B.C. A continuous flow of influences and people into east-central Europe was initiated which lasted for two millennia.

Following this collision of cultures, Old Europe was transformed, and later European prehistory and history became a "marble cake" composed of non-Indo-European and Indo-European elements. The subsequent existence of a very strong non-Indo-European linguistic and mythological substratum cannot be overlooked. To begin to understand this complex situation, it is necessary to start thinking in terms of the social and symbolic structures of cultures.

In this chapter I shall discuss the Kurgan culture of the Volga-Ural and North Pontic regions in relation to Old Europe; its influence on, infiltrations into, and destruction of the floruit of the Old European civilization. Linguistic evidence suggests that the original Indo-European homeland had to be located between the areas occupied by the Finno-Ugric, Semitic, and Caucasian linguistic families. A discussion of this problem is beyond the scope of this book and, in my belief, beyond the

reach of adequate archeological sources. The materials of the Volga-Ural interfluve and beyond the Caspian Sea prior to the 7th millennium B.C. are, so far, not sufficient for ethnographic interpretation. More substantive evidence emerges only around 5000 B.C. We can begin to speak of "Kurgan people" when they conquered the steppe region north of the Black Sea around 4500 B.C.

The Russian word "kurgan" (itself borrowed from the Turkish) means literally a "barrow" or "tumulus" and the term "Kurgan tradition" was introduced by the author in 1956 as a blanket term for the culture of these seminomadic pastoralists who built round funeral mounds.[1]

No weapons except implements for hunting are found among grave goods in Europe until c. 4500–4300 B.C., nor is there evidence of hilltop fortification of Old European settlements. The gentle agriculturalists, therefore, were easy prey to the warlike Kurgan horsemen who swarmed down upon them. These invaders were armed with thrusting and cutting weapons: long dagger-knives, spears, halberds, and bows and arrows.

The Kurgan tradition represents a stark contrast to the civilization of Old Europe which was, in the main, peaceful, sedentary, matrifocal, matrilineal, and sex egalitarian. The Kurgans were a warlike, patriarchal, and hierarchical culture with distinctive burial rites that included pit graves with tent- or hutlike structures of wood or stone, covered by a low cairn or earthen mound. Their economy was essentially pastoral with a rudimentary agriculture and seasonal, transient settlements of semi-subterranean houses.

The Kurgan tradition became manifest in Old European territories during three waves of infiltration: I at c. 4400–4300 B.C., II at c. 3500 B.C., and III soon after 3000 B.C. This chronology does not represent the evolution of a single group but of a number of various steppe peoples who shared a common tradition, extending over broad temporal and spacial parameters. Kurgan I people were from the Volga steppe; Kurgan II, who were culturally more advanced, developed in the North Pontic area

between the Lower Dniester and the Caucasus mountains; Kurgan III people were again from the Volga steppe.

Russian archeologists use the terms "early Yamna" for Kurgan I; "Mikhailovka I" or "Maikop" culture for Kurgan II; and "late Yamna" for Kurgan III. (Yamna comes from yama, "pit," i.e., "pit grave" under a barrow.)

The livelihood and mobility of the Kurgan people depended on the domesticated horse, in sharp contrast to the Old European agriculturalists to whom the horse was unknown. Pastoral economy, growing herds of large animals, horse riding, and the need for male strength to control the animals must have contributed to the transition from matrism to armored patrism in southern Russia and beyond at the latest around 5000 B.C. (Although the accurate date of this process as yet is difficult to establish, it certainly started much earlier than 4000 B.C., the date used for the transition to patrism and violence in Saharasia caused by the pressures of severe desertification; see Demeo 1991.)

The Kurgan Pastoralists of South Russia and Their Extension to the Eastern Ukraine

The Domestication of the Horse

The large horses of the Pleistocene became extinct during the drastic climatic changes that followed the last glacial period. The medium-sized horses that survived belong to one single species, *Equus ferus Boddaert,* and can be divided into two subspecies, the *tarpan* (*Equus ferus gmelini Antonius*) and the *taki* (*Przewalski* type). Of the two, the tarpan, a small but strongly built animal with a short head, tail, and mane, was domesticated. Small groups of the wild tarpan continued to live in eastern Europe until the end of the 19th century when unbridled hunting caused their extinction.

Horse domestication may have taken place in the area between the eastern Ukraine and the northern Kazakhstan around 5000 B.C. or earlier, most likely at forest edges and close to rivers whose basins were also forested. It is not surprising that the earliest evidence for the presence of the domesticated horse comes from the forest steppe of the Middle Volga basin where a Neolithic economy—stock breeding and small-scale farming—was present from the end of the 7th millennium B.C.

The earliest artifacts associated with the cult of the horse and evidence for horse sacrifice have been discovered in the Middle Volga region from this time, i.e., around 5000 B.C. In the cemetery at S'ezzhee on the bank of the Samara River, district of Kuybyshev, miniature horse figurines were found carved out of flat bone. (FIGURE 10–1) These were perforated, suggesting that they were worn as pendants and must have had symbolic meaning. Horse skulls and long bones were found above the burials in sacrificial hearths.[2] This cemetery predates the Khvalynsk period in the Lower Volga basin, dated by radiocarbon to the first half of the 5th millennium B.C. (see the following section on Khvalynsk).

Bones from a domesticated horse have been analyzed at Dereivka in the Lower Dnieper basin, 70 kilometers from the town of Kremenchug.[3] Dereivka belongs to the Sredniy Stog II group of the Kurgan culture which entered the Dnieper steppe around 4500 B.C. or somewhat earlier (Sredniy Stog I is a Dnieper-Donets site). Fifteen fragments of sexable horse mandibles found at this site were those of young adult or juvenile males, which suggests an advanced stage of domestication.

By the middle of the 5th millennium B.C., large herds of horses were kept in the forest steppe and steppe zone between the Lower Dnieper on the west and northern Kazakhstan. The analysis of animal bones in the settlement at Repin on the bank of the Don River has shown that 80 percent of all domesticated animal bones belonged to the horse.[4] Great numbers of horse bones (more than 100,000) have also been discovered near Petropavlovsk in the northern Kazakhstan in a site having Kurgan I (Early Yamna) affinities. There, horse bones constitute about 90 percent of all domesticated animal bones.[5]

One motive for the domestication of the horse may have been its use for meat and milk which continues among steppe peoples to the present day. Of greater importance, however, was its ability to be ridden, which must have occurred from the initial domestication. Although cattle, sheep, and goats can be easily herded on foot, riding was essential for large-scale horse breeding. Antler-tine cheek pieces, possibly used as bridle equipment, have been found in the Sredniy Stog sites of the middle of the 5th millennium B.C. (six occurred at Dereivka). Pairs of cheek pieces were found in graves or were associated with a ritual pit which included the skull, mandible, and leg bones of a stallion and the skulls and foreparts of two dogs.

The situation of initial domestication may have been similar to a practice known from Siberia several centuries ago. During the 18th century, Russian colonists found pastoralists between the Caspian Sea and the Altai Mountains who practiced little cultivation but kept herds of horses, cattle, sheep, and goats. Their herding was done on horseback

FIGURE 10–1

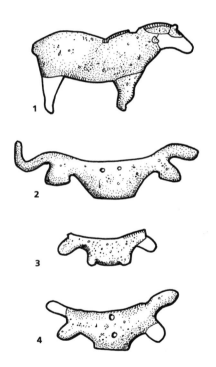

FIGURE 10–1 Earliest sculptures associated with the horse and oxen cult. (1,3) Horse, double-headed horse and (2,4) oxen figurines carved out of bone from the cemetery of S'ezzhee on R. Samara, tributary of Middle Volga, district of Kuybyshev. The pendants with double oxen heads were found in a child's grave under the sacrificial area of horses. Samara culture; early Eneolithic of the Volga region, c. 5000–early 5th mill. B.C. L of horse 11 cm; L of oxen heads 12 cm.

and the horse held a prominent position in their society. Geldings were ridden, and the main herds of horses were kept more or less wild under a stallion whose mares were milked and kept hobbled near the tents.[6]

The bovine remained the main draft animal of the Volga Neolithic as evidenced by figurines of probably yoked oxen (FIGURE 10-1, 2, 4) while the swift horse became the "motor" of transport. This innovation cut traveling time by a factor of five or more, nullifying whatever territorial boundaries had previously existed. These developments largely affected the exploitation of steppe resources and virtually all other aspects of life. Riding provided the ability to strike out across great distances, instigated cattle-looting or horse-stealing raids, the accumulation of wealth, trading capacities, and the development of violence and warfare. Once the steppe was conquered, it inevitably became a source of outward migration.

Material remains of the first half of the 5th millennium B.C. show that in an enormous territory east of the Don River and between the Middle Volga, the Caucasus Mountains, and the Ural Mountains there spread a uniform culture. Almost identical ornaments, tools, and weapons in sites thousands of kilometers apart speak for an unprecedented mobility between the tribal groups. The first incursion into the Dnieper steppe by these horse-riding peoples is dated before the middle of the 5th millennium B.C. Not much later, Kurgan I horse-riding warriors appeared in the heart of Europe.

Horse riding changed the course of European prehistory. Coupled with the use of weapons, the mounted warrior became a deadly menace to the peaceful, unarmed agriculturalists. From the middle of the 5th millennium B.C., the swift horse became a carrier of unrest that continued for millennia. If we look back at European history, at the routine massacres by horse-riding Scythians, Sarmatians, Huns, Avars, Romans, Slavs, and Vikings and the horse-drawn chariots of the Celts and those described by Homer—even the Christian Crusaders—

we see how violence, abetted by the rise of the swift horse, became a dominant aspect of life.

Culture Groups in the Forest-Steppe Region of the Middle and Lower Volga Basin

The Volga culture of the 5th millennium B.C., referred to as Eneolithic in Soviet literature (meaning "Copper-Stone Age" or "Chalcolithic"), developed from the local Volga Neolithic culture.[7] Its territory covered the southern zones of the steppe areas between the lower Don, middle Volga, and the lower Ural, bordered by the Caucasus Mountains and the Caspian Sea farther south. The Neolithic and Eneolithic of this large area has been discovered only during the last twenty years, and several regional groups and chronological phases have already been recognized. The Eneolithic is subdivided into three periods: early, middle (or "developed"), and late.

The Samara Period of c. 5000 B.C.

The Early Eneolithic is known as "the Samara culture" in the forest steppe area of the Middle Volga and "the north Caspian culture" in the Lower Volga basin. The discovery, in 1973, of the cemetery of S'ezzhee on the bank of the River Samara, a tributary of the Middle Volga in the district of Kuybyshev,[8] began an understanding of this culture which, until then, was almost entirely unknown. The cemetery was partly destroyed, and the remaining six single graves and one triple grave were in pits, 0.70–1.0 m deep, a few of which were covered with a cairn or a low earthen mound. The striking discovery here was the evidence of horse sacrifice in association with burials and the bone figurines of horses, double-headed horses, and double-headed oxen.

A sacrificial area was uncovered 40 cm below the surface in the central part of the cemetery in which two skulls of horses were found surrounded with broken pots, shell beads, sweet water shells, and harpoons all sprinkled with ochre. Another sacrificial area of this cemetery yielded an accumulation of horse and cattle leg bones. Under the

first sacrificial area, the richest graves of the cemetery were found, several containing children, all lying on a layer of ochre and sprinkled intensively with it. The most outstanding of all was the grave of a 1.5 to 2-year-old child (No. 6) equipped with a long flint dagger (FIGURE 10-2, 1), two flat figurines of double-headed oxen made of boar's tusk (FIGURE 10-1, 2, 4), three spoon-shaped objects with sculptured heads of ducks at the ends, pendants and laminae of shell, a necklace or belt of shell beads, animal teeth, and two large gouges and adzes of polished stone. These grave gifts suggest an upper-class, probably royal, burial. The deposition of a dagger and sculptures in a grave of such a young child is unusual, although symbolic. From later archeological materials and comparative Indo-European mythology, it is known that the dagger and the yoked oxen pulling carts are attributes of the sovereign God of the Shining Sky. It is likely that the sacrifice of horses was associated with the death of a royal male child.

Two figurines of horses (FIGURE 10-1, 1, 3) are from destroyed graves, as are many gouges and adzes of polished stone, large bone spears, daggers, flint points, arrowheads, and scrapers. Daggers were of flint and bone, some as long as 56 cm, which were truly formidable weapons. Flint or quartzite blades were set into shafts of bone on two sides. (FIGURE 10-2, 3)

Pots were not laid in graves but are found mostly in sacrificial areas. S'ezzhee pots were tempered with crushed shells, as all later pottery of Kurgan tradition. Most were made in a truncated egg shape with a narrow end, a flattened base, and a thickened, outwardly turned rim. The whole surface, or just the upper part, was decorated in horizontal or zigzag lines. These were executed by stabbing or stamping, by making comb impressions, and had pitted or "button" designs below the rim. (FIGURE 10-3) Similar pottery occurred in a number of settlements recently discovered between the Lower Don and Lower Ural.[9]

FIGURE 10–2

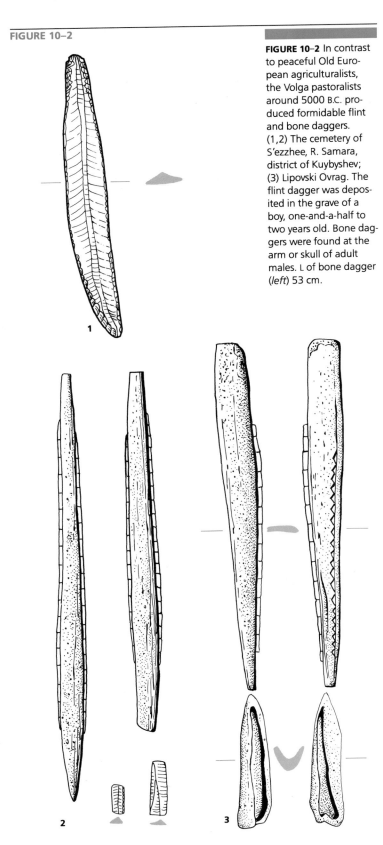

1

2

3

FIGURE 10–2 In contrast to peaceful Old European agriculturalists, the Volga pastoralists around 5000 B.C. produced formidable flint and bone daggers. (1,2) The cemetery of S'ezzhee, R. Samara, district of Kuybyshev; (3) Lipovski Ovrag. The flint dagger was deposited in the grave of a boy, one-and-a-half to two years old. Bone daggers were found at the arm or skull of adult males. L of bone dagger (*left*) 53 cm.

FIGURE 10–3

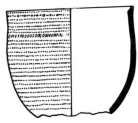

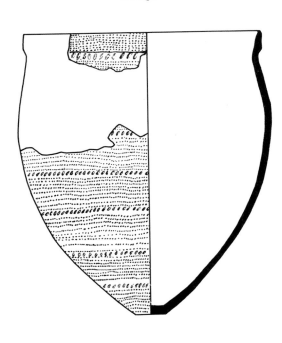

FIGURE 10–3 When painted pottery art florished in southeast and east-central Europe, Volga pastoralists produced primitive egg-shaped beakers with thickened rims decorated with horizontal lines by stabbing, incision, comb impression, and pits. Clay was tempered with crushed shells. S'ezzhee cemetery, district of Kuybyshev, Samara period, c. 5000 B.C. Scale 1:3.

Not much is known about the settlements. All are small and thin layered and have yielded only potsherds, flint scrapers, quartzite tools, and polished stone adzes and gouges. Since there are no radiocarbon dates for the S'ezzhee cemetery or other sites with similar materials, their chronology rests on typological comparisons. For instance, laminae of boar's tusks are known from the Dnieper-Donets sites and from the Samara culture. In the former area they precede the Sredniy Stog II period; in the latter, the Khvalynsk. If Khvalynsk, on the basis of radiocarbon dates, belongs to the first half of the 5th millennium B.C., the Samara culture should be placed around 5000 B.C. or early 5th millennium B.C.

The Khvalynsk Period, First Half of the 5th Millennium B.C.

The "developed Eneolithic" in the Volga basin is represented by the cemetery of Khvalynsk, located on the bank of the Volga in the district of Saratov, excavated by Vasil'ev and others.[10] One hundred and fifty-eight skeletons were unearthed in an area of 30 by 26 m, mostly from single graves, although some held two to five skeletons or more. The dead were buried in pits in a contracted position, lying on their backs with their knees upward. Twelve graves were covered with stone cairns. As in S'ezzhee, sacrificial areas were unearthed with remains of horse, cattle, and sheep sacrifices, while animal bones were also found in graves and deposited separately (leg bones of a horse and a calf, skulls of cattle, and sheep bones). The inventory of grave finds include about forty metal artifacts (rings and spiral rings), large pendants of boar's tusk, bone and shell beads and bracelets, a perforated and polished lugged axe, a schematized horse-head sculpture which was probably a scepter, bifacially retouched flint points and daggers, stone adzes, and bone harpoons. A very similar inventory was brought to light in a grave of a rich individual accidentally discovered in 1929 at Krivoluchie, in the district of Samara. The body lay in a contracted position on ground scattered with ochre and was equipped with a lugged axe of porphyry, six flint points of fine workmanship, a flint dagger, a scraper, bracelets of polished stone and bone, beads of deer teeth, and annular and cylindrical beads of pectunculus shell.[11] (FIGURE 10-4) This individual must have been an important member of the society.

In the south, related finds and burial rituals were discovered at Nalchik in the northern Caucasus in the region of Kabardino-Balkaria. One hundred and twenty-one graves were excavated under a low kurgan, 0.67 m high and 30 m across. The contracted bodies lay in groups of five to eight, on layers of ochre, and were covered with stones. Among the most common grave goods were beads of pectunculus shell, stone, and the teeth of deer, wolf, bear, boar, and other animals, stone or bone bracelets, pendants of boar's tusk, long flint daggers, arrowheads, and points. The latter were bifacially retouched.[12]

The astonishing similarity of grave goods in sites separated by thousands of kilometers suggest the existence of phenomenal mobility and intertribal relationships between Samara and the Caucasus. On the west, sites with related materials extend to the Sea of Azov and on the east to the River Ural. The types of stone tools, weapons, ornaments, and pottery of the Khvalynsk phase continued from the Samara period. The chronology of the Khvalynsk phase is indicated roughly by similarity with the finds of the Sredniy Stog II sites in the Lower Dnieper basin, dated by radiocarbon and contacts with the Karanovo and Cucuteni cultures to the middle of the 5th millennium B.C. The first radiocarbon dates for the Khvalynsk materials (analyzed by the laboratory of the Ural Institute of Education) fall within the early 4th millennium B.C. When calibrated, they must belong to the period *before* the middle of the 5th millennium B.C.[13]

The Early Yamna Period, Middle of the 5th Millennium B.C.

The "Late Eneolithic" period of the Lower Volga basin is the Early Yamna (Early Pit-grave) culture, characterized by a number of kurgans and settlements. In all respects it is a continuation from the Khvalynsk period. The excavated settlements have revealed the same tradition of ceramic craft and of flint, quartzite, and bone industry, indicating no changes in art or technology. The egg-shaped pots with out-turned rims (FIGURE 10-5), stone-tool kits dominated by adzes, gouges, and weapons—flint arrowheads, points, and daggers—continued to be produced. The continuity of the material culture is well documented by excavations in the same areas where Khvalynsk sites previously existed—by the settlement of Alekseevo near Khvalynsk, for instance, located on the terrace of a small river, a tributary of the Middle Volga.[14]

Before the discovery of the Samara and Khvalynsk cemeteries of the Volga culture, the Early Yamna kurgans with burials in pits under earthen barrows were considered to be the earliest. Their origin was nebulous. Examples of such Early Yamna kurgans were known from excavations during the fifties and sixties: Berezhnovka I,[15] Politotdel'sk,[16] and Arkhara.[17] Low earthen barrows above pit graves became the most characteristic and universal feature. During the Khvalynsk period, graves were rarely covered with an earthen mound, more often with a stone cairn or a mound which accumulated because of the sacrificial activities above the graves. The earliest earthen kurgans could have started in the Khvalynsk period in the steppe territories and may have existed side by side with flat graves of the forest-steppe region.[18] The kurgan is a feature of the steppe.

The site of this period, in the region between the Lower Don and Lower Ural, is Repin, located on the bank of the Don, excavated in the fifties by I. V. Sinitsyn.[19] This settlement yielded the greatest numbers of pots and horse bones which, as mentioned above, constituted 80 percent of all domesticated animal bones. Ten other sites with similar materials are known now in this region.

Chronologically, the Late Eneolithic follows the Khvalynsk period which belongs to the middle of the 5th millennium B.C. This is the Kurgan I period

FIGURE 10–4

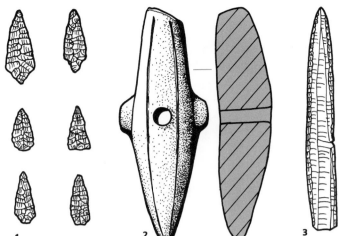

FIGURE 10–4 Prestige weapons from a chieftains's grave: (1) Flint arrowheads. (2) Lugged axe of porphyry. (3) Carefully retouched flint dagger. This grave, found at Krivoluchie, R. Samara, district of Kuybyshev, also included stone and bone bracelets, shell pendants, beads of deer teeth and shell. Scale 1/3. Khvalynsk period, first half 5th mill. B.C.

FIGURE 10–5

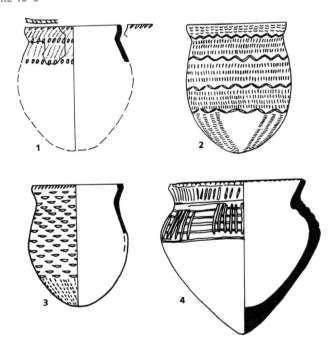

FIGURE 10–5 Pottery from the early "Yamna" (Kurgan I) kurgans in the Lower Volga area. (1) Arkhara. (2) Berezhnovka. (3) Politotdel'sk. (4) Altata. Mid-5th mill. B.C. H (1) 26 cm; (2) 28 cm; (3) 14 cm; (4) 18 cm.

in which the Kurgan people expanded into east-central Europe as far as the Karanovo culture in Bulgaria and in the Danube valley. (FIGURE 10–6)

Kurgan I Sites in the Lower Dnieper Basin: The Emergence of New Types of Burials, Pottery, and Weapons, and the Prominence of Males

The Kurgan people first entered European prehistory during the mid-5th millennium B.C. when they streamed into the basin of the Lower Dnieper and west of the Black Sea. (FIGURE 10–6)

In the Dnieper rapids region, the Dnieper-Donets settlement of Sredniy Stog I was found overlain around 4500 B.C. or earlier by a new cultural complex, Sredniy Stog II, whose people practiced single burial in cairn-covered shaft or cist graves. The bodies in these later graves were supine, either contracted or extended, and were usually supplied with flint daggers, arrowheads, spear points, and beakers with pointed bases in the Kurgan tradition. (FIGURES 10–7A, B) The skeletal remains, moreover, are dolichomesocranial, taller statured, and of a more slender physical type than those of their Dnieper-Donets predecessors,[20] who were of robust Cro-Magnon type. (FIGURE 10–7C).

In contrast to the vegetal-temper characteristic of the earlier Dnieper-Donets ceramics, the pots of these new inhabitants were tempered with crushed shells, and their stamped, pitted, or cord-impressed decorations present a solar motif. Local evolution cannot account for such abrupt changes.

FIGURE 10–6A

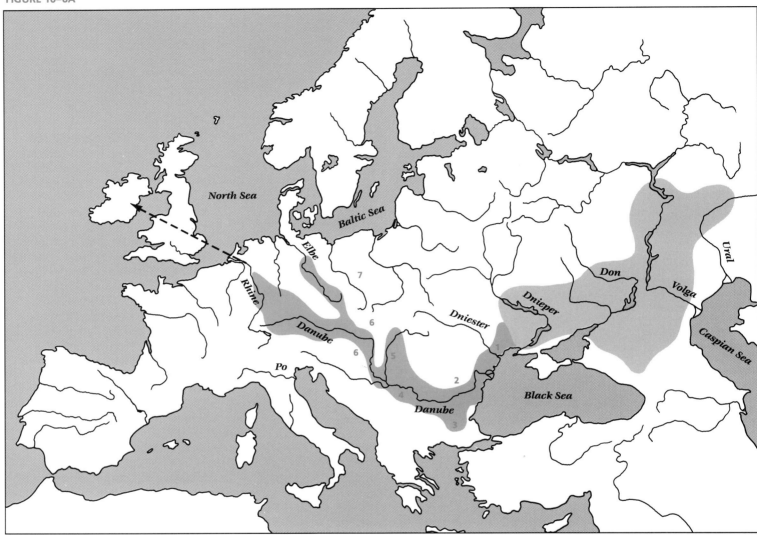

KEY

Origin of Kurgan influence in
Lower Volga-Don steppes and
distribution of Kurgan I (Early
Yamna) culture

Cultures transformed by Kurgan
elements

FIGURE 10–6B

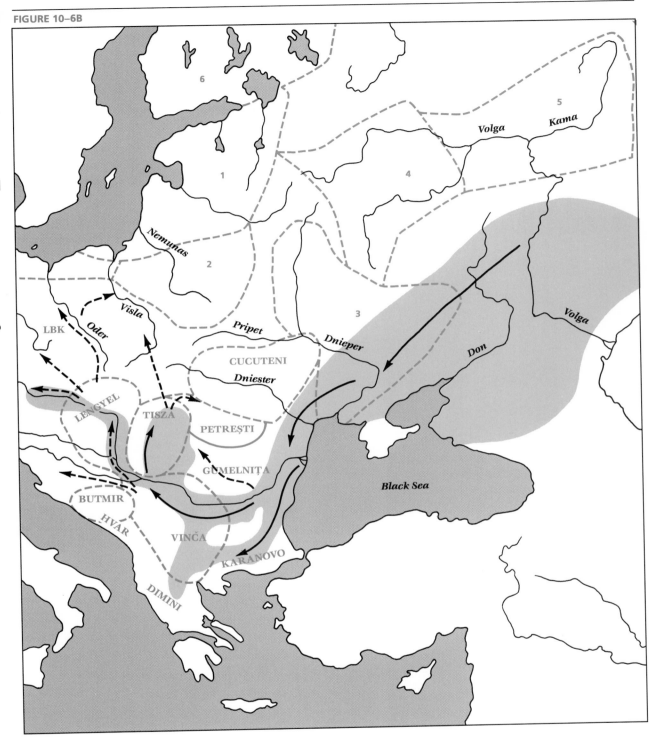

FIGURE 10–6A Kurgan thrust into east-central Europe and its influence on the Danube basin and beyond in the period between 4300 and 3500 B.C. This influence is traceable even in England and eastern Ireland in the middle of the 4th mill. B.C.

FIGURE 10–6B Kurgan I thrust (arrows) into east-central Europe c. 4400–4300 B.C. Wave No. 1 moved from the Lower Volga to the Lower Dnieper region, then infiltrated the territory west of the Black Sea. It spread across the Danubian plain, and also to the Marica plain in Bulgaria, as well as to Macedonia. Following the Danube or crossing Transylvania, it reached the east Hungarian grasslands.

KEY

Distribution of Kurgan I sites

→ Kurgan

---► Old European

Contemporary groups in northern Europe:
1. Narva
2. Nemunas
3. Dnieper-Donets
4. Volosovo
5. Volga-Kama
6. Sperrings

FIGURE 10–7A

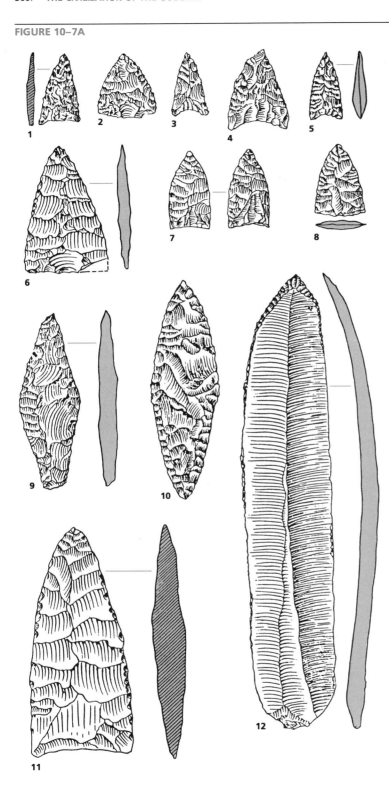

FIGURE 10–7B

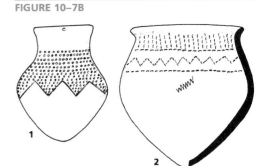

FIGURE 10–7C

FIGURE 10–7A In the Lower Dnieper basin, Kurgan I flint weapons—dagger, arrowheads, spearpoints—and beakers with stabbed decoration appeared in the mid-5th mill. B.C. (1) Aleksandriya. (2–5, 9) Dereivka. (6) Yama. (7) Stril'cha Skela. (8,10, 12) Petro Svistunovo. (11) Goncharivka. H of flint dagger 45 cm; H of largest spearpoint 15 cm.

FIGURE 10–7B Kurgan I (Sredniy Stog II) beakers from the Lower Dnieper region. When viewed from the top, the stabbed decoration forms a solar design. (1) Domotkan. (2) Mayorka. H of larger pot 13 cm.

FIGURE 10–7C Reconstruction of Kurgan I (Sredniy Stog II) male skull from Aleksandriya, Lower Dnieper, mid-5th mill. B.C.

The Sredniy Stog II complex represents an extension of the Volga pastoralists into the Dnieper basin which occurred at the end of the Khvalynsk period. Their horse cult and burials are related to those found in the Middle Volga forest steppe region. At Dereivka in the Lower Dnieper region, tombs contain remains of sacrificed horses and dogs. Graves of a man and woman, perhaps the widow, and of a man and one or two children in one grave, buried at the same time, are frequent. As the Kurgans moved into Old Europe, however, certain influences were inevitably absorbed from the local indigenous cultures. The hundred sites in the lower Dnieper-Don interfluve are primarily cemeteries, and their grave goods reflect this influence and are enriched by copper and gold objects from the west.[21]

Chisels, scrapers, and often long (to 22 cm) pointed flint daggers were placed at the man's hand and even in the cairn above. Occasionally as many as fifteen such daggerlike blades occur in a grave. Bifacially worked spearpoints, triangular flint arrowheads, narrow-butted flint and polished stone axes and daggers form the prototypical Indo-European weaponry. These were usable from horseback and are still seen later in the Bronze and Early Iron ages.

Exceptionally rich male graves include thousands of pectunculus or other shells (originally attached to disintegrated leather or woven belts); copper bead and animal tooth necklaces; shell and copper pendants; spiral arm rings and finger rings of copper; long, thin spiral-headed copper pins and tubes. Presumably, this copper came from the Ai-Bunar mines in central Bulgaria via barter with the Cucuteni. Some of the copper artifacts, however, such as the spiral arm rings, tubes, and shell-shaped pendants, are unparalleled in the west and may have been the product of local craftsmen.

The presence of antler hoes and querns is conclusive proof of agricultural activity in Sredniy Stog II, although no grains have thus far been identified. Awls, picks, polishers, and hammer-axes of bone and antler are found in the settlements in considerable numbers.

At Dereivka, the bones of 55 horses were counted within a settlement of three dwellings, representing 63 percent of the total number of domesticated animal remains. Antler cheek pieces and the depiction of possible bridle equipment on stone sculptures is fairly convincing evidence of horse riding. (FIGURE 10–8) Radiocarbon determinations for Dereivka in calibrated chronology are within the second half of the 5th millennium B.C. (UCLA 1466 : 4570–4150 B.C.; Kiev 466 : 4460–4000 B.C.; Kiev 465 : 4340–3810 B.C.).

The First Wave of Kurgans Into East-Central Europe c. 4400–4300 B.C. and Its Repercussions

The Emergence of Warrior Elite Graves, the Custom of Suttee, and the Horse Cult

After penetrating the Dnieper rapids region and the area north of the Sea of Azov, the Kurgans struck central Europe (see fig. 10–6). Actual Kurgan graves (round barrows with pit graves) found in Moldavia, southern Romania, and east Hungary are eloquent witnesses of these incursions. The earliest Kurgan graves in Moldavia date from Cucuteni A2–A3 phase, c. 4400–4300 B.C. Their graves were almost exclusively for male burials, a distinct contrast to the even ratio of male-female burials in contemporary Old European cemeteries. In contrast to the simple pit graves of Old Europe, the Kurgan tombs were cairn- or earth-covered and were reserved for the warrior elite with their favorite war gear, the spear, bow and arrow, and flint dagger or long knife. (FIGURES 10–7, 10–8, 10–9)

Burial excavations reveal two aspects of Indo-European ideology, found for the first time in east-central Europe at Suvorovo in Moldavia and at Casimcea on the Lower Danube. These two graves demonstrate the Kurgan religious concepts of the worship of the horse as a divine animal and the custom of suttee or sacrifice of the female consort or wife. (FIGURE 10–9) At Suvorovo, a chieftain was buried in a deep rectangular pit

FIGURE 10–8

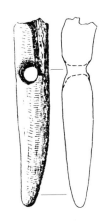
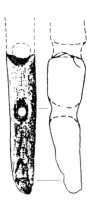

FIGURE 10–8 Antler cheek pieces from Dereivka, Lower Dnieper area. Second half 5th mill. B.C. Scale 1:3.

lined with stones containing a horse-headed scepter of porphyry, his symbol of power, and other objects deemed necessary in afterlife. (FIGURE 10-9, 2, 3) A woman, presumably his widow, was apparently put to death at this time and laid to rest beside her dead lord. Remnants of a garment covered with mother-of-pearl laminae and a necklace of unio shell beads express her relatively elevated station in life, but the only gift accorded her was a flint scraper. The double grave was covered by a massive barrow and surrounded by a circle 13 m in diameter of upright stones. The practice of suttee is also documented in Sredniy Stog II tombs at Yama and Aleksandriya in the Lower Dnieper area of the same period. A Casimcea chieftain in Romania was buried with a horse-head scepter of porphyry, his power symbol, along with five flint axe heads, fifteen arrow points and three daggers. Arrows must have been placed in a skin quiver.

The Suvorovo and Casimcea horse-headed scepters are paralleled elsewhere by finds in Moldavia, southern Romania, Transylvania, Bulgaria, and Macedonia.[22] These wands, with a carved horse head, are strikingly similar to those recovered from the Volga region, the north Caucasian steppe, and northeastern Dagestan.

An important aspect of Indo-European religious ritual was the horse sacrifice, especially in Indic (ašvamedha), Roman (*October Equus*), and Celtic traditions. The archeological indications of equine sacrifice are found at Kherson in the Ukraine where a Kurgan tomb was flanked by a pit containing a horse skull.[23] In the Kurgan cemetery north of the Danube delta, near Odessa, there was a ritual hearth and a central grave containing pairs of horse and bull skulls.[24] In 1986, a complete horse skull cut from the neck was found in a Tiszapolgár pit in northeastern Hungary dating from the end of the 5th millennium B.C. This is the earliest evidence in central Europe.[25]

The Coexistence of Kurgan Pastoralists and Cucuteni Agriculturalists

The Cucuteni civilization survived the first wave of Kurgan incursions intact. Its ceramic tradition continued undisturbed, although Kurgan elements within Cucuteni settlements (1 to 10 percent of Cucuteni A and AB pottery) indicate some sort of interaction between the two groups. This intrusive shell-tempered pottery (referred to by some as Cucuteni C) is nearly identical in shape to that of the Sredniy Stog II

FIGURE 10-9

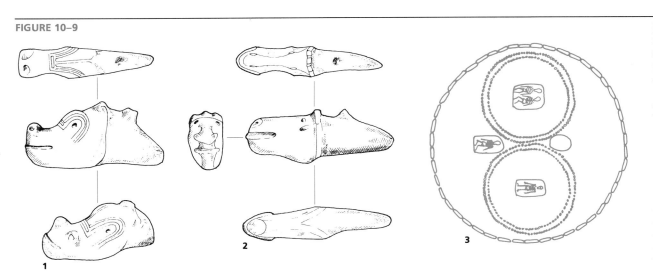

1 **2** **3**

FIGURE 10-9 Horse-head scepters made of semi-precious stone (1,2) appeared in east-central Europe in rich male graves in kurgans after the middle of the 5th mill. B.C. (1) Casimcea, Dobruja, E Romania. L 16 cm. (2) Suvorovo, Moldavia. L 17 cm. (3) Plan of the Suvorovo kurgan including a double grave of a man and a woman, probably a suttee burial, and two other graves prepared at the same time. Diameter of the kurgan 13 m.

(Kurgan I) level of the Lower Dnieper. Petrographic analysis has shown that all Cucuteni and Kurgan (Sredniy Stog II) samples were of similar mineralogical composition. This indicates that both peoples exploited similar clay types, but the respective technology was very different: the Cucuteni ware was well fired, completely oxidized, and without temper, whereas the Kurgan ceramics were low-fired and contained quantities of crushed shell, organic residues, and plant material.[26]

At the time of Cucuteni B in the early 4th millennium B.C., the local populace had relocated into areas more naturally defensible. In a few instances, an additional rampart was built across the river from a settlement. The villages and towns continued to grow, and boundaries of Cucuteni sites in the district of Uman, identified by aerial photography and magnetometry, show towns more than two kilometers long, laid out in a dozen or so concentric elipses radially cut by streets (figs. 3–63 to 3–65).[27] The density of Cucuteni sites indicates no massive dislocations in the wake of the first wave of relatively small groups of Kurgan infiltrators; nor is there evidence of amalgamation of the two groups throughout these approximately 800 years of coexistence, at least not until the mid-4th millennium B.C.

The Displacement and Amalgamation of the Varna, Karanovo, Vinča, and Lengyel Cultures

For the Karanovo-Gumelniţa civilization, the Kurgan incursions proved catastrophic. The small farming villages and townships were easily overrun, and Karanovo groups must have fled from the Lower Danube basin westward.

The Salcuţa group of southwestern Romania took refuge in Transylvanian caves or on Danubian islands.[28] Layer after layer of habitation material similar to Salcuţa IV indicates that the refugees maintained a semblance of cultural identity for yet another four or five hundred years.[29]

In the first half of the 4th millennium B.C., the Black Sea coastal Varna culture was replaced, in east Romania

and Bulgaria, by a Kurganish complex designated as Cernavoda I.[30] The fortified Cernavoda sites, in contrast to the Karanovo-Gumelniţa and Varna settlements on the open plain, were strategically located on high river terraces and consisted of a few small surface or semisubterranean dwellings on sites generally covering no more than 100 by 200 m. These people bred stock (including the horse) and engaged in hunting, fishing, and primitive agriculture, and their antler and bone tools are identical to finds in the steppe north of the Black Sea. They produced gray, badly baked, crushed-shell tempered ceramics, unmistakably related to the Kurganoid wares in Moldavia and in the Ukraine, having the characteristic decor of stab-and-drag, knobs, and impressions of cord, fingernail, and shell. No painted pottery occurs at this time, although substratum influence may account for certain untempered, occasionally brown-slipped and burnished ceramics. Only a few stylized figurines were recovered from Cernavoda I, and Old European symbolic designs had disappeared. No cereal grains were found, despite the presence of antler and bone hoes, grinding stones, and sickle blades. Horse bones were ubiquitous among the remnant heaps of domesticated animals. Tools were predominantly of bone but included maceheads and perforated hammer axes of antler and stone, flint scrapers and knives, a few copper awls and chisels.

The Kurgan disruption of Varna, Karanovo, and Vinča jolted a succession of dislocations in Yugoslavia, Hungary, Czechoslovakia, and as far west as the Upper Danube, Upper Elbe, and Upper Oder basins. Cultural boundaries disintegrated as elements of Vinča populations moved into western Hungary (to eventually become the "Balaton" complex), and into Croatia, Bosnia, and Slovenia (to become the "Lasinja" group).[31] The Lengyel people migrated west and north along the Upper Danube into Germany and Poland. Furthermore, sites of the probable Vinča refugees are also found in regions where no human community had settled since Paleolithic times, such as the eastern Alps and the

central part of Slovenia and Croatian Karst. In this hilly terrain, the location of settlements in the highest places, surrounded by cliffs or girded by rivers, suggest an extreme concern for defense. In a number of sites, traces of rectangular houses built of timber posts and thick clay walls testify to a certain retention of the Vinča architectural traditions. At the same time, caves were also occupied. The occupation of caves and of heretofore uninhabited lands suggests that the movement of the Vinča people to the northwest and west took place in times of stress.

There are no radiocarbon dates for the Balaton-Lasinja I complex. Its chronology is based on a typological relationship with the latest Vinča materials in Yugoslavia. The subsequent phase, labeled Balaton-Lasinja II–III, yielded two C-14 dates, the true age of which falls between 3900 and 3400 B.C., placing the Balaton-Lasinja I complex before 4000 B.C. By the end of the 5th millennium B.C., the Vinča traditions with their temples, figurines and exquisite pottery are no longer found. There is no continuity of habitation on the Vinča mound after c. 4300 B.C.

The Tiszapolgár complex, an offshoot of late Tisza, emerged in northeastern Hungary, eastern Slovakia, and western Transylvania. The continuity of their settlement to the mid-4th millennium B.C. indicates that these people survived and did not merge with the Kurgan culture. However, major social changes are observable and may reflect a Kurgan influence. In contrast to the Tisza and Lengyel pattern, where the majority of known sites are villages, the Tiszapolgár sites (about 100 reported) are cemeteries that suggest small communities of thirty to forty people. This situation does not reflect a normal growth of population as in Lengyel, Vinča, Karanovo, and other groups during the period before the first Kurgan wave. Also, the social role of the male had risen, indicated by several graves of males buried with more than usual care and equipped with status symbols such as maceheads. Significantly, the skeletons of these men were of proto-Europid type, whereas the majority of the population was of Mediterranean type.[32] In the cemetery of Basatanya, of 75 graves (belonging to two phases),[33] a small group of male burials included maceheads, whereas the majority of the burials in this cemetery shows Old European features.[34] In the mountainous east Slovakia, the Tiszapolgár complex persisted through the mid-4th millennium B.C. Several cemeteries of the Lažn'any group in the Carpathian foothills exemplify the last vestiges of this complex, which were finally submerged under the Kurganized Baden culture in the second half of the 4th millennium B.C.[35]

North of Budapest and in western Slovakia, Lengyel disappears after c. 4400–4300 B.C. and reemerges in Bavaria, central Germany, and western Poland, where characteristic biconic and footed vessels with warts show up in graves and in settlements.[36]

The Emergence of Kurgan Elements in the Milieu of the LBK Culture

The discontinuity of the Varna, Karanovo, Vinča, and Lengyel cultures in their main territories and the large scale population shifts to the north and northwest are indirect evidence of a catastrophe of such proportions that cannot be explained by possible climatic change, land exhaustion, or epidemics (for which there is no evidence in the second half of the 5th millennium B.C.). Direct evidence of the incursion of horse-riding warriors is found, not only in single burials of males under barrows, but in the emergence of *a whole complex* of Kurgan cultural traits: hilltop settlements, the presence of horses, the predominance of a pastoral economy, signs of violence and patriarchy, and religious symbols that emphasize a sun cult. These elements are tightly knit within the social, economic, and religious structure of the Kurgan culture.

A chain of hill forts that appeared on high riverbanks in the Middle and Upper Danube basin, in Hungary, Austria, western Slovakia, Moravia, Bohemia, and Bavaria[37] is a new phenomenon in European prehistory. The earliest hill forts are contemporary with late Lengyel and Rössen materials or immediately follow

them. Radiocarbon dates place this period between 4400 and 3900 B.C.[38]

Pit dwellings are found that sharply contrast with the solid above-ground long-houses of Lengyel and LBK type. These contain pottery decorated with solar designs, usually executed by stab and drag technique (in German called *Furchenstich*) along incisions of herringbone design and stabbings. Hanging triangles and parallel lines are typical motifs, with rows of dots above and below the shoulders. In the Upper Danube/Upper Rhine region, in Württemberg and Bavaria, this pottery is characteristic of the Rössen culture, considered to be a "mixed culture" or an LBK culture "with oriental elements."[39] This is a transformed culture, which did not simply develop from the Stroked Pottery stage of the LBK. Solar-decorated pottery is known from dwelling pits of classical Rössen and from Rössen of Wauwil type (found in Wauwilermoos, Lucerne, Switzerland). In Bavaria, a classical example of a fortified hilltop site with subterranean huts, is Goldberg in Nördlingen Ries, systematically excavated by G. Bersu in the late 1920s.[40] These pit dwellings measured from 4.2 by 3.2 m to 5.2 by 4.9 m.

Solar decorated pottery from subterranean dwellings is known from the Middle Neckar basin around Stuttgart, Pfullingen, and Tübingen, north of Schwäbische Alb, and more than twenty localities of the Aichbühl-Schwieberdingen group north of Switzerland. In Rheinpfalz, on the Lower Main, nearly identical materials are known from Bischheim and Bischoffingen-Leiselheim on the Upper Rhine.[41] Further south, in Switzerland, Rössen wares have been recovered from peat bog sites and graves, including Wauwil, Saint-Léonard in Valais, Cravanche at Belfort, and Gonvillars in eastern France.[42] In the north, Rössen sites are found on alluvial sand dunes on the eastern bank of the River Elbe, with ample pastureland around. The inferior soil of this region was not cultivated by Neolithic agriculturalists.

East of Magdeburg, the hilltop site of Wahlitz was systematically excavated.[43] This settlement, of two hectares, was surrounded by a ditch within which

were five larger houses and ten small houses. Club wheat was the main crop and cattle the dominant species of domesticated animals. The flint industry shows much relationship with the Stroked Pottery phase of the LBK, but the pottery is decorated with solar patterns characteristic of the classical Rössen culture. The radiocarbon date from Wahlitz indicates the last centuries of the 5th millennium B.C. (5300 ±200 BP, calibrated 4380–3950 B.C.)

The most impressive hilltop sites belong to the Salzmünde phase, dated to a period before the middle of the 4th millennium B.C. The name-giving site is a hilltop settlement on the River Saale near Halle. Others (such as Kahlenberg at Quenstedt, Goldberg at Mötzlich, and Oberwerschen) are located on the highest places in their vicinity, naturally protected on two or three sides by water and by extremely steep, rocky hillsides.[44] Five small rectangular houses of wattle-and-daub, built of timber uprights, three to a wall, came to light on the hilltop of Salzmünde. One of the houses, 3–5 m by 6–7 m, had a rectangular hearth in the center.

Alongside the fortified hills, a change of culture can be seen in the emergence of Kurgan type burials in the Elbe-Saale basin, dated to the first half of the 4th millennium B.C. Single graves in stone-lined and stone-covered pits under round barrows emerged in the Baalberge group in the Upper Elbe basin. These contrast with the local tradition of collective burial.[45] (FIGURE 10–10) About twenty earthen barrows have been excavated in the Elbe-Saale region; each contains a central grave in a pit below the surface and a mortuary house, usually built of stone or stone slabs. The radiocarbon dates for Baalberge and the following Salzmünde burials are within the first half of the 4th millennium B.C., between c. 3900 to 3400 B.C.

Signs of violence—evidence of people murdered with spears or axes—appear in this period and continue in the subsequent millennia. In the above-mentioned Goldberg hill fort, four individuals were found with unhealed wounds in their skulls, made with spearpoints. In Talheim, east of River Neckar in southwestern Germany, thirty-four skeletons of murdered people—men, women and children—were uncovered in a pit dug into the settlement area of the LBK (several potsherds of late LBK were found in the debris, but no other finds were associated with the skeletons). At least eighteen skulls had large holes in the back or top from thrusts of stone axes or flint points, which suggests that the people were killed from behind, perhaps as they fled. Skeletons were found in a pit 1.5 by 3.1 m across and 1.5 m deep in chaotic order and positions, with females, males, and children mixed together.[46] Since murdered people were buried in the cultural layer of the LBK culture with radiocarbon dates indicating early 5th millennium B.C., the massacre must have happened after this time, probably within the Rössen period.

The emergence of single-male burials under round mounds in eastern Ireland and central England in the middle of the 4th millennium B.C. contrasts sharply with the local tradition of communal burials. This signals the arrival of the first people carrying Kurgan traditions across the Channel or North Sea from the continent, most probably coming from the Rhine basin (see chapter 6, the description of Linkardstown type burials in eastern Ireland and related round mounds with single burials in Derbyshire, Dorset, and other locations in England). At the same time, signs of warfare and violence appear.

It is readily apparent that a portion of central Europe was Kurganized to varying degrees soon after the first Kurgan wave. While the civilization of Old Europe was agricultural, matricentric, and matrilineal, a transformation took place around 4000 B.C. to a mixed agricultural-pastoral economy and a classed patriarchal society which I interpret as a successful process of Indo-Europeanization. There was a considerable increase in husbandry over tillage. The change of social structure, religion,

FIGURE 10–10

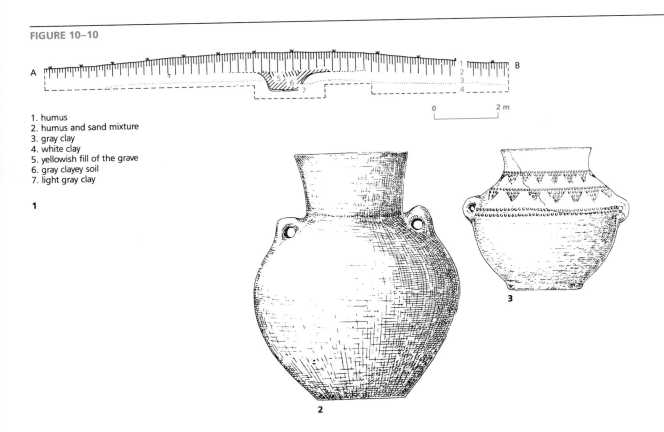

1. humus
2. humus and sand mixture
3. gray clay
4. white clay
5. yellowish fill of the grave
6. gray clayey soil
7. light gray clay

1

2

3

FIGURE 10–10 (1) Early round barrow—a typical kurgan in central Germany. Profile and detail of the grave in pit. (2,3) Vases found in the grave (skeleton did not survive); (2) of Baalberge workmanship; (3) prototypical of the Globular Amphora style. Dölauer Heide, Halle, Saale. Mid-4th mill. B.C. Scale 1:3.

and economy was not a gradual indigenous development from Old Europe, but a collision and gradual hybridization of two societies and of two ideologies.

Not all of central Europe was converted to the Kurgan way of life as an outcome of Wave No. 1, but it is clear that most of the Danube basin began to be ruled from hill forts. It took many successive generations for the Old European traditions to become gradually replaced. The indigenous populations either coexisted but remained separate from the Kurgan immigrants or were overrun and subjected to domination by a few Kurgan warriors.

A considerable number of Old European culture groups—the Cucuteni, TRB, and the western portion of the LBK—continued their existence throughout the first half of the 4th millennium B.C. or even longer. An increased Kurganization occurred during the second half of the 4th millennium B.C., which is treated in the section below.

The Second Wave, c. 3500 B.C., and the Transformation of Central Europe After the Middle of the 4th Millennium B.C.

The Kurgan tribal leaders of the north Pontic region turned to the Cucuteni area not later than the middle of the 4th millennium B.C. There they encountered a flourishing civilization which had survived the first Kurgan infiltration. This time it succumbed and was transformed through a process of amalgamation with Kurgan elements. This change can in no way be attributed to a natural evolution of indigenous elements. What continued of the indigenous culture was a pale reflection of earlier times.

The lords of the area can be recognized in royal or other elite tombs contained in mortuary houses covered with stone cupolas under barrows with stone rings. (FIGURES 10–11, 10–12) Around 3500 B.C., the culture south and north of the Carpathian Mountains was transformed beyond recognition. The transition from a matristic to a patriarchal era, in some territories of central

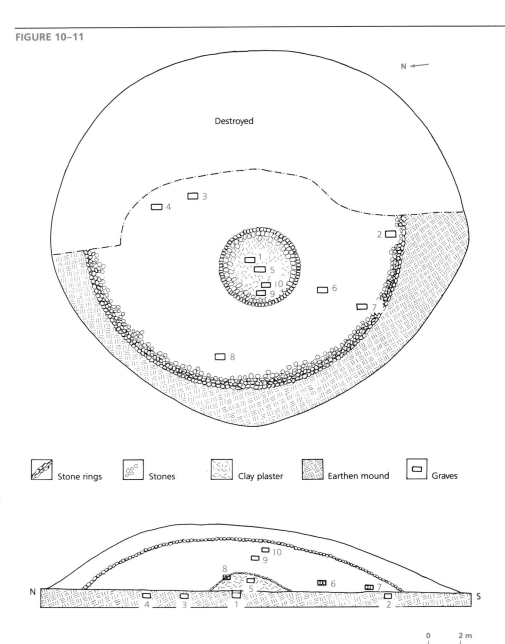

FIGURE 10–11

Destroyed

Stone rings   Stones   Clay plaster   Earthen mound   Graves

FIGURE 10–12

FIGURE 10–11 North Pontic kurgan (plan and section) consisting of a small inner tumulus covered with stones and an outer tumulus, also solidly covered with stones. A round platform in the middle was plastered with clay. The earliest graves (1–4) were lower in the ground. All other graves above the central tumulus were secondary interments. Tsareva Mogila near Kherson, NW of the Black Sea. Second half of the 4th mill. B.C. Diameter 34 m.

FIGURE 10–12 Typical North Pontic kurgan in east-central Europe. Tarnava near Vraca, NW Bulgaria. It consists of several superimposed barrows and secondary interments of several phases: (1) cross-section; (2) plan; (3) central grave of the second barrow containing two shaft-graves surrounded by a massive stone wall (Grave No. 5 cremated male; No. 6 inhumed female); (4) vases of Coțofeni craftsmanship from Grave No. 5. Second half 4th mill. B.C. Diameter 26 m.

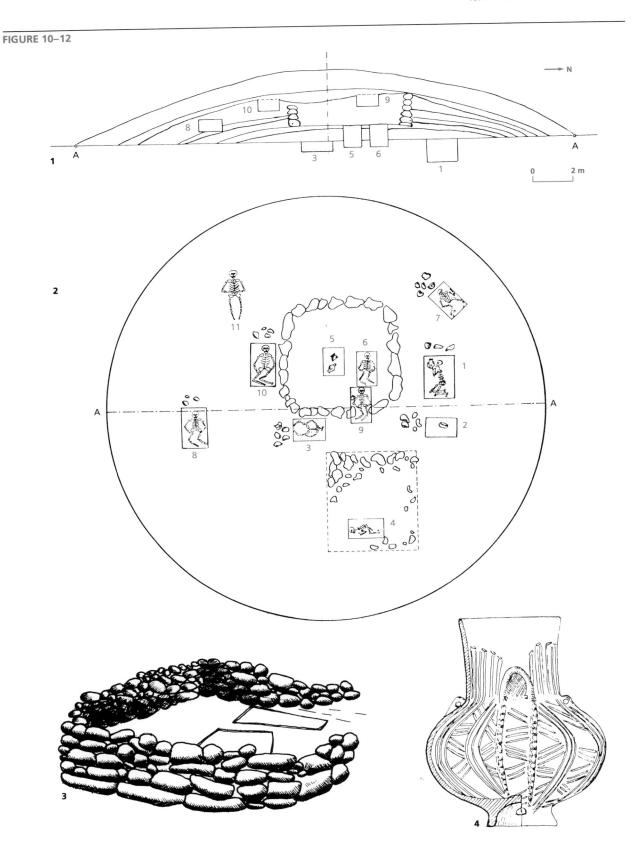

FIGURE 10–13

FIGURE 10–13 Culture groups c. 3500–3000 B.C. New formations in central Europe influenced by North Pontic culture.

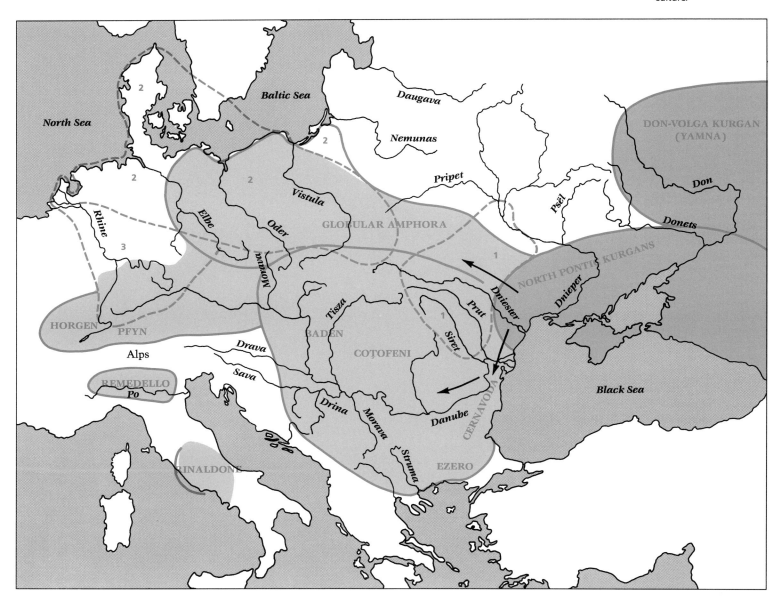

KEY

Yamna in the Don-Volga basin and North Pontic Kurgan groups

Kurganized territories in Central Europe

Limits of Kurgan territories north of the Black Sea and the Volga basin

Kurgan Wave #2 influences from the North Pontic area

Numbers mark the substratum culture groups; 1. Cucuteni; 2. TRB; 3. Michelsberg

Europe, was completed by the end of the 4th millennium B.C. New cultural groups emerged, formed of Old European and Kurgan elements. (FIGURE 10–13)

This period of transformation coincides with changes in metal technology and the beginning of the Early Bronze Age in the circum-Pontic region. The new metallurgy is characterized by bronzes of copper and arsenic, copper and tin, and copper with arsenic-tin (As, Sn, As-Sn bronze) which replaced the pure copper metallurgy of the Old European Copper Age.[47] Tests made on arsenical bronze prove it to have been reasonably hard and durable, but a side effect must have been the slow and sure poisoning of the smith. The complex of tools and weapons that emerged north and west of the Black Sea—daggers, knives, halberds, chisels, flat axes, shafthole axes—does not show a continuity from Old European local types. Rather, the shapes of bronze artifacts have analogies in the north Caucasus, in Transcaucasia, and the Near East.

The tomb structure of Kurgan Wave No. 2 points to its origin in the North Pontic area. The main monuments of the Kurgan culture north of the Black Sea are surveyed below.

The Source: The North Pontic Maikop Culture

The North Pontic culture is typified by hill forts and hundreds of Kurgan tumuli (grave mounds) with mortuary houses built of stones or wood. Royal burials share a characteristic monumental style in which the tumuli are surrounded by orthostats and stelae, then by an outermost ring of stones; within and below the tumulus is a stone- or wood-lined pit (mortuary house), covered with stone slabs and topped by a stone cupola. Models of wagons and daggers of hard metal accompany the males of the elite. Large apsidal houses, exclusively on hilltops, are an architectural innovation.

Hill forts with enormous fortifications and outstanding tumuli, including exceptionally well-built tombs of stone slabs, suggest a hierarchic society of consolidated tribal units ruled by leading families. The similarity of fortified set-

tlements, burial rites, and ceramic, stone, and metal artifacts recovered northeast and northwest of the Black Sea suggests the unification of this region, not only by commercial contacts but also by political power. The North Pontic region had at this stage diverged from its Kurgan cousin of the Volga. The Kurgan elements that appear west of the Black Sea are clearly connected with the North Pontic, not with the Volga Steppe and have analogies in the Kuro-Araks valley of Transcaucasia.

Known from the end of the 19th century, the royal tomb at Maikop in the River Kuban basin, northwestern Caucasus, is the richest and most familiar of this culture. Although it dates from the early 3rd millennium B.C., the place name has become eponymic of the whole North Pontic culture which began c. 3500 B.C.

The early phase of the Maikop culture in the Lower Dnieper area is best represented by the lowest layer of the Mikhailovka hill fort, surrounded by several walls of limestone boulders, which undoubtedly functioned as a strategic center.[48] The finds from Mikhailovka I show close affinities to those from Crimean and north Caucasian stone cists as well as to the Usatovo kurgans around Odessa. The chronology of this phase, the second half of the 4th millennium B.C., is based on radiocarbon dates from Mikhailovka. (TABLE 25) There were two wattle-and-daub houses with apsidal ends at the Mikhailovka I hilltop. One measured 5 m by 16.5 m, and the other, which was partly subterranean, was 5.7 m by 12 m. In the center of each was a round, clay-daubed stone hearth. Arrowheads, points, and scrapers of flint, bone awls, and pottery were gathered in the work area of the north apse.

Rock engravings from Kamennaya Mogila at Melitopol, north of the Sea of Azov, depict human and horse silhouettes and yoked oxen pulling a cart.[49] (FIGURE 10–14, 2) Large-horned oxen pulling a plow appear also on the wall of a cist grave at Züschen, central Germany,[50] and on the rocks at Valcamonica, northern Italy.[51] (FIGURE 10–14, 1, 3, 4) These engravings provide graphic evidence that plow agriculture was

FIGURE 10–14

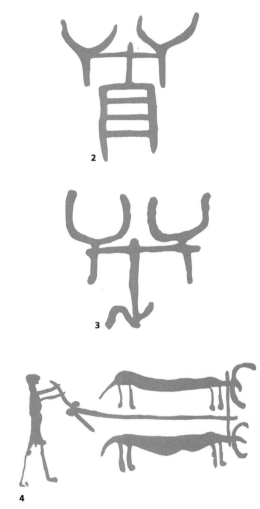

FIGURE 10–14 Rock engravings of yoked oxen pulling a vehicle and a plow, c. 3500–3000 B.C. from the North Pontic area and central Germany. (1) Züschen, C Germany. (3,4) Valcamonica, N Italy. Scale: various sizes. (2) Kamennaya Mogila, north of the Sea of Azov.

practiced and that yoked oxen were used to pull both cart and plow. After 3500 B.C., pairs of oxen appear in male graves in the Baden and Globular Amphora cultures of central Europe together with a host of other Kurgan elements (see the next section).

Mikhailovka I ceramics are typified by globular amphorae with rounded or flat bases and cylindrical necks wound with cord impressions; semiglobular tureens also occur. Pottery was brushed, stabbed, pitted, and beaded about the mouth, neck, and shoulder, and four-legged braziers were ornamented with the solar motif. (FIGURE 10–15) Ordinary pots were plain and rough, while fine ware was usually brown or blackish, polished and burnished, tempered with crushed shell or limestone and sand. This characteristic pottery is found in Pontic area kurgans concentrated south of the River Kuban in the western Caucasus where some 1,500 houselike structures of stone slabs have been counted.[52] These fairly uniform burial sites occur in the Crimea[53] and in the Lower Don, Lower Dnieper, Ingul, and Ingulets valleys.[54] Stone cists were surrounded by orthostats and an outer ring of stones. Cist walls were engraved with figures of men and male animals or painted in red ochre with zigzag, cross, and solar designs.[55]

Royal burials and hoards of the late Maikop culture in the River Kuban basin, northwestern Caucasus, express the fabulous riches of tribal leaders and their contacts with Mesopotamia in the early 3rd millennium B.C. The most lavishly equipped are those of Maikop and Tsarskaya (now Novosvobodnaya) excavated by N.I. Veselovskii at the end of the 19th century (both are known from the publications by Rostovtzeff 1920; Tallgren 1934; Hančar 1937; Childe 1936; Iessen 1950; and myself 1956).[56] These outstanding kurgans and their treasures throw much light on the social structure, kingship, religion, and art of this period. The Maikop tomb, as well as the series of others in the northern Caucasus[57] and in the south Caspian area[58] speak of the campaigns and raids south of the Caucasus Mountains and the Caspian Sea.

FIGURE 10–15

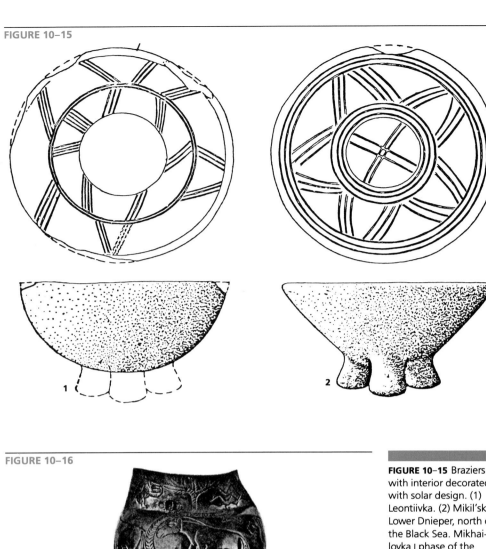

FIGURE 10–16

FIGURE 10–15 Braziers with interior decorated with solar design. (1) Leontiivka. (2) Mikil'ske, Lower Dnieper, north of the Black Sea. Mikhailovka I phase of the North Pontic culture. c. 3500–3000 B.C. H 6 cm.

FIGURE 10–16 Symbolic scene on silver vase I from Maikop northwest of the Caucasus Mts. Early 3rd mill. B.C. Scale 1:3.

An Amalgam of Kurgan and Cucuteni Traditions: The Usatovo Complex Northwest of the Black Sea

Typically, kurgans line the highest ridges along the rivers of the area. Outstanding sites are Usatovo near Odessa[59] and Tudorovo in Moldavia.[60] Characteristically, a tumulus of the Usatovo culture had a cist with uniform orthostats, an entrance corridor, a cupola-shaped cairn above the central grave, semicircles of stelae with engravings and reliefs, and inner and outer rings of stone. The richest graves were those of the leading member of the tribe and his suttee while graves of other adults and children were contrastingly poor. Near the settlement and tumuli at Usatovo there is a contemporaneous cemetery of the indigenous Cucuteni culture consisting of simple, unmarked (flat) pit graves, arranged in rows.

Contrasting burial rites of the Cucuteni and Kurgan populations are paralleled by differences in their respective habitation sites. Cucuteni dwellings were on wide river terraces, while the Kurgans located their semisubterranean dwellings on spurs, dunes, and steep hills along rivers. The houses at Gorodsk, on the bank of the River Teterev in the western Ukraine, are small, about 5 m in length with a round hearth in the center;[61] close analogies are found in the Lower Dnieper basin.

A list of radiocarbon dates obtained by analysis of charcoal and animal bones from the Usatovo and Mayaki sites of the Usatovo complex is in table 26. The calibration of dates suggests the period between the 34th and 29th centuries B.C.

A Kurgan-Influenced Culture in East-Central Europe: The Baden-Vučedol and Ezero Groups

The second Kurgan infiltration headed south from the North Pontic region toward the Lower Danube area and beyond. At the fortified hill at Cernavoda, in Dobruja, radiocarbon dates from the second phase of the hill give the age as c. 3400–3200 B.C.[62] By that time, a chain of acropolises along the Danube, in the Marica (Bulgaria) plain, and in the area north of the Aegean, reflected the spread of a ruling power. The finest recently excavated tells, converted to hill forts, are at Ezero in central Bulgaria,[63] and Sitagroi on the Drama Plain of Greek Macedonia.[64] Radiocarbon dates are given in tables 27 and 28.

In the Lower Danube, Marica, and Macedonian plains, many Karanovo tells indicate that the indigenous occupation of these sites was disrupted, and many were surmounted by fortifications (such are the Ezero, Sitagroi IV, Karanovo VII, Nova Zagora, Veselinovo, and Bikovo). In other areas, steep river banks and almost inaccessible promontories were selected as seats of the ruling class.

A cultural change of the same nature as in the Danubian basin is evident as far west as the Alpine valleys of Italy and Switzerland and the Po River basin (the Remedello group), where hill forts (such as Columare, north of Verona)[65] are known on steep hills. This change in social structure was accompanied by a change in religion. The beginning of a new era in religious concepts is manifested in the Alpine valleys by a series of stelae engraved with a set of symbols alien to the indigenous Cortaillod and Lagozza cultures. We shall return to these at the end of this chapter.

An Amalgamation of the Old European and the Kurgan Cultural Systems

During the second half of the 4th millennium B.C., the new regime seems to have successfully eliminated or changed whatever remained of the old social system. Hill forts were the foci of power and cultural life, while the surrounding area supported either pastoral or agricultural populations, depending on the environment and the numbers of indigenous people who remained. Villages were small, the houses usually semisubterranean. But in the economy, an amalgamation of the Old European and the Kurgan cultural systems is clearly evident. In some areas, such as in central Bulgaria, cultivation of emmer, barley, vetch, and pea continued intact, probably carried on by the remaining indigenous population. In other territories, seasonal camps of a pastoral economy prevailed.

The new metallurgy, with links to the circum-Pontic region, was now practiced all over east-central Europe, concentrating on the production of the dagger, the shaft-hole axe, and the flat axe of arsenic bronze; metal workshops (including clay bivalve molds) are found on hill forts.[66] The ceramic artifacts, however, continue to manifest certain Old European traditions: anthropomorphic, zoomorphic, and ornithomorphic vases of beautiful workmanship were apparently produced by surviving Old European craftsmen. Such exceptional creations are typically found in the hill forts and rich tombs under large tumuli (cf. vases from Tarnava, fig. 10–11), although they are no longer found in the ordinary villages or graves. This situation seems analogous to that of Mycenaean Greece where surviving Minoan craftsmen continued to produce masterpieces of ceramic, gold, and stone for their new lords. The Old European symbolism largely vanished from popular artifacts, giving way to the ubiquitous solar design.

Toward the end of the 4th millennium B.C., only isolated islands of the Old European tradition persisted. Such was the Coţofeni complex in the Danube valley in Oltenia, western Muntenia, southern Banat, and Transylvania.[67] (TABLE 29) The Coţofeni were sedentary agriculturalists, living in solidly built houses, using copper tools, and still producing burnished red and white painted ceramics. Large numbers of bird-shaped vases attest the continuing worship of the Bird Goddess.

The Baden-Vučedol Culture in the Middle Danube Basin

Hundreds of sites in the best explored area, the Middle Danube basin, particularly in Hungary and western Slovakia, afford a good opportunity to follow the cultural development at this critical period of European prehistory. Although treated as a separate culture, the Baden (also called Pécel or Radial-decorated Pottery) culture is actually a western branch of the overall culture complex between western Anatolia and Poland.

The Baden complex, composed of indigenous and alien elements, covered the Middle Danube basin, with northern limits in Bohemia and southern Poland. In the south, it is known in the Morava-Vardar valleys of Yugoslavia, Bosnia, and even Albania.[68] The available radiocarbon dates range between the 34th and 29th centuries B.C. (TABLE 30).

The eponymous site of Baden-Königshöhle, near Vienna, was excavated more than sixty years ago.[69] According to presently available radiocarbon dates, Baden lasted some 500 years. This period is subdivided into three phases: early (Boleraz), middle (classical Baden), and late (Bošaca). Almost a thousand Baden sites (counting surface finds) are recorded.[70]

Hilltop Sites with Apsidal Houses

The hill sites at Vučedol and Sarvaš in northwestern Yugoslavia[71] (FIGURE 10-17), Nitrianski Hrádok near Nitra and Levoča in western Slovakia,[72] a number near Vienna and Melk in Austria, and those in southern Poland, must have served as seats of chieftains. They each bear a strong resemblance to the difficult-to-access and heavily fortified hills at Mikhailovka in the Lower Dnieper, and Liventsovka at Rostov on the River Don in the Ukraine.

Atop the Vučedol hill stood two apsidal houses of the classical Baden phase. One is considered to be the chief's house and the other a storage place and kitchen. These houses were built of vertical posts and clay daub, the floors were clay plastered and dividing walls separated the rooms, each with its rectangular hearth. Apsidal houses are known also in Bulgaria (Karanovo VII and Nova Zagora), in Macedonia, northeastern Greece (Sitagroi V: figure 10-18), central and southern Greece (Lerna IV, Thebes, Asine), and in Turkey (Troy Ib and Karatas in Lycia). Baden-Ezero apsidal houses were exclusive to the leading hill forts. Moreover, apsidal houses in Palestine during the 34th–33rd centuries B.C. (at Megiddo, Meser, Jericho VII–VI, Beth Shan XVI, Rosh Hannigra II, Khirbet Kerah I, Tell Yarmuth B, II, and Byblos III) emerged together with other foreign culture elements (gray pottery, tournettes, and copper tools),[73] and are probably connected with Wave No. 2, which did not stop at the Dardanelles but proceeded to the eastern Mediterranean area as well.

Villages

The typical Baden village was set on a river terrace or promontory. The houses were small (the largest were 3.5 by 4.5 m), rectangular, and semisubterranean with pitched roofs supported by timber posts. Their clay-plastered hearths were either round or rectangular. Aboveground dwellings occur most often in western Slovakia and Hungary. Baden settlements were both permanent and seasonal. Stable settlements were more or less confined to the uplands and the northwestern portion of this culture, whereas small short-lived settlements are found in the lowlands of eastern Hungary and Yugoslavia. The pattern of permanent settlement is clearly linked to the tradition of the Old European populations.

Economy

The economy was not uniform through the entire Baden territory; farming predominated in the northwest,[74] while a pastoral economy predominated in other areas, particularly in eastern Hungary and northern Yugoslavia. Botanists have identified wheat (with emmer wheat as the most important cereal), barley, millet, oats, pulses, and perhaps rye among plant remains,[75] while hazelnuts, shells, cherry stones, and carbonized dried apples give evidence of gathering activities. Cattle led the inventory of domesticated animal bones, followed by sheep, goats, pigs, and horses. Cattle pens have been identified in areas 500–600 meters square, enclosed by ditches with crude fencing of branches and various-sized posts.[76] Sheep and roe deer bones are found in greater proportion in the debris of larger and wealthier homes.[77] Food production was heavily supplemented by fishing and hunting, shown by fish hooks and deposits of fish bones, and by bones of bear, boar, aurochs, roe deer, wolf, fox, and hare.

Local metallurgy is known from classical Baden. At Sarvaš (northern Yugoslavia) there is evidence of open sandstone molds for a tanged dagger and a flat axe.[78] Deposits of triangular dagger blades with rivet holes occur in male graves.

FIGURE 10–17

FIGURE 10–18

FIGURE 10–18 The burnt house with an apsidal end which contained the kitchen and storage area. Length c. 17 m. Sitagroi V, NE Greece, c. 29th cent. B.C.

FIGURE 10–19

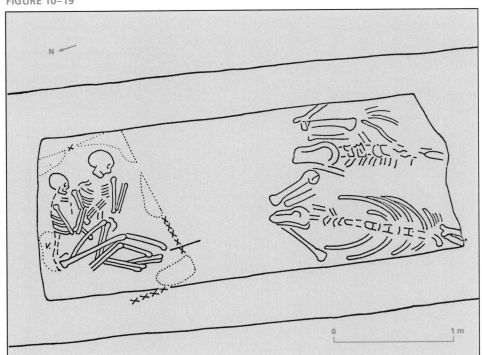

FIGURE 10-19 FIGURE **10**-19 Oxen team (right) buried with male and female in one grave. Budakalász at Budapest. Baden culture, c. 3000 B.C. L of grave pit 3.4 m.

FIGURE 10–20

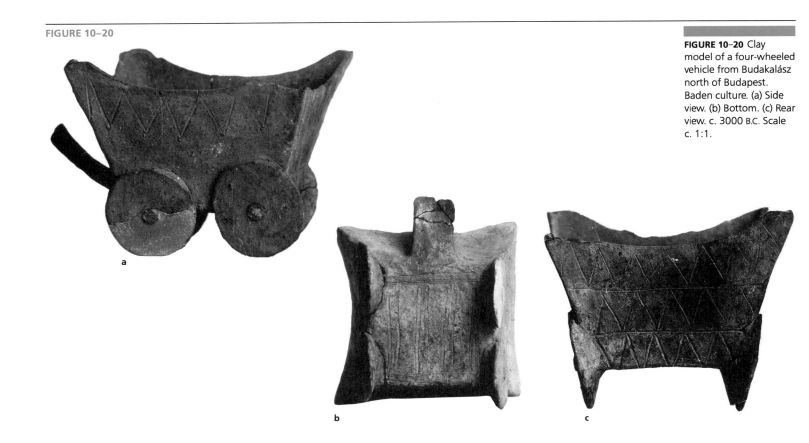

a

b

c

FIGURE **10**-20 Clay model of a four-wheeled vehicle from Budakalász north of Budapest. Baden culture. (a) Side view. (b) Bottom. (c) Rear view. c. 3000 B.C. Scale c. 1:1.

Burials with Sacrificed Animals and Vehicles

Baden cemeteries show the typical Kurgan social inequality and the practice of human and animal sacrifice, the latter by the presence of cattle, dog, and horse bones included in ritual burials. At Alsónemedi and Budakalász near Budapest, several ox teams had been sacrificed at the graves. (FIGURE 10–19) Grave goods of the wealthy include braziers and models of vehicles. At Budakalász, a cenotaph included the clay model of a four-wheeled vehicle (FIGURE 10–20) not unlike the one in an inhumation burial at Szigetszentmárton, south of Budapest.[79] The burial of a cart with the dead of high social status was customary in late prehistoric and early historic times, and a copper crown on a male skull also suggests his high social status. (FIGURE 10–21) In multiple burials, the male skeleton is found in the center while women and children are at the edge. (FIGURE 10–22)

Physical Type of Population

The physical type of Baden was predominantly Mediterranean, as was to be expected from the Vinča substratum. A steppe type was also identified, however, and a certain facial flatness in some individuals seems to reflect eastern relations. At Budakalász, the steppe type predominated, while at Alsónemedi the Mediterranean was mixed with a European brachycranial type.[80]

FIGURE 10–21

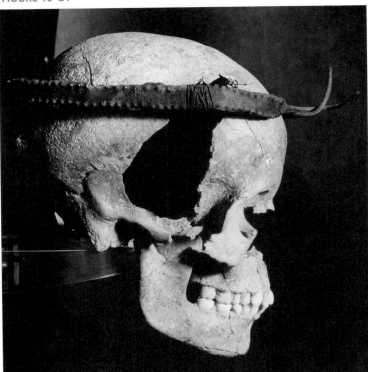

FIGURE 10–21 Skull of a male with a copper crown. Vörs, Hungary, Baden, c. 3000 B.C.

FIGURE 10–22 Multiple sacrificial burial of the Baden culture. Seventeen human skeletons (four adult and thirteen child) found in a pit. The oldest male (approximately 25 years old) lies in the center of the pit while the women and children are at the edge. Perforated horse teeth were deposited only with male skeletons. Bronocice, district of Kielce, S Poland. Radiocarbon calibrated date: 3100–2960/2870 B.C.

FIGURE 10–22

Lingering Old European Traditions in Ceramics and Symbolism

The Old European symbols recur in the Baden culture on bird vases, on winged anthropomorphic urns, and on other fine-quality ceramics decorated with a breast motif and panels of chevron, ladder, and net patterns. The finishing of ceramics by burnishing and channelling are the last flutter of the Old European way in conflict with the new Indo-European ideology reflected in the rows of pits, zigzags, and solar patterns on beakers, braziers, tureens, and wagon models. (FIGURE 10-23)

The Baden complex represents the process of amalgamation of two culture systems with contrasting economies, ideologies, racial types, and modes of living.

The Late Baden ("Kostolac") Expansion into Bosnia

The Late Baden or "Kostolac" culture continued in northern Yugoslavia and made a strong thrust south into the Tuzla and Bila valleys of Bosnia. The richest and best explored site of the Kostolac type in Bosnia is a hilltop settlement at Pivnica near Odžak situated in a strategic place overlooking the Bosna River valley. There was a large apsidal house, 15 m long, on the eastern part of the hill and traces of other houses on the other part.[81]

The Vučedol Culture

In the early 3rd millennium B.C., the Vučedol culture followed the Baden in the northwestern Balkans and the east Alpine area. This culture is named after the Vučedol hill fort at Vukovar on the Danube, northwestern Yugoslavia, excavated by R. R. Schmidt.[82] In Hungary it is called the "Zók culture" with several subgroups: "Zók" proper in southwestern Hungary, "Makó" in the Körös and Maros basins of southeastern Hungary, and "Nyirseg" in northeastern Hungary.[83] In the eastern Alpine area, it is better known as "Laibach-Ljubljana culture," after the peat-bog site excavated at Ljubljana in 1878–79 by K. Deschmann.[84]

About 500 Vučedol sites have been reported, all clustered in essentially the same territory as the Baden sites. A number of hill forts contain both Baden and Vučedol deposits, and in the hill fort of Vučedol, two successive Vučedol strata overlie the late Baden (Kostolac) phase. A similar sequence was indicated in the stratified settlements of Sarvaš, Gomolava, and Belegiš in Syrmia and Slovenia, Brno-Lišen in Moravia, Zók-Varhegy at Pecs in southwestern Hungary, and elsewhere. Vučedol materials are found diffused as far as the Adriatic islands in the south and Bohemia and central Germany in the northwest.

An Intensive Defense System of Hill Forts

An intensive defense system is seen in the chain of impressive fortresses and fortified hilltop villages. Particular concentrations of settlements occur around Vukovar and Osijek in northwestern Yugoslavia; near Pecs in southwestern Hungary; around Ljubljana in Slovenia, south of Vienna, and in western Slovakia. These hill forts functioned as administrative centers, as in the Baden period, and were located on very steep river banks, usually at the confluence with a smaller river, and were heavily defended by ramparts, palisades, and ditches on the inland side. Other settlements are also found on river banks and elevations, or on lake shores, where people lived in pile dwellings (Ljubljana and Ig, at Ljubljana).

Metallurgy

Most of the metallurgical activities took place in these locations. The Vučedol hill fort yielded several smelting ovens, copper slags, and clay and sandstone molds. The metal-tool kit consisted of awls, tanged or riveted daggers, spiral tubes used for necklaces, weapons, and ornaments, in addition to shaft-hole axes, celts, and chisels. The ruling families had their own smiths who produced the best tools and weapons of the time. Metal, however, was still rare and most of the inventory was of bone and wood.

Pottery

The Vučedol ceramics are mostly memorable for the well-polished vases in dark brown or gray, excised and encrusted with white chalk (of crushed shell), which were stamped and impressed with geometric designs, typically in zones and metopes. Their shapes include a variety of forms—footed dishes which served as braziers, large bowls, handled pots and amphorae, flat and elongated dishes with a rim, miniature pots, and jars with broom-brushed surfaces. Much of the ceramic art reflects, as in Baden, the lingering of Old European traditions. This is strikingly evident in the presence of ornithomorphic vases. The Bird Goddess of the Vinča tradition and her symbols continued to be represented, but most of the symbolic signs and decorative motifs, especially those on the interior of dishes and braziers, are not in the Old European tradition. The dominant designs, instead, are sun and star motifs alien to Old Europe. Clearly, both traditions contributed to Vučedol art and symbolism.

Burial

A variety of grave types is reported—cremation, urn graves, inhumation, pits under round earthen barrows, stone cists, and oven-shaped tombs favored for members of leading families. A rich double grave was found in the Vučedol hill fort, presumed to belong to a ruler and his wife. Both skeletons were in a contracted position. The man's left arm lay over the thigh bone of the woman and his right arm held a leather bottle near his mouth. At his side lay two spears with socketed bronze heads, and at his feet were a hammer-axe of antler, a perforated dog's incisor tooth, and a perforated Mediterranean shell. A whole lamb had been dedicated to the royal couple, and there were many bones about of cattle, stag, and pig. Other gifts had been deposited in large storage vessels, amphorae, bowls, and dishes, some of which still contained organic substances. The woman's head was covered with an exceedingly beautiful, white crusted terrine. In an adjacent oven-shaped grave, five skeletons of children had been placed in a

FIGURE 10–23

1

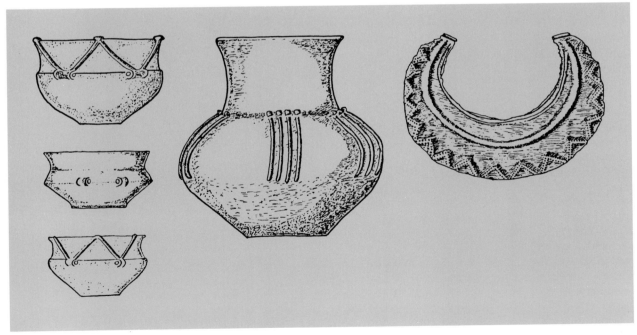

2

FIGURE 10–23 (1) Solar motifs on Baden pots. (2) Pots and a copper breast plate found in a stone cist grave at Velvary, Bohemia. Vases (*left*) have tubular handles used for suspension of the vessel (note: strings are shown in relief). Breast plates of Velvary type reappear engraved on stone stelae (see figs. 10–43, 10–44). Second half 4th mill. B.C. H of large vase 13 cm.

circle; three were newborn babies, one was half a year old, and one was four years of age. The bone analysis of the latter showed that the buried chieftain was the father.

The Ezero Culture in Bulgaria, the Northern Aegean, and Western Anatolia

Ezero is a tell in central Bulgaria located three kilometers southeast of Nova Zagora.[85] The excavations of a Bulgarian-Soviet team in this location during 1961–71 revealed an unusually complete picture of the Early Bronze Age life and chronology of the Ezero culture. Although there are a number of important settlements in central Bulgaria (Michalič, Veselinovo, Bikovo, Karanovo) as well as in the north Aegean and western Anatolia that have yielded material related to Ezero (Sitagroi IV and V, Troy I–II, Yortan, Alişar), none can compare with its scope and completeness of information. For this reason, the name *Ezero* is applied as a label for the entire culture in Bulgaria, northern Aegean, and western Anatolia. This is not a separate culture, however, but is part of one widely spread Baden-Ezero culture united by a standard repertoire of finds, and similar administrative system and settlement pattern.

Originally, the tell of Ezero, as also Karanovo, Veselinovo, Sitagroi, and others, was occupied by the Karanovo people. The continuity of this remarkable civilization, as we have seen in chapters 2 and 3, is well attested for almost two thousand years, c. 6000–4200 B.C. Then, as a result of Kurgan Wave No. 1, the continuity of the Karanovo life was truncated. After a hiatus, a hybrid culture emerged which was an amalgamation of Old European traditions overlaid with new Kurgan influences. The tell was converted into an acropolis.

The Early Bronze Age layer of Ezero above the Karanovo tell had a thickness of 3.80 m. In the central section, thirteen building horizons were excavated, all of which are of one cultural tradition beginning in the middle of the 4th and ending in the middle of the 3rd millen-

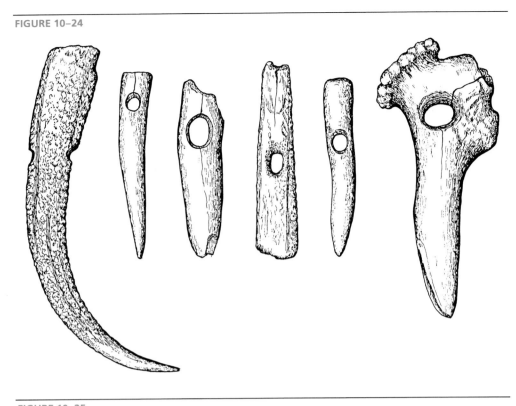

FIGURE 10–24

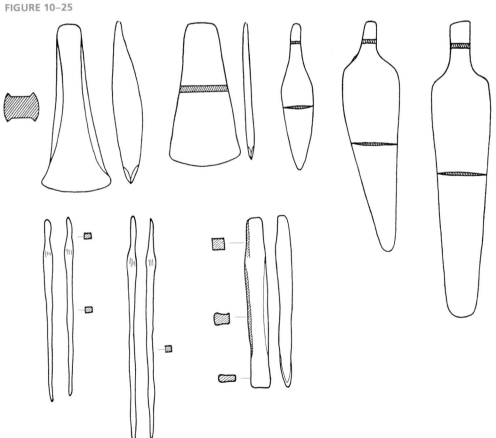

FIGURE 10–25

nium B.C. Each horizon yielded rectangular houses built of timber uprights interspersed with latticed branches and covered with a thin layer of clay daub. Some structures of lighter construction built of timber posts hardly survived although their ground plans are traced from postholes. From nearly fifty houses uncovered, twenty had apsidal ends which appeared in the earliest horizon (Horizon XIII) and continued through the duration of this culture. Larger houses consisted of two rooms, living quarters and a working area, having ovens, hearths, platforms, and silo pits for drying and storing grain. The buildings stood in groups, about twenty houses in each horizon, around an open center. This central area had direct access to a corridor-like gate, 2 to 2.5 m wide and 8 m long, which was connected with the settlement's fortification.

The hill was surrounded by two stone walls. The inner wall was 80 m in diameter, 1.5 to 2 m thick, built of large undressed stones, 60 to 80 cm in size, while the outer was double in size. Such Cyclopean walls of larger boulders were strengthened with smaller stones at the bottom and glued with clay. This acropolis, which could have held up to two hundred people, must have served as a fortress for the small, unprotected villages around it.

Who lived on this hill? The chieftain with his council of war leaders, the craftsmen and their families? Unfortunately we do not know, although the pattern appears to be proto-typical of the later Bronze Age Mycenaean acropolises.

Tools and Weapons

The acropolis was the center of many activities including the manufacture of tools and weapons of stone, bone, antler, copper, and bronze, typical throughout the Baden-Ezero culture. Flint was obtained from the Rhodope Mountains while other stones were gathered from south and north of Ezero. Stone artifacts include pestles, hammers, polishers, grinding stones, querns, axes, and chisels, also globular and cylindrical maceheads and ritual battle-axes. Bone and antler tools were found by the hundreds,

mostly awls, chisels, polishers, digging sticks, hoes (some of which were possibly used as plowshares), axes, and hammer-axes. (FIGURE 10–24) Metal artifacts were not abundant since the total number from all horizons was 37 (awls, knives or knife-daggers, chisels, needles, a.o.). (FIGURE 10–25) In addition, three stone molds for casting axes were discovered which belong to the later phases of the Ezero sequence. In the earliest horizons, awls were made of pure copper or arsenical copper, while in later horizons the percentage of arsenic was much higher suggesting progress in metal work.

Pottery

Jugs, jars, bowls, and cups with high handles were of surprisingly similar forms all over the Baden-Ezero area. Only a close interaction between the various districts, the mobility of the people, and the same social structure could result in such a uniformity of products. From the onset of this culture, there was an overall decline in the quality of pottery which, in shape, make, and decoration, cannot be compared with the exquisite Karanovo VI pottery. Although the Baden-Ezero ceramics absorbed certain elements of the local cultures, this in no way represents a continuity of the Vinča or Karanovo. If the channeling technique for decoration was used on early Baden, Ezero, and Sitagroi IV bowls, or if chevrons or zigzag designs occasionally appeared on vases, this only shows that there were local elements in the population, probably female, that continued to apply long-used motifs from memory.

The main set of prestige pottery types is a group of vessels concerned with communal eating and drinking—jug, cup, dipper, bowl—which is a distinctive feature of elite burials. In later phases of the Bronze Age such drinking vessels were either made of metal or were imitated in clay. No doubt a variety of intoxicating drinks were used. Thus, the complex of drinking vessels used primarily by males, by the male entourage of the ruler or by his warriors, replaced the symbolically decorated libation vessels or water containers used by women in temples.

FIGURE 10–26

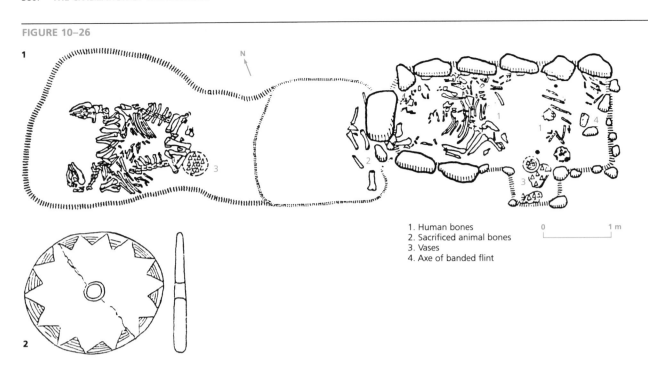

1. Human bones
2. Sacrificed animal bones
3. Vases
4. Axe of banded flint

0   1 m

FIGURE 10–26 (1) An ox team (left) buried next to the stone cist with human skeletons (right). Zdrojówka, district of Koło, Poland. (2) Bone plate with an engraved star design originally attached to the forehead of an ox. Brześć Kujawski, district of Włocławek, Poland. Diameter 8 cm.

FIGURE 10–27

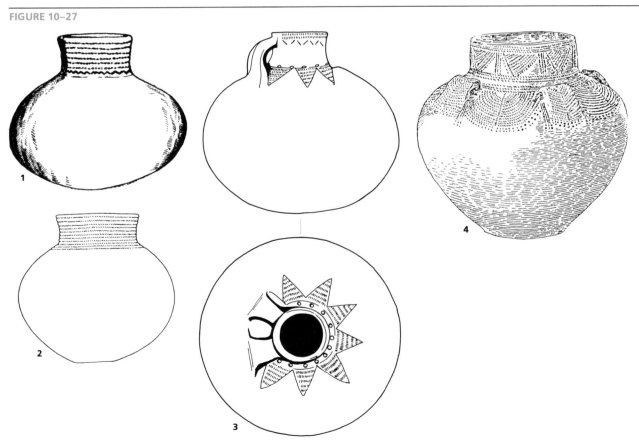

FIGURE 10–27 Globular amphorae decorated with cord impressions from Poland and the Lower Dnieper basin. (1) Kalsk, district of Swiebodzin, Poland. (2) Mikhailovka I hill fort, Lower Dnieper. (3) Strzelce, Mogilno, W Poland. (4) Rębków-Parcele, Garwolin, Poland. Second half 4th mill. B.C. Scale c. 1:4.

The Globular Amphora Culture in the Northern European Plain Between Central Germany and East Romania

The Globular Amphora culture emerged on the northern European plain and north of the Carpathians—the present territories of central Germany, Poland, Volynia, Podolia, and Moldavia—in the middle of the 4th millennium B.C.[86] (Table 31) It is known from hundreds of graves and from a few seasonal camps on sand dunes, small villages, and hilltop sites. The Globular Amphora culture was preceded by the Funnel-necked Beaker culture (TRB) and by the Cucuteni in the western Ukraine and Romania. In spite of a different substratum, the Globular Amphora culture was remarkably uniform.

There is similarity between the burial rites of the Globular Amphora people and those of the Kurgans of the Maikop culture in the North Pontic region. Both used mortuary houses built of stone slabs and practiced the ritual burial of horses, cattle, and dogs, as well as human sacrifice in connection with funeral rites honoring high-ranking males. (FIGURES 10-26, 10-29)

The typical vessel for which the culture is named is an amphora with a flat or rounded base (FIGURE 10-27), with or without two or four small handles above the shoulder for suspension. Other vases that accompanied the dead include a globular pot (a tureen or wide-mouthed beaker) and occasionally a cup. (FIGURES 10-28A, B) The clay was tempered with crushed shells and some sand or vegetable matter. In shape and construction, this pottery, particularly that from Volynia and Poland, is much the same as that from Mikhailovka I sites. The cord-impressed, incised, or stabbed decoration is restricted to the neck and shoulder.

FIGURE 10-28A

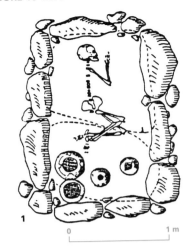

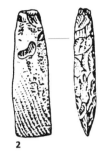

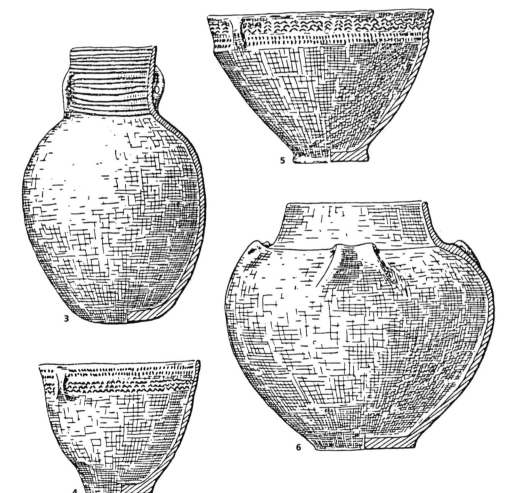

FIGURE 10-28A Stone cist grave inventories of the Globular Amphora culture. (1) A man lying on the left side in a contracted position was equipped with (2) an axe made of banded flint and (3-6) four pots. Przybysław, district of Inowrocław, W Poland. H of vase (*left*) 28 cm.

FIGURE 10-28B

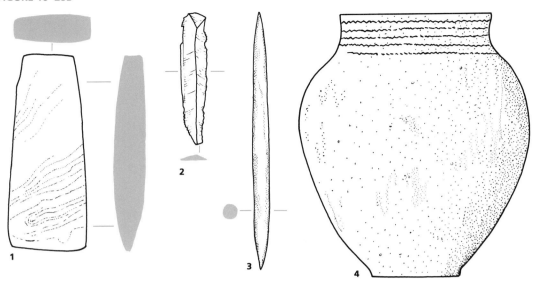

1

2

3

4

FIGURE 10-28B (1) Banded flint axe; (2) flint knife; (3) double pointed bone spear; (4) corded pot from a Globular Amphora grave at Malice, district of Sandomierz, S Poland. Second half of the 4th mill. B.C.

FIGURE 10-29

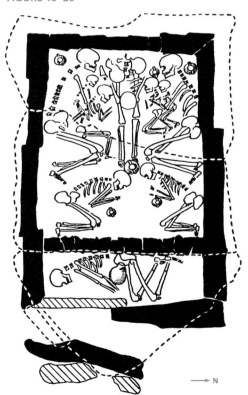

→ N

FIGURE 10-29 Plan of a Globular Amphora mortuary house. Stone slab cist with a porch covered by three large slabs. In the center at the western wall, skeleton of a male 40 to 50 years old, flanked by two females and two children on each side (children from c. 1 year to c. 8 years old). Two other skeletons are at his feet: a boy, c. 15 and a girl, c. 17. The porch area contained the skeleton of a man c. 30 years old (a leg showed signs of injury). Skeletons covered with ochre lay on the stone-slab floor daubed with a 4 cm thick layer of yellow clay. Among the funeral gifts were four axes, a chisel, daggers, arrowheads, a bone point, eight vases, three jaws of a boar, and pig bones. Voytsekhivka, district of Zhitomir, Volynia. Second half of the 4th mill. B.C.

FIGURE 10-30

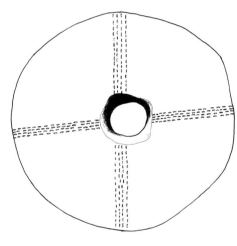

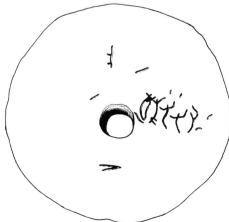

FIGURE 10-30 Engraved amber disc found in a stone cist as a gift to an important male at Ivanne near Rovno, NW Ukraine c. 600 km from the amber source area at the Baltic Sea. End 4th mill. B.C.

Male Graves with Sacrificed Humans and Animals

A classed social structure and the dominant position of men is demonstrated by richly equipped graves that contained astounding numbers of sacrificed human beings and animals. The chief adult male occupied the central position in the stone cist and was accompanied into the afterlife by family members, servants, oxen, horses, and dogs as well as boars and other game animals. These extraordinary burials contained from three to ten human skeletons buried at the same time. The sex, age, and the position of the skeletons suggest that one or more young children, an adult female, and one or two attendants were put to death to accompany their father, husband, or master to the other world. The important male skeleton is usually found at the end of the cist grave, while two or more other individuals, perhaps immediate family members, are beside him in the same room or are grouped at the opposite end. The other escorts are within the porch or in a smaller room of the mortuary house.[87]

At Klementowice, eastern Poland, the male skeleton in the center of the north end of the stone cist was equipped with as many as thirty-five artifacts including thirteen vases, four flint axes, three daggers of boar tusk, and the jawbone of a boar. A young woman, seated upright in the southern end of the cist, was equipped with only a small amphora, while the bones of an old man and of a headless individual were in the southeastern corner of the cist.[88] Generally, rich male graves contain only one female skeleton and one or two of children. One exceptional instance is the cist grave at Voytsekhivka in Volynia, containing a male skeleton flanked by two women and four children, with a young man and a woman at his feet.[89] (FIGURE 10–29)

In a number of cases, skeletal remains of adult males and children are found in separate stone cists together with sacrificed animals. The sacrificed human beings are headless or without legs, or are represented by heads alone. Often a double-pointed bone spear is found among the bones, suggesting the means of their death. At many Polish sites, a draft team of two oxen is buried near a cist with a human skeleton, as in the Baden complex (see fig. 10–26). They were laid sidewise, legs contracted, foreheads almost touching as if buried yoked, with bone disks in a star design around their necks. Near one such pair at Pikutkowo, central Poland, were two clay drums in a large dish. Other animal graves contained only cows or horses, or a combination including cows, pigs or boars, a stag, a fox, and a chamois. Pits filled with black-stained earth, perhaps remains of blood, have been noted at the animal burials.

The religious and social traditions of the Globular Amphora culture demonstrate that the grave structure was unrelated to that of the TRB culture. TRB graves contain extended burials arranged in long-barrows or megalithic passage graves which occasionally underlie Globular Amphora graves.

Sun Symbolism and the Quest for Amber

The extension of Globular Amphora sites into the area of the Nemunas and Narva cultures is explained by their quest for amber to which they attached great ideological importance. Its golden hue was symbolically significant to these sun-worshiping people, and amber discs, plain or with carved solar designs (star or cross patterns), are found in important male graves.[90] The largest amber sun disc, 10 cm in diameter (FIGURE 10–30) was discovered in a rich cist grave at Ivanne, near Rovno, northern Ukraine, some 600 km from the amber source area in East Prussia or Lithuania.[91] On it, an engraved scene shows schematic human figures holding a large bow with upraised arms. A schematic animal, possibly a horse, is separated by two dashes from the group of human figures. This engraving is closely related in style to those on Crimean stone-cist walls and North Pontic stelae.

Economy, Tools, and Weapons

The Globular Amphora people were seminomadic herders living in small groups who practiced a limited seasonal movement documented by seasonal settlements of two or three rectangular semisubterranean huts, or a singular above-ground timber house. (FIGURE 10–31) Hill forts and permanent settlements constituted the cultural focus for a tribe or clan. Agricultural tools, generally quern stones, stone hoes, and wooden plowshares, indicate farming. The evidence of domesticated plants comes from impressions of barley, wheat, and pulses found in clay daub. Finds of carbonized acorns indicate their use either for human consumption or as fodder for swine. Agriculture, however, seems to have been only supplementary to an essentially stock breeding economy in which cattle were of paramount importance. They also bred pigs, horses, dogs, sheep, and goats and hunted, fished, and gathered wild plants.

Frequently present in their grave goods are two major wood-working tools: a trapezoidal flint axe, quadrangular in cross-section, and a flint chisel. These stone tools are replicas of a pair of metal tools, which in the west were very scarce. Flint, therefore, was universally cherished and the industry was intensive. At the impressive flint mine at Krzemionki in the Upper Vistula area at Opatów, some thousand shafts bear witness to the quantities of banded flint that were removed.[92] For the Globular Amphora people, this was the primary choice for the axes and chisels. Other tools and weapons—arrowheads, points, knives, and scrapers—were made of gray or chocolate flint from other sources. Bone was used for awls and needles as well as for ornaments. Composite bows, known from engravings on stone stelae (see fig. 10–46), on walls of stone cist graves (Göhlitzsh, River Saale basin in central Germany), and from actual finds of burnt bows laid in graves (cf. grave at Bożejewice at Strzelno in western Poland) were made of wood, most likely of ash, as supported by linguistic evidence.[93] The composite bow evidenced from around the end of the 4th millennium B.C., between central Germany and the Lower Dnieper, has close analogies in central Asia, particularly in the Siberian-Mongolian steppe.

Physical Type of Population

The physical type of this population is not yet satisfactorily known. In Romania, only seven skeletons have been examined which were characterized by Olga Necrasov as "attenuated proto-Europid with some brachylization."[94] The broad-headed skulls from the stone-cist graves in western Ukraine are very similar to those from Romanian Moldavia, and the skulls from Poland are also broad-headed. Multivariate comparisons made between seventeen male skulls from central Germany, Czechoslovakia, and Poland by Ilse Schwidetzky has shown affinities with the substratum TRB population. Although the number of individuals examined is still very small, it is interesting to note that Schwidetzky sees a certain gradation within the Globular Amphora population in which breadth measurements decrease from east to west. The eastern groups are very similar to the Kurgan type, while the western resemble the central German TRB people.[95] We have yet to discover the amount of population influx and how much crossing took place between various types.

Nevertheless, it is apparent that the emergence of the Globular Amphora culture in the north European plain is crucial to an understanding of the Indo-Europeanization of this part of Europe. We must bear in mind that the fundamental social, religious, and economic components of the Globular Amphora culture link it to the North Pontic area. The fact that the Globular Amphora culture is more homogeneous than the Baden suggests that if these people were indeed Indo-European speakers, they completely succeeded in subverting the indigenous population or in converting them to their own creeds, customs, and language.

FIGURE 10–31

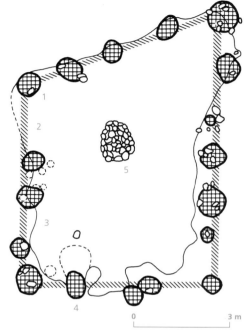

FIGURE 10–31 Plan of a Globular Amphora semi-subterranean dwelling. Biedrzychowice, district of Prudnik, Poland. L of the longest wall 10.5 m.

1. Postholes
2. Outline of the walls
3. Contours of a dwelling pit
4. Hearth
5. Stone hearth in the center

The Third Wave, c. 3000 B.C.: The Intrusion of the "Yamna" Kurgans of South Russia into East-Central Europe and Their Impact

The Kurgan Wave No. 3, c. 3000 B.C., was a massive infiltration that caused drastic changes in the ethnic configurations of Europe. (FIGURE 10–32) Population shifts to western, northern, and northeastern Europe, as well as to the Adriatic region and Greece, account for the final Indo-Europeanization of Europe.

Late Yamna Graves in Romania, Bulgaria, Yugoslavia, and Eastern Hungary

The third Kurgan thrust is identified by hundreds of graves in Romania, Bulgaria, Yugoslavia (south Banat), and eastern Hungary, which are identical to Late Yamna (pit grave) burials in the Lower Dnieper, the Lower Don, and Lower Volga basins.[96] Diagnostic features are: male burials in deep pits; timber-hut construction within the grave roofed with oak or birch beams; floor covering of wood mats, bast, or ashes; grave walls hung with rugs or other textiles; predominantly western orientation of the dead; and supine skeletal position with contracted legs (lateral in later graves). (FIGURES 10–33, 10–34) Ochre was scattered with the dead. Round and low barrows, usually no higher than one meter, were surrounded by stone rings or ditches. Stone cists, orthostats, and stelae, common in the North Pontic Mikhailovka I complex, are not characteristic of Yamna architecture. Graves were poorly equipped, but important males were furnished with a hammer-head pin of bone or copper, a round copper plate, spiral hair rings or earrings of silver or copper, cord-impressed and stabbed beakers, chains or necklaces of copper wire tubes and canine teeth, flint arrowheads, tanged daggers of arsenic copper or flint, awls and flat axes of stone or copper. Evidence abounds for the sacrifice of human beings and animals. Among the animals sacrificed were horses, cattle, sheep, goats, deer, boar, and dogs.

FIGURE 10–32

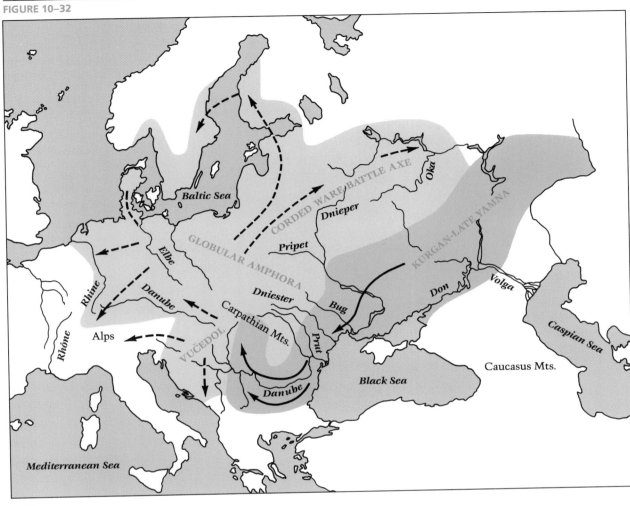

FIGURE 10–32 Kurgan Wave No. 3 c. 3000 B.C. (or soon thereafter) and its repercussions. The Late Globular Amphora-Early Corded Pottery culture shifted to the west, north, and north-east. The Vučedol shifted to western Bosnia and the Adriatic coast and ultimately reached the Peloponnese.

KEY

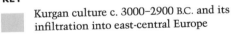 Kurgan culture c. 3000–2900 B.C. and its infiltration into east-central Europe

Globular Amphora and Early Corded Pottery culture before Kurgan Wave No. 3. Vučedol culture and its extension west and south in the early 3rd mill. B.C.

Arrows indicate directions of expansion.

FIGURE 10–33

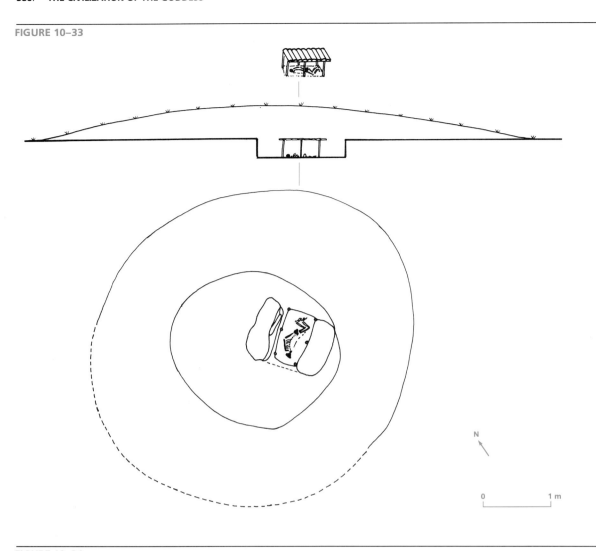

FIGURE 10–33 The third Kurgan wave is traced by hundreds of low kurgans with timber huts in pits (*yamna*, ''pit''). This is a cross-section and plan of a Yamna type kurgan in northern Yugoslavia (Vojlovica at Pančevo, east of Belgrade). The mortuary timber hut in the pit was built of six wooden posts supporting horizontal beams and had a timber floor covering. Inside the hut was a male in a contracted position lying on the right side, head pointing to the west. Two silver hair-rings were found at his head. c. 3000–2900 B.C. Kurgan is 8 m across.

FIGURE 10–34

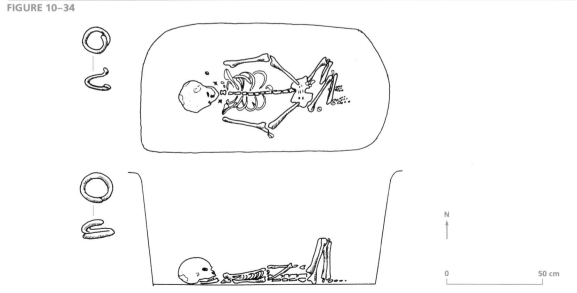

FIGURE 10–34 A pit grave (two views) from a Yamna kurgan in SW Romania. The skeleton lies on the back with contracted legs. Two silver earrings and red ochre were found at the head. Plenița, near Craiova, S Romania, c. 3000–2900 B.C.

FIGURE 10–35

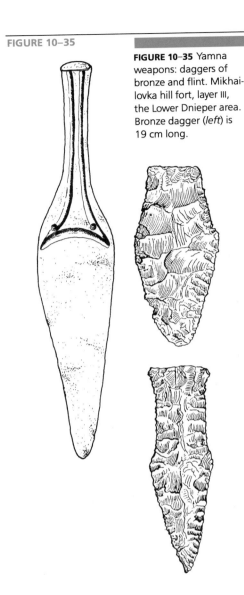

FIGURE 10–35 Yamna weapons: daggers of bronze and flint. Mikhailovka hill fort, layer III, the Lower Dnieper area. Bronze dagger (*left*) is 19 cm long.

Chronology

One of the most informative monuments north of the Black Sea is the Mikhailovka hill fort in the Lower Dnieper region, with its three layers of cultural deposits. The lower layer, Mikhailovka I, which belongs to the early Maikop culture, was overlain, after a hiatus, by two layers of the Yamna culture, Mikhailovka II and III.[97] Fortifications of stone walls, 2 m high, belong to Mikhailovka III. Bronze and flint daggers (FIGURE 10–35) and tall beakers with rounded bases, decorated with horizontal cord impressions, comb-stamped herringbone design, and cord-impressed or incised hanging striated triangles are typical of the Yamna layers. In addition to beakers, there are bowls, dishes, and three- or four-legged braziers. This type of pottery is also found in the Yamna graves of the Lower Volga.

In Moldavia and the western Ukraine, Wave No. 3 barrows are stratigraphically situated above the Usatovo-Folteşti settlements and graves. Most of the calibrated radiocarbon dates for the Yamna graves west of the Black Sea range shortly after 3000 B.C. (TABLE 32)

Yamna graves from the Lower Dnieper, Don, and Lower Volga steppe date from the same time and also from a later period. A number of earlier Yamna radiocarbon dates from the Ukraine and southern Russia are given for comparison in table 33. The chronological link is obvious.

Physical Type of Population

Eighty skeletons from Yamna graves have been examined in Romania alone, a sufficient number for some conclusions about the physical type. The Yamna people in Romania were tall statured and strongly built, with predominantly dolichocephalic skulls, medium cranial height and rounded occipital, with variable facial mass, pronounced nose, and a robust mandible.[98] This type corresponds to that of the Yamna graves in the Ukraine and south Russia.[99]

The Impact on the Balkans and Greece: The Vučedol Shift Northwest and South

The Vučedol shift from its core area into the peripheries caused changes in the whole Balkan peninsula, as well as in central Europe. Vučedol sites virtually disappeared from Hungary and the Danube lands in Yugoslavia. The migration to the northwest and south must have started c. 3000–2800 B.C. and was obviously connected with the Yamna movement from the east.

In central and northwestern Bohemia, the new settlers established a series of hilltop villages and are known under the name "Řivnac," so called after a hilltop site nine kilometers northwest of Prague, excavated in 1882–84.[100] The major source of information derives from the hilltop village at Homolka northeast of Kladno in central Bohemia.[101]

Dalmatia, western Bosnia, and Albania were reached from the eastern Alpine region. Along the Sana River in western Bosnia, the Vučedol people occupied areas not previously inhabited. Their settlements in the newly acquired lands consisted of naturally protected hill forts and caves, usually difficult to access.[102] Cemeteries of tumuli, including stone cists, were discovered at the Cetina River and at Rumen near Sinj near the Adriatic coast.[103] At Mala Gruda, Tivat, a royal tomb in a tumulus came to light equipped with a silver axe, a gold dagger of Early Helladic II type (2900–2500 B.C.), gold rings, copper plate, and Vučedol vases.[104] (FIGURE 10–36) This tumulus was nearly 4 m high and 30 m across. At the base was a round platform built of river pebbles, and the central grave, a mortuary house built of stone slabs, was lowered into the ground. The male skeleton was in a contracted position with a silver axe and gold dagger deposited at his waist, with five gold rings and a copper plate at his head. A beaker and a conical dish stood at his feet. The tomb architecture and burial rites at Mala Gruda are the same as those of the North Pontic Maikop culture. Mala Gruda is located halfway between northwestern Yugoslavia and

FIGURE 10–36

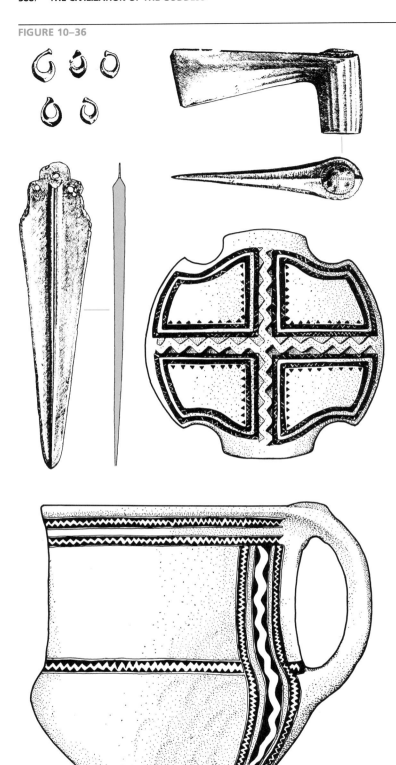

FIGURE 10–36 Halfway between the north Adriatic-east Alpine area and the Peloponnese, kurgans girded with stone rings and with stone cist graves were discovered which belong to the North Pontic Kurgan (Maikop) tradition. Royal burials were equipped with elaborate vases and prestige items. This illustration depicts grave gifts from the royal burial at Mala Gruda at Tivat on the Adriatic coast: gold rings and dagger, silver axe, beaker, and dish with encrusted design of Vučedol type. Early 3rd mill. B.C.

western Greece, where kurgans of the same tradition also emerged in the early 3rd millennium B.C.

The migration of the Vučedol south to the mountainous regions and to the inhospitable and stony Dalmatian coast cannot be explained as a normal territorial extension occasioned by a population increase. This was caused by the intrusion of Yamna people into Yugoslavia and Hungary. There was a conspicuous occupation of a series of caves, both on the continent (Hruštovaca, Dabar Pečina, Zelena Pečina in Dalmatia and Hercegovina) and on the Adriatic islands (Grapčeva Spilja on the island of Hvar, Jamina Sredi on Cres, Vela Spilja on Korčula). Ample evidence from the islands of Leucas and the northwestern Peloponnese suggests that the Kurgans arriving in Greece at the beginning of the 3rd millennium B.C., perhaps via Albania and the Adriatic, were descendants of the Indo-Europeanized east-central Europeans, i.e., the Baden-Vučedol people.

The cemetery of Steno on the island of Leucas, consisting of 33 kurgans, is a good example of the changed customs in Greece.[105] These tumuli belong to several phases, dating from the Early Helladic II and III, c. 2900–2250 B.C., and the buried chieftains and warriors were probably members of the dynasty ruling the island. The earliest and largest tumulus, encircled by a stone retaining wall, stood apart from the others (FIGURE 10–37, 2); its mortuary chamber was exceptionally large and well made, with walls of large round stones. This contained the skeletons of a man and a woman and pieces of a sheep and a lamb amid ash in the soil which suggest the remains of a funerary feast.

Other early tumuli contained inhumation graves in shafts covered by stone slabs, under a cairn of stones and a pile of earth. In some, stone cists had been inserted into the tumulus. This type of grave architecture and burial practice go back to the Maikop traditions which were diffused into east-central Europe by Kurgan Wave No. 2. Analogies are seen in the splendid kurgans northwest of the Black Sea (see fig. 10–10), the Tarnava kurgans in northwestern Bulgaria (see fig. 10–11), and the Belotić tumuli in Serbia. Other close parallels are in Albania[106] and Dalmatia.[107] The Early Helladic II date of the early or R group of the Steno tumuli is indicated by bird-shaped vases ("sauce boats"), typical of Early Helladic II. Triangular copper dagger blades, with or without the mid-rib and with two rivet holes and halberds, are known from the engravings on Valcamonica stelae (see figs. 10–41, 10–42, 10–43). Also found were slotted spearheads and poignards. But the most prestigious weapon of the elite class was the dagger which was a routine accoutrement of leading males (usually held in the right hand) found in all the rich tumuli. (FIGURE 10–37,2)

Tumuli on round stone platforms surrounded by stone rings, as well as apsidal houses, are also reported from the end of the Early Helladic period at Olympia and were continuous in the later, Middle Helladic period. Many other tumuli from the western Peloponnese are reported as Early Helladic III or Middle Helladic, i.e., the second half of the 3rd to the beginning of the 2nd millennium B.C.[108] Thus, in the middle and late 3rd millennium B.C., the Kurgan tradition seems already to have been firmly established. A series of destroyed Early Helladic II sites in the Argolid speaks for a gruesome takeover. Destruction is evidenced at Lerna, Tiryns, Asine, Zygouries, and Aghios Kosmas. At Lerna, the burned house of Tiles was not rebuilt, apsidal structures appeared, and the settlement plan changed.[109]

The takeover in Greece was apparently analogous to that of east-central Europe which entailed a transformation of the basic social structure and administrative system by the establishment of a ruling class in hill forts. A study of the physical types of the population shows that the Kurgan warrior groups were not massive in numbers and did not eradicate the local inhabitants.[110] They came in small migrating bands and established themselves forcefully as a small ruling elite.

FIGURE 10–37

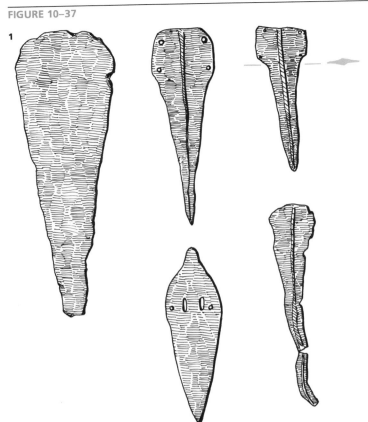

1

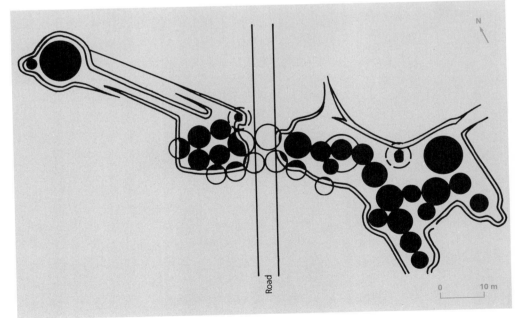

2

FIGURE 10–37 (1) Dagger, halberd, spear, and poignard blades from Steno kurgans. Scale 1:2. (2) The representative kurgan (round barrow) cemetery in Greece indicating cultural change at Steno, on the island of Leucas, west of Peloponnese. Early Helladic II–III, early 3rd mill. B.C. Kurgans had stone cairns and rings as in the North Pontic area. Stone cist graves were lowered into the ground. The royal tomb is on the left, separated from the rest. Outlines of 33 round barrows are shown (white circles mean destroyed barrows).

The Impact on Western Europe: The Bell Beaker Folk—Descendants of the Amalgamated Yamna and Vučedol Culture in the Middle Danube Basin—and Their Exodus to the West

The Bell Beaker culture of western Europe which diffused between 2500 and 2100 B.C. between central Europe, the British Isles, and the Iberian Peninsula, could not have arisen in a vacuum. The mobile horse-riding and warrior people who buried their dead in Yamna type kurgans certainly could not have developed out of any west European culture. We must ask what sort of ecology and ideology created these people, and where are the roots of the specific Bell Beaker equipment and their burial rites. In my view, the Bell Beaker cultural elements derive from Vučedol and Kurgan (Late Yamna) traditions.

The specific correspondence between the Yamna, Late Vučedol, and Bell Beaker complexes is visible in burial rites which include grave pits under round barrows, the coexistence of cremation and inhumation rites, and the construction of mortuary houses. (FIGURE 10–38) In armaments we see tanged or riveted triangular daggers made of arsenic copper, spear points of arsenic copper and flint, concave-based or tanged triangular arrowheads of flint, and arrow straighteners. In ornaments there are necklaces of canine teeth, copper tubes, or bird bones; boar tusks; and crescent-shaped pendants resembling breast plates.[111] In solar symbolism we find sun or star motifs excised and white encrusted on the inside of braziers, or incised on bone or amber button-shaped beads. Techniques of ceramic decoration include stamping or gouging in zoned

FIGURE 10–38

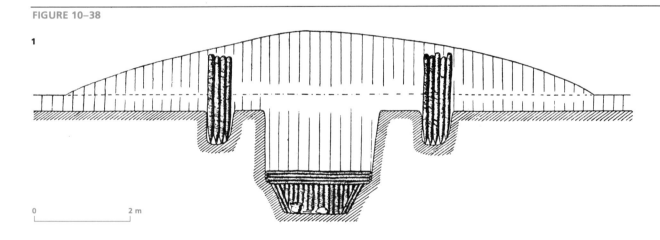

1

0   2 m

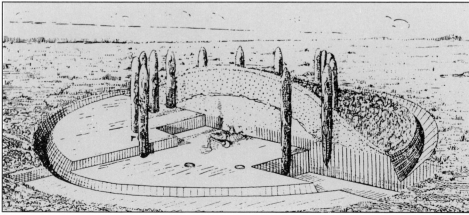

2

FIGURE 10–38 Bell Beaker kurgans from central and western Europe, a continuous Kurgan burial tradition. (1) Cross-section of a kurgan with a pit-grave surrounded by a palisade. Smolin near Breclav, Moravia. (2) Bell Beaker kurgan with a contracted skeleton in the center surrounded with wooden posts. Langedijk, Friesland, the Netherlands. Diameter of the barrows: (1) 11 m; (2) 9 m.

metopes, encrustation with white paste of delicate geometric motifs, zigzags, dashes, nets, lozenges, and dots or circles (a Baden-Kostolac-Vučedol tradition). Certain ceramic forms placed in graves, such as braziers and beakers, are from the Kurgan tradition. The Bell Beaker people, wherever they spread, continued the traditional ceramic art connected with their faith. Only the ritual importance of their uniquely beautiful stereotyped beakers could have motivated their production for hundreds of years in lands far from the homeland. The correspondences linking the Bell Beaker and Yamna with the Vučedol—in armament, costume, funeral rites, beliefs in life after death, and in symbolism—are precisely the most significant and revealing. It is very likely that the Bell Beaker complex is an amalgam of Vučedol and Yamna traditions formed after the incursion of the Yamna people into the milieu of the Vučedol culture, i.e., in the course of 300 to 400 years after 3000–2900 B.C.

Horse-Riding Warriors and Pastoralists

Horse bones in a series of sites provide a clue to the mobility of the Bell Beaker people. Analysis of animal bones from the sites at Budapest (Czepel Hollandiut and Czepel-Haros) have shown that the horse was the foremost species of the domestic fauna, constituting more than 60 percent of the total animal bones.[112] This suggests a large-scale domestication of the horse in the Carpathian basin. Bell Beaker migrations were carried out on horseback from central Europe as far as Spain (where horse bones have also been found in Bell Beaker contexts).[113] The horse also played a significant role in religion, as can be seen from the remains of the horse sacrifice where skulls are found in cremation graves.

The Bell Beaker people were primarily herders of domestic animals since cattle, sheep, goats, pigs, and dog bones consistently occur in their habitation sites. House remains are scarce, but several surface structures with stake walls daubed with clay (the largest measuring 6 by 10 m) are reported from Czechoslovakia.[114] Local metallurgy is evidenced by sandstone molds for daggers.

Kurgan Type Burials

The striking similarity of burial practices ties the Bell Beaker complex to the Kurgan (Late Yamna) tradition. Individual burials were in pit-built mortuary houses, variously constructed, some with four posts in the corners, sometimes roofed, sometimes not, or stone lined. A ditch surrounded the central grave in which several rows of stakes were set (as shown in the reconstruction of the burial at Smolin in Moravia),[115] which was then covered by an earthen barrow. Individuals lay in a crouched position facing the rising sun. A great number of half-burned or dismembered child burials in cemeteries may imply sacrifice, not simple burial. The practice of cremation was inherited from the Vučedol culture; in Hungary, cremation burials constitute nearly 90 percent of all Bell Beaker burials.

The quantitative analysis of grave material indicates that the Bell Beaker people had a social composition approximating a ranked society.[116] Three strata are represented: warriors (or rulers), craftsmen, and common folk (peasants). The richest graves are those of mature males. Grave goods indicating status are items such as earrings, button-shaped beads of amber, jet, and gold, belt rings, and weapons.

Chronology

The great majority of Bell Beaker radiocarbon dates from western Europe cluster between the 25th and 21st centuries B.C., while a few precede the middle of the 3rd millennium B.C. The earliest date comes from the habitation pit of the Czepel Hollandiut site at Budapest.[117] (TABLE 34)

The Vinkovci-Samogyvár Culture: Successors of the Vučedol and Kurgan (Late Yamna) in the Middle Danube Basin

The culture that succeeds Vučedol and Yamna in Yugoslavia and Hungary is known under two names: Vinkovci and Samogyvár. The first comes from the excavation of a settlement at Trznica near Vinkovci in Srem, northern Yugoslavia,[118] the latter from an excavation at the site of Samogyvár in southwestern

Hungary.[119] Nearly 150 sites have been excavated or recorded in the last twenty years: hill forts, kurgans, and pits containing pottery (the sole remains of habitation sites). The stratigraphy from these excavations has shown that this culture superseded the late Vučedol culture. One of the best stratigraphies was uncovered in a settlement located on a high plateau at Pecina near Vrdnik, Srem. There, the Vinkovci pits were found dug into the late Vučedol cultural layer and the latter was above the Baden-Kostolac layer.[120] The distribution of Vinkovci-Samogyvár sites covers western Hungary north up to Slovakia, western Romania, Slavonia, Srem, western Serbia, Bosnia down to Montenegro, and the Morava River basin of central Yugoslavia down to the Svetozarevo and Kruševac region. (FIGURE 10–39)

So far, archeologists have not linked the Vinkovci-Samogyvár culture with the Bell Beaker, in spite of the identity of burial rites, settlement type, and ceramics. There is hardly any reason to treat these groups as separate cultures. The repertoire of ceramic forms is inherited from the preceding late Vučedol-Makó culture of Yugoslavia and Hungary.

In western Hungary and western Yugoslavia, the Vinkovci-Samogyvár traditions continued into the 2nd millennium B.C., to be typified by hill forts and by the absence of tells, eventually developing into the "Encrusted Pottery Culture" of western Hungary and northwestern Yugoslavia, and the "Gradina culture" of Bosnia and Dalmatia (from gradina, meaning "hill forts").

FIGURE 10–39

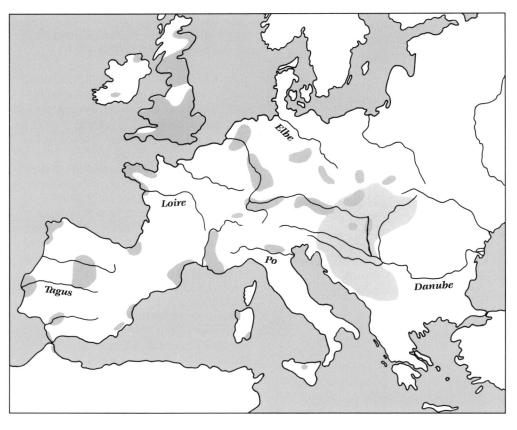

FIGURE 10–39 The area of distribution of the Vinkovci-Samogyvár sites, the possible homeland of the Bell Beaker culture in the middle of the 3rd mill. B.C. Dotted areas indicate the spread of the Bell Beaker culture in western Europe.

KEY

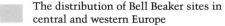
The distribution of Bell Beaker sites in central and western Europe

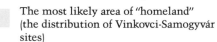
The most likely area of "homeland" (the distribution of Vinkovci-Samogyvár sites)

The Impact on Northern Europe: The Corded Pottery Culture of Central Europe and Its Expansion Northwest and Northeast

The Corded Pottery (also called Battle Axe) complex is known not only from the north-central European plain in Germany and Poland but also from Holland, Denmark, southern Sweden, southern Norway, and the East Baltic countries as far as southern Finland in the northeast; the easternmost branch (Fat'yanovo) reached the Upper Volga basin in central Russia (see fig.10–32). According to radiocarbon dates, expansion into northwestern and northeastern Europe, territories previously occupied by TRB, Nemunas, Narva, and Volosovo cultures, took place before the middle of the 3rd millennium B.C. Migration on so large a scale seems to have been a repercussion of a new push from the east— Kurgan Wave No. 3.

In the earliest phase, grave equipment throughout this area exhibits features closely related to that of central Europe. Characteristic constituents are a beaker with horizontal cord impressions around the neck, a globular amphora with a radial pattern over the shoulder, a flint axe, a chisel, a blade or flake, and a stone battle axe (Type A).[121] (FIGURE 10–40) The early phase is therefore called the "Common European Horizon." Burial in timber or stone mortuary houses under a low earthen barrow is universal. The striking uniformity in all areas where Corded Pottery graves are found is a strong argument for a more or less simultaneous dispersion.

Social Inequality and the Privileged Position of Males in Northwestern and Northeastern Europe

The social structure of the early Corded Pottery people is related to that of both the Globular Amphora and the Yamna of the Dnieper-Volga steppe. The barrows of the early phase contain only male skeletons and the central grave with mortuary pit-house structure probably honored a privileged individual. Apart from the primary burial, there are usually other graves dug into the earthen mounds that are close in time to that of

FIGURE 10–40

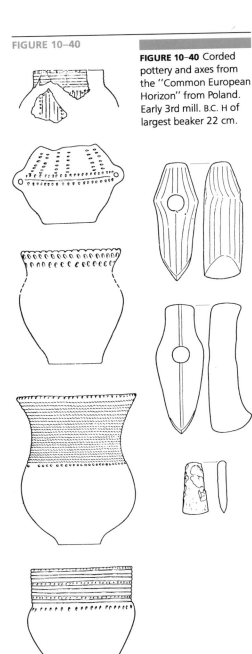

FIGURE 10–40 Corded pottery and axes from the "Common European Horizon" from Poland. Early 3rd mill. B.C. H of largest beaker 22 cm.

the primary grave, and point to the existence of at least two social categories. It is of interest that the dug-in graves outnumber the central sub-barrow graves. The lower social stratum is also represented by males. Not much is known about the burial of women and children in this period. Corded Pottery graves of the later period, however, show a normal constituency of females and juveniles.

Physical Type

Who were the Corded Pottery people? Do they represent an intrusion of a new Kurgan (i.e., Yamna) people from the east? Or does this period simply represent a later phase of the Globular Amphora complex, pushed to the north and northeast by the influx of the Yamna people? The latter seems likely. Both the Globular Amphora and Corded Pottery complexes contain components of the local TRB substratum and the Pontic steppe element. The TRB component is predominant in the physical type of the Corded Pottery population of Germany and Czechoslovakia, with the exception of some individuals who are considered to be of the steppe type.[122] Analysis of the skeletal material from Poland shows a steppe origin.[123] Elsewhere the bulk of the population were indigenous remnants of the Old Europeans.

Chronology

The Corded Pottery culture has two main periods. During the first, c. 3000–2600 B.C., the Common European Horizon, the practice of nomadic movement and the short occupation of any one spot have left very few preserved habitation sites. The simultaneous existence of the nomadic Corded Pottery pastoralists and the indigenous agriculturalists has been demonstrated by studies of Corded Pottery sites in southern Poland. The second period is characterized by the crystallization of local units. A number of radiocarbon dates from various parts of this culture fix this period between 2600–2200 B.C. (TABLE 35)

The Proto-Indo-European Economic and Social Tradition

The proto-Indo-European (PIE) culture, as reconstructed on the basis of comparative Indo-European linguistics and mythology and supported by early historic records, coincides well with archeological data. In this section I shall touch upon the linguistic and mythological evidence relevant to the question of identity between the Kurgan and proto-Indo-European traditions.

Languages, like cultures, act as living organisms: they constantly change and live through periods of convergence and divergence. Although we cannot go back much further than Volga Neolithic and Eneolithic of the 6th and 5th millennia B.C., we can reconstruct certain characteristics of this culture that are in agreement with linguistic and mythological elements. The period around 5000–4500 B.C. is marked by incessantly growing mobility and trade. I therefore assume the possibility of linguistic consolidation in process at this period, just before the proto-Indo-European outburst into Europe. The hypothetical PIE language does not reflect preagricultural conditions. As linguistically reconstructed, domesticated animals (including the horse), mobility, and the classed patriarchal society, are among the most characteristic phenomena of the PIE culture. The Kurgan culture of the 5th millennium B.C. in the Volga forest-steppe and steppe and its newly acquired territory north of the Black Sea agrees with much that is reconstructed on a linguistic basis as PIE.

Domesticated Animals

Domesticated animals played a paramount role in the PIE culture as shown by the common names for sheep (*owis*), cattle (*gwows*), steer (*(s)tauro*), pig (*sus* and *porkos*), horse (*ekwo-ekwa*), goat (*aigis, os*), and dog (*kwon-kun-*) in most of the Indo-European languages. There is another name for "cows and sheep": *peku(s)*: Latin *pecus*, Old Indic *paśu*, Baltic *peku*. Since this word has a family of related words connected with the meaning "fleece," "hair," and "to comb" (Greek *pekos*, "fleece"; Old High German *fahs*, "skin hair"; Latin *pectere*, "to comb"), it is assumed that *peku* originally connoted a woolly animal, probably a sheep, and that there was a stage when only sheep were domesticated and the other animals were not. The words for wool and weaving are clearly PIE (Old Church Slavic *vluna*, Lithuanian *vilna*, German *Wolle*, Old Indic *wina*; German *weben*, "weave," Old Indic *vabh-*) and may date back to the early phase of animal domestication.

Cattle must have been the treasured possession of a family, clan, or tribe and were used in exchange, the trend also attested by words and early historic records. In Sanskrit, the term for *lord* means "lord of cattle." The earliest written sources, the Iliad and the Rigveda, speak of how a bride or weapons are obtained in exchange for cattle. Cattle (*pecus*) were the main possession that had the meaning of our word money. Hence, the Latin name for money, *pecunia*. This role of cattle continued up to the 20th century (as dowry, for instance, in rural areas). Activities associated with cattle in Indo-European mythic and epic literature very clearly illustrate the importance of cattle raiding. The growth of private ownership derived a powerful impetus from the domestication of cattle.

The name for the domesticated horse is preserved as Latin *equos*, Gothic *aihva-*, Lithuanian *ašva*. The PIE form is reconstructed as **ekwos* or **ekwa*. Comparative Indo-European mythological research indicates the unquestionably prime role of the horse (particularly the white horse) as a sacred and sacrificial animal, the incarnation of divine power of the God of the Shining Sky. Archeology supports the linguistic and mythological evidence for an early date of horse domestication, probably no later than the end of the 6th millennium B.C. The horse was a sacrificial and riding animal and as such was used in warfare from at least the middle of the 5th millennium B.C. The earliest warriors were equipped with spear points, daggers, bows and arrows, and were able to shoot from horseback much like the historic Indo-Europeans, Scythians, Sarmatians, and others. In cult, the horse as a divine and sacrificial animal is attested as early as its known use for riding.

Metallurgy

Linguistics has failed to reconstruct a common word for metallurgy. This should not be surprising since the early Kurgans (Kurgan I) did not have this technology. Copper items were introduced to them by the Old Europeans through barter with the Cucutenians. Metallurgy was acquired considerably later, in the second half of the 4th millennium B.C. from Transcaucasia when it was transmitted north of the Black Sea, and with Wave No. 2 to east-central Europe.

Weapons

The following words can be reconstructed from original Indo-European terms for weapons.[124]

*(H)nsi, a cutting and slashing weapon, "sword," originally a flint knife or dagger (Germanic *xsaxsaz* "sword" often substitutes for "knife"); Old Indic *asi-*, Lat. *ensis*

*keru, "spearhead," "blade," or some sort of casting weapon (Vedic *saru-* meant "dart," "arrow," or "spear"; Germanic cognate is **xeruz*)

*Eengh-es-u, "spear," thrusting weapon; and **ghai-so-s*, "casting spear," "a javelin" (the source of Old Irish *gae* and Proto Germanic **zaizas*, Old Indic *hesas*, "missile")

*taqso-m, "bow"; Greek *tokson*, M Persian *taxs*, Latin *taxus*

*isu- arrow(head)

*gwiH, "bowstring" (Old Indic *jya*, Avestan *jya*, Lith. *gija* "thread," "sinew")

*Aek-on, "slingstone"

*Aek-mon-, "stone hammer"

These words support an early use of weapons which is in agreement with archeological evidence (see figs. 10-2, 10-4, 10-7, 10-35, 10-41, 10-42, 10-43, 10-45, 10-46).

Vehicles

Mobility is unquestionably a PIE characteristic, since horse riding was the prime means of Kurgan mobility. The reconstructed PIE form for vehicle (German *Wagen*, Lithuanian *vežimas*, Polish *wóz*) is a form with the root **wegh-*. Even parts of the vehicle are reconstructable: wheel—**rotha* (Lithuanian *ratas*, German *Rad*, Old Indic *rathah*, "chariot," Latin *rota*); axis—**ak'sis*, lynch **pin* (*tulis* in Lithuanian, Greek, and Germanic); and yoke—*yugom* (very well attested). The family of the root *wegh-* is associated with words for lifting, carrying, lever, and sleigh. This may imply that the original "vehicle" was for weight lifting or levering, or was a sledge. Even if it was not a four-wheeled cart in its original form, the proto-Indo-Europeans must have been acquainted with wheeled wagons from Kurgan I times. So far, the earliest evidence for the existence of wheels are miniature clay models of wheels found in Old European settlements (Cucuteni A and Karanovo VI phases) dating from the middle of the 5th millennium B.C. No parts of actual vehicles of this period have ever been found. The question as to who first invented the vehicle cannot as yet be solved.

The mobility of the Kurgans before their infiltration into Europe was probably similar to that of the later inhabitants of the steppe—the Scythians, Sarmatians, and others. Herodotus describes the Scythians as having no permanent structures or crops to defend, free to move about with their wagons, their possessions, and their livestock, and able to elude an enemy or to shoot at him from horseback whenever they chose. Indeed, it was easy for the Kurgans to burn their pit dwellings and set out for the next territory.

Social Structure

The PIE culture, as shown by comparative Indo-European linguistics and historical evidence and supported by archeology, can be described as a patrilineal society under the patriarchal leadership of a warrior chief. Age was the determining factor for leadership by this chief, who may have played an active role only in times of stress when greater group cohesion was necessary. Exogamous marriage occurred between small, mobile patrilocal families, members of a larger clan or tribe. A separate class of priests is unlikely to have been established by the proto period. Females possessed inferior status, elevated only by association with their male relations. The husband's strong rights over his wife is evidenced by epic songs and legal texts. Under the influence of the Indo-European culture, Neolithic women's influence collapsed and they became private property in the new trading and raiding society.

The evidence for patriliny, patrilocality, and patripotency furnished by proto-Indo-European kinship terminology is excellent.[125] There is general agreement among philologists and linguists that the PIE terms which concern familial and marital relationships describe a system of patrilineal inheritance and post-marital residence. For example, the basic terms that exist for one's parents' generation imply the domination of the male relations: father—*pHte:r; mother—*maHte:r; mother's brother or mother's father—*awyos; and father's brother—*pHtrwos. Common terms for both the maternal and paternal aunts are conspicuously absent. The terms for a person's own generation include: the brother—*bhraHte:r, which comprises a wide range of male peers (who traditionally form a patrilineal group with important ritual and political functions); the sister—*sweso:r which means "own" ("the woman of my clan"); the son—*swHnws (*swH, "to give birth," suggesting a strong tie between mother and son); and daughter—*dhwgHte:r (which seems to be related to milking, "to milk" or "milkmaid"). Words also exist for the husband's parents (*swekwHs and *swekwros), the husband's siblings (*gHlows, feminine; *daHywe:r, masculine), in addition to the son's wife (*snwsos) and daughter/sister's husband (*genHr). The widow (*wydh, meaning "to be empty, inadequate") is recognized as a discrete status, where the widower is not.

There is no corresponding similarity of terms for the bride's family. The Indo-European wife would have joined her husband's household where she lived together with his father and brothers. This can further be interpreted as evidence of an exogamous pattern of marriage.

The proto-Indo-European *pot denotes the male family head, patri potestas, or chief. An additional pair of correspondences, *genH-os/*genH-r provides further evidence of a patriarchal society: *genH-os is used to describe the patrilineal group into which an individual married, while the masculine noun *genH-r refers to the most prominent member of that group. The picture of an Indo-European community leader (*pot or *dompoti) painted by mythological and legal texts appears to be a despotic, and probably polygynous, warrior-patriarch who ruled his family or clan with absolute power over life and death.

The status of women was clearly inferior. The term for "bride price" derives from *wedh, "to lead" evocative of chattel. It has been suggested that females represent a "positive nuisance" to the stability of a mobile, warlike tribe.

Linguistic paleontology has provided evidence for the social organization above the immediate family. The *domos (*dreb in western PIE) or house belonging to a single family, also belonged to a small patrilocal extended family, or *weik. Residents of a *weik might further identify themselves as members of a common descent group, the *gen or clan, and chose marriage partners from within their largest ethnic group or tribe, the *teuta.

Agriculture and Its Increase in the European Branch

In the Kurgan culture of the steppe, agriculture was secondary to a pastoral economy. However, considerable knowledge of agricultural terminology in the European branch of the Indo-Europeans is suggested by lexical studies. It follows that the increase of agriculture is synchronous with a decrease of nomadism after the incursion of the Kurgan (Maikop) people into Europe, and especially into the territories where agriculture was a millennial tradition.

Some agriculture was practiced by the proto-Indo-Europeans. There are common names for "grain," "grinding" and "quern," "to sow," and "to cut"; and the word for "hoe," mat(e)ya, is widespread. Of great importance is the preservation of the names for millet (*meli, *melyom, *melya) for a lesser kind of wheat or grass, couch grass, sedge, spelt, rye grass: *puras,os; and for cereal used for fermentation and brewing: *yewos, pl. *yewoi. The root yew- is associated with the family of words having the meaning to gush or emanate, boil, ferment, agitate, rouse.

So far only millet has been identified in Kurgan sites of the Dnieper-Volga steppe. There is no trace of einkorn and emmer wheat, barley, oats, or rye, although stone hoes, sickle blades of flint, and quern stones have been found in settlements. Large hoe-like tools known from several settlements are considered to be primitive plowshares. It seems that the Kurgan people in their original home engaged in an extensive form of wild-grass economy. Except for millet, a "ground" cereal; *yewos, a cereal used for fermentation; and *puris, a grass or spelt wheat, there are no other well-attested words for cereals, and there is no archeological evidence for their existence.

Common names for rye, barley, and oats are found only in the European branch of the Indo-European languages. *rughis "rye" is known in Slavic, Baltic, Germanic, and Celtic. The word for "oats" with the root *aw- is known in Slavic, Baltic, and Latin. "Barley" apparently designated "food derived from cereals" as Latin, Germanic, and Slavic forms suggest: Latin far and farina; Old Nardic barr, "barley"; Gothic barizeins, "of barley"; Old Church Slavic brašno, "food"; Serbian brašno, "flour"; and Russian borošno, "rye flour."

Some names are common to the Indo-European speakers in southern Europe: beans, peas, vetch, and poppies are attested in Latin, Albanian, and Greek. All of these plants are well known from the Neolithic in southeastern Europe, and it is quite possible that their names were later inherited by Indo-European speakers. The name for flax, *linum*, is known in Latin, Greek, Slavic, Baltic, and Germanic. The word for hemp, *kannabis*, is preserved in Greek, Albanian, Germanic, Slavic, and Baltic, but is not known among the eastern Indo-European speakers. The above suggest that Indo-European speakers *in Europe* were acquainted with many cereals and pulses and with flax and hemp. Some of the names are common to a larger group of languages and therefore may hark back in time to the formative period as an after-effect of Wave No. 2, to the second half of the 4th millennium B.C. The pulses were apparently inherited from the Old European population of southeastern Europe. It is clear that the agricultural terminology became enriched as Indo-European speakers moved west.

The Collision of Two Ideologies

The Old European and Indo-European belief systems are diametrically opposed. The Indo-European society was warlike, exogamic, patriarchal, patrilineal, and patrilocal, with a strong clanic organization and social hierarchy which gave prominence to the warrior class. Their main gods were male and depicted as warriors. There is no possibility that this pattern of social organization could have developed out of the Old European matrilineal, matricentric, and endogamic balanced society. Therefore, the appearance of the Indo-Europeans in Europe represent a collision of two ideologies, not an evolution.

The building of temples, a long-lasting tradition of Old Europe, stopped with the Kurgan incursions into Europe, except in the Aegean and Mediterranean regions. The masterfully produced religious paraphernalia—beautiful vases, sacrificial containers, models of temples, altars, sculptures, and sacred script—disappeared as well. Not a single temple directly associated with the Kurgan people is known, either in the north Pontic or Volga steppe nor in the Kurgan influenced zone of Europe during and after the migrations. The absence of any temples or even structured altars is consistent with the life of pastoralists.

The New Symbols and Deities of Europe

The Old European worship of the Goddess was partially truncated by Kurgan Wave No. 1 toward the end of the 5th millennium B.C. Horse-head scepters and cord-impressed solar motifs on pots appeared in Dobruja and in almost the whole Danube basin, but the Old European religion continued to be practiced in the Aegean and the Mediterranean, in the Cucuteni culture of Moldavia and the western Ukraine, in the TRB of northwestern and central Europe, and in all parts of the western European Neolithic.

A renewed change of symbolism and mythical imagery occurred in the second half of the 4th millennium B.C. Not only did sun and horse symbols appear, but images of male gods with their weapons and animals also emerged. The Goddess religion of the still extant Old European population was subdued. A completely new symbolic system with no roots in Europe is one of the strongest arguments for the presence in central Europe of new lords and their creeds.

The best witness of a new religion in Europe, typified by male gods, weapons, and solar symbols, are engraved stone stelae from the second half of the 4th millennium B.C. found in the Alpine valleys, in Bulgaria, in Romania with close analogs north of the Black Sea, and in the Caucasus. Their symbolism differs sharply from those of the French and Italian statue-menhirs which portray the owl-faced female goddess before she was masculinized in the Bronze Age. The Kurgan stelae display solar symbols and masculine paraphernalia, including daggers, halberds, axes, bows, quivers and arrows, belts, breast plates, double-spiral pendants; male horses, stags, and he-goats; vehicles, and ox teams pulling a plow. (FIGURES 10–41 to 10–44) These are a prime source for the reconstruction of mythical imagery and are a great value in the accurate representation of

FIGURE 10–41

FIGURE 10–41 Representation of an Indo-European warrior god with multiple arms as halberds. Daggers are shown below the throat, in the chest area, and below the belt. A vehicle drawn by oxen is shown on the lower part. The head is not preserved. Stone stela from Lagundo, Alto Adige, N Italy, c. 3000 B.C. H 3 m.

FIGURE 10–42 Two compositions engraved on rocks from Valcamonica, northern Italy, including solar symbols (in place of the head), halberds, daggers, a belt, and a horse and stag. (1) Cemmo. H 1.15 m. (2) Papardo. Rock c. 0.60 × 1.20 m; c. 3000 B.C.

FIGURE 10–43 Stela from Bagnolo, Valcamonica, northern Italy (0.80 ×1.30 m) engraved with a radiating sun (head), a breast plate (upside down), perhaps a symbol of shining (daylight) sky, a double-spiral pendant (a symbol of morning and evening light), two daggers and two axes with long shafts, a ploughing scene with a pair of yoked oxen, and seven animals (perhaps horses, dogs, or deer). c. 3000 B.C.

FIGURE 10–42

1

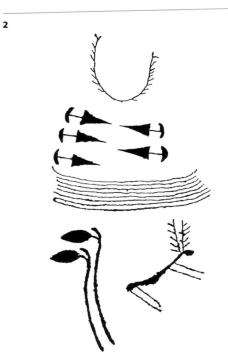

2

FIGURE 10–43

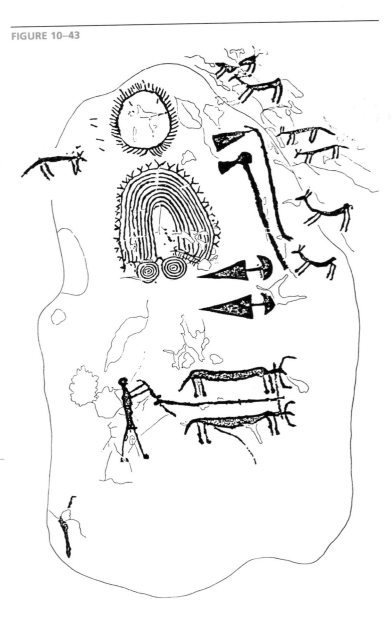

FIGURE 10–44

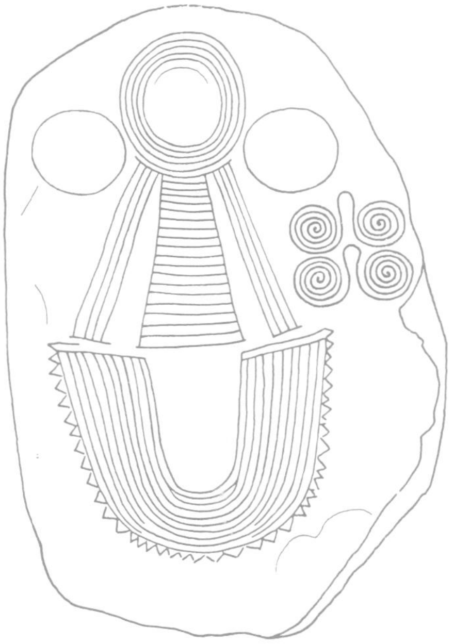

FIGURE 10–45

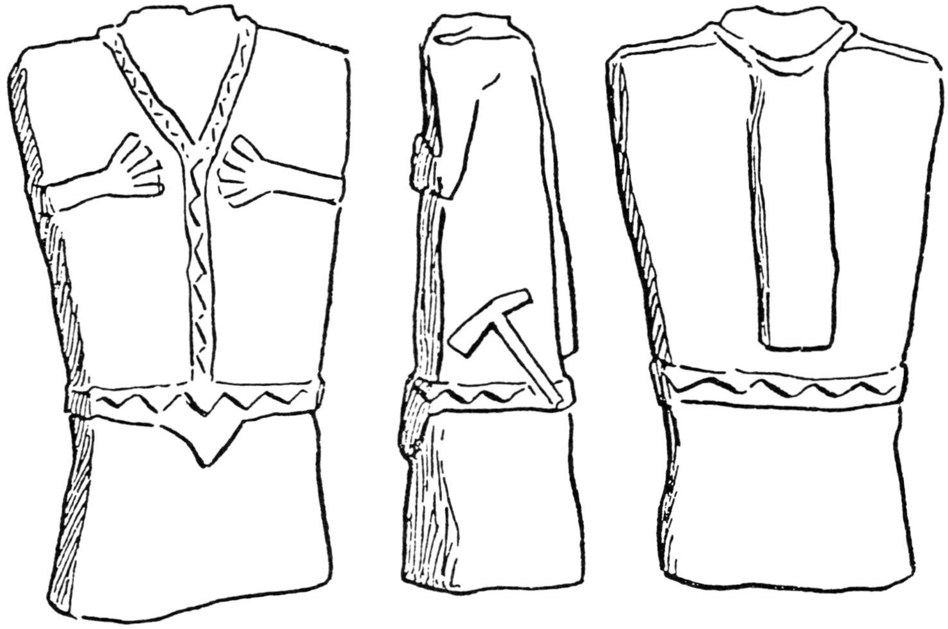

FIGURE 10–46

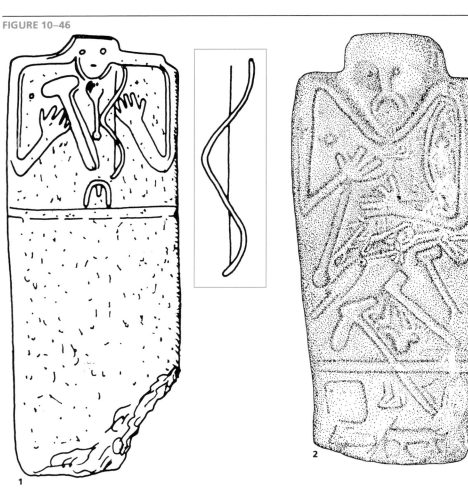

FIGURE 10–44 Stela from Caven at Teglio, Valtellina, N Italy. Radiating sun (for head) with two circles on both sides, two double-spiral pendants, and a breast plate. c. 3000 B.C. H 50 cm.

FIGURE 10–45 Anthropomorphic stela from Baia de Criș, district of Hunedoara, Transylvania, Romania. A shafted axe is shown attached at the belt on the side. The head is lost, arms are indicated. In front, a triangular collar extends down to the belt; on the back, a thong hangs attached to the collar. Tentative date c. 3000 B.C. H 70 cm.

FIGURE 10–46 Portrayals of a thunder god with an axe, mace, and bow engraved between the hands and at the belt. (1) Stone stela from Natalivka, Lower Dnieper area. Tentative date c. 3000 B.C. H 144 cm. (2) Stone stela from Kernosovka, Lower Dnieper region. Tentative date, end 4th mill. B.C. H c. 1.5 m.

1

2

hilted daggers, shafted halberds and axes, bows, quivers, vehicles, belts, and breast plates, objects rarely preserved in graves. Double-spiral pendants, breast plates, bronze daggers with triangular blades, flat axes, and flint halberd blades such as appear engraved on stelae are known from depots and graves of the Baden and Remedello (Po River Valley) cultures.

The engravings on stelae reveal a great deal about the new ideology. In fact, they constitute the richest source for the study of the earliest Indo-European symbolism and god images. These symbols are characteristically grouped, making possible the study of their interrelationships. Their consistent association on the roughly anthropomorphic stelae leaves no doubt that the engraved weapons, animals, and solar symbols are linked, that their concurrence is not accidental.

The following symbols are recorded: solar signs (circles, radiating suns, and a circle with groups of long rays) engraved in the area of the head; breast plate (a semicircle of multiple concentric lines); double-spiral pendant, one or a pair, on the chest or at the solar sign; a circle at either side of the radiating sun; hilted dagger—one, two, five, seven daggers or more—shown in the middle part of the stela; shafted halberd, one or many; shafted axe, one or more; belt of parallel lines (beaded fabric?) or of zigzag or diamond pattern (woven?); four-wheeled vehicle (shown below the belt); bow, quiver, and arrows; footprints; plow pulled by two yoked oxen; horse(s), stag(s), and he-goat(s).

The content and association of the symbolic groups are of particular interest. The most frequent are the solar groups: the radiating sun, the circle on either side of the radiating sun, the double spiral pendants, and the breast plate. This group of symbols is further associated with the belt, dagger, halberd, horse, stag, plowing scene, and a vehicle. To the specialist in comparative Indo-European mythology, such combinations of symbols will certainly recall the image of the God of the Shining Sky, who bestows progeny and promotes vegetation. This deity is known in various Indo-European groups from early

historic records and is still extant in folklore: the Indic Mitra, Baltic Dievas, Roman Dius Fidius, Janus, and Mars, Celtic Lug (called "Sun faced"), German *Tiwaz (from *deiuos), Anglo Saxon Tiw, German Ziu, Icelandic Tyr, northwestern Slavic Jarovit-Sventovit, and others. This god is associated with morning and daylight, and with the spring, summer, autumn, and winter sun. His powers are transmitted by his weapon, the dagger (or sword, later in prehistory and early history); by his animals, the stag and horse; and by the shining vehicle in which he travels. As protector of vegetation, particularly of the grain, he is associated with his pair of oxen and with plowing.

Other compositions and groupings represent other Indo-European deities. The axe is connected with the Thunder God; the club, bow, quiver, and arrows are also his. (FIGURES 10–45, 10–46)

Present knowledge of stelae would indicate that the majority represent the God of the Shining Sky. In Indo-European mythology, the image of this god is linked with kingship. The erection of stelae, therefore, may have marked the death of important personages, either chieftains or fallen heroes; a hero may substitute for a god and his weapons became divine. The second of importance was the Thunder God, the hunter and warrior, fighting with the evil and adversary of the God of Death and Underworld, the purifier and fructifier of earth. This god is best preserved in all Indo-European mythologies. The representations of male gods on stelae are quite overwhelmingly Indo-European.

The Contrasting Sets of Goddesses and Gods

The main theme of Old European goddess symbolism is the cyclic mystery of birth, death, and the renewal of life, involving not only human life but all life on earth. Symbols and images cluster around the parthenogenetic (self-generating) Goddess who is the single source of all life. Her energy is manifest in springs and wells, in the moon, sun, and earth, and in all animals and plants.

She is the Giver-of-Life, Wielder-of-Death, Regeneratrix, and the Earth Fertility Goddess, rising and dying with the plants. Male gods also exist, not as creators but as guardians of wild nature, or as metaphors of life energy and the spirits of seasonal vegetation.

The proto-Indo-European pantheon of gods was a socially and economically oriented ideology. This system was well suited to a pastoralist/mixed farming economy with prominent sovereign and warrior classes which had mastered the horse and weapons of war. The life-creating and death-wielding functions belonged to the principal male gods who also rode horses and brandished weapons. Female goddesses, like the Dawn and Sun Maiden, were not creatrixes but were simply brides or wives of male deities. This religion was oriented toward the rotating sun and other sky phenomena such as thunder and lightning. Their sky gods shone as "bright as the sky" and, in Bronze Age representations, carried shining weapons—daggers, swords, and shields—and were adorned with copper or gold chest plates, gold or amber discs, and copper-plated belts. The Indo-Europeans worshiped the swiftness of arrow and spear and the sharpness of the blade. The touch of the axe blade was thought to awaken the powers of nature and transmit the fecundity of the Thunder God. The frightening black God of Death and the Underworld marked the warrior for death with the touch of his spear tip, glorifying him as a fallen hero.

Differing Beliefs in an Afterlife

These two systems exhibit very different sets of beliefs concerning an afterlife. The Old Europeans had a strong belief in cyclic regeneration in which the main idea in grave architecture is "tomb is womb." Graves are egg shaped, uterus shaped, or anthropomorphic, the latter being conceived as the body of the Goddess. The generative triangle also figures in grave and shrine outlines and architecture. Engravings on stones of megalithic graves are symbols of regeneration, life-giving water and life energy (cupmarks, concentric circles with central dot, concentric arcs, winding snakes, snake coils, bull heads as uteri, triangles, lozenges, hourglass shapes, zigzags, lunar cycles); or images of the Goddess of Regeneration herself engraved with labyrinths, vulvas, and breasts. It was thought that the afterworld was in the West, and that a barrier of water existed between this world and the next that was crossed by ships, themselves symbols of regeneration.

Communal burials were a typical Old European practice. The megaliths of western Europe were sacred centers of the community, and the burial of de-fleshed bones to these central shrines meant a return to the ancestors. Furthermore, the bones were compared to seed which produced rebirth. Indeed, all Old European burials were, in various forms, a return to the body of the Mother for regeneration within the womb of nature.

The Indo-Europeans believed in a linear continuity of the individual from this world into another "life" in the world of the dead. Therefore, mortuary houses were built in which the dead took their belongings—tools, weapons, and ornaments that represented their rank—to the afterworld. Royal tombs and those of other important members of the society were lavishly equipped, providing the dead with status. Death in battle was particularly glorified. Kings and chieftains were often buried with their entire households—wives, servants, children—and animals, including horses, teams of oxen, and dogs. Gifts of food continued to be made after the funeral, considered necessary for the well-being of the shades.

From comparative Indo-European mythologies and beliefs we know that the world of the dead was imagined as a cold, swampy, underground realm ruled by the sovereign male god. The journey to the gloomy underworld involved a road or a river, usually a three-day period of walking, riding, or travel in chariots. Souls drifted there in a pale and passive manner, and there was no belief in the possibility of rebirth.

These radically different beliefs could not have developed from the Old Europeans. With the formation of the Baden-Ezero culture in east-central Europe and

Examples of Contrasting Symbols in Old European and Indo-European Mythologies

	OLD EUROPEAN	INDO-EUROPEAN
The Color Black	Color of fertility and Mother Earth	Color of death and of the God of Death and the Underworld, called "Black God" (in Slavic and Baltic mythology)
The Color White	Color of bone, symbolic of death related to yellow, gold, amber, marble, alabaster	Color of the God of the Shining Sky, related to yellow, gold, amber
The Serpent	Benevolent snake, symbol of life energy in humans, animals and plants; stimulating and protecting the life powers of the family and domestic animals; poisonous snake an epiphany of the Goddess of Death	Symbol of evil, especially lurking in whirlwinds; epiphany of the God of Death and the Underworld, adversary of the Thunder God
The Bull, the Bucranium	Source of life, symbol of regeneration, simulacrum of woman's uterus	Epiphany of the Thunder God, symbol of strength and maleness
The Sun	Symbol of regeneration and one of the manifestations of the Goddess of Regeneration (feminine gender for the sun in Celtic, Germanic, Baltic, and Slavic languages is inherited from Old Europe)	The dominant symbol of the Indo-Europeans: life-giving symbol associated with the God of the Shining Sky who is a year-god representing the birth of the sun, the young sun (spring), the triumphant sun (summer), and the old sun (autumn)
The Horse	Nonexistent in pre-Indo-European Europe	Sacred animal and epiphany of the main gods; white or gray—epiphany of the God of the Shining Sky, Twins, and Moon God; black—the epiphany of the God of Death and the underworld; mare—epiphany of the Dawn Goddess; gods are portrayed riding horses, or horses pull their chariots

the Globular Amphora culture in northern central Europe in the second half of the 4th millennium B.C., the Indo-European mode of burial and beliefs in the other world took root in Europe and gradually replaced the burials of the Old European type.

The Contrast Between Old European and Indo-European Symbols

The analysis of Old European and Indo-European symbols shows that these two religions and mythologies had entirely different sets of symbols which are still extant today in the mythologies and folklore of Europe. I shall give just a few examples, not the whole glossary of symbols (see chart on facing page). Examples are taken from the animal world, sky bodies, and colors.

Conclusion

East-central Europe in the period of 4500–2500 B.C. was in a constant state of transformation, due to repeated Kurgan incursions from the Volga and North Pontic steppe zone.

There were several major stages of changing ethnic configurations.

1. Around 4300 B.C., horse-riding pastoralists from south Russia (Wave No. 1) created the first shock wave and population shifts in the Danube basin. The flowering of Old Europe was truncated and the hybridization of two very different culture systems began. Most affected were the Black Sea littoral (Varna), Karanovo-Gumelniţa, Vinča, Lengyel, and LBK cultures. The Cucuteni culture survived. In the west, signs of Kurgan elements (single burials under round mounds) appeared in England and in eastern Ireland before 3500 B.C.

2. In the second half of the 4th millennium B.C., from the North Pontic-North Caucasus region, strong influences increased the transformation of central Europe. The conversion of what was still Old European into an Indo-European social structure and ideology was remarkably successful. Central Europe was now ruled from hill forts and by daggers made of hard metal (copper-

arsenic alloy). The transition from a matricentric and matrilineal to a patrilineal and patriarchal system was in process.

3. The massive Kurgan Wave No. 3, from the lower Volga region after 3000 B.C. into east-central Europe, caused new ethnic shifts. The Indo-Europeanized populations of central Europe migrated northeast to East Baltic and central Russia, northwest to southern Scandinavia, and south to Greece (Corded Pottery and Vučedol extensions).

4. The warlike and horse-riding Bell Beaker people of the middle and second half of the 3rd millennium B.C., who diffused over western Europe, are likely to have originated from an amalgam of remnants of the Vučedol people with the Yamna colonists (after Wave No. 3) in Yugoslavia and Hungary. Their parent culture is called Vinkovci-Samogyvár. This was the largest and last outmigration, from east-central Europe into western Europe, up to the west Mediterranean and the British Isles, before the onset of a more stable period, and the formations of Bronze Age cultural units.

By the third quarter of the 3rd millennium B.C., almost all parts of Old Europe were transformed economically and socially. Pastoralism and seminomadism increased and tillage decreased. Old European patterns of habitation vanished except for territories and islands which were never completely Indo-Europeanized. The Indo-European religion became official, but the Old European Goddess religion was carried on to the present day through fragments of Old European culture.

The functions and images of Old European and Indo-European deities, beliefs in an afterlife, and the entirely different sets of symbols prove the existence of two contrasting religions and mythologies. Their collision in Europe resulted in the hybridization of two symbolic structures in which the Indo-European prevailed while the Old European survived as an undercurrent. Without this insight into different symbolic structures, the ideologies of European peoples and the genesis and meaning of their symbols, beliefs, and myths cannot be comprehended.

The clash between these two ideologies and social and economic structures led to the drastic transformation of Old Europe. These changes were expressed as the transition from matrilineal to patrilineal order, from a learned theacracy to a militant patriarchy, from a sexually balanced society to a male dominated hierarchy, and from a chthonic goddess religion to the Indo-European sky-oriented pantheon of gods.

NOTES

Preface

1. James Mellaart, *Çatal Hüyük and Anatolian Kilims*, vol. 2 of *The Goddess from Anatolia* by James Mellaart, Udo Hirsch, and Belkis Balpinar. (Milan: Eskenazi, 1989): 11.

Chapter 1

1. Rudoplh Musil, "The First Known Domestication of Wolves in Central Europe," *Animals and Archaeology. Husbandry in Europe*, ed. by Caroline Grigson and Juliet Clutton-Block. BAR International Series 227 (1984): 23–27.

2. Sándor Bökönyi, "Development of Early Stock Rearing in the Near East," *Nature* 224 (1976): 19–23. Peter J. Ucko and G. W. Dimbleby, eds. *The Domestication of Plants and Animals* (Chicago: Aldine, 1969).

3. Jack R. Harlan, "The Origins of Cereal Agriculture in the Old World," *Origins of Agriculture*, ed. by Charles Reed (The Hague: Mouton, 1977). Robin Dennell, *European Economic Prehistory* (London-New York-Sydney: Academic Press, 1985): 158–68. E. S. Higgs and M. R. Jarman, "The Origins of Animal and Plant Husbandry," *Papers in Economic Prehistory*, ed. by E. S. Higgs (Cambridge University Press, 1972). Daniel Zohary, "The Progenitors of Wheat and Barley in Relation to Domestication and Agricultural Dispersal in the Old World," in *The Domestication and Exploitation of Plants and Animals*, ed. Peter Ucko and G. W. Dimbleby (Chicago: Aldine, 1969).

4. Jean Perrot, "Palestine-Syria-Cilicia," *Courses Toward Urban Life*, ed. by Robert J. Braidwood and Gordon Willey (Chicago: Aldine, 1962). Charles L. Redman, *The Rise of Civilization* (San Francisco: W. H. Freeman, 1978): 71–82.

5. J. Courtin, *Le Mésolithique de la Baume Fontbrégoua à Salernes (Var)*, Cahiers ligures de Préhistoire et d'Archéologie 24 (1975). D. Vaquer, D. Geddes, J. Barbaza, and J. Erroux, "Mesolithic plant exploitation at the Balma Abeurador, France," *Oxford Journal of Archaeology* 5 (1986):1–18. J. Roussot-Larroque, "Imported problems and home-made solutions: late foragers and pioneer farmers seen from the west," *Neolithic of Southeastern Europe and its Near Eastern Connections*, ed. C. Bálint. Varia Archaeologica Hungarica 2 (Budapest, 1989): 253–71.

6. J. K. Kozlowski, "The Neolithization of South-East Europe: An Alternative Approach," Varia Archaeologica Hungarica 2 (Budapest, 1989): 131–48.

7. T. W. Jacobsen, "Excavations in the Franchthi Cave 1969–1971," *Hesperia* 42:45–88, 253–83. J. L. Angel, "Early Neolithic People of Nea Nikomedeia," I. Schwidetzky, ed. Anthropologie 1, in *Die Anfänge des Neolithikums vom Orient bis Nordeuropa*, 8a, H. Schwabedissen, ed. (Cologne: Böhlan, 1973):101–12.

8. V. Boroneant, "Recherches archéologiques sur la culture Schela Cladovei de la zone des 'Portes de Fer'," *Dacia* 17:5–39. B. Jovanović, "The Autochthonous and the Migrational Components of the Early Neolithic in the Iron Gate," *Balcanica* 3:49–58. Dragoslav Srejović and Zagorka Letica, *Vlasac: A Mesolithic Settlement in the Iron Gates 1*, Serbian Academy of Sciences and Arts Monographs 512 (Belgrade, 1978).

9. J. Nemeskéri, L. Szatmáry, et al., "Anthropology," *Vlasac* 2, ed. Milutin Garašanin (Belgrade, 1978): 69–425. Roland Menk and János Nemeskéri, in I. Hershkovits, ed., *People and Culture in Change* (Oxford, British Archaeological Reports, 1989).

10. Augustus Sordinas, "Investigations of the Prehistory of Corfu during 1964–1966," *Balkan Studies* 10,2 (Thessaloniki 1969): 402. T. W. Jacobsen, "Excavations at Porto Cheli and Vicinity, Preliminary Report II: The Franchthi Cave, 1967–1968," *Hesperia* (Athens, 1969): 355–76. Obsidian was found here in the upper part of the Mesolithic layer.

11. J. R. Cann and Colin Renfrew, "The characterization of obsidian and its application to the Mediterranean region," *Proceedings of Prehistoric Society* 30 (London, 1964): 111–25. Colin Renfrew, "Obsidian in the Aegean," *B.S.A. Annual* 60 (1965): 225–47. Christoph Willms, "Obsidian im Neolithikum und Aneolithikum Europas," *Germania* 61, Beilage 5 (1983): 327–51.

12. Oxygen isotope analyses have shown that the spondylus shell had been transported the long distance from the Aegean. Nicholas Shackleton and Colin Renfrew, "Neolithic trade routes re-aligned by oxygen isotope analyses," *Nature* 228 (London, 1970): 1062–65.

13. James Mellaart, *Çatal Hüyük: A Neolithic Town in Anatolia* (New York: McGraw-Hill, 1967). Ibid., *The Goddess of Anatolia* vol. 1 (illustrations), vol. 2 (text). (Milan: Eskenázi, 1989). Ibid., Excava-tion report. *Anatolian Studies* 12–14 (1962–64), vol. 16 (1966).

14. James Mellaart, "L'art sur plaquettes from earliest Çatal Hüyük: A contribution to the beginning of Anatolian religion." Paper presented in the Conference on Culture Change in Europe and Anatolia 4500–2500 B.C., Dublin, Sept. 1989.

15. Bar-Yosef, "The Walls of Jericho: An Alternative Interpretation," *Current Anthropology* 27, 2 (1986): 157–62.

16. James Mellaart, *Excavations at Hacilar*, vols. 1 and 2 (Edinburgh University Press, 1970).

17. Colin Renfrew, *Archaeology and Language. The Puzzle of Indo-European Origins.* (London: Jonathan Cape, 1987).

Chapter 2

1. Marija Gimbutas, Shan Winn, and D. Shimabuku, *Achilleion, A Neolithic Village in Northern Greece, 6400–5600 B.C.* Monumenta Archaeologica 14 (Institute of Archaeology, U. of Calif., Los Angeles, 1989).

2. Chrestos Tsountas, *Ai Proistorikai Akropoleis Diminiou kai Sesklou.* (Athens, 1908).

3. Saul S. Weinberg, "Excavations at Prehistoric Elateia, 1959." *Hesperia* 31 (1962): 63–83.

4. R. J. Rodden, "An Early Neolithic Village in Greece." *Scientific American* 212 (1965): 82–92.

5. V. Milojčić, J. Boessneck, and M. Hopf, *Die deutschen Ausgrabungen auf der Argissa-Magula in Thessalien. I. Das präkeramische Neolithikum sowie Tier- und Pflanzenreste* (Bonn: Habelt, 1962).

6. T. W. Jacobsen, "Excavation at Porto Cheli and Vicinity. Preliminary Report 2: The Franchthi Cave 1967–68." *Hesperia* 38/3 (1969): 343–81. "Excavation in the Franchthi Cave 1969–71. Part 1." *Hesperia* 42/1 (1973):45–88. "Excavation in the Franchthi Cave 1969–71. Part 2." *Hesperia* 42/3 (1973): 253–82. "New Radiocarbon Dates from Franchthi Cave," *Journal of Field Archaeology* I, (1974): 303–4.

7. The three subphases of the Early Neolithic are traditionally called: I. "Early Pottery," II. "Proto-Sesklo," and III. "Early Sesklo." In fact, all three belong to Early Sesklo or Early Neolithic, representing three consecutive phases of one culture. Early Neolithic classification and radiocarbon dates are given in the book by M-H., J., M., N. Wijnen, *The Early Neolithic I Settlement at Sesklo: an Early*

Farming Community in Thessaly, Greece (Leiden, 1982).

8. Demetrios Theocharis, in *Neolithic Greece*, S. A. Papadopoulos, ed. (Athens: National Bank of Greece, 1973): 17–130.

9. J. Renfrew, "Agriculture," in *Neolithic Greece*, S. A. Papadopoulos, ed. (Athens, 1973): 147ff.

10. Sándor Bökönyi, "Animal Bones of Achilleion," in *Achilleion*; see note 1.

11. Chrestos Tsountas, *Ai Proistorikai Akropoleis Diminiou kai Seklou* (Athens, 1908).

12. Vladimir Milojčić et al., "Magulen um Larissa in Thessalien," *Beiträge zur Ur- und Frühgeschichtlichen Archäologie des Mittelmeer-Kulturraumes* 15 (Bonn, 1976). A. J. B. Wace and M. S. Thompson, *Prehistoric Thessaly* (Cambridge University Press, 1912). H. Hauptman and V. Milojčić, "Die Funde der frühen Dimini-Zeit aus der Arapi-Magula," *Thessalien* (Bonn, 1969). Konstantinou I. Gallis, *Cremation Burials from the Neolithic Period in Thessaly* (in Greek with English summary). Athens, 1982.

13. Stratigraphies and typological comparisons with the Vinča and Karanovo III–VI cultures place the Dimini sequence within 5500–4000 B.C. The following phases are distinguished:

4000 B.C.: Phase VII (Rakhmani)
Phase VI (Larisa)
Phase V (Dimini proper)
4500 B.C.: Phase IV (Otzaki II)
Phase III (Otzaki I)
Phase II (Arapi)
5500 B.C.: Phase I (Tsangli)

Phase II, the Arapi Phase, can be paralleled with Early Vinča and Karanovo III, c. 5300–5000 B.C., since considerable influence from the north is indicated by the appearance of black pottery and typical Karanovo III handles with cylindrical protuberances. Phase VII (Rakhmani) must have been contemporaneous with the late Karanovo VI as is shown by the gold pendant found in the Rakhmani layer of Demetrias-Pevkakia at Volos.

14. Nicole Lambert, "Grotte de Kitsos 1970," *Archaiologikon Deltion* 26 (Athens, 1971): 41–61.

15. J. D. Evans and Colin Renfrew, *Excavations at Saliagos near Antiparos* (London, 1968).

16. John E. Coleman, Keos I. Kephala, *A Late Neolithic Settlement and Cemetery*, American School of Classical Studies at Athens (Princeton, N.J.: 1977).

17. Draga Garašanin, *Starčevo Kultura* (Ljubljana, 1954). V. G. Fewkes, et al., "Excavations at Starčevo, Yugoslavia. A Preliminary Report," Peabody Museum, American School of Prehistoric Research, Bulletin No. 9 (Cambridge: Harvard University, 1932): 1–21.

18. I. Bognár-Kutzián, *The Körös Culture* 1 (1944), 2 (1947) (Budapest).

19. Marija Gimbutas, ed., *Neolithic Macedonia*. Monumenta Archaeologica 1, Institute of Archaeology, U. of Calif. at Los Angeles: 1976.

20. Cf. earliest Neolithic sites with white on red painted pottery in Transylvania and Oltenia. N. Vlassa, "Eine frühneolithische Kultur mit bemalter Keramik der Vor-Starčevo-Körös Zeit in Cluj-Gura Baciului, Siebenbürgen," *Prähistorische Zeitschrift* 47, H.2 (1972): 174–97. Marin Nica, "Cîrcea, cea mai veche asezare neolica de la sud de Carpati," *Studii şi Cercetari de Istorie Veche şi Arheologie* 27, 4, (1976): 435–63.

21. J. Nemeskéri, "Die wichstigsten anthropologischen Fragen der Urgeschichte in Ungarn," *Anthropol. Közlemenyek* 5 (Budapest, 1961): 39ff. Nemeskéri and Lengyel, in Gimbutas, ed., *Neolithic Macedonia*: 375–411. Zsuzsanna K. Zoffman, "Human Skeletal Remains from Divostin," in Alan McPherron and Dragoslav Srejović, eds., *Divostin and the Neolithic of Central Serbia*, Ethnology Monographs No. 10, Dept. of Anthropology, University of Pittsburgh (1988): 447–55. Olga Necrasov, "Nouvelles données anthropologiques concernant la population de la culture néolithique Starčevo-Criş," *Ann. Roum. Anthropol.* 2 (1965): 9–17.

22. J. Nemeskéri, "Populacija Lepenskog Vira," in D. Srejović, *Lepenski Vir, nova praistorijska kultura u Podunavlju* (Belgrade, 1969): 239–63.

23. Sándor Bökönyi, *Animal Domestication in Europe* (Budapest, 1974).

24. Sándor Bökönyi, "The Obre Vertebrate Fauna," *Wissenschaftliche Mitteilungen des Bosnisch-Herzegowinischen Landesmuseums* 4 (1974): 55–154. Alojz Benac, "Obre I," *Wissenschaftliche Mitteilungen des Bosnisch-Herzegowinischen Landesmuseums* 3 (1973): 344.

25. Benac, ibid.: 334–43

26. Benac, ibid.: 336

27. As shown by the analysis of Obre I obsidian tools by J. Rasson.

28. Nándor Kalicz and János Makkay, *A Méhteleki agyagistenek* (Nyiregyhaza, 1974).

29. Marija Gimbutas, "Chronology of Obre I and Obre II," in *Obre and its Place in Old Europe: Wissenschaftliche Mitteilungen des Bosnisch-Herzegowinischen Landesmuseums*, Band IV A (Sarajevo, 1974): 15–24.

30. The tell of Karanovo was first excavated by V. Mikov in 1936–37. Extensive excavations continued in 1947 to 1957 by V. Mikov together with G. I. Georgiev. Subsequently the very important tell at Azmak was excavated by G. I. Georgiev. Full accounts of excavations at both sites were never published except for a survey article: Georgi I. Georgiev, "Kulturgruppen der Jungstein-und-Kupferzeit in der Ebene von Thrazien (Südbulgarien)," *L'Europe à la fin de l'âge de la pierre* (1961): 45–100.

In the 1980s excavations at Karanovo were carried out by Stefan Hiller of the University of Salzburg in conjunction with the Bulgarian Academy of Sciences. The reports *Karanovo 1984, 1985, 1986, and 1988* appeared in the series published by the Institut für Alte Geschichte und Altertumskunde der Universität Salzburg.

31. Kazanlak (or Kazanluk) in the town of the same name was excavated by G. I. Georgiev and R. Katinčarov in 1966–70. The finds are in the museum of Kazanlak. Final reports of excavations are not published.

32. In the area of Plovdiv of Central Bulgaria, a tell with a rich layer of early Karanovo materials was excavated at Muldava by Detev, published in the Plovdiv Archaeological Museum Series *Godišnik* 6 (1968). The tell Ezero (Dipsis) 3 km south of Nova Zagora, famous for its Early Bronze Age deposits, at the bottom yielded layers of Karanovo I, III, IV, and VI culture. East of Sofia, Čavdar tell was excavated by G. I. Georgiev and R. H. Dennel. G. I. Georgiev, "Die neolithische Kultur in Čavdar und ihre Stellung im Balkan-Neolithikum," Actes du VIIIe Congrès International des Sciences Préhistoriques, 1971 (Belgrade: 1973): 263–72.

33. G. I. Georgiev, R. W. Dennel, and D. Webley, "Prehistoric settlement and land use in southern Bulgaria," *Paleoeconomy*, ed. E. S. Higgs (Cambridge, 1975): 97–109.

34. These conclusions on grain processing are based on Dennell's research in Čevdar and Kazanlak. See Robin W. Dennell, "Archaeobotany and early farming in Europe," *Archaeology* 31, 1 (New York, 1978): 8–13.

35. Karanovo marble figurines are reproduced in: Marija Gimbutas, *Goddesses and Gods*, 1982: 144 and R. R. Katinčarov, "Neolitna mramorna figurka ot gr. Kazanlak," *Arkheologija* 2, 2 (1969): 51–54, and in *Arkheologija* 3 (1973): 29, fig. 12.

36. Rudolf Tichý, "Osidleni s volutovou keramikou na Moravè; Die Besiedlung mit Voluten/Linearbandkeramik in Mähren." *Památky Archeologické* 53 (1962): 245–305.

37. Wolfram Bernhard, "Anthropologie der Bandkeramik," Anthropologie 2, *Die Anfänge des Neolithikums vom Orient bis Nordeuropa* 8b (Cologne-Vienna, 1978): 128–64.

38. Graeme Barker, *Prehistoric Farming in Europe* (Cambridge University Press, 1985): 139–47. John M. Howell, "Early Farming in Northwestern Europe," *Scientific American* (November 1987): 118–26. Sarunas Milisauskas and Janusz Kruk, "Neolithic Economy in Central Europe," *Journal of World Prehistory* 3, 4 (1989): 418.

39. S. Milisauskas and J. Kruk, ibid.: 415. Lech, J., "Flint mining among the early farming communities of central Europe," part 1 (1981), part 2 (1983): 30: 47–80.

40. J. Kruk. *Studia osadnicze nad neolitem wyżyn lessowych* (Wrocław-Warsaw-Cracow-Gdańsk, 1973).

41. For outstanding sites with LBK long-houses see B. Soudský, *Bylany: osada nejstaršich zemedelcu z mladši doby kammeni* (Prague, 1966); 143 houses have been excavated by P. J. G. Modderman, "Die geographische Lage der bandkeramischen Siedlungen in den Niederlanden." *Palaeohistoria* 6–7 (Groningen, 1958–59): 1–232. P. J. G. Modderman, "Die bandkeramische Siedlung von Sittard," ibid., 33–121. P. J. G. Modderman, "Neolithische und frühbronzezeitliche Siedlungsspuren aus Hienheim, Landkr. Kelheim, *Analecta Praehistorica Leidensia* 4 (1971): 1–25. H. T. Waterbolk and P. J. G. Modderman, "Die Grossbauten der Bandkeramik," *Palaeohistoria* 6–7 (Groningen 1958–59): 163–171. P. J. G. Modderman, *Linearbandkeramik aus Elsloo und Stein* (The Hague: Staatsuitgeverij, 1970) and *Analecta Praehistorica Leidensia*, 3

(1970). At Elsloo 95 houses were excavated. Sarunas Milisaukas, "Olszanica, An Early Farming Village in Poland." *Archaeology* 29, 1 (1976): 31–41. Hensel, Witold and Sarunas Milisaukas, *Excavations of Neolithic and Early Bronze Sites in Southeastern Poland*. Polska Akademia Nauk, Instytut Historii Kultury Materialnej (Ossolineum, 1985). M. Ilett, M. Plateaux and A. Coudart, "Analyse spatiale des habitats de Rubané recent," in J. P. Demoule and J. Guilaine, eds., *Le Néolithique de la France. Hommage à G. Bailloud*. (Paris: Picard, 1986): 131–40.

42. J. Pavúk, "Zur Problem der Gräberfelder mit der Linienbandkeramik," *Aktuelle Fragen der Bandkeramik* (Székesfehérvár, 1972). Olaf Höckman, "Zur Verteilung von Männer- und Frauengräber auf Gräberfeldern des Frühneolithikums und des ältesten Mittelneolithikums." *Jahrbuch des Römisch-Germanischen Zentralmuseums Mainz* 29 (1982): 13–74.

43. C. Constantin, "La séquence des cultures a céramique dégraissée à l'os. Néolithique de Bassin parisien et du Hainaut," J. -P. Demoule and J. Guilaine, eds., *Le Néolithique de la France. Hommage à G. Baillou* (Paris: Picard, 1986):113–27.

44. Nándor Kalicz and János Makkay, *Die Linien-bandkeramik in der grossen ungarischen Tiefebene* (Budapest, 1977): the catalog.

45. V. T. Dobosi, "Mesolithische Fundorte in Ungarn." *Aktuellen Fragen der Bandkeramik* (Székesfehérvár, 1972): 39ff.

46. János Nemeskéri, oral communication.

47. N. Kalicz and J. Makkay, "Probleme des frühen Neolithikums der nördlichen Tiefebene." *Aktuellen Fragen der Bandkeramik* (Székesfehérvár, 1972): 77–81.

48. Eugen Comşa. "Über das Neolithikum in Westrumänien," *Acta Antiqua et Archaeologica* 14 (Szeged, 1971): 31–43; 16, "Quelques problèmes concernant la civilization Ciumeşti," *Acta Archaeologica Carpatica* 13 (Krakow, 1973): 39–50.

49. Identified by S. Bökönyi from the site of Tiszavasvári-Keresztfal note 23, p. 112.

50. J. Lichardus, *Jaskiňa Domica* (Bratislava, 1968).

51. J. Korek, "Bükki kultura telepe Oroson." *Arch. Értesitö* 1951, 78: 68–72.

52. T. Kemenczei, "Boldogköváralja." *Arch. Értesitö* 1964, 91: 253 ff.

53. V. I. Markevich, "Issledovaniya neolita na srednem Dnestre," *Kratkie Soobshcheniya Instituta Arkheologii* 105 (Moscow, 1965): 85–90. V. N. Danilenko, *Neolit Ukrainy* (Kiev, 1969).

54. Z. V. Janouchevitch and V. I. Markevitch, "Espèces de plantes cultivées des stations primitives au sud-ouest de l'URSS." VIII Congrès International des Sciences Préhistoriques et Protohistoriques (Belgrade, 1971).

Chapter 3

1. At the Starčevo site of Divostin in central Yugoslavia, 45 percent of identified domesticated animal bones were cattle, whereas the Vinča assemblage contained 65 percent. In Bosnia, at Obre, the cattle bones of the Late Starčevo (Obre I) period was 47.90 percent; that of the Butmir period (Obre II) was 67.16 percent. Even in central Macedonia under considerably drier conditions, the percentage of cattle bones more than doubled in a relatively short time between the Late Starčevo (Anza III) 6.84 percent, and Early Vinča (Anza IV) 16.17 percent.

2. S. Bökönyi, *History of Domestic Mammals in Central and Eastern Europe* (Budapest, 1974): 111 ff.

3. Š. Batović, *Srednji Neolit Dalmacji* (Zadar, 1966); J. Chapman, R. Shiel, and Š. Batović, "Settlement Patterns and Land Use in Neothermal Dalmatia, Yugoslavia, 1983–84 Seasons," *Journal of Field Archaeology* 14 (1987): 123–46.

4. J. Korošec, *Danilo i Danilska Kultura* (Ljubljana, 1964).

5. G. Novak, "Problems and chronology of the finds in the cave of Grabak," *Archaeologia Yugoslavica* 3 (1960): 11–39.

6. W. Radimsky and M. Hoernes, *Die neolithische Station von Butmir* 1 (Vienna, 1895), F. Fiala and M. Hoernes 2 (Vienna, 1898).

7. Alojz Benac, "Obre I and Obre II," in *Wissenschaftliche Mitteilungen des Bosnisch-Herzegowinischen Landesmuseums* 3 A (Sarajevo, 1973); Marija Gimbutas et al., Chronology of Obre I and Obre II; outline on the anthropological finds (J. Nemeskéri); reports on cereal grains (J. Renfrew); fauna (S. Bökönyi); and quantitative analysis (E. and A. K. Sterud), *Wissentschaftliche Mitteilungen des Bosnisch-Herzegowinischen Landesmuseums* 4 A (Sarajevo, 1974).

8. Alojz Benac, *Studien zur Stein- und Kupferzeit im nordwestlichen Balkan* (Berlin: Walter de Gruyter, 1962): 49.

9. Alojz Benac, "Obre II. A neolithic settlement of the Butmir group at Gornje Polje," *Wissenschaftliche Mitteilungen des Bosnisch-Herzegowinischen Landesmuseums* 3 (Sarajevo, 1973): 30 ff.

10. Ibid. p. 56. Such objects were found in Obre II, House 15 in the wall of the auxiliary room.

11. Cultural layers at Vinča are 9.1 m thick (10.5 m if pits dug in the sterile ground are to be included). Almost two meters at the bottom belong to the Neolithic Starčevo culture and the seven meters with Vinča materials are covered with Baden-Kostolac and Vatin layers of the Bronze Age. Miloje Vasić, *Praistoriska Vinča* 1–4 (Belgrade, 1932–36). The generally accepted stratigraphy, introduced by F. Holste in *Wiener Prähistorische Zeitschrift* 1 (Vienna: 1939) is:

Vinča A, bottom layer up to 8 m (Starčevo culture)
Vinča B, 8 m to 6.5 m (Vinča culture)
Vinča C, 6.5 m to 5 m (Vinča culture)
Vinča D, 5 m 6 to 3.5 m (Vinča culture)
Vinča E, 3.4 m to 1.5 m (Baden-Kostolac culture)

A critical review of the Vinča stratigraphy was offered by B. Jovanović, "Stratigrafska podela Vinčanskog naselja" (with a résumé in French), *Starinar* 9 (Belgrade, 1960): 9–20. Another review is in John Chapman's book, *The Vinča Culture of South-East Europe*. BAR International Series 117 (1981): 6–10.

12. M. Gimbutas, ed., *Neolithic Macedonia*. Monumenta Archaeologica 1, Institute of Archaeology, U. of Calif. at Los Angeles, 1976.

13. J. Todorović and A. Cermanović, *Banjica naselje Vinčanske kulture. Banjica, Siedlung der Vinča-Gruppe* (Belgrade, 1961): 88.

14. N. Tasić and E. Tomić, *Crnokalačka Bara, Naselje Starčevačke i Vinčanske Kulture* 8, Narodni Muzej-Kruševac, Archaeološko Društvo Jugoslavija (Kruševac: Belgrade, 1969).

15. Bogdan Nikolov, *Gradechnitza* (Sofia: Nauka i Izkustvo, 1974).

16. Vladimir Dumitrescu, *The Neolithic Settlement at Rast*. BAR International Series 72 (1980).

17. N. Tasić, "Praistorisko naselje kod Valača." *Glasnik Muzeja Kosovo i Metohije* 2, 4, 5 (Priština: 1957).

18. R. Tringham and D. Krstić, *Selevac: A Neolithic Village in Yugoslavia*. Monumenta Archaeologica 15, Institute of Archaeology, U. of Calif. at Los Angeles, 1990.

19. A. McPherron and D. Srejović, eds., *Divostin and the Neolithic of Central Serbia* 1, Pittsburgh Dept. of Anthropology and National Museum Kragujevac, 1988.

20. B. Brukner, "Neolitski i rano-eneolitski zloj na Gomolava." *Rad Vojvodjanski Muzej* 14 (1965): 137–75. Ibid., "Die Siedlung der Vinča-Gruppe auf Gomolava (Die Wohnschicht des Spätneolithikums und Frühneolithikums-Gomolava Ia, Gomolava Ia-b und Gomolava Ib und der Wohnhorizont des Äneolitschen Humus Gomolava II)." *Gomolava— Chronologie und Stratigraphie der vorgeschichtlichen und antiken Kulturen der Donauniederung und Südosteuropas*, Band I. Symposium, Ruma 1986 (Novi Sad: 1986). Jelka Petrović, *Gomolava arheološko nalazište*. Novi sad (Vojvodjanski Muzej), 1984.

21. John Chapman, *The Vinča Culture of South-East Europe*. BAR International Series 117 (1981), part 2, appendix A and map.

22. Ibid. part 1: 43–51.

23. Dimensions of Vinča and Near East tells are given in ibid., part 1: 45.

24. M. Bogdanović, "Architecture and other Structures," in McPherron and Srejović, *Divostin* (see note 19).

25. B. Brukner, "Siedlung der Vinča-Gruppe," p. 23.

26. M. Gimbutas, *Neolithic Macedonia* (see note 12) 34, p. 316.

27. G. Lazarovici, "Das neolithische Heiligtum von Parţa," *Varia Archaeologica Hungarica*, 2 (Budapest, 1989): 149–74.

28. Srboljub Živanović, "Vinča skeletons studied in situ at the Gomolava site, Yugoslavia," *Current Anthropology* 18, 3 (1977): 533–34. K. Zoffman, *Das anthropologische Material des spätneolithischen Gräberfeldes von Hrtkovci-Gomolava* (Rad Vojvodjanski Muzej 30, 1987). Ibid., "Physical

anthropological study of Divostin Burial No. 1," in McPherron and Srejović, *Divostin* (see note 19).

29. The chronological classification of the Vinča culture was for a long time based on typology and stratigraphy of the Vinča tell, subdivided into A, B, C, and D phases. Early A is the Starčevo period and Early Vinča equals A2-B. Late (Classical) Vinča equals B2-C and D. Next was the subdivision into two periods: I, Vinča-Tordoš and II, Vinča-Pločnik, based on Early Vinča and Later Vinča settlements Tordoš and Pločnik, introduced by M. Garašanin, *Hronologija vinčanske grupe* (Ljubljana, 1951). For other classification see Vinča classifications by various authors given in tabular form in Vladimir Markotić, *The Vinča Culture* (Calgary: Western Publishers, 1984): pl. 1.

30. M. Gimbutas, *Neolithic Macedonia* (see note 12), pp. 34, 48, 119.

31. E. Gardner, in Gimbutas, *Neolithic Macedonia* (see note 12), p. 173.

32. D. Srejović, "Neolitska plastika centralnobalkanskog podruchja." *Neolit centralnog Balkana* (Belgrade: Radisa Timotić, 1973).

33. M. Gimbutas, *Neolithic Macedonia* (see note 12), pp. 140, 234, 241.

34. Pal Raczky, ed., *The Late Neolithic of the Tisza Region* (Budapest: Szolnok, 1987).

35. J. Banner, "A kökénydomb neolithkori telep: Die neolithische Ansiedlung von Kökénydomb," *Dolg* 6 (1930): 49–158. Id., "Anthropomorphe Gefässe der Theisskultur von der Siedlung Kökénydomb bei Hódmezővásárhely (Ungarn)." *Germania* 37 (1959): 14–35.

36. J. Csalog, "Die anthropomorphen Gefässe und Idolpastiken von Szegvár-Tüzköves." *Acta. Arch. Hung.* 11 (1959): 7–38.

37. K. Hegedüs and J. Makkay, "Vésztő-Mágor: A Settlement of the Tisza Culture," in Raczky, ed., *Late Neolithic of the Tisza Region* (1987):85–103.

38. G. Szénaszky, "A szakálhati csoport idoltöredéke Battonyáról—Das Idolfragment der Szakálhát-Gruppe aus Battonya-Godrosok. Eine neolithische Siedlung in Südostungarn." *Békéscsaba* 1984.

39. N. Kalicz and P. Raczky, "Berettyóújfalu-Herpály. A Settlement of the Herpály Culture," in P. Raczky, ed., *Late Neolithic of the Tisza Region* (1987): 105–25. V. S. Titov, *Archeologia Vengrii*, The Neolithic of Hungary (Moscow, 1980).

40. F. Horvath, "Hódmezővásárhely-Gorzsa," in P. Raczky, ed. *Late Neolithic of the Tisza Region,* (1987) pp. 31–47.

41. I. Bognár-Kutzián, "Das Neolithikum in Ungarn." *Arch. Anzeiger* 40 (1966): 249–80.

42. N. Kalicz and P. Raczky, "Berettyóújfalu-Herpály," in P. Raczky, ed. (see note 40), p. 15.

43. K. Hegedüs and J. Makkay, "Vésztő-Mágor," in P. Raczky, ed., (see note 40), p. 89–94.

44. N. Kalicz and P. Raczky, "Berettyóújfalu-Herpály," in P. Raczky, ed., op. cit., p. 200.

45. S. Siška, "Tiszapolgárska kultura na Slovensku." *Slovenská Archeológia* 16 (Nitra, 1968): 61–175.

46. Stojan Dimitrijević, *Starčevačka kultura u Slavonsko-Srijemskom prostoru i problem prijelaza starijeg u srednji Neolit u sprskom i hrvatskom podunaviju.* Simpozij Neolit i Eneolit u Slavoniji, Vukovar, 4–5 lipnja 1966 (Gradskij Muzej Vukovar, 1969).

47. V. Podborský, "Současny stav vyskumu kultury s moravskou keramikou" (résumé in German). *Slovenská Archeologia* 18, 2 (Nitra, 1970). J. Pavúk, "Nové nálezy lengyelskej kultury zo Slovenska" (résumé in German). *Slovenská Archeológia* 13, 1 (Nitra, 1965); Id., 1986. "Siedlungswesen der Lengyel-Kultur in der Slowakei." *A Béri Balogh Ádam Múzeum Évkönyve* 13 (1986): 213–44; Id., "Siedlung der Lengyel-Kultur mit Palisadenanlagen in Žlkovce, Westslowakei, *Jahresschrift für Mitteldeutsche Vorgeschichte* 73 (1990): 137–42; Id., "Lengyel-culture fortified settlements in Slovakia," *Antiquity* 65 (1991): 348–57. J. Kamienska, "Frühe Entwicklungsphasen der Lengyel-Kultur in Kleinpolen." *Studijne Zvesti* 17 (Nitra, 1969): 207–18.

48. Lengyel I: red and yellow painted type site is Lužianky; Lengyel II: painted and incised decoration, yellow color predominates but white also appears. Type site is Nitrianski Hrádok; Lengyel III: white painted pottery predominates; Lengyel IV: unpainted pottery, double-handled amphorae appear. Type site is Bodžany-Nitra; Lengyel V: unpainted and polished pottery, Ludanice type. A. Točik, "Erforschungsstand der Lengyel-Kultur in der Slowakei." *Študijné Zvesti* 17 (Nitra, 1969): 451–2.

49. Lengyel-based complexes in these territories carry various labels: in central Germany and Bohemia, Gatersleben; in western Poland and eastern Germany, Ocice (or Ottitz), Jordanów (or Jordansmühl), and Brześć Kujawski; in Bavaria, Münchshof; in Württemberg, Aichbühl I. Lengyel habitation also occurred in caves of the Alpine region and the Upper Danube.

50. J. Dombay, "Die Siedlung und das Gräberfeld in Zengövárkony." Archaeologia Hungarica 37 (Budapest, 1960).

51. Nándor Kalicz, *Kökori falu Aszódon (Neolithisches Dorf in Aszód)* (Aszód: Petofi Muzeum, 1985).

52. B. Novotný, *Lužianska skupina a počiatky malóvanej keramiky na Slovensku* (Bratislava: Slovenská Akadémia Vied, 1962).

53. V. Němejcová-Pavúková, "Vorbericht über die Ergebnisse der systematischen Grabung in Svodín in der Jahren 1971–83." *Slovenská Árcheológia* 34 (1986): 133–73. Id., "Siedlung und Kreisgrabenanlagen der Lengyel-Kultur in Svodín (Südslowakei)," in Němejcová-Pavúková, ed. *Internationales Symposiùm über die Lengyel-Kultur.* Nitra-Wien: Archäologisches Institut der Slovakischen Akademie der Wissenschaften, Institut für Ur- und Frühgeschichte der Universität (1986): 177–83.

54. Kalicz (see note 51): 96.

55. Peter I. Bogucki, *Early Neolithic Subsistence and Settlement in the Polish Lowlands.* BAR International Series 150 (1982). Ryszard Grygiel, "The Household Cluster as a Fundamental Social Unit of the Brześć Kujawski Group of the Lengyel Culture in the Polish Lowlands." *Prace i Materialy Muzeum Archeologicznego i Etnograficznego w Łodzi,* Seria Arch. 31 (1986): 43–271.

56. Ibid., p. 124.

57. Ibid., p. 129.

58. Excavated by V. Cristescu in 1924 and published in *Dacia* 3, 1925. Excavations were resumed in 1956–59 by E. Comşa, results published in *Materiale şi Cercetari Arheologie* 5–8, 1959–62.

59. D. Berciu, *Contribuţii la problemele neoliticului in Romînia in lumina noilor cercetari* (Editura Academie RPR. 1961): 367 ff.

60. E. Comşa, "Quelques donnés relatives à périodisation et à l'évolution de la civilisation Boian." *Dacia* 1 (1957): 61–71.

61. E. Comşa, "Quelques problèmes relatives au complexe néolithique de Radovanu." *Dacia* 16 (1972): 39–51. Id., "Der neolithische Wohnverband in Radovanu." *Das Altertum* 25, 2 (1979): 113–16.

62. G. Cantacuzino and S. Morintz, "Die jungsteinzeitliche Funde in Cernica (Bucharest)." *Dacia* N.S. 7 (1963): 27–89. G. Cantacuzino, "Necropola preistorica de la Cernica si locul ei in neoliticul românesc şi european." *Studii şi Cercetari de Istorie Veche* 18,3 (1967): 379–97. E. Comşa, "Die Bestattungssitten im rumänischen Neolithikum," *Jahresschrift mitteld. Vorgesch.* 58 (Halle 1974): 122–24. Olga Necrasov, Maria Cristescu, D. Botezatu, and Georgeta Miu, "Sur les caractéristiques anthropologiques de la population néolithiques de Cernica, appartenant à la culture Boian." *Ann. Roum. Anthropol.* 1983, 20: 3–15.

63. D. Berciu, *Cultura Hamangia* (Editura Academiei R.P.R., 1966).

64. O. I. Necrasov, M. Cristescu, C. Maximilian, and D. Nicolaescu-Plopşor, "Studii antropologice ale scheletelor neolitice descoperite in cimitirul de la Cernavoda." *Probleme de antropologie* 4 (1959): 21–45. O. Necrasov, M. Cristescu, D. Botezatu and G. Miu, "Aspects démographiques et caractères anthropologiques de la population néolithique de Cernavoda (Columbia) appartenant a la culture Hamangia," *Ann. Roum. Anthropol.,* 1982, 19:11–24. Olga Necrasov, Maria Cristescu, Dan Botezatu, and Georgia Miu, "Recherches paléoanthropologiques concernant les populations qui vecurent sur le territoire de la Romanie." *Arheologia Moldovei* 13 (1990): 173–206.

65. H. Todorova and T. Dimov, "Ausgrabungen in Durankulak, 1974–1987," *Varia Archaeologica Hungarica 2,* Budapest, 1989: 291–310.

66. Colin Renfrew, Marija Gimbutas, and Ernestine S. Elster, eds., *Excavations at Sitagroi. A Prehistoric Village in Northeast Greece,* vol. 1. Monumenta Archaeologica 13, Institute of Archaeology, U. of Calif. at Los Angeles, 1986.

67. J. Deshayes, "Travaux de l'Ecole Française en 1969: Dikili Tash." *Bulletin de Correspondance Hellénique* 94 (1970): 799–808. M. Seferiades, "Dikili Tash: introduction à la préhistoire de la Macédoine orientale," *Bulletin de Correspondance Hellénique* 107 (1983).

68. Henrieta Todorova, *The Eneolithic in Bulgaria.* BAR International Series 49 (1978). This work summarizes the results published elsewhere in Bulgaria.

69. H. Todorova and G. Tončeva, "Die äneolithische Pfahlbausiedlung bei Ezero in Varnasee." *Germania* 53 (1975): 30–46. H. Todorova, *The Eneolithic in Bulgaria*, p. 38.

70. H. Todorova, et al., *Seliŝtnata mogila pri Goljamo Delčevo* (Sofia, 1975): 20–52. Ana Radunčeva. *Vinica. Eneolitno selište i nekropol* (Sofia, 1976): 10 ff. H. Todorova, *Ovčarovo. Praistoričeska selišČna mogila* (Sofia, 1976): 36–39.

71. H. Todorova, S. Ivanov, V. Vasiliev, M. Hopf, H. Quitta, and G. Kohl, *Seliŝtnata mogila pri Goljamo Delčevo* (Bulgarian Academy of Sciences: Sofia. 1975): 69–100.

72. H. Todorova, *The Eneolithic in Bulgaria*, pp. 61–62.

73. The sculpture is in the Naturhistorisches Museum, Vienna. It is reproduced in author's *Gods and Goddesses of Old Europe*, 1974 (1982): 207–9.

74. Dinu V. Rosetti, "Steinkupferzeitliche Plastik aus einem Wohnhugel bei Bukarest." *IPEK* 12 (1938): 29–50, Taf. 21 and 22.

75. Marija Gimbutas, "Mythical Imagery of Sitagroi Society," *Excavations at Sitagroi* (see note 66): 225–303.

76. D. Berciu and I. Berciu, "Sapaturi și cercetari arheologice in anii 1944–1947." *Apulum* 3 (Alba Iulia 1947–49): 9ff.

77. Iuliu Paul, "Der Forschungsstand über die Petreşti-Kultur." *Študijne Zvesti* 17 (Nitra, 1969): 325–44.

78. Id., "Ein Hockergrab der bemalten Keramik bei Salzburg (Ocna Sibiului)." *Forchungen zur Volks- und Landeskunde* 6 (Bucharest, 1963): 123–38.

79. Id., "In legatura cu problema locuintelor de suprafata cu platforma din asezarile culturilor Petreşti și Cucuteni-Tripolie." *Studii și Cercetari de Istorie Veche* 18, 1 (Bucharest, 1967): 3–24.

80. V. Dumitrescu, "La civilisation de Cucuteni," *Berichten von de rijksdienst voor het oudheidkundig bodemonderzoek. Jaargang* 9 (Amersfoort, 1959): 7–48. M. Petrescu-Dimbovița, *Cucuteni* (Bucharest, 1966). H. Schmidt, *Cucuteni in der oberen Moldau, Rumänien. Die befestigte Siedlung mit bemalter Keramik von der Steinkupferzeit bis in die vollentwickelte Bronzezeit* (Berlin, 1932). T. S. Passek, "Periodizatsiya tripol'skihk poselenii." *Materialy i Issledovanija po Arkheologii SSSR* No. 10 (Moscow, 1949). T. S. Passek, "La céramique tripolienne." *Bulletin de l'Académie de la Culture Matérielle* (Moscow, 1935).

81. Silvia Marinescu-Bîlcu, *Cultura Precucuteni pe teritoriul Romaniei* (Bucharest, 1974).

82. V. Dumitrescu, *Habaşeşti* (Bucharest, 1954). M. Petrescu-Dimovița, "Die wichtigsten Ergebnisse der archäologischen Ausgrabungen in der neolithischen Siedlung von Truşeşti (Moldau)." *Prähistorische Zeitschrift* (Berlin, 1963): 172–86. Other important site monographs include: V. Dumitrescu, "La station préhistorique de Traian fouilles de 1936, 1938 et 1940," reprinted from *Dacia* Nos. 9–10 (1941–44). R. Vulpe, "Izvoare: Sapaturile din 1936–1948" (summaries in Russian and French: "Izvoare: Les Fouilles de 1936–1948). *Biblioteca de Arheologie* 1 (Bucharest, 1957). T. S. Passek, 1949 (see note 80).

83. C. Adrian Florescu, "Befestigungsanlagen der spätneolithischen Siedlungen im Donau-Karpaten-raum." *Študijné Zvesti* 17 (Nitra, 1969): 111–24.

84. M. M. Šmagliy, V. P. Dudkin, and K. V. Zinkovsky, "Pro kompleksne vyvčenniya trypil's'kykh posilen." *Arkheolohiya* (Kiev) 10:23–31.

85. V. I. Markevič, *Pozdne-tripol'skie plemena severnoi Moldavii* (Kišenev, 1981).

86. K. V. Šiškin, "Z praktyky dešyfruvannya aerofotoznimkiv u arkheolohičnyh tsilyakh," *Arkheolohiya* (Kiev) 10:32–41.

87. Markevič (see note 85).

88. Linda Ellis, *The Cucuteni-Tripolye Culture*. BAR International Series 217, 1984: 162, citing E. von Stern, "Südrussland," in *Realexicon der Vorgeschichte*, ed. M. Ebert, vol. 13, pp. 32–50.

89. Linda Ellis, ibid., pp. 81ff., 119ff., 159.

90. D. Ya. Telegin and I. D. Potekhina, *Neolithic Cemeteries and Populations in the Dnieper Basin*, ed. J. P. Mallory. BAR International Series 383 (1987): 182ff. D. Ya. Telegin, *Dniepro-Donetskaya kultura* (Kiev, 1968). The earliest discovered large cemetery was Mariupol north of the Sea of Azov: M. Makarenko, *Mariyupil'skii mogil'nik* (Kiev, 1933). This culture is therefore also called Mariupol.

91. I. I. Gokhman, *Naselenie Ukrainy u épokhu mezolita i neolita* (Moscow, 1966).

92. Borislav Jovanović, *Rudna Glava, Najstaršije rudarstvo bakra na centralnom Balkanu.* Résumé in German: *Rudna Glava, Der älteste Kupferbau im Zentralbalkan.* Bor-Belgrade, Institute of Archaeology Publication 17 (1982). Martin Kuna, "Zur neolithischen und äneolithischen Kupferverarbeitung im Gebiet Jugoslawien." *Godišnjak* 19 (Sarajevo, 1981): 13–81, pls.

93. E. N. Chernykh, *Istoriya drevneishei metallurgii vostochnoi evropy* (Moscow, 1976).

94. M. Gimbutas, "Gold Treasure at Varna," *Archaeology* 30, 1 (New York, 1977): 44–51. Id., "Varna, a sensationally rich cemetery of the Karanovo Civilization, about 4500 B.C." *Expedition* 19, 4 (Philadelphia, 1977): 93–47. I. S. Ivanov, "Les fouilles archéologiques de la nécropole chalcolithique à Varna (1972–75)." *Studia Praehistorica* 1–2 (Sofia, 1978): 13–27.

95. A. Hartman, "Ergebnisse der spektralanalytischen Untersuchung äneolithischer Goldfunde aus Bulgarien." *Studia Praehistorica* 1–2 (Sofa, 1978): 27–46; Idem., "Die Goldsorten des Äneolithikums und der Frühbronzezeit im Donauraum." *Studia Praehistorica* 1:2 (Sofia, 1978): 182–92. Ann Dodd-Oprițescu, "Les éléments 'steppiques' dans l'énéolithique de Transylvanie." *Dacia* 22: 87–97.

96. B. Jovanović, "Early Gold and Eneolithic Copper Mining and Metallurgy of the Balkans and Danube Basin." *Studia Praehistorica* 1:2 (Sofia, 1978): 194ff.

97. A. Bukowski, "Die Salzgewinnung auf polnischem Gebiet in vorgeschichtlicher Zeit und im Altertum." In Gediga, B., ed., *Surowce mineralne w pradziejach i we wczesnym średniowieczu Europy środkowej* (Ossolineum, Wrocław, 1988): 107–32.

98. Found at Sesklo, Rakhmani, Pefkakia at Volos, and the cave of Alepotrypa at Mani, southern end of the Peloponnese. Sesklo pendant and copper axes are illustrated in: Colin Renfrew, *The Emergence of Civilization. The Cyclades and the Aegean in the Third Millennium B.C.* (London 1972): 312, fig. 16.2. Gold bracelets and beads and a silver anthropomorphic pendant from the cave of Alepotrypa. H. Hauptmann, "Forschungsbericht über die Ausgrabungen und Neufunde zur ägaischen Frühzeit, 1961–65." *Archäologischer Anzeiger* 3 (Berlin, 1971): 359.

99. G. P. Sergeev, "Rannertripolskiy klad u.s. Karbuna," *Sovetskaya Arkheologiya* 1 (Moscow, 1962): 131–51. L. S. Klejn, "O date Karbunskogo klada," *Problemy Arkheologii* 1 (Leningrad, 1968): 5–75.

100. N. Angelov, "Zlatnoto sakrovishche ot Hotnica," *Arkheologiya* 1, 1–2 (Sofia, 1959): 38–46.

101. D. Galbenu, "Neoliticheskaya masterskaya dlya obrabotki ukrashenii v Khyrshove." *Dacia* N.S. 7 (Bucharest, 1963): 501–10. Here a pot with unfinished and broken bracelets and rectangular beads of spondylus shell was found near which lay a copper awl, a wedge-shaped tool, and four rings.

102. I. Bognár-Kutzián, *Tiszapolgár-Basatanya* (Budapest, 1963).

103. Linda Ellis, *The Cucuteni-Tripolye Culture* BAR International Series 217 (1984): 115ff.

104. Ibid., p. 133.

105. Ibid., p. 157.

Chapter 4

1. K. Jażdżewski, *Kultura Pucharów Lejkowatych w Polsce Zachodniej i Środkowej* (Poznań, 1936). Id., "Wzajemny stosunek do siebie elementów poŁnochych poŁudniowych i zachodnich w obrębie kultury pucharów lejkowatych," *Prace i Materiały Muzeum Archeologicznego i Etnograficznego w Łodzi*, 17 (1970): 49–76. H. Schwabedissen, "Das Beginn des Neolithikums im nordwestlichen Deutschland," ed. H. Schirnig. *Grossteingräber in Niedersachsen:* 203–22; T. Wiślański, "Kształtowanie się miejscowych kultur rolniczo-hodowlanych. Plemiona kultury pucharów lejkowatych," eds. W. Hensel and T. Wiślański. *Prahistoria Ziem Polskich*, vol. *Neolit*. 165–260 (Wrocław, 1979). Lars Larsson, *The Early Neolithic Funnel-Beaker Culture in Southwest Scania, Sweden*. BAR International Series 264 (1985).

2. T. Wiślański, "Plemiona kultury pucharów lejkowatych." *Prahistoria Ziem Polskich* 2 (1979). W. Hensel and T. Wiślański, eds., pp. 213–14.

3. Ibid., p. 217.

4. Ibid., p. 215.

5. B. Balcer, "A study of socio-economic aspects of Neolithic flint working on the example of the Funnel Beaker Culture," R. Schild, ed. *Unconventional Archaeology. New Approaches and Goals in Polish Archaeology* 87–107 (Wrocław, 1980). Id., "Wyniki badań nad krzemieniarstwem kultury pucharów lejkowatych na ziemiach Polski." T. Wiślański, ed., *Kultura Pucharów Lejkowatych w Polsce* (Poznań, 1981): 59–79.

6. T. Wiślański (see note 5), pp. 217ff.

7. Z. Podkowińska, "Spichrze ziemne w osadzie kultury pucharów lejkowatych na Gawrońcu-Pałydze w Cmielowie pow. Opatów." *Archeologia Polski* 6 (1961): 21–63. Id., "Village énéolithique de Cmielów, District Opatów, Voivodie de Kielce." *Archeologia Polona* 4 (1962): 98–110.

8. W. Haio Zimmermann, "Ein trichterbecherzeitlicher Hausgrundriss von Flögeln—im Örtjen, Kr. Cuxhaven." *Materialhefte zur Ur- und Frühgeschichte* 16: 479–88.

9. Magdalena S. Midgley, *The Origin and Function of the Eastern Long Barrows in Northern Europe.* BAR International Series 259 (1985). (Includes extensive bibliography.)

10. J. Skaarup, *Stengade. Ein langeländischer Wohnplatz mit Hausreste aus der frühneolitischen Zeit* (Rudkøbing, 1975).

11. C. Fischer, "Tidlig-neolitske anlaeg ved Rustrup." *Kuml* (1975): 29–72. Torsten Madsen, "Earthen long barrows and timber structures: aspects of the Early Neolithic mortuary practice in Denmark." *Proceedings of the Prehistoric Society* 45 (1979). Id., "En tidligneolitisk langhøj ved Rude i Østjylland." *Kuml* (1980).

12. P. V. Glob, "Barkaer. Danmarks aeldste landsby." *Nationalmuseets arbejdsmark* 1949, pp. 1–12. Id., "Do dødes lange huse." *Skalk* (1975) 6: 10–14. Midgley (see note 9), pp. 144–45.

13. Madsen 1979 (see note 11).

14. Midgley (see note 9), pp. 190–98.

15. Z. Kapica, "Różnicowanie się składów antropologicznych ludności Kujaw w czasie od neolitu do współczesności na podstawie materiałów z terenu powiatu włocławskiego." *Przegląd Antropologiczny* 34 (1968): 325–39.

16. Midgley (see note 9), p. 193.

17. E. Sprockhoff, *Die nordische Megalithkultur* (Berlin, 1938). Lili Kaelas, "The megalithic tombs in south Scandinavia—migration or cultural influence?" Symposium on the origins and interrelations of Neolithic cultures of W. Europe. *Paleohistoria* 12 (1967). "Megaliths of the Funnel Beaker culture in Germany and Scandinavia." *The Megalithic Monuments of Western Europe*, Colin Renfrew, ed. (London: Thames and Hudson, 1983):77–91. E. Schuldt, *Die mecklenburgischen Megalithigräber* (Berlin, 1972). K. Ebbesen, *Die jüngere Trichterbecherkultur auf den dänischen Inseln.* Arkaeologiske Studier 2 (København, 1975). J. A. Bakker, *The TRB West Group. Studies in the Chronology and Geography of the Makers of Hunebeds and Tiefstich Pottery* (Amsterdam, 1979).

18. Sven Thorsen, "Klokkehøj at Bojden. A dolmen with a preserved primary grave from southwest Fünen." *Kuml* 1980.

19. Kaelas 1983 (see note 17), p. 84.

20. Christopher Tilley, "Ideology and the legitimation of power in the Middle Neolithic of southern Sweden." *Ideology, Power, and Prehistory*, Daniel Miller and Christopher Tilley, eds. (Cambridge University Press, 1984): 125.

21. Ibid.

22. Poul Kjaerum, "Mortuary houses and funeral rites in Denmark." *Antiquity* 41 (1967).

23. Lars Larsson, "A causewayed enclosure and a site with Valby pottery at Stävie, western Scania." *Meddelanden från Lunds universitets Historiska Museet* (Lund, 1982).

24. Ibid.

25. Kjaerum (see note 22).

26. Jan Kowalczyk, *Zmierzch epoki kamienia* (Ossolineum, 1971): 100–101.

27. R. Rimantienė, *Akmens amžius Lietuvoje.* (Vilnius: Mokslas, 1984): 69–84.

28. H. Gross, "Moorgeologische Untersuchung der vorgeschichtlichen Dörfer in Zedmar-Bruch." *Prussia* 33: 100–68. J. Okulicz, *Pradzieje ziem pruskich od późnego paleolitu do VII w. n. e.* (Wrocław, 1973).

29. V. F. Isaenko, *Neolit Pripyatskogo Poles'ya* (Minsk, 1976).

30. R. Rimantienė (see note 27), pp. 112ff.

31. D. Bohnsack, "Ein Steinzeitgrab mit Röttelbestattung aus Braynicken, Kr. Neidenburg." *Altpreussen* 1939, 4,2, pp. 35–38.

32. T. Wiślański, "Krąg ludów subneolitycznych w Polsce." *Prahistoria Ziem Polskich* 2, Neolit (Ossilneum, 1979): 323.

33. T. Wiślański, ibid.; R. Rimantienė (see note 27) p. 180.

34. A brachycephalic skull from the peat bog at Turlojiškė, southern Lithuania, had a somewhat flattened face, a feature considered by K. Yu. Mark (in *Voprosy etnicheskoy istorii estonskogo naroda*, Talin, 1956: 219–42) to be Mongoloid. P. Ya. Denisova (in *Antropologiya drevnikh baltov*, Riga, 1975:75) and G. Česnys (see R. Rimantienė, note 27, p. 189) regard it to be a weak and fragmentary evidence for far reaching conclusions.

35. R. Rimantienė, *Akmens amžius Lietuvoje* (Vilnius: Mokslas, 1984): 189–90. G. Česnys, A. Girininkas, R. Jankauskas, and I. Papreckienė-Balčiunienė, "Kretuono 1-os gyvenvietės vidurinio neolito kapai." *Lietuvos archeologija* 4 (1985). F. Zagorskis, "Zvejnieku akmens laikmeta kapulauka apbedijumu tipologija un hronologija." *Archeologija un Etnografija* 11 (1974): 7–24.

36. F. Zagorskis, *Zvejnieku akmens laikmeta kapulauks.* (Riga: Zinatne, 1987).

37. R. Rimantienė (see note 27).

38. R. Rimantienė, *Šventoji I. Narvos kultūros gyvenvietės* (Vilnius: Mokslas, 1979). L. V. Vankina, *Torfyanikovaya stoyanka Sarnate* (Riga: Zinatne, 1970). I. A. Loze, *Pozdniy Neolit i Rannyaya Bronza Lubanskoy Ravniny* (Riga: Zinatne, 1979).

39. A. Girininkas, "Pakretuonės 3-čia gyvenvietė." *Archeologiniai tyrinėjimai Lietuvoje 1986 ir 1987 metais.* Lietuvos TSR Mokslų Akademija, Istorijos Institutas (Vilnius, 1988): 7–10.

40. I. Loze, "Novyi centr yantar'a epokhi neolita v Vostočnoy Pribaltike," (résumé in French: "Un nouveau centre du travail de l'ambre a l'époque néolithique dans les pays Baltique est"). *Sovetskaya Arkheologiya* 3 (1969): 124–34. "Neolithic amber ornaments in the eastern part of Latvia." *Przegląd Archeologiczny* 23 (1975): 49–82. *Akmens laikmets Lubana klanos.* (Latvian Academy of Sciences, Institute of History, Riga, 1979). M. Gimbutas, "East Baltic Amber in the Fourth and Third Millennium B.C," *Studies in Baltic Amber*, special issue of *The Journal of Baltic Studies* 16: 3, 1985.

41. T. Wiślański, "Dalszy rozwój ludów neolitycznych. Plemiona kultury amfor kulistych." *Prahistoria Ziem Polskich* 2, Neolit. (Wrocław-Warsaw-Cracow-Gdańsk, 1979): 289, fig. 169.

42. R. Rimantienė (see note 35), pp. 181–83.

43. Ibid., "Ariau, ariau, ariau . . ." *Mokslas ir Gyvenimas*, No. 3 (Vilnius, 1980): 22–23.

44. R. Rimantienė and G. Česnys, "The Late Globular Amphora Culture and its Creators in the Baltic Area from Archaeological and Anthropological Points of View," *The Journal of Indo-European Studies*, 1990 (Proceedings of the Conference on Transformation of European and Anatolian Culture 4500–2500 B.C., ed. by M. Gimbutas.)

Chapter 5

1. The Mesolithic shell mound, about 0.90 m thick and rich in microlithic flints, has given a C-14 date of 7770 ± 340 B.P., about 68–66th cent. B.C. The 20 cm thick layer overlying the shell mound contained the earliest pottery as well as flints. It has given a C-14 date of 7670 ± 120 B.P., approx. 67–66th cent. B.C. Above this, a sterile level 70–80 cm thick separated the Early Ceramic layer from that of the settlement with Impressed Pottery. The last layer, only 15 cm thick, is dated by a single C-14 date: 7340 ± 180 B.P., about 64–63rd cent. B.C. Augustus Sordinas, "Investigations of the Prehistory of Corfu during 1964–1966," *Balkan Studies* 10, 2 (Thessaloniki, 1969): 401–14. Id., "Radiocarbon dates from Corfu, Greece." *Antiquity* 41 (London, 1967): 64.

2. The La Porta Mesolithic site of Campania in Italy has given a C-14 date of 8619 ± 200 B.P. (6669 b.c.), with a true age most likely within the second half of the 8th mill. B.C.

3. Alojz Benac, *Studien zur Stein- und Kupferzeit im nordwestlichen Balkan.* (Berlin: Bericht der Römisch-Germanischen Kommission No. 42, 1962).

4. Šime Batović, *Stariji Neolit u Dalmaciji.* (Zadar: Societas Archeologiae Iugoslaviae, Museum Archaeologicum, 1966).

5. D. H. Trump, *Central and Southern Italy Before Rome.* (London: Thames and Hudson, 1966).

6. J. Bradford, "Buried landscapes in Southern Italy," *Antiquity* 23 (London, 1949).

7. S. M. Puglisi, "Lo strato neolitico de Coppa Nevigata." *Civiltà Preistoriche e Protostoriche della Daunia* (1975): 112–16. An exception is a date from Coppa Nevigata, a site situated on a lagoon not far from the sea: 8150 B.P. If calibrated, the true age should be in the vicinity of 7000 B.C. This date is from an animal bone and probably is too high. The site is on deep brown alluvium which is very difficult to work with stone tools. The people of Coppa Nevigata were apparently not concerned with crop growing but rather with the exploitation of shell fish from the lake. A seven-foot-deep midden is filled with cockle shells and flint awls used for their exploitation.

8. R. Jarman and D. Webley, "Settlement and land use in Capitanata, Italy," in Higgs, E. C., ed., *Paleo-economy* (Cambridge, 1975): 177–216. A. Sargent, "Exploitation Territory and Economy in the Tavoliere of Apulia." *Studi sul Neolitico del Tavoliere della Puglia.* Selene M. Cassano and Alessandra Manfredini, eds. BAR International Series 160 (1983): 223–36.

9. S. Tinè, "La civiltà neolitica del Tavoliere." *Civiltà Preistoriche e Protostoriche della Daunia* (1975): 99–112. Id., *Passo di Corvo e la Civiltà neolitica del Tavoliere* (Genoa: Sagep Editrice, 1983).

10. Daniel Evett and Jane Renfrew, "L'agricoltura neolitica italiana: una nota sui ceredi." *Rivista di Scienze Preistoriche* 26, 2 (Rome, 1971): 403–9. M. Follieri, "Cereali del villaggio neolitico di Passo di Corvo (Foggia)," *Annali di Botanica* 32 (Rome, 1973): 49–59.

11. Sándor Bökönyi, "Animal Bones from the Excavations of Early Neolithic Ditched Villages on the Tavoliere, South Italy." *Studi sul neolitico del Tavoliere della Puglia*, Selene M. Cassano and Alessandra Manfredini, eds. BAR International Series 160 (1983): 237–48.

12. M. Cipolloni, "Nuovi dati dello scavo del villaggio di Rendina pressa Melfi." *Civiltà Preistoriche e Protostoriche della Daunia* (1975). Mirella Cipolloni Sampo, *Scavi nel villaggio neolitico di Rendina* (1970–76). Reprint from *Origini* 9, 1977–82: 183–354.

13. A. Sargent (see note 8), p. 226.

14. A. Mosso, "La necropoli neolitica di Molfetta." *Monumenti Antichi* 20 (1910): 237–356. R. D. Whitehouse, "Prehistoric settlement patterns in southeast Italy." *Archaeology and Italian Society*, G. Barker and R. Hodges, eds. BAR International Series 102: 157–65.

15. Tinè 1983 (see note 9), p. 185.

16. D. Ridola, "Le grande trincee preistoriche di Matera." *Bollettino di Paletnologia Italiana* 54 (1926): 134.

17. L. H. Barfield, "Patterns of North Italian Trade 5000–2000 B.C." *Archaeology and Italian Society. Prehistoric, Roman and Medieval Studies.* BAR International Series 102 (1981): 32.

18. Ibid., p. 35. G. Tanda, "Gli anelloni litici italiani." *Preistoria Alpina* 13 (1977): 111–55.

19. G. Bailloud, "Fouille d'un habitat néolithique et torréen à Basi, Serra di Ferro, Corse." *Bulletin de la Société Préhistorique Française* 66 (1969). François de Lanfranchi and Michel-Claude Weiss, *La Civilisation des Corses. Les origines* (Ajaccio: Editions Cyrnos et Meditérranée, 1973). The date of Basi, 7700 ± 150 B.P. and Curacchiaghiu 7600 ± 180 and 7300 ± 180 B.P. are one millennium earlier than those from Filiestru, Sardinia, which seem to be too high. The pottery in both islands is related.

20. David H. Trump, *La grotta di Filiestru a Bonu Ighinu, Mara (SS)*. Dessi-Sassari 1983 (Ministero per i Beni Culturali e Ambientali, Quaderni 13, directed by F. Lo Schiavo).

21. C. Puxeddu, "Giacimenti di aossidiana del Monte Arci in Sardegna e sua irradiazione." *Studi Sardi* 14–15 (1955–57): 10–66.

22. R. Loria and D. H. Trump, "Le scoperte à Sa Ucca de Su Tintirriolu e il neolitico sardo." *Monumenta At.*, serie misc. vol. 2-2 (1978).

23. Enrico Atzeni, "Aspetti e sviluppi culturali del neolitico e delle prime età dei metalli in Sardegna." *Ichnussa. La Sardegna dalle origini all'età classica* (Milano: Libri Scheiwiller, 1981) 27–41.

24. Ibid., xxviii, fig. 5.

25. Ibid., pp. 21–51.

26. J. D. Evans, *Malta. Ancient People and Places.* (London: Thames and Hudson, 1959).

27. J. D. Evans, *The Prehistoric Antiquities of the Maltese Islands: A Survey.* (London: The Athlone Press, 1971).

28. D. H. Trump, *Skorba*. Reports of the Research Committee of the Society of Antiquaries of London 22. Oxford University Press and the National Museum of Malta, 1966.

Chapter 6

1. P. Ducos, "L'élevage en Méditerranée occidentale." Actes du Colloque Intern. de l'Institute de Recherches Méditerranées, C.N.R.S., 1976:77ff. J. Roche, *Le gisement mésolitique de Moita do sebastiao, Muge, Portugal.* Instittuto de Alta Cultura (Lisbon, 1972). Jean Guilaine and Jean-Louis Roudil, "Les civilisations néolithiques en Languedoc." *La Préhistoire Française*, 2, J. Guilaine, ed. (Paris, 1976), Editions du Centre National de la Recherche Scientifique, p. 267. F. Poplin, Th. Poulain, P. Méniel, J.-D. Vigne, D. Geddes, and D. Helmer, "Les débuts de l'élevage en France." *Le Néolithique de la France, Hommage à G. Bailloud.* J.-P. Demoule and J. Guilaine, eds. (Paris: Picard, 1986): 37–51.

2. Nigel Mills, "The Neolithic of Brittany," *Ancient France*, Chr. Scarre, ed. (Edinburgh University Press, 1984): 109.

3. Jean Guilaine, "The earliest Neolithic in the West Mediterranean: A New appraisal." *Antiquity* 53 (1979): 22–30. Patricia Phillips, *Early Farmers of West Mediterranean Europe.* (London: Hutchinson, 1975): 48.

4. Paul Bahn, "The Neolithic in the French Pyrenees." *Ancient France*, Chr. Scarre, ed. (Edinburgh University Press, 1984):184–222.

5. Carme Olària, *Cova Fosca. Un asentamiento meso-neolítico de cazadores y pastores en la serrania del Alto Maestrazgo, Castellon.* 1988. Monografies de Prehistoria i Arqueologia Castellonenques 3.

6. H. Schubart and V. Pascual, "Datacion por el C-14 de los estratos con ceramica cardial de la Coveta de l'Or." *Archivo de Prehistoria Levantina* 9 (Valencia): 45–51. B. Marti, "Cova de l'Or (Beniares, Alicante)," *Trabajos Varios del S.I.P.* (Valencia, 1977).

7. M. Hopf, "Triticum monococcum L. y Triticum dicoccum Schübl, en el Neolitico antiguo español," *Archivo de Prehistoria Levantina* 11 (Valencia, 1966): 53–73.

8. A. M. Vicent and A. M. Muñoz, "Secunda Campana de Excavationes. La Cueva de Los Murcielagos, Zuheros (Cordoba) 1969." *Excavaciones Arqueolog-*

ica en España 77 (1973). P. Lopez, "La problematica cronologica del neolitico peninsular." *C-14 y Prehistoria de la Peninsula Iberica.* Reunion 1978 (Madrid, Serie Universitaria, 77): 51.

9. P. Lopez, ibid., p. 53.

10. Jean Guilaine and Octavio da Veiga Ferreira "Le Néolithique ancien au Portugal." *Bulletin de la Société Préhistorique Française* 67 (1970): 304–22. P. Phillips (see note 3), p. 71.

11. Chr. Scarre, "The Neolithic of West-Central France." *Ancient France*, Chr. Scarre, ed. (Edinburgh, 1984): 327.

12. Antonio Beltran, *Da cacciatori ad allevatori. L'arte rupestre del Levante Spagnolo.* (Milano: Jaca Book, 1979). H. N. Savory, *Spain and Portugal.* (London: Thames and Hudson, 1968): 57. Carme Olària (see note 5), pp. 423–24.

13. M. Pelicer, "El neolitico y el bronce de la Cueva de la Cariguela del Piñar." *Trabajos de Prehistoria* 15 (Madrid, 1966).

14. D. Binder and J. Courtin, "Les styles céramiques du Néolithique ancien provençal." *Le Néolithique de la France. Hommage à G. Bailloud*, J. P. Demoule and J. Guilaine, eds. (Paris: Picard, 1986): 83–93. J. Guilaine, "Le Néolithique ancien en Languedoc et Catalogne." Id., pp. 71–82. F. Treinen-Claustre, "Le groupe de Montbol dans son contexte pyrénéen." Id., pp. 217–32.

15. A. Niederlander, R. Lacam, and J. Arnal, *Le gisement néolithique de Roucadour*, 3rd Supplement to Gallia Préhistoire (Paris, 1966). Chr. Scarre, "The Neolithic of West-Central France." *Ancient France*, (1984): 228.

16. P. -R. Giot, J. L'Helgouach, and J. Monnier, *Préhistoire de la Bretagne.* (Rennes, Ouest France, 1979).

17. J. Vaquer, "Le Chasséen meridional. État de la question." *Le Néolithique de la France, Hommage à G. Bailloud*, J.-P. Demoule and J. Guilaine, eds. (Paris: Picard, 1986):33–44.

18. L. Meroc and G. Simonnet, "Le village néolithique Chasséen de Saint-Michel-du-Touch, commune Toulouse (Haute Garonne)." *Bulletin de la Société Mériodionale de Spéléologie et de Préhistoire*, 1969: 14–15, 27–37; Id., "Le Chasséen de la haute et de la mayonne vallée de la Garonne." *Les Civilisations Néolithiques du Midi de la France*, J. Guilaine, ed., 1970. Another village was excavated at Villeneuve-Tolosane: J. Clottes, J.-P. Giraud, F. Rouzand, and J. Vaquer, "Le village néolithique de Villeneuve-Tolosane." *Archaeologia* 130 (1978): 6–13.

19. J. Arnal and G. Rodriquez, "Le gisement saintponien de Dorio. Félines-Minervois (Herault)." *Bulletin du Musée d'Anthropologie Préhistorique de Monaco* 17 (1971): 171–90.

20. L. Barfield, *Northern Italy Before Rome.* (London: Thames and Hudson, 1971). B. Bagolini, L. Barfield, and A. Broglio, "Notizie preliminari sulle ricerche nell' insediamento neolitico di Fimon-Molino, Casaretto (Vicenza) 1969–72." *Rivista Sci. Preist.* 27-1 (1973): 161–215.

21. P. Castelfranco, *Cimeli dei Museo Ponti nell'Isola Virginia Lago Varese* (Milan, 1916).

22. Barfield, ibid., p. 52.

23. M. R. Sauter, "Sepultures à cistes du Bassin du Rhône." *Sibrium* 2 (1955). Also verbal communication by Prof. Sauter in 1979.

24. Victorine von Gonzenbach, *Die Cortaillod-kultur in der Schweiz.* Monographien zur Ur- und Frühgeschichte der Schweiz 7 (Basel, 1949).

25. Emil Vogt, "Das steinzeitliche Uferdorf Egolzwil. Kr. Luzern." *Zeitschrift Schweizerischer Archäologie* 4, Kunstgeschichte 12 (1951): 193–215. René Wyss, *Das jungsteinzeitliche jäger-Bauerndorf von Egolzwil 5 im Wauwilermoos.* Archaeologische Forschungen, Schweizerisches Landesmuseum (Zurich, 1976).

26. Hans-Georg Bandi and Hansjürgen Müller-Beck, eds. *Seeberg Burgäschisee-Süd.* Acta Bernensia 2, 1963–69. (Bern: Stampfli and Cie.)

27. Emil Vogt in W. U. Guyan, ed., *Das Pfahlbauproblem* (Basel: Birkhausen, 1955). Id., "Der Stand der neolithischen Forschung in der Schweiz." *L'Europe à la fin de l'âge de la pierre.* J. Böhm and S. J. De Laet, eds. (Prague: Czechoslovak Academy of Sciences, 1961).

28. J. Boesneck, "Die Tierreste," in *Seeberg Burgäschisee-Süd.* Acta Bernensia 2,3 (1963).

29. Hansjürgen Müller-Beck, "Prehistoric Swiss Lake Dwellers," *Scientific American* 205, 4 (1961): 138–47.

30. H. Müller-Beck, "Jahrringchronologische Synchronisierung der jungsteinzeitlichen Siedlungen Thayngen-Weier und Burgäschisee-Süd und Südwest." *Germania* 41, 7 (1963).

31. Bruno Huber, "Seeberg, Burgäschisee-Süd, Dendrochronologie." *Seeberg, Burgäschisee-Süd* 2, 4. H.-G Bandi and H. Müller-Beck, eds. C. W. Ferguson, B. Huber, and H. Suess, "Determination of the Age of Swiss Lake Dwellings as an Example of Dendrochronologically-Calibrated Radiocarbon Dating." *Zeitschrift für Naturforschung* 21, 7 (1966): 1173–77.

32. J. L. Helgouach and Ch.-T. Le Roux, "Morphologie et chronologie des grandes architectures de l'Ouest de la France." *Le Néolithique de la France,* J. O. Demoule and J. Guilaine, eds. (Paris: Picard, 1986):181–91.

33. P-R. Giot, J. L. Helgouach, and J. Monnier, *Préhistoire de la Bretagne* (Rennes: Ouest France, 1979). Elizabeth Shee Twohig, *The Megalithic Art of Western Europe* (Oxford: Clarendon Press, 1981): 162. Aubrey Burl, *Megalithic Brittany* (London: Thames and Hudson, 1985).

34. Twohig (see note 33), p. 178.

35. J. L. Helgouach and Ch.-T. Roux (see note 32), p. 190.

36. Ch.-T. Le Roux, "Informations archéologiques." *Gallia Préhistoire* 24 (1981): 395–423; Id., "Le tumulus de Gavrinis, état des recherches." *Bulletin Société préhist. française* 80 (1983): 131.

37. J. Lecornec, "Le cairn de Petit-Mont à Arzon (Morbihan)." *Bulletin Société préhist. française* 80 (1983): 131.

38. A. Thom and A. S. Thom, *Megalithic Remains in Britain and Brittany* (Oxford University Press, 1978).

39. M. Almagro and A. Arribas, *El poblado y la necrópolis megalitica de Los Millares.* Bibliotheca Praehistorica España 3 (Madrid, 1963). G. and V. Leisner, *Die Megalithgräber der iberischen Halbinsel. Der Westen* (Berlin: de Gruyter). 1956–65.

40. A. Whittle, "Earlier Neolithic Enclosures in North-West Europe." *Proceedings of the Prehistoric Society* 43 (1977): 329–48.

41. A. ApSimon, "An Early Neolithic House in Co. Tyrone." *Journal of the Royal Society of Antiquaries of Ireland* 99, part 2 (1969): 165–68.

42. Ibid., p. 167.

43. F. Pryor, *Excavation at Fengate, Peterborough, England. The First Report.* Royal Ontario Museum Archaeology Monograph 3, 1974. C. H. Houlder, "A Neolithic Settlement on Hazard Totnes." *Trans. Devon Arch. Explor. Soc.* 21:2–31.

44. Michael J. O'Kelly, *Early Ireland* (Cambridge University Press, 1989).

45. S. Caufield, "Neolithic Fields: The Irish Evidence." *Early Land Allotment in British Isles,* H. C. Bowen and P. J. Fowler, eds. Oxford: BAR British Series 48 (1978): 137–43.

46. D. V. Clark and N. Sharples, "Settlement and Subsistence in the Third Millennium B.C." *The Prehistory of Orkney,* Colin Renfrew, ed. (Edinburgh University Press, 1985): 54–82.

47. Ibid., 68.

48. A. Whittle (see note 40), pp. 337, 339.

49. P. Ashbee, *The Ancient British Causewayed Enclosures* (Norwich: Geo Abstracts Ltd., 1978): 71.

50. J. D. Hedges and D. G. Buckley, "Excavations at a Neolithic Causewayed Enclosure, Orsett, Essex, 1975." *Proceedings of Prehistoric Society* 44 (1978): 219–308.

51. P. Drewett, "The excavation of a Neolithic causewayed enclosure on Offham Hill, East Sussex, 1976." *Proceedings of Prehistoric Society* 43 (1977): 201–42.

52. Rey Robertson-Mckay, "The Neolithic Causeway Enclosures at Staines. Survey; Excavations 1961–63." *Proceedings of Prehistoric Society* 53:23–128.

53. I. F. Smith, "Windmill Hill and its Implications," *Palaeohistoria* 12 (1966): 469–481. "The Neolithic" in *British Prehistory,* Colin Renfrew, ed. (London: Duckworth): 100–36.

54. P. Drewett (see note 51).

55. A. Thom and A. S. Thom (see note 38).

56. G. T. Meaden, *Circles in the Age of Stonehenge,* 1991.

57. G. de G. Sieveking, et al., "The New Survey of Grimes Graves, Norfolk." *Proceedings of Prehistoric Society* 39 (1973): 182–218.

58. C. Renfrew, ed., "The Neolithic." *British Prehistory* (London: Duckworth, 1974): 100–36.

59. W. A. Cummins, "Stone Axes as a Guide to Neolithic Communications and Boundaries in England and Wales." *Proceedings of Preh. Soc.* 46 (1980): 45–60.

60. J. M. Coles, F. A. Hibbert, and B. J. Orme, "Prehistoric Roads and Tracks in Somerset: 3. The Sweet Track." *Proceedings of Preh. Soc.* 39 (1973): 256–98.

61. S. Piggott, *Neolithic Cultures of the British Isles* (Cambridge University Press, 1954). C. Renfrew, ed., "The Neolithic." *British Prehistory* (London: Duckworth, 1974): 100–36.

62. D. P. S. Peacock, "Neolithic Pottery Production in Cornwall." *Antiquity* 43:170 (1969): 145–49.

63. A. L. Brindley, J. N. Lanting, and W. G. Mook, "Radiocarbon Dates from the Neolithic Burials at Ballintruer More, Co. Wicklow and Ardcrony, Co. Tipperary." *Journal of Irish Archaeology* (1983): 19.

64. D. V. Clarke, "Rinyo and the Orcadian Neolithic." *From the Stone Age to the Forty-Five,* Anne O'Connor and D. V. Clarke, eds. (Edinburgh: John Donald Publishers Ltd., 1983): 45–56.

65. R. de Valera and Sean O Nualláin, *Survey of the Megalithic Tombs of Ireland,* Dublin: Stationery Office: vol. 1, 1961; vol. 2, 1964; vol. 3, 1972; vol. 4, 1982.

66. A. Lynch. "Poulnabrone—A Stone in Time . . ." *Archaeology of Ireland* 2, 3 (1988): 105–7.

67. George Eogan, *Knowth and the Passage-Tombs of Ireland* (London: Thames and Hudson, 1986).

68. Michael J. O'Kelly, *Newgrange: Archaeology, Art, and Legend* (London: Thames and Hudson, 1982).

69. K. J. Bley, *The Earliest Indo-European Burial Tradition in Neolithic Ireland.* Ph.D. dissertation, UCLA, 1989. Ann Arbor: University of Michigan Microfilms Int.

70. F. Lynch, "Towards a Chronology of Megalithic Tombs in Wales." *Welsh Antiquity,* George C. Boon and J. M. Lewis, eds. (Cardiff: National Museum of Wales, 1976): 63–80.

71. *The Earthen Long Barrows of Britain,* 2nd ed. (Norwich: Geo Books, 1984).

72. R. J. C. Atkinson, "Wayland's Smithy." *Antiquity* 34 (1965): 126–33.

73. Stuart Piggott, *The West Kennet Long Barrow Excavations 1955–56.* (London: Her Majesty's Stationery Office, 1962).

74. A. Henshall, *Chambered Tombs of Scotland,* 2 vols. (Edinburgh University Press, 1963, 1972).

75. C. Renfrew, ed., "Scottish Chambered Tombs and Long Mounds." *British Prehistory: A New Outline* (London: Duckworth, 1974): 137–64.

76. K. J. Masters, "The Lochhill Long Cairn." *Antiquity* 57 (1973): 96–100.

77. "Excavation of the Dalladies Long Barrow, Fettercain, Kincardinshire." *Proc. Soc. Antiq. Scot.* 104 (1974): 23–47.

78. T. C. M. Brewster, *The Excavations of Whitegrounds Barrow, Burythorpe.* Wintringham: The Last Riding Archaeological Research Committee, 1984.

Chapter 7

1. Lithic sculptures and symbolic marks are present from the Acheullean and Mousterian periods; see J. E. Musch, "Animal Farm Paleolithic Sculptures from the Northwest European Plains," Paper presented at the World Archaeology Congress in Southhampton, 1986. Also "Bilderbuch der Steinzeit." *Archäologische Berichten* 20 (1991).

2. See the splendid book on Upper Paleolithic cave and sanctuaries and their art: A. Leroi-Gourhan, *Treasures of Prehistoric Art* (New York: Harry N. Abrams, 1967).

3. N. Delporte, *L'image de la femme dans l'art préhistorique* (Paris: Picard, 1979).

4. Marija Gimbutas, *The Language of the Goddess. Unearthing the Hidden Symbols of Western Civilization* (San Francisco: Harper and Row, 1989).

5. John Onians, "On the Origins of Art," published jointly with Desmond Collins in *Art History. Journal of the Association of Art Historians* 1, 1 (1978): 1–25.

6. Leslie G. Freeman, Richard G. Klein, and Joaquin G. Echegaray, "A Stone Age Sanctuary." *Natural History* 92, no. 8 (1983): 47–52.

7. J. G. D. Clark, *Star Carr: A Case of Study in Bioarchaeology.* McMaleb Module No. 10 (1974): 1–42.

8. P. Graziosi, "Nuove manifestazioni d'arte mesolitica e neolitica nel riparo Gaban presso Trento." *Rivista di Scienze Preistoriche* 30, 1–2 (1973): 237–78.

9. Mentioned by B. A. Uspenski, "Kult Nikoly na Rusi. . . ." *Trudy po znakovym sistemam* 10 (1978): 86–140.

10. G. Thomson, "The Arkoudiotissa." *Kretika Chronika* 15–16, pt. 3 (1962): 93–96.

11. Martin P. Nilsson, *Griechische Feste von religiöser Bedeutung*, 1st. ed. (Leipzig, 1906): 312.

12. W. Mannhardt, *Letto-preussische Götterlehre* (Riga, 1936): 442–52.

13. Pamela Berger, *The Goddess Obscured. Transformation of the Grain Protectress from Goddess to Saint* (Boston: Beacon Press, 1985): 49–70.

14. See more illustrations of figurines of Lespugue and Willendorf type in Leroi-Gourhan, 1967, pp. 44–45, charts.

15. M. Gimbutas, "Senosios Europos deivės ir dievai." *Metmenys* 48 (1984): 28–57.

16. A. J. Greimas, *Apie dievus ir žmones* (Chicago: A and M Publication, 1979): 317–19.

17. Carmichael, 1900 (reprint 1983), p. 169.

18. S. Rüttner-Cova, *Frau Holle. Die gestürzte Göttin* (Basel: Sphinx Verlag, 1986).

19. Michael Shapiro, "Baba-Jaga: A Search for Mythopoeic Origins and Affinities." *International Journal of Slavic Linguistics and Poetics* 27 (1983).

20. J. Doan, "Five Breton Cantiques from Pardons." *Folklore* 91 (1980): 35.

21. Joseph Cassar-Pullicino, *Studies in Maltese Folklore* (Malta University Publication, 1976): 238.

22. Marija Gimbutas, Shan Winn, and Daniel Shimabuku, *Achilleion. A Neolithic Settlement in Thessaly, Northern Greece, 6400–5600 B.C.* Monumenta Archaeologica 14, Institute of Archaeology, U. of Calif. at Los Angeles, 1989.

23. J. S. Mellaart, *Çatal Hüyük: A Neolithic Town in Anatolia* (Edinburgh University Press, 1967). D. O. Cameron, *Symbols of Birth and Death in the Neolithic Era* (London: Kenyon Deane, 1981): 4–14. James Mellaart, *The Goddess from Anatolia*, vol. 1 (wall paintings), vol. 2 (text) (Milan: Eskenazi, 1989).

24. Marija Gimbutas, "The Temples of Old Europe." *Archaeology* 33 (December 1980): 41–50.

25. M. Grbić, et al. *Porodin. Kasnoneolitsko naselje na Tumbi kod Bitolja* (Bitola, 1960).

26. The temple of Radingrad was excavated by Totju Ivanov in 1974; not yet published.

27. V. Dumitrescu, "Cascioarele." *Archaeology* 18 (1965): 34. Idem., "Edifice destiné au culte dans la couche Boian-Spanţov de la station-tell de Căscioarele." *Dacia* 15 (1970): 5–24.

28. G. Lazarovici, "Das neolithische Heiligtum von Parţa." *Neolithic of Southeastern Europe and its Near Eastern Connections.* Varia Archaeologica Hungarica 2 (Budapest, 1989): 149–74.

29. B. Kitanovski, D. Simoska, and B. Jovanović, "Kultno mesto na nalazištu Vrbjanska Čuka (s. Slavej) kod Prilepa." *Vinča and its World* (Belgrade: Serbian Academy of Sciences and Arts Symposia, 1990): 107–11. V. Sanev, "Neolitsko svetilište od tumba vo Macari, Skopsko," *Macedoniae acta archaeologica* (Prilep, 1988): 9.

30. J. D. Evans, *The Antiquities of the Maltese Islands: A Survey* (London: The Athlone Press, 1971). D. H. Trump, *Skorba.* Excavations carried out on behalf of the National Museum of Malta 1961–63, The Society of Antiquities London and the National Museum of Malta (1966). T. Zammit, "Neolithic Representations of the Human Form from the Islands of Malta and Gozo." *The Journal of the Royal Anthropological Institute of Great Britain and Ireland* 54 (1924): 67–100, illustrations.

31. J. D. Evans, *Malta. Ancient People and Places* (London: Thames and Hudson, 1959): 148.

32. M. P. Malmer, *Words and Objects* (1983): 91–110.

33. S-J. Péquart, M. Péquart, M. Boule, and H. Vallois, *Téviec: Station nécropole mésolithique du Morbihan.* Archives de l'Institut de paléontologie humaine 18 (1937). S-J. Péquart and M. Péquart, *Hoedic. Deuxième station nécropole mésolithique du Morbihan* (Anvers, 1954). James Hibbs, "The Neolithic of Brittany and Normandy." *Ancient France*, Christopher Scarre, ed. (Edinburgh: University Press, 1983): 312–3.

34. Evidence from Macedonia Early Neolithic, Starčevo, and Karanovo cultures (Anza I, Macedonia, Obre I in Bosnia, and Karanovo in Central Bulgaria), cf. Chapman, J. C., "Meaning and Illusion in the Study of Burial in Balkan Prehistory," A. C. Poulter, ed. *Ancient Bulgaria* (1983): 1–42.

35. T. W. Jocobsen and T. Cullen, "A Consideration of Mortuary Practices in Neolithic Greece: Burials from Franchthi Cave." *Mortality and Immortality. The Anthropology and Archaeology of Death*, S. C. Humphreys and Kelen King, eds., pp. 79–103.

36. K. Kenyon, *Digging Up Jericho* (London: Benn, 1957).

37. F. Zagorskis, *Zvejnieku akmens laikmeta kapulauks* (Riga: Zinatne, 1987).

38. D. Srejović, *Lepenski Vir* (Belgrade: Srpska Književna zadruga, 1969). Id., "Europe's First Monumental Sculpture: New Discoveries at Lepenski Vir." *New Aspects of Antiquity*, M. Wheeler, ed. (London: Thames and Hudson, 1972). Srejović, D. and L. Babović, *Umetnost Lepenskog Vira* (Beograd: Narodni Muzej, 1983).

39. S. Bökönyi, "Animal Remains from Lepenski Vir: The Vertebrate Fauna of this Early Center of Domestication Represent an Atypical Animal Husbandry." *Science* 167, no. 3926 (1970): 1702–4.

40. D. Srejović and Z. Letica, *Vlasac: A Mesolithic Settlement in the Iron Gates* (Serbo-Croatian with a summary in English). Belgrade: Serbian Academy of Sciences and Arts 12, 1978.

41. See note 30.

42. Excavated with Shan Winn and Daniel Shimabuku. The skeletal analysis has been done by János Nemeskéri of Budapest, but his illness and death in 1989 precluded the publication of the results.

43. John W. Hedges, *Tomb of the Eagles* (London: J. Murray, 1984).

44. Judson T. Chesterman, "Investigations of the Human Bones from Quanterness," in Colin Renfrew, *Investigations in Orkney* (London: Thames and Hudson, 1979): 103.

45. Hedges (see note 43): 135.

46. Hedges (see note 43): 140.

47. Hedges (see note 43): 155.

48. J. D. G. Clark, *Star Carr.* See note 7.

49. S. Gallus, "Die figuralverzierten Urnen vom Soproner Burgstall." *Archaeologica Hungarica* 3 (1934).

50. Colin Renfrew, *Approaches to Social Archaeology* (Cambridge: Harvard University Press, 1984): 180.

51. M. Bloch, "Tombs and states." *Mortality and immortality: the Anthropology and Archaeology of Death*, S. C. Humphreys and H. King, eds. (London: Academic Press, 1981). Id., "Death, women and power." *Death and the Regeneration of Life*, M. Bloch and J. Parry, eds. (Cambridge University Press, 1982).

52. W. A. Douglas, *Death in Murelaga: Funerary Rituals in a Spanish Basque Village* (Seattle: University of Washington Press, 1969).

53. Loring Danforth, "Judgement of the Bones." *Science Digest* (1981): 92–97. Photographs by Alexander Tsiaras.

54. Idem.

55. E. Gasparini, *Il matriarcato slavo. Antropologia culturale dei protoslavi* (Florence: Sansoni, 1973): 597–630.

56. E. S. Twohig, *The Megalithic Art of Western Europe* (Oxford: Clarendon Press, 1981).

57. M. Brennan, *The Stars and the Stones: Ancient Art and Astronomy in Ireland* (London: Thames and Hudson, 1983).

58. M. J. O'Kelley, *Newgrange: Archaeology, Art, and Legend* (London: Thames and Hudson, 1982): figs. 45–47.

59. G. Eogan, *Knowth and the Passage-Tombs of Ireland* (Ireland: Thames and Hudson, 1986): 147 ff.

60. C. T. Le Roux, *Gavrinis et les îles du Morbihan. Les mégalithes du golfe.* Guides Archéologiques de la France. Impr. Nationale, 1985. For more illustrations see Twohig 1981 (note 56), pp. 172–75.

Chapter 8

1. N. Vlassa, "Chronology of the Neolithic in Transylvania in the Light of the Tartaria Settlements Stratigraphy." *Dacia* N.S., vol. 7 (1963): 485–94. A. Falkenstein, "Zu den Tontafeln aus Tartaria." *Germania* 43:2 (1965): 269–73. V. Milojčić, "Die Tontafeln von Tartaria (Siebenbürgen) und die absolute Chronologie des mitteleuropäischen Neolithikums." *Germania* 43. Heft 2 (1966): 261–68. M. S. F. Hood, "The Tartaria tablets." *Antiquity* 51 (1967): 99–113. Id., "The Tartaria tablets." *Scientific American* (May 1968): 30–37. J. Makkay, "The Late Neolithic Tordos Group Signs." *Alba Regia* (Annales Musei Stephani Regis) 10 (1969): 9–49. D. Whipp, "The Tartaria tablets." *Antiquity* 57 (June 1973): 147–49.

2. Shan M. M. Winn. *Pre-writing in Southeastern Europe: the Sign System of the Vinča Culture, ca. 4000 B.C.* (Calgary: Western Publishers, 1981).

3. Harold Haarmann, "Writing from Old Europe." *The Journal of Indo-European Studies.* 17 (1990). Also *Universalgeschichte der Schrift* (Frankfurt-New York: Campus Verlag, 1990): 69–94.

Chapter 9

1. J. J. Bachofen. *Versuch über die Gräbersymbolik der Alten* (Basel, 1859). Reprinted with a Foreword by C. A. Bernoulli and an Appreciation by Ludwig Klages (Basel, 1925). *Das Mutterrecht: Eine Untersuchung über die Gynaikokratie der alten Welt nach ihrer religiösen und rechtlichen Natur* (Stuttgart, 1861, reprinted Basel, 1897). *Die Sage von Tanaquil* (Heidelberg, 1870). *Myth, Religion, and Mother's Right. Selected Writings.* Translated by Ralph Manheim (Bollinger: Princeton University Press, 1973), Series 84. Robert Briffault, *The Mothers. A Study of the Origins of Sentiment and Institutions*, three volumes, first published in 1927; *The Mothers*, abridged, with an introduction by Gordon Rattray Taylor (London: George Allen and Unwin, 1959, and New York: Atheneum, 1977).

2. George Thomson, *The Prehistoric Aegean. Studies in Ancient Greek Society* (London: Lawrence and Wishart, 1949).

3. David Fraser, *Land and Society in Neolithic Orkney.* BAR British Series 117 (1983). John Bintliff, *European Social Evolution. Archaeological Perspectives* (University of Bradford, 1984). Colin Renfrew, *Approaches to Social Archaeology* (Cambridge: Harvard University Press, 1984).

4. Pieter van de Velde, "The Social Anthropology . . . a Neolithic Cemetery in the Netherlands." *Current Anthropology* 5 (1979): 37–58. S. Skomal, *Wealth Distribution as a Measure of Prehistoric Change: Chalcolithic to Copper Age Cultures in Hungary* (Ann Arbor: University Microfilms International, 1983). See also notes 24, 31, 32, 34.

5. J. J. Bachofen, *Myth, Religion and Mother Right* (see note 1): 81.

6. Riane Eisler, *Chalice and the Blade* (San Francisco: Harper and Row, 1987).

7. Demetrios R. Theocharis, "Development and Diversification: The Middle Neolithic of Thessaly and the Southern Region." *Neolithic Greece* (Athens, National Bank of Greece): 65.

8. Ibid.

9. R. J. Rodden, "Recent Discoveries from Prehistoric Macedonia." *Balkan Studies* 5 (1964): 109–24.

10. Cited by S. Tabaczyński, *Neolit środkowo Europejski. Podstawy gospodarcze* (Warsaw-Cracow-Wrocław: Ossolineum, 1970): 242.

11. John Bintliff, *European Social Evolution. Archaeological Perspectives* (University of Bradford, 1984): 101.

12. T. S. Passek, *Periodizatsiya tripolskikh poselenii*. Materialy i Issledovaniya po Arkheologii SSSR, 10 (1949): 149–50.

13. J. Lüning, "Research into the Bandkeramik Settlement of the Aldenhovener Platte in the Rhineland." *Analecta Praehistorica Leidensia* 15 (1982): 19.

14. Ibid., 16–19.

15. Bintliff (see note 11), p. 86.

16. S. Milisauskas, "Olszanica, an early farming village in Poland." *Archaeology* 29:30–41.

17. Pieter van de Velde, "On Bandkeramik Social Structure: Analysis of Pot Decoration and Hut Distribution from the Central European Neolithic Communities of Elsloo and Hienheim." *Analecta Praehistorica Leidensia* 12 (1979). Repeated in *Current Anthropology* 20 (1979): 37–58.

18. A. Patricia Phillips, "Attribute Analysis and Social Structure of Chassey-Cortaillod-Lagozza Populations." *Man* 6 (1971): 341–52.

19. A. Benac, "Obre I," in *Wissenschaftliche Mitteilungen des Bosnisch-Herzegowinischen Landesmuseums* 3A (Sarajevo, 1973): 347–59. J. Nemeskéri, "Outline on the anthropological finds of a neolithic site," in M. Gimbutas, ed., *Obre I & II, Wissenschaftliche Mitteilungen des Bosnisch-Herzegowinischen Landesmuseums* 6A (Sarajevo, 1974): 37–46.

20. J. C. Chapman, "Meaning and Illusion in the Study of Burial," in *Balkan Prehistory. Ancient Bulgaria.* Papers presented to the International Symposium on the Ancient History and Archaeology of Bulgaria, 1981, A. G. Poulter, ed., Part I (University of Nottingham), p. 8.

21. T. W. Jacobsen and T. Cullen, "A Consideration of Mortuary Practices in Neolithic Greece: Burials from Franchthi Cave." *Mortality and Immortality. The Anthropology and Archaeology of Death*, S. C. Humphreys and K. King, eds., p. 88.

22. The total number of cemeteries dating from the fifth millennium B.C. is about 80. The following largest were excavated: Cernica at Bucharest with 362 graves of the Boian group. Gh. Cantacuzino, "The prehistoric necropolis of Cernica and its place in the neolithic cultures of Romania and of Europe in the light of recent discoveries." *Dacia* 13 (Bucharest, 1969): 45–59; Cernavoda at Constanța of the Hamangia culture with about 600 graves (400 were excavated): D. Berciu and S. Morintz. "Santierul arheologic Cernavoda." *Materiale și Cercetari Arheologice* 3 (Bucharest, 1957): 83–92; also D. Berciu, *Cultura Hamangia* (Bucharest, 1966); Zengövarkóny of the Lengyel culture with 368 graves uncovered: J. Dombay, *Die Siedlung und das Gräberfeld in Zengövarkóny* (Budapest, 1960); Tiszapolgár-Basatanya with 200 graves in northeastern Hungary: I. Bognár-Kutzián, *Tiszapolgár-Basatanya* (Budapest, 1963); Azód with 220 graves of the Lengyel culture: N. Kalicz, *Kökori falu Aszódon* (Aszód: Petőfi Muzeum, 1985).

23. Rudolf Feustel and Herbert Ullrich, "Totenhütten der neolithischen Walternienburger Gruppe." *Alt-Thüringen*, (1965): 105–202.

24. Olaf Höckmann, "Zur Verteilung von Männer- und Frauengräbern auf Gräberfeldern des Frühneolithikums und des älteren Mittelneolithikums." *Jahrbuch des Römisch-Germanischen Zentralmuseums.* Mainz 29 (1982): 13–74.

25. J. Pavúk, "Zur Problem der Gräberfelder mit der Linienbandkeramik." *Actuelle Fragen der Bandkeramik.* Székesfehérvár (1972): 23–129.

26. Höckmann (see note 24), p. 30.

27. Pavúk (see note 25) and Höckmann (see note 24), p. 18.

28. G. Gallay and R. Schweizer, "Das bandkeramische Gräberfeld von Rixheim." *Archäologisches Korrespondenzblatt.* Mainz (1971): 15–22.

29. A. Kulczycka-Leciejewiczowa, "The Linear and Stroked Pottery Cultures." *The Neolithic of Poland*, T. Wiślański, ed. Instytut Historii Kultury Materialnej Polskiej Akademii Nauk (Warsaw, 1970).

30. N. Kalicz, *Kökori falu Aszódon.* Aszód, (1985): 103.

31. István Zalai-Gaál, Sozialarchäologische Untersuchungen des mitteleuropäischen Neolithikums aufgrund der Gräberanalyse (Béri Balogh Ádám Múzeum évkönyvéböl 14 (Szekszárd 1988).

32. I. Lengyel, "Sozialarchäologische Deutung der Ergebnisse von Laboruntersuchungen unter besonderer Berücksichtigung der spätneolithischen Gräbergruppe von Mórágy-Tüzködomb." In International Prehistoric Conference Szekszárd, 1985. A Béri Balogh Ádám Múzeum Évkönyve 13 (1986): 155–69.

33. Settlement and graves were excavated by K. Jażdżewski in the 1930s and by R. Grygiel and P. Bogucki in the 1970s. See R. Grygiel, "The household cluster as a fundamental social unit of the Lengyel Culture in the Polish Lowlands." *Prace i Materialy* (Lódź) 31:43–271.

34. S. Skomal, *Wealth Distribution as a Measure of Prehistoric Change: Chalcolithic to Copper Age Cultures in Hungary*, UCLA PhD dissertation, 1983. University Microfilms International: 94ff.,

201 ff. Marita Meisenheimer, *Das Totenritual, geprägt durch Jenseitsvorstellungen und Gesellschaftsrealität. Theorie der Totenrituals eines kupferzeitlichen Friedhofs zu Tiszapolgár-Basatanya (Ungarn).* BAR International Series 475 (1989).

35. V. A. Dergachev, *Vykhvatinskiy mogil'nik* (Kishenev, 1978).

36. H. Wiklak, "Podsumowanie wyników badań wykopaliskowych w obrębie grobowca 9 w Sarnowie, województwo włocławskie." *Prace i Materiały Muzeum Archeologii i Etnografii w Łodzi* 33 (1986): 5–19.

37. M. S. Midgley, *The Origin and Function of the Earthen Long Barrows of Northern Europe.* BAR International Series 259 (1985): 192.

38. M. Gimbutas, *The Language of the Goddess.* (San Francisco: Harper and Row, 1989): 237–40.

39. Chapman; (see note 20) p. 32.

40. H. Todorova, *The Eneolithic in Bulgaria.* BAR International Series 49 (1978): 77.

41. M. Gimbutas, "Gold Treasures at Varna." *Archaeology* 30 (1977): 44–51. I. Ivanov, "Les fouilles archéologiques de la nécropole chalcolithique de Varna (1972–1975)," pp. 13–26, in "Varnenski nekropol i problemi chalkolita," *Studia Praehistorica* 1–2 (Sofia, 1978).

42. H. Todorova, *Kusnoeneolitnyat nekropol kraj gr. Devnja.* Izvestiya Nat. Mus. Varna 7 (1971): 3–40.

43. A. Radunčeva, *Vinica—eneolitno selište i nekropol.* RP (Excavations and Research) 6 (Sofia, 1976).

44. A. Colin Renfrew, "Megalith, territories and populations." *Acculturation and Continuity in Atlantic Europe*, S. J. De Laet., ed. Diss. Arch. Gandenses (Brugge, De Tempel), 1976: 200, 206. Colin Renfrew, *Approaches to Social Archaeology* (Cambridge: Harvard University Press, 1984): 160.

45. Robert Chapman, "The emergence of formal disposal areas and the problem of megalithic tombs in prehistoric Europe." *The Archaeology of Death* (1979): 72, 80.

46. David Fraser, *Land and Society in Neolithic Orkney* 2. BAR British Series 117 (1983): 356.

47. Ibid., 431–2.

48. Renfrew 1984 (see note 44), pp. 182, 234.

49. Hermann Behrens, "The first 'Woodhenge' in Middle Europe." *Antiquity* 50 (1981): 172–77.

50. G. Wainright, "Durrington Walls: A Ceremonial Enclosure of the 2nd millennium B.C." *Antiquity* 42 (1968): 20–26. Id., "Woodhenge." *Scientific American* 233 (1970): 30–38.

51. R. A. Maier, "Fragen zur neolithischen Erdwerken Südbayerns." *Jahresbericht der Bayerischen Bodendenkmalpflege* (1962):5–21.

52. G. Wainright (see note 50).

53. R. J. C. Atkinson, *Stonehenge*, rev. ed. (Harmonds-Worth: Penguin Books, 1979).

54. E. Joassaume, *Dolmen for the Dead* (Batsford: Hatchette, 1987).

55. David Fraser (see note 46), p. 329.

56. Colin Renfrew, *Investigations in Orkney.* Society of Antiquaries (London, 1979). See J.T. Chesterman: 97–111, 162–172.

57. David Fraser (see note 46), pp. 338–39. Information from J. W. Hedges "Isbister: A chambered tomb in Orkney," British Arch. Reports, International Series 115, 1983.

58. J. T. Chesterman (see note 56).

59. James Mellaart, *Çatal Hüyük, A Neolithic Town in Anatolia* (New York: McGraw-Hill, 1967): pl. 83.

60. Francis J. Byrne, *Irish Kings and High Kings* (London: Batsford, 1973) 7–27. Myles Dillon, *The Cyles of the Kings* (London: Oxford University Press, 1946): 38–41. Proinsias Mac Cana, "Aspects of the Theme of King and Goddess in Irish Literature." *Études Celtiques* 7 (1955–56): 76–114, and 8 (1958) 59–65. Ulrike Roider, "The Celtic Myth of Sacral Kingship." *The Journal of Indo-European Studies* 18 (1990).

61. Roslyn M. Frank and D. P. Metzger, *The Mother Goddess in Basque Oral Tradition* (Iowa City: University of Iowa, 1982).

62. Robert Briffault, *The Mothers*, 1977 ed., p. 87.

63. Roslyn M. Frank and D. P. Metzger (see note 61).

64. P. L. Henry, "Interpreting the Gaulish Inscription of Chamalières." *Études Celtiques* 21 (1984): 141–50. Eric P. Hamp, "The Rebirth of Gaulish." *Celtic Studies*, Association of North America Newsletter 5.2 (1986): 3.

65. J. J. Tierney, "The Celtic Ethnography of Posidonius," *Proceedings of the Royal Irish Academy* 60C2 (1960): 189–275.

66. James E. Doan, "Woman and Goddesses in Early Celtic History, Myth, and Legend." *Irish Studies Program* (Boston: Northeastern University, 1987): 20.

67. Marcel Detienne, "The Violence of Wellborn Ladies: Women in the Thesmophoria." *The Cuisine of Sacrifice among the Greeks*, translated by P. Wissing (The University of Chicago Press, 1989): 138–9.

68. John Hawkins, quoted by George Thomson in *The Prehistoric Aegean Studies in Ancient Greek Society* (London: Lawrence and Wishart, 1949): 202–3.

69. Quote from Jacquetta Hawkes, *Dawn of the Gods: Minoan and Mycenaean Origins of Greece* (New York: Random House, 1969): 73–74.

70. Keith Branigan, "Early Minoan Society—The evidence of the Mesara Tholoi reviewed," C. Nicolet, ed. *Aux Origines de L'Hellénisme* (Paris, 1984): 29–37. J. Coles, "Social ranking in prepalatial cemeteries." *Problems in Greek Prehistory*, E. French and K. Wardle, eds. (Bristol, 1988): 49–61.

71. Robert Briffault, *The Mothers*. Abridged by G. R. Taylor (New York: Atheneum, 1977): 86.

72. Thomson (see note 68), p. 99.

73. Briffault (see note 71), p. 88.

74. Thomson (see note 68), p. 145.

75. Herodotus, *The Histories* I, 173.

76. Thomson (see note 68), p. 122.

77. Ibid., p. 164.

78. Herodotus (see note 75), p. 146.

79. Thomson (see note 68), p. 164.

80. Ibid.

81. J. J. Bachofen, *Myth, Religion and Mother Right* (see note 1): 84; "The Myth of Tanaquil" (see note 1): 211–46.

82. J. Heurgon, *Daily Life of the Etruscans* (London, 1964): 95–122.

83. Larissa Bonfante Warren, "The Women of Etruria." *Arethusa* 6, 1 (Spring, 1973): 91ff.

84. Thomson (see note 68), p. 98.

85. A. Tovar, *The Ancient Languages of Spain and Portugal* (New York: Vanni, 1961): 127.

86. T. Wilbur, "Indo-Europeanization of the Western Pyrenees." *Journal of Indo-European Studies* 8, 1–2 (1980): 4.

87. José Miguel de Baradiarán, *Mitologia Vasca* I (1960).

88. Julio Caro Baroja, *Los pueblos del norte de la peninsula hispánica* (Madrid Burgos: Imprenta Aldecoa, 1943). Angel Montenegro Duque, "Las Orígenes de los vascos." *Hispania Antiqua* 1: 271ff.

89. Ibid.

90. Jacques Poumarède, *Les Successions dans le sud-ouest de la France au Moyen Age* (Presses Universitaires de France, 1972): 243–49; 257–61. Frank M. Roslyn, Monique Laxalt, and Nancy Vosburg, "Inheritance, Marriage and Dowry Rights in the Navarrese and French Basque Law Codes," in *IV Proceedings of the Western Society of French Historians* (ABC-Clio Press, 1977): 22–42. M. Frank Roslyn and Shelley Lowenberg, "The Role of the Basque Woman as Etxeko-Andrea, the Mistress of the House." *Proceedings of the Fourth Annual Meeting of the Western Society for French History 1977* (Santa Barbara, California): 14–16.

91. Robert Briffault (see note 62), p. 86.

92. Ibid, p. 92. H. Zimmer, "Das Mutterrecht der Pikten und seine Bedeutung für die arische Altertumswissenschaft." *Zeitschrift für Savigny Stiftung für Rechtsgeschichte*, Band XV (Weimar: Hermann Böhlan, 1894): 209–40. Marjorie Anderson, *Kings and Kingship in Early Scotland* (Edinburgh: Scottish Academic Press, 1973).

93. J. J. Tierney, "The Celtic Ethnography of Posidonius," *Proceedings of the Royal Irish Academy* 1960: 252.

94. Mentioned in *Roman History* 62, 2, 6. Quoted by James E. Doan, "Women and Goddesses in Early Celtic History, Myth and Legend." *Working Papers in Irish Studies* (Boston: Northeastern University, 1987): 28.

95. Doan (see note 66), p. 92.

96. Ibid.

97. H. M. Chadwick, *Origin of the English Nation* (Cambridge University Press, 1907): 328–40. Bertha Philpotts, *Kindred and Clan in the Middle Ages and After* (Cambridge University Press, 1913): 270. E. A. Thompson, *The Early Germans* (Oxford: Clarendon Press, 1965): 17. Briffault (see note 62), pp. 90ff.

98. Herbert Schultz, *The Prehistory of Germanic Europe* (New Haven: Yale University Press, 1983): 320.

99. Aija Veldre Beldavs, "Goddesses in a Man's World: Latvian Matricentricity in Culture and Spheres of Influence in Society." *Journal of Baltic Studies* 8, 2 (1977): 105–129.

100. E. Gasparini, *Il matriarcato slavo. Antropologia culturale dei protoslavi* (Florence: Sansoni, 1973): 597–630.

Chapter 10

1. Marija Gimbutas, *Prehistory of Eastern Europe. Mesolithic, Neolithic and Copper Age Culture in Russia and the Baltic Area.* Peabody Museum, Harvard University, Bulletin No. 20. (Cambridge, 1956).

2. I. B. Vasil'ev, and G. I. Matveeva, "Poselenie i mogil'nik u sela S'ezzhee." *Ocherki istorii i kul'tury Povolzh'ya* 2 (Kuybyshev, 1976): 73–96. I. B. Vasil'ev, *Eneolit Povolzh'ya: Step' i lesostep'.* Kuybyshevskiy Gosudarstvenny Pedagogicheskiy Institut (Kuybyshev, 1981).

3. V. I. Bibikova, "K Izucheniu drevneishikh domashnikh loshadey Vostochnoy Europy," 2 (Study of ancient domestic horses of East Europe). 1. *Biulleten Boskovskogo Obshchestva Ispitatelei Prirody Otd. Biologicheski* 5:118–26. S. Bökönyi, "Horses and sheep in East Europe in the Copper and Bronze Ages." *Proto-Indo-European: the Archaeology of a Linguistic Problem.* Studies in Honor of Marija Gimbutas, S. N. Skomal and E. C. Polomé, eds. Institute for the Study of Man (Washington, D.C., 1987): 137–44.

4. V. P. Shilov, *Ocherki po istorii drevnikh plemen Nizhnego Povolzh'ya* (Leningrad, 1975): 13.

5. A. G. Petrenko, *Drevnee i srednevekovoe zhivotnovodstvo srednevo Povolzh'ya i Predural'ya* (Moscow: Nauka, 1984).

6. V. V. Radlov, *Sibirskie drevnosti* (St. Peterburg, 1888) 1: 249ff., 404ff. A. M. Khazanov, *Nomads and the Outside World* (Cambridge University Press, 1984).

7. I. B. Vasil'ev, *Eneolit Povolzh'ya: Step' i lesostep'.* Kuybyshevskiy Gosudarstvenny Pedagogicheskiy Institut (Kuybyshev, 1981): 19ff.

8. I. B. Vasil'ev and G. I. Matveeva, "Poselenie i mogil'nik u sela S'ezzhee." *Ocherki istorii i kul'tury Povolzh'ya* 2 (Kuybyshev, 1976): 73–96. I. B. Vasil'ev, *Lesostepnoe Povolzh'e v epokhu eneolita i rannei bronzy.* Diss. Institute of Archaeology, Academy of Sciences (Moscow, 1979). I. B. Vasil'ev, *Eneolit Povolzh'ya: Step' i lesostep'.* Kuybyshevskiy Gosudarstvenny Pedagogicheskiy Institut (Kuybyshev, 1981).

9. I. B. Vasil'ev, *Eneolit Povolzh'ya: Step' i lesostep'.* Kuybyshevskiy Gosudarstevenny Pedagogicheskiy Institut (Kuybyshev, 1981): 12–20.

10. Ibid., pp. 23ff.

11. V. V. Golmsten, "Pogrebenie iz Krivoluchya" (Burial at Krivoluchie). *Soobshcheniya GAIMK* (1931) 6: 7–12.

12. A. P. Kruglov, B. B. Piotrovski, and G. V. Podgaetski, "Mogilnik v g. Nal'chike" (Cemetery in the city of Nalchik). *Materialy i Issledovaniya po Arkheologii SSSR* (1941) 3:67–147.

13. I. B. Vasil'ev, *Eneolit Povolzh'ya: Step' i lesostep'.* Kuybyshevskiy Gosudarstvenny Pedagogicheskiy Institut (Kuybyshev, 1981): 631; unfortunately exact dates obtained by the analysis have not been published.

14. Ibid., pp. 45ff.

15. I. V. Sinitsyn, "Pam'yatniki yamnoy kul'tury Nizhnego Povol'zhya: ikh s'vyaz s Pridneprovem." *Kratkie Soobshcheniya Instituta Arkheologii* (Kiev) 7: 32–36.

16. K. F. Smirnov, "Bykovskie kurgany," *Materialy i Issledovaniya po Arkheologii SSSR* 78 (1960):235.

17. Sinitsyn (see note 15).

18. I. B. Vasil'ev, *Eneolit Povolzh'ya: Step' i lesostep'.* Kuybyshevskiy Gosudarstvenny Pedagogicheskiy Institut (Kuybyshev, 1981): 43.

19. Sinitsyn (see note 15).

20. T. P. Zinevich and S. Kruts, *Antropologichna kharakeristika davn'ogo naseleni'ya teritorii Ukrainy.* Novaya dushla (Kiev, 1968): 13–39. S. I. Kruts, *Naselenie territorii Ukrainy epokhi medibronzy* (Kiev, 1972): 125.

21. D. Ya. Telegin, *Seredn'o-Stogivs'ka kul'tura epokhi midi* (Kiev, 1973): 111.

22. M. Gimbutas, "The First Wave of Eurasian Steppe Pastoralists into Copper Age Europe." *Journal of Indo-European Studies* 5, 4 (1977): 277–339. V. A. Dergachev, *Moldavia i Sosednie teritorii v epokhu eneolita* (Kishenev: Shtiintsa).

23. R. I. Viezzhev, "Roboti na dilyanitsi v poseleniya v s. Zolotiy Baltsi." *Arkheologicheskie Pamyatniki* (Kiev, 1960).

24. N. M. Shmagliy and I. T. Chernyakov, "Kurgany stepnoy chasti mezhdurechya Dunaya i Dnestra." *Materialy po Arkheologii Severnogo Prichernomor'ya* 6 (Odessa, 1970).

25. Verbal information by S. Bökönyi, 1987.

26. T. G. Movsha, "O svyazyakh plemen tripol'skoy kul'tury so stepnymi plemenami mednogo veka." *Sovetskaya Arkheologiya* 2 (Moscow, 1961): 186–99. Linda Ellis, "Analysis of Cucuteni-Tripolye and Kurgan Pottery and the Implications for Ceramic Technology." *The Journal of Indo-European Studies* 8 (1980): 211–30.

27. M. M. Shmagliy, V. P. Dudkin, and K. V. Zin'kous'kiy, "Pro vivchennya tripil'skikh poselen." *Arkheologiya* 8 (Kiev, 1973): 23–39.

28. Sebastian Morintz and Petre Roman, "Aspekte des Ausgangs des Aeneolithikums und der Übergangstufe zur Bronzezeit im Raum der Niederdonau." *Dacia* N.S. 12 (Bucharest).

29. Morintz and Roman (see note 28), pp. 47–80.

30. Named after the eponymous fortified hill in the district of Constanța, Dobruja, Cernavoda II dates from a second site in the same area. D. Berciu, "Quelques données préliminaires concernant la civilisation de Cernavoda." *Slovenská Arkheológia* 20, 1: 268–80.

31. The name "Lasinja" was given to a Croatian site by Dimitrijević in 1961 and is used for similar complexes in western Hungary and eastern Austria. The term Balaton I, used by Kalicz, is a synonym for Lasinja. Nándor Kalicz, "Über die chronologische Stellung der Balaton-Gruppe in Ungarn." *Symposium über die Entstehung und Chronologie der Badener Kultur* (Bratislava, 1973): 131–63. Ibid., "The Problems of the Balaton-Lasinja Culture." *The Journal of Indo-European Studies* 8, 3–4 (1980): 245–73. For Lasinja complex see Franz Leben, "Zur Kenntnis der Lasinja-Kultur in Slowenien." *Symposium* (see note 31), pp. 187–97.

32. Pal Patay, "Gräber von Sippen-Häuptlinge aus Kupferzeit." *A Móra Ferenc Muzeum Évkonyve* 2 (1966–67): 49–55.

33. Of the total skeletons suitable for analysis, 28 belonged to the early phase; 11 were Proto-Europid, of which eight were male and three female. J. Nemeskéri, in I. Bognár-Kutzián, *The Cemetery of Tiszapolgár Basatanya* (Budapest, 1963).

34. Susan Nacev Skomal, "The Social Organization of the Tiszapolgár Group at Basatanya-Carpathian Basin Copper Age." *The Journal of Indo-European Studies* 8, 1–2 (1980): 75–93.

35. Stanislav Šiška, "Gräberfelder der Lažn'any-Gruppe in der Slowakei." *Slovenská Archeológia* 20, 1 (Nitra): 107–75.

36. The Lengyel-derived complexes are variously labeled: *Gatersleben* in central Germany and Bohemia; *Ocice* (Ottitz), *Jordanów,* or *Jordansmühl,* and *Brześć Kujawski* in eastern Germany and western Poland; *Münchshofen* in Bavaria; and *Aichbühl* in Württemberg. Jan Lichardus, "Zu Problemen der Ludanice-Gruppe in der Slowakei—k problémom ludanickej skupini na Slovensku," *Slovenská Archeológia* 12, 1 (Nitra, 1964): 69–162.

37. The important sites are Békasmegyer at Budapest, Koroncó at Gyor, Esztergom, Pfaffstetten, Retz, and Waltrahöhle at Jamm. O. Seewald, "Die jungneolithische Siedlung in Retz (Niederdonau)." *Praehistorica* 7 (Vienna, 1940). Richard Pittioni, *Urgeschichte des österreichischen Raumes* (Vienna, 1954): 177–87. Nitrianski Hrádok, Vysoki Breh, and Bajč-Vlkanovo near Nitra, Jesišovice at Znojmo, Staré Zamky at Lišen near Brno, Cimburk at Kutná Hora ((Bohemia). Halle A. Točik, "Záchranny vyskum v Bajči-Vlkanove v rokach 1959–1960." *Študijné Zvesti* 12 (Nitra, 1964): 15–185. A. Medunová, "Eneoliticke sidlište Stare Zámky v Brne-Lišni." *Památky Archeologicke* 50 (Praha, 1964): 91–155. F. Benesch, *Die Festung Hutberg* (Halle, 1941).

38. Marija Gimbutas, "The First Wave of Steppe Pastoralists into Copper Age Europe." *The Journal of Indo-European Studies* 5, 4 (1977): 299–301.

39. E. Sangmeister, "Zur kulturellen und zeitlichen Stellung der Rössener Kultur." *Festschrift für W. -H. Schuchhardt* (Baden-Baden, 1960): 199–207. Bertold Schmidt, "Die Landschaft östlich von Magdeburg im Neolithikum." *Jahresschrift für mitteldeutsche Vorgeschichte* 54 (1970): 88. A. Gallay, "Signification culturelle et chronologique du Néolithique de Cravanche (Territoire de Belfort, France)." *Homo* 72, H.1/2 (1972): 36–50.

40. G. Bersu, "Vorgeschichtliche Siedlungen auf dem Goldberg bei Nördlingen." *Neue deutsche Ausgrabungen, Deutschtum und Ausland,* H. 23/24 (1930): 130–43. Idem. "Rössener Wohnhäuser vom Goldberg, Württemberg." *Germania* 20 (1936): 229–43.

41. J. Lüning, "Aichbühl, Schwieberdingen, Bischheim." *Študijné Zvesti* 17 (Nitra, 1969): 233–47.

42. E. Vogt, "Ein Schema des schweizerischen Neolithikums." *Germania* 45 (1967): 1–20. A. and G. Gallay, "Eléments de la civilisation de Rössen à Saint-Léonard, Valais, Suisse." *Archive suisses d'Anthropologie générale* 31 (Genève, 1966): 28–41. P. Petrequin, "La grotte de la Baume de Gonvillars." *Annuaire litt. de l'Université de Besançon* 107 (1970): 1–185.

43. Th. Voigt, "Funde der Einzelgrabkultur auf dem Taubenberg bei Wahlitz, Kr. Burg." *Jahresschrift für mitteldeutsche Vorgeschichte* 37 (Halle, 1953): 109–53.

44. Paul Grimm, "Die Salzmünder Kultur in Mitteldeutschland." *Jahresschrift der Vorgeschichte der sächsisch-thüringischen Länder* 19 (Halle, 1939): 1–104.

45. J. Preuss, "Die Baalberger Gruppe in Mitteldeutschland." *Veröffentlichungen des Landesmuseums für Vorgeschichte in Halle* 21 (Halle, 1966). H. Behrens, "Die Jungsteinzeit im Mittelelbe-Saale Gebiet." *Veröffentlichungen des Landesmuseums für Vorgeschichte in Halle* 27 (Halle 1973). Jan Lichardus, *Rössen-Gatersleben-Baalberge* (Bonn, 1976): 99–135. Ulrich Fischer, *Die Gräber der Steinzeit im Saalegebiet* (Berlin, 1956): 48–66.

46. Joachim Wahl and Hans Günter König, "Anthropologische-traumatologiche Untersuchung der menschlichen Skelettreste aus dem bandkeramischen Massengrab bei Talheim, Kreis Heilbronn." *Fundberichte aus Baden-Württemberg* 12:65–195.

47. M. Gimbutas, "The beginning of the Bronze Age in Europe and the Indo-Europeans, 3500–2500 B.C." *The Journal of Indo-European Studies* 1 (1973): 163–214. E. N. Chernykh, "Metallurgical provinces of the 5th–2nd Millennia in Eastern Europe in Relation to the Process of Indo-Europeanization." *The Journal of Indo-European Studies* 8, 3–4 (1980): 317–37.

48. O. F. Lahodovska, O. G. Shaposhnikova, and M. L. Makarevich, *Mikhailivs'ke poseleni'ya* (Kiev, 1962): 22–38.

49. M. J. Rudinski, "Kamennaya Mogila." *Kratkie Soobshcheniya Instituta Arkheologii* 1 (Kiev, 1952):21–31. Alexander Häusler, "Südrussische und nordkaukasische Petroglyphen." *Wissenschaftliche Zeitschrift der Martin-Luther-Universität Halle-Wittenberg* 12, 11 (Halle, 1963): 889–921.

50. W. Schrickel, *Westeuropäische Elemente im Neolithikum und in der frühen Bronzezeit Mitteldeutschlands* (Leipzig, 1957).

51. Emmanuel Anati, *Evolution and Style in Camunian Rock Art* (Capo di Ponte, Brescia, 1976), figs. 57, 64, 75.

52. A. M. Tallgren, "Sur les monuments mégalithiques du Caucase occidental." *Eurasia Septemtrionalis Antiqua* 9 (Helsinki, 1934): 1–45.

53. A. A. Shchepinskiy, "Pamyatniki iskustva epokhi rannego metala v Krymu." *Sovetskaya Arkheologiya* 3 (Moscow, 1963). Alexander Häusler, "Innenverzierte Steinkammergräber der Krim."

Jahresschrift für mitteldeutsche Vorgeschichte (Berlin, 1964): 59–82.

54. D. Ja. Telegin, "Eneolitichni steli i pamyatki nizhne Mikhailivs'kogo tipu." *Arkheologiya* 4 (Kiev, 1971): 3–17.

55. I. M. Chechenov, "Grobnitsa épokhi ranney bronzy v g. Nal'chike." *Sovetskaya Arkheologiya* 1 (1970): 109–124.

56. M. I. Rostovzeff, "The Sumerian Treasure of Astrabad." *The Journal of Egyptian Archaeology* 6, 1 (1920): 4–27. Rostovtzeff, "L'âge de cuivre dans le Caucase et les civilisations de Soumer et de l'Egypte-Protodynastique." *Revue archéologique* 5 ser., vol. 12 (1920a): 1–37. Rostovtzeff, *Iranians and Greeks in South Russia* (Oxford, 1922): 17–34. Tallgren (see note 52). F. Hančar, "Urgeschichte Kaukasiens von den Anfängen seiner Besiedlung bis in die Zeit seiner frühen Metallurgie." *Bücher zur Ur- und Frühgeschichte* bd. 6 (1937): 448. V. G. Childe, "The axes from Maikop and Caucasian metallurgy." *Annals of Archaeology and Anthropology* 23 (1936): 113–19. A. A. Iessen, "K khronologii Bolshykh Kubanskikh Kurganov" (Contribution to the problem of chronology of the Great Kuban Kurgans) *Sovetskaya Arkheologiya* 12 (1950): 157–200.

57. Gimbutas (see note 1). A. M. Tallgren, "Staromy-shastovskaya." *Reallexicon* Bd. 12 (1928): 389, pl. 94. A. M. Tallgren, "Zu der nordkaukasischen frühen Bronzezeit." *Eurasia Septemtrionalis Antiqua* 6 (1931): 126–45, pl. 141.

58. E. G. Schmidt, *Excavations at Tepe Hisar Damghan* (The University Museum, Philadelphia, 1937).

59. O. F. Lahodovska, "Raskopki Usativskogo kurgana 1–11." *Naukovi Zapiski* 2 (Kiev 1946). Id., "Pamyatki usativskogo tipa." *Arkheologiya* 8 (Kiev 1953): 95–109. T. D. Passek, "Periodizatsiya tripol'skikh poselenii." *Materialy i Issledovaniya po Arkheologii SSSR* 10 (Moscow 1949): 194–275.

60. A. I. Melyukova, "Kurgan usatovskogo tipa u sela Tudorovo." *Kratkie Soobshcheniya Instituta Arkheologii* 88 (Moscow 1962): 74–83.

61. T. Passek (see note 59), 158ff.

62. Petre I. Roman, "Strukturänderungen des End-neolithikums im Donau-Karpatenraum." *Dacia* 15: 31–169.

63. G. I. Georgiev, N. Ya. Merpert, R. V. Katinčarov, and D. G. Dimitrov, eds. *Ezero. Rannobronzovoto Selišče* (Sofia, Bulgarian Academy of Sciences, 1979).

64. Colin Renfrew, Marija Gimbutas, and Ernestine Elster, *Excavations at Sitagroi. A Prehistoric Village in Northeast Greece* 1 (1986). On the apsidal house, Colin Renfrew, "The burnt house at Sitagroi." *Antiquity* 54, 174 (1970): 131–34.

65. For northern Italy: F. Zorzi, "Resti di un abitato capannicolo eneolitico alle Colombare di Negrar." *Actes du IV Congrès International du Quaternaire* 2 (Roma 1953): 782–98. Emmanuel Anati, *I Camuni* (Milan 1979): 103.

66. D. Berciu, "Rezultatele primelor sapaturi de la Crivaţ." *Studii și Cercetari de Istorie Veche* 17, 3 (Bucharest 1966): 527.

67. See note 28.

68. N. Tasić, *Der Badener und Vučedoler Kultur-Komplex in Jugoslavien.* Dissertationes (Belgrade-Novi Sad).

69. Richard Pittioni, *Urgeschichte des Österreichischen Raumes* (Vienna 1954): 195.

70. János Banner, *Die Peceler Kultur* (Budapest 1956). Richard Pittioni, *Urgeschichte des Österreichischen Raumes* (Vienna 1954): 191ff. Zdzisław Sochacki, "The Radial-decorated Pottery Culture." *The Neolithic in Poland* (Wrocław-Warsaw-Cracow 1970): 319ff.

71. R. R. Schmidt, *Die Burg Vučedol* (Zagreb) 1945.

72. A. Točik in *Študijné Zvesti* (Nitra 1964), 12.

73. Jayne Warner, "The Megaron and Apsidal House in Early Bronze Age Western Anatolia: New Evidence from Karataş." *American Journal of Archaeology* 83, 2 (April 1979): 133–47. Jan G. P. Best, "The Foreign Relations of the Apsis-House Culture in Palestine." *Pulpudeva* (Plovdiv 1976): 205–9.

74. J. Bayer, "Die Ossarner Kultur, eine äneolithische Mischkultur im östlichen Mitteleuropa." *Eiszeit und Urgeschichte* 5 (Vienna 1928): 60–120.

75. Z. Sochacki (see note 70), p. 329. The analysis done by W. Gizbert. Sarunas Milisauskas and Janusz Kruk, "Economy, Migration, Settlement Organization, and Welfare during the Late Neolithic in Southeastern Poland." *Germania* 67 (1989): 84.

76. Z. Sochacki (see note 70), p. 321.

77. S. Bökönyi, *History of domestic Mammals in Central and Eastern Europe* (Budapest 1974): 32, fig. 1: 15, 16.

78. R. R. Schmidt (see note 71), fig. 81a.

79. Nándor Kalicz, "Ein neues kupferzeitliches Wagenmodel aus der Umgebung von Budapest." *Festschrift für Richard Pittioni zum siebzigsten Geburtstag* (Vienna 1976): 188–202.

80. J. Nemeskéri, "Anthropologische Übersicht des Volkes der Peceler Kultur," in J. Banner, *Die Peceler Kultur* (Budapest 1956): 295–309. I. Toth, "Profilation horizontale du crane facial de la population ancienne et contemporaine de la Hongrie." *Crania Hungarica* 3, 1–2 (1958): 3–126.

81. Alojz Benac, *Studien zur Stein- und Kupferzeit im nordwestlichen Balkan* (Berlin 1962): 146–48.

82. R. R. Schmidt, *Vučedol* (Zagreb 1945). Nikola Tasić, *Badenski i vučedolski kulturni kompleks u Jugoslaviji.* Dissertations 4 (Belgrade 1967).

83. Nándor Kalicz, *Die Frühbronzezeit in Nordost-Ungarn* 4 (Budapest 1968): 62–109.

84. K. Deschmann, "Über die vorjährigen Funde im Laibacher Pfahlbau." *Mitteilungen der Altertumsgesellschaft in Wien* 8, 3–4 (Vienna 1878): 3–20. In 1963 excavations were resumed by T. Bregant.

85. See note 63.

86. Stefan Nosek, *Kultura amfor kulistych w Polsce* (Wrocław-Warsaw-Cracow 1967): 276 ff.

87. Ibid., pp. 217ff.

88. Ibid., p. 278.

89. I. F. Levistskiy, "Pamyatki megalitychnoy Kul'turi na Volyni." *Anthropologiya* 2 (Kiev 1929): 192–222.

90. T. Wiślański, *Kultura amfor kulistych w Polsce Pólnocno-Zachodniej* (Warsaw 1966). Id., "The Globular Amphora Culture." *The Neolithic in Poland* (Warsaw 1970): 178–231. Marija Gimbutas, "East Baltic Amber in the Fourth and Third Millenia B.C." *Studies in Baltic Amber: The Journal of Baltic Studies* 16, 3 (1985).

91. I. K. Sveshnikov, "Nove pokhovannya kul'turi kulyatikh amfor u Roven'skiy oblasti." *Arkheolohiya* 8 (Kiev 1973): 63–67.

92. Wiślański (see note 90).

93. Aleksander Kośko and Victor I. Klochko, "A Late Neolithic Composite Bow." *Journal of the Society of Archer-Antiquaries* 30 (1987): 15–23.

94. Olga Necrasov, "Les populations de la période de transition du Néo-Enéolithique à l'âge du Bronze romaine et leurs particularités anthropologiques." *Anthropologie et Archéologie: les cas de premiers âges des Metaux. Actes du Symposium de Sils-Maria 25–30 septembre 1978*, Roland Menk and Alain Gallay, eds. (Geneva 1981): 60–61.

95. Ilse Schwidetzky, "The Influence of the Steppe People Based on the Physical Anthropological Data." *The Journal of the Indo-European Studies* 8 (1980): 356.

96. Marin Dinu, "Le problème des tombes à ocre dans les regions orientales de la Roumanie." *Preistoria Alpina* 10 (1974): 261–75. Ecsedy, I., *The People of the Pit-Grave Kurgans in Eastern Hungary* (Budapest 1979). Borislav Jovanović, "Some Elements of the Steppe Culture in Yugoslavia." *The Journal of Indo-European Studies* 11 (1983): 31–45.

97. Lahodovska, et al. (see note 48).

98. Necrasov (see note 94), pp. 63–65.

99. G. P. Zinevich, *Ocherki paleoantropologii Ukrainy* (Kiev 1967).

100. N. Mašek, "Die Řivnac-Gruppe in Böhmen und ihre chronologische Stellung." *Symposium 1961* (Prague): 327–35.

101. Robert W. Ehrich and Emilie Pleslová-Štiková, *Homolka. An Eneolithic Site in Bohemia* (Prague 1968); also appeared as Bulletin 24 of the American School of Prehistoric Research, Peabody Museum, Harvard University, Cambridge, Mass.

102. Alojz Benac, *Studien zur Stein- und Kupferzeit im nordwestlichen Balkan* (Berlin 1962): 135–45.

103. Ibid., p. 140.

104. M. Parović, V. Pešikan, and V. Trbuhović, "Fouilles des Tumulus du l'âge du bronze ancien dans la plaine de Tivat." *Starinar* 22 (Belgrade 1974): 129–41.

105. W. Dörpfeld, *Alt-Ithaka* (Munich 1927). N. G. L. Hammond, "The Tumulus-Burials of Leucas and their Connections in the Balkans and Northern Greece." *The Annual of the British School of Archaeology at Athens* 69 (1974): 129–44.

106. Hammond (see note 105).

107. Parović, Pešikan, Trbuhović (see note 104).

108. Spiridon Marinatos, "Further Discoveries at Marathon." *Arch. Anal. Athens* (1970): 355, fig. 10.

109. John L. Caskey, "The Early Helladic Period in the Argolid." *Hesperia* 29 (1960): 301.

110. Nikolaos I. Xirotiris, "The Indo-Europeans in Greece. An Anthropological Approach to the Population of Bronze Age Greece." *The Journal of Indo-European Studies* 8, 1–2 (1980): 201–11.

111. It is doubtful that the lunula-shaped pendants represent bows as it was proposed by Stuart Piggott in "Beaker Bows: A Suggestion," *Proceedings of the Prehistoric Society* 37, 2 (London 1971): 80–94. It is likely that the crescents with a perforation worn attached to breasts symbolized breast plates. As solar symbols they must have been sacred to the God of the Shining Sky. The symbolic importance of breast plates is evidenced in the Baden period and continued throughout the Bronze Age.

112. S. Bökönyi, *History of Domestic Mammals in Central and Eastern Europe* (Budapest 1974): 242. R. Kalicz-Schreiber, "Die Probleme der Glockenbecherkultur." *Glockenbecher-symposion* (Oberried 1974): 214.

113. W. Schule, "Glockenbecher und Hauspferde," in J. Boessneck, ed., *Archäologich-biologische Zusammenarbeit in der Vor- und Frühgeschichtsforschung* (Wiesbaden 1969): 88–93.

114. Ladislav Hájek, "Die älteste Phase der Glockenbecherkultur in Böhmen und Mähren." *Památky archeologické* 57 (Prague 1966): 221.

115. Boris Novotný, "Hroby kultury zvoncovitých poharu u Smolina na Morave." *Památky archeologické* 49 (Prague 1958): 297–311.

116. Bruce A. Replogle, "Social Dimensions of British and German Bell Beaker Burials: An Explanatory Study." *The Journal of Indo-European Studies* 8, 1–2 (1980): 165–201.

117. R. Kalicz-Schreiber (see note 112).

118. S. Dimitrijević, "Arheološka iskopavanja na području Vinkovačkog muzeja, rezultati 1957–1966." *Acta Musei Cibalensis* 1, Vinkovci.

119. I. Ecsedy, "Die Siedlung der Samogyvár-Vinkovci Kultur bei Szava und einige Fragen der Frühbronzezeit in Südpannonien." *A Janus Pannonius Muzeum Evkönyve* 23 (1979): 97–136.

120. N. Tasić, "Die Vinkovci-Kultur." *Kulturen der Frühbronzezeit des Karpatenbeckens und Nordbalkans*, N. Tasić, ed. (Beograd 1984): 15–28.

121. Andrzej Kempisty, "The Corded Ware Culture in the Light of New Stratigraphic Evidence." *Przegląd Archeologiczny* 26 (Warsaw 1973): 34–35.

122. Ilse Schwidetzky, "The Information of the Steppe People Based on the Physical Anthropological Data." *The Journal of Indo-European Studies* 8 (Washington 1980): 350ff.

123. A. Wierciński, "Untersuchungen zur Antropologie des Neolithikums in Polen." Fundamenta. *Monographien zur Urgeschichte*, H. Schawbedissen, ed., series B, 3 (Cologne and Vienna): 170–85. Id., "Problem strukturalnej i procesualnej identyfikacji antropologicznej Prasłowian." *Slavia Antiqua* 24 (Warsaw 1974).

124. Based on information supplied by Martin E. Huld, 1989.

125. Paul Friedrich, "Proto-Indo-European Kinship." *Ethnology* 1 (1966): 1–36.

GLOSSARY OF CULTURES AND MAJOR SITES

(See the bibliography for complete information on most literature references.)

ACHILLEION
Neolithic site in southern Thessaly, Greece, belonging to the Sesklo culture—mid-7th to mid-6th mill. B.C. An important key to understanding the chronology (based on 42 radiocarbon dates and excellent stratigraphy), architecture, pottery evolution, and religion of the Neolithic Aegean.
Excav. by M. Gimbutas with Shan M. Winn, and D. Shimabuku in 1973 and 1974. Lit.: M. Gimbutas *et al.* 1989.

AI-BUNAR
Copper mines at Stara Zagora, central Bulgaria, main supplier of natural copper for east-central Europe. Earliest exploitation began in the early 5th mill. B.C. and continued throughout the Karanovo V and VI periods in the mid-5th mill. B.C.
Excav. by N. Y. Merpert and E. N. Chernykh, 1971–72. Lit.: E. N. Chernykh, 1978.

ANGHELU RUJU
A cemetery of underground tombs (hypogea) of the Ozieri culture, 9 km north of Alghero, Sardinia, locally called *domus de Janas*, "witches' houses." The tombs have a sloping passage, sometimes stepped, which leads to the doorway of a roofed antechamber. The second door opens into the main burial chamber. In most cases, smaller cells, egg-shaped or rectangular, open out of the end. Some chambers have two pillars, some have bucrania or bull horns in relief above the entrance or on interior walls. Burial was by collective inhumation.
Excav. in early 20th century. Lit.: A Taramelli, "Nuovi scavi nella necropole preistorica, Anghelu Ruju." *Monumenti Antichi dei Lincei* 19 (Alghero, 1909): 397ff.

ANZA
Stratified settlement located at the village of Anzabegovo, between Titov Veles and Štip, Macedonia. Anza I: Early Macedonian Neolithic, c. 6300–5900 B.C. Anza II and III: Starčevo culture, 5900–5300 B.C.; Anza IV: Early Vinča culture, c. 5300–5000 B.C.
Excav. by J. Korošec in 1960; 1969–70 by the joint Yugoslav-American team, M. Garašanin and M. Gimbutas. Museum: Štip. Lit.: M. Gimbutas, ed. *Neolithic Macedonia*, 1976.

ARGISA
A stratified tell of the Neolithic and Bronze Age at Gremnos near Larisa, Thessaly, Greece. In more than 8.5 m of cultural material, 15 strata were observed representing Early Ceramic, "Proto-Sesklo," Dimini, and Mycenaean sequences.
Excav. by V. Milojčić, 1955–58. Museum: Larisa. Lit.: V. Milojčić, J. Boessneck, M. Hopf, 1962 .

ASZÓD
A settlement and cemetery of the Lengyel culture, spread over 25 hectares, northeast of Budapest, Hungary.
Excav. by N. Kalicz in 1960–82. Museum: Petöfi in Aszód. Lit.: N. Kalicz, *Kökori falu Aszód*, 1985.

AUVERNIER
A stratified site with layers of Cortaillod, Horgen, and Corded Pottery cultures in Canton Neuchâtel, Switzerland. Cortaillod dates: c. 4000–3200 B.C.
Excav. 1919–20, 1948, 1950, 1964–65. Museums: Musée Neuchâtel and Musée de l'Homme. Lit.: P. Vouga, *Le Néolithique lacustre ancien*, Neuchâtel, 1934; J-P. Jéquier & C. Strahm, *Les fouilles archéol. d'Auvernier en 1964* (Musées neuchâtelois), 1965: 78–88; A. Gallay, "Les fouilles d'Auvernier 1964–65 et le problème des stations lacustres." *Archives suisses d'anthropologie générale* 30 (1965): 57–82.

AVEBURY
One of the largest ceremonial structures of Britain located west of Marlborough, Wiltshire. The circle of stones, ditch, and outer bank of this henge monument enclose an area of 28½ acres. On the central plateau area two smaller stone circles with arrangements of stones in the center. The ditch and bank are broken by four equally spaced entrances. At the south entrance Kennet Avenue begins, consisting of two parallel rows of sarsen stones leading to a building called the Sanctuary, c. 2 km away. The monument was used from the 4th to the 2nd mill. B.C. In the ditch were found Windmill Hill, Petersborough, Rinyo-Clacton, Beaker, and later Bronze Age potsherds.
Excav. by A. Keiller 1925–39, 1965. Lit.: I. F. Smith, *Windmill Hill and Avebury, Excavations by Alexander Keiller, 1925–39*; M. Dames, 1977; A. Burl, *Prehistoric Avebury*, 1979 (New Haven: Yale Univ. Press); Idem., *Rites of Gods*, London (Dent), 1981.

AZMAK
One of the largest stratified Karanovo tells, located near Stara Zagora, central Bulgaria. Yielded consecutive layers of Karanovo I–VI, c. 6000–4300 B.C.
Excav. by G. I. Georgiev, 1960–63. Museum: Stara Zagora. Lit.: G. I. Georgiev, 1961 and 1967.

BAALBERGE
A barrow with a single central grave in a stone cist from the mid-4th mill. B.C., distr. of Bernburg, central Germany. This is the name-giving site for a cultural group considered to be a southern variant of the TRB culture, but burial rites suggest a strong Kurgan influence.
Excav. by P. Höfer, 1901. Lit.: P. Höfer, *Jahresschrift Halle*, 1 (1902): 16ff.

BADEN Culture
A Kurgan-influenced complex, composed of contrasting indigenous post-Vinča (agricultural) and alien Kurgan (pastoral, patriarchal) elements, in the Middle Danube basin dated between the 34th and 30th centuries B.C. Also called "Pécel" or "Radial-decorated Pottery" culture. Together with Ezero (which see) it forms a large and uniform cultural complex stretching between W Anatolia and Poland.

BALATON

Post Vinča cultural complex in W Hungary. Related to the Lasinja complex in Croatia, Bosnia, and Slovenia from the first half of the 4th mill. B.C.

BANDKERAMIK

See *Linearbandkeramik*.

BANJICA

A stratified Vinča site northeast of Belgrade, with 4 m of cultural remains.

Excav. 1955–57 by J. Todorović and A. Cermanović. Lit.: J. Todorović and A. Cermanović, 1961.

BARNENEZ

An impressive stone cairn (more than 90 m long) including eleven passage graves with corbelled chambers at Plouézoc'h, Lanmeur, Finistère, NW Brittany. Possibly in use for some 500 years, the primary cairn with five tombs dates from the middle of the 5th mill. B.C.; the secondary was built 200–300 years later. A number of orthostats in chambers were engraved with symbols—wavy lines, triangles or axes, ships, and a cross.

Excav. by P.-R. Giot, 1955–68. Lit.: P.-R. Giot, *Barnenez*, Rennes; Idem., "Les leçons finales du cairn de Barnenez," in P. Kjaerum and C. E. Daniel, eds., 1973: 192–202; P.-R. Giot and J. L'Helgouach, *Bulletin Soc. Preh. Français*, 54 (1956): 358–65.

BATTLE AXE Culture

See *Corded Pottery Culture*.

BELL BEAKER Culture

A mobile and pastoral culture, an amalgam of Yamna and Vučedol traditions in east-central Europe, which diffused between 2500 and 2100 B.C. between central Europe, the British Isles, and the Iberian Peninsula.

BODROGKERESZTÚR

Type site for the middle stage of the Hungarian Copper Age, c. 4000 B.C., located at the mouth of the Bodrog River in NE Hungary; a cemetery of 50 inhumation graves.

Excavated by L. Bella 1921–26.

BOIAN Culture

Developed from the symbiosis between the Early Vinča and LBK cultures in southeastern Romania. In its second stage, stimulated the formation of the Petreşti and Cucuteni cultures. Eponymous site is on an island in Lake Boian north of the Danube, between Olteniţa and Calaraşi, SE Romania.

Excav. by V. Christescu 1924; E. Comşa 1956–59. Museum: NAM, Bucharest. Lit.: V. Christescu, *Dacia* 2 (1925); Comşa, *Materiale Cercetari Archeol.* 5–8 (1959–62).

BRONOCICE

A Funnel Beaker (TRB) and Baden-like settlement located on an elevation above the Nidzica River (tributary of the upper Vistula) floodplain, distr. of Kielce, S Poland. This site covers more than 50 hectares (120 acres). Five occupational phases are uncovered: three of TRB, c. 3770–3110 B.C.; last two of Baden-like culture, c. 3110–2400 B.C.

Excav. by J. Kruk and S. Milisauskas, 1974–78. Lit.: J. Kruk and S. Milisauskas, *Germania* 59 (1981): 1–19; *Germania* 60 (1982): 211–16; *Germania* 64 (1984): 1–30; *Archeologia Polski* 26, 1: 65–113; W. Hensel and S. Milisauskas, *Excavations of Neolithic and Early Bronze Age Sites in SE Poland* (Ossolineum), 1985: 52–78.

BRZEŚĆ KUJAWSKI

LBK site of c. 5100 B.C., and a late Lengyel settlement c. 4300–4000 B.C. in the province of Bydgoszcz, Włocławek distr., W Poland. Distinct for over 50 trapeze-shaped Lengyel houses, 15–39 m long with inhumation burials nearby.

Excav. by K. Jażdżewski 1933–36; P. Bogucki and R. Grygiel 1976–80. Lit.: K. Jażdżewski, *Wiadomości Archeologiczne* 15 (1938), 1ff.; P. Bogucki, 1982; R. Grygiel, 1986.

BUCOVAŢ

A Vinča group in W Romania named from the stratified tell of Bucovaţ, Timişoara dist. The cultural layer, 1.7 m thick, is subdivided into three phases: Bukovaţ I–III.

Excav. in 1973 and 1975. Lit.: Gheorghe Lazarovici, *Neoliticul Banatului*, 1979.

BÜKK Culture

Also called "Eastern Linearbandkeramik." A culture in the upper Tisza basin of the 6th mill. B.C. named after the Bükk Mountains, north of the Hungarian plains.

BURGÄSCHI

See *Seeberg*.

BUTMIR

Settlement in Sarajevo, the name-giving site for the Butmir culture in Bosnia, c. 5300–4300 B.C.

Excav. 1893–96. Museum: Zemaljski Muzej, Sarajevo. Lit.: W. Radimsky and M. Hoernes, 1895; F. Fiala and M. Hoernes, 1898, *Die neolithische Station von Butmir*.

BYLANY

LBK settlement near Kutná Hora, Kolin, Czechoslovakia.

Excav. 1953–61 by B. Soudský. Museums: Bylany and Prague. Lit.: B. Soudský 1958, 1959, 1960; *Antiquity* 36 (1962), 1966.

CARNAC

Stone alignments—avenues built of multiple rows of upright stones, 1–6 km long—outside Carnac in Brittany, presumed to be of the same age as passage graves. There are three separate structures: the Menec, north of Carnac composed of 1,000 stones in 11 parallel rows; the Kermario, with 10 rows; and Kerlescant with 13 rows. Each alignment originally had a circle of standing stones or other constructions at the western end. These may be the sanctuaries toward which the avenues are aimed.

Lit.: P. R. Giot, *Brittany*, London, 1960.

CĂSCIOARELE

A stratified site including late Boian and Gumelniţa settlements near Olteniţa, an island in the lower Danube. Famous for the temple with pillars, wall paintings, and the clay model of a large edifice.

Excav. in 1925 by G. Stefan; 1962–69 by H. and V. Dumitrescu. Museum: National Museum, Bucharest. Lit.: V. Dumitrescu, 1965, 1970; H. Dumitrescu, 1968.

CASTELNOVIAN

Mesolithic culture of eastern Spain and southern France.

ÇATAL HÜYÜK

Largest Neolithic town in the world, located on the Konya plateau, south-central Turkey, from the end of the 8th through the 7th mill. B.C. The excavated portion of this tell has revealed mudbrick houses and temples, wall paintings and reliefs, sculptures, and a host of other objects greatly contributing to the reconstruction of Neolithic life and religion.

Excav. by J. Mellaart, 1961–63, 1965. Lit.: J. Mellaart, 1962, 1963, 1967, 1989.

CERNAVODA

1. Cemetery site of the Hamangia culture, northwest of Constanţa, Danube delta, Romania. 2. Fortified hilltop settlement of a Kurganized culture, early 4th mill. B.C.

Excav. by D. Berciu in 1957. Museum: National Museum, Bucharest. Lit.: D. Berciu, 1966.

CERNICA

Cemetery at Bucharest, Romania, from the Early Boian phases, early 5th mill. B.C., in which 362 inhumation burials were uncovered.

Excav. by G. Cantacuzino and S. Morintz, 1960–67. Museum: National Museum, Bucharest. Lit.: C. Cantacuzino and S. Morintz, *Dacia* N.S. 7 (1963): 27ff; G. Cantacuzino, *Dacia* N.S. 9 (1965): 45ff; *Dacia* N.S. 13 (1969): 45–59.

CHAERONEA
Sesklo settlement in Boeotia, central Greece, with 6 m of cultural material.
Excav. by G. Sotiriadis, 1902–7. Museum: Chaeronea. Lit.: Sotiriadis, *Athen. Mitt.* 30 (1905); *Ephem. Arch.* (1908); *Rev. Études Greques* 25 (1925).

CHASSÉE Culture
An advanced Neolithic post-Cardial culture in France, related to the Cortaillod in Switzerland and the Lagozza in Italy. Practiced intensive horticulture with technologically advanced ceramics and lithics. Dated to the 5th and early 4th mill. B.C.

CORDED POTTERY Culture
Pastoral, patriarchal, single-grave culture of the first half of the 3rd mill. B.C. in the Upper Danube, Elbe, Oder, and Vistula basins. From C Europe it spread to NW Germany, S Scandinavia, the East Baltic area, the Upper Dnieper basin, and C Russia. Also known as the Battle Axe culture.

CORTAILLOD
A culture of lakeshore dwellers of the 5th and 4th mill. B.C. in western and central Switzerland and eastern France. Ceramics were bag-shaped with little decoration. Agriculture is attested by grain crops as well as apples, pears, plums, cabbage, flax, and opium poppy. There is ample evidence of a highly developed tool kit, weaving technology, and animal domestication.

COȚOFENI Culture
A cultural complex representing remnants of Old European traditions in the Danube valley, western Muntenia, southern Banat, and Transylvania toward the end of the 4th mill. B.C. These sedentary agriculturalists used copper tools and still produced burnished red and white painted ceramics.

CRIȘ Culture
Same as Körös. The Starčevo culture in Romania, named after the Criș River.

CUCUTENI
A stratified settlement near Tirgu-Frumoș, distr. of Iași, Moldavia, NE Romania with Cucuteni A, A-B, and B phases, which gave its name to the Cucuteni civilization in Moldavia.
Excav. by H. Schmidt in 1909–10, and by M. Petrescu-Dimbovița in 1961–68. Museums: Berlin and Bucharest, Iași and Birlad. Lit.: Schmidt, *Cucuteni*, 1932; Petrescu-Dimbovița, *Cucuteni*, 1966.

CUCUTENI Culture
A culture in Moldavia and the western Ukraine, dated from c. 4800 to c. 3500 B.C. Originated from an amalgam of the colonizing Boian people with the Neolithic LBK culture in Moldavia to become one of the richest cultures of Old Europe. The largest settlements of the Late Cucuteni period contained as many as 2,000 houses arranged in concentric ellipses covering 400 hectares. Cucuteni ceramic art is one of the finest of Old Europe.

COVA FOSCA
A stratified cave site in Castellon near Alto Maestrazgo, E Spain, indicating an early and gradual transition from a food gathering to a food producing economy in the west Mediterranean area. Its earliest layer, from the 8th mill. B.C., contained sheep but no domesticated plants. The lithic industry was mesolithic. Pottery—deep egg-shaped bowls —appeared during the next period, c. 6500–6000 B.C.
Excav. by Carme Olària and F. Gusi in 1975–79. Lit.: C. Olària, *Cova Fosca*, 1988.

DANILO
A settlement near Šibenik, W Yugoslavia, the eponymous site of the Danilo culture.
Excav. by D. Rendić-Miočević in 1952; by J. Korošec 1953–55. Museum: Šibenik. Lit.: J. Korošec, 1964.

DANILO-HVAR Culture
A culture which lived along the Adriatic coast in Dalmatia c. 5500–4000 B.C.

DIKILITASH
A tell settlement at Philipi, Macedonia, NE Greece, with Neolithic and Early Bronze Age layers dating from late 6th to early 3rd mill. B.C.
Excav. by J. Deshayes and D. Theocharis 1965, 1968–70. Lit.: J. Deshayes, *Bulletin de Correspondance Hellénique* 86, 2: 912–33.

DIMINI Culture
Late Neolithic culture of Thessaly, c. 5500–4000 B.C. Dimini derives from the eponymous settlement near Volos.
Excav. by C. Tsountas 1901-2. Lit.: Tsountas, 1980.

DIVOSTIN
Starčevo and Late Vinča settlements near Kragujevac, C Yugoslavia.
Excav. by A. McPherron and D. Srejović 1968–69. Museum: Kragujevac. Lit.: A. McPherron and D. Srejović, *Divostin*, 1988.

DNIEPER-DONETS Culture
Neolithic culture of the Dnieper basin, represented by a massive (robust) Cro-Magnon population, descended from the Upper and Middle Dnieper basin. Three developmental phases, distinct for practicing collective burial, are recognized between 5500 and 4500 B.C. This culture was supplanted in the middle of the 5th mill. B.C. by a steppe population from the Volga basin.

DNIESTER-BUG Culture
An early Neolithic culture in Moldavia and the western Ukraine, 6500–5000 B.C. Independent experiments in animal and plant domestication by groups indigenous from the Mesolithic, 500 years before contacts with Starčevo (Criș) agriculturalists. Influences from Starčevo and LBK culture in later phases.

DONJA BRANJEVINA
A Starčevo settlement near Deronj, northern Yugoslavia, distinct for its Starčevo ritual objects.
Excav. by S. Karmanski 1968. Museum: Odžaci. Lit.: S. Karmanski, *Žtrvenici, statuete i amuleti sa lokalitela D. Branjevina kod' Deronja*, Odžaci, 1968.

DOMICA
A cave, 5 km long, which begins near Kečovo, distr. of Šafárikovo, Slovakia, and extends into NE Hungary at Barydla, where it is called Aggtelek. Ritual structures and deposits of the Bükk culture were found within.
Excav. by L. V. Marton and O. Kadić 1910; by J. Böhm 1933–34. Lit.: F. V. Tompa, *Die Bandkeramik in Ungarn*, 1929; B. Novotný, 1958.

DOWTH
One of the three large circular mounds in the funerary complex of the Boyne Valley, Co. Meath, E Ireland. The mound is 85 m in diameter and 15 m in height. The base is surrounded by kerbstones. There are two chambers on its western side. The larger has a passage 8 m long, a cruciform chamber with a corbelled roof, and a large stone basin in the center. The smaller one has a short passage and a circular chamber. Some orthostats in both tombs were pecked with symbols.
Lit.: George Coffey, *Newgrange and other Incised Tumuli in Ireland*, Dublin, 1912.

DURRINGTON WALLS
A ceremonial monument at Amesbury, Wiltshire from the Middle and Late Neolithic of S England, late 4th and 3rd mill. B.C. This is a twin-entrance henge with a diameter of more than 500 m (1600 ft.). Two timber structures of concentric rings were within the enclosure, one of them approached by an avenue of timber uprights.

EGOLZWIL 1–5
Small Neolithic lakeshore villages of cattle breeders in Canton Luzern, Switzerland, of the Egolzwil group, related to the Cortaillod culture of the 1st half of the 4th mill. B.C. Distinct for its well-preserved rectangular

timber houses, bark and wooden tools and vessels, data for forest history, and vegetation studies.

Excav. by E. Vogt 1950, 1952, 1954–64 (Egolzwil 3 and 4); by R. Wyss 1956 (Egolzwil 5). Lit.: E. Vogt 1951, 1954, 1967; R. Wyss 1976.

EHRENSTEIN
Late Neolithic villages from the 4th mill. B.C. of the Michelsberg and Schussenried groups, with well-preserved timber houses of one or two rooms in the distr. of Ulm on the Danube, Baden-Württemberg, Germany. Distinct for the good preservation of wooden artifacts and quantities of grain.

Excav. in 1962 and 1960 by O. Paret and H. Zürn. Lit.: O. Paret, *Das steinzeitdorf Ehrenstein bei Ulm*, Stuttgart, 1955; H. Zürn, *Germania* 40 (1962).

ELATEIA (DRAKHMANI)
Two Sesklo tells rich in ceramic finds, Phokis, Greece.

Excav. by G. Sotiriadis 1909–10; by S. Weinberg 1959. Museum: Chaeronea. Lit.: G. Sotiriadis, *Athen. Mitt.* 30 (1905), 31 (1906); *Ephem. Arch.* (1908); *Rev. Études Greques* 25 (1912); Wace and Thompson, *Prehistoric Thessaly*, 1912; Weinberg *AJA* 65 (1961); *Hesperia* 31 (1962).

ELLERBEK Culture
A Mesolithic culture inhabiting northwestern Germany throughout the 5th mill. B.C.

ELSLOO
An LBK settlement and graves in the province of Limburg, The Netherlands. Ten hectares yielded 95 long-houses of various phases within c. 5500–5000 B.C. Of 110 graves, 70 were inhumations in contracted position and 40 were cremations.

Excav. by P. J. R. Modderman 1950, 1958–59, 1966; by R. S. Hulst 1963. Lit.: P. J. R. Modderman, *Palaeohistoria* 6–7 (1958–59), 1970.

ERTEBØLLE Culture
Indigenous Mesolithic food-gatherers inhabiting the coastal regions of Denmark and southern Sweden throughout the 5th mill. B.C.

EZERO
A stratified tell in central Bulgaria near Nova Zagora, originally occupied by the Karanovo people between 6000 and 4300 B.C. The hybrid culture which emerged after a hiatus following Kurgan Wave No. 1, was an amalgamation of Old European and Kurgan influences and is related to Baden. Habitation continued through most of the 4th mill. B.C.

Excav. by N. Ya. Merpert, G. I. Georgiev, et al., through the 1970s. Lit: Georgiev, G. I., N. Ya. Merpert, R. V. Katinčarov, and D. G. Dimitrov, 1919, *Ezero*.

FAFOS
Vinča settlements at Kosovska Mitrovica, S Yugoslavia. Fafos I (Early) and Fafos II (Late Vinča) are known for Vinča art and ritual objects.

Excav. by B. Jovanović in 1956 and 1959–61. Museum: Priština. Lit.: B. Jovanović and J. Glišic, *Arheološki Pregled* 3, 1961.

FILIESTRU
A stratified cave site in Sardinia, province of Mara, 30 km south of Sassari, which yielded a sequence of Neolithic and Bronze Age deposits: Impresso (Cardial), Filiestru, Bonu Ighinu, Ozieri, Monte Claro, Bonnanaro, and Sa Turricula, all with radiocarbon dates.

First explored by R. Loria in 1969 and 1972 and excav. by D. Trump in 1979 and 1980. Lit.: D. Trump, 1983.

FRUMUŞICA
Classical Cucuteni settlement from the mid-5th mill. B.C. near Peatra Neamţ, Moldavia, noted for its exquisite painted vases.

Excav. by C. Matasă. Museum: Peatra Neamţ. Lit.: C. Matasă, 1946.

FUNNEL-NECKED BEAKER Culture
A fully agricultural society, also called TRB, dated from the end of the 5th mill. B.C. to the middle of the 3rd mill. B.C. It moved into the Ertebølle and Ellerbek territories and later colonized the lower Vistula region of northern Poland and the Nemunas basin to western Belorussia.

GAVRINIS
One of the most elaborately decorated passage graves in Brittany, located on an island (former peninsula) in Morbihan. The designs pecked on 23 stone slabs of the passage reveal the theme of regeneration expressed by rising concentric arcs, spirals, axes, and bulls.

Lit.: C.-T. LeRoux, 1985; E. S. Twohig, 1981.

ĠGANTIJA ("Giants' Tower")
The best preserved temple complex on the island of Gozo (north of Malta) from the mid-4th mill. B.C. Consists of two anthropomorphically shaped temples, each having five egg-shaped apses (see fig. 5–25). Known from the 18th century, clearance of the site was undertaken in 1827.

Excav. by the National Museum, Valletta. Lit.: J.D. Evans 1959 and 1971.

GLOBULAR AMPHORA Culture
A culture of patriarchal pastoralists whose appearance in north-central Europe during mid-4th mill. B.C. led to the disintegration of the TRB culture. Also extended into areas of the Cucuteni as well as the Nemunas and Narva cultures. Burial rites are similar to those of the Kurgan culture in the North Pontic region.

GOLDBERG
A hilltop site with stratified deposits of Rössen, Michelsberg, and Altheim type from the end of the 5th to the 3rd mill. B.C. near Nördlingen, distr. Aalen, Württemberg, SW Germany. A number of small rectangular houses with hearths were uncovered.

Excav. by G. Bersu in the 1920s. Lit.: G. Bersu, *Neue deutsche Ausgrabungen*, 1930; *Germania* 20 (1936), 21 (1937).

GOMOLAVA
A stratified tell on the River Sava, Vojvodina, N Yugoslavia, with a mid-Vinča layer below Baden-Kostolac, Middle and Late Bronge Age, La Tène II and III, Roman, and medieval layers.

Excav. since 1904 by J. Brunšmed; by R. Rašajski and S. Nagy 1953; by B. Brukner and B. Jovanović 1965–71. Museum: Novi Sad. Lit.: B. Brukner, "Die Siedlung der Vinča-Gruppe auf Gomolava," in B. Brukner, D. Dejić, M. Girić, B. Jovanović, B. Mitrović, et al., *Gomolava Simpozium*, Ruma (Novi Sad, 1986): 19–38.

GORSZA
One of the largest tell-like settlements, located at the confluence of the Tisza and Maros rivers on the Hungarian plain, near Hódmezövásárhely, SE Hungary. The 3 m thick cultural deposits yielded Late Neolithic, Early and Late Copper Age, and Early and Middle Bronze Age materials. Most significant were levels of the Tisza culture, 2 m thick, subdivided into five phases. Of these, level C revealed houses and house complexes arranged in an open central area, some with interior and exterior walls decorated with incisions and red and yellow painting, ritual vases richly decorated with meanders, altars, tables, figurines, and such.

Excav. by E. Zabotay in 1953; by G. Gazdapusztai 1955–57 and 1963; by F. Horváth 1978 to present. Museum: Hódmezövásárhely. Lit.: F. Horvath, "Hódmesövásárhely-Gorzsa. A Settlement of the Tisza culture," P. Raczky, ed. *The Late Neolithic of the Tisza Region*, 1987: 31–46.

GRADEŠNICA (GRADECHNITZA)
Several Neolithic and Chalcolithic stratified settlements in the vicinity of the Gradešnica village near Vraca, NW Bulgaria. Cultural remains date from the end of the 7th to the early 5th mill. B.C. and belong to the west Bulgarian branch of the Starčevo and Early Vinča cultures, parallel to Karanovo I–III in C Bulgaria. Excavations revealed the remains

of many rectangular houses built of timber uprights with wattle-and-daub walls. Among the finds were 200 clay figurines, temple models, offering tables, exquisite painted pottery, and the finest examples of inscribed plaques, figurines, and other ritual objects with Old European script signs from the end of the 6th mill. B.C.

Excav. by B. Nikolov between 1963 and 1973. Publ.: B. Nikolov, 1974.

GRIMES GRAVES
Neolithic flint mines near Brandon, on the Norfolk-Suffolk border, England. In 346 mine shafts, good quality flint was discovered from which axe blades were produced and traded in semifinished condition. One shaft included an altar of flint lumps surrounded by piled deer antlers. At its base was a chalk lamp and in front were chalk balls, the chalk figurine of a goddess, and a phallus. Lit.: R. R. Clarke, *Grimes Graves*, 1964.

GUMELNIŢA
A tell settlement near Olteniţa, S Romania.
Excav. by V. Dumitrescu in 1925 and 1960. Museum: National Museum, Bucharest. Lit.: V. Dumitrescu, *Dacia* 2 (1925), 7–8 (1937/40), 4 N.S. (1960); *Archaeology* (1966).

GUMELNIŢA Culture
A culture in southern Romania in the mid-5th mill. B.C. related to and synchronous with Karanovo VI in C Bulgaria, which produced magnificent ceramics and sculptural art.

HĂBĂŞEŞTI
A large Classical Cucuteni settlement of c. 4300 B.C. near Tîrgu-Frumoş, Moldavia, NE Romania.
Excav. by V. Dumitrescu 1949–50. Museum: National Museum, Bucharest. Lit.: V. Dumitrescu, 1954.

HACILAR
A Neolithic village in SW Turkey, including a pre-pottery layer of the 8th mill. B.C., followed by 6th mill. Neolithic layers with pottery (Levels IX–VI, Late Neolithic) with substantial mudbrick houses, and by Chalcolithic levels (V–I).
Excav. and publ. by J. Mellaart, 1970.

HAĠAR QIM
A temple complex in S Malta near the sea built of globigerina limestone from the end of the 4th mill. B.C. Consists of six double-egg-shaped temples surrounded by a wall (see fig. 5–26). In one niche beneath a step in a break in the corner, statues of the Goddess were having egg-shaped buttocks and legs. (PLATE 20) Figures of the same shape with egg-shaped calves appear on a wall in relief.

These represent the same temple Goddess as the gigantic goddess of Tarxien. At the outer wall of one of the temples is a great upright stone, standing more than 4.5 m high, possibly a Goddess's menhir.
Excav. began in 1839 by J. G. Vance; National Museum of Valletta 1944, 1954. Museum: Nat. Museum, Valletta. Lit.: J. D. Evans, 1959 and 1971.

HAL SAFLIENI
Large, unique Maltese hypogeum in the outskirts of Valletta, consisting of 33 egg-shaped, rock-cut tombs and halls on three levels reaching 10 m below the surface. Red-ochre-painted egg-shaped cells, ceilings painted with ivy-spirals and discs, bull frescoes on walls, axe- and double-egg-shaped amulets, and figurines of fish and ladies with egg-shaped buttocks lying on beds speak for the prevalence of regeneration symbolism. It is presumed that funerary rituals took place continually between c. 4000–2500 B.C.
Excav. by T. Zammit 1905–9. Lit.: J. D. Evans 1959, 1971; D. Trump, *Malta, An Archaeological Guide* (London, 1972): 58–65.

HAMANGIA Culture
A Neolithic culture on the Black Sea coast with a distinctive art style of black-burnished pottery with white-encrusted designs and individualistic figurine types. Five phases of cultural development parallel to Boian and Karanovo III–IV, 5500–4700 B.C. The treasured finds are clay sculptures of a pair of gods found in a grave, cemetery of Cernavoda.

HERPÁLY
Tell settlement in the Berettyö valley and name-giving site for the cultural group in E Hungary, related to Tisza. The mound contained 3 m of Late Neolithic Herpály materials and a Bronze Age layer 1.2 m thick. Five building horizons were unearthed within the Herpály culture which yielded large tripartite houses, including two-storied buildings, probably used for worship, with elaborately built rectangular bread ovens with bucrania on four corners, walls decorated with bull heads in clay, clay basins on both floors, a great many biconical and pedestalled vases, and more; c. 4700–4400 B.C..
Trial excav. by L. Zoltas and J. Söregi 1921–22; by J. Korek and P. Patay 1955; large scale excav. by N. Kalicz and P. Raczky 1977–82. Lit.: J. Korek and P. Patay, *Folia Arch.* 8 (1956): 23–42; N. Kalicz and P. Raczky, "Berettyöújfalu-Herpály. A Settlement of the Herpály Culture," in P. Raczky, ed., *The Late Neolithic of the Tisza Region*, 1987: 105–25.

HLUBOKÉ MAŠŮVKY
Settlements of LBK and Lengyel cultures near Znojmo, Moravia. Noted for Lengyel painted pottery and statuary.
Excav. by F. Vildomec 1927–39; by J. Neustupný 1949–50. Lit.: F. Vildomec and Salm, *Ipek* 11 (1931–37); *Obzor Prehist.* 13 (1946); J. Neustupný, *Arch. Rozhl.* 2 (1950); 3 (1951); *Časopis Nár. Mus. Prag.* (1948–50).

HÓDMESÖVÁSÁRHELY
See *Gorzsa, Kökenydomb.*

HÖEDIC
A kitchen midden and graves of premegalithic Brittany located on an island south of Vannes, distr. of Morbihan. Includes 9 graves with 14 inhumation burials, 4 of which were covered with deer antlers. Important for insight into the beginnings of collective burials.
Excav. by M. & S.-J. Péquart, 1931–34. Lit.: S.-J. Péquart, *Hoëdic, deuxième station nécropole du mésolithique cotier Armoricain*, 1954.

HORGEN
Late Neolithic, post-Cortaillod lakeshore settlements on Lake Neuchâtel, Canton Zürich, Switzerland. Eponymous site for cultural group related to Seine-Oise-Marne in E France.
Excav. in 1923. Lit.: E. Vogt, "Horgener Kultur, Seine-Oise-Marne Kultur und nordische Steinkiste." *Anzeiger für Schweizerische Altertumskunde*, Zürich, 1938.

HURBANOVO
A stratified settlement with layers of LBK (Želiezovce variant), Lengyel, Tisza, and Bükk cultures near Hurbanovo, Komárno, Slovakia.
Excav. 1953–8. Museum: Nitra. Lit.: C. Ambros and B. Novotný, *Arch. Rozhl.* 5 (1953); P. Čaplovič, *Arch. Rozhl.* 8 (1956); B. Novotný, *Počiatky vytvarneho prejavu na Slovensku* (1958); H. Quitta, *Prähist. Zeitschrift* 36 (1960).

HVAR
Island cave site at Grapčeva spilja, eponymous for the Late Neolithic culture along the Adriatic coast, Yugoslavia. Excav. and publ. by G. Novak, *Hvar* (1955). Museum: Zagreb.

ISBISTER
A megalithic tomb of S Orkney from the late 4th to early 3rd. mill. B.C. which yielded important information on burial rites. Hundreds of disarticulated human skeletons (after excarnation by birds) were found, as well as fish skeletons and carcasses of sea eagles and other birds of prey, probable incarnations of the Goddess of Regeneration.
Excav. by R. Simison. Lit.: J. W. Hedges, 1984.

IZVOARE

Early Cucuteni settlement on the Bistriţa River near Bacău, Moldavia, NE Romania, with five horizons belonging to Proto-Cucuteni and Cucuteni A.

Excav. by R. Vulpe 1936–38. Museum: National Museum, Bucharest.

KARANOVO

Tell near Nova Zagora, C Bulgaria, eponymous site of the Karanovo culture which provides the backbone of the east Balkan cultural sequence: Karanovo I–IV, 6th to 1st half of the 6th mill. B.C. Karanova V–VI: early and mid-5th mill. B.C. Layer VII is from the Early Bronze Age which does not show continuity from layer VI.

Excav. by V. Mikov and G. I. Georgiev 1936–57. Museums: Nova Zagora and Sofia. Lit.: V. Mikov, *Izvestija* 5 (1937), *Antiquity* 13 (1939), *Sovetskaya Arkheologiya* 1 (1958); G .I. Georgiev, 1961; S. Hiller and G. I. Georgiev, *Tell Karanovo* 1984–86; S. Hiller and V. Nikolov, *Tell Karanovo* 1988–89 (Salzburg: Universität, Institut für Alte Geschichte und Altertumsforschung).

KARBUNA

Find of 852 objects in a vase attributed to the Pre-Cucuteni (Tripolye A) culture from the Čimišli distr., Soviet Moldavia, USSR. More than half of the objects were of copper and more than 250 were of shell.

Lit.: Sergeev, *Sovetskaya Arkheologiya* 1 (1962).

KNOSSOS

Best known for its palace-temple from the Bronze Age on Crete, 5 km SE from Herakleion, discovered by Arthur Evans at the beginning of the 20th century. First settled by Neolithic farmers around 7000 B.C. Neolithic deposits below the Early Minoan Bronze Age layer are 4 m thick.

Excav. by J. D. Evans in the early 1960s. Lit.: J. D. Evans, 1964.

KNOWTH

The principal and most spectacular monument of the Boyne Valley funerary complex, Co. Meath, E Ireland, from the middle of the 4th mill. B.C. The central mound, which covers an acre and a half and is 9.9 m in height, was surrounded by 16 smaller satellite tombs. There are two passage graves within the large mound placed back to back. The eastern one has a corbel-vaulted burial chamber with three niches in which cremation deposits were found. One niche contained a stone basin decorated with grooves and circles. The stones forming the kerb around the mound and the passage grave orthostats are pecked with symbols.

Excav. by G. Eogan 1962–1980s. Lit.: G. Eogan, *Knowth*, 1985.

KODŽADERMEN

A tell 7 m high with remains of the Boian culture, followed by Gumelniţa, near Šumen, NE Bulgaria.

Excav. by R. Popov in 1914. Museum: Sofia. Lit.: R. Popov, *Izvestija Bulg. Arh. Druž.* 6 (The Bulgarian Archeol. Society), 1916–18.

KÖKÉNYDOMB

A tell settlement in Hódmezővásárhely, SE Hungary, covering 1.5 hectares with burials of the Tisza culture. Noted for rich sculptural art. First half of the 5th mill. B.C.

Excav. by J. Banner in 1929, 1940–42, and 1944. Museum: Hódmezővásárhely. Lit.: J. Banner, "A Kökénydombi neolithkori telep," *Dolgozatok* 6 (1930): 49–158; 1958.

KÖLN-LINDENTHAL

A typical LBK settlement with long-houses on the outskirts of Cologne, Germany, with 7 phases of occupation. Over 30 houses uncovered in 30,000 sq m of excavation. The last village was surrounded by a ditch.

Excav. in 1929–32. Lit.: W. Buttler and W. Haberey, *Die bandkeramische Ansiedlung von Köln-Lindenthal*. Röm-Germ. Forschungen 11 (1936).

KÖRÖS Culture

A Neolithic culture of the 1st half of the 6th mill. B.C. in SE Hungary, named after the Körös River. A northern branch of the central Balkan Starčevo culture.

KOSTOLAC Culture

A late Baden branch in northern Yugoslavia and Bosnia.

KURGAN Culture

A warlike, patriarchal, and hierarchical culture of S Russia with a pastoral economy augmented by a rudimentary agriculture with transient settlements of semisubterranean houses. Their burials, which reveal concentrations of wealth among ruling males, include pit graves with tent- or houselike structures of wood or stone covered by a low cairn or earthen mound. The term *Kurgan* was coined by the author in 1956 to designate a Proto-Indo-European (PIE) culture. In Russian, the Kurgan culture of the Volga steppe and forest steppe, c. 4500–3500 B.C., is called *early Yamna*; its extension into the lower Dnieper steppe is called *Sredniy Stog* II, followed by the Maikop culture north of the Black Sea and the Caucasus Mts., and *late Yamna* in the Volga basin, c. 3500–2500 B.C.

LAGOZZA Period

Middle to late 4th mill. B.C. lakeshore villages of northern Italy, following the Square-Mouth Pottery stage, related to Chassean.

LARGA-JIJIEI

Multiple settlement site in the distr. of Iaşi, Moldavia, NE Romania, with Early ("Pre-Cucuteni") and Late Cucuteni (Cucuteni B) material.

Excav. by A. D. Alexandrescu. Lit.: A. D. Alexandrescu, *Dacia* V (1961) and *SCIV* 12, 2 (1961).

LASINJA Culture

See *Balaton*.

LAŽN'ANY

Last stage of the dying and isolated Tisza culture known only from inhumation and cremation graves in eastern Slovakia. Diminished copper and obsidian industries and a diminished ceramic style.

LENGYEL Culture

A clearly distinct cultural group from the Danube basin, formed around 5000 B.C. from a Starčevo core through intensified relations with Bosnia and the Adriatic area. After c. 4300 B.C. emerges in Bavaria, C Germany, and W Poland, colonizing the central areas of the LBK culture.

LENGYEL

Name-giving settlement and cemetery near Szekszárd, Tolna, Hungary.

Excav. 1882–88 by M. Wosinszky. Museum: Szekszárd. Lit.: M. Wosinszky, *Das prähistorische Schanzwerk von Lengyel*, 1888.

LEPENSKI VIR Culture

The indigenous culture of the Iron Gate region of N Yugoslavia and S Romania, transitional between the Upper Paleolithic Gravettian and the Starčevo culture, 11th to 6th mill. B.C. Fourteen sites explored, including Cuina Turcului, Vlasac, Padina, and Lepenski Vir.

LEPENSKI VIR

A locus of 50 triangular/trapezoidal temples and graves on the bank of the Danube River at the Iron Gate, N Yugoslavia, 6500–5500 B.C. The temples revealed red plastered floors, rectangular stone-walled altars, 54 monumental egg-shaped sculptures, some with Fish Goddess characteristics, and many other objects of ritual significance.

Excav. by D. Srejović and Z. Letica 1965–69. Museum: Univ. of Belgrade. Lit.: D. Srejović 1969; D. Srejović and L. Babović, 1983.

LERNA
A stratified site near Argos, E Peloponnese, Greece, consisting of two Neolithic layers, followed by Early Bronze Age remains.

Excav. by J. L. Caskey 1956–59. Museum: Argos. Lit.: J. L. Caskey, *Hesperia* 23 (1954), 25 (1956), 26 (1957), 27 (1958), 28 (1959).

LEȚ
Tell at St. Gheorghe, Transylvania, consisting of two phases of the Starčevo (Criş) culture, followed by the Boian and Cucuteni-Ariuşd layers.

Excav. by Z. Székely, I. Nestor, and E. Zaharia 1949–55. Museum: NAM, Bucharest. Lit.: E. Zaharia, *Dacia* N.S. 6 (1962).

LINEARBANDKERAMIK (LBK) Culture
Located between eastern France and Romania c. 5500–4500/4300 B.C. Also called "Danubian," "Linear Pottery," and "Bandkeramik."

LIPARI
Islands north of Sicily, source of obsidian. Castello di Lipari yielded Late Neolithic (Diana culture), Copper Age, and Early Bronze Age occupation materials.

Excav. by L. Bernabó Brea and M. Cavalier began in 1950 and continued for several decades. Materials in local museum; part exposed in situ in front of the cathedral. Lit.: M. Cavalier, *Costello de Lipari*, 1958.

LISIČIĆI
Hvar settlement near Konjic, Hercegovina, Yugoslavia, divided into three living horizons.

Excav. by A. Benac 1952–54. Museum: Zemaljski Muzej, Sarajevo. Lit.: A. Benac, *Neolitsko naselje u Lisičićima kod Konjica*, Sarajevo, 1958.

LUKA-VRUBLEVETSKAYA
Early Cucuteni (Tripolye A) settlement, located in the Upper Dniester valley, distr. of Kamenec-Podolski, Ukraine, USSR.

Excav. 1946–50 by S.N. Bibikov. Museum: Moscow, Inst. Arch. Lit.: S.N. Bibikov, *Materialy i Issledovaniya po Arkhelogii SSSR* 38: 1–408.

LUŽIANKY
Settlement and cemetery of the Lengyel culture with painted pottery, on the bank of the Nitra River, 6 km NW of Nitra, Slovakia. The name is used to designate highly advanced, early Lengyel red and yellow painted pottery.

Excav. by V. Budinský-Krička 1942; by B. Novotný 1956. Lit.: B. Novotný, 1962.

MAES HOWE
A magnificent passage grave from Orkney, Scotland, with a squared burial chamber roofed by corbelling covered by a circular cairn surrounded by a ring ditch; looted by the Vikings. The affinities with Newgrange suggest that this tomb was built at the end of the 4th mill. B.C.

Lit.: V. Gordon Childe, "Excavations at Maes Howe," *Preh. Soc. AS* 82, 1947–48; A. S. Henshall, *The Chambered Tombs of Scotland* 1 (1963): 219–22.

MAIKOP Culture
The Kurgan culture, more advanced than Kurgan I, which developed in the North Pontic area between the Lower Dniester and the Caucasus mountains. The early stage is represented in the lowest layer of Mikhailovka, c. 3500 B.C., in the Lower Dnieper basin. Royal burials and hoards of the late Maikop culture of the early 3rd mill. B.C. in the northwestern Caucasus area express the fabulous riches of tribal leaders and their contacts with Mesopotamia.

MARICA
A tell near the town of Marica, distr. of Časkovo, C Bulgaria, with cultural remains of the Karanovo V period, early 5th mill. B.C. Used unnecessarily as a culture name, representing a period of the Karanovo culture.

Lit.: H. Vajsová, *Slovenská Arheológia* 14 (1966).

MĠARR (TA' ḤAĠRAT)
A temple complex in N Malta, 1 km west of Skorba. This is a double temple consisting of two adjacent trefoils. The larger is from the Ġgantija phase, the smaller is from the Hal Saflieni phase, middle and 2nd half of the 4th mill. B.C.

Excav. by T. Zammit in 1923–26. Lit.: J. D. Evans, 1971.

MICHELSBERG Culture
A Late Neolithic culture of the 4th mill. B.C. of the Upper and Middle Rhine basin, extending to Bohemia and Austria in the east. It occupies a frontier zone between the W European Neolithic and TRB, with cultural elements related to both. The name comes from a hilltop site northeast of Karlsruhe, Germany.

Excav. since 1888. Lit.: J. Lüning, 1968.

MNAJDRA
One of the most attractively located temple complexes in S Malta. Built in a hollow at the bottom of a hill which opens out to give a view of the sea, 100 m. away. The Ħaġar Qim complex is 500 m. up the hill. Consists of two main buildings, anthropomorphic in shape, of the Tarxien period, c. 3000 B.C. (see fig. 5–27), and a smaller trefoil temple from the Ġgantija phase, mid-4th mill. B.C.

Temples were built of coralline limestone blocks and slabs, with globigerina limestone used exclusively for the interior. Among the finds are figurines with exposed vulvas and pregnant bellies representing a birth-giving function.

Excav. by J. G. Vance 1840; by the Nat. Museum of Valletta 1944, 1954, which contains the finds. Lit.: J. D. Evans, 1959 and 1971.

MOHELNICE
LBK settlement followed by a Lengyel settlement at Zábřeh, Šumperk, Moravia.

Excav. by R. Tichý 1953. Museum: Brno. Lit.: R. Tichý, *Arch. Rozhl.* 8 (1956); *Sbornik Arch. Ust. Brno* I (1960); 2–3 (1961–62); *Přehled Výzkumu Brno* 1960; 1962; *Pam. Arch.* 49 (1958); 53 (1962).

MOLFETTA
An Impresso settlement with 50 excavated burials at Bari, Puglia, Italy.

Excav. by A. Mosso and M. Gervasio 1908–10. Museums: Museo Archeologico di Bari and Seminario di Molfetta. Lit.: M. Mayer, *Le stazioni preistoriche di Molfetta*, 1904; M. Mayer, *Molfetta and Matera*, 1924; A. Mosso, "La necropoli neolitica di Molfetta," *Monumenti Antichi* 20 (1910): 237ff.

MONTE D'ACCODDI
A pyramid-shaped ritual place, 6 m high and 30–37 m wide, near Sassari, N Sardinia, from the Ozieri culture, c. 4000 B.C. This structure of earth and stones has a ramp 41.5 m long leading to it. Among the finds are exquisite vessels, marble figurines, and large stone altar tables. Southeast of the structure stood two menhirs, and to the west was a multiroom building with a hearth, quernstones, and figurines, among other finds.

Excav. by E. Contu 1952–60. Lit.: E. Contu, *Bollettino di Paletnologia Italiana* n.s. 8 V (1953): 174ff.; *Rivista di Scienze Preist.* 8 (1953): 199ff.; 15 (1960): 236ff.; G. Liliu, *Bollettino PI*, 66 (1957): 11, 39ff.

NARVA Culture
East Baltic Neolithic culture, from the 5th to early 3rd mill. B.C. Fishing was main occupation; agriculture was practiced in later settlements around 3000 B.C.

NEA NIKOMEDEIA
Settlement site near Verroia, Macedonia, consisting of two levels: Early Neolithic (Proto-Sesklo) and Late Neolithic.

Excav. by R. J. Rodden 1961–63. Museum: Verroia. Lit.: R.J. Rodden, *Proceedings of Preh. Society* 28 (1962); *Scientific American* (April, 1965).

NEBO

A Butmir settlement near Travnik, Bosnia, Yugoslavia.

Excav. 1948–49 by A Benac. Museum: Zemaljski Muzej, Sarajevo. Lit.: A. Benac, *Prehistorijsko naselje Nebo i Problem Butmirske Kulture*, 1952; *Glasnik Sarajevo Arh.* NF 8 (1953).

NEMUNAS Culture

Indigenous culture of the Nemunas basin in S Lithuania and NE Poland during the Mesolithic and Neolithic. Also known as *Zedmar* in German and *Serowo* in Polish. Colonized by the TRB around the middle of the 4th mill. B.C. and the Globular Amphora people around 3000 B.C., resulting in hybridization of traditions and final disappearance of Nemunas features.

NEWGRANGE

One of the finest passage graves of Ireland, 25 km north of Dublin, in the religious complex of the Boyne Valley. Built around 3200 B.C., the mound of stones and turf layers is delimited by 97 kerbstones, covers about one acre, and is about 11 m in height. The 19 m long interior passage ends with a cruciform chamber with a corbelled roof. The largest capstones weigh between six and eight tons. Many stones of the entrance, chamber, and passage carry exquisite pecked designs including the triple snake spiral, concentric circles and arcs, rhombs, triangles, snakes, and cup marks, all consistent with the symbolism of regeneration. Traces of cremation burials were found in the chamber cells.

Excav. and publ. by M.J. O'Kelly, *Newgrange*, 1982.

NITRA

An Early Linear Pottery cemetery with 77 graves located on the left bank of the Nitra River, Slovakia, and a Lengyel village with preserved houses.

Excav. by J. Lichardus and J. Vladár. Lit.: J. Vladár, *Slovenská Archeológia* 18–2 (1970).

OBRE I

A Starčevo (Kakanj) settlement near Kakanj, Bosnia, consisting of four habitation horizons. The earliest represents a Starčevo complex with geometrically painted black on red ware; the upper three belong to an end of the same culture, locally called "Kakanj." 6th mill. B.C.

Excav. 1968 by A. Benac and M. Gimbutas. Museum: Zemaljski Muzej. Lit.: M. Gimbutas, *Archaeology* 23, 4 (1970); A. Benac, *Wiss. Mitt. des Bosnisch-Herzegowinischen Landesmuseums* (Sarajevo), 3, Heft A (1973): 327–430.

OBRE II

Butmir settlement near Kakanj, Bosnia with nine habitation horizons and three developmental phases. Early and middle Butmir dated within 5000–4500 B.C.

Excav. by A. Benac and M. Gimbutas 1967–68. Museum: Zemaljski Muzej, Sarajevo. Lit.: M. Gimbutas, *Archaeology* 23-4 (1970); A. Benac, "Obre II, Neolithic Settlement of the Butmir group at Gornje Polje." *Wiss. Mitt. des Bosnisch-Herzegowinischen Landesmuseums* (Sarajevo) 3, Heft A (1973): 1–327; M. Gimbutas, et al., Wiss. Mitt. 4, Heft A (1974).

ÖCSÖD-KOVÁSHALOM

A Tisza settlement located in the loop of the lower Körös River, SE Hungary, contemporary with Szegvár-Tüzköves which lies c. 40 km to the south. The occupation area covers 21 hectares and is composed of three larger and two smaller settlement nuclei, each covering 3–5 hectares. The cultural layer of 1.30–1.60 m thickness is composed of two continuous layers, Tisza I and II, from the 1st half of the 5th mill. B.C.

Excav. by P. Raczky 1982–83. Lit.: P. Raczky, "Öcsöd-Kováshalom, A Settlement of the Tisza Culture." *The Late Neolithic of the Tisza Region*, P. Raczky, ed., 1987: 61–83.

OLSZANICA

An LBK settlement at the western edge of the city of Cracow, S Poland, located on a loess elevation above the Rudawa River. The LBK occupation covers 50 hectares, with 1½ hectares uncovered, revealing the remains of more than 20 long-houses from various phases ranging from 7 to 41.5 m in length. Radiocarbon dates place the settlement between the end of the 6th and mid-5th mill. B.C.

Excav. by S. Milisauskas with the Institute of History of Material Culture, Polish Acad. of Sciences 1967–73. Lit.: W. Hensel and S. Milisauskas, *Excavations of Neolithic and Early Bronze Age Sites in SE Poland* (Ossolineum), 1985: 10–51.

OTZAKI

Tell near Larisa, Thessaly, with four cultural layers of the Sesklo culture.

Excav. by V. Milojčić 1953–55. Museum: Larisa. Lit.: V. Milojčić, *Arch. Anzeiger* 1954, 1955, 1959; *Jb. Römisch-Germ. Zentral Museum*, 1959; V. Milojčić and J. Milojčić von Zumbusch, 1971.

OVČAROVO

Neolithic and Chalcolithic settlements SE of Trgovište, N Bulgaria. An Early Neolithic site with subterranean dwellings was found at Ovčarovo-Zemnika I. A Chalcolithic tell with 13 habitation horizons lies west of the Neolithic site at the Kalaidžidere River. Distinct for 500 years of continuous habitation, divided into periods I–IV, parallel to Karanovo V–VI and late Boian-Gumelniţa, c. 4750–4250 B.C. Ample information on the structure of a small township and architecture. Finds from the 9th habitation horizon include two-story buildings (temples), temple models, ceramic workshops, exquisite graphite-painted and white-encrusted pottery, spondylus jewelry, and a ritual tableau consisting of 26 miniature clay objects representing altars, female figurines, tables, vases, chairs, and drums. A cemetery of inhumation graves lies near the tell.

Excav. by H. Todorova 1972–75. Lit.: H. Todorova, *Ovčarovo*, Sofia, 1976.

OZIERI Culture

A burgeoning Late Neolithic Sardinian culture, end of the 5th and early 4th mill. B.C., characterized by hypogea (underground tombs) and an extraordinary ceramic tradition. Vases in a great assortment of shapes were incised and painted with a rich variety of symbols and mythical images, similar in value to Late Cucuteni paintings of the same period.

PADINA

Site in the Iron Gate Gorge, N Yugoslavia, related to Lepenski Vir.

Excav. by B. Jovanović 1968–71. Lit.: B. Jovanović, *Arh. Pregl.* 10 (1968); *Stare Kulture u Djerdapu* (1969); *Arch. Iugoslavica* 9 (1971).

PARŢA

Early and Classical Vinča settlement SW of Timişoara, SW Romania. Noted for two temples with monumental sculptures and bucrania.

Excav. by I. Miloia 1931; M. Moga 1943 and 1951; M. Moga and O. Radu 1962–63; from 1980 to present by G. Lazarovici. Museum: Timişoara. Lit.: G. Lazarovici 1979; *Varia Arch. Hungarica* 2 (1989): 149–74.

PASSO DI CORVO

The largest ditched village in the Tavoliere Plain, located 5 km north of Foggia, SE Italy, from the 2nd half of the 6th mill. B.C. Consists of some 100 compounds of C-shaped ditches, girded by an outer ditch of c. 1 km across. The center part with several C-shaped ditches has been explored, revealing a small rectangular house on a stone foundation with an apsidal end. The settlement is typified by exquisite painted pottery and black-burnished round and egg-shaped vessels of Scaloria type. The treasured find is a Goddess figurine marked with M signs and butterflies.

Excav. by S. Tinè 1965–80. Lit.: S. Tinè, *Passo di Corvo*, 1983.

PÉCEL
See *Baden.*

PETREȘTI Culture
From the Mureș basin in Transylvania dated to the middle 5th and early 4th mill. B.C., related to classical Cucuteni. Trichrome painted pottery is typical.

PFYN
A lakeshore village with nine houses from c. 3000 B.C., Canton Thurgau, Switzerland. A name-giving site for the Late Neolithic in E Switzerland.
Excav. 1944 by K. Keller-Tarnuzzer. Lit.: O. Tschumi, *Urgeschichte der Schweiz* I (1949): 717ff.

PLOČNIK
Late Vinča settlement at Prokuplje, S Yugoslavia with c. 3 m of cultural deposits. The name is used to designate late Vinča.
Excav. by M. Grbić 1927; by B. Stalio 1968-70. Museum: National Museum, Belgrade. Lit.: M. Grbić, *Äneolithiche Ansiedlung*, Belgrade (NM), 1929.

POLJANICA (POLYANICA)
A Chalcolithic tell south of Trgovište, N Bulgaria, with eight consecutive building levels forming a cultural layer 3 m thick, from the end of the 6th throughout the 1st half of the 5th mill. B.C. Distinct for its well-organized settlement plan surrounded by wooden palisades. Buildings are from one to three rooms, symmetrically and compactly grouped according to the four cardinal points. Entrances through the palisades were half way in each side.
Excav. by H. Todorova 1972. Lit.: H. Todorova, 1978: 48-51, tables 18-21.

PORODIN
Tell settlement near Bitola, S Yugoslavia. Macedonian Early Neolithic, c. 6000 to early 6th mill. B.C. Noted for temple models of clay, sculptured art, and exquisite painted pottery.
Excav. by M. Grbić, et. al. 1953-54. Lit.: M. Grbić, et al., 1960.

RADIAL-DECORATED POTTERY
See *Baden.*

RAST
A stratified tell with Early and Classical Vinča materials on the bank of Țifarului stream, less than 300 m from the Danube, S of Craiova, W Romania, covering more than 10,000 sq m. Although partly destroyed, it yielded quantities of ceramic and stone objects. Noted for the richly decorated and inscribed figurines, offering vessels, and other ritual objects.

Excav. by V. Dumitrescu et. al. 1943, 1950. Lit.: V. Dumitrescu, 1980.

RENDINA
A stratified Early Neolithic settlement of a ditched village type in the Ofanto River valley, SE Italy, dated from the end of the 7th to the mid-6th mill. B.C. The site yielded three phases (I–III) of the late Impresso culture of S Italy, revealing a gradual sequence of culture. Period III ceramics included anthropomorphic vases, vases decorated with symbols, figurines, and seals. Cereals, pulses, and five domestic animal species—cattle, sheep, goat, pig, and dog—were present.
Excav. by M. Cippolloni Sampò 1970-76. Lit.: M.C. Sampò, 1982.

RÖSSEN
Late phase of the LBK culture with elements deriving from Kurgan I. The name comes from the cemetery near Merseburg, C Germany.
Excav. 1882-90. Lit.: F. Niquet, *Das Gräberfeld von Rössen*, Museum Halle Publications 9, 1938.

RUDNA GLAVA
Vinča copper mines in the mountainous region of NE Serbia near the towns of Rudna Glava and Donje Milanovec, from the first half of the 5th mill. B.C. Thirty shafts were uncovered which yielded stone tools and ceramic objects of the Vinča culture (including fine black-channeled vases and an offering table with ram's head protome.
Excav. by B. Jovanović 1968-79. Lit.: B. Jovanović, 1986; 1980; 1982.

SALCUȚA
A stratified settlement site in Oltenia, north of the Danube, distr. of Craiova, SW Romania, with Starčevo materials at the bottom, followed after a sterile layer by classical and late Vinča, then by Coțofeni, and topped with Bronze Age deposits. Eponymous site for the 5th mill. population from Oltenia and Banat, a variant of the Vinča culture, related to Gumelnița and Karanovo V–VI.
Excav. by I. Andrieșescu 1916-20; H. Dumitrescu 1947; D. Berciu 1961. Lit.: D. Berciu, *Contribuții la problemele neoliticului in Romînia,* (Bucharest, 1961): 158ff.

SALZMÜNDE
A fortified hilltop settlement and non-megalithic inhumation graves from the end of the 4th mill. B.C. on the middle Saale River, NW of Halle, C Germany. Eponymous site for a culture group in C Germany and Bohemia following Baalberge phase. A Kurganized group, with patriarchal elements and warlike character, contemporary with the

megalith builders of the Walternienburg group in the Elbe basin.
Lit.: P. Grimm, "Salzmünder Kultur," *Jahreschrift Halle* 29 (1938).

SAMARA Culture
An early Eneolithic culture of c. 5000 B.C. from the forest-steppe area of the Middle Volga region showing evidence of horse sacrifice, sculptures of horses and oxen, and the use of flint and bone daggers.

SAMOGYVÁR
See *Vinkovci.*

SARNATE
A peat bog site of the Narva culture from the end of the 4th mill. B.C. in the distr. of Alsunga, W Latvia, which yielded timber-frame, above-ground rectangular houses, quantities of wooden utensils, fishing tools and nets, ladles in a waterbird shape, a large Goddess sculpture, a boat, amber workshop, layers of nuts, large Narva-type pots, etc.
Excav. by E. Šturms and L. Vankina. Lit: L. Vankina, 1970.

SARNOWO
A cemetery of long triangular barrows (30-60 m long) from the mid-4th mill. B.C., distr. Włocławek, Kujawia, W Poland. Barrow 9 was built for a woman 70 years old who was buried in a coffin under a ritual wooden structure.
Excav. by Królikowska 1947. Lit.: W. Chmielewski, *Zagadnienie grobowców Kujawskich* (Warsaw, 1952); H. Wikłak, *Prace i Materiály Muzeum Arch. i Etnogr. w Łodzi* 33 (1986): 5-19.

SAVA
A tell settlement near Varna, E Bulgaria. Eponymous site for cultural group on the Black Sea coast, preceding the cemetery of Varna and contemporary with Karanovo V (or "Marica") in C Bulgaria; early 5th mill. B.C.
Lit.: M. Mirčev and D. Zlatarski, "Selištnata mogila pri selo Sava." *Izvestija na Varnenskoto Archeol. Družestvo* 11 (1960); H. Vaisová (Todorova), *Slovenská Arheológia* 14 (1966).

SCALORIA
Cave at Manfredonia, SE Italy, with deposits from the Upper Paleolithic, Early Neolithic Impresso, and Middle Neolithic ("Scaloria") period, with exquisite painted pottery from the second half of the 6th mill. B.C. Consists of wide upper and narrow lower caves with stalagmites and stalactites. Whole vases and sherds of 1500 painted vases are recorded with designs associated with the theme of regeneration; 137 whole and disarticulated skeletons were found at the entrance to the

lower cave. Spring water is found at the bottom of the sleeve-shaped lower cave, clearly the holiest area. Vases were deposited at the stalagmites.

Excav. by Q. Quagliati 1930; M. Gimbutas, S.M. Winn, D.M. Shimabuku 1978–80. Lit.: U. Rellini, *La piu antica ceramica dipinta in Italia*, 1934; *Bollettino Palaeoist. Italiana* 56–57 (1936–37); S.M. Winn and D.M. Shimabuku, "The Heritage of Two Subsistence Strategies: Preliminary Report on the Excavations at Grotta Scaloria, Southeastern Italy, 1978," *Anthropology 9*, Dept. of Anthrop., Saint Mary's Univ., Halifax, N. Sc., Canada.

SEEBERG-BURGÄSCHI SÜD
One of the best explored Swiss lakeshore villages of the Cortaillod culture, mid 4th mill B.C., located at Lake Burgäschi in the Swiss midlands. Remarkable for the preservation of pile dwellings and wooden implements. Excavations by Bern Historical Museum in 1952, 1957, and 1958. From 1957 excavated by Hansjürgen Müller-Beck.

Lit.: 9 vols. in *Acta Bernensia-Seeberg, Burgäschi-Süd*, 1963–73. Hansjürgen Müller-Beck, 1961, 1965.

SEINE-OISE-MARNE (SOM)
The final Neolithic-Copper Age culture of the Paris basin, early 3rd mill. B.C., best known for its gallery-grave-type megaliths and rock-cut tombs.

SELEVAC
A Vinča settlement in the Lower Morava valley between Smederovo and Smederevska Palanka, Serbia, Yugoslavia. Cultural deposits with nine habitation horizons yielded classical Vinča materials of three phases from between 5000 and 4400 B.C.

Excav. by R. Tringham and D. Krstić 1976–78. Lit.: R. Tringham and D. Krstić, eds., *Selevac*, 1990.

SERRA D'ALTO
Settlement and cemetery site near Matera, Basilicata, Italy. Type site of the Middle Neolithic of S Italy, 5th mill. B.C.

Excav. by D. Ridola and U. Rellini 1919. Museum: Museo di Matera. Lit.: Mayer, *Molfetta und Matera*, 1924.

SESKLO Culture
A Neolithic culture of Thessaly and southern Macedonia, c. 6500–5500 B.C. which reached its climax by 6000 B.C. The name-giving site is a stratified settlement west of Volos, Thessaly, which includes early, middle, and late Sesklo layers, followed by Dimini layer.

Excav. by C. Tsountas 1901–02; D. R. Theocharis 1957–77. Museum: Volos. Lit.: C. Tsountas 1908; D.R. Theocharis, *Praktika*

32 (1957); *Thessalika 1* (1958); *Neolithic Greece*, 1973.

SILBURY HILL
The largest human constructed mound in Neolithic Europe, 5.5 miles west of Marlborough, Wiltshire. Its base has a turf core covered by layers of soil and chalk rubble, dated to c. 2600 B.C. It is 130 ft. high and covers 5.25 acres, surrounded by a silted ditch.

Lit.: R. J. C. Atkinson, *Silbury Hill* (London, 1969); Idem., *Antiquity* 42: 299; *Antiquity* 43: 216; M. Dames, 1956.

SIPINTSI (SCHIPENITZ)
A late Cucuteni settlement northwest of Chernovitsi on the bank of the Prut River, W Ukraine (Bukovina), USSR, noted for pictorial vase painting.

Lit.: O. Kandyba, *Schipenitz*, 1947.

SITAGROI
Tell in the Drama Plain, NW Greece, with 12 m of cultural debris representing five periods, 5500–2500 B.C. Periods I and II: Late Neolithic (synchronous with Karanovo III and IV); period III: Chalcolithic (synchronous with Karanovo V–VI); periods IV and V: Balkano-Danubian culture of the Early Bronze Age.

Excav. by C. Renfrew and M. Gimbutas 1968–69. Lit.: C. Renfrew, M. Gimbutas, E. Elster, *Sitagroi*, 1986.

SITTARD
An LBK settlement in the province of Limburg, The Netherlands, 2nd half of the 6th mill. B.C. In an occupied area over 600 m long, 22 complete and 26 incomplete longhouses were found. Ceramics of several phases and c. 800 flint tools were uncovered from pits.

Excav. by P.J.R. Modderman 1953–58. Lit.: *Palaeohistoria* 6–7 (1958–59): 33ff.

SKORBA
Site of a settlement and the ruins of temples from the Ġgantija to Tarxien phases, mid-4th to mid-3rd mill. B.C. in N Malta. A two-room building from the end of the 5th mill. B.C. (Red Skorba period) which had a religious function contained a group of figurines with triangular masks. A village from the pre-temple period yielded important information on the domestication of plants and animals, with evidence of lentils, barley, emmer and club wheat, sheep, goats, and cattle.

Excav. by D. Trump, 1960–63; Museum: National Museum, Valletta. Lit.: D. Trump, *Skorba*, 1966.

SMILČIĆ
Settlement of the Impresso culture overlaid by Danilo layers near Zadar, Dalmatia, W Yugoslavia.

Excav. 1957–59 by Š. Batović 1962. Museum: Zadar. Lit.: Š. Batović, *Diadora* 2 (1960–61); 1966.

STARČEVO Culture
Neolithic culture of C Yugoslavia, S Romania, and SE Hungary, c. 6300–5300 B.C., whose traditions are closely related to the cultures of Thessaly and Macedonia. Name-giving settlement of the Starčevo culture is near Belgrade, Yugoslavia.

Excav. by M. Grbić; by V. Fewkes, H. Goldman, and R. W. Ehrich 1931–32. Museum: National Museum, Belgrade. Lit.: V. Fewkes, *Bull. Am. School Preh. Research* 9 (1936); D. Arandjelović-Garašanin, *Starčevacka Kultura* (1954).

STEIN
LBK settlement in the Province of Limburg. In an area of one hectare, 50 houses of various LBK phases were uncovered. The largest was 37 m long and 7.5 m wide.

Excav. by P. J. R. Modderman 1962–63. Lit.: P. J. R. Modderman, 1970.

STENTINELLO
Late Impresso settlement at Syracuse, Sicily. The name is also used to designate Sicilian Early Neolithic.

Excav. by P. Orsi 1890, 1912, 1920; by S. Tinè 1961. Museum: Museo di Siracusa. Lit.: P. Orsi, *BPI* 16 (1890); 36 (1910); S. Tinè, *Arch. Stor. Siracusano* 7 (1961).

STONEHENGE
The most celebrated henge monument in Britain, located in the Salisbury Plain near Amesbury, Wiltshire. Reconstructed many times, Stonehenge I, c. 3000 B.C., was a circular monument, 107 m in diameter, with a wooden building in the center. Inside the ditch and bank is a circle with 56 holes which contained human cremations. About 1800 B.C. or earlier, the monument was altered: two concentric rings of sockets were dug in the center for the erection of 82 bluestones imported from the Prescelly Mountains in Pembrokeshire, Wales. To Stonehenge II belongs the avenue of two parallel banks leading to the Avon River more than 3 km away. Stonehenge III belongs to the Wessex culture of the Bronze Age. The bluestones were replaced by huge predressed sarsen stones set as a circle of uprights with a continuous, curving lintel enclosing a U-shaped arrangement of five trilithons. There has been much discussion on its association with megalithic astronomy.

Lit.: R. J. C. Atkinson, *Stonehenge*, 1956; A. Burl, D. C. Heggie, *Megalithic Science* (London, 1981); C. L. N. Ruggles, *Megalithic Astronomy*, BAR 123 (London, 1984).

STŘELICE
Lengyel settlement at Jevišovice, Znojmo, S Moravia, Czechoslovakia, noted for painted pottery and figurines. Early 5th mill. B.C.

Excav. by J. Palliardi and J. Vildomec, late 19th to early 20th cent. Museum: Boskovštejn near Znojmo and Brno. Lit.: J. Palliardi, *MPC* I (Vienna, 1897); I (1914); J. Vildomec, *OP* 7/8 (Prague, 1928–29); 12 (Prague, 1940); J. Neustupný, *AR* 3 (1951).

STROKED POTTERY
Later phase of the LBK culture, c. 4700–4400 B.C.

ŠVENTOJI
A peatbog site of the Narva culture near the Baltic Sea, north of Palanga, end of the 4th–early 3rd mill. B.C. Excavated by R. Rimantienė for more than 20 years since 1966. Forty localities were explored. Distinct for exceptional preservation of wooden artifacts, nets, cords, bark, quantities of wooden oars, hoes, pounders, house and fence posts. Workshops, amber artifacts, wooden sculptures, including a 2 m high post with an Owl Goddess face, were also found. The same area yielded a settlement of the early Corded Pottery (Baltic Coast Variant) period.

Lit.: R. Rimantienė, *Šventoji I*, Vilnius (Mokslas), 1979; *Šventoji II*, Vilnius (Mokslas), 1980.

SZATMAR Culture
Earliest Neolithic complex in the Upper Tisza basin.

SZEGVÁR-TÜZKÖVES
Settlement and burials of the Tisza culture at Szentes, SE Hungary. A classic example of two coexistent settlement types: a central tell-like mound flanked by a single-layer settlement. The tell measures 400 × 100 m and is 2.5 m in height; the settlement covered 11 hectares. Excavations of the central mound yielded two phases: early Tisza and classical Tisza, c. 5000–4500 B.C. The site is famous for its clay sculptures of female and male gods, anthropomorphic vases, and pedestalled bowls, among other finds. Although this is a major center of the Tisza culture, it has been recklessly damaged by modern building activities of agricultural cooperatives.

Excav. by J. Czalog 1956–57; J. Korek 1970; M. Seleanu 1978. Museums: Szentes and Nat. Museum, Budapest. Lit.: J. Czalog, 1959, 1972; J. Korek, "Szegvár-Tüzköves. A Settlement of the Tisza Culture," P. Raczky, ed. *The Late Neolithic of the Tisza Region*, 1987: 47–60.

TABLE DES MARCHANDS
A passage grave on the Locmariaquer peninsula, Morbihan, Brittany, distinct for its chamber-facing, 3 m high triangular stone with convex sides and protruding head, decorated in relief with 49 hooks and a cup mark or vulva in the center, symbolic of the Goddess of Regeneration. This is one of the earliest recorded megalithic tombs in Brittany, described since the 18th cent.

Lit.: E. Twohig, (1981): 170.

TANGÎRU
Stratified tell with 12 levels of the Boian and 9 of the Gumelnița periods near Giurgiu, Lower Danube, Romania.

Excav. by D. Berciu 1933–35, 1956, 1957. Lit.: D. Berciu, *Contribuții la problemele neoliticului in Rominia*, (Bucharest, 1961).

TARTARIA
A stratified tell with deposits 3–4 m thick of Early Vinča (Turdaș), Petrești, and Coțofeni cultures in the distr. of Orastie, Transylvania, W Romania. A shaft associated with the earliest (Early Vinča) layer contained the skeleton of a man, 35–40 years old, lying on a layer of ashes, accompanied by 26 schematic figurines of clay and two of alabaster, a spondylus armring, and three baked clay plaques incised with Old European script signs.

Excav. by K. Horedt 1942–43; N. Vlassa 1961. Lit.: K. Horedt, *Apulum* 3 (1947–49): 44ff; N. Vlassa, *Dacia* NS 7 (1963): 485ff.

TARXIEN
One of the finest temple complexes of Malta, located 400 m east of the Hal Saflieni hypogeum in Valletta, dating from c. 3300 B.C. (earliest temple) to 3000–2500 B.C. (main temples). Consists of double and triple temples with egg-shaped chambers and a semicircular forecourt (see figs. 5–28, 5–29). Distinct for a statue of the Goddess, originally 2.5–3 m in height (fig. 7–64), beautifully carved altar blocks with plant spiral motifs, an animal procession, relief carvings of two bulls, and a probable bitch with 13 puppies. A cremation cemetery superimposed on the site is post-Tarxien, dating from c. 2500–2000 B.C.

Museum: Archaeological Mus., Valletta. Lit.: T. Zammit, *Prehistoric Malta, the Tarxien Temples*, (Oxford, 1930); J. D. Evans, 1959 and 1971; D. Trump, *Malta, Archaeological Guide*, (London, 1972): 65–75.

TÉVIEC
Pre-Pottery kitchen midden site and graves, representing predecessors of the megalith builders, on a small island, distr. of Morbihan, Brittany. Some collective graves were uncovered, up to 6 burials together, and 23 inhumation graves. Burials were covered with ritual hearths, the jawbones of stag and boar, and stone mounds; jaws and antlers were found deposited with the skeletons.

Excav. by M. and S.-J. Péquart 1928–30. Lit.: Péquart, *L'Anthropologie* 38 (1928); 39 (1929).

THAYNGEN
A stratified settlement in Kanton Schaffhausen, N Switzerland, with cultural deposits of Michelsberg I and II and Pfyn III cultures from the 2nd half of the 4th mill. B.C. Distinct for the preservation of rectangular timber houses and wooden artifacts. Various building horizons yielded from 5 to 9 houses.

Excav. by K. Sulzberger 1914–22; W. Guyan 1950–63. Lit.: W. Guyan, *Das Pfahlbauproblem* (1955): 221ff; *Helvetia Antiqua* (1966): 21ff.

TIRPEȘTI
Early Cucuteni ("Pre-Cucuteni III") settlement in the distr. of Tg. Neamț, region of Bacău, NE Romania.

Excav. by V. Dumitrescu and S. Marinescu-Bîlcu in the early 1960s. Museums: Nat. Mus. Bucharest and Bacău. Lit.: S. Marinescu-Bîlcu, 1974.

TISZA Culture
Chalcolithic culture located along the Lower Tisza River basin in eastern Hungary and northern Yugoslavia, descended from the Starčevo (Körös) culture, c. 5300–4300 B.C.

TISZADOB
An early phase of the Bükk culture.

TISZAPOLGÁR-BASATANYA
Late Tisza cemetery site (166 graves excav.) at the village of Polgár near Tiszalök, NE Hungary; Early and Middle Copper Age of the Carpathian Basin.

Excav. by F. Tompa 1929; I. Bognár-Kutzián 1946. Museum: Nat. Museum, Budapest. Lit.: I. Bognár-Kutzián, 1963.

TISZAPOLGÁR
End phase of the Tisza culture in NE Hungary, E Slovakia, and W Transylvania, 44th to 39th centuries B.C. The name derives from the cemetery at Polgár, NE Hungary.

TRAIAN
LBK and Cucuteni settlements in N Moldavia, NE Romania, which include: Dealul Fîntînilor with LBK and Early and Classical (Cucuteni A-B) remains; and Dealul Viei with a single layer from the Early Cucuteni ("Pre-Cucuteni I") culture.

Excav. by H. Dumitrescu 1951–59. Museum: Nat. Museum, Bucharest. Lit.: H. Dumitrescu, *SCIV* 3 (1952); 4 (1953); 5 (1954); 6 (1955); *Materiale și Cercetari Arh.* 3 (1957); 5 (1959); H. and V. Dumitrescu, *Mat. Cerc. Arh.* 6 (1959).

TRB

Abbreviated from the Danish *Tragtbaegerkultur* and the German *Trichterbecherkultur*. See *Funnel-necked Beaker* culture.

TRIPOLYE

Classical Cucuteni settlement near Kiev, W Ukraine, eponymous for the Cucuteni civilization in Soviet Moldavia and the W Ukraine.

Excav. by V. V. Khvojka 1899. Museum: Kiev. Lit.: V. V. Khvojka, *Trudy XI Arkh. sjezd* (Kiev, 1901).

TRUȘEȘTI

Cucuteni settlement near Botoşani, N Moldavia. Most of the 98 houses uncovered belong to the Classical Cucuteni (Cucuteni A2) period, mid-5th mill. B.C.

Excav. in 1951–59; by M. Petrescu-Dîmboviţa 1961. Museum: Iaşi. Lit.: M. Petrescu-Dîmboviţa, *Truşeşti*, 1963.

TURDAȘ (Tordos)

Early Vinča settlement on the south bank of the Mureş River, Transylvania, Hunedoara, W Romania. Eponymous for the early Vinča culture, c. 5300–4900 B.C.

Unsystematic excav. end of 19th cent. Museum: Institute of History, Cluj. Lit.: H. Schmidt, *Zeitschrift für Ethnologie*, 1903; M. Roska, *Torma collection*, 1941.

USATOVO-GORODSK-FOLTEȘTI

An amalgam of Kurgan and Cucuteni traditions composed of Usatovo in the steppe region near Odessa, Gorodsk, in the northwestern Ukraine, and Folteşti I in Romanian Moldavia; dated between the 34th and 29th centuries B.C.

VĂDASTRA

Early Vinča settlement near Corabia, Oltenia, SW Romania. The name is also used for the culture in Oltenia.

Excav. by V. Christescu 1926; D. Berciu 1934; C. Mateescu 1946–62. Museum: NAM, Bucharest. Lit.: V. Christescu, *Dacia* 3–4 (1927–33); C. Mateescu, *SCIV* 6 (1955); *Cerc. Arh.* 5–6 (1959); *Arch. Rozhl.* 14 (1962).

VALAČ

Late Vinča settlement near Kosovska Mitrovica, S Yugoslavia, from the first half of the 5th mill. B.C.

Excav. by N. Tasić and J. Glišić 1957. Museum: Kosovska Mitrovica. Lit.: N. Tasić, 1957; N. Tasić, *Glasnik muzeja Kosovo i Metohija* 4–5 (1960): 11–82.

VALCAMONICA

The area of rock engravings in the Alpine Valley of Camonica, particularly concentrated in the vicinity of Capo da Ponte, 55 km north of Brescia, N Italy. A variety of designs and symbols are engraved and pecked, beginning with the Neolithic (Phase I) and ending with the Iron Age (Phase IV). Phase II, c. 3000 B.C., is distinct for the appearance of daggers, halberds, horses, wagons, suns, and sun-worshiping scenes. Compositions of these motifs occur on stelae (see chap. 10) which represent characteristic traits of the Indo-European religion. Many stelae seem to be monuments dedicated to the God of the Shining Sky.

Research on rock engravings has been carried out from the early 1960s to the present by Emmanuel Anati. Lit.: E. Anati, *The Camonica Valley* (London, 1964); 1976.

VALEA LUPULUI

Late Cucuteni (Cucuteni B) settlement on the terrace of the Bahlui River, distr. of Iaşi, NE Romania.

Excav. by M. Petrescu-Dîmboviţa and M. Dinu 1953–57. Museum: Iaşi. Lit.: Petrescu-Dîmboviţa, *SCIV* 5 (1954); 6 (1955); D. Marin, *Materiale Cercetari Arh.* 3 (1957); 5 (1959).

VARNA

Enormously rich cemetery of inhumation graves in the outskirts of the city of Varna, Bulgaria, at the Black Sea, from the mid-5th mill. B.C., revealing thousands of gold, copper, shell, and marble objects.

Excav. by Ivan Ivanov 1972–76. Lit.: I. Ivanov, *Treasures of the Varna Chalcholithic Necropolis* (Sofia, Septemvri 1978); M. Gimbutas, *Archaeology* 30.1 (1977): 44–51; M. Gimbutas, *Expedition* 19.4 (1977): 39–46.

VARVAROVKA (VARVARIVKA)

Late Cucuteni (Tripolye) settlement near Kishenev, Moldavia.

Excav. by V.I. Makarevich 1967. Museum: Kishenev.

VESELINOVO

Karanovo tell of the Karanovo III period, distr. of Jambol, E Bulgaria. Name also used for the culture of this period.

Excav. by V. Mikov. Lit.: V. Mikov, *Izvestija* 13 (Sofia, 1939).

VÉSZTÖ-MÁGOR

One of the impressive tell settlements of the Tisza culture in E Hungary, covering 4.5 hectares; 230 sq m excavated. Nine cultural levels revealed deposits of the Szakálhát type (early Tisza, transitional between Körös and classical Tisza), three levels of Tisza proper (with 44 burials), and a Copper Age (Tiszapolgár) level which was covered, after a hiatus, with three Middle Bronze Age levels. The site is distinct for the remains of large two-room houses, including a possible temple which held a rich ritual assemblage of monumental sculptures, tables, vases, etc.

Excav. by K. Hegedüs 1972–76. Lit.: K. Hegedüs and J. Makkay, "Vésztö-Mágor. A Settlement of the Tisza Culture," *The Late Neolithic of the Tisza Region*, P. Raczky, ed. 1987: 82–103.

VIDRA

Settlement near Giurgiu, southeast of Bucharest, noted for its figurine and plastic art. Lowest level belongs to the Boian-Giuleşti phase, followed by the Boian-Vidra and Gumelniţa layers.

Excav. by V. Rosetti 1931–33 and 1958. Museum: Bucharest City. Lit.: V. Rosetti, *Săpăturile de la Vidra*, 1934; *Publ. Muz. Municip. Buchreşti* 1–2 (1935–36); *Ipek* 12 (1938); *Materiale Cercetari Arh.* 7 (1961).

VINČA

Settlement site with a mound of cultural remains 10.5 m deep, 14 km SE of Belgrade on the Danube River, Belo Brdo distr., Yugoslavia. The two earliest settlements (below 8 m) belong to the Starčevo culture, above which were 7 m of deposits characteristic of the Vinča civilization, subdivided into four consecutive phases.

Excav. by M. Vasić 1908–12, 1924, 1928–32. Museum: National Museum, Belgrade, and University of Belgrade. Lit.: M. Vasić, *Preistoriska Vinča* I–IV (1932–36).

VINKOVCI

Symbiosis of local Post-Vučedol and intrusive Yamna pastoral culture in C Yugoslavia and Hungary, possible parent to the Bell Beaker Culture. Also known as Samogyvár.

VLADIMIROVKA (VLADIMIRIVKA)

Classical Cucuteni (Tripolye B) settlement with c. 200 houses in the S Bug valley, W Ukraine.

Excav. by B. Bezvenglinski 1927–28; T.S. Passek 1940. Lit.: T. S. Passek, *Céramique tripolienne*, 1935; 1949.

VLASAC

One of the best explored Mesolithic sites of the Lepenski Vir culture in the Iron Gate region, 9th–8th mill. B.C. including trapezoidal structures and egg-shaped sculptures.

Excav. by D. Srejović and Z. Letica in the 1970s. Lit: Srejović and Letica, 1978 (includes extensive reports on human and animal bones by J. Nemeskéri and S. Bökönyi).

VUČEDOL

A Kurganized culture which followed the Baden culture in the NW Balkans in the early 3rd mill. B.C. Called the "Zók" culture in

Hungary and the "Laibach-Ljubljana" culture in the E Alpine area. Vučedol materials are found as far south as the Adriatic islands and in Bohemia and C Germany in the northwest. Migration to the northwest and south which began c. 3000–2800 B.C. was caused by the intrusion of Yamna people into Yugoslavia and Hungary.

WALTERNIENBURG
A cemetery of late passage-grave tombs in the R. Elbe basin, distr. of Magdeburg, Germany. Eponymous site for the "Walternienburg-Bernburg" culture, a variant of TRB.
Lit.: N. Niklasson, *Jahres Schrift Halle* 13 (1925); U. Fischer, *Die Gräber der Steinzeit*, 1956.

WEST KENNET
One of the longest barrows in Britain, 8 km west of Marlborough, Wiltshire. The burial chamber has five niches at the end of tomb with a crescent-shaped forecourt. Burial deposits consisted of approximately 40 disarticulated inhumations dating from the late 4th mill. B.C.
Excav. by S. Piggott 1955–56. Lit.: S. Piggott, *The West Kennet Long Barrow* (London, 1962).

WINDMILL HILL
A causewayed camp in Britain, 1.6 km north of Avebury, Wiltshire, enclosed by three discontinuous ditches, the outer having a diameter of 1200 ft. (c. 400 m). Occupation began before the mid-4th mill. B.C., and the monument was used from the later 4th throughout the 3rd mill. B.C. as shown by Windmill Hill, Peterborough, Rinyo-Clacton, and Beaker sherds found in the outer ditch.
Lit.: I. F. Smith, 1965.

XEMXIJA
Egg- or kidney-shaped, rock-cut tombs with collective burials in N Malta from the pre-temple period, considered to be prototypes for the shape of Maltese temples. Some tombs have several recesses and partitions of stone. Human bones were found in disorder, mixed with animal bones.
Excav. in 1955. Museum: National Museum, Valletta. Lit.: J. D. Evans, 1959 and 1971.

YAMNA
See *Kurgan culture*.

ZEDMAR
See *Nemunas culture*.

ZENGÖVÁRKONY
Settlement and cemetery of the Lengyel culture near Pécs, SW Hungary. The cemetery held 368 burials, most of which were single inhumations.
Excav. by J. Dombay 1936–48. Museum: Pécs. Lit.: J. Dombay, "A Zengövárkonyi öskori telep es temetö," *Arch. Hung.* 23 (1939); "Die Siedlung und das Gräberfeld in Zengövárkony," *Arch. Hung.* 37 (1960).

ZÓK
See *Vučedol*.

ZWENKAU
LBK settlement near Leipzig, Germany. In an area of 7,000 sq m, 24 complete and 3 incomplete houses were uncovered which varied in sizes from 12 to 36.5 m in length (smaller houses in later phases).
Excav. by K. Tackenberg 1935; H. Quitta 1952–57. Lit.: K. Tackenberg, *Germania* 21 (1937): 217ff; H. Quitta, *Germania* 31 (1935): 119ff; *Neue Ausgrabungen in Deutschland* (1958): 68ff.

GLOSSARY OF TECHNICAL TERMS

aceramic
A pre-ceramic stage of Neolithic culture.

acropolis
A citadel or fortified site on an elevated location.

allée couverte
(See *gallery grave*.)

alluviation
The deposit of sediment through the flow of water.

Anatolia
The former name of Asia Minor, the western peninsula of Asia, including Turkey, lying between the Black Sea and the Mediterranean.

anthropomorphic
In human form.

apse, apsidal end
A semicircular recess in a building.

askos
Bird-shaped vase.

Atlantic period
Warm and moist climatic period, c. 5500–3000 B.C.

Aurignacian
The Upper Paleolithic period associated with Cro-Magnon populations and the first cave art, characterized by Aurignacian flint industry, dated c. 43,000–31,000 B.C.

blade
A long parallel-sided flake struck from a specially prepared core.

Bonu Ighinu period
Middle Neolithic of Sardinia, mid-5th millennium B.C. Oven or egg-shaped rock-cut tombs are distinctive of this period. Stiff Nude sculptures in the Sardinian style were placed with the dead. Pottery is well burnished in a variety of shapes, incised or dotted, including symbols of horns and vulvas.

Boreal period
Postglacial subdivision of climate with rising temperature; continental (dry). Start of mixed oak forests; c. 7700–5500 B.C.

Brachycephalic
"Short headed" with a cephalic index above 80, having a breadth of head at least four-fifths as great as the length from front to back.

Bronze Age
The second of the three-stage system (stone, bronze, iron), typified by the use of bronzes of copper and arsenic, copper and tin, and copper with arsenic-tin (As, Sn, As-An bronze). Bronze was harder than copper. Its beginning in Europe during the second half of the 4th mill. B.C. is linked with the Black Sea region (Circum-Pontic zone) and coincides with the first evidence of weapons of hard metal.

bucranium
Bull/ox/cow skull rendered in clay or other material, symbolizing the regenerative uterus. Found throughout Old Europe and the Near East, particularly in temples and hypogea dedicated to rituals of regeneration.

burin
A pointed tool made of chipped flint or stone used to engrave antler, bone, ivory, and other materials.

cairn
A mound of stones covering a burial chamber.

calibrated chronology
Radiocarbon chronology calibrated (checked) with dendrochronology which determines the true age of an object. Calibration has shown that uncalibrated radiocarbon dates are too low.

caprovines
Animals with cloven hooves—goats and sheep (*capra* and *ovis*).

cardial pottery
Pottery impressed with the edge of cardium shells.

cardium edule shells
Shells used in the decoration of impresso or cardial pottery, widely found in the central and western Mediterranean area.

carination
A sharp break in the curve of a vessel's profile.

causewayed camps or **enclosures**
Earthworks, located near megalithic tombs or long-barrows, consisting of roughly oval areas surrounded by ditches broken at intervals by earthen causeways. These may have served as sites for seasonal celebrations, the cremation of human bodies, and rituals associated with death and regeneration. Causewayed camps are particularly rich in southern Britain and Wales and are also found in Denmark and Sweden during the passage-grave period.

Chalcolithic
(See *Eneolithic*.)

chambered tombs
Found in western England, southern Wales, and Scotland, these are related to the court tombs of Ireland and to passage graves. A stone mortuary hut is incorporated into a long-barrow mound which was opened for ritual deposits and successive interments. The chambered tombs of the Orkney are dated between the end of the 4th and the mid-3rd mill. B.C.

channelled decoration
Grooved decoration, typical of Vinča ware.

cist
A stone coffin.

Common European Horizon
The earliest phase of the Corded Pottery complex, c. 3000–2600 B.C.

Copper Age
Use of pure copper metallurgy in east-central Europe, 5500–3500 B.C.

cordon
A strip of clay applied to the surface of a pot before firing.

cord ornament
Pottery decoration produced by impressing a twisted cord into the surface of the soft clay. The Corded Ware culture of the early and mid-3rd mill. B.C. in central and northern Europe takes its name from this mode of decoration.

court tombs
Irish tombs, also called "horned tombs," possibly dated to the first half of the 4th mill. B.C. These consist of a large court and chambers covered by a triangular, trapezoidal, or somewhat rectangular stone cairn.

Cro-Magnon
An early form of Homo sapiens with a robust physique, known from skeletal parts found in the Cro-Magnon cave in the Dordogne, southern France, associated with Upper Paleolithic tools.

crosta soil
a calcarious stratum, resistant to water penetration, usually found on slight rises or hills.

cup mark
A cup-shaped pit, often surrounded by a circle or concentric circles, carved on megaliths, menhirs, and other stones. Water gathered in these "cups" is to this day considered to have healing properties.

cursus
A structure consisting of a long avenue defined by two parallel earthen banks with quarry ditches outside them. Found in Late Neolithic Britain.

dendrochronology
The science dealing with the study of the annual rings of trees determining the dates and chronological order of past events. In 1929, A. E. Douglass showed how this method could be used to date archeological material. Recent studies based on California bristlecone pine established a floating chronology going back to 7210 B.C. which is applicable for the Neolithic. This method checks the validity of radiocarbon chronology. (See *radiocarbon*.)

dentalium shell
Any tooth shell of the genus *Dentalium*.

Diana period
Final Neolithic of southern Italy; end of the 5th and early 4th millennia B.C. Typical are round vessels with shining surfaces. Also called "Bellavista type."

dolichocephalic
Long headed, with a cephalic index below 75, having a breadth of head which is small in proportion to the length from front to back. The index is obtained by expressing the maximum breadth as a percentage of maximum length.

dolmen
A megalithic structure consisting of two or more upright stones covered with a capstone typically forming a chamber. Dolmen is also used as a descriptive term for megalithic chamber tombs.

domus de Janas
"Witches house" or subterranean tomb of the Ozieri period of Sardinia. Consists of simple egg-shaped rooms as well as elaborate complexes of halls and chambers painted with red, purple, and yellow ochre and symbols of regeneration.

earthen long-barrows
(See *long-barrows*.)

Eneolithic
"Copper and stone culture," from Latin *eneos*, "copper," and *Lithos*, "stone." Same as *Chalcolithic*, from Greek *chalcos*, "copper."

endogamy
Marriage within the same kin-group, as opposed to exogamy.

Epicardial
Late Cardial pottery of the fully agricultural society of the 6th mill. B.C. in southern France and eastern Spain. This includes not only shell-impressed pottery (rare) but also applied cordons, channelling, punctuations, incisions, beaded decoration, and other techniques.

Epipaleolithic
Latest Paleolithic culture, used also to express the continuation of these traditions into the Mesolithic.

eponymous
In archeology, the name given to a place, tribe, or culture derived from the representative site where it is first discovered.

ex voto
(See *votive*.)

excarnation
The exposure of human bodies to birds of prey to remove the flesh.

exogamy
Marriage, usually by the woman, outside of her kin-group.

figulina pottery
Delicate ceramics from the Late Neolithic Serra d'Alto culture in southern Italy, mid-5th mill. B.C. Made of fine orange or cream-colored clay, either left plain or painted in dark brown or red. Geometric motifs and inventive handles in the shapes of animals or spirals. Required refined kiln firing. Widely traded.

fruitstand
An open bowl having a high pedestal base produced for the purpose of ritual offerings, often exquisitely decorated by painting and incision. Particularly rich examples are known from the Lengyel, Tisza, Petreşti, and Cucuteni cultures.

gallery grave
A megalithic chambered tomb dating to the late 4th and early 3rd millennia B.C. consisting of an elongated room built of massive boulders.

greenstone
A loose term comprising a variety of rocks such as serpentine, olivine, jade, jadeite, and nephrite, used for the production of Neolithic axes and jewelry.

gylany
A term coined by Riane Eisler to represent a balance and equality between the sexes. *Gy* is from the Greek root word *gyne*, meaning "woman," *an* is from *andros*, "man," and the letter *l* stands for "linking."

henge monuments
Huge circular banked enclosures with internal ditches having one or more entrances, constructed as ceremonial gathering places. The central area can be empty or contain a circle of stones, remains of wooden posts, or pits. Henges are found in Britain and in central Europe. Henges from the Lengyel (often misinterpreted as fortified settlements) and LBK cultures belong to the 5th mill. B.C., a tradition continuous in Old Europe for several millennia.

hill fort
A fortified hilltop enclosed by one or more ramparts of stone, or earth and ditches. Not known to Europe before the Kurgan I influence.

hüyük
Tell, in Turkish.

hypogeum
An underground tomb, usually with one or more egg-shaped chambers. The largest cluster is the hypogeum at Hal Saflieni in eastern Malta in which the dead were buried from

the 4th mill. until around 2500 B.C. Great numbers of hypogea are known from the Ozieri culture in Sardinia.

Iberia
Ancient name for Portugal and Spain.

impresso pottery
Pottery whose outer surface is smoothed and decorated with impressions of cardial edule shell or fingernail. Same as cardial pottery. Found in the Adriatic and the West Mediterranean area between 6500–5500 B.C.

Indo-European (IDE)
A family of languages characterized by basic vocabularies that have many correspondences of inflection, grammatical number, gender, and ablaut, including Indo-Iranian, Slavic, Baltic, Germanic, Celtic, Romance, Greek, Albanian, Armenian branches, and a number of dead languages. The term *Indo-Germanic* is used in German; *Aryan* applies for Indo-Iranian but is also used as a generic term for IDE. See **Proto-Indo-European** for the pre-historic parent language and culture.

in situ
Found in its original location.

kerbstone, -s; curbstone, -s
One of the stones or a range of stones forming a curb along the outer edge of an earthen mound.

kernos, *pl.* kernoi
A ceramic piece usually in the form of a ring to which a number of cups or miniature vases were attached, used for offerings.

kurgan
A Turkic loanword meaning a *barrow* or *tumulus* in Russian, used by the author to designate the round barrows including single burials of the seminomadic patriarchal pastoralists of southern Russia, expressing burial rites which are different from Old European long-barrows and other mounds. The kurgan is a feature of the steppe.

Kurgan tradition
A term applied to Proto-Indo-European (PIE) traditions linked with the Kurgan culture which spread into Europe during the period of 4300–2800 B.C.

Linkardstown barrows
A type of tomb from east-central Ireland consisting of stone cists under round mounds used for single burials only. These date to the mid-4th mill. B.C. and signal the arrival of the first people of Kurgan tradition as far west as Ireland.

lithic
Pertaining to the use of stone, from Greek *lithos,* "stone."

loess
A wind-borne rock dust carried from moraines and outwash deposits, laid down as a stratum during periglacial conditions in the area surrounding the ice sheets in central Europe. Early farmers of the LBK culture found it rich and easy to till.

long-barrows
Triangular or trapezoidal earthen burial enclosures, often found in clusters, retained by either stone or timber frames with entrances in the middle of the wide end, opening to the rising sun. Most barrows range from 25 to 45 m, or are as long as 170 m. They are found in Denmark, northern Germany, and western and southern Poland and are associated with the TRB population of the 4th mill. B.C., except for their extension into England where they range from southern England to southern Scotland.

Los Millares type tomb
A passage grave with a short corridor and circular chamber or tholos, covered with a round, earthen mound surrounded by a ring of stones. These continued in Iberia throughout the late 4th and early 3rd mill. B.C. The name comes from Los Millares cemetery and township near the coast in Almeria, southeastern Spain, dated to c. 3000 B.C.

Magdalenian
The final Paleolithic culture of western Europe, 15,000–9,000 B.C., famous for its cave and mobiliary art. Named after the site of La Madeleine, Dordogne, France.

magula
The Greek term used for a tell, or mound-shaped layers of settlement debris from the Neolithic and Early Bronze Age in the Aegean area, particularly Thessaly and Macedonia.

matriarchy
A social system in which the dominant authority is held by women.

matriliny, matrilineal
A social structure in which ancestral descent and inheritance is traced through the female line.

matrilocal
The home territory of a matrilineal kin group.

matristic society
A matrilineal "partnership" society in which women are honored but do not subjugate men.

megalith
A huge stone, erected singly or as part of a burial monument.

megalithic culture
A term used for western European matrilineal societies using megalithic structures as sacred ossuaries and ceremonial centers.

megalithic monuments
Ritual structures composed of huge stones found in Western Europe, primarily in France, Iberia, England, Ireland, Denmark, northwestern Germany, and southern Sweden, as well as on the islands of Malta. These include standing stones called menhirs, tombs for the collective deposition of bones (passage graves, gallery graves, and circular chambers), and temples (in Malta). The earliest date is from Brittany (c. 4700 B.C.) showing a duration of at least 2000 years. Megalithic tombs are often in the shape of a vagina and uterus, or in the anthropomorphic shape of the body of the Goddess, symbols of regeneration.

megaron
A building consisting of a rectangular room with a central hearth and porch, as found during the Bronze Age, used by a chieftain or the warrior elite. Not to be confused with Neolithic temples which consist of two rooms, temple proper and workshop.

menhir
A standing stone associated with megalithic tombs, some representing the Goddess of Death and Regeneration in the form of the Owl Goddess.

metronymy
Naming through the female line. The father is not formally recognized.

Mesolithic
Literally "middle stone" age between the Upper Paleolithic and Neolithic. A hunting and collecting way of life persisted in the new environment created by the withdrawal of the ice sheets around 8300 B.C. Flint industries are often distinguished by microliths.

Millares, Los
(See *Los Millares.*)

microlithic tools
Small tools less than 2 cm long, made on a blade or flake. These often occur in geometric shapes.

mother-kinship system
A matrilineal, matristic social structure which recognizes women as progenators of the clan. Woman as mother is the social center. The society is usually endogamous.

Mousterian epoch
Middle Paleolithic, roughly 100,000 years ago, associated with Neanderthal populations.

mudbrick
Unbaked brick.

Neolithic
Literally "new stone" age in which humans lived a settled life, used ground stone tools, and produced their own food by the cultivation of crops and the domestication of animals.

obsidian
A natural glass of gray to black color found in volcanic areas. Obsidian was a main trade item for millennia during the Neolithic used for tools, particularly sickle blades. Spectrographic analysis of trace elements allow most of the sources to be identified. The most important sites in Europe were the Melos island in the Aegean, Monte Arci in Sardinia, Lipari off Sicily, and the Carpathian Mountains in northeast Hungary and eastern Slovakia.

ochre
Red, orange, or yellow oxides of iron.

ornithomorphic
Bird shaped.

orthostats
Upright side stones which often surround a megalithic tomb.

ossuary
Tomb or other site for the deposition of bones. Neolithic ossuaries functioned as sacred communal centers, providing a link between the living kin and the ancestors.

Paleolithic
Literally "old stone" age, beginning with the emergence of humans and the manufacture of tools, some three million years ago. Divided into Lower, Middle, and Upper, the Paleolithic lasted until the final retreat of the ice sheets from northern Europe c. 8300 B.C.

passage grave
A passage that ends in a chamber, covered by a mound of soil or a stone cairn. One or more tombs may be found under a single mound. Unlike other types, these are found in cemetery settings, sometimes with one great tomb surrounded by smaller ones, such as at Knowth, Ireland. The earliest passage graves of the 5th mill. B.C. in Brittany, had circular chambers which later included other forms: rectangular, angled, lateral, and V shaped. Radiocarbon dates for Newgrange and Knowth are from the mid- to late 4th millennium B.C.

patriarchy
A form of social organization in which the father (*pater*) is the supreme authority in the family, clan, or tribe.

patrilocal
The home territory of the husband's family or tribe.

patrilineal
Tracing descent and inheritance through the male line.

petroglyph
A rock engraving or painting.

pisé (terre pisé or pisé de terre)
Rammed earth, a durable form of construction using soils with high sand and low clay contents, usually compacted in molds.

pithos, *pl.* pithoi
Large ceramic jar.

portal tomb, portal dolmen
A form of megalithic chamber tomb found mainly in Ireland but also in Wales and Cornwall. It is usually found without a covering mound, consisting of a single chamber of six stones: a pair of portal stones, two side stones, a back stone, and a capstone.

Pre-Pottery Neolithic
Food-producing culture without pottery. Same as *aceramic*.

proto
Earliest form of.

Proto-Indo-European (PIE)
The hypothetically reconstructed parent form of the Indo-European linguistic family. By means of comparative linguistics, mythology, and archeology, PIE is reconstructed as a patriarchal, patrilineal, pastoral, mobile, and warlike culture with a pantheon of dominant male gods which is in direct contrast with the social structure, economy, and religion of Old Europe.

protome
The sculpted protrusion on an offering vessel in reduced anthropomorphic or zoomorphic form, usually symbolic of a divinity.

radiocarbon or C-14
A dating method, first suggested by W. F. Libby in 1946, based on a determination of the radioactivity of carbon from a sample. When organic matter dies, it ceases to exchange its carbon with the atmosphere and its C-14 dwindles by decay. The known rate of decay of C-14, based on a half-life of 5568 ± 30 years, will give the time elapsed since the death of the sample. The calibration with tree-ring counting chronology (see *dendro-*

chronology) has shown that true solar-year dates of samples are substantially earlier than the radiocarbon dates. The true age for samples from the Neolithic period is established through calibration with dendrochronology (see radiocarbon dates and their calibration in the Appendix).

rhyton
A deep, conical libation vessel, usually carved of marble in Old Europe.

Rinyo-Clacton
A Late Neolithic pottery style in Britain, known from the South English coast near Clacton and from Scotland at Rinyo. The characteristic vessel shape is a flat-based pot with straight flaring sides.

secondary burial
The interment of defleshed, disarticulated bones or skulls in special tombs or ossuaries, typical of Neolithic communal burials.

sepulcros de fosa
Stone-cist graves in pits dated to the 4th and early 3rd mill. B.C. Many are found in the Barcelona area of Catalonia.

Serra d'Alto style
Figulina pottery with fantastic handles.

shrine
Any structure or place consecrated to a deity, as an altar or temple.

spondylus
Spondylus gaederopus, a Mediterranean seashell from which beads, pendants, diadems, and bracelets were cut. Widely traded into central Europe between the 7th and 5th mill. B.C.

Square-Mouth Pottery period
Dated around the 5th millennium B.C. in northern Italy.

stela, *pl.* stelae
An upright stone or slab with an engraved or sculptured surface.

Stiff Nude
Anthropomorphic White Goddess of Death and Regeneration made of bone, alabaster, marble, soft stone, or clay; usually with folded arms, schematized head (with nose only or indicating a mask related to the Bird Goddess), small or absent breasts, and legs reduced to cones. These were placed with the dead in tombs. Sardinian Nudes of the 6th and 5th mill. B.C. are rounded in form, while the Cycladic of the 4th and early 3rd mill. are slim and abstracted. All have large pubic triangles in the center of their form. The White Goddess of Karanovo wears a mask with

round eyes and teeth, representing a poisonous snake.

strata
Layers of cultural debris representing various periods of development.

stratigraphy
A superposition, where one deposit overlies another if there has been no subsequent disturbance. One of the major tools for the establishment of chronology.

suttee burial
The immolation of a widow or children with the deceased husband, characteristic of Indo-European culture. Not known in Old Europe.

tauf
Same as *pisé, terre pisé,* or *pisé de terre.*

tell
A mound composed of accumulated layers of settlement debris. Normally found in regions where buildings were of mudbrick. The name comes from the Arabic. Same as *tepe* in Persian and *hüyük* in Turkish.

temple
An edifice dedicated to the worship of a deity or deities.

theacratic
A social structure organized around the worship of a Goddess, guided by a queen, assisted by a council of women.

tholos
A circular tomb having an elaborate entrance and ceremonial space, used for communal burials on Crete during the 3rd mill. B.C.

Tiefstich pottery
Vases decorated with deep incisions and encrustations of white paste found in northern European megaliths.

torba
A cementlike flooring material used for Maltese temples made from the local globigerina stone by crumbling, watering, and pounding; mid-4th to early 3rd mill. B.C.

two-stage burial
The reburial of gathered, disarticulated bones or skulls which have been cleaned of flesh through the process of excarnation or cremation.

votive
Offered or dedicated in accordance with a prayer or vow.

Upper Paleolithic
The last stage of the Paleolithic, beginning c. 40,000–38,000 B.C. and lasting for some 30,000 years. Associated with Homo sapiens, blade and burin industries, and cave and mobiliary art.

wattle-and-daub
A form of wall construction consisting of upright posts or stakes interwoven with twigs or tree branches, plastered with mud or clay and straw.

Yamna
Literally referring to a pit-grave (*yama,* "pit") under a barrow. Early Yamna and Late Yamna designate the periods of the Kurgan culture of the Russian steppes.

zoomorphic
The use of animal forms in symbolic or mythical representations.

CHRONOLOGIES

Chronological Outline: Major Events

7000–6500 B.C. Beginning stages of food production and settled village life in the coastal zones of the Aegean Sea and Crete.

6500–5500 B.C. Full-fledged Neolithic with pottery in the Aegean, central and east Balkan, Adriatic, and Mediterranean areas. Cultivation of wheat, barley, vetch, and peas, and evidence of all domesticated animals except the horse. Villages appear with rectangular houses built of mud brick and of timber. First two-roomed temples are constructed in SE Europe.

5500–5000 B.C. Spread of a food-producing economy from east-central to central Europe. Beginnings of copper metallurgy in Yugoslavia, Romania, and Bulgaria. Increase in size of villages and rise of the Vinča, Tisza, Lengyel, Butmir, Danilo, and Karanovo civilizations, followed by Hamangia, Petreşti, and Cucuteni. A "sacred script" appears on ceremonial objects for religious use.

5000–4300 B.C. Climax of culture in east-central and southeast Europe. Efflorescence of ceramic art, copper and gold metallurgy, and architecture (including two-story temple buildings). Megalithic tombs appear in Western Europe, first farmers in the British Islands and N Europe.

4300–3500 B.C. Patriarchal steppe pastoralist Wave No. 1 starting the disintegration of the Varna, Karanovo, Vinča, Petreşti, Lengyel, Tisza, Butmir, and Danilo-Hvar cultures. Initial Indo-Europeanization (Kurganization) of the Danube basin: marked changes in habitation patterns, social structure, economy, and religion. Dwindling of Old European art: cessation of figurines, polychrome ceramics, and temple building. Mediterranean, west and north European cultures continue Old European traditions.

3500–3000 B.C. Increased Indo-Europeanization of central Europe. New Kurgan influences

from north of the Black Sea. End of Cucuteni culture. Formation of Baden-Ezero and Globular Amphora cultures in central Europe of indigenous and Kurgan elements. Old European culture continues in the Mediterranean and western Europe. This is the temple period in Malta, the time of megalithic graves between Iberia and S Scandinavia, of extraordinary mounds with megalithic structures in Ireland (Newgrange, Knowth), and henge monuments in England.

3000–2500 B.C. Kurgan (late Yamna) wave from S Russia to east-central Europe creates further unrest: The Corded Pottery people (successors to Globular Amphora) diffuse from central to northwestern Europe, east Baltic, and central Russia. The Vučedol people migrate from NW Yugoslavia along the Adriatic coast to NW Greece, and the Bell Beaker people (possible amalgam of the Vučedol and Yamna cultures) spread c. 2500–2200 B.C. from east-central Europe to as far as Iberia and the British Isles.

Note on Chronology

Radiocarbon dating, which was implemented in the 1950s, revolutionized earlier chronological concepts and extended the time frame of the Neolithic and Copper Ages by more than three millennia. This modern dating method was further refined by comparing the radiocarbon content of charcoal or other organic samples recovered from prehistoric sites with the dendrochronologically-dated bristlecone pines of California. According to this calibration, the actual dates of the Neolithic and Copper Ages are approximately 500 to 1000 years older than those indicated by radiocarbon alone. At present, archeological dating is based on the combined techniques of radiocarbon dating and dendrochronology. In this study, the radiocarbon dates are listed as B.P. (Before Present), based upon the conventional half-life of radioactive carbon which is 5568 years; as b.c., after

subtraction of 1950 years, the conventional date for the implementation of the radiocarbon dating method (b.c. is not capitalized because it does not indicate true age); and as B.C. (approximate true age). In the tables where date distributions are present, the "approximate true age" heading of the right-hand column is meant to indicate true age within a century or more. In no case does it represent a fixed calendrical date. In this text, all archeological dates not otherwise designated are understood to be B.C.

Portions of the C–14 data are plotted graphically and follow the relevant tables.

All calibrated dates are from M. Stuiver and P. J. Reimer, *Radiocarbon* 28, 1022–1030, 1986. The program was compiled with Microsoft, Fortran version 3.3, copyright Microsoft Corporation 1985. File 2 of the program was used. This file contains a 20-year (bi-decadal) radiocarbon age dataset to 7210 cal B.C. (C–14 age circa 8200 B.P.). The A.D. 1950–2500 B.C. portion (Stuiver and Pearson, 1986, and Pearson and Stuiver, 1986) is the internationally recommended calibration curve (Mook 1986). The various sections of the complete calibration curve are:

Stuiver and Pearson, 1986 AD 1950–500 B.C.
Pearson and Stuiver, 1986 500 B.C.–2500 B.C.
Pearson, et al, 1986 2500 B.C.–5210 B.C.

Bi-decadeal weighted average of data from:
Linick et al., 1985 for 5219–5882 B.C., and 6383–7199 B.C.
Stuiver et al., 1986 for 5685–5805 B.C., 6360 B.C., and 6474–7198 B.C.
Kromer et al., 1986, for 5229–6200 B.C. and 6279–7207 B.C. and
Linick et al., 1986 for 5355–5815 B.C., and 6089–6549 B.C.

For all dates, the unaltered laboratory quoted errors were used. The dates in the tables are from grain, charcoal, or wood unless otherwise identified (bone, shell).

TABLES AND PLOTS OF RADIOCARBON DATES

TABLE 1
Aegean Neolithic and Sesklo and Dimini Cultures

SITE	LAB NUMBER	C–14 YEARS B.P.	CALIBRATED AGE RANGES B.C. Maximum (calibrated age) minimum
Early and Middle Neolithic			
Knossos, Crete	BM-124	8050±180	----(7049)----
Knossos "	BM-126	7000±180	6077 (5840) 5640
Knossos "	BM-272	7570±150	6559 (6431) 6186
Knossos "	BM-278	7910±140	7050 (6771,6742,6716) 6568
Knossos "	BM-436	7740±140	6690 (6563,6510) 6440
Sesklo, near Volos, E Thessaly	P-1675	6694±87	5644 (5616,5599,5578) 5490
Sesklo "	P-1676	6314±84	5342 (5296,5281,5242) 5224
Sesklo "	P-1678	7427±73	6401 (6225,6192,6189) 6170
Sesklo "	P-1677	6741±103	5720 (5633) 5530
Sesklo "	P-1679	7611±83	6554 (6455) 6406
Sesklo "	P-1680	7300±93	6218 (6117) 6006
Sesklo "	P-1681	7755±97	6680 (6566) 6460
Sesklo "	P-1682	7583±72	6473 (6436) 6388
Sesklo "	P-1672	6504±85	5493 (5474,5433,5428) 5342
Sesklo "	P-1674	6964±92	5970 (5815) 5730
Elateia, Phokis	GrN-3502	7040±130	6075 (5959,5890) 5790
Elateia "	GrN-3041	7190±100	6120 (6078,6056,6046,6015,6004) 5970
Elateia "	GrN-3037	7360±90	6374 (6174) 6100
Elateia "	GrN-2973	7480±70	6429 (6381,6317,6251) 6182
Antre Corycien, cave, C Greece	Gif-2339	7370±100	6381 (6177) 6100
Argisa,bone, W Thessaly	GrN-4145	7500±90	6440 (6389) 6183
Argisa,bone "	UCLA-1657A	8130±100	data exceeds calculable range
Argisa,bone "	UCLA-1657D	7990±95	7060 (7028,6979,6966,6863,6829) 6690
Franchthi, cave, Peloponnese	P-1824	6670±70	5635 (5569) 5488
Franchthi, cave "	P-1922	6790±90	5740 (5643) 5574
Franchthi, cave "	P-1922A	6730±70	5648 (5630) 5545
Nea Nikomedeia, Macedonia	P-1203A	7281±74	6176 (6107) 6606
Nea Nikomedeia "	P-1202	7557±91	6469 (6426) 6238
Nea Nikomedeia, Macedonia	Gx-679	7780±270	7050 (6600) 6390
Nea Nikomedeia "	Q-655	8180±150	data exceeds calculable range
Achilleion at Farsala, S Thessaly	P-2130	7084±91	6077 (5970) 5830
Achilleion "	UCLA-1882A	6930±155	5970 (5753) 5640
Achilleion "	UCLA-1896B	7460±177	6460 (6374,6325,6240) 6100
Achilleion "	UCLA-1896A	7180±155	6170 (6076,6059,6043,6018,6001) 5878
Achilleion "	UCLA-1896C	7330±95	6230 (6146) 6080
Achilleion "	UCLA-1896E	7280±105	6215 (6106) 5996
Achilleion "	LJ-2941	6900±100	5951 (5740) 5641
Achilleion "	LJ-2942	7170±100	6110 (6074,6063,6040,6021,5998) 5960
Achilleion "	LJ-2943	7020±150	6075 (5954,5923,5879) 5730

continued

TABLE 1 *continued*

SITE	LAB NUMBER	C–14 YEARS B.P.	CALIBRATED AGE RANGES B.C. Maximum (calibrated age) minimum
Achilleion at Farsala, S Thessaly	LJ-2944	7000 ± 100	6075 (5954,5923,5879) 5730
Achilleion "	LJ-3180	7510 ± 50	6434 (6398) 6231
Achilleion "	LJ-3181	7200 ± 50	6099 (6980,6052,6049,6012,6007) 5986
Achilleion "	LJ-3184	7280 ± 50	6172 (6106) 6082
Achilleion "	LJ-3186	7250 ± 50	6126 (6090) 6002
Achilleion "	LJ-3200	7030 ± 80	5982 (5956,5956,5884) 5766
Achilleion "	LJ-3201	7210 ± 80	6118 (6082) 5981
Achilleion "	LJ-3202	6940 ± 100	5960 (5768) 5657
Achilleion "	P-2117	7273 ± 76	6175 (6102) 6002
Achilleion "	P-2118	7471 ± 77	6427 (6378,6321,6246) 6179
Achilleion "	P-2120	7342 ± 68	6224 (6170) 6096
Achilleion "	P-2121	7181 ± 85	6105 (6076,6059,6043,6018,6001) 5970
Achilleion "	P-2122	7107 ± 86	6081 (5977) 5846
Achilleion "	P-2124	7086 ± 85	6076 (5970) 5834
Achilleion "	P-2125	6964 ± 87	5964 (5815) 5730
Late Neolithic			
Knossos, Crete	BM-273	6210 ± 150	5322 (5220) 4945
Knossos "	BM-274	6140 ± 150	5240 (5198,5175,5135,5114,5073) 4901
Antre Corycien, cave, C Greece	Gif-2124	6380 ± 90	5470 (5329) 5240
Antre Corycien, cave, "	Gif-2123	6250 ± 90	5317 (5233) 5081
Dimini, Phase V, Thessaly	Heidelberg		4711 (4468) 4350
Dimini, Phase V, "	Penn. Lab	5622 ± 80	4574 (4466) 4362
Saliagos, Cyclades	P-1311	6172 ± 74	5233 (5206,5153,5146) 5006
Saliagos, Cyclades	P-1396	6074 ± 79	5201 (5031,5029,4998,4959,4949) 4902
Saliagos, Cyclades	P-1368	5909 ± 87	4933 (4780) 4722
Saliagos, Cyclades	P-1333	5775 ± 84	4777 (4677,4630,4629) 4526
Saliagos, Cyclades	P-1393	5716 ± 85	4717 (4651,4649,4579) 4467
Franchthi cave, Peloponnese	P-1824	6170 ± 70	5232 (5205,5155,5148) 5007
Kitsos cave, Attica	Gif-1729	5750 ± 130	4780 (4664,4638,4601) 4470
Kitsos cave, Attica	Gif-1612	5700 ± 140	4772 (4572,4536,4536) 4367
Kitsos cave, Attica	Gif-1832	5650 ± 130	4711 (4496) 4360
Kitsos cave, Attica	Gif-1670	5550 ± 150	4573 (4365) 4245
Kitsos cave, Attica	Gif-1280	5470 ± 150	4470 (4345) 4155
Kitsos cave, Attica	Gif-1610	5350 ± 200	4370 (4233,4183,4167) 3980

Plot of Data from Table 1: Early and Middle Neolithic Greece

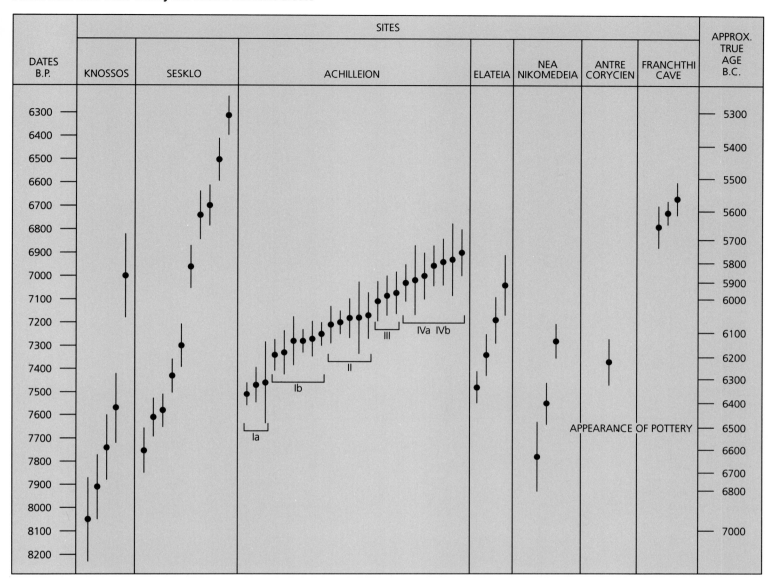

Plot of Data from Table 1: Late Neolithic Greece

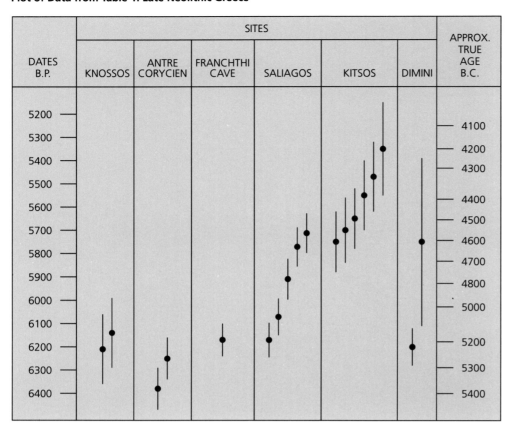

TABLE 2
Macedonian Neolithic, Starčevo-Körös, and Lepenski Vir Cultures

SITE	LAB NUMBER	C–14 YEARS B.P.	CALIBRATED AGE RANGES B.C. Maximum (calibrated age) minimum
Macedonian variant			
Anza I	LJ-2181	7270 ± 140	6222 (6101) 5980
Anza I	LJ-3032	7210 ± 50	6105 (6082) 5989
Anza I	LJ-2330/31	7170 ± 60	6089 (6074,6063,6040,6021,5998) 5973
Anza I	LJ-3183	7150 ± 50	6083 (6034,6027,5991) 5969
Anza I	LJ-3186	7140 ± 70	6085 (6031,6029,5988) 5963
Anza I	LJ-2332	7110 ± 120	6090 (5978) 5830
Anza I	LJ-2341	7230 ± 170	6218 (6086) 5960
Anza I	LJ-2339	7120 ± 80	6082 (5981) 5883
Anza I	LJ-2342	7100 ± 80	6078 (5975) 5845
Anza I	LJ-2333	6840 ± 100	5800 (5715,5677,5665) 5630
Anza I	LJ-2157	6970 ± 290	6100 (5820) 5560
Anza II	LJ-2337	7080 ± 60	6071 (5969) 5843
Anza II	LJ-2409	6850 ± 50	5747 (5721) 5642
Anza II	LJ-2405	6940 ± 80	5957 (5768) 5720
Anza II	LJ-2345	6600 ± 110	5630 (5493) 5419
Anza II	LJ-2338	6800 ± 140	5800 (5645) 5550
Anza II	LJ-2343	7050 ± 280	6160 (5961) 5640
Anza II	LJ-2344	6800 ± 270	5970 (5645) 5488
Anza III	UCLA-1705C	6700 ± 80	5644 (5619,5595,5583) 5500
Anza III	UCLA-1705B	6540 ± 120	5560 (5480) 5340
Anza III	LJ-2185	6510 ± 110	5530 (5475,5430) 5330
Vršnik	H-595/485	6865 ± 150	5954 (5730) 5620
Hissar	LE-534	8785 ± 130	data exceeds calculable range
Porodin, near Bitola, Pelagonia	H-1486/987	7110 ± 140	6090 (5978) 5810
Starčevo-Körös			
Divostin, C Yugoslavia	Bln-823	7080 ± 180	6100 (5969) 5740
Divostin "	Bln-866	7060 ± 100	6074 (5964) 5800
Divostin "	Bln-826	7020 ± 100	5988 (5954,5923,5879) 5740
Divostin "	Bln-896	6950 ± 100	5960 (5799) 5665
Divostin "	Bln-827	6910 ± 100	5954 (5744) 5650
Deszk, SE Hungary	Bln-581	6605 ± 100	5620 (5497) 5425
Deszk "	Bln-584	6540 ± 100	5550 (5480) 5350
Deszk "	Bln-583	6410 ± 120	5480 (5343) 5240
Deszk "	Bln-582a	6390 ± 100	5474 (5333) 5240
Deszk "	Bln-582	6260 ± 100	5325 (5234) 5082
Gyalaret "	Bln-75	7090 ± 100	6080 (5972) 5830
Kotacpart "	Bln-115	6450 ± 100	5480 (5378) 5246
Katalszeg "	Bln-86	6370 ± 100	5470 (5325,5251,5250) 5230
Gornja Tuzla, Bosnia	Grn-2059	6640 ± 75	5629 (5541) 5482
Gornja Tuzla "	Bln-	6390 ± 150	5480 (5333) 5230
Obre I "	UCLA-1605I	7240 ± 60	6124 (6088) 5996
Obre I "	UCLA-1605G	6710 ± 70	5644 (5623) 5533
Obre I "	UCLA-1605F	6430 ± 60	5474 (5354) 5248
Obre I "	Bln-659	6230 ± 80	5302 (5230) 5072
Obre I "	UCLA-1605H	6150 ± 60	5222 (5200,5170,5139,5102,5082) 5003
Lepenski Vir			
Level Ia, house 36	Bln-740b	7360 ± 100	6377 (6174) 6090
Level Ia, house 36	Bln-740a	7310 ± 100	6223 (6122) 6008
Level Ib/c, house 54	Z-143	7300 ± 124	6227 (6117) 5997
Level Ib/c, house 54	Bln-653	7040 ± 100	6033 (5959,5890) 5750
Level Ib/c, house 54	Z-115	6984 ± 94	5970 (5831) 5730
Level Id, house 9	BM-379	6900 ± 100	5951 (5741) 5640

continued

TABLE 2 *continued*

SITE	LAB NUMBER	C–14 YEARS B.P.	CALIBRATED AGE RANGES B.C. Maximum (calibrated age) minimum
Level Id, house 9	Bln-575	6860 ± 100	5820 (5727) 5630
Level Ie, house 16	Bln-647	6845 ± 100	5810 (5718,5671,5669) 5630
Level Ie, house 51	Bln-576	6820 ± 100	5750 (5650) 5620
Level Id, house 1	Bln-649	6800 ± 100	5740 (5645) 5575
Level II, house IX	Bln-654	6630 ± 100	5630 (5645) 5575
Level I, house 34/43	Bln-652	6620 ± 100	5630 (5510) 5480
Level II, house XXXII	Bln-655	6560 ± 100	5560 (5484) 5380

Plot of Data from Table 2: Macedonian Neolithic, Starčevo-Körös, and Lepenski Vir Cultures

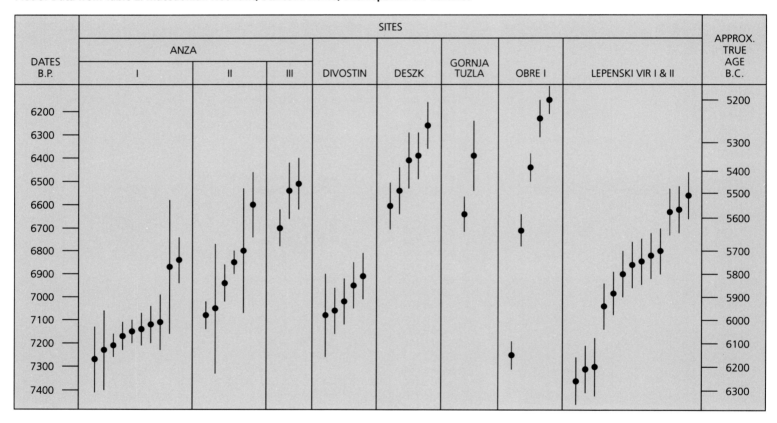

TABLE 3
Karanovo Culture

SITE	LAB NUMBER	C–14 YEARS B.P.	CALIBRATED AGE RANGES B.C. Maximum (calibrated age) minimum
Phase I			
Azmak	Bln-293	7303±150	6374 (6118) 5990
Azmak	Bln-291	7158±150	6120 (6071,6068,6036,6024,5994) 5840
Azmak	Bln-292	6878±100	5957 (5734) 5630
Azmak	Bln-296	6779±100	5740 (5641) 5560
Azmak	Bln-294	6768±100	5730 (5638) 5550
Azmak	Bln-295	6720±100	5694 (5626) 5500
Azmak	Bln-299	6812±100	5750 (5648) 5585
Azmak	Bln-297	6675±100	5640 (5563) 5480
Azmak	Bln-298	6540±100	5550 (5480) 5350
Azmak	Bln-224	6652±150	5640 (5563) 5480
Azmak	Bln-301	6483±100	5490 (5471,5443,5420) 5330
Azmak	Bln-300	6426±150	5490 (5350) 5240
Azmak	Bln-430	6279±120	5340 (5237) 5082
Phase II–III			
Karanovo	Bln-152	6807±100	5750 (5647) 5581
Karanovo	HV-14610	6800±75	5737 (5645) 5624
Karanovo	Bln-201	6573±100	5612 (5486) 5410
Karanovo	Bln-234	6500±150	5550 (5474,5435,5426) 5246
Karanovo	HV-14611	6555±60	5535 (5483) 5419
Karanovo	Bln-3458	6440±60	5476 (5366) 5249
Karanovo	HV-14609	6535±70	5508 (5479) 5380
Karanovo	HV-14181	6530±75	5508 (5479) 5368
Karanovo	Bln-3464	6500±50	5485 (5474,5435,5426) 5357
Karanovo	Bln-3465	6510±60	5488 (5475,5430) 5360
Karanovo	Bln-3461	6480±60	5483 (5470,5444,5419) 5340
Karanovo	Bln-34588	6440±60	5476 (5366) 5249
Karanovo	HV-14186	6475±65	5483 (5463,5447,5417) 5336
Karanovo	Bln-3460	6440±60	5476 (5366) 5249
Karanovo	Bln-3459	6420±60	5463 (5347) 5246
Karanovo	HV-14183	6420±60	5463 (5347) 5246
Karanovo	Bln-3465	6410±60	5471 (5343) 5245
Karanovo	HV-14181	6530±75	5508 (5479) 5368
Karanovo	Bln-3463	6350±60	5350 (5317,5259,5247) 5236
Karanovo	Bln-3587	6380±60	5414 (5329) 5239
Karanovo	HV-14184	6340±75	5352 (5313,5263,5245) 5233
Karanovo	HV-14180	6230±75	5298 (5230) 5075
Karanovo	Bln-3585	6130±60	5212 (5195,5180,5131,5126,5067) 4947
Sitagroi	Bln-778	6425±100	5480 (5350) 5242
Sitagroi	Bln-779	6625±170	5650 (5532) 5380
Sitagroi	Bln-648	6265±75	5318 (5235) 5207
Sitagroi	Bln-884	6240±100	5317 (5231) 5067
Dikili Tash	Ly-1062	6100±200	5240 (5053,5013,5008) 4790
Dikili Tash	Ly-1064	6040±120	5203 (4941) 4794

Plot of Data from Table 3: Karanovo Culture

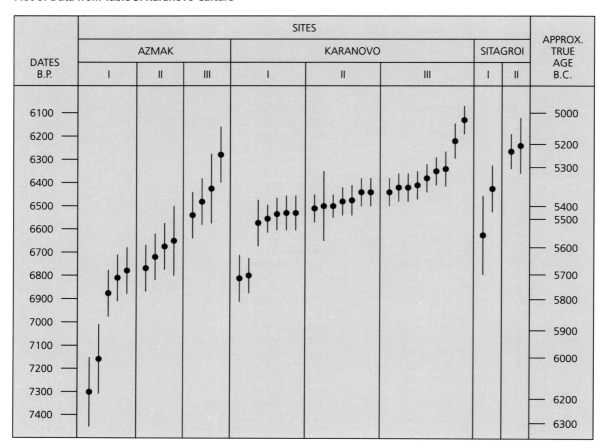

TABLE 4

Distribution of Radiocarbon Dates of the Linearbandkeramik (LBK) Culture. Early, Music-Note Decorated, and Stroked Phases

SITE	LAB NUMBER	C–14 YEARS B.P.	CALIBRATED AGE RANGES B.C. Maximum (calibrated age) minimum
Early			
Bylany	GrN-4752	6170±45	5225 (5205,5155,5148) 5062
Bylany	GrN-4754	6270±65	5317 (5236) 5211
Bylany	Grn-4755	6180±150	5310 (5208) 4908
Bylany	LJ-2032	6200±300	5474 (5215) 4790
Bylany	LJ-2037	6330±250	5490 (5308,5267,5244) 4949
Bylany	LJ-2040	6280±200	5471 (5237) 4949
Bylany	M-1896	6250±230	5471 (5233) 4906
Bylany	M-1897	6320±230	5480 (5300,5273,5243) 5003
Bylany	BM-562	6184±89	5236 (5209) 5005
Bylany	BM-563	6686±53	5636 (5613,5605,5571) 5507
Bylany	BM-566	6178±134	5295 (5207) 4940
Bylany	BM-569	6754±96	5730 (5635) 5550
Bylany	Bln-438	6400±250	5550 (5338) 5078
Chabarovice	Bln-437	6070±60	5196 (4996,4964,4948) 4904
Chabarovice	Bln-51	6310±200	5480 (5292,5286,5241) 5060
Eitzum	Hl-1487/985	6480±210	5617 (5470,5444,5419) 5230
Eitzum	Grn-2311	6510±100	5510 (5475,5430) 5340
Elsloo	Grn-2159	6320±90	5350 (5300,5273,5243) 5220
Elsloo	Grn-2160	6150±70	5227 (5200,5170,5139,5102,5082) 4949
Elsloo	Grn-2164	6270±250	5480 (5236) 4906
Elsloo	Grn-2884	6055±80	5197 (4990,4988,4945) 4859
Elsloo	GrN-996	6175±70	5233 (5206,5151,5150) 5009
Geleen	GrN-996	6370±250	5530 (5325,5251,5250) 5060
Geleen	GrN-	6125±35	5204 (5194,5183,5063) 5002
Hienheim	GrN-	6235±45	5240 (5231) 5148
Hienheim	GrN-	6155±45	5218 (5201,5167,5141,5096,5086) 5055
Hienheim	GrN-	6220±45	5236 (5225) 5145
Hienheim	GrN-	6140±45	5210 (5198,5175,5135,5114,5073) 5005
Lautereck-D	GrN-4750	6440±45	5474 (5366) 5327
Lautereck-E	GrN-4667	6285±100	5340 (5238) 5210
Mohelnice	Bln-102	6405±100	5480 (5340) 5240
Mohelnice	Bln-102a	6430±75	5477 (5354) 5246
Olszanica, Poland	GrN-5384	6300±400	5620 (5240) 5790
Olszanica	M-2011	6150±210	5321 (5200,5170,5139,5102,5082) 4841
Olszanica	M-2165	6700±220	5750 (5619,5595,5583) 5417
Olszanica D1	M-2314	6350±250	5500 (5317,5259,5247) 5007
Rosdorf	Hv-586	6100±150	5230 (5053,5013,5008) 4845
Sittard	GrN-320	6200±200	5340 (5215) 4903
Sittard	GrN-423	6170±100	5240 (5205,5155,5148) 4947
Šturovo	Bln-553	6260±100	5325 (5234) 5082
Šturovo	Bln-559	6260±60	5311 (5234) 5209
Strzeke, Poland	GrN-5087	6136±100	5230 (5197,5177,5134,5119,5070) 4909
Szamossalyi, Hungary	Mn-404	6045±100	5199 (4942) 4843
Westeregeln	Bln-42	6140±100	5230 (5198,5175,5135,9114,5073) 4940
Westeregeln	Bln-92	6200±200	5340 (5215) 4903
Westeregeln	GrN-223	6180±150	5310 (5208) 4908
Zalavár	Bln-87	6430±100	5480 (5354) 5243
Žopy	Bln-57		

continued

TABLE 4 *continued*

Music-Note Decorated (*Notenkopf*)

Bylany	BM-561	6038±87	5194 (4941) 4845
Bylany	BM-565	6023±77	5052 (4938,4915,4907) 4842
Dresden-Nickern	Bln-73	5955±100	4991 (4895,4881,4847) 4770
Dresden-Nickern	Bln-73a	5935±100	4891 (4770,4768,4727) 4586
Dresden-Nickern	Bln-77	5815±100	4832 (4721) 4580
Hienheim	GrN-4830	5910±50	4896 (4789) 4775
Hienheim	GrN-4832	5780±85	4778 (4711,4708,4680) 4529
Mold	Bln-58	5990±160	5200 (4931,4928,4901) 4720
Pulkau	Bln-83	6215±100	5301 (5223) 5060
Rehmsdorf	Bln-176	5932±100	4940 (4840,4838,4815) 4720
Winden-am-See	Bln-55	5940±100	4940 (4892,4887,4841) 4727
Winden-am-See	Bln-107	5820±100	4832 (4722) 4580
Wittislengen	GrN-	6030±110	5198 (4939,4913,4909) 4793
Zwenkau-Harth	GrN1581	6160±70	5054 (4939,4913,4909) 4848
Zwenkau-Harth	H-224/223	6000±115	5192 (4933,4925,4903) 4780
Tirpeşti	Bln-800	6170±100	5240 (5205,5155,5148) 4947
Tirpeşti	Bln-801	6245±100	5319 (5232) 5070

Stroked

Bylany	GrN-4751	5810±60	4780 (4719) 4597
Bylany	LJ-2053	5820±200	4937 (4722) 4470
Bylany	BM-564	5756±51	4720 (4667,4636,4609) 4537
Bylany	BM-568	5635±65	4573 (4469) 4369
Bylany	BM-571	5789±82	4780 (4713,4697,4686) 4541
Bylany	BM-572	5729±78	4719 (4656,4645,4585) 4494
Žalany	Bln-240	5881±100	4900 (4782) 4679
Zwenkau-Harth	Bln-66	5900±100	4933 (4787) 4720
Zwenkau-Harth	K-555	5840±20	4779 (4772,4759,4728) 4719

Rössen (with Kurgan I elements)

Dümmer	Hv-327	5510±240	4664 (4355) 4042
Dümmer	Hv-374	5420±50	4346 (4333,4273,4259) 4237
Dümmer	Hv-317	5430±80	4356 (4335) 4166
Dümmer	Hv-814	5565±85	4497 (4453,4425,4395,4377,4369) 4347
Dümmer	Hv-816	5425±350	4677 (4334) 3821
Dümmer	Hv-1220	5170±90	4211 (3991) 3822
Dümmer	Hv-1230	5175±155	4228 (3993) 3788
Gonvillars	Gif-468	5380±250	4470 (4241) 3970
Gonvillars	Gif-466	5000±250	4040 (3785) 3522
Wahlitz	GrN-433	5300±200	4350 (4220,4200,4147,4110,4088,4060,4048) 3826

Plot of Data from Table 4: Linear Pottery (LBK) Culture

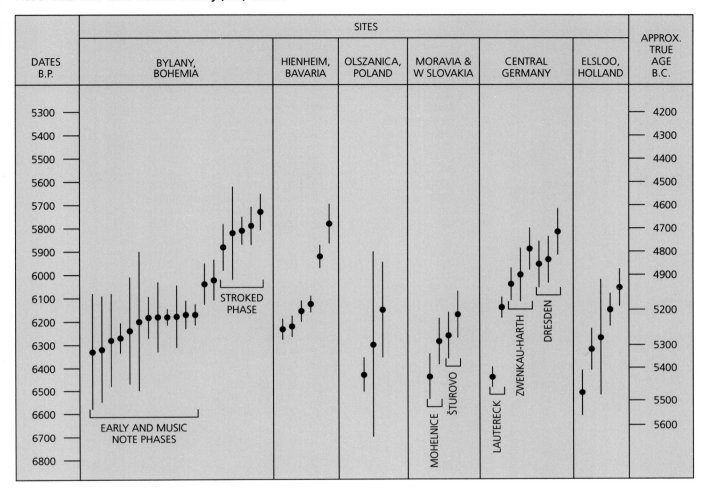

TABLE 5
Bükk Culture

SITE	LAB NUMBER	C–14 YEARS B.P.	CALIBRATED AGE RANGES B.C. Maximum (calibrated age) minimum
Tiszadob phase			
Korlat	Bln-119	6440 ± 100	5480 (5366) 5244
Tiszavasvari-Keresztfal	Bln-505	6305 ± 100	5340 (5241) 5210
Tarnabod	Bln-123	6280 ± 100	5330 (5237) 5148
Bükk proper			
Ostoros	Bln-549	6180 ± 100	5240 (5208) 4949
Tarnazsadány	Bln-676	6155 ± 100	5230 (5201,5167,5141,5096,5086) 4940
Szamossályi	Bln-404	6136 ± 100	5230 (5197,5177,5134,5119,5070) 4909
Tarnazsadány	Bln-506	6120 ± 100	5230 (5193,5185,5062) 4906
Kečovo (Domica cave)	GrN-2435	6080 ± 75	5202 (5037,5025,5000,4951,4950) 4904

TABLE 6
Dniester-Bug Culture

SITE	LAB NUMBER	C–14 YEARS B.P.	CALIBRATED AGE RANGES B.C. Maximum (calibrated age) minimum
Soroki,II 3	Bln-588	7515 ± 120	6460 (6404) 6180
Soroki,II 1	Bln-586	6825 ± 150	5830 (5653) 5560
Soroki,5	Bln-589	6495 ± 100	5500 (5473,5437,5424) 5330

TABLE 7
Butmir Culture

SITE	LAB NUMBER	C–14 YEARS B.P.	CALIBRATED AGE RANGES B.C. Maximum (calibrated age) minimum
Early and Middle Butmir			
Obre II	Bln-639	6175 ± 80	5234 (5206,5151,5150) 5005
Obre II	GrN-683	6110 ± 65	5207 (5190,5058) 4942
Obre II	GrN-5684	6106 ± 60	5205 (5056) 4942
Obre II	Bln-792	6075 ± 100	5210 (5032,5029,4998,4958,4949) 4859
Obre II	UCLA-1605A	6020 ± 60	5040 (4937,4917,4907) 4848
Obre II	LJ-2327	6020 ± 150	5205 (4937,4917,4907) 4780
Obre II	GrN-5685	5985 ± 40	4939 (4900,4870,4869) 6841
Obre II	GrN-5686	5930 ± 45	4899 (4837,4817,4803) 4782
Obre II	Bln-657	5925 ± 80	4935 (4835,4821,4799) 4729
Obre II	UCLA-1605E	5890 ± 60	4894 (4784) 4724
Obre II	UCLA-1605C	5875 ± 60	4892 (4780) 4720
Obre II	Bln-638	5850 ± 80	4838 (4774) 4620
Obre II	Bln-656	5840 ± 100	4892 (4772,4759,4728) 4589
Obre II	Bln-790	5770 ± 100	4780 (4673,4632,4624) 4510
Obre II	Bln-637	5740 ± 80	4723 (4660,4648,4590) 4501

Plot of Data from Table 5: Bükk Culture

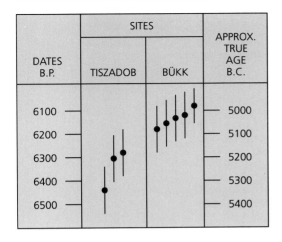

Plot of Data from Table 6: Dniester-Bug Culture

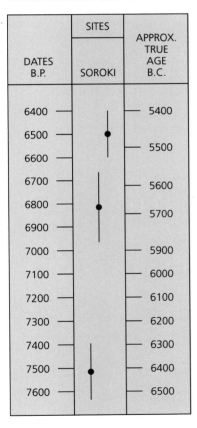

Plot of Data from Table 7: Butmir Culture

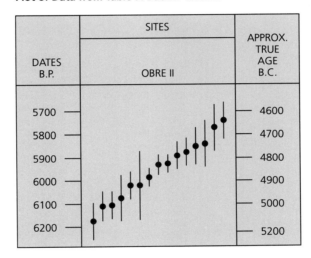

TABLE 8
Vinča Culture

SITE	LAB NUMBER	C–14 YEARS B.P.	CALIBRATED AGE RANGES B.C. Maximum (calibrated age) minimum
Early Oszentiván	Bln-477	6270±60	5315 (5236) 5213
Predionica	GrN-1546	6190±60	5234 (5210) 5063
Anza IV	LJ-2329	6210±60	5237 (5220) 5075
Anza IV	LJ-2178	6100±250	5317 (5053,5013,5008) 4770
Anza IV	LJ-2411	6070±200	5240 (4996,4964,4948) 4780
Magura Fetelor, Vadastra	UCLA-1865	6230±80	5302 (5230) 5072
Oszentivan	Bln-478	6070±100	5206 (4996,4964,4948) 4855
Oszentivan	Bln-480	6050±100	5200 (4943) 4845
Divostin	Bln-865	6020±100	5193 (4937,4917,4907) 4793
Divostin	Z-336	6005±93	5053 (4934,4923,4904) 4789
Divostin	Bln-867	5250±100	4233 (4039,4010) 3980
Divostin	Bln-868	6070±100	5206 (4996,4964,4948) 4855
Divostin	Bln-871	6190±100	5210 (5046,5019,5004) 4901
Divostin	Bln-863	5825±100	4936 (4724) 4582
Divostin	Bln-898	5860±100	4896 (4777) 4611
Divostin	BM-574	5247±80	4227 (4038,4011,4009) 3990
Bapska 2	Bln-346	5955±80	4941 (4895,4881,4847) 4780
Valač	Bln-436	5845±80	4835 (4773,4750,4729) 4615
Valač	GrN-1537	5845±160	4934 (4773,4750,4729) 4520
Bapska	Bln-348	5820±80	4787 (4722) 4588
Banjica	GrN-1542	5710±90	4717 (4577,4553,4547) 4465
Selevac	Z-233b	6152±90	5232 (5201,5169,5140,5099,5083) 4945
Selevac	Z-233a	6133±80	5223 (5196,5179,5132,5123,5069) 4944
Selevac	Har-3211	6050±70	5198 (4942) 4843
Selevac	Har-3232	6070	5194 (4941) 4845
Selevac	LJ-2521	6080±100	5210 (5037,5025,5000,4951,4950) 4863
Medvednjak	ALJ-2521	6100±100	5220 (5053,5013,5008) 4903
Gornja Tuzla	Bln-349	5710±100	4720 (4577,4553,4547) 4460
Gornja Tuzla	GrN-1974	5580±60	4490 (4456,4417,4403) 4357
Vinča	GrN-1536	5670±120	4714 (4512) 4360
Vinča	GrN-1542	6190±60	5234 (5210) 5063
Beran-Krs	Z-491	6030±160	5210 (4939,4913,4909) 4780
Gomolava Ia	GrN-7376	6010±70	5039 (4935,4921,4905) 4809
Grivac	Bln-872	5930±100	4940 (4837,4817,4803) 4728
Beran-Krs	Z-492	5870±150	4938 (4779) 4580
Gornea	Bm-1124	5869±54	4836 (4779) 4719
Vinča	GrN-1537	5845±160	4939 (4773,4750,4729) 4520
Gomolava Ib	GrN-7374	5715±75	4714 (4651,4649,4579) 4469
Lubljanica	M-2455	5660±200	4720 (4461) 4245

Plot of Data from Table 8: Vinča Culture

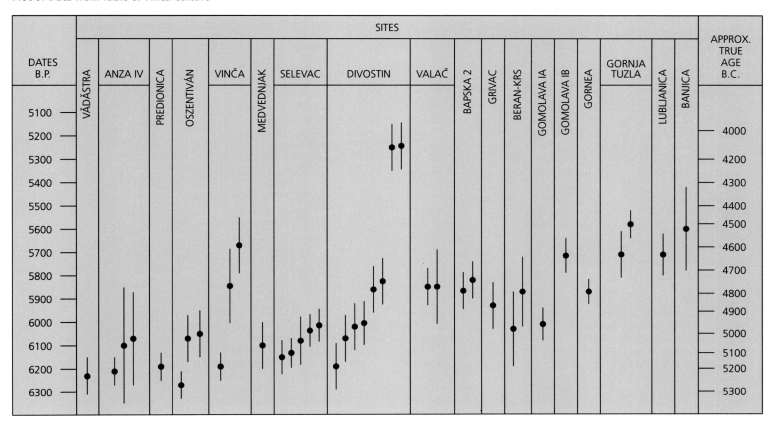

TABLE 9
Tisza Culture

SITE	LAB NUMBER	C–14 YEARS B.P.	CALIBRATED AGE RANGES B.C. Maximum (calibrated age) minimum
Szakálhát Group			
Battonya-Parázs-tanya	Bln-1966	6370 ± 60	5371 (5325,5251,5250) 5239
Battonya-Parázs-tanya	Bln-1667	6280 ± 60	5319 (5237) 5218
Battonya-Parázs-tanya	Bln-1971	6270 ± 65	5317 (5236) 5211
Battonya-Parázs-tanya	Bln-1970	6175 ± 70	5233 (5206,5151,5150) 5009
Dévaványa-Réhely	Bln-1337	5955 ± 60	4937 (4895,4881,4847) 4784
Dévaványa-Réhely	Bln-1378	5960 ± 60	4938 (4895,4879,4849) 4786
Dévaványa-Réhely	Bln-1377	5875 ± 60	4892 (4780) 4720
Dévaványa-Réhely	Bln-1339	6095 ± 60	5202 (5050,5016,5006) 4909
Vestö-Mágor	Bln-1628	6250 ± 100	5321 (5233) 5074
Vestö-Mágor	Bln-1625	6150 ± 100	5230 (5200,5170,5139,5102,5082) 5940
Esztár Group			
Berettyóújfalu-Szilhalom	Bln-5570	6330 ± 90	5360 (5308,5267,5244) 5230
Berettyóújfalu-Szilhalom	Bln-5579	6340 ± 60	5345 (5313,5263,5245) 5235
Classical Tisza			
Hódmezovásárhely-Gorsza (Level 16)	Fra-108	5970 ± 100	5345 (5313,5263,5245) 5235
Hódmezovásárhely-Gorsza (Level 10)	Fra-77	5670 ± 100	4675 (4512) 4369
Hódmezovásárhely-Gorsza (Level 10)	Fra-76	5650 ± 110	4669 (4496) 4360
Hódmezovásárhely-Gorsza (Level 1)	Fra-95	5979 ± 100	5038 (4899,4873,4864) 4780
Hódmezovásárhely-Gorsza	Bln-?	5580 ± 100	4520 (4456,4417,4403) 4350
Véstö-Mágor	Bln-1626	6000 ± 100	5054 (4933,4925,4903) 4790
Véstö-Mágor	Bln-1342	5970 ± 80	4944 (4897,4876,4857) 4783
Kisköre	Bln-179	5995 ± 80	5034 (4932,4926,4902) 4790
Kisköre	Bln-515	5890 ± 80	4898 (4784) 4718
Herpály Group			
Berettyóújfalu-Herpály (Level 9)	Bln-1934	5730 ± 80	4720 (4657,4645,4585) 4493
Berettyóújfalu-Herpály (Level 9)	Bln-2835	5790 ± 60	4775 (4713,4696,4687) 4584
Berettyóújfalu-Herpály (Level 9)	Bln-2936	5930 ± 60	4932 (4837,4817,4803) 4778
Berettyóújfalu-Herpály (Level 8)	Bln-2673	5630 ± 70	4573 (4468) 4367
Berettyóújfalu-Herpály (Level 8)	Bln-2939	5680 ± 60	4662 (4519) 4465
Berettyóújfalu-Herpály (Level 8)	Bln-2940	5640 ± 60	4787 (4772,4759,4728) 4677
Berettyóújfalu-Herpály (Level 8)	Bln-2928	5840 ± 70	4790 (4772,4759,4728) 4620
Berettyóújfalu-Herpály (Level 8)	Bln-2933	5830 ± 60	4785 (4725) 4620
Berettyóújfalu-Herpály (Level 8)	Bln-2927	5710 ± 80	4714 (4577,4553,4547) 4467
Berettyóújfalu-Herpály (Level 8-7)	Bln-2926	5770 ± 80	4775 (4673,4632,4624) 4525
Berettyóújfalu-Herpály (Level 8)	Bln-2930	5710 ± 60	4676 (4577,4553,4547) 4493
Berettyóújfalu-Herpály (Level 8-7)	Bln-2925	5830 ± 70	4787 (4725) 4610
Berettyóújfalu-Herpály (Level 8-7)	Bln-2929	5800 ± 70	4780 (4716) 4584
Berettyóújfalu-Herpály (Level 8-7)	Bln-2938	5600 ± 60	4506 (4461) 4362
Berettyóújfalu-Herpály (Level 7)	Bln-2924	5820 ± 70	4785 (4722) 4597
Berettyóújfalu-Herpály (Level 7)	Bln-2993	5520 ± 70	4459 (4358) 4340
Berettyóújfalu-Herpály (Level 7)	Bln-2931	5500 ± 70	4452 (4353) 4337
Berettyóújfalu-Herpály (Level 7)	Bln-2937	5770 ± 70	4772 (4673,4632,4624) 4533
Berettyóújfalu-Herpály (Level 7)	Bln-2706	5706 ± 60	4673 (4575,4558,4543) 4485
Berettyóújfalu-Herpály (Level 6)	Bln-2958	5630 ± 60	4529 (4468) 4369
Berettyóújfalu-Herpály (Level 6)	Bln-2923	5680 ± 80	4669 (4519) 4460
Berettyóújfalu-Herpály (Level 6)	Bln-2670	5810 ± 50	4778 (4719) 4608
Berettyóújfalu-Herpály (Level 6)	Bln-2584	5750 ± 60	4720 (4664,4638,4601)
Berettyóújfalu-Herpály (Level 6)	Bln-2494	5655 ± 50	4576 (4550) 4461
Berettyóújfalu-Herpály (Level 6-5)	Bln-2583	5490 ± 60	4450 (4350) 4335
Berettyóújfalu-Herpály (Level 6-5)	Bln-2668	5750 ± 50	4718 (4664,4638,4601) 4532

continued

SITE	LAB NUMBER	C–14 YEARS B.P.	CALIBRATED AGE RANGES B.C. Maximum (calibrated age) minimum
Berettyóújfalu-Herpály (Level 5)	Bln-2493	5645 ± 55	4574 (4492) 4407
Szilhalom	Bln-2675	5680 ± 100	4711 (4519) 4402
Esztár-Fenyvespart	Bln-1679	5770 ± 55	4725 (4673,4632,4624) 4548
Csöszhalom Group			
Csöszhalom	Bln-509 (Upper Level)	5575 ± 60	4470 (4455,4420,4401) 4356
Csöszhalom	Bln-510 (Middle Level)	5875 ± 100	4899 (4780) 4626
Csöszhalom	Bln-512 (Lower Level)	5775 ± 100	4780 (4677,4630,4629) 4510
Csöszhalom	Bln-513 (Lower Level)	5940 ± 100	4940 (4893,4883,4845) 4730
Csöszhalom	Grn-1993	5895 ± 60	4895 (4785) 4725
Csöszhalom	Bln-100	5575 ± 100	4520 (4455,4420,4401) 4350
Polgár (Tiszapolgár) Group			
Bélmegyer-Mondoki domb	Bln-?	5300 ± 70	4239 (4220,4200,4147,4110,4088,4060,4048) 4005
Méhkerék 23	Bln-2165	5385 ± 65	4341 (4242) 4154
Tiszapolgár-Basatanya	Deb-361 (Grave 5)	5350 ± 190	4360 (4233,4183,4167) 3990
Tiszapolgár-Basatanya	Deb-348 (Grave 23)	5020 ± 180	4000 (3895,3887,3810,3788) 3640
Tiszapolgár-Basatanya	Deb-348 (Grave 28)	5060 ± 170	4035 (3938,3867,3818) 3690
Tiszapolgár-Basatanya	Deb-349 (Grave 54)	5090 ± 190	4216 (3951,3842,3824) 3700

Plot of Data from Table 9: Tisza Culture

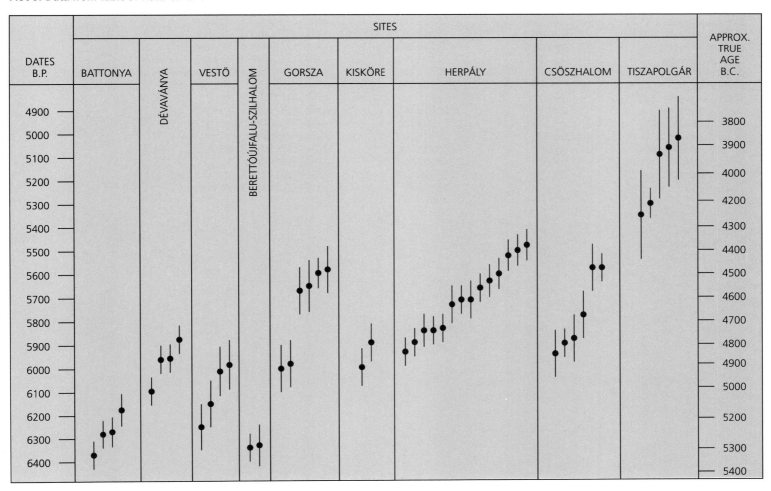

TABLE 10
Lengyel Culture

SITE	LAB NUMBER	C–14 YEARS B.P.	CALIBRATED AGE RANGES B.C. Maximum (calibrated age) minimum
Early			
Unterpullendorf	VRI-104a	5940 ± 100	4940 (4892,4887,4841) 4727
Unterpullendorf	VRI-42	6130 ± 140	5240 (5195,5180,5131,5126,5067) 4901
Lang-Enzersdorf	VRI-	5950 ± 130	5038 (4894,4883,4845) 4720
Lang-Enzersdorf	VRI-	5880 ± 120	4933 (4782) 4611
Bapska Sopot	Bln-346	5955 ± 80	4891 (4775) 4626
Bapska Sopot	Bln-348	5820 ± 80	4787 (4722) 4588
Kutna Hora	LJ-2053	5800 ± 300	5053 (4716) 4350
Aszód-Papi	Bln-1208	5750 ± 100	4770 (4664,4638,4601) 4490
Aszód-Papi	Bln-1210	5885 ± 100	4900 (4783) 4682
Aszód-Papi	Bln-1211	5990 ± 100	5048 (4931,4928,4901) 4780
Aszód-Papi	Bln-607	5620 ± 100	4653 (4465) 4360
Aszód-Papi	UCLA-1225	5100 ± 105	4031 (3957,3838,3826) 3780
Gustorzyn	Lod-174	5740 ± 140	4780 (4660,4641,4590) 4460
Late			
Letenye-Szentkeresztdomb	Bln-585	5460 ± 120	4669 (4470) 4360
Zalavár-Mekenye	Bln-502	5400 ± 80	4348 (4318,4285,4246) 4154
Kuczyna	Lod-93	5530 ± 220	4664 (4360) 4151
Brześć Kujawski	GX-6369	5525 ± 320	4773 (4359) 3999
Brześć Kujawski	Lod-167	5410 ± 340	4664 (4330,4279,4248) 3820
Brześć Kujawski	Lod-193	5400 ± 190	4459 (4318,4285,4246) 4000
Brześć Kujawski	Lod-165	5370 ± 180	4378 (4238) 4000
Brześć Kujawski	GrN-8869	5330 ± 130	4340 (4228,4194,4159) 4000
Brześć Kujawski	Lod-194	5280 ± 190	4350 (4215,4205,4138,4120,4044) 3824
Brześć Kujawski	Lod-187	5280 ± 190	4350 (4215,4205,4138,4120,4044) 3824
Brześć Kujawski	Lod-195	5260 ± 190	4340 (4210) 3820
Brześć Kujawski	Lod-173	5250 ± 180	4340 (4039,4010) 3820
Brześć Kujawski	Lod-164	5210 ± 180	4240 (4032,4026,4001) 3790
Brześć Kujawski	Lod-110	5160 ± 180	4230 (3988) 3780
Brześć Kujawski	Lod-163	5130 ± 160	4218 (3974) 3726
Brześć Kujawski	Lod-170	4930 ± 160	3950 (3773,3758,3704) 3530
Brześć Kujawski	Lod-162	4830 ± 160	3780 (3639) 3378
Krusza Zamkowa Grave 392,		5565 ± 100	4510 (4453,4425,4395,4377,4369) 4340
with diadem		5330 ± 65	4315 (4228,4194,4159) 4041

Plot of Data from Table 10: Lengyel Culture

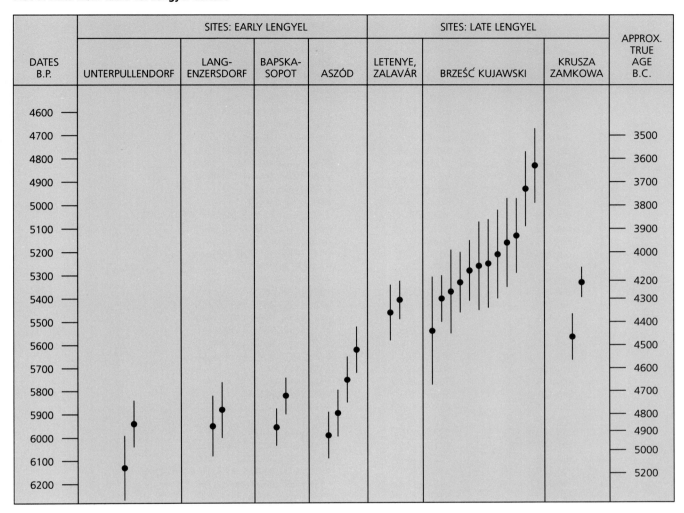

TABLE 11
Karanovo Culture (Phases IV–VI and Boian-Gumelniţa)

SITE	LAB NUMBER	C–14 YEARS B.P.	CALIBRATED AGE RANGES B.C. Maximum (calibrated age) minimum
Sitagroi III	Bln-882	5795 ± 100	4790 (4715,4690) 4530
Sitagroi III	Bln-881	5555 ± 100	4500 (4451,4438,4366) 4340
Sitagroi III	Bln-883	5545 ± 100	4490 (4364) 4340
Sitagroi III	BM-650b	5367 ± 85	4350 (4237) 4042
Sitagroi III	Bln-774	5100 ± 120	4034 (3957,3838,3826) 3780
Dikili-Tash	Gif-1424	5750 ± 140	4780 (4664,4638,4601) 4460
Dikili-Tash	Gif-1425	5750 ± 140	4780 (4664,4638,4601) 4460
Dikili-Tash	Gif-1423	5650 ± 140	4714 (4496) 4350
Dikili-Tash	Gif-1738	5600 ± 150	4664 (4461) 4340
Jasatepe	Bln-338	6080 ± 80	5203 (5037,5025,5000,4951,4950) 4903
Karanovo	Bln-154	5840 ± 250	5047 (4772,4759,4728) 4408
Azmak	Bln-149	5888 ± 100	4931 (4784) 4684
Azmak	Bln-136	5840 ± 100	4892 (4772, 4759,4728) 4589
Azmak	Bln-151	5829 ± 100	4837 (4725) 4584
Azmak	Bln-142	5803 ± 150	4894 (4717) 4500
Azmak	Bln-151	5829 ± 100	4837 (4725) 4584
Azmak	Bln-143	5737 ± 150	4780 (4659,4642,4588) 4406
Azmak	Bln-131	5717 ± 100	4720 (4652,4649,4580) 4460
Azmak	Bln-139	5703 ± 100	4720 (4573,4561,4539) 4460
Azmak	Bln-135	5700 ± 100	4720 (4572,4564,4536) 4460
Azmak	Bln-137	5697 ± 100	6669 (4571,4568,4533) 4460
Azmak	Bln-150	5630 ± 100	4657 (4468) 4360
Azmak	Bln-138	5621 ± 200	4720 (4466) 4259
Azmak	Bln-141	5620 ± 100	4653 (4465) 4360
Azmak	Bln-144	5597 ± 120	4651 (4460) 4350
Azmak	Bln-134	5520 ± 200	4653 (4358) 4155
Azmak	Bln-145	5390 ± 100	4350 (4243) 4046
Azmak	Bln-147	5219 ± 150	4240 (4033,4023,4003) 3820
Azmak	Bln-146	5035 ± 150	4000 (3906,3880,3813) 3690
Chotnica	Bln-125	5560 ± 100	4510 (4452,4428,4392,4384,4368) 4340
Goljamo Delčevo	Bln-923	5970 ± 100	4997 (4897,4876,4857) 4780
Goljamo Delčevo	Bln-925	5940 ± 100	4940 (4892,4887,4841) 4727
Goljamo Delčevo	Bln-922	5840 ± 100	4892 (4772,4759,4728) 4589
Goljamo Delčevo	Bln-924	5840 ± 100	4892 (4772,4759,4728) 4589
Goljamo Delčevo	Bln-966	5840 ± 100	4892 (4772,4759,4728) 4589
Goljamo Delčevo	Bln-920a	5640 ± 100	4661 (4470) 4360
Goljamo Delčevo	Bln-920	5590 ± 100	4530 (4459,4411,4409) 4450
Goljamo Delčevo	Bln-921	5515 ± 100	4460 (4356) 4249
Bikovo-Dončova	Bln-337	5590 ± 80	4513 (4459,4411,4409) 4355
Căscioarele	Bln-335	5985 ± 120	5060 (4900,4870,4869) 4780
Căscioarele	Bln-336	5895 ± 120	4937 (4785) 4627
Căscioarele	Bln-332	5865 ± 150	4936 (4778) 4578
Căscioarele	Bln-598	5855 ± 80	4891 (4775) 4626
Căscioarele	Bln-334	5758 ± 80	4772 (4667,4636,4611) 4516
Căscioarele	Bln-333	5740 ± 120	4780 (4660,4641,4590) 4470
Căscioarele	Bln-602	5705 ± 80	4713 (4574,4559,4542) 4466
Căscioarele	Bln-605	5675 ± 80	4667 (4515) 4459
Căscioarele	Bln-599	5670 ± 100	4675 (4512) 4369
Căscioarele	Bln-344	5620 ± 120	4661 (4465) 4350
Căscioarele	Bln-603	5620 ± 120	4661 (4665) 4350
Căscioarele	Bln-604	5580 ± 100	4520 (4456,4417,4403) 4350
Căscioarele	Bln-607	5560 ± 100	4510 (4452,4428,4392,4384,4368) 4340
Căscioarele	Bln-624	5560 ± 100	4510 (4452,4428,4392,4384,4368) 4340
Căscioarele	Bln-345	5555 ± 120	4520 (4451,4438,4366) 4340

continued

SITE	LAB NUMBER	C–14 YEARS B.P.	CALIBRATED AGE RANGES B.C. Maximum (calibrated age) minimum
Căscioarele	Bln-606	5545 ± 100	4490 (4364) 4340
Căscioarele	Bln-343	5485 ± 120	4460 (4349) 4240
Căscioarele	Bln-608	5400 ± 120	4360 (4318,4285,4246) 4044
Varaşti	GrN-1987	5360 ± 70	4336 (4235) 4046
Gumelniţa	GrN-3025	5715 ± 70	4713 (4651,4649,4579) 4481
Salcuţa	GrN-1989	5450 ± 55	4355 (4340) 4244
Salcuţa	GrN-1990	5475 ± 55	4361 (4347) 4250
Vulkaneshti II	Mo-417	5810 ± 150	4896 (4719) 4500
Vulkaneshti II	Le-640	5300 ± 60	4236 (4220,4200,4147,4110,4088,4060.4048) 4007

Plot of Data from Table 11: Boian-Gumelniţa and Karanovo IV-VI Cultures

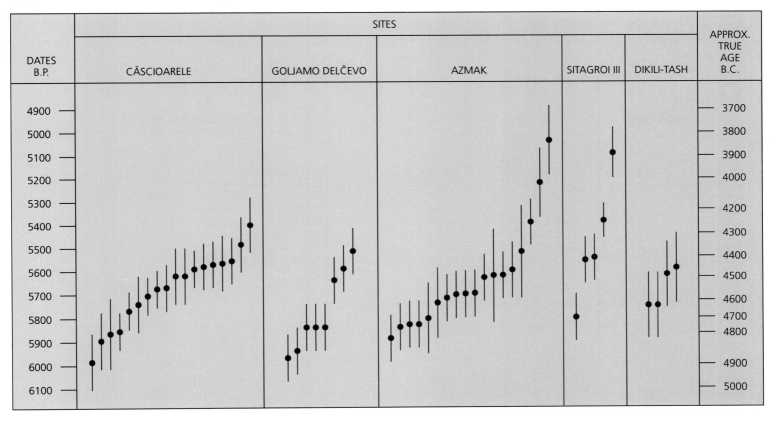

TABLE 12
Cucuteni Culture

SITE	LAB NUMBER	C–14 YEARS B.P.	CALIBRATED AGE RANGES B.C. Maximum (calibrated age) minimum
Early			
Poduri	Bln-2804	5820±50	4780 (4722) 4619
Poduri	Bln-2803	5880±150	4940 (4782) 4584
Poduri	Bln-2782	5780±50	4726 (4711,4708,4680) 4583
Novye Ruseshty I	Bln-590	5565±100	4510 (4453,4425,4395,4377,4369) 4340
Tîrpeşti I	GrN-4424	5540±85	4467 (4363) 4341
Poduri	Bln-2783	5690±50	4662 (4527) 4469
Poduri	Bln-2784	5680±60	4662 (4519) 4465
Margineni	Bln-1536	5625±50	4518 (4467) 4398
Margineni	Bln-1534	5610±55	4510 (4463) 4365
Classical			
Margineni	Bln-1535	5485±60	4365 (4349) 4264
Poduri	Bln-2802	5420±150	4454 (4333,4273,4259) 4042
Poduri	Bln-2766	5350±80	4336 (4233,4183,4167) 4042
Leca-Ungureni	Bln-795	5345±100	4340 (4232,4190,4165) 4008
Habaşeşti	GrN-1985	5330±80	4331 (4228,4194,4159) 4009
Polivanov Yar	GrN-5134	5440±70	4356 (4338) 4237
Draguşeni	Bln-1060	5355±100	4340 (4234,4174,4169) 4040
Luka-Vrublevetskaya (bone)	UCLA-1642C	5310±160	4350 (4223,4198,4151,4051,4050) 3980
Krasnostavka	Ki-882	5310±160	4350 (4223,4198,4151,4051,4050) 3980
Late			
Klishchiv	LE-1060	5100±50	3985 (3957,3838,3826) 3816
Novorozanivka II	UCLA-1642F	4915±300	4033 (3771,3768,3700) 3370
Valea Lupului	GrN-1982	4950±60	3787 (3776,3744,3708) 3694
Soroki-Ozero	BM-495	4940±105	3932 (3775,3751,3706) 3640
Soroki-Ozero	BM-494	4792±105	3700 (3626,3566,3541) 3381
Evminka (bone)	UCLA-1671B	4890±60	3780 (3695) 3537
Chapaevka (bone)	Bln-631	4870±100	3780 (3691) 3530
Evminka (bone)	UCLA-1466B	4790±100	3700 (3626,3568,3540) 3382

Cucuteni and Tripolye Classification on the Basis of Stratigraphy and Typology

PHASES	SITES
Pre-Cucuteni I	Traian-Dealul Viei
Pre-Cucuteni II (Triploye A-1)	Floreşti, Larga Jijia, Izvoare I-1, Poduri
Pre-Cucuteni III (Tripolye A-2 and A-3)	Traian-Dealul Fîntînilor, Izvoare I-2, Tîrpeşti, Poduri, Luka Vrublevetskaya, Bernovo Luka
Cucuteni A-1	Izvoare II, Tîrpeşti, N. Ruseshty I (lower), Poduri
Cucuteni A-2 (Tripolye BI-1)	Tîrpeşti, Cucuteni, Izvoare II-2, Frumuşica, Poduri, Margineni, Truşeşti, Polivanov Yar III-1
Cucuteni A-3 (Tripolye BI-2)	Cucuteni, Habaşeşti, V. Ruseshty I (upper), Leca Ungureni, Poduri, Polivanov Yar III-2
Cucuteni A-4 (Tripolye BI-3)	Ruginoasa, Draguşeni, Fedeleşeni, Yar III-3, Nezvisko (lower)
Cucuteni AB-1 (Tripolye BII-2)	Traian-Dealul Fintînilor, Corlăteni, Klishchiv, Soloncheni II, Veremie
Cucuteni AB-2 (Tripolye BII-2)	Traian-Dealul Fîntînilor, Cucuteni-Dimbul Morii, Kolomiyshchina II, Poduri-Dealul Ghindaru, Vladimirivka, Tripolye, Nezvisko (upper)
Cucuteni B-1 (Tripolye BIII-1)	Cucuteni, Petreni, Ghelăieşti-Nedeia,Cucuteni-Cetaţuia, Văleni-Piatra Neamţ, Poduri, Şipeniţ (Sipintsi), Varvarivka 8, Maidan (Màidanetskoe)
Cucuteni B-2 (Tripolye BIII-3)	Cucuteni-Cetaţuia, Valea Lupului, Podei Tg, Ocna, Stina I, Poduri
Cucuteni B-3 (Tripolye BIII-3)	Popudnia, Tomashivka, St. Buda, Sushkivka, Stina 4, Krutoborodintsi II, Tripolye B, Kolòmiyshchina I, Sadoveni-Manoleosa

continued

SITE	LAB NUMBER	C–14 YEARS B.P.	CALIBRATED AGE RANGES B.C. Maximum (calibrated age) minimum
Tripolye CI	Koshilivtsi, Novorozanivka, Bilcze Zlote, Chapaevka		
Tripolye CII-1	Zhvanets, Vikhvatintsi, Lukashi, Sofiivka II		
Horodiştea-Folteşti	Usatovo, Ternivka, Parkany, Sukleya,		
(Tripolye CII-2)	Kolodiazhnoe, Izvoare III, Horodiştea I (Gorodishche), Folteşti		

Note: Broken line indicates the end of the Cucuteni civilization. Tripolye CII-2 represents a Kurgan culture with a strong influence of the Cucuteni substratum.

Plot of Data from Table 12: Cucuteni Culture

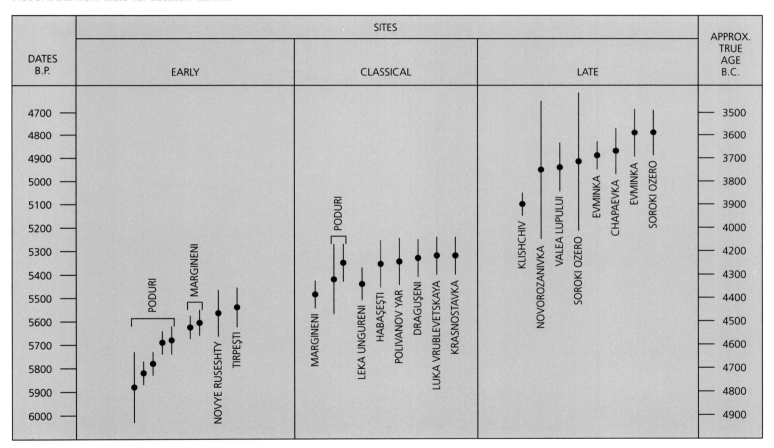

TABLE 13

Dnieper-Donets Culture

SITE	LAB NUMBER	C–14 YEARS B.P.	CALIBRATED AGE RANGES B.C. Maximum (calibrated age) minimum
Osipovka	Kiev	6075±400	5464 (5032,5029,4998,4958,4949) 4520
Osipovka	Kiev	5940±420	5321 (4892,4887,4841) 4360
Yasonovatka	Kiev	5800±300	5053 (4716) 4350
Nikolskoe	Kiev	5540±400	4892 (4363) 3980

Plot of Data from Table 13: Dnieper-Donets Culture

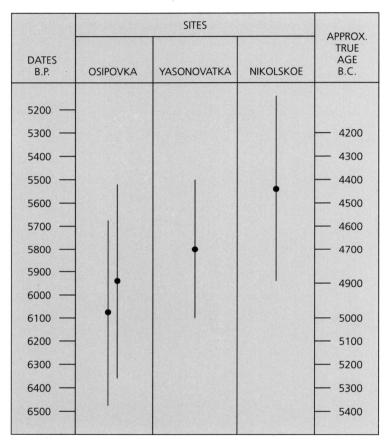

TABLE 14
Ertebølle (Mesolithic) and TRB (Neolithic) Cultures, Northern Europe

SITE	LAB NUMBER	C–14 YEARS B.P.	CALIBRATED AGE RANGES B.C. Maximum (calibrated age) minimum
Ertebølle in NW Germany and Scandinavia			
Brovst	K-1613	5610 ± 100	4577 (4463) 4350
Brovst	K-1855	5410 ± 100	4360 (4330,4279,4248) 4049
Brovst	K-1856	5500 ± 100	4460 (4353) 4245
Brovst	K-1857	5450 ± 110	4452 (4340) 4163
Brovst	K-1859	5490 ± 110	3500 (3356) 3100
Brovst	K-1861	5410 ± 110	4360 (4330,4279,4248) 4048
Brovst	K-1863	5400 ± 110	4360 (4318,4285,4246) 4046
Brovst	K-1864	5420 ± 100	4360 (4333,4273,4259) 4049
Dümmer	Hv-1220	6060 ± 115	5210 (4992,4979,4946) 4843
Elinelund	U-48	5450 ± 210	4500 (4340) 4007
Ellerbek	Y-440	6060 ± 200	5230 (4992,4979,4946) 4780
Ellerbek	KI-152	5170 ± 110	4216 (3991) 3818
Ertebølle	K-1529	5760 ± 100	4780 (4668,4635,4613) 4500
Ertebølle	K-1530	5660 ± 120	4711 (4504) 4360
Ertebølle	K-1531	5600 ± 120	4653 (4461) 4350
Ertebølle	K-1534	5580 ± 110	4530 (4456,4417,4403) 4340
Ertebølle	K-1533	5570 ± 110	4520 (4454,4423,4398,4370) 4340
Ertebølle	K-1532	5550 ± 110	4500 (4365) 4340
Ertebølle	K-1535	5110 ± 100	4032 (3963,3834,3828) 3790
Flynderhage	K-1450	5230 ± 100	4228 (4035,4018,4005) 3970
Haldrup Strand	K-1612	5630 ± 120	4665 (4468) 4350
Lietzow	Bln-560	5190 ± 120	4223 (3996) 3820
Lietzow	Bln-561	5815 ± 100	4832 (4721) 4580
Norslund	K-990	5730 ± 120	4770 (4657,4645,4585) 4460
Norslund	K-991	5680 ± 120	4720 (4519) 4367
Ølby Lyng	K-1230	5210 ± 130	4231 (4032,4026,4001) 3822
Ølby Lyng	K-1231	5320 ± 130	4340 (4225,4196,4155) 4000
Ralswiek	Bln-563	5455 ± 100	4451 (4342) 4168
Ringkloster	K-1652	5610 ± 110	4653 (4463) 4350
Ringkloster	K-1765	5500 ± 110	4460 (4353) 4240
Salpetermose	K-1232	5550 ± 120	4510 (4365) 4340
Salpetermose	K-1233	6020 ± 100	5193 (4937,4917,4907) 4793
Salpetermose	K-1234	5780 ± 120	4790 (4711,4708,4680) 4500
Salpetermose	K-1235	5410 ± 120	4366 (4330,4279,4248) 4046
Satrup-Südensee	GrN-6590	6015 ± 90	5056 (4936,4919,4906) 4797
Satrup-Südensee	GrN-6588	6024 ± 90	5192 (4938,4915,4908) 4804
Satrup-Südensee	KN-137	5960 ± 80	4942 (4895,4879,4849) 4781
Satrup-Südensee	KN-139	5880 ± 65	4893 (4782) 4720
Satrup-Rüde	Y-160	5960 ± 70	4940 (4895,4879,4849) 4783
Satrup-Rüde	Y-441a	5620 ± 200	4720 (4465) 4256
Satrup-Rüde	Y-471	5620 ± 200	4720 (4465) 4256
Sølanger	K-1723	5520 ± 110	4470 (4358) 4248
Vejlebro	K-1799	5310 ± 110	4333 (4223,4198,4151,4051,4050) 4000
Vejlebro	K-2301	5410 ± 100	4360 (4330,4279,4248) 4049
Vejlebro	K-1802	5540 ± 100	4480 (4363) 4340
Vejlebro	K-1801	5180 ± 110	4218 (3994) 3820
TRB, Poland			
Cmielów	GrN-5088	4615 ± 35	3491 (3366) 3349
Cmielów	GrN-5036	4650 ± 40	3500 (3373) 3358
Cmielów	H-566/592	4675 ± 110	3625 (3497,3423,3380) 3350
Cmielów	GrN-5090	4720 ± 40	3617 (3510,3396,3388) 3379
Cmielów	GrN-5089	4775 ± 40	3636 (3620,3574,3533) 3389
Radziejów		4680 ± 380	3938 (3498,3419,3380) 2920

continued

TABLE 14 *continued*

SITE	LAB NUMBER	C–14 YEARS B.P.	CALIBRATED AGE RANGES B.C. Maximum (calibrated age) minimum
Radziejów	GrN-5045	4710±40	3613 (3507,3401,3386) 3378
Sarnowo	GrN-5035	5570±60	4468 (4454,4423,4398,4370) 4354
Zarębowo	GrN-5044	4625±40	3496 (3370) 3351
Gródek Nadbużny	KN-243	5050±160	4032 (3933,3874,3816) 3690
Niedzwiedź I	M-2323	4640±190	3640 (3373) 3048
Niedzwiedź I	M-2322	4600±190	3626 (3360) 3040
Niedzwiedź I	M-2321	4470±190	3493 (3263,3246,3102) 2910
Niedzwiedź I	Bln-927	4715±100	3630 (3509,3398,3387) 3370
Lupawa	Bln-1814	6060±80	5198 (4992,4979,4946) 4863
Lupawa	Bln-1593	5730±45	4711 (4657,4645,4585) 4519
Lupawa	Bln-1313	4025±60	2852 (2574,2533,2508) 2474
Lupawa	Bln-927	4715±100	3630 (3509,3398,3387) 3370
Bronocice	DIC-719	5060±110	3990 (3938,3867,3818) 3708
Bronocice	DIC-362	4940±125	3871 (3580) 3460
Bronocice	DIC-542	4800±70	3692 (3629,3560,3544) 3393
Bronocice	DIC-718	4690±75	3618 (3501,3411,3382) 3365
Bronocice	DIC-716	4610±120	3596 (3364) 3107
Bronocice	DIC-360	4600±75	3498 (3360) 3145
Bronocice	DIC-363	4520±60	3352 (3331,3226,3185,3155,3143) 3098

Central German Groups with Kurgan elements

Baalberge:

Hüde	Hv-373	4840±130	3780 (3642) 3386
Postoloprty	Bln-482	4925±80	3786 (3772,3761,3703) 3643
Březno	GrN-8803	5090±45	3978 (3951,3842,3824) 3814

Salzmünde

Halle-Dölau	H-209/579	4970±90	3939 (3780,3731,3727) 3692
Halle-Dölau	Bln-53	4630±100	3596 (3371) 3147
Halle-Dölau	Bln-64	4780±100	3690 (3622,3572,3535) 3380

Bernburg

Aspenstedt	H-210/271	4560±110	3496 (3344) 3048
Halle-Dölau	Bln-838	4105±110	2884 (2856,2822,2659,2639,2671) 2497
Halle-Dölau	Bln-838a	4380±100	3296 (3028,2935,2930) 2910
Halle-Dölau	Bln-912	4340±100	3094 (2922) 2890
Pevestorf	Hv-582	4380±100	3296 (3028,2985,2930) 2910

TRB, Germany

Berlin-Heidmoor	H-29/146	5140±115	4040 (3979) 3789
Berlin-Heidmoor	H-30/145	5020±105	3970 (3895,3887,3810,3788) 3700
Grube-Rosenhof	Kn-?	5200±70	4213 (3998) 3973
Satrup Moor	Y-472	4960±50	3787 (3778,3738,3712) 3698
Schöner Mark	————	5105±70	3993 (3960,3836,3827) 3813
Satrup-Südensee	Y-472	4960±50	3787 (3778,3738,3712) 3698
Satrup-Südensee	Kn-667	4830±70	3698 (3639) 3525
Satrup-Südensee	GrN-6589	4815±85	3698 (3634) 3389
Satrup-Südensee	GrN-6592	4800±85	3695 (3629,3560,3544) 3386
Satrup-Südensee	KN-138	4740±75	3635 (3604,3585,3518) 3377
Satrup-Südensee	GrN-6591	4710±85	3628 (3507,3401,3386) 3369
Satrup-Südensee	Kn-666	4610±60	3496 (3364) 3340
Flögeln (house); charcoal from postpits	Hv-8452	4795±60	3675 (3628,3564,3542) 3514
Flögeln (house); charcoal from postpits	Hv-8454	4730±85	3635 (3594,3589,3514,3391,3390) 3373
Flögeln (house); charcoal from house wall trench	Hv-8450	4500±65	3347 (3307,3235,3177,3163,3134,3112,3110) 3043
Flögeln (house); charcoal from house wall trench	Hv-8453	4400±65	3260 (3034) 2921

continued

SITE	LAB NUMBER	C–14 YEARS B.P.	CALIBRATED AGE RANGES B.C. Maximum (calibrated age) minimum
TRB, The Netherlands			
Angelsloo	GrN-5070	4100 ± 30	2863 (2855,2824,2657,2640,2619) 2590
Angelsloo	GrN-2370	4145 ± 30	2874 (2866,2809,2771,2724,2698,2672,2669) 2623
Angelsloo	GrN-5767	4315 ± 100	3040 (2918) 2785
Angelsloo	GrN-5103	4355 ± 45	3035 (3015,3004,2925) 2916
Angelsloo	GrN-4201	4380 ± 75	3098 (3028,2985,2930) 2916
Anlo	GrN-1824	4420 ± 50	3291 (3040) 2928
Odoorn	GrN-2226	4590 ± 80	3496 (3356) 3137
TRB, Sweden			
Vätteryd	U-46	4680 ± 140	3640 (3498,3419,3380) 3200
Vätteryd	U-47	4280 ± 170	3096 (2911) 2622
Linnebjar	Lu-35	4690 ± 100	3650 (3498,3419,3380) 3138
Svenstorp	Lu-12	4780 ± 100	3690 (3622,3572,3535) 3380
Bölensvattnet	St-1661	4920 ± 80	3785 (3771,3764,3702) 3641
Värby	Lu-10	4820 ± 100	3772 (3636) 3387
Värby	Kn-103	4900 ± 120	3896 (3697) 3534
Ängdala	––––	4360 ± 70	3091 (3018,3001,2926) 2913
TRB, Denmark			
Konenhoj (A?)	K-923	5260 ± 100	4240 (4210) 3990
Mosegarden (B)	K-3463	5080 ± 90	3992 (3946,3846,3822) 3783
Lindebjerg (B)	K-1659	5010 ± 100	3960 (3786) 3700
Rustrup (C)	K-2254	4970 ± 100	3943 (3780,3731,3727) 3690
Rustrup (C)	K-2255	4920 ± 100	3896 (3771,3764,3702) 3630
Rustrup (C)	K-2253	4910 ± 100	3790 (3699) 3548
Rude (B)	K-3124	4910 ± 90	3785 (3699) 3635
Jordløse mose	K-3776	4980 ± 65	3933 (3781) 3700
Mosegarden (B?)	K-3464	4890 ± 100	3780 (3695) 3539
Konenhoj (C)	K-919	4850 ± 100	3777 (3645) 3521
Rude (B)	K-3125	4810 ± 70	3694 (3633,3552,3549) 3517
Aamosen	K-129	4940 ± 160	3960 (3775,3751,3706) 3535
Aamosen	K-128	4910 ± 160	3943 (3699) 3522
Aamosen	K-126	4880 ± 170	3934 (3693) 3386
Aamosen	K-125	4840 ± 170	3790 (3642) 3378
Aamosen	K-132	4660 ± 150	3360 (3252,3249,3099) 2920
Aamosen	K-131	4610 ± 150	3615 (3364) 3100
Aamosen	K-124	4600 ± 170	3619 (3360) 3042
Sølager	K-1724	4650 ± 100	3612 (3375) 3340
Sarrup	K-2628	4580 ± 70	3490 (3351) 3137
Sarrup	K-2630	4600 ± 90	3502 (3360) 3138
Sarrup	K-2631	4620 ± 90	3508 (3368) 3147
Toftum	K-2983	4590 ± 60	3491 (3356) 3147
Toftum	K-2979	4620 ± 90	3508 (3368) 3147
Toftum	K-2982	4550 ± 90	3373 (3341) 3098
Megalith Period in Denmark and NW Germany			
(Passage Graves, Stone Packing Graves, Cult Buildings or Offering Places)			
Vroue	K-1569	4040 ± 100	2865 (2580) 2470
Vroue	K-1574	4210 ± 100	2917 (2883,2796,2784) 2622
Vroue	K-1572	4230 ± 100	2921 (2888,2791,2789) 2665
Vroue	K-1573	4270 ± 100	3023 (2909) 2703
Vroue	K-1571	4300 ± 100	3030 (2915) 2782
Vroue	K-1567	4430 ± 100	3330 (3091,3065,3043) 2920
Vroue	K-1568	4560 ± 100	3493 (3344) 3100
Vroue	K-1566	4570 ± 100	3496 (3348) 3100
Vroue	K-1570	4980 ± 100	3950 (3781) 3690

continued

TABLE 14 *continued*

SITE	LAB NUMBER	C–14 YEARS B.P.	CALIBRATED AGE RANGES B.C. Maximum (calibrated age) minimum
Oster Ristofte	K-1789	4310 ± 100	3040 (2917) 2784
Tustrup	K-718	4390 ± 120	3320 (3031,2966,2940) 2910
Tustrup	K-727	4440 ± 120	3340 (3094,3059,3045) 2920
Katbjerg	K-978	4490 ± 120	3360 (3301,3239,3173,3167,3107) 2928
Lanum	K-1771	4510 ± 100	3360 (3318,3231,3181,3159,3139) 3040
Herrup	K-1767	4510 ± 100	3360 (3318,3231,3181,3159,3139) 3040
Herrup	K-1768	4530 ± 100	3370 (3334,3219,3189,3152,3148) 3042
Herrup	K-1769	4530 ± 100	3370 (3334,3219,3189,3152,3148) 3032
Herrup	K-1766	4650 ± 100	3612 (3375) 3340
Fovlum	K-1602	4530 ± 100	3370 (3334,3219,3189,3152,3148) 3042
Fovlum	K-1601	4540 ± 110	3380 (3338,3213,3203) 3042
Mecklenburg: Frauenmark	Bln-432	4010 ± 100	2858 (4569,2538,2503) 2460
Gnewitz	Bln-472	4250 ± 100	3013 (2897) 2699
Katelbogen	Bln-554	3800 ± 120	2460 (2278,2234,2209) 2042
Lancken-Granitz	Bln-991	3990 ± 120	2858 (2559,2544,2495) 2354
Lancken-Granitz	Bln-992	3885 ± 100	2556 (2454,2420,2402) 2203
Liepen	Bln-473	4080 ± 100	2875 (2850,2845,2652,2647,2612) 2491
Poggendorfer F.	Bln-990	3795 ± 100	2456 (2276,2239,2207) 2046

Summary TRB Chronology

CALENDAR YEARS	PHASES	REGIONAL CHRONOLOGICAL LABELS
3000 B.C.	Phase 5	Megalithic graves in Holland, northwestern Germany, Denmark, and southern Sweden, "Tiefstich" pottery Middle Neolithic in Denmark
3500 B.C.	Phase 4	Virum in Denmark, Fuchsberg in northern Germany, Salzmünde in central Germany, Luboń in Poland, Michelsberg V in the Rhine basin
3700 B.C.	Phase 3	Early Neolithic C in Denmark, Satrup in N Germany, Younger Baalberge in central Germany, Wiórek in Poland, Michelsberg IV
4000 B.C.	Phase 2	Early Neolithic B in Denmark, Rosenhof in N Germany, Pikutkowo in Poland, Michelsberg III
4300 B.C.	Phase 1	Early Neolithic A in Denmark and N Germany, Early Baalberge in central Germany, Sarnowo in Poland, Michelsberg I and II in the Upper Rhine area

Plot of Data from Table 14: TRB Culture in Poland and Germany

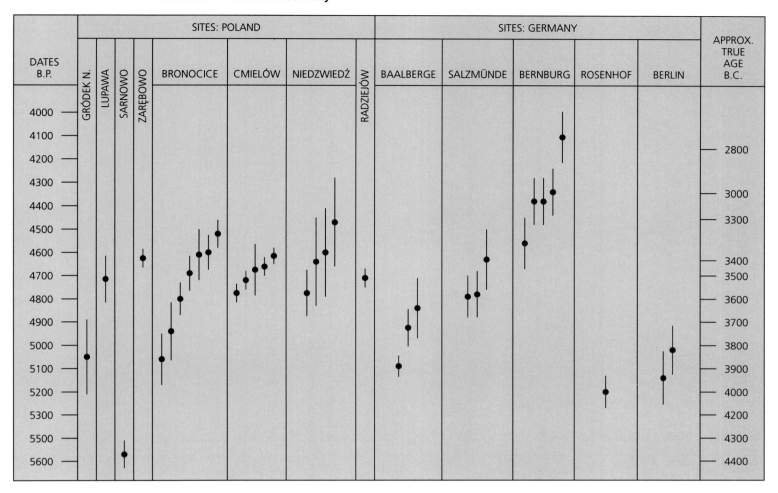

Plot of Data from Table 14: Mesolithic Ertebølle *(lower)* and TRB cultures in NW Germany, Holland, Denmark, and Sweden

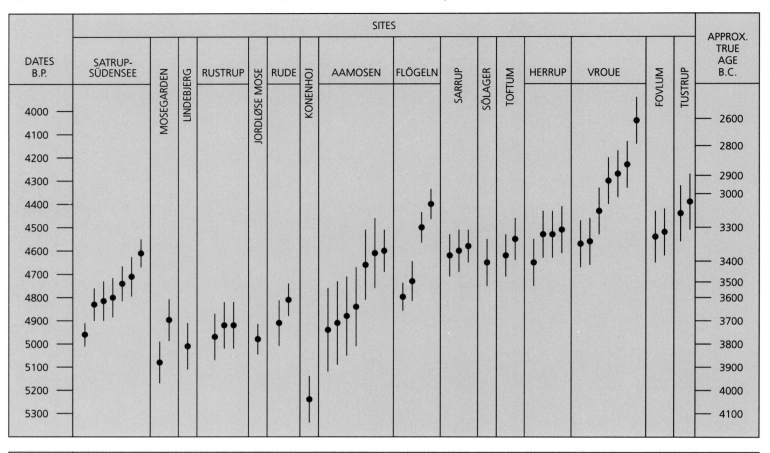

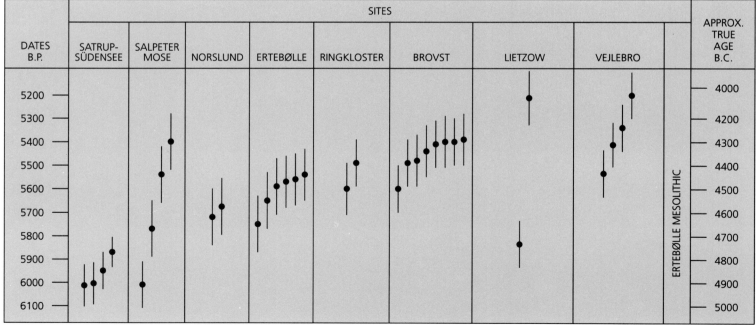

TABLE 15
Nemunas Culture

SITE	LAB NUMBER	C–14 YEARS B.P.	CALIBRATED AGE RANGES B.C. Maximum (calibrated age) minimum
Zedmar (Serowo)	Bln-2162	5280±50	4229 (4215,4205,4138,4120,4044) 4004
Zedmar	LE-1387	4900±80	3782 (3697) 3635
Zedmar	LE-1386	4870±80	3777 (3691) 3538

Plot of Data from Table 15: Nemunas Culture

DATES B.P.	SITES ZEDMAR (SEROWO)	APPROX. TRUE AGE B.C.
4800		3600
4900		3700
5000		3800
5100		3900
5200		4000
5300		4200

TABLE 16

East Baltic Narva Culture

SITE	LAB NUMBER	C–14 YEARS B.P.	CALIBRATED AGE RANGES B.C. Maximum (calibrated age) minimum
Narva, Estonia	TA-33	5820±200	4937 (4722) 4470
Narva, Estonia	TA-7	5300±250	4370 (4220,4200,4147,4110,4088,4060) 3816
Osa, Latvia	LE-961	5880±80	4896 (4782) 4715
Osa, Latvia	LE-962	5780±70	4775 (4711,4708,4680) 4544
Osa, Latvia	LE-850	5730±50	4712 (4657,4645,4585) 4516
Osa, Latvia	LE-758	4000±60	2588 (2564,2541,2499) 2465
Zacene, Belorussia	LE-960	5450±75	4359 (4340) 4239
Kääpa, Estonia	TA-5	4865±235	3960 (3686,3650) 3370
Kääpa, Estonia	TA-6	4480±225	3510 (3295,3242,3104) 2900
Kääpa, Estonia	TA-4	4350±220	3350 (3013,3007,2924) 2665
Sarnate, Latvia	TA-26	4700±250	3777 (3504,3406,3384) 3048
Sarnate, Latvia	Bln-769	4640±100	3606 (3373) 3200
Sarnate, Latvia	TA-265	4510±70	3352 (3318,3231,3181,3159,3139) 3045
Sarnate, Latvia	LE-814	4501±110	3370 (3308,3235,3178,3163,3134,3110) 2939
Šventoji 2B, Lithuania	LJ-2523	4730±100	3640 (3594,3589,3514,3391,3390) 3370
Šventoji 1B, Lithuania	LJ-2628	4640±60	3505 (3373) 3350
Šventoji 1B, Lithuania	TA-247	4440±90	3335 (3094,3059,3045) 2924
Šventoji 2B, Lithuania	Vs-23	4440±90	3335 (3094,3059,3045) 2924
Šventoji 1B, Lithuania	LE-904	4225±70	2915 (2887,2792,2788) 2700
Šventoji 1B, Lithuania	LE-833	4100±60	2870 (2855,2824,2657,2640,2619) 2579
Šventoji 3B, Lithuania	Vib-9	4410±70	3296 (3037) 2922
Piestiņa, Latvia	LE-750	4670±150	3640 (3496,3427,3379) 3143
Piestiņa, Latvia	LE-748	4520±120	3370 (3331,3226,3185,3155,3143) 3030
Piestiņa, Latvia	LE-867	4240±50	2914 (2892) 2708

Plot of Data from Table 16: East Baltic Narva Culture

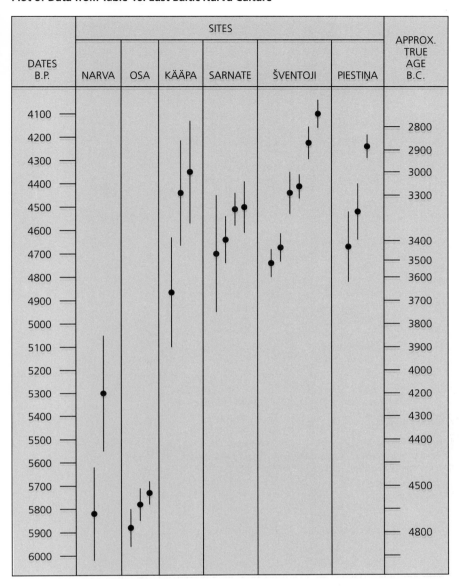

TABLE 17

Central Mediterranean (Dalmatia, S. Italy, Sardinia, Corsica, Malta) Cultures

SITE	LAB NUMBER	C–14 YEARS B.P.	CALIBRATED AGE RANGES B.C. Maximum (calibrated age) minimum
East Adriatic			
IMPRESSO			
Sidari, Corfu island	Gxo-771	7670±120	6610 (6474) 6420
Sidari, Corfu island	Gxo-772	7340±180	6410 (6170) 5993
Gudnja, cave, I, Dalmatia	GrN-10315	7170±70	6072 (6074,6063,6040,6021,5998) 5971
Gudnja, cave, I "	GrN-10314	6935±50	5841 (5761) 5731
Gudnja, cave, I/II "	GrN-10311	6560±40	5514 (5484) 5426
Vela, cave, IA	––––	7200±120	6140 (6080,6052,6049,6012,6007) 5970
Vela, cave, IA	––––	7000±120	5980 (5840) 5730
Gospodska pecina, cave	Z-579	7010±90	5980 (5951,5941,5873,5862,5846) 5740
Pokrovnik I, I		7000±100	5980 (5840) 5740
Pokrovnik I, II	Z-895	6300±150	5410 (5240) 5076
Škarin Samograd, cave, I	HD-11773	6740±50	5647 (5632) 5562
Škarin Samograd, cave, I	HD-12094	6750±55	5650 (5635) 5566
Škarin Samograd, cave, I	HD-11950	6780±50	5719 (5641) 5624
Škarin Samograd, cave, I	HD-11952	6600±100	5620 (5493) 5423
Tinj-Podlicade, I, open site	GrN-15236	6980±160	6032 (5828) 5650
Tinj-Podlicade, I, open site	GrN-15237	6670±260	5760 (5560) 5340
Tinj-Podlicade, I, open site	GrN-15238	6280±210	5473 (5237) 4947
Medulin-Vižula, I, open site	HD-12093	6850±180	5958 (5721) 5560
Medulin-Vižula, I, open site	HD-11733	6140±65	5219 (5198,5175,5135,5114,5073) 4948
DANILO CULTURE			
Gudnja cave	GrN-1031	6560±40	5514 (5484) 5426
Pokrovnik I open site	Z-895	6300±150	5410 (5240) 5076
South Italy			
IMPRESSO			
Coppa Nevigata	Pisa	8150 (uncertain)	data exceed calculable range
Madonna, cave, Calabria Sanctuary (Praia a Mare)	R-285	7555±85	6464 (6425) 6239
Scaramella di San Vito (Final Impresso-early painted)	Pisa	7000±100	5980 (5840) 5740
Rendina II near Melfi	LJ-4548	7110±140	6090 (5978) 5810
Rendina II near Melfi	LJ-4551	6900±150	5960 (5741) 5630
Rendina II near Melfi	LJ-4549	6760±100	5730 (5637) 5550
Rendina II near Melfi	LJ-4550	6440±150	5490 (5366) 5240
SCALORIA PERIOD			
Scaloria cave at Manfredonia	LJ-4649	6720±100	5694 (5626) 5500
Scaloria cave at Manfredonia	LJ-4981	6530±260	5640 (5479) 5240
Scaloria cave at Manfredonia	LJ-4650	6490±100	5490 (5472,5440,5423) 5330
Scaloria cave at Manfredonia	LJ-4651	6330±90	5360 (5308,5267,5244) 5230
Scaloria cave at Manfredonia	LJ-5096	6290±80	5330 (5238) 5214
Scaloria cave at Manfredonia	LJ-5097	6290±90	5330 (5338) 5210
Scaloria cave at Manfredonia	LJ-5095	6400±80	5472 (5338) 5241
Scaloria cave at Manfredonia (except the two last, all other charcoal samples date burials within the upper cave)	LJ-4983	6120±80	5217 (5193,5185,5062) 4941
Passo di Corvo, near Foggia	R(Tinè 1983)	6540±65	5509 (5480) 5412
Passo di Corvo, near Foggia	R(Tinè 1983)	6140±120	5230 (5198,5175,5135,5114,5073) 4906
Piccioni, Abruzzi	R	6247±130	5330 (5232) 5060
RIPOLI			
Ripoli	R	5630±80	4578 (4468) 4364
Ripoli	R	5630±150	4711 (4468) 4350

continued

SITE	LAB NUMBER	C–14 YEARS B.P.	CALIBRATED AGE RANGES B.C. Maximum (calibrated age) minimum
SERRA D'ALTO			
Lipari island	R	5200 ± 60	4211 (3998) 3977
Scaloria cave, Manfredonia	R	5480 ± 70	4450 (4348) 4248
Madonna cave, Calabria, Level VI	R	5555 ± 75	4468 (4451,4438,4366) 4347
DIANA			
Madonna cave, Level V	R	5110 ± 70	3994 (3963,3834,3828) 3814
Lipari	R	5000 ± 200	4000 (3785) 3544
Contrada Diana, XXI	R	4885 ± 55	3775 (3694) 3638
Sardinia			
IMPRESSO PERIOD			
Filiestru, Mara, SS	Q-3020	6710 ± 75	5645 (5623) 5531
Filiestru, Mara, SS	Q-3021	6615 ± 75	5620 (5506) 5478
Filiestru, Mara, SS	Q-3022	6515 ± 65	5490 (5476) 5361
Filiestru, Mara, SS	Q-3023	6470 ± 65	5482 (5454,5449,5415) 5334
FILIESTRU PERIOD			
Filiestru	Q-3024	6120 ± 55	5207 (5193,5185,5062) 4946
Filiestru	Q-3025	5900 ± 50	4894 (4787) 4729
BONU IGHINU PERIOD			
Filiestru	Q-3026	5625 ± 65	4529 (4467) 4367
Su Tintirriolu	R-882	5680 ± 160	4772 (4519) 4360
OZIERI PERIOD			
Filiestru	Q-3027	5250 ± 60	4223 (4039,4010) 3996
Filiestru	Q-3028	4950 ± 50	3786 (3776,3744,3708) 3696
Gr.D. Guano, Oliena	R-884	5090 ± 50	3980 (3951,3842,3824) 3813
Gr.D. Guano, Oliena	R-883	4900–4830 ± 50	3777 (3697) 3644
Gr.D. Guano, Oliena	R-879	4900–4830 ± 50	3777 (3697) 3644
MONTE CLARO PERIOD			
Filiestru	Q-3029	4430 ± 50	3297 (3091,3065,3043) 2929
Corsica			
IMPRESSO EARLY NEOLITHIC			
Basi VII		7700 ± 150	6680 (6553,6542,6487) 6420
Araguina			
Sennola XVII		7650 ± 150	6620 (6464) 6265
Curacchiaghiu 6		7600 ± 180	6600 (6441) 6186
Curacchiaghiu 6		7280 ± 160	6355 (6106) 5980
Aléria Casabianda		6670 ± 130	5650 (5560) 5480
Strette XXb		6420 ± 300	5630 (5347) 5060
Strette XXb		6480 ± 480	5810 (5470,5444,5419) 4903
MIDDLE AND LATE NEOLITHIC			
Basi VI		5200 ± 120	4226 (3998) 3822
Basi VI		5250 ± 120	4240 (4039,4010) 3970
Curacchiaghiu 5		4930 ± 140	3943 (3773,3758,3704) 3539
Scaffa Diana 21-22		5330 ± 100	4340 (4228,4194,4159) 4005
Scaffa Diana 21-22		5360 ± 100	4340 (4235) 4040
Scaffa Diana 18-19		4775 ± 90	3690 (3662,3574,3533) 3381
Malta			
Skorba (Red Skorba Phase)	BM-148	5175 ± 150	4227 (3993) 3789
Skorba (Zebbuġ Phase)	Bm-147	5000 ± 150	3980 (3785) 3640
Skorba (Zebbuġ Phase)	BM-145	5140 ± 150	4218 (3979) 3780
Mgarr	BM-100	4640 ± 150	3626 (3373) 3107
Skorba (Ġgantija Phase)	BM-142	5240 ± 150	4240 (4037,4014,4008) 3824
Skorba (Tarxien Phase)	BM-143	4380 ± 150	3330 (3028,2985,2930) 2788
Tarxien	BM-101	4485 ± 150	3370 (3298,3240,3171,3106) 2920

Plot of Data from Table 17: Central Mediterranean Early Neolithic

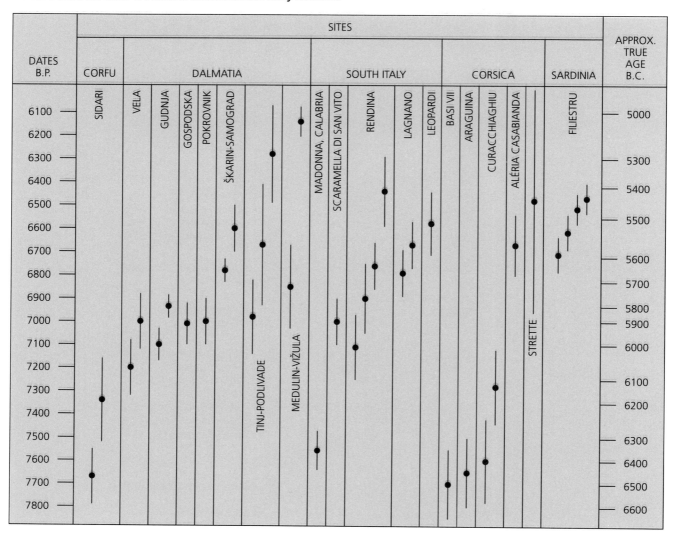

Plot of Data from Table 17: Central Mediterranean Middle and Late Neolithic

TABLE 18
West Mediterranean Early Neolithic, Cardial (Impresso) and Epicardial Cultures

SITE	LAB NUMBER	C-14 YEARS B.P.	CALIBRATED AGE RANGES B.C. Maximum (calibrated age) minimum
Spain			
Cova Fosca I, (Castellon)	CSIC-356	7100 ± 70	6076 (5975) 5849
Cova Fosca I　　"	CSIC-357	7210 ± 70	6113 (6082) 5984
Cova Fosca II　　"	CSIC-353	7460 ± 110	6430 (6374,6325,6240) 6170
Cova Fosca III (Aceramic)	I-9868	8880 ± 200	data exceeds calculable range
Cova de l'Or (Alicante)	H-1754/1208	6265 ± 75	5318 (5235) 5207
Cova de l'Or　　"	Kn-51	6510 ± 160	5560 (5475,5430) 5246
Cova de l'Or　　"	C11-M1	5980 ± 260	5230 (4899,4872,4865) 4580
Cova de l'Or　　"	C12-M2	6630 ± 290	5750 (5535) 5245
Murcielagos de Zuhueros (Cordoba) L.IV	CSIC-59	5930 ± 130	4993 (4837,4817,4803) 4720
Murcielagos de Zuhueros (Cordoba) L.IV	CSIC-54	6190 ± 130	5304 (5210) 4945
Murcielagos de Zuhueros (Cordoba) L.IV	CSIC-53	6190 ± 130	5304 (5210) 4945
Murcielagos de Zuhueros (Cordoba) L.IV	CSIC-55	6170 ± 130	4240 (5205,5155,5148) 4940
Murcielagos de Zuhueros (Cordoba) L.V	CSIC-56	5960 ± 130	5048 (4895,4879,4849) 4720
Murcielagos de Zuhueros (cereal) (Cordoba) L.V	CSIC-57	5980 ± 130	5191 (4899,4872,4865) 4770
Murcielagos de Zuhueros (Cordoba) L.IV	CSIC-58	6100 ± 130	5230 (5053,5013,5008) 4855
Murcielagos de Zuhueros (cereal) (Cordoba) L.IV	GrN-6640	6196 ± 45	5233 (5213) 5073
Murcielagos de Zuhueros (cereal) (Cordoba) L.II	GrN-6639	6025 ± 45	5031 (4938,4915,4908) 4862
Murcielagos de Zuhueros (Cordoba) L.V	GrN-6638	6240 ± 35	5239 (5231) 5208
Montbolo (Catalonia)	Gif-1209	6450 ± 170	5530 (5378) 5240
Ereta del Pedregal en Navarres (Valencia)	M-754	6130 ± 300	5360 (5195,5180,5131,5126,5067) 4720
Cueva del Nacimiento (Jaen)	Gif-1368	6780	5653 (5641) 5631
Cueva del Nacimiento (Jaen)	Gif-3471	7620	6472 (6448) 6433
Abrigo Grande del Barranco de los Grajos en Cieza (Murcia)	HAR-179	7200 ± 160	6180 (6080,6052,6049,6012,6007) 5886
Cardial (Impresso) and Epicardial culture in southern France			
COASTAL PROVENCE			
Cap Ragnon cave (Bouches-du-Rhône)	MC-500A(Shell)	7970 ± 150	(7019,6994,6959,6935,6916,6906,6821) sigmas beyond calculable range
Ile Riou Bouches-du-Rhône), open air site	MC-500B(Shell)	7650 ± 150	6620 (6464) 6265
	MC-440(Shell)	7600 ± 150	6570 (6441) 6230
Châteauneuf-les-Martigues series (Bouches-du-Rhône):			
Cailloutis 8C	Ly-438	7830 ± 170	7030 (6675,6651,6648) 6470
Foyer 7	Ly-624	6780 ± 240	5955 (5641) 5480
Cailloutis 6	Ly-446	6430 ± 140	5490 (5354) 5240
Cailloutis 7	Ly-447	6420 ± 120	5480 (5347) 5240
Foyer 5	Ly-623	6070 ± 490	5480 (4996,4964,4948) 4403
Foyer 1	Ly-622	5940 ± 290	5230 (4892,4887,4841) 4490
Cave	MC-531L(Shell)	6780 ± 100	5740 (4641) 5560
Cave	MC-531T(Shell)	6760 ± 100	5730 (5637) 5550
Le Baratin (Vaucluse), open air site	Gif-1855	6600 ± 140	5230 (5053,5013,5008) 4849
Baume Fontbrégoua, cave	Gif-2990	6700 ± 100	5650 (5619,5595,5583) 5490
Baume Fontbrégoua, cave	Gif-2989	6180 ± 120	5240 (5208) 4945
Baume Fontbrégoua, cave	Gif-2988	5800 ± 150	4894 (4716) 4490
Baume Fontbrégoua cave	Gif-2757	5690 ± 190	4780 (4527) 4350
Baume Fontbrégoua cave	Gif-2756	5690 ± 190	4780 (4527) 4350
Roucadour, Level C	Gsy-36a	5850 ± 150	4933 (4774) 4535
Grotte Gazel (Aude)	Grn-6702	6850 ± 90	5800 (5721) 5630
Grotte Gazel (Aude)	Kn.s.m.	6780 ± 200	5830 (5641) 5490
Grotte Gazel (Aude)	Gif-3575	6600 ± 130	5630 (5493) 5410
Grotte Gazel (Aude)	Gif-218	6540 ± 300	5717 (5480) 5230
Grotte Gazel (Aude)	Gif-218	6400 ± 300	5620 (5338) 5007

continued

SITE	LAB NUMBER	C–14 YEARS B.P.	CALIBRATED AGE RANGES B.C. Maximum (calibrated age) minimum
Grotte Gazel (Aude)	Kn.s.m.	6540 ± 200	5630 (5480) 5245
Grotte Gazel (Aude)	GrN-6707	6305 ± 55	5327 (5241) 5231
Grotte Gazel (Aude)	GrN-6706	6095 ± 65	5203 (5050,5016,5006) 4908
Grotte Gazel (Aude)	GrN-6705	6040 ± 65	5056 (4941) 4859
Grotte Gazel (Aude)	Gif-1273	5050 ± 150	4000 (3933,3874,3816) 3700
Saint Mitre Cave, (Haute Provence) III,Y II	MC-264	6700 ± 130	5713 (5619,5595,5583) 5480
Saint Mitre Cave, (Haute Provence) III,3	MC-263	6400 ± 100	5475 (5338) 5240
Saint Mitre Cave, (Haute Provence) H III,3	MC-265	6100 ± 120	5230 (5053,5013,5008) 4864
Saint Mitre Cave, (Haute Provence) III,12,2	MC-202	5950 ± 200	5200 (4894,4883,4845) 4600
Saint Mitre 2	M-203	5150 ± 200	4233 (3983) 3708
Grotte Bourbon C5, (Gard)	Ly-538	6180 ± 180	5321 (5208) 4903
Grotte Bourbon C2, (Gard)	Ly-412	6050 ± 120	5205 (4943) 4802
Shelter Jean Cros	Gif-218	6500 ± 150	5550 (5474,5435,5426) 5246
Labastide-en-Val (Aude) Grotto de Combe Obscure	Ly-423	6400 ± 160	5480 (5338) 5230
"Abri du Capitaine," Sainte-Croix-de-Verdon (Basses-Alpes)	Gif-1111	6050 ± 150	5220 (4943) 4790
Camprafaud, Level 19, Hérault	Gif-1491	6300 ± 140	5370 (5240) 5084
Camprafaud, Level 17, Hérault	Gif-1489	5900 ± 140	4940 (4787) 4611
Camprafaud, Level 16, Hérault	Gif-1488	5900 ± 140	4940 (4787) 4611
Camprafaud, Level 18, Hérault	Gif-1490	5800 ± 140	3775 (3629,3560,3544) 3380
Font-Juvénal, C 12, (Aude)	MC-499	5850 ± 100	4894 (4774) 4598

Cardial (Impresso) and Epicardial in Liguria, N. Italy

RIPARO ARMA DI NASINO SERIES, SAVONA

Arma di Nasino IXs-66	R-315	6280 ± 70	5322 (5237) 5214
Arma di Nasino IXm-66	R-316	6015 ± 65	5039 (4936,4919,4906) 4844
Arma di Nasino IXm-66	R-316a	5955 ± 65	4938 (4895,4881,4847) 4783
Arma di Nasino IXi-63	R-267	6470 ± 120	5490 (5454,5449,5415) 5246
Arma di Nasino IXs-63	R-265	6280 ± 120	5340 (5237) 5083
Arma di Nasino VIII-66	R-313	6420 ± 65	5473 (5347) 5246
Arma di Nasino VIII-66	R-313a	6400 ± 105	5480 (5338) 5240
Arma di Nasino VIIIa-63	R-263	6140 ± 110	5230 (5198,5175,5135,5114,5073) 4808

CAVERNA DELLE ARENE CANDIDE SERIES, LIGURIA

Arene Candide	VR-101	6220 ± 55	5238 (5225) 5087
Arene Candide Level 12	LJ-4136	5960 ± 140	5054 (4895,4879,4849) 4720
Arene Candide Level 12	LJ-4137	5730 ± 90	4723 (4657,4645,4585) 4469
Arene Candide (Fiorano) Level 13A	LJ-4138	5970 ± 120	5048 (4897,4876,4857) 4770
Arene Candide Level 13B	LJ-4139	6260 ± 90	5321 (5234) 5089
Arene Candide Level 13B	LJ-4140	6120 ± 100	5230 (5193,5185,5062) 4906
Arene Candide Level 13C	LJ-4141	6250 ± 100	5321 (5233) 5074
Arene Candide Level 13C	LJ-4142	6100 ± 90	5212 (5053,5013,5008) 4904
Arene Candide Level 14	LJ-4144	6520 ± 100	5540 (5477) 5340

Plot of Data from Table 18: Early Neolithic Spain

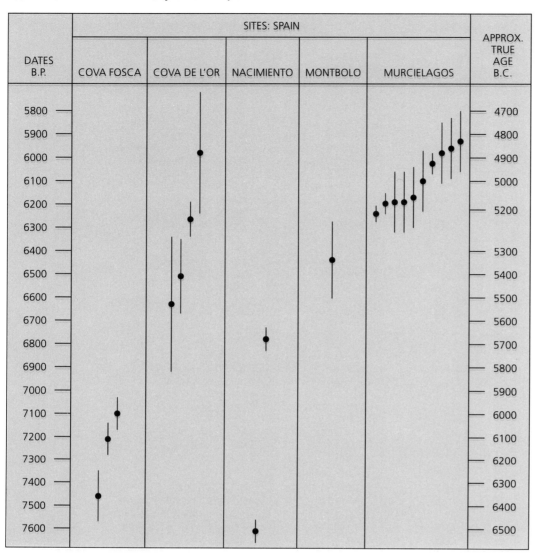

Plot of Data from Table 18: Early Neolithic South France and North Italy

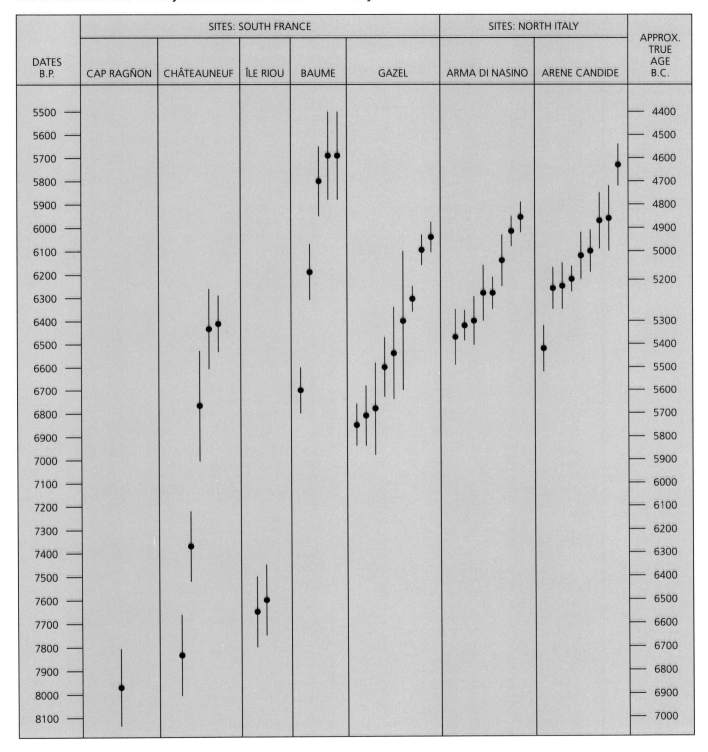

TABLE 19

Middle and Late Neolithic: Fiorano, Square-Mouth Pottery, and Lagozza Cultures

SITE	LAB NUMBER	C–14 YEARS B.P.	CALIBRATED AGE RANGES B.C. Maximum (calibrated age) minimum
Grotta Arma dello Stefanin series, Savona, Liguria			
Arma dello Stefanin IIIa	R-124	5600±80	4521 (4461) 4357
Arma dello Stefanin IIIb	R-143	5180±70	4039 (3994) 3828
Arma dello Stefanin IIIc	R-143D	5480±80	4452 (4348) 4245
Romagnano, Adige Valley series			
Romagnano III, 13-14, T1	R-776	5560±50	4464 (4452,4428,4392,4384,4368) 4354
Romagnano III, 15, T1	R-777	5530±50	4457 (4360) 4347
Romagnano III, 17, T2	R-779	5470±50	4359 (4345) 4250
Romagnano III, 19-20, T4 (Fiorano)	R-781	5810±50	4778 (4719) 4608
Romagnano III, 19-20, T4 "	R-781a	6006±50	4992 (4934,4922,4904) 4846
Romagnano III, AA1-2	R-1136	6480±50	5482 (5470,5444,5419) 5344
Square-Mouth Pottery Period			
Arene Candide III	R-104	5075±45	3970 (3944,3848,3821) 3789
Arene Candide IV-2	R-103	5465±50	4357 (4344) 4249
Arene Candide IV-1	R-102	5335±50	4243 (4229,4193,4161) 4044
Molino Casarotto series			
Molino Casarotto	Birm-261	5780±135	4831 (4711,4708,4680) 4990
Molino Casarotto	Birm-262	5820±135	4895 (4722) 4520
Molino Casarotto	Birm-263	5525±200	4655 (4359) 4157
Molino Casarotto	Birm-264	5750±135	4780 (4664,4638,4601) 4460
Molino Casarotto	Birm-265	5930±130	4993 (4837,4817,4803) 4720
Molino Casarotto	Birm-266	5555±130	4520 (4451,4438,4366) 4330
Molino Casarotto	Birm-267	5700±130	4730 (4572,4564,4536) 4370
Isola Virginia series, Lombardy			
Isola Virginia I	Pi-4	5534±144	4520 (4361) 4240
Isola Virginia 2	Pi-38	5326±180	4350 (4227,4195,4158) 3980
Pertusello IV	R-157	5400±90	4351 (4318,4285,4246) 4049
Cava Serrelle	R-1046	5290±50	4231 (4218,4203,4143,4115,4073,4068,4046) 4007
Monte Rocca series, Verona, NE Italy			
Site L	Birm-616	5070±100	3990 (3942,3850,3820) 3725
Site L	Birm-617	5370±70	4339 (4238) 4047
Petescia, Italy	Pi-28	5398±145	4360 (4315,4286,4245) 4040
Luni 7, Tre Erici, Trl,Str 10	St-1344	5395±80	4547 (4310,4288,4244) 4152
Grotta Aisone	R-95	5825±75	4787 (4724) 4598
Lagozza series			
Lagozza di Besnate 1	R-78	4735±50	3626 (3599,3587,3516) 3380
Lagozza di Besnate 1a	R-78a	4580±50	3372 (3351) 3146
Lagozza di Besnate 1b	R-338	4980±50	3906 (3781) 3703
Lagozza di Besnate 2	R-337	4805±50	3677 (3631,3556,3546) 3522
Lagozza di Besnate	Pi-34	4794±90	3694 (3627,3565,3542) 3384
Toppo Daguzzo 3a	LJ-4	4650±60	3508 (3375) 3354
Toppo Daguzzo 3b	LJ-4545	4710±80	3627 (3507,3401,3386) 3371
Toppo Daguzzo 4a	LJ-4546	4560±80	3373 (3344) 3104
Toppo Daguzzo 4b	LJ-4547	4440±70	3322 (3094,3059,3045) 2928
Pertusello III	R-115	4390±70	3254 (3031,2966,2940) 2918
Pertusello III	R-155	4390±70	3254 (3031,2966,2940) 2918
Arma di Nasino VIII-62	R-332	4705±70	3622 (3506,3403,3385) 3371
Arma di Nasino VIII-63	R-262	4220±90	2917 (2885,2794,2786) 2629

Plot of Data from Table 19: Middle and Late Neolithic Italy

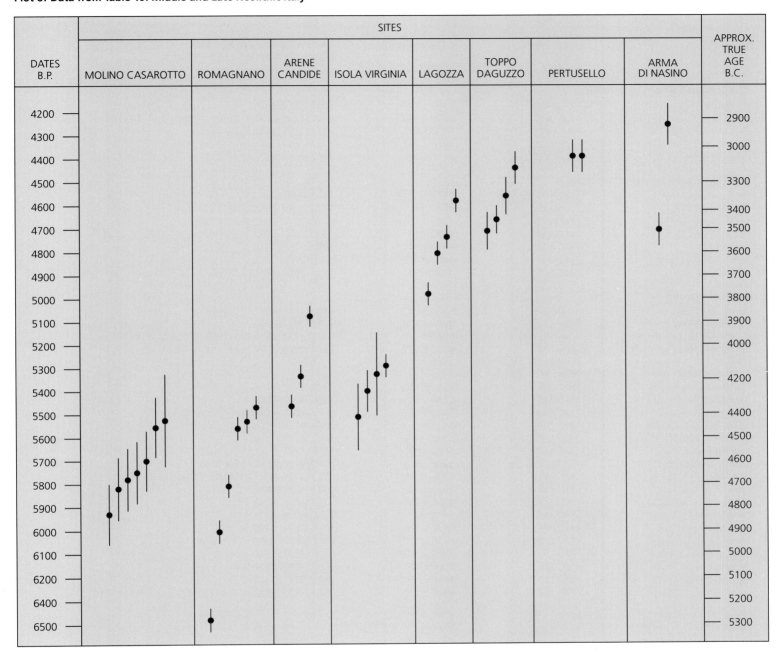

TABLE 20

Middle and Late Neolithic (Chassée) Culture in France

SITE	LAB NUMBER	C–14 YEARS B.P.	CALIBRATED AGE RANGES B.C. Maximum (calibrated age) minimum
Camprafaud (Hérault) cave series			
Camprafaud, Level 14	Gif-1486	5450 ± 130	4457 (4340) 4155
Camprafaud, Level 15	Gif-1487	5300 ± 130	4340 (4220,4200,4147,4110,4088,4060,4048) 3990
Camprafaud, Level 13	Gif-1485	5100 ± 130	4035 (3957,3838,3826) 3725
Camprafaud, Level 12	Gif-1484	4900 ± 130	3904 (3697) 3530
Camprafaud, Level 10	Gif-1157	4350 ± 140	3302 (3013,3007,2924) 2784
Font-Juvénal (Aude) Rock Shelter series			
Font-Juvénal C11	MC-498	5540 ± 100	4480 (4363) 4340
Font-Juvénal C7a	MC-495	4860 ± 90	3777 (3676,3663,3648) 3530
Font-Juvénal C8	MC-496	4800 ± 150	3777 (3629,3560,3544) 3370
Font-Juvénal C5	MC-493	4490 ± 80	3348 (3301,3239,3173,3167,3107) 3036
Font-Juvénal C12	MC-494	4570 ± 90	3493 (3348) 3104
Font-Juvénal C12b	MC-490	4400 ± 100	3308 (3034) 2910
Font-Juvénal C3	MC-491	4200 ± 90	2914 (2800,2798,2782) 2622
Eglise cave series			
Grotte de l'Eglise, Level 8A	Gif-1333	5500 ± 140	4480 (4353) 4240
Grotte de l'Eglise, Layer 9	Gsy-112B	4825 ± 130	3778 (3637) 3383
Grotte de l'Eglise, Layer 5	Gsy-112A	4510 ± 125	3370 (3318,3231,3181,3159,3139) 2933
Grotte de l'Eglise, Level 15	Gsy-1332	4200 ± 130	2920 (2880,2798,2782) 2590
Saint-Michel-du Touch (Haute-Garonne) settlement			
Saint-Michel-du Touch	MC-2092	5510 ± 100	4460 (4355) 4248
Saint-Michel-du Touch	MC-843	5460 ± 90	4366 (4343) 4237
Saint-Michel-du Touch	MC-848	5440 ± 90	4361 (4338) 4166
Saint-Michel-du Touch	MC-2089	5440 ± 130	4454 (4338) 4050
Saint-Michel-du Touch	MC-109	5380 ± 200	4457 (4241) 3990
Saint-Michel-du Touch	MC-844	5350 ± 90	4339 (4233,4183,4167) 4040
Saint-Michel-du Touch	MC-2091	5330 ± 100	4340 (4228,4194,4159) 4005
Saint-Michel-du Touch	MC-2216	5270 ± 140	4331 (4213,4207,4134,4125,4043) 3970
Saint-Michel-du Touch	MC-104	5260 ± 200	4340 (4210) 3818
Saint-Michel-du Touch	MC-2215	5250 ± 150	4319 (4039,4010) 3826
Saint-Michel-du Touch	MC-845	5190 ± 90	4216 (3996) 3826
Saint-Michel-du Touch	MC-846	5130 ± 100	4036 (3874) 3790
Saint-Michel-du Touch	MC-2217	5130 ± 100	4036 (3874) 3790
Saint-Michel-du Touch	MC-105	4900 ± 190	3950 (3697) 3386
Saint-Michel-du Touch	MC-106	4900 ± 130	3904 (3697) 3530
Saint-Michel-du Touch	MC-103	4580 ± 120	3505 (3351) 3100
Saint-Michel-du Touch	MC-102	4500 ± 200	3504 (3307,3235,3177,3163,3134,3112,3110) 2910
Le Curnic	Gsy-47 B	5980 ± 150	5196 (4899,4872,4865) 4720
Vailly-sur-Aisne	Sa-57	5470 ± 300	4674 (4345) 3990
Boutigny-sur-Essonne	Sa-79	5410 ± 300	4571 (4330,4279,4248) 3828
Seuil des Chèvres D7	Ly-69	5240 ± 100	4231 (4037,4014,4008) 3980
Abri Gay, Poncin, Ain	Ly-513	5490 ± 110	4460 (4350) 4240
Lempdes, Puy de Dome	Sa-208	5400 ± 300	4572 (4318,4285,4246) 3826
Seuil des Chèvres	Ly-388	5300 ± 180	4350 (4220,4200,4147,4110,4088,4060,4048) 3970
Abris de Saint Mitre 2	MC-203	5150 ± 200	4233 (3983) 3708
La Breche au Diable, Calvados	Gsy-39	4790 ± 150	3775 (3626,3568,3540) 3370
Les Matigons, Charente	Gsy-32	4570 ± 200	3619 (3348) 2928
Saint-Etienne de Gourgas F.22	Gif-154i	4570 ± 300	3690 (3348) 2910
Videlles II	GrN-4676	4500 ± 50	3342 (3307,3235,3117,3163,3134,3112,3110) 3047
Videlles I	GrN-4675	4500 ± 60	3345 (3307,3235,3177,3134,3112,3110) 3045
Montavne de Lumbres, Pas de Calais	Gsy-49	4470 ± 200	3496 (3263,3246,3102) 2910

continued

SITE	LAB NUMBER	C–14 YEARS B.P.	CALIBRATED AGE RANGES B.C. Maximum (calibrated age) minimum
Biard, Charent	Gsy-71	4435 ± 200	3370 (3092,3062,3044) 2789
Fort-Harrouard, Eure de Loir	Gsy-97	4400 ± 125	3330 (3034) 2910
Abris de Saint Mitre I	MC-201	4350 ± 150	3308 (3013,3007,2924) 2782
Richardmenil, Meurthe-et-Moselle	Ny-4	4280 ± ?	2914 (2911) 2906
Perte du Cros	Gsy-35 A	4201 ± 150	3013 (2880,2797,2783) 2580
Perte du Cros	Gsy-35B	4800 ± 130	3773 (3629,3560,3544) 3378
Trou Arnaud, Drome	Gsy-77	4140 ± 135	2910 (2865,2810,2747,2725,2697, 2674, 2668) 2500

Paris basin

JONQUIÈRES, (LE MONT-D'HUETTE) (OISE)

Jonquières S XIV	Ly-2970	5300 ± 140	4340 (4220,4200,4147,4110,4088,4060,4048) 3990
Jonquières S XIV	Gif-2919	5120 ± 130	4040 (3969) 3780
Jonquières S XXII	Gif-2918	4290 ± 100	3032 (2913) 2708

CATENOY, (LE CAMP CÉSAR) (OISE)

Catenoy S IV, C 5a	Ly-2967	4550 ± 160	3510 (3341) 2939
Catenoy S IV, C 5a	Ly-2965	4620 ± 120	3606 (3368) 3109
Catenoy S IV, C 5b	Ly-2968	4820 ± 150	3780 (3636) 3378
Catenoy S IV, C 5?	Ly-2713	4930 ± 120	3934 (3773,3758,3704) 3548
Catenoy S IV, C 5c	Ly-2966	5280 ± 140	4333 (4215,4205,4138,4120,4044) 3980

BOURY-EN-VEXIN (LE CUL-FROID) (OISE)

Boury-en-Vexin, T.4, C.D.	Ly-2712	4570 ± 130	3505 (3348) 3045
Boury-en-Vexin, T.3, C.E.	Ly-2711	5180 ± 100	4216 (3994) 3822
Boury-en-Vexin, ST 1,D.A.	Ly-2961	5240 ± 150	4240 (4037,4014,4008) 3824

COMPIÈGNE, (LE COQ GALLEUX) (OISE)

Compiègne ST 14	Ly-2718	5330 ± 110	4340 (4228,4194,4159) 4003
Compiègne Coupe 9 ca	Ly-2714	4950 ± 160	3960 (3776,3744,3708) 3539
Compiègne Fossé 2	Ly-2715	4450 ± 140	3360 (3096,3053,3048) 2920

Plot of Data from Table 20: Chassée Culture in France

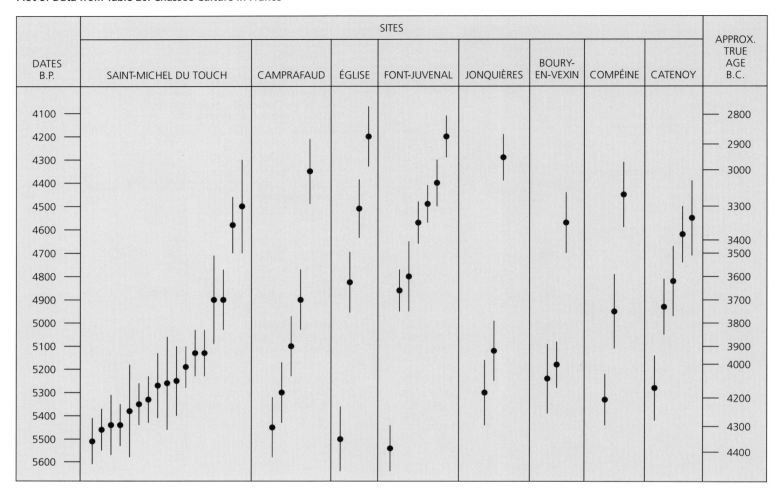

TABLE 21
Cortaillod Culture, Switzerland

SITE	LAB NUMBER	C–14 YEARS B.P.	CALIBRATED AGE RANGES B.C. Maximum (calibrated age) minimum
Auvernier-Port	B-2559	5130±120	4040 (3974) 3790
Auvernier-Port	B-2560	5100±80	3994 (3957,3838,3826) 3788
Auvernier-Port	B-2561	4980±110	3950 (3781) 3690
Auvernier-Port	B-2557	4360±110	3265 (3018,3001,2926) 2990
Auvernier-Port	B-2558	4390±70	3254 (3031,2966,2940) 2918
Lac Chalain	GrN-672	4180±130	2920 (2875,2802,2778,2715,2706) 2580
Lac Chalain	GrN-970	4590±80	3496 (3356) 3137
Chavannes	B-659a	5150±120	4213 (3983) 3790
Chavannes	B-659b	5120±120	4037 (3969) 3780
Chavannes	B-659	5180±120	4221 (3994) 3818
Chavannes	GrN-5610	4930±40	3781 (3773,3758,3704) 3694
Egolzwil 3	VRI-28	5620±130	4669 (4468) 4350
Egolzwil 3	K-115	4700±150	3650 (3504,3406,3384) 3340
Egolzwil 3	K-116	5280±280	4452 (4215,4205,4138,4120,4044) 3780
Egolzwil 3	K-118	4980±140	3970 (3781) 3640
Egolzwil 3	K-121	4920±130	3934 (3771,3764,3702) 3539
Egolzwil 3	GL-18	4650±110	3616 (3375) 3220
Egolzwil 3	F-17	4650±110	3616 (3375) 3200
Egolzwil 4	VRI-29	5360±150	4360 (4235) 4000
Egolzwil 4	KN-21	5370±160	4360 (4238) 4000
Egolzwil 4	H-228/276	5150±100	4040 (3983) 3816
Egolzwil 4	H-227/277	5040±100	3980 (3910,3878,3814) 3706
Saint-Leonard	B-232	4750±100	3650 (3611,3582,3523) 3370
Seeberg-B-Süd	B-118B	4630±180	3633 (3371) 3048
Seeberg-B-Süd	B-119A	4750±100	3650 (3611,3582,3523) 3370
Seeberg-B-Süd	B-119B	4800±130	3373 (3629,3560,3544) 3378
Seeberg-B-Süd	B-120	4500±100	3360 (3307,3235,3177,3163,3134,3112,3110) 2949
Seeberg-B-Süd	B-121	4680±100	3623 (3498,3419,3380) 3350
Seeberg-B-Süd	B-122	4750±100	3650 (3611,3582,3523) 3370
Seeberg-B-Süd	B-123	4530±100	3370 (3334,3219,3189,3152,3148) 3042
Seeberg-B-Süd	B-125	4550±100	3380 (3341) 3048
Seeberg-B-Süd	B-126	4500±100	3380 (3341) 3048
Seeberg-B-Süd	B-244	4790±120	3700 (3626,3568,3540) 3378
Seeberg-B-Süd	B-245	4630±120	3612 (3371) 3038
Seeberg-B-Süd	LJ-1293	5060±35	3956 (3938,3867,3818) 3788
Seeberg-B-Süd	B-114	4390±80	3290 (3031,2966,2940) 2917
Seeberg-B-Süd	B-115	4950±90	3930 (3776,3744,3708) 3648
Seeberg-B-Süd	B-116	4840±110	3777 (3642) 3389
Seeberg-B-Süd	B-118A	4490±90	3352 (3301,3239,3173,3167,3107) 2949
Sion-Petit Chasseur	B-2110	5130±100	4036 (3974) 3790
Sion-Petit Chasseur	B-2111	5100±70	3992 (3957,3838,3826) 3789
Zürich-Kl. Haffner	UCLA-1664A	4800±100	3700 (3629,3560,3544) 3384
Zürich-Gr. Haffner	UCLA-1722B	5145±70	4033 (3981) 3821
Zürich-Kl. Haffner	UCLA-1764A	4690±60	3613 (3501,3411,3382) 3370
Zürich-Gr. Haffner	UCLA-1722C	4640±70	3508 (3373) 3347

Plot of Data from Table 21: Cortaillod Culture, Switzerland

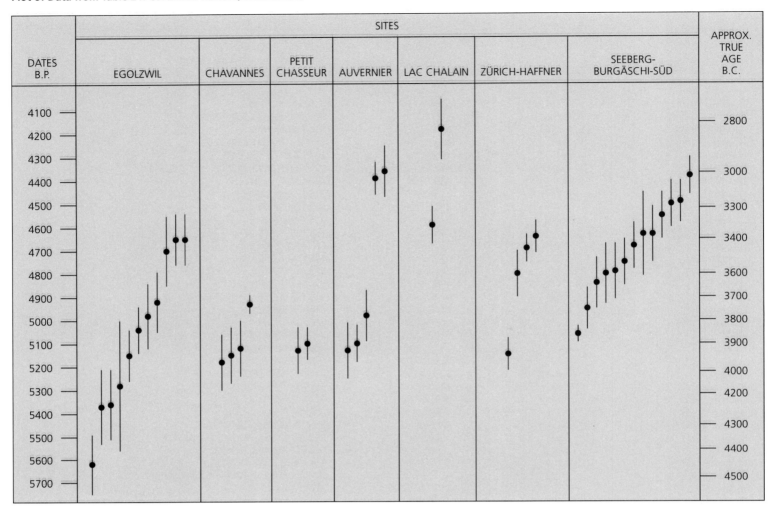

TABLE 22

Passage Graves in Portugal, Spain, and Brittany

SITE	LAB NUMBER	C–14 YEARS B.P.	CALIBRATED AGE RANGES B.C. Maximum (calibrated age) minimum
Portgual and Spain			
Orca dos Castenairos (Fragoes)	GrN-4294	5060±50	3964 (3938,3867,3818) 3786
Orca dos Castenairos (Fragoes)	GrN-4295	4610±50	3494 (3364) 3343
Carapito I (Guarda) Beire Alte	GrN-5110	4850±40	3697 (3645) 3545
Carapito I (Guarda) Beire Alte	GrN-5111	4590±65	3492 (3356) 3144
Orca das Seixas dolmen	GrN-5754	4900±40	3776 (3697) 3647
Lapa do Burgio	GrN-5628	4850±45	3697 (3645) 3544
Praia das Marcas (Sintra) passage grave	KN	4250±60	2919 (2903) 2782
Praia das Marcas (Sintra) passage grave	H	4160±110	2910 (2879,2806,2774,2720,2702) 2580
Poco da Gratiera Evora (Alentejo)	TL	6460±280	5630 (5411) 5210
Polygonal Chamber at Gorinos 2 Evora, Alentejo	TL	6390±260	5550 (5333) 5070
Fragoas, Conillio VIla Nova de Paiva (Beira)	GrN-4924	5060±50	3964 (3938,3867,3818) 3786
Praia das Marcas (Sintra) Tholos type (related to Los Millares)	H	3650±100	2192 (2034) 1890
Praia das Marcas (Sintra)	KN	3640±60	2133 (2032) 1935
Los Millares (Almeria)	H-204/247	4295±85	3028 (2914) 2784
Los Millares (Almeria)	KN-72	4380±120	3308 (3028,2985,2930) 2900
Baranquete, El (Almeria)	CSIC-81	4280±130	3040 (2911) 2699
Brittany			
Île Bono Finistère (charcoal in basal layer of chamber)	Gsy-64A	5380±135	4360 (4241) 4008
Kercado, Carnac, Morbihan	Sa-95	5840±300	5198 (4772,4759,4728) 4360
Île Guennoc III, Landéda Finistère	Gif-165	5800±300	5053 (4716) 4350
Île Guennoc III, Landéda Finistère	Gif-1879	5075±140	4033 (3944,3848,3821) 3705
Île Guennoc III, Landéda Finistère	Gif-813	4505±120	3370 (3310,3233,3179,3161,3136) 2933
Île Guennoc, Cairn II, tomb B hearth in chamber	Gsy-164B	4350±200	3340(3013,3007,2924) 2669
Barnenez, Plouesoc'h, Finistère	Gif-1309	5750±150	4790 (4664,4638,4601) 4460
Barnenez, Plouesoc'h, Finistère	Gif-1556	5550±150	4573 (4365) 4245
Barnenez, Plouesoc'h, Finistère	Gif-1310	5450±150	4460 (4340) 4048
Barnenez, Plouesoc'h, Finistère	Gif-1116	5100±140	4037 (3957,3838,3826) 3710
Ty Floc'h, Saint Thois, Finistère	Gif-5234	5580±120	4573 (4456,4417,4403) 4340
Ty Floc'h, Saint Thois, Finistère	Gif-5233	4670±120	3626 (3496,3427,3379) 3340
La Hoguette Fontenay-le-Marmion, Calvados	Ly-131	5560±150	4577 (4452,4428,4392,4384,4368) 4248
La Hoguette Fontenay-le-Marmion, Calvados (Bone)	Ly-421	5160±190	4233 (3988) 3726
La Hoguette Fontenay-le-Marmion, Calvados (Bone)	Ly-420	5050±260	4223 (3933,3874,3816) 3540
La Hoguette Fontenay-le-Marmion, Calvados	Gif-1345	5000±130	3970 (3785) 3690
La Hoguette Fontenay-le-Marmion, Calvados	Ly-132	4580±150	3595 (3351) 3042
Île Carn, Ploudalmezeau, Finistère	Gif-1362	5390±150	4360 (4243) 4007
Île Carn, Ploudalmezeau, Finistère	Gif-414	5340±250	4459 (4230,4191,4163) 3824
Île Carn, Ploudalmezeau, Finistère	GrN-1968	5230±75	4222 (4035,4018,4005) 3988
Île Carn, Ploudalmezeau, Finistère	Gif-1363	4840±150	3780 (3642) 3382
Kerléven, Finistère	Gsy-111	4825±125	3777 (3637) 3384

Plot of Data from Table 22: Passage graves, Brittany

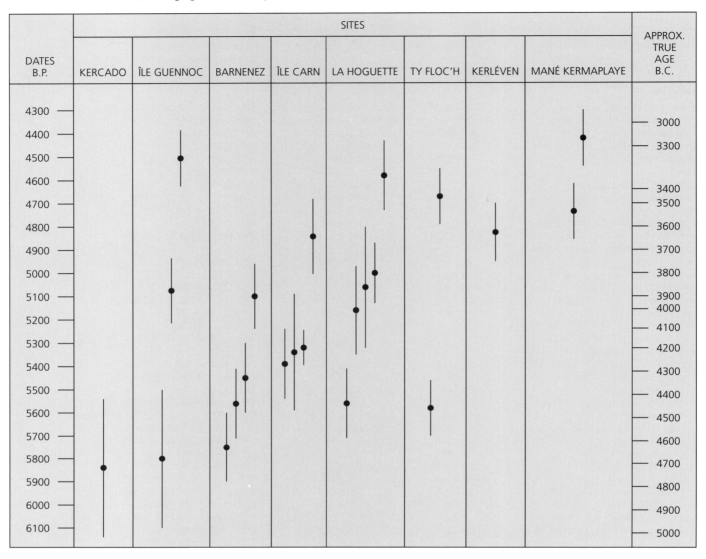

TABLE 23
Great Britain and the Orkney Islands

SITE	LAB NUMBER	C–14 YEARS B.P.	CALIBRATED AGE RANGES B.C. Maximum (calibrated age) minimum
Long Barrows, Great Britain			
Lambourn (burnt wood)	GX-1178	5365 ± 180	4360 (4237) 3990
Beckingham Road (antler)	NPL-138	5200 ± 160	4240 (3998) 3814
Dalladies (charred wood)	I-6113	5190 ± 105	4219 (3996) 3823
Fussell's Lodge (charcoal)	BM-134	5180 ± 150	4228 (3994) 3790
Kilham (charcoal)	BM-293	4830 ± 125	3778 (3639) 3385
South Street (charcoal)	BM-356	4760 ± 130	3700 (3615,3579,3527) 3370
South Street (charcoal)	BM-357	4700 ± 135	3640 (3504,3406,3384) 3350
Nutbane (charcoal)	Bm-49	4680 ± 150	3640 (3498,3419,3380) 3147
Dalladies (charcoal)	SRR-289	4660 ± 50	3508 (3493,3480,3377) 3362
South Street (charcoal)	BM-358a	4620 ± 140	3615 (3368) 3100
Dalladies (charcoal)	SRR-290	4532 ± 55	3355 (3335,3218,3190,3151,3149) 3103
South Street (antler)	BM-358b	4530 ± 110	3370 (3334,3219,3189,3152,3148) 3040
Beckhampton Road (antler)	BM-506b	4467 ± 90	3344 (3260,3247,3101) 2929
Giant's Hills (antler)	BM-191	4410 ± 150	3340 (3037) 2900
Giant's Hills (antler)	BM-192	4320 ± 150	3264 (2919) 2704
Beckhampton Road (antler)	BM-506a	4257 ± 90	3012 (2901) 2703
Megalithic Chamber Tombs and other Structures from the Orkney Islands			
Knap of Howar	SRR-348	4765 ± 70	3642 (3617,3577,3529) 3383
Knap of Howar	SRR-346	4532 ± 70	3362 (3335,3218,3190,3151,3149) 3099
Knap of Howar	SRR-344	4451 ± 70	3332 (3096,3053,3049) 2930
Knap of Howar	SRR-349	4422 ± 70	3304 (3073,3069,3040) 2924
Knap of Howar	SRR-345	4448 ± 75	3333 (3096,3055,3048) 2928
Knap of Howar	SRR-452	4081 ± 65	2867 (2850,2840,2652,2647,2612) 2504
Skara Brae	Birm-637	4430 ± 100	3330 (3091,3065,3043) 2920
Skara Brae	Birm-638	4430 ± 120	3340 (3091,3065,3043) 2920
Skara Brae	Birm-639	4400 ± 100	3308 (3034) 2910
Skara Brae	Birm-636	4350 ± 130	3296 (3013,3007,2924) 2786
Skara Brae	Birm-438	4140 ± 120	2900 (2865,2810,2747,2725,2697,2674,2668) 2506
Skara Brae	Birm-436	4040 ± 110	2867 (2580) 2460
Skara Brae	Birm-434	4020 ± 110	2863 (2573,2535,2506) 2460
Skara Brae	Birm-435	3870 ± 110	2554 (2451,2433,2392,2384,2356) 2147
Skara Brae	Birm-433	3830 ± 110	2470 (2299) 2140
Grandtully	GaK-1398	4080 ± 90	2872 (2850,2845,2652,2647,2612) 2495
Grandtully	GaK-1396	3920 ± 100	2573 (2462) 2290
Townhead	GaK-1714	4070 ± 100	2873 (2598) 2480
Rinyo	Q-1226	3850 ± 100	2470 (2334) 2144
Llandegai	NPL-220	4740 ± 150	3700 (3604,3585,3518) 3350
Llandegai	NPL-224	4480 ± 145	3370 (3295,3242,3104) 2920
Llandegai	NPL-221	4420 ± 140	3340 (3040) 2910
Stones of Stenness	Srr-350	4506 ± 65	3349 (3312,3233,3180,3161,3137) 3045
Stones of Stenness	SRR-357	4188 ± 70	2903 (2877,2800,2780,2713,2708) 2625
Monamore I	Q-675	5110 ± 110	4034 (3963,3834,3828) 3780
Monamore II	Q-676	4190 ± 110	2920 (2877,2800,2780,2712,2708) 2611
Lochhill	I-6409	5070 ± 105	3990 (3942,3850,3829) 3717
Glenvoidean	I-5974	4860 ± 115	3780 (3676,3663,3648) 3519
Pitnacree	GaK-601	4810 ± 90	3698 (3633,3552,3549) 3387
Pitnacree	GaK-602	4220 ± 90	2917 (2885,2794,2786) 2629
Quanterness	Q-1294	4590 ± 75	3495 (3356) 3140
Quanterness	Q-1363	4540 ± 110	3380 (3338,3213,3203) 3042
Quanterness	SRR-754	4360 ± 50	3038 (3018,3001,2926) 2916
Quanterness	Q-1479	4150 ± 75	2887 (2867,2808,2772,2723,2699) 2606
Quanterness	Q-1480	3945 ± 70	2571 (2767) 2364
Quanterness	SRR-755	3870 ± 55	2463 (2451,2433,2392,2384,2356) 2285

continued

TABLE 23 *continued*

SITE	LAB NUMBER	C–14 YEARS B.P.	CALIBRATED AGE RANGES B.C. Maximum (calibrated age) minimum
Knowe of Ramsay	Q-1221	4305 ± 69	3025 (2916) 2789
Knowe of Ramsay	Q-1227	4005 ± 60	2590 (2566,2540,2501) 2466
Quoyness	SRR-752	4190 ± 50	2893 (2877,2800,2780,2712,2708) 2667
Quoyness	SRR-753	4365 ± 50	3039 (3020,2998,2927) 2917
Knowe of Yarso	Q-1225	4225 ± 60	2913 (2877,2792,2788) 2702
Maes Howe	SRR-505	4135 ± 65	2881 (2863,2812,2742,2726,2696,2677,2666) 2594
Maes Howe	Q-1482	3970 ± 70	2580 (2483) 2457
Embo	B-442	3870 ± 100	2480 (2451,2433,2392,2384,2356) 2149
Isbister	GU-1178	4245 ± 100	3011 (2895) 2669
Isbister	GU-1179	4430 ± 55	3300 (3091,3065,3043) 2928
Isbister	GU-1180	4420 ± 90	3321 (3040) 2920
Isbister	GU-1181	4410 ± 130	3340 (3037) 2910
Isbister	GU-1182	4480 ± 80	3345 (3295,3242,3104) 2949
Isbister	Q-3013	4375 ± 50	3090 (3025,2991,2929) 2919
Isbister	GU-1184	3910 ± 80	2559 (2459) 2298
Isbister	Q-3014	3830 ± 50	2454 (2299) 2201
Isbister	GU-1184	4365 ± 90	3098 (3020,2998,2927) 2910
Isbister	Q-3015	4260 ± 50	2917 (2903) 2784
Isbister	GU-1185	4420 ± 95	3329 (3040) 2919
Isbister	Q-3016	4360 ± 55	3039 (3018,3001,2926) 2916
Isbister	GU-1186	4040 ± 100	2865 (2580) 2470
Isbister	Q-3017	4030 ± 50	2851 (2576,2531,2510) 2491
Isbister	GU-1190	4260 ± 55	2918 (2903) 2783
Isbister	Q-3018	4285 ± 45	2921 (2912) 2890

Plot of Data from Table 23: Long-Barrows and Megalithic Chamber Tombs in Great Britain

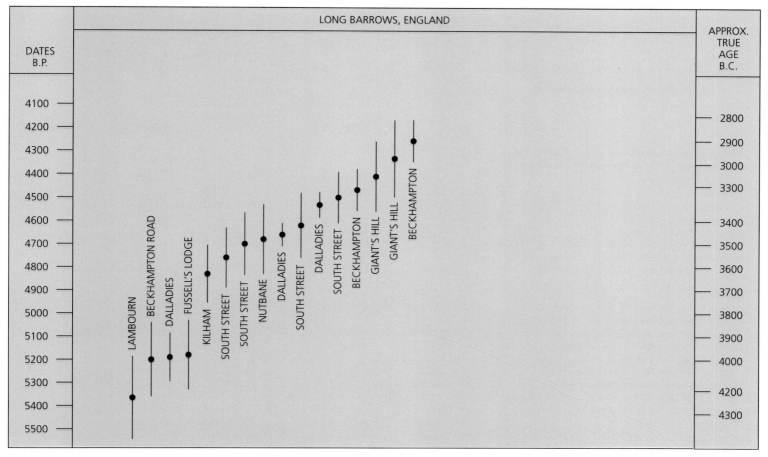

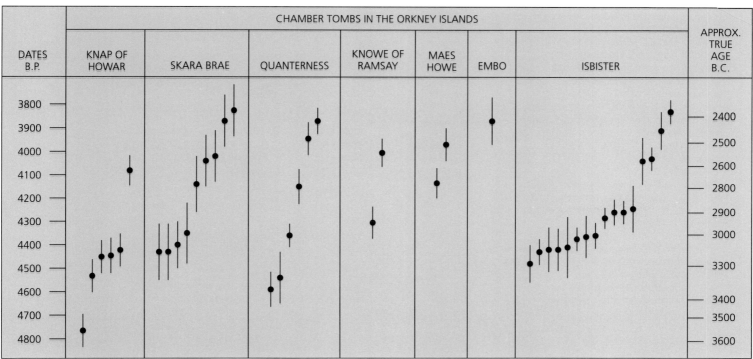

Irish Passage Tombs and Related Structures

SITE	LAB NUMBER	C–14 YEARS B.P.	CALIBRATED AGE RANGES B.C. Maximum (calibrated age) minimum
Habitation material under passage-tombs			
Knowth	BM-1076	4852±71	3773 (3646) 3534
Knowth 17	UB-318	4878±150	3902 (3692) 3389
Knowth 17	UB-319	4795±185	3780 (3628,3564,3542) 3360
Habitation sites considered to be contemporary with passage-tombs Culleenamore, Co. Sligo			
Charcoal from hearth	ST-7624	4710±100	3633 (3507,3401,3586) 3360
Charcoal from hearth	LU-1948	3970±75	2582 (2483) 2407
Charcoal from hearth	LU-1759	3780±60	2317 (2202) 2137
Hut-sites Knocknarea North	St-9030	4475±140	3370 (3292,3274,3269,3244,3103) 2920
Hut-sites Knocknarea North	St-1947	4250±75	2920 (2897) 2704
Temple na Ferta, Scotch Street, Armagh	UB-2379	4350±50	3035 (3013,3007,2924) 2915
Temple na Ferta, Charcoal from fill of a ring ditch that also contained sherds of Carrowkeel pottery	UB-2380	4090±105	2879 (2853,2828,2655,2644,2615) 2493
Tombs			
Knowth I, charcoal from mound	GrN-12357	4405±35	3094 (3036) 2927
Knowth I, charcoal from spread on old ground surface considered to be contemporary with mound building	GrN-12358	4490±60	3342 (3301,3239,3173,3167,3107) 3042
Knowth I, organic material in basal (sod) layer of mound	UB-357	4745±165	3700 (3609,3584,3520) 3350
Knowth I, Fragments of wood in basal layer of mound behind orthostat 75 of eastern tomb	GrN-12827	4465±40	3317 (3258,3248,3100) 3040
Knowth 2, Charcoal from spread in mound	BM-785	4185±126	2920 (2876,2801,2729,2714,2707) 2590
Knowth 9, Charcoal from cremation deposit in end recess	GrN ?	4415±50	3261 (3038) 2927
Knowth 16, Charcoal from spread within mound	BM-1078	4399±67	3261 (3034,2950) 2921
Newgrange	GrN-5462	4425±45	3291 (3083,3068,3041) 2929
Newgrange Both dates from charcoal from soil placed by the tomb builders between the roof slabs of the passage.	GrN-5463	4415±40	3098 (3038) 2928
Newgrange, Vegetation from redeposited sods in basal mound layer	GrN-9057	4480±60	3339 (3295,3242,3104) 3039
Carrowmore Site 4, Charcoal from 'stone fundament to Stone B'(? socket) in the central cist	Lu-1840	5750±85	4771 (4664,4638,4601) 4505
Carrowmore Site 4, Charcoal from beside second 'inner stone circle.' This is considered to be secondary by the excavator	Lu-1750	4320±75	3033 (2919) 2894
Carrowmore Site 7, Charcoal from intact bottom layer in the central chamber (post-hole, mid point of chamber and circle)	Lu-1441	5240±80	4226 (4037,4014,4008) 3987
Carrowmore Site 27	Lu-1698	5040±60	3958 (3910,3878,3814) 3781
Carrowmore Site 27	Lu-1808	5000±65	3941 (3785) 3704
Carrowmore Site 27 The foregoing three dates come from charcoal which was found in the same area between and under the lowest layer of stones in the stone-packing surrounding the central chamber.	Lu-1818	4940±85	3901 (3775,3751,3706) 3646
Sliabh Gullion The determination came from basal sandy peat below a spread of stones that may have been associated with the construction of the cairn.	UB-179	5215±195	4331 (4033,4024,4002) 3788
Sliabh Guillion, above the sandy peat layer	UB-180	3955±75	2477 (2469) 2398
Sliabh Guillion, above the sandy peat layer	UB-181	4035±75	2858 (2578) 2470

Plot of Data from Table 24: Megalithic Passage Tombs in Ireland

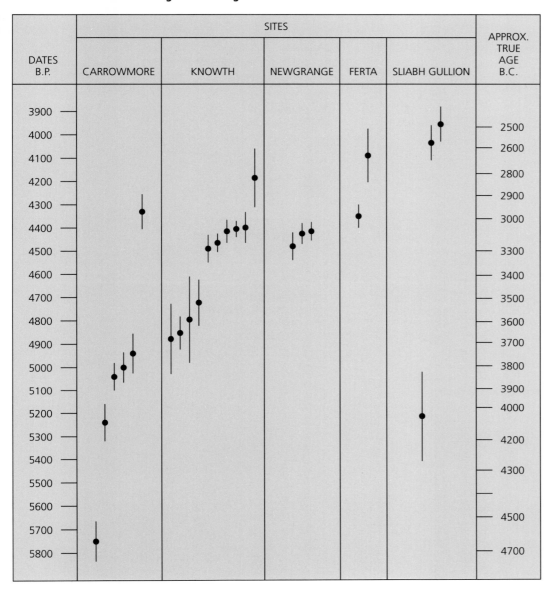

TABLE 25
Mikhailovka I, North Pontiac (Maikop) Culture

SITE	LAB NUMBER	C–14 YEARS B.P.	CALIBRATED AGE RANGES B.C. Maximum (calibrated age) minimum
Mikhailovka I	Bln-629	4400 ± 100	3308 (3034) 2910
Mikhailovka I	Le-645	4340 ± 65	3036 (2922) 2910
Mikhailovka I	Bln-630	4330 ± 100	3091 (2921) 2788

TABLE 26
Usatovo Sites

SITE	LAB NUMBER	C–14 YEARS B.P.	CALIBRATED AGE RANGES B.C. Maximum (calibrated age) minimum
Usatovo	UCLA-1642A	4300 ± 60	3018 (2915) 2891
Mayaki	Bln-629	4400 ± 100	3308 (3034) 2910
Mayaki	UCLA-1642B	4375 ± 60	3093 (3025,2991,2929) 2917
Mayaki	UCLA-1642G	4375 ± 60	3093 (3025,2991,2929) 2917
Mayaki	Leningrad	4340 ± 65	3036 (2922) 2910

Plot of Data from Tables 25 and 26: North Pontic (Mikhailovka I) and Usatovo Cultures

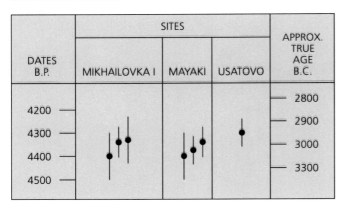

TABLE 27
Ezero I, Early Bronze Age, Bulgaria

SITE	LAB NUMBER	C–14 YEARS B.P.	CALIBRATED AGE RANGES B.C. Maximum (calibrated age) minimum
Ezero I	Bln-428	4260 ± 80	2923 (2903) 2706
Ezero I	Bln-427	4365 ± 80	3095 (3020,2998,2927) 2912
Ezero I	Bln-421	4335 ± 80	3039 (2922) 2899
Ezero I	Bln-422	4310 ± 80	3032 (2917) 2788
Ezero I	Bln-423	4440 ± 80	3332 (3094,3059,3045) 2926
Ezero I	Bln-424	4575 ± 80	3492 (3349) 3108
Ezero I	Bln-522	4455 ± 100	3340 (3098,3051,3050) 2925
Ezero I	Bln-526	4135 ± 100	2890 (2863,2812,2742,2726,2696,2677,2666) 2580
Ezero I	Bln-523	4400 ± 100	3308 (3034) 2910
Ezero I	Bln-524	4460 ± 100	3340 (3252,3249,3099) 2926
Ezero I	Bln-525	4280 ± 100	3028 (2911) 2706
Ezero I	Bln-527	4390 ± 100	3302 (3031,2966,2940) 2910

TABLE 28
Sitagroi IV, Drama Plain, NE Greece

SITE	LAB NUMBER	C–14 YEARS B.P.	CALIBRATED AGE RANGES B.C. Maximum (calibrated age) minimum
Sitagroi IV (Acorns)	Bln-773	4390 ± 100	3302 (3031,2966,2940) 2910
Sitagroi IV	Bln-879	4550 ± 100	3380 (3341) 3048
Sitagroi IV	Bln-878	4398 ± 100	3307 (3034,2952,2949) 2910
Sitagroi IV (Acorns)	Bln-651	4332 ± 79	3038 (2921) 2898
Sitagroi IV	Bln-650a	4363 ± 56	3040 (3019,2999,2927) 2916
Sitagroi IV	Bln-880	4510 ± 100	3360 (3318,3231,3181,3159,3139) 3040

TABLE 29
Coţofeni Culture in the Iron Gate Region, SW Romania

SITE	LAB NUMBER	C–14 YEARS B.P.	CALIBRATED AGE RANGES B.C. Maximum (calibrated age) minimum
Ostrovul Corbului	LJ-3797	4570 ± 60	3372 (3348) 3137
Ostrovul Corbului	LJ-3798	4420 ± 50	3291 (3040) 2928
Ostrovul Corbului	LJ-3799	4400 ± 60	3255 (3034) 2922
Baile Herculane	LJ-3533	4470 ± 50	3332 (3263,3246,3102) 3039
Baile Herculane	LJ-3534	4360 ± 60	3974 (3018,3001,2926) 2915
Baile Herculane	LJ-3535	4360 ± 60	3974 (3018,3001,2926) 2915
Baile Herculane	LJ-3536	4300 ± 60	3018 (2915) 2891

TABLE 30
Baden and Vučedol Cultures

SITE	LAB NUMBER	C–14 YEARS B.P.	CALIBRATED AGE RANGES B.C. Maximum (calibrated age) minimum
Oszentiván	Bln-476	4515 ± 80	3359 (3327,3229,3183,3157,3141) 3044
Sümeg	A-246	4520 ± 160	3499 (3331,3226,3185,3155,3143) 2926
Podolie	Bln-556	4455 ± 80	3337 (3098,3051,3050) 2929
Vučedol, Baden Phase	Z-1446	4540 ± 100	3370 (3338,3213,3203) 3045
Vučedol " "	Z-1617	4500 ± 100	3360 (3307,3235,3177,3163,3134,3112,3110) 2949
Vučedol " "	Z-1619	4400 ± 100	3308 (3034) 2910
Vučedol " "	Z-1618	4300 ± 100	3030 (2915) 2782
Iwanovice	M-2166	4375 ± 200	3350 (3025,2991,2929) 2705
Hisar	Bln-350	4290 ± 100	3032 (2913) 2708
Pivnica	Kn-145	4110 ± 160	2910 (2857,2821,2691,2689,2660,2637,2623) 2470
Hrustovača	Bln-564	4125 ± 80	2882 (2861,2815,2733,2729,2694,2681,2664,2632,2628) 2581
Homolka	GrN	4075 ± 70	2866 (2651,2649,2610) 2500
Vučedol, Vučedol phase	Z-1637	4300 ± 100	3030 (2915) 2782
Vučedol " "	Z-1621	4300 ± 100	3030 (2915) 2782
Vučedol " "	Z-1447	4290 ± 120	3040 (2913) 2703
Vučedol " "	Z-1453	4290 ± 120	3040 (2913) 2703
Vučedol " "	Z-1624	4200 ± 100	2915 (2880,2798,2782) 2619
Vučedol " "	Z-1449	4190 ± 120	2920 (2877,2800,2780,2712,2708) 2590
Vučedol " "	Z-1454	4130 ± 120	2900 (2862,2814,2738,2728,2695,2679,2665,2630) 2502
Vučedol " "	Z-1622	4100 ± 100	2880 (2855,2824,2657,2640,2619) 2498

TABLE 31
Globular Amphora Culture

SITE	LAB NUMBER	C–14 YEARS B.P.	CALIBRATED AGE RANGES B.C. Maximum (calibrated age) minimum
Gnewitz	Bln-472	4250 ± 100	3013 (2897) 2699
Katelbogen	Bln-554	3800 ± 120	2460 (2278,2234,2209) 2042
Klementowice	KN-225	4440 ± 160	3340 (3094,3059,3045) 2920
Klementowice	GrN-5046	4175 ± 30	2882 (2873,2803,2777,2716,2705) 2668
Pevestorf	Hv-582	4380 ± 100	3296 (3028,2985,2930) 2910
Poggendorfer F.	Bln-990	3795 ± 100	2456 (2276,239,2207) 2046
Serrahn	Bln-342	4170 ± 120	2910 (2872,2804,2776,2717,2704) 2580
Stehelčeves	GrN-4065	4260 ± 70	2921 (2903) 2708
Zarębowo	GrN-5044	4625 ± 40	3496 (3370) 3351

Plot of Data from Tables 27—31: Ezero, Coţofeni, Baden, and Globular Amphora Culture Groups

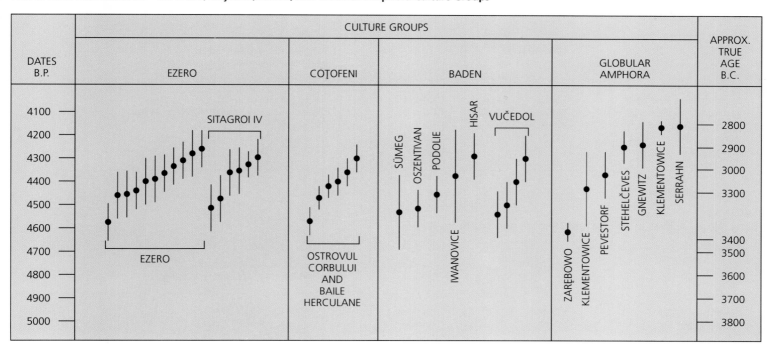

TABLE 32
Yamna Graves West of the Black Sea

SITE	LAB NUMBER	C–14 YEARS B.P.	CALIBRATED AGE RANGES B.C. Maximum (calibrated age) minimum
Baia Hamangia (Romania)	KN-38	4060±160	2886 (2587) 2460
Baia Hamangia (Romania)	Bln-29	4090±160	2900 (2853,2828,2655,2644,2615) 2460
Cernavoda (Romania)	Bln-62	4260±100	3018 (2903) 2701
Varna (Bulgaria)	KI-89	4210±60	2910 (2883,2796,2784) 2699
Ketegyhaza (E. Hungary)	Bln-609	4265±80	3011 (2906) 2707

TABLE 33
Early Yamna Graves in the Eastern Ukraine and Southern Russia

SITE	LAB NUMBER	C–14 YEARS B.P.	CALIBRATED AGE RANGES B.C. Maximum (calibrated age) minimum
Pereshchepino 1/7	Ki-100/5	4310±105	3040 (2917) 2783
Pereshchepino 1/6	Ki-100/4	4290±90	3028 (2913) 2782
Brilyuvata m.6	Ki-497	4270±120	3032 (2909) 2699
Brilyuvata m.12	Ki-497	4080±100	2875 (2850,2845,2652,2647,2612) 2491
Tsatsa 6/3	UCLA-1270	4210±80	2914 (2883,2796,2784) 2629
Kristoforovka 1/1	Ki-578	4170±170	2912 (2872,2804,2776,2717,2704) 2499
Ust'man 1/13	UCLA-1271	4150±80	2889 (2867,2808,2772,2723,2699) 2594
Svatovo 1/1	Ki-585	4000±190	2878 (2564,2541,2499) 2280
Ust'Dzhegutinskaya 32/10	LE-693	4110±60	2873 (2857,2821,2689,2660,2637,2623) 2583
Ust'Dzhegutinskaya 24/1	LE-687	4040±60	2855 (2580) 2491
Balki 1/40	LE-1168	4080±90	2872 (2850,2845,2652,2647,2612) 2495
Balki 1/40	Ki-601	3990±110	2855 (2559,2544,2535) 2398

TABLE 34
Bell Beaker Habitation Pit at Budapest

SITE	LAB NUMBER	C–14 YEARS B.P.	CALIBRATED AGE RANGES B.C. Maximum (calibrated age) minimum
Budapest	Bln-1221	4235±100	2922 (2889,2790) 2666
Budapest	Q-1122	4270±90	3018 (2909) 2706
Budapest	GrN-6900	3945±40	2557 (2467) 2458
Budapest	GrN-6901	3830±55	2455 (2299) 2200
(all samples are from the same source)			

TABLE 35
Corded Pottery Sites in the East Baltic Area

SITE	LAB NUMBER	C–14 YEARS B.P.	CALIBRATED AGE RANGES B.C. Maximum (calibrated age) minimum
Kesocha, Northern Mazovia	K-1836	3880 ± 100	2554 (2453,2423,2398) 2200
Šventoji II, Lithuania	LE-835	3860 ± 50	2460 (2343) 2283
Abora, Latvia	LE-749	3860 ± 100	2470 (2343) 2147
Eyni, Latvia	LE-751	4000 ± 60	2588 (2564,2541,2499) 2465
Leimaniški, Latvia	TA-27	3770 ± 200	2480 (2198,2151,2149) 1920
Leimaniški, Latvia	TA-23	3970 ± 250	2886 (2483) 2140
Osa, Latvia	LE-758	4000 ± 60	2588 (2564,2541,2499) 2465

Plot of Data from Tables 30, 32—35: Vučedol, Yamna, Bell Beaker, and Corded Pottery Cultures

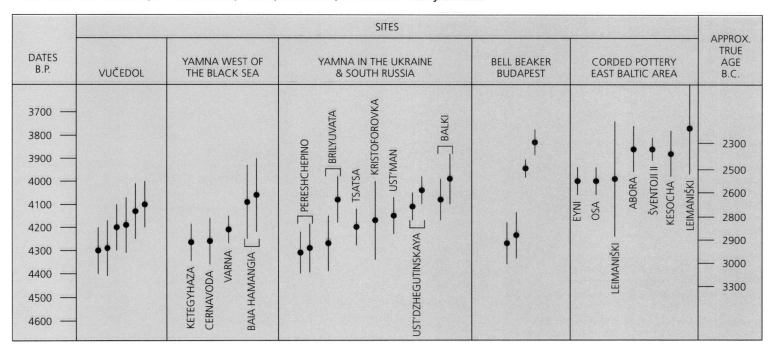

ILLUSTRATION SOURCES AND CREDITS

The abbreviations below are for bibliographical items mentioned more than three times. References for others are in *Notes* and *General Bibliography*.

Abbreviations

Benac 1973, *Obre*; Alojz Benac, "Obre I & II." *Wissenschaftliche Mitteilungen des Bosnisch-Herzegowinischen Landesmuseums*, III (1973).

Evans 1959; J. D. Evans, *Malta. Ancient People and Places*. London: Thames and Hudson, 1959.

Evans 1971; J. D. Evans, *Prehistoric Antiquities of the Maltese Islands: A Survey*. London: Athlone Press, 1971.

Gimbutas 1974, *GG*; Marija Gimbutas, 1974, *The Gods and Goddeses of Old Europe: 7000–3500 B.C.* London: Thames and Hudson, and University of California Press, Berkeley (2d ed. 1982).

Gimbutas 1976, *Anza*; Marija Gimbutas, ed., *Neolithic Macedonia*. Monumenta Archaeologica 1. Institute of Archaeology, University of California, Los Angeles, 1976.

Gimbutas 1989, *Achilleion*; Marija Gimbutas, Shan Winn, and D. Shimabuku, *Achilleion. A Neolithic Village in Northern Greece, 6400–5600 B.C.*. Monumenta Archaeologica 14, Institute of Archaeology, University of California, Los Angeles, 1989.

Gimbutas 1989, *Language*; Marija Gimbutas, *The Language of the Goddess*. San Francisco: Harper and Row, 1989.

Mellaart 1967, *Çatal*; James Mellaart, *Çatal Hüyük: A Neolithic Town in Anatolia*. New York: McGraw-Hill, 1967.

Raczky 1987, *Tisza*; P. Raczky, ed., Late Neolithic of the Tisza Region. Budapest-Szolnok, 1987.

Srejović 1969; Dragoslav Srejović, *Lepenski Vir*. Belgrade: Srpska Knijiževna zadruga, 1969.

Theocharis 1973; D. R. Theocharis, "The Neolithic Civilization in Neolithic Greece." Athens: National Bank of Athens.

Vasić 1932–36, *Vinča*; Miloje Vasić, *Praistorijska Vinča*, 1 (1932); 2–4 (1936). Belgrade: Izdanje Štamparje Drvavne.

Chapter 1

1–1 (1) Courtesy Stara Zagora Museum. Photo K. Kónya 1971. (2) Gimbutas 1989, *Achilleion*.

1–3 Mellaart 1967, *Çatal*.

1–5 Gimbutas 1989, *Achilleion*

Chapter 2

2–1 (1) Milojčič 1962; (2) Photo K. Kónya 1971.

2–3, 2–6 Gimbutas 1989, *Achilleion*.

2–4 Photo K. Kónya 1971.

2–5, 2–7, 2–9, 2–10 Theocharis 1973.

2–11 (1) Private collection, Larisa, Thessaly; (2) Volos Archeological Museum.

2–12 D. Tloupas collection, Larisa, Thessaly.

2–13 Wace and Thompson 1912.

2–15 (1) Selmeczi excav. 1969: P. Raczky 1976; reproduction from W. Meier-Arendt, "Überlegungen zur Herkunft des linienbandkeramischen Langhauses," Varia Archaeologica Hungarica 2, 1989. (2) O. Trogmayer, *Acta Antiqua et Archaeologica* X (Szeged)

2–16 (1) S. Dimitrijević 1969; (2) Gimbutas 1976, *Anza*.

2–17 Benac 1973, *Obre*.

2–18 Gimbutas 1976, *Anza*.

2–19 Kutzián 1944.

2–20 Courtesy National Museum Budapest; author's photo.

2–21 (1) Srejović 1969; (2) S. Karmanski, *Žrtvenici, statuete i amuleti sa lokaliteta Donja Branjevina kod Deronja*, Odžaci 1968.

2–22 (1) Courtesy G. Georgiev, Archaeological Museum of Sofia. (2) P. Detev 1968.

2–23, 2–24, 2–25, 2–26 Courtesy Stara Zagora Museum. Photo K. Kónya 1971.

2–29 Courtesy Moravian Museum, Brno. Photo K. Kónya 1971.

2–30 Hermann Behrens, *Die Jungsteinzeit im Mittelelbe-Saale Gebiet*, Berlin (Deutscher Verlag der Wissenschaften), 1973.

2–31A M. Ilett, M. Plateaux, and A. Coudart, "Analyse spatiale des habitats du Rubané récent," *Le Néolithique de la France*, J. P. Demoule and J. Guilaine, eds. Paris: Picard, 1986.

2–31B (1) Behrens 1973; (2) R. Tichý, Památky archeologické 53, 1962; (3) Müller-Karpe 1968.

2–32, 2–33 Soudský 1969.

2–34 Pavúk 1972.

2–35 Courtesy Moravian Museum, Brno. Photo K. Kónya 1971.

2–37 Courtesy National Museum, Budapest. Photo K. Kónya 1971.

2–36, 2–38, 2–40 V. S. Titov and I. Erdelý, *Arkheologiya Vengrii*. Moscow, 1980.

2–39 Tompa 1929.

2–41 Danilenko 1969.

Chapter 3

3–3 Novak 1955. Drawing Linda Williams.

3–4 Korošec 1958. Drawing J. Bennett.

3–5 Zadar Archaeological Museum; reproduced from *Prehistory of Yugoslavia*, A. Benac, ed., 1977.

3–6 Courtesy Zemaljski Muzej, Sarajevo. Photo K. Kónya 1971.

3–7 (1,2) V. Radimsky and M. Hoernes 1895; (3) Benac 1973, *Obre*. Drawing J. Bennett.

3–8 Gimbutas 1976, Anza. *G.G.* Drawing Linda Williams.

3–9, 3–10, 3–11 Benac 1973, *Obre*.

3–12 P. Detev 1959, *Godišnik* 3 (Plovdiv). Drawing Linda Williams.

3–13 After W. Radimsky and M. Hoernes 1895, reprinted from *Prehistory of Yugoslavia*, 1977, A. Benac, ed.

3–15 McPherron and Srejovič 1988.

3–16 Vasić 1932–36, *Vinča*.

3–17 Gimbutas 1976, *Anza*.

3–18   (1) Courtesy University Collection, Belgrade. Photo K. Kónya 1971. (2) Courtesy National Museum Belgrade (excav. B. Galović 1960).

3–19   Courtesy National Museum, Belgrade; (1,2) Photo K. Kónya 1971; (3) Photo M. Djordjević 1968.

3–20   Catalog, Belgrade National Museum, 1968. Drawing Elena Bechis.

3–21, 3–22
       Courtesy National Museum, Belgrade. Photo M. Djordjević 1969.

3–23   J. Banner, "Antropomorphe Gefässe der Theisskultur von der Siedlung Kökenydomb bei Hödmezövásárhely (Ungarn)," *Germania* 38 (1959).

3–24   After F. Horvath in Raczky 1987, *Tisza*. Drawing J. Bennett.

3–25   N. Kalicz and P. Raczky in Raczky 1987, *Tisza*. Drawing J. Bennett.

3–26   K. Hegedüs and J. Makkay in Raczky 1987, *Tisza*. Drawing J. Bennett.

3–27   K. Hegedüs and J. Makkay in Raczky 1987, *Tisza*.

3–28   Raczky 1987, *Tisza*.

3–29, 3–30
       Courtesy Koszta Jozsef Museum, Szentes. Photo K. Kónya 1971.

3–31   K. Hegedüs and J. Makkay in Raczky 1987, *Tisza*.

3–33   (1) V. S. Titov and I. Erdelý 1980 (based on Dombay 1939, 1960); (2) Drawing Linda Williams.

3–34   Courtesy Moravian Museum, Brno. Photo K. Kónya.

3–35   (1) P. I. Bogucki 1982; (2) After K. Jażdżewski, reproduced from M. Gimbutas 1956; (3) W. Hensel 1980.

3–36, 3–37, 3–38
       Courtesy Moravian Museum, Brno. Drawing Linda Williams; Photo K. Kónya.

3–39 and 3–40
       Institute of Archaeology, Budapest, courtesy N. Kalicz. Drawing J. Bennett.

3–41   Novotný 1958. The vase is housed in Piešťany Museum, Slovakia.

3–43   Courtesy E. Comşa, Institute of Archaeology, Bucharest.

3–44, 3–45, 3–47, 3–48
       Courtesy Institute of Archaeology, Bucharest. Photo K. Kónya 1971.

3–46   G. Cantacuzino, *Dacia* 13, 1969.

3–50   Todorova 1976.

3–51   Perničeva 1978.

3–52   G. Georgiev and N. Angelov, *Izvestija* 18 (1952), Bulgarian Academy of Sciences. Drawing J. Bennett.

3–53   Todorova 1976. Drawing Linda Williams.

3–54   Drawing Linda Williams.

3–55   Courtesy Archaeological Museum Varna. Author's photo.

3–56   Courtesy Olteniţa Museum. Drawing Linda Williams.

3–57   Courtesy Bucharest City Museum.

3–58, 3–59
       After Gimbutas in Renfrew, Gimbutas and Elster, 1986, *Sitagroi.*

3–62   Dumitrescu 1954. Drawing J. Bennett.

3–63   Shmaygliy, Dudkin and Zin'kovs'kiy 1973.

3–64, 3–65
       Šiškin 1973.

3–66   Passek 1949.

3–67   V. M. Masson and N. Ya. Merpert 1982, *Eneolit SSSR.* Moscow.

3–68   Courtesy Peatra Neamţ Museum. Photo K. Kónya 1971.

3–69   Courtesy Peatra Neamţ Museum. Drawing Linda Williams.

3–70   A. Crîşmaru, *Drăguşeni,* Muzeul Judeţean de Istorie, Botoşani, 1977.

3–71   A. Niţu, "Decorul zoomorf pictat pe ceramica Cucuteni-Tripolie," *Archeologia Moldovei* 8 (1975). Drawing Linda Williams.

3–72   Courtesy Peatra Neamţ Archaeological Museum. Photo K. Kónya 1971.

3–73   Courtesy Historical Museum Kishenev, Moldavia. Gimbutas 1974, G. G.

3–75 to 3–77
       Telegin 1968.

3–78, 3–79
       Telegin and Potekhina 1987.

3–80   Makarenko 1933.

3–81   Kutzián 1976.

3–82 to 3–85
       Courtesy Varna Archaeological Museum. Author's photo 1976.

3–86   Sergeev 1962. Drawing Linda Williams.

3–87, 3–88
       Markevič, 1981. Drawing J. Bennett.

3–89   Dumitrescu 1954. Drawing J. Bennett.

Chapter 4

4–2A   Nielsen 1985.

4–2B, 4–2C, 4–6, 4–7
       Wiślánski 1979 in Hensel and Wiślański 1979.

4–3   Courtesy photo: The National Museum Copenhagen.

4–4, 4–5
       Courtesy Cracow Archaeological Museum. Photo K. Kónya 1971.

4–8   Zimmerman, *Materialhefte zu Ur und Frügeschichte,* 16.

4–9   Lili Kaelas 1983 in *The Megalithic Monuments of Western Europe.* Colin Renfrew, ed. Reconstruction of a long-barrow: H. Gerdsen, 1987, *Die "Grossen Steine" von Kleinenkneten.* Wildeshausen.

4–10   H. Wikłak, *Prace i Materialy,* 33 (1986).

4–11   Midgley 1985.

4–12   After Burchard 1973, reprinted from Midgley 1985.

4–13   Courtesy photo: The National Museum Copenhagen.

4–14   Ewald Schuldt 1972, *Die mecklenburgischen Megalithgräber.* Berlin: VEB Deutscher Verlag der Wissenschaften.

4–15   Kjaerum 1967.

4–16   Courtesy photo: Forhistorisk Museum, Morsgård, Denmark.

4–17, 4–18, 4–19, 4–20, 4–21, 4–22 (1), 4–24, 4–25, 4–26, 4–27, 4–28, 4–30, 4–32 (2), 4–33, 4–34
       R. Rimantienė, Akmens amžius Lietuvoje, 1984. Drawings J. Bennett.

4–22 (2), 4–23, 4–29, and 4–32 (1, 3)
       Vankina, *Sarnate,* 1970. Drawings J. Bennett.

4–31   I. Loze, *Akmens laikmeta māksla Austrumbaltijā.* Riga (Zinatne) 1983. Drawings J. Bennett.

Chapter 5

5–3   UCLA excavation by J. Mallory. Personal information. Full report to appear in *Origini,* Rome.

5–4, 5–5, 5–6
       Tiné 1983.

5–7   Cipolloni, *Rendina* 1982.

5–8   Matera Museum; P. Graziosi, *L'arte preistorica in Italia,* 1973. Drawing J. Bennett.

5–9   After Lo Porto; reproduced from Müller-Karpe 1974.

5–10, 5–11 (1)
       Trump, 1983.

5–11 (2), 5–12, 5–13, 5–14, 5–15, 5–16, 5–17, 5–18
       Atzeni 1981.

5–19   Tanda 1984.

5–20   Ridley, *The Megalithic Art of the Maltese Islands,* 1976.

5–21   Evans 1971.

5–22   Courtesy Archaeological Museum, Valletta. Author's photo 1985. Drawing J. Bennett.

5–23   Evans 1959.

5–24   Trump 1966b.

5–25, 5–26, 5–27, 5–28
       Evans 1971. Drawings J. Bennett.

5–29   Evans 1959.

Chapter 6

6–2 and 6–3
       Beltran 1979.

6–4   D. Binder and J. Courtin in *Le Néolithique de la France.* J. P. Demoule and J. Guilaine, eds. 1986.

6–5A   J. Guilaine in *La Néolithique de la France.* 1986.

6–5B   Antonio Mario Radmilli, *La preistoria alla luce delle ultime scoperte.* Florence 1963.

6–6   Jean Courtin, *Le Néolithique de la Provence.* Paris 1974.

6–7   Hansjürgen Müller-Beck 1961, "Prehistoric Swiss Lake-Dwellers," *Scientific American* 205, 6.

6–8   Victorine von Gonzenbach, 1949.

6–9, 6–10, 6–11, 6–12, 6–13
H.-J. Müller-Beck 1965, *Seeberg-Burgäschi Süd.*

6–15, 6–16, 6–17, 6–19
P. R. Giot, *La Bretagne avant l'histoire.* Rennes, Simon c. 1975.

6–18   P. R. Giot, *Menhirs et dolmens. Monuments mégalithiques de Bretagne.* Chateaulin, Jos le Doaré, 1975.

6–20   Twohig 1981.

6–21, 6–22, 6–24, 6–25
After Leisner 1956: reproduced from Müller-Karpe 1974.

6–23   (1) Documents d'Histoire de Bretagne; (2) Twohig 1981.

6–26   Smith 1965. 6–23 (1) Documents d'Histoire de Bretagne; (2) Twohig 1981.

6–27   Hermann Behrens, "The First 'Woodhenge' in Middle Europe." *Antiquity* 4, 1981.

6–28   *Journal of the Cork Historical and Archaeological Society* 63, 1958.

6–29   R. de Valera and S. Ó. Nualáin, *Survey of the Megalithic Tombs in Ireland* 3. Dublin (Stationery Office), 1972.

6–30, 6–34
Courtesy of Commissioners of Public Works, Dublin.

6–31   O'Kelly 1989.

6–32, 6–33
Eogan 1986.

6–35   Müller-Karpe 1974.

6–36   Stuart Piggott, *West Kennet*, 1962.

6–37   Paul Ashbee, *The Earthen Long Barrow in Britain*, 1970.

Chapter 7

7–1, 7–13
Gimbutas 1989, *Achilleion.*

7–2   Evans 1959.

7–3   P. Detev, "Praistoričeskoto selišče pri selo Muldava." *Godišnik* 6 (Plovdiv 1968).

7–4   R. Rimantienė, *Šventoji*, 1969.

7–5   Courtesy Kosovka Mitrovica Museum. Drawing by E. Bechis from author's photograph.

7–6   Drawing by E. Bechis from photograph reproduced in Gimbutas 1974, *G.G.*

7–7, 7–10
Mellaart 1970, *Hacilar.* Drawing J. Bennett.

7–8   N. Marinatos, *Art and Religion in Thera*, 1984.

7–9, 7–19, 7–24, 7–25
Gimbutas 1989, *Language.*

7–11, 7–21, 7–22
Gimbutas 1974, *G.G.*

7–12, 7–20
H. Delporte, *L'image de la femme dans l'art préhistorique.* Paris (Picard) 1979.

7–14   Courtesy Svetozarevo Museum. Drawing Patricia Reis.

7–15   Courtesy National Museum Belgrade. Photo K. Kónya 1971.

7–16   K. Tloupas collection, Larisa, Thessaly. Drawing from photograph by E. Bechis.

7–17, 7–18
Gimbutas 1976, *Anza.*

7–23   Courtesy Archaeological Museum Bitolj. Drawing J. Bennett after author's photo.

7–26   Mellaart 1967, *Çatal.*

7–27   D'Anna 1977, Twohig 1981 and Gimbutas 1989, *Language.*

7–28   (1) Author's drawing from a vase in Stara Zagora Museum; (2) Atzeni 1981; (3,4) drawing from vase and steatite prism in Herakleion Museum, Crete.

7–29   (1) Gimbutas 1974, *G.G.*; (2) Dumitrescu 1974.

7–30   J. Thimme, *Antike Kunst* 8.

7–31   V. Santoni, *Scientific American* (Italian edition) 29, 170 (1982).

7–32   Courtesy Varna Archaeological Museum. Author's photo 1976.

7–33   From author's excavations in Achilleion 1973 (1) and Anza 1969 (2).

7–34   Gimbutas 1974, *G.G.*

7–35   Dorothy Cameron, *Symbols of Birth and Death in the Neolithic Era*, London: Kenyon-Deane, 1981.

7–36   Gimbutas 1989, *Language* (reproduced from J. Thimme, ed., *Art and Culture of the Cyclades*, 1977).

7–37   Courtesy Piatra Neamţ Archaeological Museum. Drawing J. Bennett.

7–38   Herakleion Museum. Drawings J. Bennett.

7–39   Courtesy Cracow Archaeological Museum. Drawing from photo reproduced in Gimbutas 1974, *G.G.*

7–40   Beltran 1979.

7–41   After P. de Mortillet, reproduced from E. Anati 1968.

7–42, 7–43, 7–44, 7–45, 7–53
Gimbutas 1974, *G.G.*

7–46, 7–47, 7–48, 7–49, 7–50
Gimbutas 1989, *Achilleion.*

7–51, 7–52
Mellaart 1967, *Çatal.* Drawing J. Bennett.

7–54   A. Benac, ed., *Prehistory of Yugoslavia*, 1977.

7–55   Gimbutas 1980, *Temples.*

7–56   (1) Gimbutas 1989, *Language* (Courtesy Cornelius Mateesco, Bucharest); (2) Nikolov, *Gradechnitza* 1974.

7–57   H. Dumitrescu 1968.

7–58, 7–59
Gimbutas 1980, *Temples.*

7–60   Photo Cristina Biaggi.

7–61, 7–62, 7–63
Evans 1971. Drawing J. Bennett.

7–64   Drawing J. Bennett after author's photo.

7–65, 7–66
Courtesy Archaeological Museum Valletta. Author's photo.

7–67   Courtesy Copenhagen National Museum.

7–68, 7–77, 7–78, and 77–80 (1)
Tloupas collection, Larisa, Thessaly. Photo D. Tloupas.

7–69   Wace and Thompson 1912.

7–70   Belgrade National Museum Catalog 1968.

7–71   *IPEK* 1927:119.

7–72   Courtesy B. Galović 1969, Belgrade National Museum.

7–73   Tasić 1973.

7–74   Courtesy Belgrade National Museum. Photo M. Djordjević 1968.

7–75, 7–76, 7–83, and 7–84
Gimbutas 1989, *Achilleion.*

7–79   Nikos Efstratiou 1985, *Agios Petros: A Neolithic Site in the Northern Sporades*, BAR Ser. 241.

7–80   (2) Vasić, *Vinča* 3.

7–81   Gimbutas 1974, *G.G.*

7–82   (1) Belgrade National Museum; (2) Štip Archaeological Museum; Photo K. Kónya 1971.

7–85   Belgrade National Museum Catalog 1968.

7–86, 7–87, 7–90, 7–91
Vasić 1932–36, *Vinča* 3, fig. 91. Photo M. Djordjević 1968.

7–88   Kandyba, 1937.

7–89   Drawing J. Bennett from author's photo. Belgrade National Museum.

7–92   Courtesy Museum Smederevska Palanka. Drawing from a slide by J. Bennett.

7–93   B. Brukner 1962, *Rad. Vojvodjanski Muzej* 11.

7–94   Todorović and Cermanović 1961, *Banjica.* Drawing J. Bennett.

7–95, 7–96
S. Cucoş, *Memoria Antiquitatis* 3 (1971).

7–97   Rosetti, *IPEK* 12, 1938.

7–98   Pavuk 1972.

7–99   Müller-Karpe 1974.

7–100, 7–101
Srejović 1969.

7–102   Srejović and Babović 1983.

7–103   Evans 1971.

7–104   L. M. Ugolini, *Malta. Origine della Civiltà Mediterranea*, Rome 1934. Drawing J. Bennett.

7–105, 7–106, 7–107
Courtesy Archaeological Museum Valletta (figs. 106, 107). Drawings by J. Bennett from author's photos.

7–108   Evans 1959.

7–109, 7–110, 7–111, 7–112
Atzeni 1981.

7–113 Tanda 1984.

7–114 Author's excavation 1979–80.

7–115 S. Gallus, *Arch. Hungarica* 3, 1934. Drawing J. Bennett.

7–116 Hedges 1984. Drawing J. Bennett.

7–117, 7–121
Twohig 1981.

7–118 Müller-Karpe 1974.

7–119, 7–126
Eogan 1986, *Knowth*.

7–120 (1–6) Leisner 1956; (7, 8) K. Ebbesen 1975, *Arkaeologiske Studier* 2 (Copenhagen).

7–121 H. Gerdsen 1987, *Die "Grossen Steine" von Kleinenkneten*. Wildeshausen.

7–122, 7–123, 7–124
O'Kelly 1983.

7–125 Brennan 1983.

7–127 Courtesy Commission of Public Works, Dublin.

7–128, 7–129
Twohig 1981. Drawing J. Bennett.

7–130 Le Roux 1985. Drawing J. Bennett.

Chapter 8

8–3 Dumitrescu 1980.

8–4 After Berciu 1961, *Contribuții la problemele neoliticului in Rominia*, Bucharest.

8–5 Tasić 1973.

8–6 Banner 1950.

8–7 (1) Letica 1967, "Miniaturne sudovi iz Vinči," *Zbornik Nar. Muzeja* V; (2) Czalog 1959, *Acta Arch. Hung.* XI; (3) Paul 1979, "Das Siegelgefäss von Daia Română," *Forschungen zur Volks-und Landeskunde* 22,2 (Bucharest). Drawing J. Bennett.

8–8 Nikolov 1974, *Gradechnitza*.

8–9 Courtesy Archaeological Museum Sibiu, Romania. See Fig. 7.3. Drawing J. Bennett.

8–10 Courtesy Museum Priština, S. Yugoslavia. Drawing J. Bennett.

8–11 Todorović-Cermanović 1961, *Banjica*.

8–12 Nikolov 1974, *Gradechnitza*.

8–13 Rudinskiy 1931, *Industrie en os de la station paléolithique de Mezin*. Kiev, Acad. Nauk.

8–14 Vasić 1933, *Vinča*.

8–15 Brukner 1962, *Rad. Vojvod. Muzeja*, 11.

8–16 Courtesy Regional Museum Priština; Gimbutas 1989, *Language*.

8–17, 8–18
Courtesy C. N. Mateesco, Institute of Archaeology, Bucharest. (1–3) Tsountas 1908; (4) Gimbutas 1976; (5,6) Rodden 1964; (7,8) Courtesy G. Georgiev, Sofia; (9,10) Kutzián 1944; (11,13,14) Wace & Thompson 1912.

8–19 F. Prendi, *Studia Albanica* 1, 1966.

8–20 Colin Renfrew 1987 in *Proto-Indo-Europeans. The Archaeology of a Linguistic Problem*. Studies in Honor of Marija Gimbutas, E. Polomé and S. Skomal, *eds*.

8–21 (1,2) Kutzián 1944; (3,4) Stara Zagora Museum.

8–22 Haarmann 1991.

Chapter 9

9–1 Tsountas 1908, reconstruction drawing by M. Korres.

9–2 R. J. Rodden 1962, *Proceedings of the Prehistoric Society*, 28.

9–3 M. Petrescu-Dîmbovița, 1963, *Prähistorische Zeitschrift*.

9–4, 9–5
Courtesy M. Petrescu-Dîmbovița, Iași, reproduced from Gimbutas 1974, G. G.

9–6 Passek 1949.

9–7 After K. Günther 1971. *Steinzeit und Ältere Bronzezeit*, Münster Westfalen: Landesmuseum für Vor-und Frühgeschichte.

9–8, 9–10
Kalicz 1985.

9–9 R. Feustel and H. Ullrich 1965, *Alt-Thüringen*.

9–11, 9–12
Grygiel 1986.

9–13 H. Wiklak, 1986, *Prace i Materiały Muzeum Arch. i Ethnogr. w Łodzi* 33.

9–14, 9–15
Frazer 1983.

9–16, 9–17
Nanno Marinatos 1984.

Chapter 10

10–1 Vasil'ev and Matveeva 1976.

10–2, 10–3, 10–5
After Vasil'ev 1981.

10–4 After V. V. Golmsten 1931, *Soobshcheniya GAIMK*, 6.

10–7, 10–8
D. Ya. Telegin 1973, *Sredno-Stogivs'ka kul'tura*, Kiev. Reproduced from James Mallory, *In Search of the Indo-Europeans*. London: Thames and Hudson, 1987.

10–9 V. M. Danilenko and M. M. Shmagliy 1972, *Arkheologiya* 1972–76. V. A. Dergachev, *Moldaviya i sosednie territorii v epokhu bronzy*. Kishinev.

10–10 E. Schröter 1966, *Ausgrabungen und Funde* 11.

10–11 B. Nikolov 1976, *Arkheologija*, Sofia, 1976, 3.

10–14 (1,2) A. Häusler 1963, "Südrussische und nordkaukasische Petroglyphen." *Wiss. Zeitschrift der Martin Luther Universität Halle-Wittenberg* 12, 11; (3,4) after E. Anati 1975, *Evoluzione e stile nell'arte rupestre Camuna*. Archivi 6, Capo di Ponte.

10–15 D. Ya. Telegin 1971, *Arkheologiya* 4, Kiev.

10–16 B. V. Farmakovskiy 1914, *materialy po Arkheologii Kavkaza* 34.

10–17 R. R. Schmidt 1945, *Die Burg Vučedol*. Zagreb.

10–18 Renfrew in Renfrew, Gimbutas, and Elster, 1986, *Sitagroi*.

10–19 M. Gimbutas 1980, "The Kurgan Wave #2 . . . ," *Journal of Indo-European Studies* 8, 3–4; Czalog 1961.

10–20, 10–21
Courtesy National Museum Budapest.

10–22 J. Kruk and S. Milisauskas 1982, *Germania* 60.

10–23 V. Moucha 1960, *Archeol. Rozsledy* 12, 4.

10–24 and 10–25
G. I. Georgiev, N. Merpert, R. V. Katinčarov and D. G. Dimitrov eds., 1979, *Ezero*, Sofia.

10–26 T. Wiślański 1979 in Hensel and Wiślański 1979.

10–27 (1) S. Nosek, 1967, *Kultura amfor kulistych w Polsce*; (2) Lahodov'ska, Shaposhnikova and Makarevich, 1962, *Mikhaylivs'ke poselennya*, Kiev.

10–28 T. Wiślański, 1966, *Kultura amfor kulistych w Polsce Północnozachodniej*, Warsaw.

10–29 I. F. Levitskiy, 1929, *Antropologiya* 2, Kiev.

10–30 I. K. Sveshnikov, *Arkheologiya* 8, Kiev.

10–31 Wiślański 1970.

10–32 B. Jovanović, 1975, "Les tumuli de la culture de steppes et fosses funéraires dans le bassin danubien," *Starinar* XXVI (Belgrade).

10–34 *Studii și Cercetări de Istorie Veche* (Bucharest), 1952, 3.

10–35 Lahodovs'ka, Shaposhnikova, and Makarevich, 1962, *Mikhaylivs'ke poselennya*, Kiev.

10–36 B. Govedarica, 1987, in *Hügelbestattung in der Karpaten-Donau-Balkan Zone. D. Srejović and N. Tasić, eds. (Belgrade).

10–37 N. G. L. Hammond, 1974, *The Annual of the British School of Archaeology at Athens* 69 (originally after Dörpfeld 1927).

10–38 (1) B. Novotný, 1958, *Památky archeologické* 49 (Prague); (2) reproduced from M. E. Mariën, Oud-België. Antwerpen: De Sikkel, 1952; after van Giffen.

10–40 Jan Machnik, 1979, "Krąg kulturowy ceramiki sznurowej," Hensel and Wiślański 1979.

10–41, 10–44
E. Anati, 1967, *Arte preistorica in Valtellina*. Sondrio: Banka Populare.

10–42 E. Anati, 1972, *I pugnali*, Archivi 4, Centro Comuno di Studi Preistorici.

10–43 E. Anati, 1976, *Evolution and Style in Camunian Rock Art*. Archivi 6, Centro Camuno di Studi Preistorici (English edition).

10–45 Foca, *Sargetia* 4.

10–46 M. Gimbutas, *Journal of Indo-European Studies*, 8 (1980), after Danilenko 1951.

10–47 J. P. Mallory, 1989.

Color Plates

1 Author's photo.

2, 5 Archaeological Museum Larisa. Photo D. Tloupas. Gimbutas 1989, Achilleion.

3 Photo K. Kónya

4 Theocharis 1973.

6 Nikolov 1974.

7 Benac 1962.

8, 9, 10
Regional Museum Priština. Photo M. Djordjević, Belgrade.

11 Photo M. Djordjević, Belgrade.

12 Koszta Jozsef Museum Szentes, Hungary. Publ. in catalog: *Idole, prähistorische Keramiken aus Ungarn*, Naturhistorisches Museum, Vienna, 1972. Author's photo.

13 Kalicz 1970. Photo K. Kónya, Budapest.

14 Museum Sáveni, courtesy V. Dumitrescu 1979.

15 Archaeological Museum Cracow. Author's photo.

16 Photo K. Kónya

17, 18 Museum of Antiquities, Syracuse, Sicily. Author's photo.

19, 20, 21
Author's photo.

22 National Museum Belgrade. Publ. in catalog *Neolit centralnog Balkana*, 1968.

23, 24 Srejović and Babović, 1983.

BIBLIOGRAPHY

General works, monographs, major excavation reports, catalogs, and articles having value for history of research or influence on research are included here. Regional bibliographies are in the Notes and in the Glossary of Cultures and Major Sites.

Almagro, M. and A. Arribas
1963. *El poblado y la necrópolis megalitica de Los Millares.* Bibliotheca Praehistorica España 3, Madrid.

Ammerman, Albert J. and
L. L. Cavalli-Sforza
1984. *The Neolithic Transformation and the Genetics of Populations in Europe.* Princeton University Press.

Anati, E.
1976. *Evolution and Style in Camunian Rock Art.* Capo di Ponte: Centro Camuno di Studi Preistorici, Archivi 6.

Arnal, Jean
1960. "Les styles céramiques du Néolithique français," in *Préhistoire* 14. Gérard Bailloud and Raymond Riquet, eds. pp. 1–211.

1976. *Les statues-menhirs, hommes et dieux.* Paris: Éditions des Hespérides.

Ashbee, P.
1966. "The Fussell's Lodge Long Barrow." *Archaeologia* 100:1–80.

1970. *The Earthen Long Barrows in Britain.* London: Dent.

Ashbee, P., I. F. Smith, and J. Evans
1979. "Excavations of Three Long Barrows Near Avebury, Wiltshire." *Proceedings of the Prehistoric Society* 45:207–300.

Atkinson, R. J. C.
1965. "Wayland's Smithy." *Antiquity,* 39:126–33.

Atzeni, Enrico
1981. "Aspetti e sviluppi culturali del neolitico e della prima età dei metalli in Sardegna." *Ichnussa. La Sardegna dalle origini all'età classica* 27–41. Milan: Libri Scheiwiller.

Bach, A.
1978. *Neolithische Populationen im Mittelelbe-Saale-Gebiet: zur Anthropologie des Neolithi-kums unter besonderer Berücksichtigung der Bandkeramiker.* Monographien zu Ur und Frühgeschichte 1, Weimer.

Bailloud, Gérard and Mieg de Boofzheim
1955. *Les civilisations néolithiques de la France dans leur contexte européen.* Paris: Picard.

Bailloud, Gérard
1964. *Le néolithique dans le Bassin parisien,* 2nd supplement to *Gallia Préhistoire* (2nd ed. 1974). Paris.

Bakels, C. C.
1978. "Four Linearbandkeramik Settlements and Their Environment: A Palaeoecological Study of Sittard, Stein, Elsloo, and Hienheim." *Analecta Praehistorica Leidensia* 11.

Banner, Janos
1959. "Anthropomorphe Gefässe der Theisskultur von der Siedlung Kökénydomb bei Hódmezővásá-hely (Ungarn)." *Germania* 37:14–35.

Barber, E. J. W.
1991 Prehistoric Textiles: *The Development of Cloth in the Neolithic and Bronze Ages.* Princeton University Press.

Barfield, Laurence
1971. *Northern Italy Before Rome.* London: Thames and Hudson.

Barker, Graeme
1981. *Landscape and Society: Prehistoric Central Italy.* London: Academic Press.

1985. *Prehistoric Farming in Europe.* Cambridge University Press.

Barker, Graeme and Clive Gamble, eds.
1985. *Beyond Domestication in Prehistoric Europe.* Orlando: Harcourt Brace Jovanovich.

Batović, Šime
1966. *Stariji Neolit u Dalmaciji.* Societas Archaeologica Iugoslaviae. Zadar: Museum Archaeologicum.

Becker, Carl Johan
1955. "The Introduction of Farming into North-ern Europe." *Journal of World History* 2, 4: 749–67.

1959. "Flint Mining in Neolithic Denmark." *Antiquity* 33:82–92.

Behrens, H.
1973. *Die Jungsteinzeit im Mittelelbe-Saale Gebiet.* Berlin: VEB Deutscher Verlag der Wissenschaften.

1981. "The First 'Woodhenge' in Middle Europe." *Antiquity* 55:72–178.

Behrens, H. and E. Schröter
1980. Siedlungen und Gräber der Trichterbecher-kultur bei Halle (Saale). Berlin: Deutsche Akademie der Wiss.

Beier, H. J.
1988. *Die Kugelamphorenkultur in Mittelelbe-Saale Gebiet und in der Altmark.* Berlin: VEB Deutscher Verlag der Wissenschaften.

Beltran, Antonio
1979. *Da cacciatori ad allevatori. L'arte rupestre del Levante Spagnolo.* Milano: Jaca Book.

Benac, Alojz
1952. *Prehistorijsko naselje Nebo i problem Butmirske kulture (La station préhistorique de Nebo et le problème de la culture butmirienne).* Ljubljana.

1958. *Neolitsko naselje u Lisičicima kod Konjica.* Sarajevo: Zemaljski Muzej, Djela, Odj. ist. fil. nauka. 10, 9.

1962. *Studien zur Stein- und Kupferzeit im Nordöstlichen Balkan.* Berlin: Berichte der Römisch-Germanischen Kommission, no. 42.

1973a. "Obre II. A Neolithic Settlement of the Butmir group at Gornje Polje." *Wissenschaftliche Mitteilungen des Bosnisch-Herzegowinischen Landesmuseums* 3A (combined ed. 1974). Sarajevo.

1973b. "Obre I. Neolitsko naselje Starčevačko-Impresso i Kakanjske kulture na Raskršcu (Obre I, A Neolithic Settlement of the Starčevo-Impresso and Kakanj Cultures at Raskršce)." *Glasnik Zemaljskog Muzeja* 5, 27/28: 5–171.

Benac, Alojz et al., eds.
1979. *Praistorija Jugoslovenskikh Zemalja* 1–4. Sarajevo: Academy of Sciences of Bosnia and Herzegovina.

Berciu, Dumitru
1966. *Cultura Hamangia.* Bucharest: Academia Populare Romine.

1967. *Romania Before Burebista.* London: Thames and Hudson.

Bernabó Brea, Luigi
1957. *Sicily Before the Greeks,* rev. ed. London: Thames and Hudson.

Bernabó Brea, L. and M. Cavalier
1956. "Civiltà preistoriche delle Isole Eolie e del territorio di Milazzo." *Bollettino di Paletnologia Italiana* 65:1–99.

1957. "Stazioni preistoriche delle Isole Eolie." *Bollettino di Paletnologia Italiana* 66:97–151.

Bernhard, Wolfram
1978. "Anthropologie der Bandkeramik." *Die Anfänge des Neolithikums vom Orient bis Nordeuropa* 8b, Anthropologie 2. Cologne-Vienna: 128–64.

Bocquet, A. and A. Houot
1982. "La vie au Néolithique, Charavines, un village au bord d'un lac, il y a 5000 ans." *Histoire et Archéologie* 64.

Boessneck, J., J. P. Jéquier, and H. R. Stampfli
1963. *Seeberg, Burgäschisee-Süd*, part 3: *Die Tierreste*. Acta Bernensia 2. Bern.

Bintliff, John
1984. *European Social Evolution*. University of Bradford.

Bognár: See Kutzián.

Bogucki, P.
1982. *Early Neolithic Subsistence and Settlement in the Polish Lowlands*. Oxford: British Archaeological Reports, International Series 150.
1984. "Patterns of Animal Exploitation in the Early Neolithic of the Polish Lowlands," in *Animals and Archaeology. Husbandry in Europe*. J. Clutton-Brock and C. Grigson, eds. Oxford: British Archaeological Reports, International Series 227:34–44.

Bogucki, P. and R. Grygiel
1983. "Early Farmers of the North European Plain." *Scientific American* 248 (4):104–112.

Böhm, J. and S. J. De Laet, eds.
1961. *L'Europe à la fin de l'âge de la pierre. Actes du Symposium consacré aux problèmes du néolithique européen. Prague-Liblice-Brno, 5–12 Octobre, 1959*. Praha: Éditions de l'Académie Tchécoslovaque des Sciences.

Bökönyi, Sándor
1970. "Animal Remains from Lepenski Vir." *Science* 167 (3926): 1702–4.
1971. "The Development and History of Domestic Animals in Hungary." *American Anthropologist* 73, 3:640–74.
1974. *History of Domestic Mammals in Central and Eastern Europe*. Budapest: Akadémiai Kiadó.
1976. "The Vertebrate Fauna of Anza," in *Neolithic Macedonia*. M. Gimbutas, ed. Monumenta Archaeologica, 1, Institute of Archaeology, U. of Calif. at Los Angeles: 313–63.
1986. "The Faunal Remains of Sitagroi," in *Excavations at Sitagroi*, I. Colin Renfrew, Marija Gimbutas, and Ernestine S. Elster, eds. Monumenta Archaeologica, 13, Institute of Archaeology, U. of Calif. at Los Angeles: 63–133.
1987. "Horses and Sheep in East Europe in the Copper and Bronze Ages," in *Proto-Indo-European: the Archaeology of a Linguistic Problem*. Studies in Honor of Marija Gimbutas. S. N. Skomal and E. C. Polomé, eds. Washington: Institute for the Study of Man: 137–44.
1989. "Animal Remains," *Achilleion. A Neolithic Settlement in Thessaly, Greece, 6400–5600 B.C.* Marija Gimbutas, Shan Winn, and Daniel Shimabuku eds. Monumenta Archaeologica 14, Institute of Archaeology, U. of Calif. at Los Angeles: 315–320.

Branigan, K.
1984. "Early Minoan Society: The Evidence of the Mesara Tholoi Reviewed." *Aux Origines de l'Hellénisme*, C. Nicolet, ed. 29–37, Paris.

Brennan, Martin
1983. *The Stars and the Stones: Ancient Art and Astronomy in Ireland*. London: Thames and Hudson.

Broglio, A.
1971. "Osservazioni sulle culture neolitiche del Veneto e del Trentino nel quadro del neolitico padano." *Origini* 5:21.

Brønsted, J.
1957. *Danmarks oldtid*, vol. 1: *Stone Age*. Copenhagen: Glydendal.

Brunnacker, R., B. Heim et al.
1967. *Seeberg, Burgäschisee-Süd*, part 4: *Chronologie und Umwelt*. Acta Bernensia 2. Bern.

Burgess, Colin, Peter Topping, Claude Mordant, and Margaret Maddison, eds.
1988. *Enclosures and Defences in the Neolithic of Western Europe*. Oxford: British Archaeological Reports, International Series 403.

Burl, Aubrey
1985. *Megalithic Brittany: A Guide*. London: Thames and Hudson.

Burnez-Lanotte, Laurence
1987. *Le Chalcolithique moyen entre la Seine et le Rhin intérieur: Étude synthétique du rituel funéraire*. Oxford: British Archaeological Reports, International Series 354.

Cameron, Dorothy O.
1981. *Symbols of Birth and Death in the Neolithic Era*. London: Kenyon Deane.

Cann, J. R. and Colin Renfrew
1964. "The Characterization of Obsidian and Its Application to the Mediterranean Region." *Proceedings of Prehistoric Society* 30:111–25.

Cassano, Selene M. and Alessandra Manfredini
1983. *Studi sul neolitico del Tavoliere della Puglia*. Oxford: British Archaeological Reports, International Series 160.

Chapman, John
1981. *The Vinča Culture of Southeast Europe*. Oxford: British Archaeological Reports, International Series 117.
1983. "Meaning and Illusion in the Study of Burial in Balkan Prehistory," in *Ancient Bulgaria*. Papers presented to the "International Symposium on the Ancient History and Archaeology of Bulgaria." University of Nottingham, 1981. A. G. Poulter, ed., part 1, p. 8. University of Nottingham.

Chernykh, E. N.
1978. *Gornoe delo i metallurgya v drevneyshey Bolgarii*. Sofia: Bulgarian Academy of Sciences.
1980. "Metallurgical Provinces of the 5th-2nd Millennia in Eastern Europe in Relation to the Process of Indo-Europeanization." *The Journal of Indo-European Studies* 8, 3–4:317–37.

Childe, V. Gordon
1925. *The Dawn of European Civilization*. London: Kegan Paul, Trech, Trubner & Co., Ltd.
1958. *The Prehistory of European Society*. London: Penguin Books.

Chmielewski, W.
1952. *Zagadnienie grobowców Kujawskich w świetle ostatnich badań*. Łódź: Biblioteka Muzeum Archaeologicznego 2.

Cipolloni Sampo, Mirella
1982. *Scavi nel villaggio neolitico di Rendina 1970-1976*. Reprint from Origini 11.

Clark, J. G. D.
1952. *Prehistoric Europe. The Economic Basis*. London: Methuen.
1966. *Prehistoric Europe*. Stanford University Press.

Clark, Grahame and Stuart Piggott
1965. *Prehistoric Societies*. London: Hutchinson.

Clutton-Brock, J.
1981. *Domesticated Animals from Early Times*. London: Heinemann and British Museum (Natural History).

Clutton-Brock, J. and C. Grigson, eds.
1984. *Animals and Archaeology*. Oxford: British Archaeological Reports, International Series.

Collins, Desmond, ed.
1975. *The Origins of Europe. From New Studies in Archaeology and History*. Apollo Editions.

Comşa, Eugen
1974. "Die Bestattungssitten im rumänischen Neolithikum." *Jahresschrift mitteldt. Vorgeschichte* 58:113–56. Halle/Saale.

Constantin, Claude
1983. *Fin du Rubané. Céramique du Limbourg et Post-Rubané. Le néolithique le plus ancien en Bassin parisien et en Hainaut*, 2 vols. Université de Paris.

Courtin, J.
1974. *Le Néolithique de la Provence*. Paris: Klincksieck.

Cremonesi, G.
1965. "Il villaggio di Ripoli alla luce dei recenti scavi." *Rivista di Scienze Preistoriche* 20:85–155.

Csálog, József
1959. "Die anthropomorphen Gefässe und Idolplastiken von Szegvár-Tüzköves." *Acta Archaeologica* 7–38. Budapest.
1972. "Thronende Frauen-Idol von Szegvár-Tuzköves." *Idole, Prähistorische Keramiken aus Ungarn* 20–24. Vienna: Naturhistorisches Museum.

Cucoş, St.
1973. "Un complex ritual cucutenian descoperit la Ghelaeşti (jud. Neamţ)." *Studi şi Cercetari de Istorie Veche* 24,2:207. Bucharest.

Dames, Michael
1976. *The Silbury Treasure. The Great Goddess Rediscovered.* London: Thames and Hudson.
1977. *The Avebury Cycle.* London: Thames and Hudson.

D'Anna, A.
1977. *Les statues-menhirs et stèles anthropomorphes du midi méditerranéen.* Editions du Centre National de la Recherche Scientifique. Paris.

Daniel, G.
1980. "Megalithic Monuments." *Scientific American* (July): 78–90.

Daniel, G. and P. Kjaerum, eds.
1973. *Megalithic Graves and Ritual.* Copenhagen.

DeLaet, S. J.
1967. *La préhistoire de l'Europe.* Bruxelles: E. Meddens.

De Laet, Sigfried, ed.
1976. *Acculturation and Continuity in Atlantic Europe, Mainly During the Neolithic Period and the Bronze Age.* Papers presented at the 4th Atlantic Colloquium, Ghent, 1975, vol. 16. Bruges: De Tempel.

Delano-Smith, C.
1979. *Western Mediterranean Europe.* London and New York: Academic Press.

Demeo, James
1991. "The Origins and Diffusion of Patrism in Saharasia, c. 4000 BCE: Evidence for a Worldwide, Climate-linked Geographical Pattern in Human Behavior." *World Futures,* 30:247–71.

Demoule, J. P. and J. Guilaine, eds.
1986. *Le Néolithique de la France.* Hommage à G. Bailloud. Paris: Picard.

Dennell, Robin
1978. *Early Farming in South Bulgaria from the VI to the III Millennia B.C.* Oxford: British Archaeological Reports, International Series (Supplementary) 45.
1983. *European Economic Prehistory.* London: Academic Press.

Dergachev, Valentin A.
1978. *Vykhvatinskiy mogil'nik.* Kishenev: Shtiintsa.
1986. *Moldaviya i sosednie teritorii v ëpokhu eneolita.* Kishenev: Shtiintsa.

De Valera, R. and Sean O Nualláin
1961–82. *Survey of the Megalithic Tombs of Ireland,* vol. 1, 1961; vol. 2, 1964; vol. 3, 1972; vol. 4, 1982. Dublin: Stationery Office.

Dimitrijević, Stojan
1969. *Starčevačka kultura u Slavonsko-srijemskom prostoru i problem prijelaza ranog u srednji neolit u srpskom i hrvatskom podunavlju* (with résumé in German: *Die Starčevo-Kultur im slawonisch-syrmischen Raum und das Problem des Übergangs vom älteren zum mittleren Neolithikum im serbischen und kroatischen Donaugebiet).* Vukovar: Gradski Muzej.

Dixon, J. E., J. R. Cann and Colin Renfrew
1968. "Obsidian and the Origins of Trade." *Scientific American* 218, 3:38–46.

Dombay, J.
1960. *Die Siedlung und das Gräberfeld in Zengövárkony. Archaeologia Hungarica* 37. Budapest.

Driehaus, Jürgen
1960. *Die Altheimer Gruppe und das Jungneolithikum in Mitteleuropa.* Mainz: Verlag des Römisch-Germanischen Zentralmuseums.

Dumitrescu, Hortensia
1952–59. "Reports on the Excavations of the Cucuteni Site at Traian," in *Studii şi Cercetari de Istorie Veche,* vol. 3 (1952):121–40; vol. 4 (1953): 45–68; vol. 5 (1954):35–68; vol. 6 (1955):459–86; and in *Materiale şi Cercetari Archaeologice,* vol. 3 (1957):115–28; vol. 5 (1959):189–202.
1968. "Un modèle de sanctuaire découvert dans la station énéolithique de Cascioarele." *Dacia* 12:381–94.

Dumitrescu, Vladimir
1945. *La station préhistorique de Traian: fouilles de 1936, 1938, et 1940.* Reprint from *Dacia* 9–10 (Bucharest 1941–44).
1954. *Habaşeşti.* Bucharest: Institute of Archaeology.
1963. "La civilisation de Cucuteni." *Berichten van de rijksdienst voor het outheidkundig bodemonderzoek* 9 (Leiden): 7–48.
1965. "Cascioarele." *Archaeology* 18:34.
1968. *L'art néolithique en Roumanie.* Bucharest: Meridiane.
1970. "Édifice destiné au culte découvert dans la couche Boian-Şpantov de la station-tell de Cascioarele." *Dacia* 15:5–24.
1979. *Arta Culturii Cucuteni.* Bucharest: Meridiane.
1980. *The Neolithic Settlement at Rast.* Oxford: British Archaeological Reports, International Series 72.

Ecsedy, István
1979. *The People of the Pit-Grave Kurgans in Eastern Hungary.* Budapest: Akadémiai Kiadó.

Efstratiou, Nikos
1985. *Agios Petros: A Neolithic Site in the Northern Sporades.* Oxford: British Archaeological Reports, International Series 241.

Ehrich, Robert William, ed.
1965. *Chronologies in Old World Archaeology:* 3d. ed, 1991.

Erich, R. W. and E. Pleslova
1968. *Homolka: An Eneolithic Site in Bohemia.* Prague: Akademia.

Eisler, Riane
1987. The Chalice and the Blade: Our History, Our Future. San Francisco: Harper and Row.

Ellis, Linda
1984. *The Cucuteni-Tripolye Culture.* Oxford: British Archaeological Reports, International Series 217.

Eogan, George
1985. *Knowth and the Passage-Tombs of Ireland.* London: Thames and Hudson.

Escalon de Fonton, M.
1956. "Préhistoire de la Basse-Provence." *Préhistoire* 12:1–159. Paris.

Evans, J. D.
1959. *Malta. Ancient Peoples and Places.* London: Thames and Hudson.
1964. *Excavation in the Neolithic Settlement at Knossos.* Bulletin of the Institute of Archaeology 4. London.
1971a. *The Prehistoric Antiquities of the Maltese Islands: A Survey.* London: The Athlone Press.
1971b. "Neolithic Knossos: The Growth of a Settlement." Proceedings of Preh. Soc. 37:95–117.

Evans, J. D. and Colin Renfrew
1968. *Excavations at Saliagos.* London: Thames and Hudson.

Farruggia, Jean-Paul, Rudolph Kuper, Jens Lüning, and Petar Stehli
1973. "Der bandkeramische Siedlungsplatz Langweiler 2, Gemeinde Aldenhoven, Kreis Düren." *Rheinische Ausgrabungen* 13, Bonn.

Ferguson, C. W., B. Huber and H. E. Suess
1966. "Determination of the Age of Swiss Lake Dwellings As an Example of Dendrochronologically Calibrated Radiocarbon Dating." *Zeitschrift für Naturforschung.* Band 21a, Heft 7:1173–77.

Ferguson, C. W., M. Gimbutas, and H. Seuss
1976. "Historical Dates for Neolithic Sites of Southeast Europe." *Science* 191:1170–72.

Fernandes-Miranda, M.
1983. *Neolitizacion en la peninsula Iberica.* Actes du Colloque, "Premières commenautés paysannes in Méditerranée occidentale." Montpellier.

Fiala, Fr. and M. Hoernes
1898. *Die neolithische Station von Butmir,* part 2. Vienna: Verlag von Adolf Holzhausen.

Fischer, Ulrich
1956. *Die Gräber der Steinzeit im Saalegebiet.* Berlin.

Fraser, David
1983. *Land and Society in Neolithic Orkney,* 2. Oxford: British Archaeological Reports, British Series 356.

Gallay, Alain
1966. "Nouvelles recherches dans la station néolithique d'Auvernier." *Ur-Schweiz,* 30. Basel.
1975. "La Dynamique du peuplement néolithique suisse." *Bulletin d'Études préhistoriques alpines* 7:6–20.
1977. *Le Néolithique Moyen du Jura et des plaines de la Saône.* Frauenfeld: Verlag Huber.

Garašanin, M., V. Sanev, D. Simoska, and B. Kitanoski
1971. *Les Civilisations Préhistoriques de la Macédoine.* Štip, Septembre-Octobre.

Gejvall, N. G.
1969. *Lerna, a Preclassical Site in the Argolid*, 1: *The Fauna*. Princeton (N.J.) University Press.

Georgiev, Georgi I.
1961. "Kulturgruppen der Jungsteinzeit und der Kupferzeit in der Ebene von Thrazien (Südbulgarien)," in *L'Europe à la fin de l'âge de la pierre* (Symposium 1959): 45–100.

1967. "Beiträge zur Erforschung des Neolithikums und der Bronzezeit in Südbulgarien." *Archaeologia Austriaca* 41, 2:90–144.

Georgiev, Georgi I, N. Y. Merpert, R. V. Katinčarov, and D. G. Dimitrov
1979. *Ezero, rannobronzovoto selišče*. Sofia: Bulgarian Academy of Sciences.

Gerdsen, Hermann
1987. *Die "Grossen Steine" von Kleinenkneten. Zwei Grossesteingräber bei Wildeshausen. Landkreis Oldenburg*. Wildeshausen.

Gimbutas, Marija
1972. "Neolithic Cultures of the Balkan Peninsula," in *Aspects of the Balkans: Continuity and Change*. Henrik Birnbaum and Speros Vryonis, eds. The Hague and Paris: Mouton.

1973a. "The Beginning of the Bronze Age in Europe and the Indo-Europeans." *The Journal of Indo-European Studies* 1, 2:163–215.

1973b. "Old Europe c. 7000–3500 B.C.: The Earliest European Civilization before the Infiltration of the Indo-European Peoples." *Journal of Indo-European Studies* 1:1–20.

1974a. "Balkans, History of." Entry in *Encyclopaedia Britannica*, 15th ed.

1974b. *The Gods and Goddesses of Old Europe: 7000–3500 B.C.*, 2nd ed., 1982. London: Thames and Hudson, and Berkeley: University of California Press.

1977. "The First Wave of Eurasian Steppe Pastoralists into Copper Age Europe." *The Journal of Indo-European Studies*, 4, 2:277–339.

1979. "The Three Waves of the Steppe People into East Central Europe." *Archiv Suisses d'Anthropologie Générale* 43, 2:113–37.

1980a. The Kurgan Wave #2 into Europe and the Following Transformation of Culture." *Journal of Indo-European Studies* 8:273–317.

1980b. "The Temples of Old Europe." *Archaeology* 33, 6:41–50.

1886. "Remarks on the Ethnogenesis of the Indo-Europeans in Europe." Bernhard & Kandler-Pálsson, eds. *Ethnogenese europäischer Völker*. (Stuttgart-New York: Gustav Fischer Verlag): 5–20.

1989. *The Language of the Goddess*. San Francisco: Harper & Row.

Gimbutas, Marija, ed.
1976. *Neolithic Macedonia (As Reflected by Excavations at Anza, Ovče Polje)*. Monumenta Archaeologica 1, Institute of Archaeology, U. of Calif. at Los Angeles.

Gimbutas, Marija, Daniel Shimabuku, and Shann Winn
1989. *Achilleion. A Neolithic Settlement in Thessaly, Northern Greece. 6400–5600 B.C.* Monumenta Archaeologica 14, Institute of Archaeology, U. of Calif. at Los Angeles.

Giot, P. R.
1960. "Brittany." *Ancient Peoples and Places* 13. London: Thames and Hudson.

1980. *Barnenez, Carn, Guennoc*. Rennes.

1981. "The Megaliths of France," in *The Megalithic Monuments of Western Europe*, Colin Renfrew, ed., pp. 18–290. London: Thames and Hudson.

Giot, P. R., J. L'Helgouach, and J. L. Monnier
1979. *Préhistoire de la Bretagne*. Rennes.

Göttner-Abendroth, Heide
1982. *Die Tanzende Göttin. Prinzipien einer matriarchalen Ästhetik*. Munich: Frauenoffensive. In English translation: *The Dancing Goddess. Principles of a Matriarchal Aesthetic*. Boston: Beacon Press, 1991.

1983. *Die Göttin und ihr Heros. Die matriarchalen Religionen in Mythos, Märchen und Dichtung*, 3rd ed. Munich: Frauenoffensive.

Gonzenbach, Victorine, von
1949. *Die Cortaillodkultur in der Schweiz*. Monographien zur Ur- und Frühgeschichte der Schweiz, 7.

Grbić, M., et al.
1960. *Porodin, Kashoneolitsko naselje na Tumbi kod Bitola*. Bitola: Archaeological Museum.

Greenfield, Haskel J.
1988. "The Origins of Milk and Wool Production from the Central Balkans." *Current Anthropology* 29:573–93.

Grimm, Paul
1938. "Die Salzmünder Kultur in Mitteldeutschland." *Jahresschrift für die Vorgeschichte der Sächsisch-Thüringischen Länder* 29:1–104.

Grygiel, R.
1986. "The Household Cluster As a Fundamental Social Unit of The Brześć Kujawski Group of the Lengyel Culture in the Polish Lowlands." *Prace i Materialy* 31:43–271. Lódź: Museum Archaeoliczne i Etnologiazne.

Guilaine, J.
1974. *La Balma de Montbolo et Néolithique de l'Occident méditerranéen*. Toulouse: Institut pyrénéen d'études anthropologiques.

Guilaine, J., ed.
1976a. *La Préhistoire Française. 2: Civilisations Néolithiques et Protohistoriques*. Paris: Centre National Res. Sc.

1976b. *Premiers bergers et paysans de l'Occident Meditérranéen*. Civilisations et Sociétes 58. The Hague and Paris: Mouton.

Guilaine, J.
1979. "The Earliest Neolithic in the West Mediterranean: A New Appraisal." *Antiquity* 53:22–29.

Guyan, W.
1955. *Das jungsteinzeitliche Moordorf von Thayngen-Weier*. Monographien zur Ur- und Frühgeschichte der Schweiz, vol. 2. Basel: Birkhäuser Verlag.

Guyan, W., ed.
1955. *Das Pfahlbauproblem*. Basel: Birkhausen.

Haarmann, Harold
1990. "Writing from Old Europe," *The Journal of Indo-European Studies* 17.

1990. *Universalgeschichte der Schrift*. Frankfurt-New York: Campus Verlag.

Hamond, F.
1981. "The Colonisation of Europe: The Analysis of Settlement Processes," in *Pattern of the Past: Studies in Honour of David Clarke*. I. Hodder, G. Isaac, and N. Hammond, eds., pp. 211–78. Cambridge University Press.

Hauptmann, H. and V. Milojčić
1969. *Die Funde der frühen Dimini-Zeit aus der Arapi-Magula, Thessalien*. Bonn.

Hawkes, Christopher
1940. *The Prehistoric Foundation of Europe*. London: Methuen and Co.

Hawkes, J.
1968. "The Proper Study of Mankind." *Antiquity* 42:255–62.

1969. *Dawn of the Gods: Minoan and Mycenaean Origins of Greece*. New York: Random House.

Hedges, John W.
1983. *Isbister. A Chambered Tomb in Orkney*. Oxford: British Archaeological Reports, International Series 115.

1984. *Tomb of the Eagles*. London: J. Murray.

Heggie, Douglas C.
1981. *Megalithic Science. Ancient Mathematics and Astronomy in Northwest Europe*. London: Thames and Hudson.

Hensel, W. and T. Wiślański, eds.
1979. *Prahistoria Ziem Polskich. Neolit*. Wrocław: Ossolineum.

Henshall, A. S.
1963. *The Chambered Tombs of Scotland*, vol. 1. Edinburgh University Press.

1972. *The Chambered Tombs of Scotland*, vol. 2. Edinburgh University Press.

Herity, Michael
1974. *Irish Passage Graves. Neolithic Tomb-Builders in Ireland and Britain, 2500–2000 B.C.* Dublin: Irish University Press, and New York: Barnes and Noble.

Herity, Michael and George Eogan
1977. *Ireland in Prehistory*. London: Routledge & Kegan Paul.

Higgs, E. S., ed.
1975. *Paleoeconomy*. London: Cambridge University Press.

Höckmann, O.
1975. "Das Neolithikum Südosteuropas und des südöstlichen Mitteleuropa," in *Handbuch der Urgeschichte* 2, K. J. Narr, ed. pp. 161–97 Bern: Franke Verlag.

Howell, John M.
1983. *Settlement and Economy in Neolithic Northern France*. Oxford: British Archaeological Reports, International Series 157.

Ivanov, Ivan S.
1978. "Les fouilles archéologiques de la nécropole chalcolithique à Varna, 1972–1975." *Studia Praehistorica* 1–2:13–27.

Jarman, M. R. and H. N. Jarman
1968. "The Fauna and Economy of Early Neolithic Knossos." *Annual of the British School of Archaeology at Athens* 63:241–64.

Jażdżewski, K.
1936. *Kultura pucharów lejkowatych w Polsce zachodniej i środkowej (Die Trichterbecherkultur in West- und Mittelpolen)*. Łódź: Bibljoteka Prehistoryczna, 2.

Jones, G. D. B.
1987. *Apulia*. vol. 1, *Neolithic Settlement in the Tavoliere*. Society of Antiquaries Research Report 44. London: Thames and Hudson.

Joassaume, E.
1987. *Dolmen for the Dead*. Batsford: Hatchette.

Jovanović, Borislav
1969. "Chronological Frames of the Iron Gate Group of the Early Neolithic Period." *Archaeologia Iugoslavica* 10:23–38.

1978a. "Early Gold and Eneolithic Copper Mining and Metallurgy of the Balkans and Danube Basin." *Studia Praehistorica* 1–2:192–97. Sofia.

1978b. "The Oldest Copper Metallurgy in the Balkans." *Expedition* 21, 1:9–19. Philadelphia.

1980. "The Origins of Copper Mining in Europe." *Scientific American* 242, 5:152–68.

1982. *Rudna Glava. Najstaršije rudarstvo bakra na centralnom Balkanu (résumé in German: Rudna Glava. Der älteste Kupferbau im Zentralbalkan.)* Institute of Archaeology Publication 17. Bor-Belgrade.

Kaelas, Lili
1956. "Dolmen und Ganggräber in Schweden." *Offa* 15:5–24.

1981. "Megaliths of the Funnel Beaker Culture in Germany and Scandinavia," in *The Megalithic Monuments of Western Europe*. Colin Renfrew, ed. 2nd ed. pp. 77–91. London: Thames and Hudson.

Kalicz, Nándor
1970. *Dieux d'argile*. Budapest: Corrina.

1985. *Kökörfalu Aszódon. (summary in German: Neolithisches Dorf in Aszód.)* Aszód: Petöfi Museum.

Kalicz, Nándor and János Makkay.
1972. "Gefässe mit Gesichtsdarstellungen der Linienbandkeramik in Ungarn." *Idole, prähistorische Keramiken aus Ungarn*. Naturhistorisches Museum, N.F. 7:9–15. Vienna.

1977. *Die Linienbandkeramik in der grossen Ungarischen Tiefebene*. Budapest: Akadémiai Kiadó.

Kandyba, O.
1937. *Schipenitz. Kunst und Geräte eines neolitischen Dorfes*. Bücher zur Ur- und Frühgeschichte 5. Vienna and Leipzig.

Kinnes, Ian
1981. "Dialogues With Death," in *The Archaeology of Death*, R. Chapman and K. Randsborg, eds. London: Cambridge University Press.

Korošec, Josip
1959. "Prehistorijska glinena plastika u Jugoslaviji (Prehistoric Plastic Art in Yugoslavia)." *Arheol. Radovi i Rosprave* I (Ljubljana): 61–117.

1964. *Danilo i Danilska Kultura (with a German translation: Danilo und die Danilo-Kulturgruppe)*. Ljubljana.

Kruk, Janusz
1980. *The Neolithic Settlement of Southern Poland*. J. M. Howell and N. J. Starling, eds. Oxford: British Archaeological Reports, International Series 93.

Kutzián, Ida Bognár
1944, 1947. *The Körös Culture*. 2 vols. Dissertationes Pannonicae, 2, 23. Budapest.

1963. *The Copper Age Cemetery of Tiszapolgár-Basatanya*. Budapest: Akadémiai Kiádó.

1968. *The Early Copper Age in Hungary*. Budapest: Akadémiai Kiádó.

1972. *The Early Copper Age Tiszapolgár Culture in the Carpathian Basin*. Budapest: Akadémiai Kiádó.

Lagodovska, O. F., O. G. Shaposhnikova, and M. L. Makarevich
1962. *Mikhailivsk'e poseleniya*. Kiev.

Lamberg-Karlovsky, C. C., ed.
1972. *Old World Archaeology: Foundations of Civilization*. Readings from *Scientific American*. San Francisco: W. H. Freeman and Co.

Lambert, M.
1973. "Cave Kitsos." *Bulletin of the Hellenic Correspondence* 97, 2:413–63.

Lanfranchi, François de and Michel-Claude Weiss
1973. *La Civilisation des Corses. Les origines*. Ajaccio: Editions Cyrnos et Méditerranée.

Larsson, L.
1978. *Ageröd I:B—Ageröd I:D. A Study of Early Atlantic Settlement in Scania*. Acta Archaeologica Lundensia 12.

Larsson, Mats
1985. *The Early Neolithic Funnel-Beaker Culture in Southwest Scania, Sweden. Social and Economic Change, 3000–2500 B.C.* Oxford: British Archaeological Reports, International Series 264.

Lazarovici, Gheorge
1979. *Neoliticul Banatului*. Cluj: Napoca.

Leisner, Georg and Vera
1943. *Die Megalithgräber der Iberischen Halbinsel. 1: Der Süden*. Berlin: Walter de Gruyter.

1956, 1959. *Die Megalithgräber der Iberischen Halbinsel. 2: Der Westen*. Berlin: Walter de Gruyter.

Leisner, Vera
1965. *Die Megalithgräber der Iberischen Halbinsel. Der Westen*. Berlin: Walter de Gruyter.

Leisner, Vera, G. Zbyszewski and Veiga Ferreira
1969. "Les Monuments préhistoriques de Praia das Macas et de Casainhos." *Servicos Geologicos de Lisboa* (Lisbon).

Le Rouzic, Z.
1930. *Les cromlechs de Er, Lannic*. Vannes.

Le Roux, C.-T.
1983. "Circonscription de Bretagne." *Gallia Préhistoire* 24:395–423.

1985. *Gavrinis et les îles du Morbihan. Les mégalithes du golfe*. Guides Archéolgiques de la France. Impr. National.

L'Helgouach, J.
1965. *Les sépultures mégalithiques en Armorique, dolmens à couloir et allées couvertes*. Rennes, Ouest-France: Travaux du Laboratoire d'Anthropolgie Préhistorique de la Faculté des Sciences.

1976. "Les civilisations néolithiques en Armorique," in *La Préhistoire Française, 2. Civilisations Néolithiques et Protohistoriques*. CNRS, 365–74. Paris.

Lichardus, Ján
1986. "Le rituel funéraire de la culture de Michelsberg, dans la région du Rhin supérieur et moyen," in *Le Néolithique de la France*, J.-P Demoule and J. Guilaine, eds. pp. 343–59. Paris.

Lichardus, Ján and Josef Vladár
1970. "Neskorolengyelské sídliskove hrobové nalezy z Nitry (résumé in German: Spätlengyelzeitliche Siedlung- und Grabfunde aus Nitra)." *Slovenská Archeológia* 18, 2:373–421.

Lichardus, J., M. Lichardus-Itten, G. Bailloud, and J. Cauvin
1985. *La Protohistoire de l'Europe: Le Néolithique et le Chalcolithique entre la Méditerranée et la mer Baltique*. Paris: Nouvelle Clio.

Lüning, J.
1968. *Die Michelsberger Kultur. Ihre Funde in zeitlicher und räumlicher Gliederung*. Berichten der Römisch-Germanischen Kommission 48.

1982. "Research Into the Bandkeramik Settlement of the Aldenhovener Platte in the Rhineland." *Analecta Praehistorica Leidensia* 15:1–29.

1982. "Siedlung und Siedlungslandschaft in Bandkeramischer und Rössener Zeit." *Offa* 39:9–33.

MacKie, Euan
1977. *The Megalith Builders*. Oxford: Phaidon.

Madsen, T.
1979. "Earthen Long Barrows and Timber Structures: Aspects of the Early Neolithic Mortuary Practice in Denmark." *Proceedings of the Prehistoric Society* 45:301–20.

Malmer, M.
1962. *Jung-neolithische Studien*. *Acta Archaeologica Lundensia*, 36.

Mallory, J. P.
1989. *In Search of the Indo-Europeans. Language, Archaeology and Myth*. London: Thames and Hudson.

Manfredini, A.
1972. "Il villaggio trincerato di Monte Acquilone nel quadro del Neolitico dell'Italia meridionale." *Origini* 6:29–154.

Marinatos, Nanno
1984. *Art and Religion in Thera. Reconstructing a Bronze Age Society*. Athens: Mathioulakis.

Marinescu-Bîlcu, Silvia
1974. *Cultura Precucuteni pe Teritoriul României*. Bucharest: Institutul de Arheologie.

Marinescu-Bîlcu, Silvia and Barbu Ionescu
1968. *Catalogue sculpturilor eneolitice din Muzeul raional Olteniţa*. Olteniţa.

Markevich, V. I.
1970. "Mnogosloinoe poselenie Novye Ruseshty I." *Kratkie soobshcheniya Instituta arkheologii* 123:58–68. Moscow.

1981. *Pozdne-Tripol'skie plemena severnoy Moldavii*. Kishinev: Institute of Archaeology.

Marković, Cedomir
1985. *Neolit Crne Gore (The Neolithic of Montenegro)*. University of Belgrade, Department of Philosophy.

Markotić, Vladimir
1984. *The Vinča Culture*. Calgary: Western Publishers.

Mataşa, C.
1946. *Frumuşica. Village préistorique à céramique peinte dans la Moldavia du Nord*. Bucharest.

1964. "Asezarea eneolitica Cucuteni B de la Tîrgu Ocna-Podei (raionul Tîrgu Ocna, reg. Bacău)," *Arheologia Moldovei*, 2–3 (Bucharest): 166.

McPherron, Allan and D. Srejović, eds.
1988. *Divostin and the Neolithic of Central Serbia*. University of Pittsburg and National Museum, Kragujevac.

Meaden, George Terence
1991. *Goddess of the Stones: The Language of the Megaliths*. Foreword by M. Gimbutas. London: Souvenir Press.

Meisenheimer, Marita
1989. *Das Totenritual geprägt durch Jenseitsvorstellungen und Gesellschaftsrealität. Theorie der Totenrituals eines kupferzeitlichen Friedhofs zu Tiszapolgár-Basatanya (Ungarn)*. Oxford: British Archaeological Reports, International Series 475.

Mellaart, James
1962. "Excavations at Çatal Hüyük. Second Preliminary Report." *Anatolian Studies* 13.

1963. "Deities and Shrines of Neolithic Anatolia." *Archaeology* 16, 1:29–38.

1963. "Excavations at Çatal Hüyük. Third Preliminary Report." *Anatolian Studies* 14.

1967. *Çatal Hüyük: A Neolithic Town in Anatolia*. New York: McGraw-Hill.

1970. *Excavations at Hacilar* 1 (text), 2 (illustrations). Edinburgh University Press.

1970. "Prehistory of Anatolia and Its Relations with the Balkans," *Symposium International sur l'Ethnogenese des Balkaniques, Plovdiv, 1969*.

1975. *The Neolithic of the Near East*. New York: Scribner.

Mellaart, James, Udo Hirsch, and Belkis Balpinar
1989. *The Goddess from Anatolia*, 1–4. Milan: Eskenazi.

Mellars, P. A., ed.
1978. *The Early Postglacial Settlement of Northern Europe*. London: Duckworth.

Midgley, M. S.
1985. *The Origin and Function of the Earthen Long Barrows of Northern Europe*. Oxford: British Archaeological Reports, International Series 259.

Milisauskas, Sarunas
1978. *European Prehistory*. New York, San Francisco, and London: Academic Press.

Milisauskas, Sarunas and Janusz Kruk
1984. "Settlement Organization and the Appearance of Low Level Hierarchical Societies During the Neolithic in the Bronocice Microregion, Southeastern Poland." *Germania* 64:1–30.

1989. "Neolithic Economy in Central Europe," *Journal of World Prehistory* 3, 4:403–46.

Milojčić, Vladimir, J. Boessneck, and M. Hopf
1962. *Die deutschen Ausgrabungen auf der Argissa Magula in Thessalien*. Beiträge zur ur- und frühgeschichtlichen Archäologie des Mittelmeer-Kulturraumes. Bonn.

Milojčić, Vladimir and Johanna Milojčić-von Zumbusch
1971. *Die deutschen Ausgrabungen auf der Otzaki-Magula in Thessalien*. Beiträge zur ur- und frühgeschichtlichen Archäolgie des Mittelmeer-Kulturraumes. Bonn.

Modderman, P. J. G.
1958–9. "Die geographische Lage der bandkeramischen Siedlungen in den Niederlanden." *Palaeohistoria* 6–7 (Groningen): 1–232.

1970. *Linearbandkeramik aus Elsloo und Stein*. The Hague: Staatsuitgeverij; and *Analecta Praehistorica Leidensia* 3.

1971. "Neolithische und frühbronzezeitliche Siedlungsspuren aus Hienheim Landkr. Kelheim." *Analecta Praehistorica Leidensia* 4.

Movsha, T. G.
1971. "Sviatilishcha tripol'skoy kul'tury." *Sovetskaya Arkheologiya* 1:201–5.

Müller-Beck, Hansjürgen
1961. "Prehistoric Swiss Lake Dwellers." *Scientific American* 205, 6:138–47.

1965. *Seeberg, Burgäschisee-Süd*, part 5: *Holzgeräte und Holzbearbeitung*. Acta Bernensia, 2. Bern.

Müller-Karpe, Hermann
1968. *Handbuch der Vorgeschichte 2: Jungsteinzeit*.

1974. *Handbuch der Vorgeschichte 3: Kupferzeit*. Munich: C. H. Beck.

Muñoz Amilibia, Ana Maria
1965. *La Cultura Neolitica Catalana de los "Sepulcros de Fosa."* Publicaciones Eventuales 9. Barcelona.

Murray, Jacqueline
1970. *The First European Agriculture*. Edinburgh University Press.

Nandris, John
1970. "The Development and Relationships of the Earlier Greek Neolithic." *Man* 15, 2:192–213.

Nemeskéri, János
1978. "Demographic Structure of the Vlasac Epipaleothic Population," in *Vlasac, Mezolitsko naselje u Džerdapu*, 2. M. Garašanin, ed., pp. 97–133. Belgrade.

Necrasov, Olga
1981. "Les populations de la période de transition du Néo-Enéolithique à l'âge du Bronze romaine et leurs particularités anthropologiques." *Anthropologie et Archéolgie: les cas de premiers âges des Metaux. Actes du Symposium de Sils-Maria 25–30 septembre 1979*. Roland Menk and Alain Gallay, eds. Geneva.

Nica, Marin
1977. Nouvelles données sur le Néolithique ancien d'Olténie." *Dacia* 21:13–53.

Nielsen, Poul Otton
1985. "The First Farmers from the Early TRB Culture at Sigerstad" (Danish, with English summary). *Tilegnet Carl Johan Becker. Aarbøger for nordisk Oldkyndighed og Historie 1984*. Copenhagen.

Nikolov, Bogdan
1974. *Gradechnitza*. Sofia: Nauka i Iskustvo.

Nosek, Stefan
1967. *Kultura amfor kulistych w Polsce*. Wroclaw-Warsaw-Cracow: Osslineum.

Nosek, Stefan, ed.
1964. *Studia i materiały do badan nad neolitem małopolski*. Warsaw, Polska Akademia Nauk, prace komisii archaeologii.

Novotný, Bohuslav
1958. *Slovensko v mladšej dobe kamennej (Die Slowakei in der Jungsteinzeit)*. Bratislava.

1962. *Lužianska Skupina a počiatky malovanej keramiky na Slovensku (The Lužianky Group and the Beginnings of Painted Pottery in Slovakia)*. Bratislava.

O'Kelly, Michael J.
1982. *Newgrange. Archaeology, Art, and Legend*. London: Thames and Hudson.

1989. *Early Ireland*. London: Cambridge University Press.

Olària, Carme
1988. *Cova Fosca. Un asentamiento meso-neolítico de cazadores y pastores en la serrania del Alto Maestrazgo, Castellon.* Monografies de Prehistorica i Arquelogia Castellonenques 3.

Papadopoulos, Stelios A., ed.
1973. *Neolithic Greece.* Athens: National Bank of Athens.

Papathanassopoulos, G.
1981. *Neolithic and Cycladic Civilization.* Athens: National Archaeological Museum ("Melissa" Publishing House).

Pape, W.
1979. "Histogramme neolithischer C 14-Daten." *Germania* 57:1–51.

Passek, T. S.
1949. "Periodizatsiya tripol'skikh poselenii." *Materialy i issledovaniya po arkheologii SSSR* 10. Moscow.

1961. "Rannezemledel'cheskie (tripol'skie) plemena podnestrov'ia." *Materialy i issledovaniya po arkheologii SSSR* 84. Moscow.

1962. "Neolit i eneolit jugoevropeiskoy chasti SSR" (Neolithic and Chalcolithic Periods in the Southern Part of the European USSR)." *Materialy i issledovaniya po arkheologii SSSR* 102. Moscow.

Pavúk, Juraj
1991. "Lengyel-culture fortified settlements in Slovakia."*Antiquity* 65:348–57.

Peroni, Renato
1963. "La Romita di Asciano (Pisa). Riparo sotto roccia utilizzato dell'età neolitica alla barbarica." *Bollettino Preistoriche Italiano* 71–72:251–442.

Pétrequin, P. and J.-F. Piningre
1976. "Les sépultures collectives mégalithiques de Franche-Comté." *Gallia Préhistoire* 19:287–394.

Petrescu-Dîmbovița, Mircea
1963. "Die wichtigsten Ergebnisse der archäologischen Ausgrabungen in der neolithischen Siedlung von Trușești (Moldau)." *Prähistorische Zeitschrift* 51 (Berlin): 172–86.

1966. *Cucuteni. Monumentele Patriei Nostre.* Bucharest.

Petrescu-Dîmbovița, Mircea et al., eds.
1987. *La civilisation de Cucuteni en contexte européen.* (Proceedings of the Conference on Cucuteni Culture in Iași and Peatra Neamț, 1984). Iași: Université Al. I. Cuza.

Phillips, Patricia
1975. *Early Farmers of West Mediterranean Europe.* London: Hutchinson.

1980. *The Prehistory of Europe,* chap. 5: The Neolithic. London: Allen Lane.

1982. *The Middle Neolithic in Southern France: Chasseen Farming and Culture Process.* Oxford: British Archaeological Reports, International Series 142.

Piggott, Stuart
1954. *The Neolithic Cultures of the British Isles.* London: Cambridge University Press.

1955. "Windmill—East or West?" *Proceedings of Prehistoric Society* 21:96–102.

1962. *The West Kennet Long Barrow.* London: Her Majesty's Stationery Office.

1965. *Ancient Europe, from the Beginnings of Agriculture to Classical Antiquity.* University of Chicago Press.

1982. *Scotland Before History.* Edinburgh University Press.

1983. *The Earliest Wheeled Transport: From the Atlantic Coast to the Caspian Sea.* London: Thames and Hudson.

Piggott, Stuart, Glyn Daniel, and Charles McBurney, eds.
1974. *France Before the Romans.* Park Ridge, N.J.: Noyes Press.

Pittioni, R.
1954. *Urgeschichte des Österreichischen Raumes.* Vienna: Denticke.

Prendi, Frano
1966. "La civilisation préhistorique de Malik." *Studia Albanica* (Tirana) 1:255–72.

1972. "Traits du Néolithique Récent en Albanie à la lumière de nouvelles découvertes (La civilisation Maliq-Kamnik)." *Studia Albanica* (Tirana) 9, 1:1–13.

Preuss, J.
1966. *Die Baalberger Gruppe im Mitteldeutsch-land.* Publications of Landesmuseum für Vorgeschichte, Halle, 21. Berlin.

Raczky, Pal, ed.
1987. *The Late Neolithic of the Tisza Region.* Budapest-S. Szolnok: Kossuth Press.

Radimsky, W. and M. Hoernes
1895. *Die neolithische Station von Butmir,* part 1. Vienna: Verlag von Adolf Holzhausen.

Radmilli, Antonio
1962. *Piccola quida della preistoria italiana.* Firenze: Sonsoni.

Reed, Charles A., ed.
1978. *Origins of Agriculture.* The Hague and Paris: Mouton.

Renfrew, Colin
1969. "The Autonomy of the Southeast European Copper Age." *Proceedings of the Prehistoric Society for 1969* 35:12–47.

1972. *The Emergence of Civilization: The Cyclades and the Aegean in the Third Millennium B.C.* London: Methuen.

1973. *Before Civilization: The Radiocarbon Revolution and Prehistoric Europe.* New York: Knopf.

Renfrew, Colin, et al.
1973. *The Explanation of Culture Change—Models in Prehistory.* London: Duckworth.

1976. *British Prehistory, a New Outline.* Park Ridge, N.J.: Noyes Press.

1979. *Investigations in Orkney.* London: Society of Antiquaries.

1983. *The Megalithic Monuments of Western Europe.* London: Thames and Hudson.

1984. *Approaches to Social Archaeology.* Cambridge: Harvard University Press.

Renfrew, Colin, Marija Gimbutas, and Ernestine S. Elster, eds.
1986. *Excavations at Sitagroi. A Prehistoric Village in Northeast Greece,* vol. 1. Monumenta Archaeologica 13, Institute of Archaeology, U. of Calif. at Los Angeles.

Renfrew, Jane M.
1973. *Palaeoethnobotany. The Prehistoric Food-plant of the Near East and Europe.* London: Methuen and Co.

Richards, Colin and Julian Thomas
1984. "Ritual Activity and Structured Deposition in Later Neolithic Wessex." *British Archaeological Reports, International Series* 133:189–215.

Ritchie, Anna and Graham Ritchie
1978. *The Ancient Monuments of Orkney.* Edinburgh: Her Majesty's Stationery Office.

Rimantienė, Rimutė
1979. *Šventoji* I. Vilnius: Mokslas.

1980. "The East Baltic Area in the Fourth and the Third Millennia B.C." *The Journal of Indo-European Studies* 8, 3–4:407–141.

1984. *Akmens amžius Lietuvoje.* Vilnius: Mokslas.

Ripoll, E. and M. Llongueras
1963. "La cultura neolitica de los sepulcros de fosa en Catalunya." *Ampurias* 21:1–90.

Rodden, R. J.
1965. "An Early Neolithic Village in Greece." *Scientific American* 212:82–92.

Rosetti, D.
1934. "Sapaturile dela Vidra." *Museului Municipiului Bucuresti* 1:1–31.

Ruggles, C. L. N.
1984. *Megalithic Astronomy. A New Archaeological and Statistical Study of 300 Western Scottish Sites.* Oxford: British Archaeological Reports, British Series 123.

Runnels, Curtis, and Tjeerd H. van Andel
1988. "Trade and the Origins of Agriculture in the Eastern Mediterranean." *Journal of Mediterranean Archaeology,* 1 (1):83–109.

Sakellaridis, Margaret
1979. *The Economic Exploitation of the Swiss Area in the Mesolithic and Neolithic Periods.* Oxford: British Archaeological Reports, International Series 67.

Sangmeister, E. and Ch. Strahm
1973. "Die Funde aus Kupfer in Seeberg, Burgäschisee-Süd." *Seeberg Burgäschissee-Süd* 6, Steingeräte und Kupferfunde, Bern, Stämpfli (Acta Bernensia 2): 189–272.

Sauter, Marc-R.
1955. "Sépultures à cistes du bassin du Rhône et civilisations palafittiques." *Sibrium* 2:133–39.

1973. "Anthropologie du Néolithique, la Suisse. Présentation critique de la documentation." *Die Anfänge des Neolithikums von Orient bis*

Nordeurope, 7a, Anthropoligie, 1. Cologne and Vienna, Böhlau (Fundamenta, B, 3): 235–46.

1977. *Swisse préhistorique, des origines aux Helvètes* (Prehistoric Switzerland, from the origins to the Helvetians). Boudry, Switzerland: Éditions de la Baconnièrre.

Savory, H. N.
1968. *Spain and Portugal. The Prehistory of the Iberian Peninsula.* Ancient Peoples and Places 61. London: Thames and Hudson.

Scarre, Christopher, ed.
1984. *The Neolithic of France.* Edinburgh University Press.

Schachermeyr, Fritz
1976. *Die Agäische Frühzeit.* 1: *Die Vormykenischen Perioden.* Vienna: Verlag der Österreichischen Akademie der Wissenschaften.

Schackleton, N. and Colin Renfrew
1970. "Neolithic Trade Routes." *Nature* 288:1062–65.

Schmidt, H.
1932. *Cucuteni in der oberen Moldau, Rumänien, Die befestigte Siedlung mit bemalter Keramik von der Stein-Kupferzeit bis in die vollentwickelte Bronzezeit.* Berlin: Walter de Gruyter.

Schmidt, R. R.
1945. *Die Burg Vučedol.* Zagreb.

Schwabedissen, H.
1980. "Ertebølle/Ellerbek-Mesolithikum oder Neolithikum?" In *Mesolithikum in Europa.* B. Gramsch, ed., pp. 129–42. Potsdam: Museum für Ur- und Frühgeschicte.

Schwidetzky, I., K. Gerhardt, and W. E. Mühlmann
1990. "Sonderheft Neolithikum." *Homo* 40.

Sjøø, M. and B. Mor
1987. *The Great Cosmic Mother: Rediscovering the Religion of the Earth.* San Francisco: Harper & Row.

Skomal, S.
1983. *Wealth Distribution as a Measure of Prehistoric Change: Chalcolithic to Copper Age Cultures in Hungary.* UCLA, Unpublished Ph.D. Dissertation. University Microfilms International. Ann Arbor, Michigan.

Simoska, Dragica and Vojislav Sanev
1976. *Praistorija vo centralna Pelagonija.* Bitola: Naroden Muzej.

Šiška, S.
1968. "Tiszapolgárska kultura na Slovensku." *Slovenská Archeológia* 16:61–175.

Smith, Isobel F., ed.
1965. *Windmill Hill and Avebury. Excavations by Alexander Keiller 1925–1939.* Oxford University Press.

Soudský, B.
1969. "Étude de la maison néolithique," *Slovenská Archeológia* 17:5–96.

Srejović, Dragoslav
1966. "Neolithic Anthropomorphic Figurines from Yugoslavia," IPEK (Berlin), 21 (1964–65):28–41.

1969. "The Roots of the Lepenski Vir Culture." *Archaeologia Iugoslavica* 10:13–21.

1972. *Europe's First Monumental Sculpture: New Discoveries at Lepenski Vir.* London: Thames and Hudson.

Srejović, Dragoslav and L. Babović
1983. *Umetnost Lepenskog Vira.* Belgrade: Narodni Muzej.

Srejović, Dragoslav and Z. Letica
1978. *Vlasac: A Mesolithic Settlement in the Iron Gates* (Serbo-Croatian with a summary in English). Belgrade: Serbian Academy of Sciences and Arts.

Srejović, Dragoslav and Nikola Tasić
1990. *Vinča and its World.* Belgrade: Serbian Academy of Sciences and Arts Symposia 51.

Starling, N.
1983. "Neolithic Settlement Patterns in Central Germany." *Oxford Journal of Archaeology* 2 (1):1–11.

Tanda, Giuseppa
1984. *Arte e religione della Sardegna preistorica nella necropoli di Sos Furrighesos-Anela (SS),* vol. 1–2. Sassari: Chiarella.

Tasić, N.
1957. "Praistorisko naselje kod Valača" (Prehistoric Settlement at Valac)." *Glasnik Muzeja Kosova i Metohije,* vols. 2, 4–5. Priština.

Tasić, N. and E. Tomić
1969. *Crnokalačka Bara Naselje Starčevačke i Vinčanske Kulture.* Dissertationes, vol. 3. Narodni Muzej Kruševac. Kruševac and Belgrade: Archeološko Društvo Jugoslavije.

Telegin, D. Ia.
1973. *Seredn'o-Stogivs'ka kul'tura ėpokhi midi.* Kiev.

Telegin, D. Ia. and I. D. Potekhina
1987. *Neolithic Cemeteries and Populations in the Dnieper Basin.* J. P. Mallory, ed. Oxford: British Archaeological Reports, International Series 383.

Theocharis, D. R.
1956. "Nea Makri: Eine Grosse Neolithische Siedlung in der Nähe von Marathon." *Athenische Mitteilungen* 71:1–29.

1973. "The Neolithic Civilization: A Brief Survey," in *Neolithic Greece.* S. Papadopoulous, ed. Athens: National Bank of Athens.

Thimme, Jürgen, ed.
1980. *Kunst und Kultur Sardiniens von Neolithikum bis zum Ende der Nuraghenzeit.* Catalog of the Exhibit.

Thom, A. and A. S. Thom
1978. *Megalithic Remains in Britain and Brittany.* Oxford: Clarendon Press.

Thom, A., A. S. Thom, and A. Burl
1980. *Megalithic Rings.* Oxford: British Archaeological Reports, British Series 80.

Thomas, Julian
1988. "The Social Significance of Cotswold-Severn Burial Practices." *Man* 23, 3. London, Royal Archaeological Institute.

Thorpe, I. J.
1984. "Ritual, Power, and Ideology—Reconstruction of Earlier Neolithic Rituals in Wessex." Oxford, British Archaeological Reports, British Series 133:41–60.

Tinè, Santo
1983. *Passo di Corvo e la civiltà neolitica del Tavoliere.* Genoa: Sagep Editrice.

Titov, V. S.
1969. *Neolit Gretsii. Periodizatsiya i khronologiya.* Moscow: Nauka.

Titov, V. S. and I. Erdeli
1980. *Arkheologiya Vengrii.* Moscow: Nauka.

Todd, Ian A.
1976. *Çatal Hüyük in Perspective.* Menlo Park, Calif.: Benjamin Cummings Publishing Co.

1980. *The Prehistory of Central Anatolia,* vol. 1, *The Neolithic Period.* Studies in Mediterranean Archaeology 60. Göteborg: Paul Åströms Förlag.

Todorova, Henrieta
1974. "Kultszene und Hausmodell aus Ovčarovo, Bez. Targoviste," *Thracia* (Sofia) 3:39–46.

1976. *Ovčarovo. Praistoričeska selišna mogila.* Sofia: Bulgarian Academy of Sciences.

1978. *The Eneolithic Period in Bulgaria in the Fifth Millennium B.C.* (translated from the Bulgarian by Vessela Zhelyaskova). Oxford: British Archaeological Reports, International Series (Supplementary) 49.

Todorova, Henrieta, St. Ivanov, V. Vasilev, H. Hopf, H. Quitta, and G. Kohl
1975. *Seliščnata Mogila pri Goljamo Delčevo.* Sofia: Bulgarian Academy of Sciences.

Todorović, Jovan and Aleksandrina Cermanović
1961. *Banjica, naselje vinčanske kulture* (Banjica, Siedlung der Vinča-Gruppe). Belgrade: City Museum.

Torrence, Robin
1986. *The Prehistoric Obsidian Trade in the Aegean.* London: Cambridge University Press.

Treuil, René, Pascal Darque, Jean-Claude Poursat, and Gilles Touchais
1989. *Les civilisations égéennes du Néolithique et de lÂge du Bronze.* Nouvelle Clio. L'histoire et ses problèmes 1. Presses Universitaires de France, Paris.

Tringham, Ruth
1971. *Hunters, Fishers, and Farmers of Eastern Europe, 6000–3000 B.C.* London: Hutchinson University Library.

Tringham, Ruth and Dušan Krstić
1990. *Selevac. A Neolithic Village in Yugoslavia.* Los Angeles, UCLA, Institute of Archaeology. Monuments Archaeologica 15.

Trump, D. H.
1966a. *Central and Southern Italy Before Rome. Ancient People and Places.* London: Thames and Hudson.

1966b. *Skorba.* Reports of the Research Committee of the Society of Antiquaries of London 22. Oxford University Press and the National Museum of Malta.

1980. *The Prehistory of the Mediterranean.* New Haven: Yale University Press.

1981. "Megalithic Architecture in Malta," in *The Megalithic Monuments of Western Europe,* Colin Renfrew, ed., pp. 64–76. London: Thames and Hudson.

1983. *La Grotta di Filiestru a Bonu Ighinu. Mara (SS).* Dessi-Sassari.

Tsountas, Christos
1908. *Proistorikae Akropolis Diminiou kai Sesklou* (The Prehistoric Acropolis of Dimini and Sesklo). Athens: A. D. Sakellariou.

Twohig, Elizabeth Shee
1981. *The Megalithic Art of Western Europe.* Oxford: Clarendon Press.

Van de Velde, Pieter
1979. "On Bandkeramik Social Structure: Analysis of Pot Decoration and Hut Distributions from the Central European Neolithic Communities of Elsloo and Hienheim." *Analecta Praehistorica Leidensia* 12. Leiden University Press.

Vankina, L. V.
1970. *Torfyanikovaya stoyanka Sarnate.* Riga: Zinatne.

Vasić, Miloje M.
1932–36. *Praistorijska Vinča,* 1, 1952; 2–4, 1936. Belgrade: Izdanje Drvavne Štamparje.

Vasil'ev, I. B.
1981. *Eneolit Povolzh'ya: step' i lesotep'.* Kuybyshev: Kuybyshevskii gosudarstvennyi pedagogicheskiy institut.

Vasil'ev, I. B. and G. Matveeva
1976. "Poselenie i mogil'nik u sela S'ezzhee," *Ocherki istorii i kul'tury Povolzh'ya.* Kuybyshev: Kuybyshevskii gosudarstvennyi universitet.

1984. *Vinča u praistorije i srednem veku.* Catalog, Gallery of Serbian Academy of Sciences and Art (with summaries in German by M. Garasanin, Draga Garasanin, Borislav Jovanovic, Blazenka Stalis, and others). Belgrade.

Vine, Philip M.
1982. *The Neolithic and Bronze Age Culture of the Middle and Upper Trent Basin.* Oxford: British Archaeological Reports, International Series 105.

Vlassa, Nicolae
1972. "Eine frühneolithische Kultur mit bemalter Keramik der Vor-Starčevo-Körös-Zeit im Cluj-Gura Baciului, Siebenbürg." *Prähistorische Zeitschrift* 47, 2:174–97.

Vogt, E.
1951. "Das steinzeitliche Uferdorf Egolzwil 3 (Kt. Luzern)." *Der Zeitschrift für schweizerische Archaeologie und Kunstgeschichte* 12, 4:193–215.

1954. "Pfahlbaustudien," in *Das Pfahlbauproblem.* W. V. Guyan, ed., pp. 199–212. Birkhausen.

1967. "Ein Schema des schweizerischen Neolithikums." *Germania* 45, 1–2:1–20.

Vulpe, R.
1957. *Izvoare: Sapaturile din 1936–1948* (Summaries in Russian and French: Izvoare: Les Fouilles de 1936–1948). Bucharest: Biblioteca de Arheologie.

Wace, A. J. B. and M. S. Thompson
1912. *Prehistoric Thessaly.* London: Cambridge University Press.

Wainwright, G. J.
1969. "A Review of Henge Monuments in the Light of Recent Research." *Proceedings of Prehistoric Society* 35:112–33.

Waldren, W., R. Chapman, J. Lewthwaite, and R. Kennard
1984. *The Deya Conference of Prehistory: Early Settlement in the Western Mediterranean Islands and Their Peripheral Areas.* Oxford: British Archaeological Reports, International Series 229.

Weinberg, Saul S.
1962. "Excavations at Prehistoric Elateia, 1959." *Hesperia* 31:158–209.

Whitehouse, Ruth D.
1969. "Settlement and Economy in Southern Italy in the Neothermal Period," *Proceedings of the Prehistoric Society* 34:332–67.

Whittle, A. W. R.
1977a. *The Earlier Neolithic of S. England and Its Continental Background.* Oxford: British Archaeological Reports, Supplement 35.

Whittle, A.
1977b. "Earlier Neolithic Enclosures in North-West Europe." *Proceedings of the Prehistoric Society* 43:329–48.

1985. *Neolithic Europe: A Survey.* London: Cambridge University Press.

Wijnen, Marie-Helene Josephine Marcelle Nicole
1982. *The Early Neolithic I Settlement at Sesklo: An Early Farming Community in Thessaly, Greece.* Leiden: University Press. Also: *Analecta Praehistorica Leidensia* 14.

Willms, C.
1983. "Obsidian im Neolithikum Europas." *Germania* 61:327–51.

1985. "Neolithischer Spondylusschmuck. Hundert Jahre Forschung." *Germania* 63:331–43.

Winn, Shan M. M.
1981. *Pre-Writing in Southeast Europe: The Sign System of the Vinča Culture, ca. 4000 B.C.* Calgary: Western Publishers.

Wiślański, T., ed.
1970. *The Neolithic in Poland.* Wrocław-Warsaw-Kraków: Inst. Hist. Kultury Mat. Polsk. Akad. Nauk.

Wolkstein, Diane and Samuel Kramer
1983. *Inanna. Queen of Heaven and Earth. Her Stories and Hymns for Sumer.*

Wyss, René
1977. *Das jungsteinzeitliche Jäger-Bauerndorf von Egolzwil 5 im Wauwilermoos.* Naturwissenschaftliche Beiträge von H. R. Stampfli, S. Wegmüller, F. H. Schweingruber. Zürich: Schweizerisches Landesmuseum, Archaeologische Forschungen.

Wyss, René and Jakob Bill
1978. "An Ancient Lakeshore Settlement at Egolzwil Helps Clarify Europe's Neolithic past." *Archaeology* 31 (5):24–32.

Zagorskis, F.
1987. *Zvejnieku akmens laikmeta kapulauks.* Riga: Zinatne.

Zaharia, Eugenia
1962. "Considérations sur la civilisation de Criş à la lumière des sondages de Leţ," *Dacia* 6:5–51.

Zalai-Gaál, István
1988. *Sozialarchäologische Untersuchungen des mitteleuropäischen Neolithikums aufgrund der Gräberanalyse.* (Béri Balogh Adám Múzeum) évkönyvébol 14. Szekszárd.

Zervos, C.
1962. *La naissance de la civilisation en Grèce.* Paris: Editions "Cahiers d'Art."

Zohary, D.
1969. "The Progenitors of Wheat and Barley in Relation to Domestication and Dispersal in the Old World," in *The Domestication and Exploitation of Plants and Animals,* P. J. Ucko and G. W. Dimbleby, eds., pp. 47–66. London: Duckworth.

Zürn, Hartwig
1965. *Das jungsteinzeitliche Dorf Ehrenstein (Kreis Ulm). Ausgrabung 1960. Die Baugeschichte.* Stuttgart: Staatliches Amt für Denkmalpflege.

INDEX

References to notes are by number and page in the Notes section beginning on p. 404. Page references in italic indicate figures.

Abraham, 85
Abrigo de Verdelpino, 186
Abruzzi, 163
Acheulian, 222
Achilleion, 13–23, 56, 224, 245; temples, 17, 231, 251–55, 260, 325. *See also* Sesklo culture
Acorns, 186, 193, 383
Acropolis: Ezero, 378–79; Sesklo tell and, 325. *See also* Hill forts.
Actaeon, 251
Adelphos/Adelphe, 347
Adriatic, 4, 59, 118, 155–81; Butmir culture and, 59; Danilo-Hvar culture, 53–56; islands, 53, 55, 156, 376, 388; Impresso, 3,4; Kurgans, 376, 385, 387–88; Lengyel culture and, 77; navigation, 5, 53–55; Starčevo culture and, 29; Vinča culture and, 64. *See also* Dalmatia.
Adzes, 19, 39
Aegean, 4, 5, 48, 90–93, 325; church-house cluster, 326; Death Goddess, 242; Early Pottery Neolithic, 156; headdress, 273; islands, 4, 14, 35, 118, 237, 273, 326, 344, 347; Kurgans, 378–80; matriliny, 344, 347; religion (general), 396; script signs, 319; Sesklo culture, 12, 13–23; Snake Goddess, 236, 237; temples, 396; trade, 4, 5, 35, 64, 118; Vinča culture, 64. *See also* Greece.
African hairstyles, 272
Afterlife, 399–401
Age: at death, 341; maturity symbols, 176; social status of, 335–36
Aggtelek cave, 43, 44, 45, 46
Aghios Kosmas, 389
Aghios Pétros, 273
Agriculture, 3, 52, 222, 324, 325; beginning, *see* Domestication; biological model of diffusion, 3; Bükk, 44; Çatal Hüyük, 7, 8; Chassée, 191–92; Cortaillod,

196–99; Dniester-Bug, 47; in France (northern), 191; in Italy (southern), 160; Karanovo, 31, 95; Kurgans and, 352, 361, 363, 364, 369–72 passim, 383, 395–96; LBK, 38; Lengyel, 81–83; and male gods, 342; in Malta, 172; in Mediterranean (western), 185–86, 191; Narva, 144, 147, 152; PIE, 395–96; and Pregnant Goddess, 228–30; "revolution" theory of beginning, 3; rituals, 343–44; in Sardinia and Corsica, 166; Sesklo, 19; spreading, 2–9, 12, 25, 38, 43, 126, 127, 184, 206; Starčevo, 25, 26–27; TRB, 131; Vinča, 64. *See also* Animals; Plants.
Ai-Bunar, 52, 116, 118, 361
Aichbuhl, 407n.49, 415n.36
Aichbuhl-Schwieberdingen group, 216, 364
Ain Sakhri, 342
Aisne, River, 38
Aiterhofen, 331, 333
Akrotiri, 227, 345
Akte, 347
Alabaster, 8, 19, 64, 170–71
Alba, 312
Albania, 55, 156, 372, 387, 388, 389
Aldenhoven Plateau, 330
Aleksandriya, 360, 362
Alekseevo, 356
Alentejo, 239
Alghero, 169, 171, 290
Aliakmon River, 13
Alicante, 186
Ali̧sar, 378
Allées couvertes, 204. *See also* Gallery graves.
Almeria, 205
Almizaraque, 299
Alpine physical types, 9
Alpine region: Chassean culture, 192; Cortaillod culture, 195; Kurgans, 363, 371, 376, 387, 388, 396; Lengyel culture, 407n.49; obsidian trade, 166; regeneration symbols, 244
Alsónemedi, 375
Altai Mountains, 353
Altamira, 223

Altata, 357
Alto Adige, 397
Alto Maestrazgo, 186
Alvastra, 138, 268–69
Alzey-Worms, 331
Amber: Kurgan, 152, 382, 383; Narva, 144, 150, 152; TRB, 137, 268, 269
Amphorae, globular, 380, 381, 392
Amulets, 202, 222, 245
Ana, 305
Anatolia, 2, 4, 5–9, 12, 52; Bird Goddess, 230; double goddess, 265; Earth Mother, 228; headdress, 273; Kurgans, 378–80; matriliny, 347; Mistress of Animals, 227; script signs, 314, 319; Snake Goddess, 237; temples (general), 256. *See also* Çatal Hüyük.
Ancestors: Bird and Snake Goddesses and, 342; burial practices and, 281, 294, 295, 296
Andrea Priu, 172, 290
Androcracy, 324. *See also* Patriarchy.
Ane, 349
Anela, 291
Anghelu Ruju, 169, 171
Animals: domestication of, 2–7 passim, 12, 19, 191, 353–54, 391, 393–94; Goddess and, 9, 222, 223–40, 244; gods and, 251, 342; in Italy (southern), 160; in rock art, 187; sacrificed, *see* Animal sacrifice; in Sardinia and Corsica, 166; wild, 2, 52, 83, 131, 206 (*see also* Fishing; Hunting). *See also* individual animals.
Animal sacrifice, 244; in British islands, 208, 294; Cucuteni, 260; horses, 353, 354, 356, 362, 383, 384, 391, 394; Kurgan, 353, 354, 356, 362, 375, 381, 383, 384, 391; Lepenski Vir, 244, 286, 294; in Malta, 176, 181; TRB, 268
Ankou, 243, 305
Annia, 305
"Annia's Cave," 305
Antiparos, 23
Antler tools, 117–18, 126; Kurgan, 361, 363, 379; Nemunas, 142, 143; TRB, 131
Antrim, County, 209

Anu, 243, 305, 349
Anza (Anzabegovo): Starčevo culture at, 25, 26, 28, 29, 66, 317, 406n.1; Vinča culture at, 62, 64, 66, 67, 70, 233, 406n.1
Apples: carbonized, 196; symbol, 243
Aprons, 277, 278, 279, 280
Apulia, 157, 163, 164, 165
Aquatic animals, 2, 83, 113. *See also* Fish; Water birds.
Aquatic signs: megalithic, 297. *See also* Water.
Aquitaine, 191
Araguina Sennola, 4
Arapi, 23, 405n.13
Arc, multiple, 297–304 passim, 400
Archeomythology, 342
Architecture, 41, 49, 52; Butmir, 61; Çatal Hüyük, 7; LBK, 41; Lengyel, 81–83; Maltese, 172–73, 174–81; Petreşti, 101; Sesklo, 15–18, 325; Starčevo, 27, 61; Tisza, 73–75; Vinča, 64. *See also* Houses; Temples; Tombs.
Ardèche, 192
Ardovo, 45
Arene Candide, 190
Argisa, 12, 14, 20, 23
Argolid, 4, 389
Argonauts, 347
Argyll, 219
Arhus, 131
Aristophanes, 344
Arkhara, 356, 357
Arkose, 192
Arm rings, 118, 121, 250, 336, 361. *See also* Bracelets.
Arms closed (figurines), 98
Arnesano, 164, 165
Arron, 219
Arrowheads: Chassée, *193f.6–6*; in graves, 333; Kurgan, 356–62 passim, 369, 382, 383, 384, 390; Nemunas, 143; in rock engraving, *187f.6–2*
Arsenical bronze, 369, 379
Art, 9, 52, 222, 223, 325; "beginning of," 223; in British islands, 213–15; Butmir, 56; Cucuteni, 109; Etruscan, 347; forms, *see* Architecture; Painting; Pottery; Sculptures; Hamangia, 90; in